THE CHINESE IN SOUTHEAST ASIA was first published in 1951 and was reprinted the following year. Since then it has gained acceptance as the standard work on the subject, but has long been out of print. The author has now prepared a revised edition, giving the statistics for 1960 but bringing the text in most cases up to date to a later period, and incorporating some 50,000 words of new material. The format of the book has been changed and the size increased, but while making room for the new material has necessitated some cuts, most of the basic historical and descriptive matter has been retained. The new edition will be essential to students of Far Eastern affairs.

The author was a member of the Malayan Civil Service, 1921–46, a Consultant, United Nations, 1946–48, and Lecturer in Far Eastern History at Cambridge University, 1949–63. He was the author of many other books on the Far East, including THE CHINESE IN MALAYA (1948), CHINA (*Nations of the Modern World*) (1962), THE REVOLUTION IN SOUTHEAST ASIA (1962), and THE BOXER UPRISING (1963). He died not long after completing work on this new edition.

THE CHINESE IN SOUTHEAST ASIA

THE CHINESE
IN
SOUTHEAST ASIA

BY

VICTOR PURCELL
C.M.G., Litt.D.

Second Edition

Issued under the auspices of the
Royal Institute of International Affairs

OXFORD UNIVERSITY PRESS
LONDON   KUALA LUMPUR   HONG KONG

Oxford University Press, Ely House, London W. 1

GLASGOW NEW YORK TORONTO MELBOURNE WELLINGTON
CAPE TOWN SALISBURY IBADAN NAIROBI LUSAKA ADDIS ABABA
BOMBAY CALCUTTA MADRAS KARACHI LAHORE DACCA
KUALA LUMPUR HONG KONG

First published 1951
Second edition 1965
Reprinted 1966

PRINTED IN GREAT BRITAIN
BY R. & R. CLARK, LTD., EDINBURGH

PREFACE

THIS work was first published in 1951, was reprinted in 1952, and has since been out of print.

On accepting an invitation from Chatham House to prepare a revised edition I was faced with the task of bringing the book up to date while retaining material likely to be of continued interest to the student and general reader. Much has happened to the Overseas Chinese in the interval between the two editions and much has been written about them. New demographical material has been included throughout, though some old tables have been retained because of their historical interest. I have written a completely new Introduction and Conclusion to meet the changed situation. Into Chapter 4 I have inserted a summary of some of the recent research done in the field, and at the end of each regional study an outline of events from 1949–63 to bring the story as nearly as possible up to date. I have omitted the old appendices except the first (on dialects by R. A. D. Forrest) as being 'marginal', but have included a new one on recent archaeological research by Alastair Lamb.

I have pruned the original Bibliography and have included a selection of works in Western languages which have appeared since 1951, and have added an entirely new Bibliography of selected works in Chinese and Japanese, which is the work of Mr Hugh D. R. Baker.

To Professor Raymond Firth, Mr B. R. Pearn, and Mr O. W. Wolters I am indebted for commenting on the manuscript in considerable detail and I have endeavoured to profit by their knowledge and advice though, of course, for the text as it stands I accept full responsibility. I am grateful to Dr Alastair Lamb for providing Appendix II, to Mr Baker for his work, and to Messrs J. H. Macdonald, Giok Po Oey, T. E. Smith, Francis J. Tatu, R. E. H. Waring, and R. W. Whitney for providing me with valuable information of several kinds. One of the maps at the end of the book is reproduced by the kind permission of Professor Charles A. Fisher and the Royal Geographical Society. The editing of the manuscript was undertaken first by Miss Katharine Duff and then by Miss Hermia Oliver, whose minute care and experienced advice have saved the book from many errors and infelicities. To both I offer my best thanks. Finally, I must acknowledge my indebtedness to Mr A. S. B. Olver for his great assistance through the years and for his tactful handling of the controversies that have occasionally arisen between my advisers and myself.

Cambridge, 1964   V. P.

CONTENTS

PART IV

THE CHINESE IN VIETNAM (NORTH AND SOUTH), CAMBODIA, AND LAOS

PART V

THE CHINESE IN MALAYA AND SINGAPORE

PART VI

THE CHINESE IN BRITISH BORNEO

PART VII

THE CHINESE IN INDONESIA

PART VIII

THE CHINESE IN THE PHILIPPINES

ABBREVIATIONS AND NOTES

BEFEO   = *Bulletin de l'École Française d'Extrême Orient* (Hanoi)
FEQ   = *Far Eastern Quarterly*
JASB   = *Journal of the Asiatic Society of Bengal*
JBRS   = *Journal of the Burma Research Society*
JRASSB = *Journal of the Royal Asiatic Society, Straits Branch*
JRASMB = *Journal of the Royal Asiatic Society, Malayan Branch*
JRASNCB = *Journal of the Royal Asiatic Society, North China Branch*
JRGS   = *Journal of the Royal Geographical Society*
KMT   = Kuomintang

CURRENCY[1]

The Spanish dollar varied in value, according to the price of silver, between 3*s*. 6*d*. and 4*s*. 6*d*. 4*s*. can be taken as the mean.

The Burmese currency is now the kyat (formerly the Burma rupee) = 1*s*. 6*d*.

In 1906 the Straits Settlements dollar was fixed at 2*s*. 4*d*. It was later replaced by the Malayan dollar with the same value, but the sign SS$ was still sometimes used for convenience. M$ is now usual.

At parity there are 11 Siamese bahts (ticals) to the pound sterling.

The official parity of the South Vietnam piastre was fixed at 35 to the US$ on 1 January 1960.

The official rate of exchange for the guilder (Indonesia) was 10·691 guilders = £1 sterling before independence. The Indonesian currency is now the rupiah (£1 = Rp 126·45 (1959)).

The peso (Philippines) = 50 U.S. cents.

WEIGHTS

    1 picul = 133⅓ lb.[1]
    1 catty (kati) = 1⅓ lb.
    1 tahil (tael) = 1⅓ oz.

MEASURES

    1 hectare = 2·471 acres.
    1 mow = ⅙ of an acre.
    1 orlong = c. ⅔ of an acre.

[1] But see the *Statesman's Year-Book* for up-to-date information regarding currency, weights and measures.

INTRODUCTION

THE Overseas Chinese in Southeast Asia, during their history covering some 600 years, have passed through a number of distinct phases. The first was when these countries were still ruled by their native princes and the Chinese settlements were small—often 'ghettoes' in the principal towns, though occasionally (as in Palembang in the fifteenth century) isolated groups of Chinese were able to maintain a local independence. The second phase was when the European powers had established their colonies, and the improved trade opportunities as well as the protection provided encouraged them to immigrate into them in larger numbers. But it was only in the great period of European colonial expansion in the last quarter of the nineteenth century and onwards, when this immigration increased to a flood to meet the demand for manpower created by the 'opening up' process, that the third phase was inaugurated. The Overseas Chinese, who originally had been exclusively males, now brought their womenfolk with them from China in increasing numbers, with the result that Chinese assimilation into the local communities, when such was taking place, was now slowed down or stopped, and the immigrants formed a completely separated community on their own.

It was in the latter phase, especially during the first three decades of the twentieth century, that the spirit of Chinese nationalism began to develop among the Overseas Chinese, stimulating in opposition to itself the growth of local nationalisms. The battle between the 'reformists' and the 'revolutionaries' was fought out in the newly-born Overseas Chinese press in the years before the Revolution of 1911. Later on, the rise to power of the Kuomintang was signalized by the expression of an aggressive nationalism whose virtual claim was 'where there are Chinese, there is China', and the attempts of the KMT to form an *imperium in imperio* in each of the Southeast Asian countries not only provoked the Colonial Governments to repressive action but also aroused the abiding resentments of the indigenous peoples among whom the Chinese were living. Another complicating factor was the growth of Communism in China and its extension to the Overseas Chinese. Nevertheless the Colonial Governments remained in firm control of the situation up to the outbreak of the war with Japan at the end of 1941.

The next phase was the Japanese occupation of Southeast Asia from 1941–5, when the Overseas Chinese were very much on the defensive, and the only overt expression of their resistance to the conqueror was the Communist guerrillas in the Malayan jungle. But those guerrillas were intent not so much on fighting the Japanese as on preserving their strength for the struggle with European 'imperialism', if, and when, the Europeans were able to resume control of their colonies or protectorates.

The period after the Japanese surrender in 1945 was one in which the KMT attempted to reimpose their control over the whole of China, and the Colonial Powers reimposed—or attempted to reimpose—their authority over their liberated possessions. The Overseas Chinese at this period were submitted to violent stresses and strains. They were split by the hostility between the KMT and the Communists, and during the struggle for independence between the several nationalisms and the Colonial Governments (as in Indonesia) they often found themselves ground between the upper and nether millstones.

The simultaneous relinquishment of control of their dependencies by the Colonial Powers and the triumph of Communism in China were the two forces exerting the greatest influence on the fortunes of the Overseas Chinese, and they are the outstanding features of their history since the first edition of this work appeared. We must therefore examine the changes in some detail.

Before the Second World War the Chinese minorities in the British, Dutch, French, or American territories were dependent on the Metropolitan Power for their protection and were to a large extent utilized by it as middlemen between the Government and the native population. The rise of nationalism and the attainment of independence by these 'colonies' meant that the Chinese no longer had the 'Metropolitan Power' to protect them and were exposed to the fears and resentments of the new local nationalisms. (This was particularly the case in Indonesia, where the Chinese found themselves sandwiched in between the two belligerents, the Dutch and the insurgent nationalists.) Before the war, the Colonial Powers, with some intermissions due to 'slumps', encouraged the immigration of Chinese in large numbers, but the newly independent countries of Southeast Asia now closed their doors and all alien immigration was very strictly controlled. Moreover, the remittance of money by Overseas Chinese to China for the support of their families was also submitted to control and reduction. Southeast Asia had ceased to be an El Dorado for enterprising Chinese emigrants or a refuge for the needy.

On its rise to power from 1927 onwards the Nationalist Government of China had declared itself the protector of the Overseas Chinese, and had established consulates throughout Southeast Asia with the consent of the Colonial Governments who recognized it. The overseas policy of the KMT (as we shall see later on) was based on the principle of 'nationalism', and the nationality law of the Chinese Republic regarded all persons of Chinese race as its citizens whatever other national status they might possess. This policy inevitably led to friction with the Colonial Governments, and although the influence of the KMT among the Overseas Chinese was at this time very considerable, China was not yet strong enough to enforce its will on the Powers, whose military resources were so vastly greater than its own. Thus it was that KMT protection of Overseas Chinese nationals was more effective in arousing resentment against the Nationalist Government for attempting to create an *imperium in imperio* in the several Southeast Asian countries than in 'protecting' and establishing privileges for the Overseas Chinese.

The creation of the People's Republic in China in 1949 signalized the return of China to 'Great Power' status, since the new China was now united as it had never been since the Ch'ing dynasty and had well-trained and well-disciplined armies which were able to challenge the United Nations forces when war broke out in Korea. The People's China, however, still lacked a navy of any importance and its air power, while sufficient perhaps for defence, was still quite inadequate for any adventures far afield. Therefore it was mainly by reason of its prestige that the People's China could claim to be 'protector' of its overseas brethren.

Although the hard core of KMT supporters were dismayed by the Communist victory in China and remained hostile to the People's Government, and most of the Overseas Chinese were apprehensive of its consequences, a large number of them were undoubtedly pleased when their ancestral country once more promised to be a 'Great Power'. The Chinese in Malaya, being mainly of recent immigrant origin, were particularly affected by the Revolution since many had relatives living in China towards whose support they contributed. But as time went on a number of factors contributed to modify or diminish the earlier satisfaction.

Article 98 of the Chinese constitution states: 'The People's Republic of China protects the proper rights and interests of Chinese resident abroad'.

To deal with Overseas Chinese affairs the People's Government created machinery of somewhat bewildering complexity. As in other Chinese Government undertakings, there was a 'duality' with a 'government' and a 'party' organization working side by side—often with almost identical personnel and similar responsibilities. The Overseas Chinese Affairs Commission (OCAC) was certainly the primary authority, but it seems to have been paralleled by a shadowy body, the Overseas Work Committee of the Central Committee. The OCAC had the rank of a full ministry in the People's Government. There was also the United Front Department of the Central Committee of the CCP charged with political work among the Overseas Chinese.

To understand how the People's Government interpreted Article 98 we shall have to take note of a curious anomaly. The People's China was a Communist State and as such recognized the equality of all races politically and economically. Thus, by its constitution, the People's China was 'a unified, multi-national State'. 'All the nationalities', the constitution went on, 'are equal.' From this it followed that no special superiority or privileges could be claimed by the 'Han' Chinese (Sun Yat-sen's 'single pure race'), and if it was to be consistent the People's Government had to apply the same principle overseas. Consequently in its appeals to the new nationalities of Southeast Asia, Chinese official propaganda never insisted on the special rights of the Chinese minorities as against those of the remainder of the population but stressed the unity and solidarity of 'the People' of the country in question as against the foreign 'imperialists' or the forces of 'neo-colonialism'. Hence, the Communist insurrection in Malaya (1948–60) was always referred to on Peking Radio as a struggle of the Malayan 'People' against imperialism and capitalism, although in point of fact 99 per cent of the guerrillas in the jungle were Chinese.

However effective this Communist theory of the unity of the many nationalities and the identity of their interest might be in securing sympathy for the People's China, it was obviously unsuited as a rallying cry for the Overseas Chinese. For the fact was that the Overseas Chinese were very often industrialists, merchants, traders, mine-owners, &c, and, when labourers, were employed by capitalist undertakings. They operated, in short, within a capitalistic framework. Moreover, many of the laws passed against the Chinese in Indonesia, Thailand, Vietnam, &c, were passed, not against them as a race or community, but as 'capitalists', 'monopolists', even when the majority of them were only petty traders, or to exclude them as 'aliens' from minor occupations reserved for 'nationals' (as in Thailand and the Philippines). Thus the People's Government, even when it had diplomatic representation in the country concerned (and it was not yet recognized by Thailand, South Vietnam, Malaya, and the Philippines), submitted to local anti-Chinese measures which could be represented as 'anti-capitalistic'.

Where, however, the number of Chinese discriminated against by local legislation was so great that the People's China could not ignore it, it was placed in a difficult position. This was the case when, in the late 1950s, the operation of the nationality laws in Indonesia and of the nationality treaty between China and Indonesia deprived some hundreds of thousands of Chinese in that country of their livelihood owing to the operation of laws forbidding 'aliens' to carry on trade in country districts and small towns, and the People's Government felt compelled to intervene. Nevertheless, it accepted the Indonesian Government's explanation that the laws in question were intended to restrict the anti-social operation of private enterprise and not as discrimination against Chinese as such, and instead of demanding that the offending legislation should be rescinded, undertook to repatriate the persons without livelihood to China (even though, in some cases, their ancestors had left China a hundred years or more previously).

The People's China thus made it plain that it valued the good will of the newly independent Southeast Asian States more than the solidarity and protection of the Overseas Chinese. It was thus successful in obtaining 'treaties of amity and non-aggression' both with Indonesia and Burma, though Thailand and the Philippines, as members of SEATO, remained impervious to this approach.

But of even greater potential importance than the adherence of the People's China to Communist economic theory was the line which it adopted over the dual-nationality question. The Communists were perfectly aware of the friction and resentments created in Southeast Asian countries by the KMT policy, and decided on an entirely new approach to the question of dual citizenship, and in the new regulations regarding Overseas Chinese remittances and investments. The new approach to dual citizenship was a feature of the Asian-African Conference at Bandung in 1955.

In September 1954 Mr Chou En-lai, the Chinese Premier, expressed the readiness of his Government to solve the question of the nationality of 'some 12 million Chinese' residing outside the country by mutual negotiations with the Governments concerned. The one country which showed an interest in the proposal was Indonesia. Discussions between China and Indonesia began in Peking in November 1954 and were concluded in the last week of December. Finally the treaty was signed on 22 April 1955 between Mr Sunario, the Indonesian Foreign Minister, and Mr Chou En-lai, in the middle of the Asian-African (or Afro-Asian) Conference.

The main provisions of the treaty were these. All persons who held simultaneously the nationalities of the People's Republic of China and the Republic of Indonesia must choose between the two nationalities within a period of two years. The wives of those holding dual nationality should choose their own nationality. In the case of those who failed to choose within two years, if their fathers were of Chinese origin they should be deemed to have chosen Chinese nationality, and *mutatis mutandis* for Indonesians.

Article XI was of key importance:

With a view to improving the conditions under which citizens of one country reside in the other, each of the high contracting parties agrees to encourage its own citizens residing in the other country to respect the laws and social customs of the country in which they reside and not to take part in political activities in that country. . . .

Owing, however, to delay on the part of Indonesia, arising from its internal difficulties over the citizenship question and with its Chinese minority (which have been referred to already), this treaty was not ratified for five years. The repercussions of its application are dealt with in due place (see Chapter 49). But the principle incorporated in the treaty that the signatories should encourage their nationals residing in the other country 'not to take part in political activities in that country' was a signal departure in the attitude of China towards the Overseas Chinese. If the principle could be implemented and extended to the other countries of Southeast Asia it promised to end the long-standing friction and to do something to allay the fears of 'Chinese expansion'.[1]

It was this fear of 'Chinese expansion' which dominated the international scene in Southeast Asia in the 1950s and 1960s, though the fear was shared by the potential victims of this expansion in very varying degrees. While naturally conscious of the presence of a powerful neighbour, the Burmese relied on their neutrality to keep them secure; the Indonesians were aware, it seemed, only of the Chinese grip on the local retail business and not of any contemplated descent *en masse* into Indonesia; while the Thais regarded the threat in all seriousness and formed their international alliances accordingly, the Filipinos did likewise (though not with the same sense of urgency), and the Malays of the Federation favoured the creation of Malaysia to offset the concentration of Chinese Communist activity in Singapore with secret extensions to the mainland and to 'British' Borneo.

The above outline indicates some of the main preoccupations of Southeast Asia with the question of China and the Overseas Chinese in the 1960s. In our Conclusion we shall be called upon to assess the policy of the People's China towards Southeast Asia and the likelihood that it will attempt to restore the traditional imperial 'suzerainty' over the region and whether the pressure of internal population will lead to a mass overspilling into the region. We shall also discuss the prospects of assimilation. But before we are in a position to do this we must review the history of the Overseas Chinese from the beginning, taking account of them both in the aggregate and country by country, since the record of the past is written indelibly into the happenings of the present.

[1] At a meeting with Mr David Marshall, former Singapore Chief Minister, in October 1956 in Peking, Mr Chou En-lai reiterated his belief that Chinese living in Singapore should, if they wished, be able to surrender their nationality and assume Singapore citizenship when the country became independent. He also made these points:

1. Any Chinese residing in Singapore who voluntarily adopted Singapore citizenship would immediately cease to have Chinese citizenship, although his racial and cultural affinity would remain.

2. Chinese acquiring Singapore citizenship might, if they wished, later adopt Chinese citizenship in accordance with the laws of Singapore.

3. While Chinese citizens living in Singapore should respect the local laws and refrain from taking part in political activities, their proper rights and interests should be safeguarded against any discrimination (*Manchester Guardian*, 13 Oct. 1956).

PART I

THE AREA AS A WHOLE

I

THE DISTRIBUTION OF THE CHINESE
IN SOUTHEAST ASIA

IN compiling the figures of the distribution of ethnic Chinese in South-east Asia in 1960, the writer adopted the same interpretation of 'ethnic' as he had in compiling the figures for 1947, namely as a term to describe those persons who regarded themselves as being Chinese irrespective of national status or of ability to speak the Chinese language. This seem-ingly was the test applied by the Census authorities in enumerating Chinese in the Federation of Malaya (1957), Singapore (1957), Sarawak (1960), North Borneo (1960), and Brunei (1960). In some of the other countries (e.g. Thailand (1960) and Cambodia (1950)) Chinese 'nationals' had been separately enumerated, but this did not cover those of Chinese race or custom who were nationals of their country of residence. In Burma, Laos, and Vietnam (now divided into North and South) there had been no recent censuses and the writer was thrown back on estimates —sometimes of the most unsatisfactory kind.

When this new edition was nearly ready for press, the Provincial Reports of the Philiphines for 1960 were becoming available. In these returns the people resident in the Philippines were enumerated accord-ing to their 'citizenship' ('A person's citizenship depends on the country to which he owes allegiance') and 'mother tongue' ('the language spoken in the person's home in childhood'). (At the time of going to press the provisional totals for the Philippines as a whole were available for Chinese 'citizens', but not for all persons who had Chinese for their mother tongue. The details are set out in Chapter 50.)

The special significance of the returns for the Philippines is that they revealed for certain that a much greater number of persons claimed to be Chinese nationals than spoke Chinese as their mother tongue. This was no doubt true also for Malaya, Indonesia, and elsewhere, although no figures were available for these countries. This curious phenomenon might be used as an argument against the assimilability of the Overseas Chinese and is discussed in the Conclusion to this work.

For Burma the returns of the 1941 Census (excepting the gross totals) were lost during the Japanese invasion. For Burma, North and South Vietnam, and for Laos the writer had to adopt estimates, and it was in relation to these countries that the greatest chance of error existed. For Thailand and Indonesia he had again to adopt estimates, but in the case of these countries he could at least profit from the work of specialists who had gone as carefully into the matter as the available information permitted. For Cambodia a census was in progress at the time when this edition was being prepared, but the returns were not available in time for incorporation. An estimate had therefore to be adopted. (Should, however, any 'stop-press' returns come to hand they will be included in a note.)

In estimating what the totals of ethnic Chinese were likely to be on the basis of figures acceptable for an earlier period, the writer had to attempt to ascertain the probable annual rate of increase of Chinese in the region. To help him do this he consulted a demographer with considerable experience in the field of Southeast Asia, namely Mr T. E. Smith, late of the Malayan Civil Service, now Secretary of the Institute of Commonwealth Studies of the University of London, who very kindly provided him with some valuable material. In reply to an inquiry by the writer, Mr Smith wrote:

If you are considering the South-East Asian region as a whole, I think that the annual rate of increase of the Chinese population in the region during the decade 1950–60 would be about 3 per cent per annum. As regards the Federation of Malaya and Singapore, (which need to be considered together in view of the amount of undocumented movement between them) the growth rate for the decade (after correction of census figures) was over 3 per cent. (See the UN *Economic Bulletin for Asia and the Far East*, Vol. xiii, no. 2, September 1962, for an evaluation of population data of Malaya and Singapore.) In Sarawak and North Borneo the growth rates between censuses were 3·5 and 3·7 per cent per annum respectively. All these figures relate to Chinese population only.

The rate of growth of the Chinese population of Indonesia was probably somewhat lower than 3 per cent per annum during the decade if the movement (admittedly on a fairly small scale) of Chinese from Indonesia back to China is taken into account. I have not, however, as yet seen separate Chinese figures from the recent Indonesian census.[1]

Assuming the 1947 estimate of the numbers of ethnic Chinese at 8,500,000 to have been correct, and disregarding migration (which, except from Indonesia to China after 1960, was comparatively small as compared with the pre-war period), at an annual rate of increase at 2½ per

[1] A 'preliminary census' is understood to have been held in 1961, but no detailed figures are yet to hand (V.P.).

cent their number would be 11,717,000 in 1960, and at 3 per cent the figure would be 12,500,000. The figure actually adopted in the table below is 11,300,000.[2]

Commenting on the Census reports for Southeast Asian countries, Mr Smith, in a letter to the writer, says: 'There are, of course, always small differences according to whether visitors temporarily resident in a country are included or excluded and I would suggest that any figure you quote should be to the nearest 10,000.' I had this in mind in drawing up my table, but I have thought it appropriate to quote the precise Census figure when such was available for 1960.

Ethnic Chinese in Southeast Asia
(*Census figures in ordinary type; estimates in italics*)

	Chinese		Total Population	Chinese	Total Population
	1931 or circa	*1947*	*1947*	*1960*	*1960*
Burma	194,000	*300,000*	*17,000,000*	*350,000*	20,662,000
Siam (Thailand)	445,000 (1929)	*2,500,000*	*17,359,000*	*2,670,000*	26,257,916
N. Vietnam				55,000	15,916,955
S. Vietnam	418,000	*850,000*	*27,000,000*	800,000	14,214,000
Cambodia		(French Indochina)		*350,000*	*5,347,000*
Laos				*35,000*	*1,805,000*
Federation of Malaya	1,704,000	2,615,000	5,849,000	2,552,276	6,909,009
Singapore		(Malaya)		1,230,700	*1,634,000*
Sarawak				236,473	744,529
North Borneo	..	*220,000*	*878,000*	104,542	454,421
Brunei				21,745	83,877
Indonesia	1,233,000 (1930)	*1,900,000*	*69,000,000*	*2,690,000*	93,506,000
Portuguese Timor				*5,000*	517,079
Philippines	72,000 (1933)	*120,000*	*19,511,000*	181,626	27,087,685
	1947 Total Ethnic Chinese		*8,505,000*	1960 Total Ethnic Chinese	*11,282,362*
	Total (all races)		*156,597,000*	Total (all races)	*215,139,471*

---

[2] How widely the estimates of the number of Chinese in Southeast Asia vary can be gathered from the following references:

Burma, 320,000 (*New York Times*, 29 Nov. 1959); 350,000 ('A Guide to Overseas Chinese', *The Times*, 8 May 1956); 750,000 (*Japan Times*, 5 Nov. 1957).

North Vietnam, 50,000 (*New York Times*, 14 May 1961); 100,000 ('A Guide to Overseas Chinese', *The Times*, 8 May 1956); 30,000 (*Statesman's Year-Book, 1961*).

Laos, 15,000 (*The Times*, 28 Sept. 1956); 40,000 (*Bulletin statistique de Laos, 1958*).

Thailand, 3,690,000 (*Free China Information*, 14 Feb. 1957); 3 million (*Christian Science Monitor*, 3 June 1957); 2,315,000 (Skinner, 1955 (see p. 82)).

Philippines, 300,000 (Reuter's Correspondent to *Japan Times*, 13 Jan. 1961); 200,000 (*The Times*, 28 Sept. 1956); 130,000 (*Philippines Economic Handbook, 1960*).

There are equally variant estimates for Indonesian Chinese.

In Southeast Asia in the mid-twentieth century the Chinese were scattered through the countries in which they lived, in large towns, villages, peasant farms, plantations, and mining communities. Sometimes they had come to an area already well populated and developed; sometimes they had opened up an almost uninhabited region. Java, perhaps the most densely populated area in the world, had in 1947 at least three-quarters of a million Chinese, if not considerably more; the coast-lands of Western Borneo, almost uninhabited before Chinese immigration, were also the site of a large Chinese immigrant community. Burma and Siam exhibited similar contrasts within themselves: between the densely settled delta of the Irrawaddy and the almost uninhabited Northern Shan States (where the Bawdwin mines were located), the two focuses of Chinese settlement in Burma; in Siam, between the thickly populated Menam delta and the Isthmus of Kra, almost empty until the advent of the Chinese.[3] In central Siam the Chinese lived closely associated with the Siamese people by whom, until recent decades, they were completely absorbed within a few generations. In Siam about half the Chinese lived in the lower delta of the Menam, in the neighbourhood of Bangkok; the remainder of the race were scattered through the country, living in villages and towns rather than rural communities and tending to concentrate in the more commercialized districts. A notable concentration of Chinese, consisting of the more recent immigrants, was to the southwest of Siam, where they worked in the mines, on the rubber plantations, and as merchants in the villages.

Apart from the concentration in the Kra Isthmus region, the chief occupations of the Chinese in Siam were the various forms of retail and wholesale trade. The Chinese, in fact, controlled most of the retail trade in the country. In particular they had the lion's share in rice distribution and milling, and there was scarcely a commodity from pepper to sugar in which they were not interested as middlemen. They also made up a large part of the class of skilled craftsmen.

Most of the Chinese in Siam originally came from Hainan, Mei Hsien, and Chao Chou (including the city of Swatow) in east Kwangtung. The last-named group was apparently in the majority, especially those from Chin Hai, Yao P'ing, Chi Yang, and Chao An.

In Malaya the Chinese had a special significance in that they were here the majority community and had been so since before 1941. In that year there were for the whole of Malaya 2,379,000 Chinese as compared with 2,279,000 Malays, though, excluding Singapore, which was virtually a Chinese city, the Malays still outnumbered them. By 1947 they had still further strengthened their position so that they accounted for 2,615,000 of the population, whereas the Malays were now 2,544,000. This outnumbering of the native population (though the Malays themselves have

[3] Leonard Unger, 'The Chinese in Southeast Asia', *Geographical R.*, xxxiv/2 (1944).

multiplied their numbers several-fold within the last few decades by natural increase and by the reinforcement of Indonesians, mostly Javanese) had given rise to one of the most perplexing political problems in the Far East.

Malaya's Chinese were largely urban and were occupied in trade, but they also supplied the bulk of the labour in the tin mines of which they owned about one-third. There was a large Chinese labour force on the rubber estates where, however, before the war with Japan, they were out-numbered by the Indians. In addition to these occupations, the Malayan Chinese were actively engaged in every branch of the trades and crafts, from agriculture (squatters) and pig keeping and poultry rearing (which they almost monopolized) to the building and skilled artisan trades, tailoring, dressmaking, and cobbling, and managing or working in oil mills, soap factories, shipping firms, sawmills, and many other undertakings. The pineapple industry was entirely a Chinese enter-prise.

Most numerous of the Chinese tribes in Malaya were the Hokkiens, after them came the Cantonese, followed by the Hakkas (Khehs), Teochius, and Hailams (Hainanese), and in much smaller numbers by the Kwongsai, Hokchius, Hokchias, and others. The Hokkiens, being the pioneer community in Malaya and the principal merchants, were more numerous in the Settlements of Singapore, Penang, and Malacca, and the Cantonese more numerous in the remainder of the country.

In Java the Chinese lived throughout the island, usually in cities and towns rather than in the rural areas, and they were the middle-class merchants who controlled much of the wholesale and retail trade. Commerce and transport occupied 61 per cent of the Chinese in Java in 1930: sugar processing, food industries, and timber were next among their occupations. In Batavia the Chinese formed 15 per cent of the total population.

The people of south Fukien were among the earliest immigrants to Indonesia, especially Java. Some of the families had been there for almost two centuries (the founder of the Tsai (Tsoa) house landed in Java five generations ago, in 1753).[4] The Hakkas and the people from Chao Chou (including the city of Swatow), the Teochius, and from southern Kwangtung, followed the Hokkiens. The Hakkas began to settle in West Borneo between 1740 and 1745, and were followed thither by Teochius. At first they were employed in gold-mining or were agri-culturists, engaged in cultivation of rubber, pepper, and tobacco; but towards the end of the nineteenth century, when both plantations and mines grew up under European management, the Teochius and many Hakkas moved on to colonize Bangka, Billiton, and east Sumatra.

The Chinese of Indonesia, especially those of Java, had a much more

[4] Ta Chen, *Emigrant Communities in South China* (1940), p. 266.

noticeable admixture of native blood than had the Chinese of the other Southeast Asian countries.[5]

Chinese immigration into Indochina was directed principally towards Cochinchina and Cambodia and comparatively little towards Annam and Tongking which were already thickly populated, or towards Laos which was hard of access and little developed. In Cochinchina and Cambodia,

The Hakkas often inhabit the same areas as the Cantonese, Hokkien, and other tribes.
The following authorities, among others, have been followed: (1) Linguistic Map of China, *Geographical J.* cii/2 (August 1943), p. 5; (2) Ta Chen, *Emigrant Communities*, p. 23; (3) W. J. Cator, *The Economic Position of the Chinese in the Netherlands Indies* (1936), p. 28 (map).

however, the Chinese pervaded every phase of economic life. The largest concentration of them was in the city-continuum of Saigon-Cholon. In these countries they had a virtual monopoly of the rice trade, just as they had in Siam (though attempts had been made to limit their share of the trade in both countries, especially in Siam). They were also engaged in pepper planting and vegetable gardening, but had taken practically no part in the newer estate agriculture of rubber, cotton, tea, and palm oil —indeed as aliens they were barred from the lands most suitable for this purpose.

[5] When attending a meeting of the Chung Hua Hui at Leyden in 1946, at which a hundred or so Indonesian Chinese resident in the Netherlands were present, the writer was struck with the dark complexion so common among them which was in marked contrast with the lighter complexion of the Chinese of most of Malaya, except parts of Penang and Malacca.

As in other countries of the area, the trade depression of 1929–32 had a greatly restricting effect on immigration to Indochina, but in the few years before the Pacific War this was recovering.

It has been convenient to summarize the distribution and occupation of the overseas Chinese country by country, but it should be remarked that this distribution was always dictated by economic considerations, as, for example, the belt of mining activity which extends from Burma round about Moulmein to the southward along the west coast of the Malay Peninsula through Siam and Malaya and then crops up again in the Indonesian islands of Bangka and Billiton, among the bauxite deposits of the Rhio Archipelago off Singapore, and finally among the oil wells of Palembang in Sumatra.

The Chinese of the Philippines formed a group somewhat isolated from the main body, so to speak. They had traded with and emigrated to these islands for some centuries and they persevered in their intercourse in spite of the intermittent severity and grudging tolerance of the Spanish. When, however, in 1898 the Americans assumed control of the islands, they extended to them the exclusion laws against Chinese immigration which were already in force in the United States. When the Filipinos took over the administration of their own country the term 'exclusion' (which had been subject at least to some liberal exceptions under the Americans) was more and more literally interpreted. But although their numbers were at present not very great in comparison with the Filipinos, the economic position of the Chinese in the Philippines based, as ever, on their control of trade (they owned, before 1941 at least, three-quarters of the rice-mills), had been maintained in the face of determined attempts by Filipino nationalists to oust them from it.

So much will serve as a general introductory survey of the distribution of the Chinese in Southeast Asia: in the first chapter of each country study contained in the successive parts of this survey, the subject will be dealt with in much greater detail.

The sketch-map of the principal places of origin in China of the Chinese in Southeast Asia, reproduced on p. 6, has been designed by the author and executed by Regmarad, and is subject to the following considerations. The shading indicates roughly the distribution in China of the several tribes represented overseas, but in the case of the Hakkas, of whom small communities are to be found throughout Kwangtung intermingled with the Cantonese,[6] only the areas most densely populated by them are shown in the map. Nor must it be assumed that the overseas Chinese come equally from all over the shaded areas.

[6] See L. Richard, *Comprehensive Geography of the Chinese Empire and Dependencies* (Shanghai, 1908), p. 207.

2

EARLY CHINESE CONTACTS WITH
SOUTHEAST ASIA[1]

CHINA's intercourse overland with the countries on its southern border is of a much greater order of antiquity than its contacts by sea. Its soldiers were in Tongking and Annam in the third century B.C.; thereafter they penetrated to Cambodia, then to Siam, the last-named being reached by sea. Here there was a halt for a considerable time before its navigators went on to Malaya, Sumatra, and Java. The process took many centuries, and for long intervals there is a complete lack of information regarding the Southeast Asian countries.[2] Merchants from the West passed across Central Asia into China in the Han and later dynasties by routes that skirted the northern and southern slopes of the Tarim river basin, but they also came into the empire by way of the south, up the rivers of what is now Burma and across the hills into the present Yunnan, and by the longer sea route to the south coast. As early as the second century B.C. there appear to have been Chinese trade routes through Yunnan to the Irrawaddy and Salween valleys. For a time the main port in the south was in the future Tongking, and it was not until later centuries that it was supplanted by Canton. It was to Loyang that in A.D. 166 came an embassy of Westerners claiming to be sent by their King, who is supposed to have been the Roman Emperor Marcus Aurelius Antoninus (An-tun).[3]

Our earliest and surest information is of the Chinese intercourse with the countries sharing a land frontier with China on the southwest, and first of all in point of time comes Annam.

During the Han dynasty there existed a kingdom known as Nan-Yüeh (Nam-Viet) which extended from the region of Canton far into the

---

[1] The existing state of knowledge and theory regarding early Chinese contacts with Southeast Asia is set out in Paul Wheatley, *The Golden Khersonese* (1961). See also App. II of the present work.

[2] This seems to be true as a generalization, though the *Han Shu*, vol. xxviii, speaks of voyages in the Han dynasty to Jihnan and Hsüwenhopu taking five months, to Touyüankuo taking four months, and to Ilumeikuo taking about twenty days. See Feng Ch'eng-chün, *Nan Yang Chiao T'ung Shih* (History of Chinese Relations with the Nanyang) (Shanghai, 1937), p. 1.

[3] See K. S. Latourette, *The Chinese: their History and Culture*, 3rd ed. (N.Y., 1946), p. 123. Among the recent finds at Go Oc Eo was a gold medal bearing an image of Antoninus Pius with a date which corresponds to A.D. 152, showing that at an early date Funan (the ancient State in southern Annam) had connexions, direct or indirect, with the western Mediterranean See G. Coedès, *Les États hindouisés d'Indochine et d'Indonésie* (Paris, 1948), pp. 38–39, 89).

Indochinese peninsula to the present central Annam.[4] In 111 B.C. this kingdom was conquered by the Chinese and was divided into nine districts, one of which, Chiuchen (Annamese Cu'uchan), corresponds roughly to the present province of Thanhhoa in northern Annam.[5] It is likely that Chinese suzerainty extended even farther south, though in an indefinite way. However, to date there has been no archaeological evidence of any Chinese settlement of the Han dynasty farther south than a spot immediately below Thanhhoa in the provinces of Nghean and Hatinh.

After the native chief of Chiuchen had yielded to the Chinese without putting up any resistance, he was retained in his position with the title of T'aishou.[6]

The new masters of the southern territory, the 'Sons of Han' as they called themselves, ruled at first with moderation, allowing to the natives a considerable degree of freedom, but about the beginning of the Christian era they adopted a sterner attitude. At least this was so in the case of Tongking where, according to Chinese records, the Emperor Hsi Kuang (A.D. 1–25)[7] 'transformed the people through the rites and by justice', and it is most probable that the Chinese attitude towards the natives of Chiuchen was the same. It was this heavier hand of alien government, aiming at securing the rapid sinicization of the subdued barbarians, which no doubt aroused the spirit of resistance, for in A.D. 40 Cheng-Tse (Tr'ung-Trac in Annamese), the daughter of a native chief of Tongking from Mileng (Annamese, Milinh), stirred up a rebellion which succeeded temporarily in driving out the Chinese, and the native chiefs of Chiuchen joined in the struggle.

In the present state of knowledge it is impossible to establish with precision the dates of the earlier Chinese settlements in Chiuchen, but Professor Janse thinks it very likely that some pioneers ventured to immigrate thither in the third century B.C., and this is the time when the

---

[4] The work of Prof. Olov R. T. Janse, *Archaeological Research in Indo-China* (1947), greatly extends our existing knowledge of the Chinese remains in the region. Professor Janse's historical summary is here followed.

[5] É. Chavannes, trans., *Les Mémoires historiques de Se-Ma T'sien* (Paris, 1895–1905), i. 87 and ii. 168, cited by Janse, p. xvi. And Léonard Aurousseau, 'La Première Conquête des Pays Annamites', *BEFEO*, xxii. 137–264, and xiv. 9, 13 (cited by Janse at same place). Wang Wen-yuan (p. 4), citing Wang Ton-lin, *Histoire du peuple chinois* (in Chinese), and H. Maspero, 'Étude d'histoire d'Annam, III: Commanderie de Siang', *BEFEO*, iii (1918), pp. 11–28, gives a somewhat different account of this early period. He says that in the year 214 B.C. the first Emperor of the Chin dynasty, Shih Huangti, sent 500,000 Chinese—soldiers, peasants, and those condemned to banishment—to take possession of Nam-Viet, 'the land beyond the southern border'. After the conquest the country was divided into three commands, that of Nanhai, corresponding probably to the present province of Kwangtung, that of Kweilin in the present-day Kwangsi, and that of Shiang in Tongking and north Annam. These (says Wang Wen-yuan) marked the foundation of the first important Chinese colony in Indochina.

[6] Maspero, *BEFEO*, xxxvii. 263, 264 n. 5, cited by Janse.

[7] This is the period of the usurpation of Wang Mang (A.D. 9–23). Hsi Kuang does not appear to be historical.

Chinese began to infiltrate into northern Indochina, especially Tongking. In any case there must have been a considerable intercourse between southern China and Thanhhoa at the end of the third or at least at the beginning of the second century B.C. To a certain extent this supposition can be corroborated by archaeology (e.g. from examples in the 'Huai Valley' style).

Professor Janse makes the following interesting observations on the period:[8]

It can be assumed that the first Chinese who ventured into the country and mingled with the natives were journeying merchants or artisans. Even to-day Chinese peddlers are highly regarded among the natives because of their skill in commerce and craftsmanship. As they are generally fairly well-to-do, they are much sought after by the families of the aboriginal chieftains. Thus many of these modern settlers bring with them into Tongking and Northern Annam Chinese crafts and customs. What is happening to-day in this respect has certainly been going on not merely for centuries but for millennia. . . . In the wake of these tradesmen certainly came the civil and military mandarins, accompanied by the less welcome tax-collector, and by political refugees.

At this early time (Henri Maspero points out) the entire territory was covered with marshes and forests in which elephants, rhinoceroses, and tigers abounded and in which the aboriginals lived by hunting and fishing, eating pythons and wild beasts killed by their bone-tipped arrows. To this diet they added small crops from their primitive rice-fields which they prepared by burning down a part of the forest before the rainy season, without cultivating or irrigating the area. Only around the centres of administration, under the influence of the Chinese governors, especially the prefect Jen Yen, had they begun to till the soil in the manner of the Chinese.[9]

Such was the land which the Chinese called the 'Kingdom of the Naked'. It was not until after the victorious campaign of Ma Yuan at the beginning of the Christian era that the Chinese settled on any large scale. Archaeological evidence of this is to be found on the brick tombs of the later Han discovered in Thanhhoa. Among the most fascinating funerary objects unearthed by Dr Janse are models of farm-houses or, in some cases, probably manor-houses, consisting of quadrangular yards surrounded by walls and a variety of buildings. Some are even provided with furniture, such as ovens, troughs, &c. They give an excellent picture of early Chinese settlements in Annam.

It will be convenient here to discontinue the outline of Sino-Annamese contacts and to resume it in the part of this survey dealing with Indochina, turning our attention to the question of the antiquity of Chinese intercourse with Malaysia far away to the south. According to the consensus of opinion, the date of the first Chinese association with these

---

[8] p. xvi.   [9] Maspero, p. 12, cited by Janse, p. xvi.

regions goes back to the third and even fourth centuries B.C. Dr Heine-Geldern in 1934 pointed out the stylistic similarities between some of the prehistoric stone sculptures of the Pasemah region in southern Sumatra and those standing at the tomb of the Chinese general Huo K'iu-ping in Shensi province in China, erected in 117 B.C. This, he says, seemed to indicate more or less intimate contacts with China, to be dated probably in the second and first centuries B.C. A decade later the same authority again referred to his own statement and pointed out that since then Chinese objects of the Han dynasty had actually been found in Indonesia. Moreover, a considerable number of Chinese sepulchral pottery vessels of the Han period had been excavated in Sumatra, Java, and Borneo, and one of them, from Sumatra, bore an inscription dating it 45 B.C.[10] From these finds, De Flines inferred, no doubt correctly, that Chinese colonists or merchants must have lived in Indonesia as early as the Han period. Also from Sumatra comes a bowl engraved with designs of persons in Chinese dresses and of horses in Han style, and other pieces of evidence included a Chinese bronze dagger-axe (*ko*) which was said to have come from Sumatra, and another from Java.

Taking all into account [Dr Heine-Geldern writes] one may come to the conclusion that direct Chinese influence in Indonesia goes back at least to the early Han period, that is at the very latest to the 1st century B.C. However, the ornamental designs of the Dyak tribes of Borneo and of the Ngada of Flores are so clearly related to Chinese designs of the late Chou period that one can hardly avoid the inference that Chinese contacts started as early as the beginning of the third century B.C., and probably earlier.

The investigation of this very early period of intercourse is almost exclusively a monopoly of the archaeologist and of the anthropologist, and what conclusions are to be drawn from the finds must remain a matter of some delicacy to the non-expert in these fields. Nevertheless it is important to note the difference of opinion between some of the schools of thought concerning the degree of Chinese influence on the regions of Southeast Asia. Speaking of the intercourse of a much later period, the second Sung dynasty onwards, Fay Cooper Cole remarks:

These early contacts were primarily for trade and, while they did help to shape the history of Malaysia, they seldom were intimate enough to introduce Chinese methods, such as the potter's wheel; few Chinese words entered the language; and the influence of their political and religious ideas was nil.[11]

To this we may object that Chinese methods of agriculture, at least, through these same contacts had a profound effect on the economy of the Southeast Asian countries. None the less, Hindu influence upon Southeast Asia has been culturally much more important than Chinese, and in

10 R. Heine-Geldern, *Prehistoric Research in the Netherlands Indies* (N.Y., 1945), p. 147. See also his *The Archaeology and Art of Sumatra*.
11 *The Peoples of Malaysia* (N.Y., 1945), p. 27.

the sphere of navigation in the first centuries of the Christian era it was the Arabs, the Indians, and the Persians who made their way to China and the Chinese who, generally speaking, stayed at home. There was a colony of Arabs in Sumatra at a very early date, and they had a counting-house at Canton as early as A.D. 300.[12]

Latourette says that 'Chinese merchants seem not to have ventured very far afield, and to have left chiefly to strangers the initiative in foreign trade, but outsiders found China a profitable country with which to deal'. Lack of enterprise is also attributed to the Chinese by Groeneveldt, the pioneer writer on Chinese intercourse with Southeast Asia, who remarks:

> A careful perusal of the geographical literature of the ancient Chinese has shown that they have not gained their knowledge of Southeastern Asia by bold voyages of discovery: slowly and cautiously they have crept along its shores, probably not venturing to a country before they have become acquainted with it through others.[13]

And Kuwabara (cited by Braddell) says, 'the Chinese trading ships before the T'ang era were inferior in all respects to those of the South Sea countries'. Although it must be conceded that the Chinese were behind the Middle Eastern races in enterprise or curiosity, the remarks of Groeneveldt apply in a measure to all other peoples who have come into Southeast Asia. Were their explorations of the coasts of Borneo (asks Mr Tom Harrisson) any slower or more cautious than those of the Portuguese? On the contrary there is every indication that there was a regular trade on a mass scale for centuries back. Certainly by the fourth and fifth centuries Chinese ships were feeling their way along the coasts and over the seas to meet the Arabs, Persians, and Indians part way.

The reason for Chinese comparative dilatoriness in utilizing the sea routes on their own account may have been their sense of national sufficiency, and the feeling that they had nothing of great value to obtain from the regions of the south, but none the less their influence spread out over the land routes through the agency of the Arab and Indian traders. 'It is clear that at the time when the European barbarians of the north were conquering Rome, a southward movement in the Far East was taking place—the flow of the cultured Chinese into Malay lands, and the spread of Chinese civilization in Malaysia.'[14] At the same time the main colonizing activity was by Indians. Individual Chinese pilgrims and travellers, such as the Buddhist monk, Fa Hsien (or Fa Hien), went overland to India, visited Ceylon by sea, and arrived in what was either Java or Malaya in A.D. 413, and I-tsing, much later, in A.D. 692, reached Lang-

---

[12] Braddell, *JRASMB*, xx/2 (1947), p. 8.
[13] W. P. Groeneveldt, *Notes on the Malay Archipelago and Malacca; Miscellaneous papers relating to the Indian Archipelago* (London, 1887), i. 126–262.
[14] G. Nye Steiger, H. Otley Beyer, and Conrado Benitez, *A History of the Orient* (Boston, 1926), pp. 202 and *passim*.

ya-si, identified as Langkasuka, a kingdom in the Malay peninsula. Fa Hsien found no Chinese in Java or Malaya (whichever it may have been), though his eyes filled with tears, he tells us, at the sight of a Chinese taffeta fan, for he had been away from home for thirteen years.[15]

It is not perhaps remarkable that the Chinese of the fourth, fifth, and sixth centuries left most of the colonizing initiative to others, for, quite apart from their self-sufficiency, these were the Dark Ages of Chinese history when warfare and foreign invasion were almost incessant. Nevertheless, in the first Sung dynasty (A.D. 420–79) missions from these southeastern countries made their appearance in China, and after the Liang dynasty (A.D. 502–57) envoys came from over the sea every year for the purpose of getting an almanac and of acquitting themselves of the duty of tribute in greater number than in any former time.[16]

Reference in Chinese history to countries and places in these territories does not necessarily mean that they were known to the Chinese by direct contact. An early voyage, however, was in A.D. 607 when the Emperor Sui Yang-ti sent a mission by sea to Siam to open up commercial relations with that country.[17] But the sprinkling of references to places, probably in this Southeast Asian area, of obscure identity which may be found in the History of the Liang Dynasty (502–57) is succeeded in the History of the T'ang Dynasty (618–907) by information regarding definite countries which has a much surer feel. For example, we hear (and believe) that between 756 and 779 three envoys of Java arrived in China and that in the year 813 further envoys arrived at the capital with presents of four negro slaves, parrots of different colours, pinka-birds (not identified), and other gay trifles. The Emperor honoured the envoy with the title of Left Defender of the Office of the Four Inner Gates, and when the recipient wanted to waive the title in favour of his younger brother, the Emperor praised him for his unselfishness and bestowed a title on both of them.[18]

We are now definitely in the era of the tribute-bearing missions which soon took on the character of trading expeditions since the Emperor

---

[15] *Fa Hsien Fo Kuo Chi*, the record of Fa Hsien's voyages, has been translated by Samuel Beal as 'An Account of the Buddhist Countries' (1869), by J. Legge (1866), and re-translated by H. A. Giles (1923). Rémusat's French translation is earlier (1836). Giles gives the track of the voyage of Fa Hsien from Ceylon to China as being via the Straits of Sunda, whereas W. A. Grimes (*JRASMB*, xix/1 (February 1941)), a meteorologist, basing his views on a study of the winds near the equator, considers that he went via the Straits of Malacca. This is also the view of Braddell, who thinks that Fa Hsien's *Ye-po-ti* was not Java but Malaya. (*JRASMB*, xix/1 (1947), p. 25.) But see Wheatley, *Golden Khersonese*, pp. 37–41, 108. Wheatley follows A. Grimes in identifying *Ye-po-ti* with north-west Borneo instead of Java as accepted hitherto.

[16] Braddell, *JRASMB*, xix/1 (1941), p. 21.

[17] *Chau* [sic] *Ju-kua* (late Sung Dynasty): *His work on the Chinese and Arab trade in the Twelfth and Thirteenth Centuries*, translated from the Chinese and annotated by Friedrich Hirth and W. W. Rockhill (St Petersburg, 1911), p. 8. The name of the work in Chinese is *Chu Fan Chi*. [18] *T'ang History*, Book 222/2; Groeneveldt, p. 140.

invariably presented to the envoys gifts equal to or greater in value than
those they had brought. The missions were very numerous and a mere
recital of them would not add much to our enlightenment. They had
always, of course, a purely diplomatic appearance, especially those sent on
the accession of a new Emperor or a new dynasty.

Between 1209 and 1214 a book was written by Chao Ju-kua, a member
of the imperial family of the Sung dynasty (960–1280) and superintendent
and commissioner of customs at Ch'üanchowfu, a coast town to the
north of Amoy. This book, based on information gained from merchants
from India, Persia, Syria, and Arabia, gives facts concerning the countries
and peoples of the West, including Spain, and of the Chinese trade with
the Malaysian islands. (Some details from this work are cited both above
and later in this chapter.)

In the History of the Sung Dynasty we have a detailed account of
Java, including the observation: 'Their houses are handsome and are
adorned with yellow and green tiles: when Chinese merchants arrive
they are received as guests in a public building and what they eat and
drink is copious and clean.'[19]

In 1291 Angkor was visited by Marco Polo and the Lady Kutai, whom
the Mongol Emperor of China was sending as a bride for the Khan of
Persia, there to behold the fast-fading glories of the Khmer empire.[20]
Five years later, one Chou Ta-kwan was a member of the Chinese
mission sent to acquaint the King of Cambodia with the accession of
Yüan Cheng, the new Emperor of China and grandson and successor of
Kublai Khan. To this same Chou Ta-kwan we owe a vivid and detailed
account of the Khmer empire.[21] What concerns us here, however, is his
remarks concerning his own countrymen who visited or were resident in
Cambodia. Here are some of them rendered into English from Pelliot's
translation.

The Chinese who follow the sea as a profession take advantage of their being in
this country to dispense with wearing clothes. Rice is easy to obtain, women are
easy to find, the houses are easy to run, personal property is easy to come by,
commerce is easy to engage in. Thus there are constantly those who direct themselves towards this country.

In this country it is the women who are skilful in commerce. Thus a Chinese who
arrives down there and takes a wife profits in addition by her commercial aptitude.

This Chinese chronicler (says Mr Brodrick), with the typical prejudice of his people against frequent washing, wrote that, 'the people are
often ill, owing to their too frequent baths and the incessant wasting of
the heat'.

[19] Book 489; Groeneveldt, p. 141.
[20] A. H. Brodrick, *Little Vehicle* (London, [1949?]), p. 156.
[21] 'Tcheou-Ta-Kouan, Mémoires sur les coutumes de Cambodge' (trans. by Paul Pelliot),
BEFEO, ii/2 (1902).

According to Chou Ta-kwan, the embassy to Cambodia in 1296 was entirely successful and homage was rendered to China, but (says Pelliot) 'peut-être est-il trop intéressé dans l'affaire pour que nous accordions pleine créance à ses dires. En fait il n'y a aucune trace que des relations officielles régulières aient suivi la mission de 1296.'

There is certainly no mention of Cambodia in the History of the Yüan dynasty.

It is first in the Yüan dynasty (A.D. 1280–1368) that action combines with colour to make real the machinations of Chinese imperial politics in these waters. In the year 1292 the Emperor Kublai Khan, no doubt envious of the growing influence of Java in further India and the eastern part of the archipelago, sent an expedition against the Javanese State of Singosari. He ordered the Governor of Fukien to send Shih Pi, Ike Mese, and Hau Hsing to collect from Kiangsi and Kiukiang soldiers to the number of 20,000 who were to be embarked in a thousand ships for the Southern Ocean. Shih Pi sailed with 5,000 men from Ch'üanchow, probably via the Paracel Islands, Macclesfield Bank (to give them their modern names), Annam (Giau-chi), and Champa, encountering bad weather on the way, and in the first moon of the following year they passed the Natuna Islands to a place which was probably Billiton in Java where the fleet stopped to cut timber to make small boats suitable for going up the rivers. An internal feud was in progress between native potentates and in this Shih Pi took sides, routing the army of Daha (Kediri).[22]

But Shih Pi lost 3,000 of his men (largely, it seems, through sickness) and for this he was disgraced and ordered to receive seventeen strokes. But in 1295 he was restored to favour, and he died, high in honours, at the age of eighty-six.

The Ming History records that at this time Java was subdued,[23] but the truth is that the great expedition had failed and no new one was undertaken. The military expeditions of the Mongols had nowhere more than a temporary influence.

The empire of Sri Vijaya, which endured for many centuries, had its capital in Sumatra in the neighbourhood of Palembang. It included the Malay Peninsula under its sway. Eventually it decayed under Chola (Coromandel) raids, the revolt of Melayu (Jambi), and attacks from neighbouring kingdoms. The Sung chronicles have many references to Sri Vijaya's wars. The empire eventually disappeared and was succeeded by Jambi. Jambi in turn (between 1338 and 1365) succumbed to Majapahit, whose seat of government was in Java. Majapahit was war-like and destructive: it sacked ports in Borneo, Surabaya, Ceram,

[22] For an account of the complex politics and strategy of this expedition see E. S. de Klerck, *History of the Netherlands Indies* (Rotterdam, 1938), i. 139–40.

[23] Book 324. It appears from Chinese records and the account of Marco Polo that Tuban, Sedayu, and Tjanggu were at that time prosperous commercial towns (De Klerck, p. 140).

and Lombok, and finally subjected Sri Vijaya's colonies in the Malay Peninsula.[24]

Palembang, near the east coast of Sumatra, fell into Chinese hands on the decay of Sri Vijaya and remained under them for about two hundred years. The Chinese who lived there followed piracy as a calling, using the port as a retreat and strongpoint. This town, then, was one of the earliest places in Southeast Asia where the Chinese settled in any numbers. San-fo-ts'i is a rival for the distinction (if, indeed, it were a Malayan territory distinct from Sri Vijaya), and when it faded in importance about the same time as Sri Vijaya, several thousand Chinese from Fukien and Canton who lived there began to govern themselves. In 1377 they had as their leader a man named Liang Tau-ming from Namhoi in Kwangtung.

Meanwhile, in 1349, Wang Ta-yuan, a Chinese merchant, writes of Tumasik, or Old Singapore.[25] His account gives the very definite impression that here also was a fairly large settlement of Chinese. This is the first colony of Chinese in the Malay Peninsula of which we have any record.

In a later chapter in the history of the Chinese in Malaya we shall discuss the question whether the Chinese formed any permanent settlement in the Malay kingdom of Malacca, which was founded about A.D. 1400 and endured until the Portuguese conquest of 1511. The chances are (we shall decide) that the merchants who visited the place were merely seasonal visitors, coming down from China with one monsoon and going back with the other. But it was in the early years of the Malay kingdom that the Emperors of the Ming dynasty began to send expeditions to the Southern Ocean and beyond on a grand scale.[26]

In 1403, says the Ming History,[27] the Emperor sent the eunuch Yin Ch'ing as envoy to Malacca with presents of silk brocade.[28] But more noteworthy was the visit a few years afterwards by the famous Grand Eunuch, Cheng Ho, later deified as Sam-po-kung.

Altogether Cheng Ho and his colleagues, the Grand Eunuch Wang Chin, and the assistant envoys, the Grand Eunuchs Hung Pao and Yung Chen, together with the Senior Lesser Eunuch Chang Ta, commanding the fleet, made seven voyages, in 1405, 1407, 1409, 1414, 1417, 1421, and 1431 (these being the years in which the expeditions set

[24] See Sir Richard Winstedt, *Malaya and its History* (London, 1948), p. 29 ff. There are maps showing the probable extent of Sri Vijaya and Majapahit accompanying H. Otley Beyer, 'The Philippines before Magellan', *Asia*, xxi (1921).   [25] See p. 235.
[26] In summarizing the Ming voyages the writer has to be much on his guard. The facts and translations of the authorities of last century, particularly Rockhill, have been subjected to the searching scrutiny of Professor Duyvendak, and many errors and slips have been revealed.
[27] J. J. L. Duyvendak, 'The True Dates of the Chinese Maritime Expeditions in the Early Fifteenth Century', *T'oung Pao*, xxxiv (1939).
[28] Ming History, Book 325.

out).[29] The account published by them in 1431 is in their collective name, but it is not clear which of them took part in the several voyages. The following is abstracted from their account as quoted by Professor Duyvendak:

Voyage I

In the third year of Yung Lo (1405), 'commanding the fleet', we went to Ku-li (Calicut) and other countries. At that time the pirate Ch'en Tsu-yi and his followers were assembled at San-fo-ts'i (Palembang) where they plundered the native merchants. We captured the leader alive and returned in the fifth year (1407).

Voyage II

In the fifth year of Yung Lo (1407) ,'commanding the fleet', we went to Kua-Wa (Java), Ku-li (Calicut), Ko-chih (Cochin), and Hsien-lo (Siam). The kings of these countries all presented us as tribute with local products, precious birds, and (rare) animals. We returned in the seventh year (1409).

Voyage III

In the seventh year of Yung Lo (1409), 'commanding the fleet', we went to the countries visited before and took our route by the country of Hsi-lan-shan (Ceylon). Its king Ya-lieh-jo-nai-erh (Alagakkonara) was guilty of a gross lack of respect and plotted against the fleet. Owing to the manifest answer (to prayer) of the divine power (the plot) was discovered and thereupon the king was captured alive. In the ninth year (1411), on our return, he was presented (to the throne as a prisoner). Subsequently he received the imperial favour of returning to his own country.

The fourth voyage (1414) was to Ormuz and other places and the fleet returned in 1415. In that year the king of the country of Man-la-chia (Malacca) came in person with his wife and son to present tribute. On the fifth voyage (1417–19) the envoys visited Ormuz again and also Aden, Mogadisho, Calicut, &c, bringing back zebras, lions, camels, and ostriches. Ormuz figured once more in the sixth voyage (1421–2) and in the sixth year of Hsüan-ti (1431), 'starting once more for the barbarian (countries) in order to make known the imperial commands', the fleet sailed for the Western Ocean, returning in 1433.

The object of the voyages was to enhance the prestige of the Ming dynasty and, incidentally, to keep a look out for any rebels against the dynasty who might have taken refuge in the Nanyang. 'The Imperial Ming dynasty', proclaimed the high envoys, 'in unifying seas and continents, surpasses the Three Dynasties and even goes beyond the Han and the T'ang. The countries beyond the horizon and from the ends of

[29] 'What are today called the Indian Ocean or the Nanyang were formerly called the Nan Hai (Southern Sea) or the Nan-hsi Hai (Southwestern Sea). The sea to the south of the Gulf of Siam was given the special name of Ch'ang Hai' (Feng Ch'eng-chün, p. 91).

C.S.E.A.—B

the earth have all become subjects (of the Imperial Ming). . . . The barbarians from beyond the seas . . ., have come to audience bearing precious objects and presents.'

Says Professor Duyvendak in another place:[30]

These embassies must have been stupendous undertakings; fleets are described of 62 vessels carrying 37,000 soldiers; more than 20 countries in the Indian archipelago and the Indian Ocean were visited; chiefs and kings, like those of Palembang and of Ceylon, were deposed and sent as captives to China, and members of the expeditions went as far as Aden and Mecca, bringing messages from the Chinese court. Most surprising of all, these fleets were commanded by eunuchs, of whom none is more famous than Cheng Ho, known as San-Pao-T'ai-Chien.

The dynastic histories have a good deal to say of Java during the period of Cheng Ho's voyages. The denizens of the country were divided into three kinds of people—first, the Chinese who resided there temporarily and whose clothes and food were fine and nice; secondly, the traders from other countries, who resided there for a longer time, and who also were quite civilized and clean; and thirdly, the natives of the country, who were very dirty and were fond of eating snakes, insects, and worms, and who slept and ate together with the dogs. From Grissé, in 1411, a Chinese from Canton sent representatives to the Chinese court and a letter offering produce of the country as tribute. Tuban was the native name of a place near Grissé where more than a thousand families lived, all under one chief. Amongst them were many Chinese from Canton and Changchow (near Amoy) who were settled there. Fowls, goats, fish, and vegetables were cheap there. Surabaya was another place where there were many Chinese. Later it seems that Tuban was deserted by them because of its insecurity (there being numerous robbers) and all trade went to a new place, Yortan (situated in the present district of Paduran), but it subsequently disappeared.

There is in the Chinese records a large number of references to the Chinese in Java and Sumatra in the fifteen and sixteenth centuries on the eve of the European incursions into these waters. Many pirates are mentioned, including Ch'en Tsu-yi who was seized by Cheng Ho. Later on, in the reign of Chia Ching (1522–66), another notorious Cantonese robber flourished. Besides his main business of robbery, he had a large commercial establishment in which many Hokkiens were employed.

Regarding the Chinese navigation of these seas, it has been remarked that their junks always sailed with the trade winds, going with the northeast monsoon and returning home with the southwest monsoon. On the outward voyage it was the custom to follow the Asiatic coast, but on the home trip the ships of Amoy probably sailed along the west coasts of Borneo, Palawan, Luzon, and Formosa. Moreover, the sailing directions in Chinese books indicate that ships bound for the Sulu Archipelago,

[30] *Ma Huan Re-examined* (1933). (On the *Ying yai sheng lan*, ascribed to Ma Huan.)

eastern Borneo, and, in later centuries, even for Banjermassin and Java, first crossed over to the island of Luzon and sailed southwards through the Philippines.[31]

This opinion is consistent with that of Sir Roland Braddell who says:

Summarizing, we suggest that both *a priori* reasoning and such data as we possess lead to a very early knowledge of Borneo on the part of the Indians and Chinese and that in the case of both of them probably, but the latter certainly, they must have been familiar with Borneo before they became familiar with Java, the navigation to which was far more difficult and more dangerous.[32]

Let us now go back for a while and consider the early history of the Chinese contacts with Borneo in more detail, keeping in mind the implications raised by Dr Heine-Geldern's revelations of the finds there and in Indonesia.

The credit for bringing Brunei to the official notice of China seems to have been due to neither the Chinese nor the Borneans, but rather to the enterprising Arab traders of Canton and Ch'üan-chow. It is not known just how early these Arabs began trading in Brunei, but in 977 a certain Abu Ali and two other Arabs came to the Chinese court as envoys from the king of Brunei. From the twelfth to the fifteenth century accounts of Brunei, Sulu, Mindoro, and others of the Philippine Islands became more numerous. Before 1225 Chinese vessels were making trading trips to nearly all parts of the Philippines. Apart from Sulu, which had always maintained closer relations with Borneo than with the Philippines, the most important trade centre appears to have been Mindoro.[33]

The traditions of Borneo and Sulu indicate that a Chinese province was established some centuries ago in the neighbourhood of the Kinabatangan River, and the province had dominion over the Sulu River. It is mainly accepted, too, that a daughter of a Chinese 'prince', who was in all probability the governor of the province referred to, came from the Kinabatangan River to marry the second sultan of Brunei, and from that couple originated the royal family of Brunei of the present day.

The statement that the Dusuns are 'half-Chinese' is frequently made by residents of Borneo. This theory has led to much controversy. In the middle of the last century a traveller in Sarawak, a Mr Witti, expressed himself strongly against any supposed Chinese mixture in the blood of the Dusuns, saying, 'I think no Chinese colonies ever existed in the north of Borneo', but the same traveller in a journey up the Pagalan River speaks of a tribe that was 'probably the result of an infusion of Chinese blood with the aboriginal races of Borneo'.[34] Regarding the

[31] Steiger, *History of the Far East* (Boston, 1936), pp. 202, 203. See also p. 8 n.1 of this Survey, and the remarks on Chinese navigation of Southeast Asian waters in J. V. Mills, 'Malaya in the Wu-pei-chih Charts', *JRASMB*, xv/3 (Dec. 1937).
[32] *JRASMB*, xix/1 (Feb. 1941), p. 72.   [33] Steiger, *Hist. of Orient*, p. 205.
[34] Cited by Ling Roth, *The Natives of Sarawak and British North Borneo* (London, 1896), i. 24.

Dyaks, Earl remarks that the Chinese of his time supposed them to be descended from a large body of their countrymen left by accident on the island, but this belief, he says, was entertained solely on the basis of the Chinese legend of the Kuni Balu snake whose stone was stolen by the Emperor of China by the agency of Chinese who formed a chain from the snake's lair to waiting junks. The stone was recovered by the snake, but the human chain of Chinese remained to colonize the country. Another legend of this nature concerned the origin of the Bolupih race from a Chinese native union. C. A. de Crespigny could see no similarity between the natives and the Chinese except a turning-in of the upper eyelid in childhood, whereas St John observed that the 'features of many are very like the Chinese—perhaps a trace of that ancient kingdom that tradition fixes in this neighbourhood'.[35] In the present century I. H. N. Evans has pronounced strongly against the theory of Chinese admixture with the Dusuns though he admits Chinese admixtures on the Klias Peninsula and the Kinabatangan River.[36]

But whatever the truth regarding the Chinese colonization of Borneo in remoter times, it is certain that by the early nineteenth century a considerable admixture of the races was in progress. Intermarriage between Chinese men and Dyak women was common and St John, at the request of the Raja, opened a school for the benefit of the offspring of such unions.

Truly speaking [St John adds] the Chinese women up here are themselves the offspring of mixed marriages, but having been brought up in all the manners and customs of the Chinese, are looked upon as Chinese. The settled agricultural tribes between the Brunei and Murudu Rivers were considered good examples of Chinese and natives intermarrying.

Of special interest to the students of Chinese contacts with Borneo is the evidence afforded by native agricultural methods and the 'sacred jars'.

Sir Spenser St John describes the methods used by the native people of Tumposok where he first saw natives ploughing. The plough was of a very simple construction, serving rather to scratch the ground than to turn it over, was entirely of wood, and was drawn by a buffalo, and its action was the same as if a pointed stick had been dragged through the land to a depth of about four inches. After ploughing, they used a rough kind of harrow. 'I think this superior agriculture', says St John, 'is obviously a remnant of Chinese civilization.'[37]

Tangible evidence of Chinese contact with Sarawak is afforded by the

---

[35] Ling Roth, *Natives of Sarawak*, i. 57 and 59.
[36] I. H. N. Evans, *Among Primitive Peoples in Borneo* (London, 1932), p. 274 ff.
[37] It is interesting to compare this description with that of a native plough of supposedly Chinese origin in the Philippines (see p. 530), and there is a reference to another plough not of local design in Malaya (see p. 261).

'sacred jars', undoubtedly of Chinese origin. The 'jar cult' played an important role not only in Borneo but also among the Moi of southern Indochina, in the Philippines, in Formosa, and various other parts of the Indonesian region. (Dr Heine-Geldern remarks that Professor Janse's recent discoveries in Indochina may help to solve the origin of this cult.) St John describes the several kinds of jars existing in Sarawak. The best known were the Gusi, the Rusa, and the Naga. The most valuable, the Gusi, was a green colour, about 18 inches in height, and was, from its medicinal properties, exceedingly sought after. One fetched at Tawaran the price of £400 to be paid in produce. The Naga was a jar two feet in height ornamented with Chinese dragons. This was at this time worth only £7–8; while the Rusa, covered with the figures of some kind of deer, was worth £15–16.[38] Another jar, the Ningkah, mentioned in another contemporary account, fetched $150.[39]

These jars were the principal commodity in the Chinese trade with Borneo and other islands. This trade may have been of the 'silent' variety, when Chinese junks, laden with silk, beads, iron, copper pots, and many kinds of jars arrived off the coast and made their presence known by beating on gongs. The natives would bring to the beach whatever they had to trade and then retire to a distance. The traders would take ashore what they considered the proper equivalent in terms of their own goods, and if this proved satisfactory they took the native articles and moved on to the next settlement.[40] But whether or no this method of trading was usual in later times, it seems that in the time spoken of by Chao Ju-kua (12th–13th centuries) buying and selling were carried on in a more friendly and civilized way. After a ship had arrived and had been boarded by the natives they mingled freely with the ship's folk. The custom was for native traders to assemble in crowds and carry the goods away with them in baskets, 'and even if one cannot at first know them and can but slowly distinguish the men who remove the goods there will be no loss'.[41]

More impressive, aesthetically speaking, than the jars are the pottery and china revealed by the pick and spade in mineral exploration. Mr Helms records that on one occasion his party found a number of paving tiles four inches thick, 'beautifully made of pebbles, concrete, quartz,

[38] Ling Roth, *Natives of Sarawak*, ii. 284. Every Dyak tribe possessed some jars according to their riches or importance, though, as one European lady remarks, 'no one would suppose from their appearance that they were worth more than the common earthenware water-pots we use in our bath-houses'. They were, in fact (to judge from examples in the Sarawak Museum), of as cheap a quality as the Chinese trader could persuade the natives to purchase. Examples of these jars are illustrated in Plate 159 of N. Ottema, *Ceramiek Handboek*, 2nd ed. (Amsterdam, 1946). One special jar, owned by the Sultan of Brunei, was supposed to have magical qualities, and Bisayas used to come with presents for the Sultan to obtain in return a little water from the jar with which to sprinkle their rice-fields to ensure good crops.
[39] L. W. Helms, *Pioneering in the Far East* (London, 1882), p. 153, cited by Ling Roth, ii. 280.   [40] Cole, *Peoples of Malaysia*, p. 28.
[41] Steiger, *Hist. of Far East*, p. 205.

etc. They had been polished, were clearly very old, and made by people of a higher civilization.' Were these, by any chance, relics of Chinese settlement?

The coming of the Europeans caused a break in the trading relations between China, Borneo, and the other Malaysian islands which had gone on for so long. In the year 1530 one of the functionaries in the capital addressed a memorial to the throne respecting the discontinuance of the tribute from Borneo. This memorial says: 'During the period Cheng-te (1506–1521) the Franks (Portuguese) had been violently spreading their influence and the tribute had ceased. A few years afterwards the natives had tried to begin sending it again, but it was evident that their regard for the Chinese empire had suffered very much.'

Finally, let us summarize what is known of Chinese intercourse with the Philippines prior to the Spanish period.

It is at a comparatively late date that the Philippines are first mentioned in Chinese history; and the fact is the more striking (says Laufer) since some of the adjacent isles to the south are touched upon much earlier. In the fifth year of Hung-wu (1372) the first embassy arrived in China with tribute, and the Emperor reciprocated by dispatching an official with presents of silk gauze woven of gold and coloured threads to the king of the country. But (Laufer warns us):

From this first mention of the Philippines in Chinese history we should not be so narrow-minded as to infer that Chinese intercourse with the Philippines dates from just the year 1372; on the contrary, the fact that there was a Philippine embassy in that year points to a long commercial intercourse between the two peoples which had escaped the knowledge of the court historiographers at Peking.[42]

The statement made in the Imperial Geography of the Ming (*Ta Ming I Feng Chi*) that no investigation of Luzon had been made by previous generations is contradicted by the fact that Philippine tribes are described in Chao Ju-kua's work of the thirteenth century.

Since Laufer wrote there has been considerable further investigation of the subject, and the present state of knowledge can best be summarized in the words of Dr H. Otley Beyer:

It is improbable that many Chinese ships were engaged in this trade with the Philippines during the early period (at least before the late 11th–12th century part of it) and it is unlikely that there were any Chinese residents in the islands at that time . . . [re 12th–14th centuries] Chinese merchant colonies began to establish themselves in a few places where a fairly strong or well-organized native government gave prospect of protection. . . . With the death of Cheng Ho, however, and the passing of the Yung Lo regime, this Chinese attempt at dominions overseas also passed away . . . [re A.D. 1430–1450]. As Mohammedan influence spread eastward through the southern Philippines, and northward from Borneo into Luzon, the

---

[42] Berthold Laufer, 'The Relations of the Chinese to the Philippine Islands', *Smithsonian Miscellaneous Collections* (quarterly issue), i (Sept. 1907), p. 251.

Siam and Indo-China trade was at first cut off, while the Chinese merchant vessels were forced to seek new trading routes leading around the eastern side of Luzon, and into the eastern Visayan Islands etc., where Islamic beliefs had not yet penetrated. . . . While the Chinese settlers intermarried freely in the country, built good houses, and taught their families better ways of living, they were not otherwise interested in converting or spreading new ideas among the native folk. Their influence was chiefly economic, and aside from the brief period of Yung Lo's empire, made no attempt to meddle or interfere with native political constitutions, social customs, or beliefs. . . .[43]

What has been given above is only a brief outline of a vast subject of which the facts are, for many periods, largely unprecipitated. In an attempt to confine this survey to manageable proportions and to give it a contemporary focus, we have adopted the principle that our interest in the Chinese of Southeast Asia begins in earnest only when they had formed permanent settlements, and it is true to say that the majority of such settlements still remaining, outside Annam and Tongking, were founded within the last 350 years. Nevertheless, we should not forget that the stream of Chinese immigration into the region, swelling into spate in the second and third decades of the present century, was but an expansion of long pre-existing rivulets of intercourse.

After the great military expeditions of the early Mings, the urge to imperial expansion overseas appears to have gone out of the Chinese. The self-contained spirit of the Middle Kingdom reasserted itself and the Emperors were content with adventures by land. It would indeed be harder to explain why the urge arose at all than why it subsided so soon. The fact remains that whereas the colonization of the Europeans followed in the wake of their fleets and soldiers or to lands obtained by treaty from the native rulers, the Chinese in the last three and a half centuries have entered Southeast Asia either as visiting merchants or as suppliants for permission to remain from the Javanese Sultans, or from the Spanish, Dutch, British, or French. They came no more as haughty emissaries of the Dragon Throne, armed to the teeth to enforce the imperial will, but as humble and peaceable shiploads of traders, artisans, or coolies, waiting, like Czech or Italian peasants on Ellis Island, for permission to enter the land of promise. But their meekness and peaceableness were in the long run to be far more forceful than the militancy of the Europeans; for where the latter came in their tens the Chinese came in their thousands, and when the Europeans had gone, they remained.

[43] H. Otley Beyer, *Early History of Philippine Relationships to Foreign Countries, especially China* (1948).

3

EMIGRATION TO THE 'NANYANG'

THE Overseas Chinese are almost exclusively drawn from the south-eastern provinces of Kwangtung, Fukien, and Kwangsi—the great majority from the first two. This has mainly been due to population pressure and to the contiguity of these provinces to Southeast Asia.[1] This emigration was accentuated by internal troubles in China. In the Ming dynasty there had already been substantial emigration to the Nanyang, but a new wave was set up by the civil strife consequent on the change-over from the Ming to the Ch'ing, or Manchu, dynasty.[2] For example, the anti-Manchu pirate and patriot Koxinga, who had occupied Formosa, made descents on the coasts of Fukien in order to replenish his stores and at the same time embarrass the Manchu Government. Partly to cut off his supplies and partly to intimidate the population of these regions whose sympathies were anti-dynastic, the Manchus made the latter forsake a zone of country from about eight to thirty miles deep on the coasts of Kwangtung, Fukien, and Chekiang. This zone was de-nuded of its crops and its villages were burnt down. A reference was made to this in the reign of the first Manchu Emperor when governors were ordered to give houses and land to such persons who had moved into the interior 'so that they might be satisfied'. The harsh treatment they received was undoubtedly an encouragement to many in these parts of China to seek refuge overseas.

Contacts with Europeans were also a subsidiary encouragement to emigration. The first European efforts to trade were centred in Kwang-tung. In 1516 Perestrello came from Malacca to China; in 1517 de Andrada arrived in Canton and received permission from the viceroy to trade. The attitude of the Portuguese soon aroused the hostility of the Chinese and their trading depot was attacked and destroyed in 1522. They retired to Lampa in Kwangtung where they maintained a trading post for the next fifty years. Another expedition reached the coast of Fukien in 1518 and established depots at Ch'üanchowfu, north of Amoy, at Foochow, and at Ningpo in Chekiang. Between 1545 and 1549 an imperial edict for the extermination of the Portuguese was enforced

[1] Population pressure in China, especially in the nineteenth century, is instructively dealt with by G. E. Tyler, 'The Taiping Rebellion, its economic background and social theory', *Chinese Social & Pol. Science R.*, xvi (1933), pp. 545–614.
[2] See Duyvendak, 'Chinese in the Dutch East Indies', ibid. xi (1927), pp. 1–15.

wherever possible. Nevertheless Macao was founded as a trading post in 1557. The Portuguese paid rent for the Macao Peninsula until 1849. During the eighteenth century Macao was the chief port for the Western trade in China. The Spanish next opened up direct relations with the Chinese, using Manila as their base, but the trade between the Philippines and Amoy was almost entirely in Chinese hands. The port of Amoy from 1730 to 1842 was closed to all foreigners except Spaniards. The Dutch made attempts to open up trade at Canton in 1604 and 1607 but were defeated by the Portuguese interests at Macao. Though they eventually occupied Formosa, they were driven out by Koxinga in 1661. Further efforts made by the Dutch to obtain recognition of their trade were without success, and it was not until 1762 that they were able to establish a factory at Canton. The English made their first essay to join in the trade in 1596, but it was a failure. They tried in 1647 to operate under Portuguese auspices, meeting, however, with little success. The East India Company renewed the attempt to trade with Canton in 1664 and 1674, but were foiled, mainly by the Portuguese. The Company did, however, succeed in 1667 and 1670 in trading at Amoy and Formosa, but their factory in the latter place was closed in 1681. In 1685 an imperial decree opened all the ports of China to foreign trade; but Canton and Amoy remained the principal trading entrepôts.

A circumstance which tended towards centring the foreign trade on Canton and eventually confining it to this one port was the establishment of a monopoly by the Chinese Government. In 1702 an official called a Hoppo, or emperor's merchant, was appointed at Canton and became the sole broker for all purchases and sales. Two years later the Hoppo had to admit certain other merchants into a share of his monopoly. Henceforth the trade increased in bulk and flourished, though subject to very severe restrictions and a rigorous disciplining of the foreign merchants, most of whom had to withdraw to Macao in the non-trading season. In 1757 an imperial edict prohibited all foreign trade at any port other than Canton. Attempts to improve the conditions of trade and to establish relations on a proper footing led to the sending of embassies to Peking by the Dutch and the British, but without concrete result. The situation continued down to the First China War of 1839–42.

It will be seen, then, that Chinese contacts with foreign traders were practically confined to the Kwangtung and Fukien ports, though the intercourse was even then a restricted one. It was not the policy of the Spanish or of the Dutch (except at the beginning) to attract the Chinese to their colonies; it was only after 1786, when the British began to make settlements in the Malay Peninsula, that the Chinese found an unqualified welcome. The capitalistic development of colonies in the nineteenth and twentieth centuries had not yet begun, and there was no demand for coolie labour on a large scale before then. The Americans first traded with Canton in 1784, but it was not until 1848 that the first Chinese immigrants arrived at San Francisco.[3]

Such were some of the circumstances which induced, or paved the way for, Chinese emigration to the Nanyang. Our task must now be to investigate the factors which discouraged this emigration.

Ancestor worship was a strong force in discouraging the Chinese from emigrating. The spirits of the dead needed the constant attendance of the living to ensure their welfare, and those who deserted the vicinity of the graves of their ancestors and left their spirits without sacrificial offerings and ritual attention were guilty of unfilial conduct. Thus it was at all times that only those who were forced by dire necessity left their native villages, and they were regarded as outcasts and vagabonds. It was natural, therefore, that a great many refugees and criminals should have been included among the emigrants.[4]

Religion was reinforced by Government policy. The Emperors took the view that the loss of subjects was not a loss to be compensated for by any trade advantages. Under the Mings the law was not so strict as it became later under the Ch'ings (the Manchus were also more orthodox Confucians than the Mings—and aliens are frequently more orthodox and conservative than the people they live amongst). The Laws of the Ch'ing dynasty, section ccxxv, are explicit:[5]

> All officers of government, soldiers, and private citizens, who clandestinely proceed to sea to trade, or who remove to foreign islands for the purpose of inhabiting and cultivating the same, shall be punished according to the law against communicating with rebels and enemies and consequently suffer death by being beheaded. The governors of cities of the second and third orders shall likewise be beheaded, when found guilty of combining with, or artfully conniving at the conduct of such persons . . .

Thereupon ensues a long list of penalties, but the officials who had offended by allowing the emigration to occur were to be pardoned if they afterwards succeeded in securing the offenders and bringing them to condign punishment.

The Manchu policy was dictated largely by the consideration that emigrants from the disaffected south would almost certainly be anti-Manchu and, once out of reach of the Manchu officials, would undoubtedly be plotting among themselves and with their friends inside the country for the overthrow of the dynasty. Those who enlisted under

---

[3] So it is commonly stated, but in the correspondence relating to a project to send Chinese to Trinidad in 1806 ('Notices of Pinang', *J. of Indian Archipelago*, vi (1852), pp. 145–72) it is mentioned that Chinese had already been taken to Nootka Sound in North America. The writer has so far been unable to discover the facts of this matter.

[4] H. Gottwaldt, *Die überseeische Auswanderung der Chinesen* (1903), insists that 'only the scum of the Chinese go abroad'.

[5] Sir George Thomas Staunton, *Ta Tsing Leu Lee; being the Fundamental Laws of the Penal Code of China* (London, 1810).

Koxinga would be a case in point. And in maintaining this policy the officials were helped by the sentiment of the Chinese that all beyond the confines of the Middle Kingdom were barbarians and were not to be consorted with. The law could never be enforced because economic stress and hope of gain were the more powerful forces, but the principle was held in theory until 1860 when it was disposed of in the treaties with foreign Powers, though the law was not actually repealed until 1894. The officials reaped a big harvest from it, for they collected large sums from returning immigrants as a price of inaction, and they also made levies on the same account on the families in China of emigrants overseas; for in China responsibility is a very far-reaching principle.

The attitude of the Government being as it was, it can readily be understood that little attention was paid to the misfortunes and persecutions of overseas Chinese. The massacre of the Chinese in the Philippines in 1603 and 1639, and in Java in 1740, caused no great concern to the Chinese Emperors. There are instances of reprisals in the Ming dynasty, but even these are few and far between.

We shall see how the value of the foreign trade was too great an inducement for officials and others to ignore, and the profits to be obtained by the Chinese themselves when they made trading voyages led to connivance on the part of the Governors: in 1567 the Governor of Fukien allowed his provincials to go abroad to trade with all foreigners except the Japanese, who were the arch-pirates of the period and who ravaged the Chinese coasts. Traders had, however, to get licences to leave the country.

In 1717 the Emperor K'ang Hsi summoned those of his subjects who had been residing in foreign countries to return to their homes, but consented to pardon all who had been abroad since the beginning of his reign some fifty-six years before. His successor, Yung Cheng, allowed the inhabitants of the coast provinces to go abroad to trade under licence on condition that they subsequently returned home; but in 1728 he forbade those who were unlicensed to come back at all.

A proclamation by Ch'en Hung-mou, Governor of Fukien, in 1754, continues the story of the official attitude towards emigration:[6]

. . . A large proportion of the maritime population of Fukien is beholden for its subsistence to trade beyond the sea. The southern seas having at an earlier period been closed to trade (by a law that) provided that all persons who had gone abroad before its enactment might return home within three years, but that no one who should go abroad after its enactment should be allowed to return at all. In the fifth year of the reign of Yung Cheng (1727) this interdict was removed, and there has been, from that time, a movement of traders from the Inner Land abroad unceasing as the welling of a spring. Feeling, however, that there must be some who, with sea

---

[6] Sir Thomas Francis Wade, *Tzŭ Erh Chih*, Documentary Series (London, 1867), gives the Chinese original of the proclamation and a translation on p. 33 of the Key.

upon sea between (China, and) the distant (land where they were), could not have returned home within the appointed time, the late Governor-General, Hao, first in one memorial, and then in a second, moved His Majesty to allow such persons to return; which proposition was sanctioned. But in the 14th year of Ch'ien Lung (1749) there occurred the case of Chen I-lao. . . .

Chen I-lao was a native of the district of Lung-ch'i, who having un-authorizedly proceeded from Kwangtung to Batavia had become head-man of the Chinese at that port, and had there collected duties on foreign trade. As he could not belong to the class of honest trader (says the proc-lamation), but was the sort of man who would be laying hold of some pretext or other to give trouble, as soon as this came out he was tried (by the Chinese authorities) and sentenced to banishment; and since then such traders who are still detained abroad, being filled by his trial with doubt and fears, have not ventured to return home.

. . . the Governor, humbly reflecting [the proclamation goes on] that it is because of our Emperor's treatment of the natives and foreigners as one, that the trade of the foreigner is enabled to continue, as thread joined to thread, uninterrupted; that alike cherishing those from afar, and benefiting by his bounty the (native) merchant, his Majesty shows a consideration that leaves nothing untouched, did (as the records show) explain the matter in a memorial. . . .

The result of which was that those Chinese residing abroad, providing that their reason for not returning within the allotted time was 'the in-ability to close their accounts' were to be permitted to return to their homes and to bring with them any wives or concubines they had ac-quired abroad, together with their children.

This represents the situation until the First China War of 1839–42. The war has been stigmatized as the 'Opium War', and indeed opium was its occasion, but among the objects of the British was to force the Chinese Government to permit diplomatic contacts and to improve the insupportable conditions under which foreigners were required to trade. The Nanking Treaty which followed the war was unilateral; that is to say, the Chinese undertook to make concessions to the British without obtaining corresponding advantages. The Chinese gained no right to send consuls abroad, but at this time they did not want to do so. Treaty ports were established under the treaty, but the determination of the Chinese Government not to allow diplomatic intercourse led to a further war in 1858–60, in which Great Britain was partnered by France.

Morse[7] and MacNair[8] give in detail the history of how the Chinese were eventually brought to recognize the principle that their nationals had a right to emigrate. The Second China War was concluded by the Treaty of Tientsin. The French made their own separate treaty, and the Americans, though not participants in the war, also obtained a treaty of

[7] See H. B. Morse, *International Relations of the Chinese Empire: The Period of Conflict 1834–60* (London, 1910), *passim*.   [8] H. F. MacNair, *The Chinese Abroad* (Shanghai, 1925).

their own. The Chinese recognition to the three Powers of the right of their people to emigrate took place about the same time (by the two conventions of Peking, 1860), but, owing to some complications and difference in procedure, the first incorporation of the principle in a treaty was in the Burlingame Treaty of 1870 with America when the Chinese Emperor 'cordially recognised the inherent and inalienable right of man to change his home and allegiance, and also the mutual advantage of the free migration of aliens and subjects respectively from one country to another for the purpose of curiosity, of trade, or as permanent residence'. A similar principle was embodied in agreements with Great Britain and France, but the method of promulgation was to be by imperial decree to the high authorities in every province, who should issue proclamations within their jurisdiction. The first official recognition of the right of the Chinese to leave their homeland is found in these proclamations.[9]

It was but slowly that the Chinese began to see the advantages of having diplomatic and consular representatives in foreign countries where they had nationals or with which they had trading relations. The first permanent legation was established in London in 1877. The minister was accredited both to London and Paris. A Chinese legation was opened at Washington in 1878, in Tokyo in the same year, and in 1879 at St Petersburg. Consuls were established at various ports in the next decade or so.

But the sentiment of the Chinese against emigration persisted throughout the nineteenth century and into the twentieth, and it still persists. The popular attitude can well be illustrated by extracts from two American writers—the first referring to about the middle of the nineteenth century and the second to its last quarter:

I

... if they [the Chinese emigrants] return with wealth enough to live upon, they are liable to the vexatious extortions of needy relatives, sharpers, and police, who have a handle for their fleecing whip in the law against leaving the country, although this clause has been neutralized by subsequent acts, and is not in force, the power of public opinion is against going.[10]

---

[9] George F. Seward, *Chinese Immigration* (N.Y., 1881), chap. vi, discusses the emigration of Chinese to the Nanyang and the question of their disposition to emigrate. His thesis is that, through growing northern influences and more amalgamation with northern stock, the people of the southern part of China are losing their migratory tendency. When they are not recruited, as for the more distant continents, they go only to nearby countries. Emigration to California was an episode only; the Chinese naturally go where the native peoples are less vigorous than they. In spite of great inducements held out to them, their numbers in the Dutch East Indies have remained small. During the same period in which Europeans changed the face of America, the Chinese in Java had made a lodgement only. They have not mongolized it. This was written before the large-scale emigrations of the twentieth century, and the 'loss of migratory tendency' has certainly not been true so far as Southeast Asia is concerned. Nevertheless the thesis is worthy of consideration in the other respects.

[10] S. Wells Williams, *The Middle Kingdom* (London, 1883), i. 279.

II

To the foreigner, acquainted with the experience of other lands in modern times, the simple, obvious, indispensable recipe for the relief of many of the ills to which the Chinese are subject, is emigration. . . . But this is an expedient which the Chinese themselves will never adopt, for the reason that it will take them away from the graves of their ancestors, to which, by the theory of Confucianism, they are inexorably linked. Generally speaking, no Chinese will leave his home to seek a fortune at a distance unless he is in some way driven to do so. His ideal in life is to be

'Fixed like a plant on his peculiar spot,
To draw nutrition, propagate, and rot.'

Generally speaking, no Chinese leaves his home not intending to return. His hope is always to come back rich, to die and be buried where his ancestors are buried.[11]

But in noting these impressions of competent observers we should bear in mind that they are speaking of China as a whole: the sentiment against emigration in the specifically emigrant communities of the Kwangtung and Fukien seaboard was certainly not great, if it existed at all: indeed there is reason to believe that, in the last few decades at least, they regarded themselves as having a privileged entrée to the good things that came from the Nanyang.

After the Second World War, Chinese emigration into Southeast Asia, however, virtually came to an end with the imposition of strict controls.

4

SOME SPECIAL ASPECTS OF CHINESE SOCIETY IN SOUTHEAST ASIA

THE outstanding feature of the European approach to the Overseas Chinese in the last decade or so has been the way in which the methods of the social sciences have largely replaced the older historical or political ones. This is exemplified in the work of Maurice Freedman on the Chinese in Malaya, G. William Skinner and R. J. Coughlin on those in Thailand, of Donald Earl Willmott on those in Indonesia, and of T'ien Ju-k'ang on those in Sarawak. Space does not permit of a summary of the investigations of the works of other writers (which are listed in the Bibliography), but some of their conclusions are also mentioned in this chapter.

Freedman, in his *Chinese Family and Marriage in Singapore* (1957), first of all describes the social background of the community (family organization in China, migration to the Nanyang, &c), then the structure

---

[11] A. H. Smith, *Chinese Characteristics* (N.Y., 1894), pp. 165-6.

and composition of the household, the kinship system, the structure of marriage, the formation of marriage, marriage disrupted, and death and its cult. He concludes that while Chinese society to be seen in Singapore takes its culture directly from Southeastern China, the economic and political conditions of the Colony are totally alien to those of the home setting, and the social organization of Chinese in Singapore cannot be understood simply as a branch of society in China. 'At the same time as agnatic kinship is reinterpreted in Singapore, the powerful bias of the homeland system in favour of the patriline is modified overseas by the removal of local groups based on kinship' (p. 225).

Marriage in Singapore (says Freedman) no longer represents a link between two corporate groups, and Chinese in the Colony, while preferring to seek their wives within their own dialect-groups (and often within narrower divisions of those groups), treat the new marriage as a matter concerning only the bridal couple and their fellow household-members. In Singapore there has been a change in the relative status of primary and secondary wives (the 'principal wives' and 'concubines' of the older European literature on China) such that the latter have often assumed a significance probably unknown in China. At the same time the definition of secondary wife has become much blurred, and there is a shading of polygamy into mistress-keeping. The forms of marriage have proliferated, and various versions and combinations of traditional and modernist ceremonial make it difficult to arrive at any general statement of the essentials for Chinese marriage at the present time.

In the disruption of Chinese marriage (Freedman continues) the inadequacy of Chinese mechanisms to control domestic disputes is very apparent. Since there are no clearly defined larger kinship units, no local units in urban life, and no formal structure of authority in the rural settlements, marital quarrels tend frequently to find their way to persons and bodies standing outside the limits of Chinese society itself. It is at this point that 'government', in the shape of the magistrates' courts and the Department of Social Welfare (succeeding the old Chinese Protectorate), intervenes decisively in Chinese life. Divorce among Chinese is essentially a matter of mutual agreement between spouses.

The fate of ancestor worship in a version of Chinese society from which much of the traditional kinship organization has disappeared presents some interesting theoretical problems. The ritual attention to ancestors has survived in Singapore but, unsupported by an integrated agnatic system, the worship of ancestors has little significance for the religious grouping of kinsmen beyond the limits of the individual household. What Chinese practise in Singapore is 'memorialism' rather than rites of ancestor worship as rites of kinship solidarity.

Freedman concludes by saying that the new Social Research Unit of the University of Malaya (since split into the Universities of Malaya and

Singapore) must clearly be in the future the focus for any co-operation
between the field-workers. In his opinion, the development of a Research
Section in the Singapore Department of Social Welfare would be a great
advantage to students of society in Malaya.

In his *Chinese Society in Thailand* (1957), G. William Skinner subjects
the local Chinese community to analysis in terms of his own social
anthropological discipline. He begins by describing the Chinese in 'Old
Siam', Chinese migration and population growth up to 1917, the position
of the Chinese in their economy in the reigns of Rama IV (1851–68) and
Rama V (1868–1910), the 'Pattern of Instability', namely Chinese society
in Thailand from Rama III to Rama V (including intermarriage and
assimilation), the transition to nationalism with consequent cohesion,
demographic trends from 1918–55, 'conflicting interests' in Chinese Thai
society up to 1938, the community during the Second World War and its
aftermath, and 'Repression and Reconsideration' of the Chinese problem
under the second Phibun Administration (1948–56).

Skinner's work is illustrated with maps, tables, and charts. The tables
give migrational statistics for Chinese at various periods, population by
monthon, a model of the probable growth of the Chinese population in
Thailand, 1917–55, &c, and a number of tables showing economic and
social change—i.e. growth in the number of rice-mills, representative
wages of Chinese skilled labourers, occupational stratification, ethnic
occupational specialization by major categories, occupational classes, and
occupational specialization by Chinese speech group.

The author is interested above all in the possibilities of the assimilation of the Chinese in Thailand to the Thai community as a whole.
There was, he thinks, once a possibility that a local-born Chinese society,
intermediate in culture between Chinese immigrant society and Thai
society, might develop in Siam. However, such a development has not in
fact occurred. There are thousands of intermediate individuals who are
identified as Chinese in some social situations and as Thai in others, who
have both a Chinese and a Thai name, either of which is used according
to the suitability of the occasion, and who can speak Thai or Chinese with
equal fluency. But such individuals were not developing relationships
among themselves closer than those with pure Chinese or Thai society.
Their private relations might, for example, be with Chinese and their
public relations with Thai, or their elder associates might be Thai and
their younger associates Chinese. The wider society in Thailand's cities
and towns was still polarized by its unmistakable Thai and Chinese
elements.

Considerable attention is given in the book to the question of social
mobility, to the opportunities for and tendencies to social improvement
with the Chinese Communists of Thailand.

Skinner's final conclusion was that the chief factors influencing the rate of Chinese assimilation in Thailand were the nature and amount of education in the Chinese language available to local-born Chinese, the proportion of the China-born to the total in the ethnic total, the amount of legal discrimination between their nationals and aliens, the scope and effectiveness of Chinese agencies promoting nationalism, and the degree of influence on the local Chinese of the People's Government of China. All those factors could be influenced to some extent by their Government's policy. Should the Thai Government have no choice but to recognize Peking and allow the establishment of Communist Chinese diplomatic and consular offices in Thailand, or should there be a general Communist victory in Southeast Asia, those events would certainly retard the assimilation of the Chinese into the Thai population.

The thesis of R. J. Coughlin's *Double Identity: the Chinese in Modern Thailand* (1960) is that the Overseas Chinese have a double identity, both Chinese and Southeast Asian; 'rather than a withering ethnic group, they may in fact be the present-day image of the future Southeast Asian'. The author asks whether Thailand can resist the tremendous pressures exerted by China's expanding population, and if so, whether it can resist the extraordinary cultural dynamic that China represents in Asia today. 'We have been so conditioned to think of the inevitable assimilation of an immigrant minority group by the host society that we overlook too easily the likelihood of the host society itself being overwhelmed, demographically and culturally, by its great neighbour' (p. 205).

The technique adopted by Donald Earl Willmott in *The Chinese of Semarang: a Changing Minority Community in Indonesia* (1961) is to subject a chosen section of the Chinese community in Indonesia to detailed analysis and hence to arrive at conclusions which have application, *mutatis mutandis*, to the community as a whole. His book (he states) 'attempts to present a comprehensive picture of a minority community in a rapidly changing, non-Western, urban setting' (p. vii). To do this he describes the city of Semarang and its people, the sources of new currents in the Chinese community, their occupations and economic activities, ethnic group relations, Chinese community structure, organizations, leadership, schools and education, religion and magic, and family and kinship. From these surveys Willmott attempts to formulate a theory of socio-cultural change.

The general theory here presented draws upon the work of many sociologists and anthropologists. The author analyses existing theories of socio-cultural change and then formulates the hypotheses which emerged from his study of the Semarang Chinese community. This is done under a number of headings—structure (type of group, stability factors, change readiness factors), innovation, purposive change, emergent change, necessitated change, imposed change, emulative change, &c. The object is to formulate a method for the scientific study of communities such as the

Chinese of Semarang, but the writer concedes that much more work is required before the method can be applied with any exactness.

In the course of his survey, Willmott has a number of interesting things to say regarding the difference between Peranakans (Indonesian-born Chinese) and the Totoks (newcomers or *Sinkheh*), which probably apply in some degree to the Overseas Chinese as a whole, and on family and kinship (the latter can be profitably compared with Freedman and Skinner's observations regarding the Chinese in Singapore and Thailand). Although about one-half of the Semarang Chinese families are still of the 'joint' or 'stem' types, the 'conjugal' type is preferred by an increasingly large majority. The traditional patrilinear system has been largely replaced by a bilateral system, in which the wife's relations are as important as the husband's. 'The training and treatment of children has become increasingly lenient' (p. 77), and while filial piety is still widely accepted, 'it has been somewhat redefined, with greater emphasis on love, respect, and mutuality, and less on obedience and subservience' (p. 277). 'Women have been emancipated from the seclusion and complete submission of their traditional role, but they still usually centre their interests and activities within the household.' Marriage is now a matter for consultation between parents and young people, usually on the initiative of the latter. Divorce is still rare, but is not as strongly disapproved as formerly. Though concubinage still occasionally occurs, it is widely condemned in the Chinese community. 'Mutual obligations and social relations among kin are much less important than they used to be.'

One striking observation in Willmott's work relates to Christianity. Whereas Christianity in the People's China is greatly on the decline, Willmott states that Catholicism and Protestantism have both spread very rapidly in the Chinese community of Semarang. In 1926 it was reported that there were less than 3,000 Chinese Protestants and only about 300 Chinese Catholics in the whole of Java, but in 1955 there were probably about 5,000 Protestants and 2,000 Catholics in the Chinese community of Semarang alone (total ethnic Chinese 60,000, in a total population of all races of 360,000 (1955)). Nevertheless, religious belief among the Chinese community generally seemed to be on the decline. A questionnaire survey by Willmott in 1955 showed that the religious preferences among the students in non-Christian Chinese schools in Semarang were 'no religion' 59 per cent, 'Chinese religions' 22 per cent, and 'Christian' 19 per cent; in Christian Chinese schools in Semarang the preferences were 39, 5, and 56 per cent respectively.

Lea Williams, in *Overseas Chinese and Nationalism; the Genesis of the Pan-Chinese Movement in Indonesia* (Glencoe, Ill., 1960), discusses the many aspects of the broadening base of Chinese group life during the period 1900–16. The traditional organizations based on separate speech-groups or assuming the underground form of 'secret societies' were replaced by all kinds of modern unions, encompassing the Chinese living throughout Java and uniting into nation-wide organizations.

An important study incorporating the results of anthropological field work is T'ien Ju-k'ang, *The Chinese of Sarawak; a Study of Social Structure* (1955). Dr T'ien discusses the warp and woof of Chinese associations, clanship, the bazaar economy and the rubber trade, and relations with the mother country. He emphasizes the problem of power in Chinese society in Sarawak—at the bottom there was the huge majority of Chinese planters and labourers, in the middle was the fairly numerous class of small and smallish merchants, the middlemen, who gathered the local products and distributed the imported goods, and at the top the few big *towkays*. Patronage was highly concentrated. Dr T'ien says:

> Social conditions in Sarawak are such that a few individuals are able to make their influence penetrate into almost every aspect of social life thus bringing the general Chinese public almost completely under their control. No one in the Chinese community can advance without a 'back mountain' as it is called.

In the 1950s control by the big *towkays* over the rural areas seemed to be on the increase. Subject to the overall control of the British administrative officers, the 'Capitans China' (an institution which had died out in most other parts of Southeast Asia) ran the local Chinese communities. In the First Division four new Capitans China had recently (1954) been appointed.

Account should also be taken of the work of a Russian scholar on the Overseas Chinese, Mr N. A. Simoniya of the Institute of International Relations of the Soviet Academy of Sciences, Moscow, who, however, relies on secondary authorities. It illustrates the Marxist approach to the subject.[1] This is a summary of his conclusions.

The programme of construction now under way in the Chinese People's Republic means that the poverty and hunger which forced hundreds of thousands of Chinese peasants and artisans to abandon their native land is now a thing of the past. The People's Government has been successful in providing employment for 200,000 returning emigrants in the last few years. Over 10 million Chinese belonging to Overseas Chinese families are taking an active part in the socialist construction of China. In framing its policy towards the Overseas Chinese, the People's Government is guided by the fact that they are participating in the economic development of the countries in which they live within the framework of the local laws and customs. This policy is in keeping with the spirit of Bandung. The legacy of colonialism in Southeast Asia was an underdeveloped

---

[1] N. A. Simoniya, *Overseas Chinese in Southeast Asia; a Russian Study*, trans. by U.S. Joint Publications Research Service (Dec. 1961). In his Introduction the author criticizes the views of the 'imperialist' writers on the overseas Chinese, e.g. Cator, Skinner, and Purcell (p. 6).

(or practically undeveloped) industry on the one hand and an excessively developed colonial-type middleman trade tying the region's trade to the world capitalist market on the other. A heritage of colonialism in Southeast Asia is the continuing domination of the monopolies.

The Chinese bourgeoisie could play a very appreciable part in a solution of outstanding problems, given a positive attitude on the part of the several Southeast Asian Governments. The large-scale participation of the Chinese bourgeoisie in the construction of the national economy could be all the more useful since it has acquired a great deal of experience in the field of entrepreneurship. Moreover, it still maintains its old-established connexions with the markets of Southeast Asia and the Far East.

The wide scope of socialist transformations taking place in China in 1955–6 made it necessary to work out new regulations governing the Chinese emigrants' capital investments in China. These provided for the organization of Government companies to administer Overseas Chinese investments in China. Under the regulations, the capital invested in such companies by the Chinese immigrants would remain under their ownership even after the construction of Socialism had been completed in China. The emigrants might withdraw their capital after twelve years; they would receive an annual interest of 8 per cent, and might transfer 50 per cent of their annual profit abroad.

Thus (Mr Simoniya concludes) the policy of the Chinese Government towards the Overseas Chinese took into account the interests of Socialist construction in the People's Republic on the one hand and the interests of the Overseas Chinese on the other, besides serving the cause of peaceful coexistence and meeting the vital national economic requirements of the Southeast Asian countries.[2]

Finally, the observations of a well-known commentator on Chinese affairs can be summarized to indicate the general situation of the Chinese in Southeast Asia in the third quarter of the twentieth century. He, however, writes rather from the historical and economic than from the sociological angle.

The great underlying question of Southeast Asia, as of many other parts of the world (says C. P. FitzGerald) was how the uneven and backward economy of these countries could be modernized and developed to a point where the standard of living approached that achieved in the stable countries of the West. Could this be done by free enterprise, tempered perhaps by some State socialism and primed with foreign aid? Or could it only be achieved, as it was being achieved in China, by the forceful compulsion and mass enthusiasm of the Communist regime? Free enterprise must mean that capitalists were given scope to carry out

[2] An interesting study of a Teochiu community in Province Wellesley, Malaya, from the sociological angle, which came to hand after the above was written, is W. H. Newell, *Treacherous River* (1962). It deals with the problem of assimilation.

their operations, restrained from too great an exploitation of the workers, but unhampered by racist ideologies and excessive nationalist policies. In Southeast Asia the capitalists were the Chinese. It was not possible to discriminate against capitalists because they were Chinese and at the same time successfully to oppose Communism, because that too was backed by China. In the long run Southeast Asian countries must decide whether they wanted Chinese capitalism or Chinese Communism, and the run was not going to be very long.[3]

Education

In the first edition of this work (pp. 46–47) the rapid extension of education, both in China and among the Overseas Chinese, consequent on the adoption of *Kuo Yü* (the National Language) as the medium of instruction was described. This movement is now well known to all students of China, and all that it is necessary to add here is that education through *Kuo Yü* was extended greatly in China after the coming into power of the People's Government and has simultaneously been vigorously developed among the Overseas Chinese.

The partiality of so many Overseas Chinese for education through the medium of the Chinese language, however, can be said to be the greatest barrier to the assimilation of the Overseas Chinese into the communities of the Southeast Asian countries, and has been the occasion of political action among the local nationalist parties to check and offset it. In Thailand the Government has made continuous efforts to control Chinese education since the 1930s; in Indonesia since independence the liberty of Chinese, whether China- or local-born, to run their own schools has been progressively curtailed. In the Federation of Malaya the policy is to make Malay, the 'national language', the main medium of instruction in schools and the Chinese members of the Alliance Government have acquiesced in this policy. It has nevertheless been the subject of protests and demonstrations on the part of teachers and pupils in Chinese schools. In Singapore efforts have been made to promote the use of Malay, the official language, in education, and Malay middle schools have now been established there for the first time. Nevertheless, education was one of the subjects reserved to the State of Singapore under the Malaysia constitution, and this is no doubt because Singapore's population was predominantly Chinese and a majority of them wished to ensure that their children were educated through the medium of the Chinese language.

The political and social consequences of the continued existence of Chinese schools in Southeast Asia are considered in the Conclusion to this work.

[3] C. P. FitzGerald, 'Overseas Chinese in South East Asia', *Australian J. of Pol. & Hist.*, viii/1 (May 1962).

Religion

On going overseas to the Nanyang the Chinese took with them their religious beliefs. Be the principle of Buddhism, Taoism, or Confucianism effective or ossified, there can be no doubt at all that the world of spirits, demons, gods, and heroes is still a very real thing to the majority of Chinese and goes with them wherever they go. Dr Ta Chen[4] notes that among the items of household expenditure other than food, clothing, and shelter, that for religious practices predominates over all others both in the emigrant and non-emigrant families of east Kwangtung and south Fukien. ('These expenditures', he says, 'are a good index of the prevalence of religious concern.') Scepticism has assuredly grown with the advance of education, but for the majority it would seem that 'keeping in' with the Great Unseen was as much a matter of insurance as of piety and ethics.

Broadly speaking, the religion of the villagers of south China consists of the worship of Shen, Fu, and Yao in addition to the cult of their own ancestors. Shen and Fu are spirits from Buddhism and Taoism (especially the popular, corrupted, and confused aspects of the two religious systems); whereas Yao, a ghost, is from primitive ancestor worship via Confucianism. In one emigrant community in south Fukien Dr Ta Chen's investigators found that of 224 persons questioned, 154 expressed belief in Shen and Fu, 60 had no religious preferences, 5 believed in Christianity, and 5 seemed to be wavering between acceptance and rejection of Shen and Fu. Comparative popularity would, we may be sure, depend largely on results; for, like the Roman gods, a Chinese god is expected to render a return for respect accorded and the offerings made to him. A Roman observed his rites with scrupulous adherence to the letter of the law, expecting that if he did not the gods would make it an excuse to wriggle out of the bargain, and the Chinese regard their gods in much the same spirit.[5]

Amongst the most popular goddesses in the Buddhist pantheon both in China and overseas is Kwan Yin, the goddess of mercy, 'she who hears the sounds (prayers) of mortals—she who looks down on the world and hears its cries'. She is the counterpart of the Taoist goddess T'ien Hou Sheng Mu, Holy Mother, queen of heaven, and she is credited with attributes similar to those of the Virgin Mary. Kwan Yin was originally the Buddhist male god, Avalokiteswara, who changed his sex to female some centuries after his arrival in China.

Another popular god among the Overseas Chinese is Kwan Ti, the god of war.

---

[4] *Emigrant Communities.*

[5] Ibid. chap. x, and Purcell, *The Chinese in Malaya* (1948), chap. vi. There is an instructive article, 'Chinese Contemporary Cults', by Clarence Burton Day in *FEQ*, vi/3 (May 1947), which covers a number of the gods and heroes worshipped in south China and the Nanyang.

Each craft or guild has its own patron saint—Wu Ku Lao Yeh for farmers, Chiao Sheng Lao Yeh (whose festival is on the 7th or the 5th moon) for carpenters, Shui Hsin Lao Yeh for incense-stick makers, Kwan Ti, the god of war, in his capacity of god of wealth, for tradesmen, and T'ien Hou Sheng Mu, the Taoist queen of heaven, for fishermen and sailors (but overseas her name is changed to Ma Tsu (Ma Chew Poh)), which is also popular in Amoy. In many Cantonese houses the image of the household god of the earth, T'o Yei Shan or Tei Chu, is placed *underneath* a table! The god is not worshipped in Hokkien households.

In addition to the worship of the standard deities of the Buddhist and Taoist cults, the Chinese of the Nanyang have special deities of their own which are worshipped by them only overseas or in the emigrant communities from which they sprang. The outstanding examples are Sam Po Tai Shan for the Shen, and Toh Peh Kong (Hokkien), Ta Pai Kung (Mandarin), or Tai Pak Kung (Cantonese) for the Fu.

Sam Po Tai Shan is none other than the spirit of the famous Grand Eunuch Cheng Ho of the Ming dynasty who visited Malacca in the early years of the fifteenth century.[6] He is particularly worshipped in Malacca. Crawfurd remarks, 'Sam Po Kung (Sam Po Tai Shan) is evidently a name to be conjured with among the illiterate classes. The miracles which he performed to save his countrymen from the perils of their travels in unknown lands are among the marvels of romance, illustrating, in a striking way, one of the factors in a genesis of a myth.'

Toh Peh Kong, however, is the most popular hero among the Overseas Chinese. But one may search for him in vain in the standard books on Chinese religion.[7] In Siam he is known as Pan Tou Kung. He probably derives from Tu Ti (earth god), but overseas he is primarily the spirit of the pioneers. The Chinese pioneers of the early days suffered terrible hardships and were honoured in memory by those who came after them. Toh Peh Kong seems to be the personification of the pioneer spirit generally and is not the deification of a special person as Sam Po Tai Shan is of Cheng Ho.[8]

A worship of very long standing in Malaya is that of Wang Yeh, who has the spiritual function of visiting the universe as the representative of heaven. The early settlers brought the worship with them from Fukien province.[9]

[6] See pp. 17, 18.
[7] In particular the monumental work by Henri F. S. Doré, *Recherches sur les superstitions en Chine* (Shanghai, 1911–28).   [8] See Skinner, *Chinese Society in Thailand*, pp. 129–30.
[9] Wang Yeh was worshipped from early days but the Wang Kang Festival in Malacca wherein five images of this deity were carried does not seem to have originated until 1886.

Chinese Mohammedans exist in the Shan States and in Indonesia, though in the latter country their numbers are not great. Chinese Christians are comparatively few in Southeast Asia, though in Malaya, for example, they increased between 1901 and 1931 by one-half (50·2 per cent) to 30,738, while during the same period the Chinese population increased by only 45·5 per cent. Among the Churches the Roman Catholic Church has the strongest hold.

PART II

THE CHINESE IN BURMA

5

DEMOGRAPHY

A CENSUS of Burma was last taken in 1941 but the detailed returns were lost during the Japanese occupation of the country. The gross returns gave the total population as 16,824,798. Since then we have only estimates to guide us. The *Statesman's Year-Book, 1956* gives 19,242,000 as the estimated total population in 1954; the UN *Demographic Yearbook, 1961* gives the estimate of 20,662,000 for mid-1960 (stating that a sample census was taken on 1 February 1953 of 252 towns only, approximating to the urban area of the Union, in which the population counted was 2,940,704); the UN *Demographic Yearbook, 1962* gives an estimate of 21,527,000 for 1961. The number of Chinese in Burma by the Census of 1931 was 193,594, 127,099 being males and 66,545 females.

In the first edition of this work reasons were given for estimating the number of ethnic Chinese in Burma in 1947 at 300,000. Tinker, referring to this estimate, says, 'The author was assured by an independent and authoritative source that this represents the minimum figure'.[1] He goes on to observe:

Today the numbers of Chinese in the country are rising rapidly: before the war the total was 193,594; the immigration figures show a present-day total of 157,000, but this is definitely far short of the actual total which must number about 350,000. Whereas there were 30,626 Chinese in Rangoon in pre-war days, 70,366 were enumerated at the 1953 census. The all-Burma figures must bear some relation to the increase of 133 per cent.

The same author later on in his book says:

The infiltration of Chinese into Burma presents a more serious problem [than that of frontier demarcation]: Chinese overland immigration has substantially increased since the Second World War but received little attention until the KMT

---

[1] Hugh Tinker, *The Union of Burma*, 2nd ed. (London, 1959), p. 189 and n. 2.

question became serious; the Burma Government then took steps to watch the border, closing all entry routes between the Shwel and Salween Rivers (i.e. the frontier east of Bhamo). Frontier officials have been unable to prevent illegal entry, and a steady stream of immigration continues. Many are refugees from Communist oppression; others, possibly, are Communist agents.[2]

Mr B. Ward-Perkins, I.C.S. (Retd), to whom I referred this point, considered that 350,000 was too high and supported this view from his experience, but I have felt myself constrained to accept it with some reserve as representing the most recent informed opinion.

Many persons of Chinese *race* in Burma had for long regarded them-selves as Burmese citizens and had no more interest in China than U.S. citizens of the second or third generations have in their European ancestral homes.[3] One authority stated in June 1948:[4] '. . . The best information based on information given by various Chinese Guilds would place the total number of Chinese through the whole of Burma at approximately 300,000. In the absence of any reliable census, this has generally been accepted as the closest possible estimate.'

Another person entitled to speak with authority states:

From personal observation in 1946–7, I should say that the Chinese in Burma were no more numerous than they had been in 1939. Most of the racketeers brought in by the Burma Road had gone off to Shanghai. . . . I should think that 19,000 is an underestimate of the numbers that left in 1942. I saw many thousands on all the trains and stations going north from Rangoon to Myitkyina. If 200,000 was a correct figure in the 1930s I should think 300,000 is the top figure in the 1940s.[5]

In mid-1948 the Burmese Government announced that the registration of all foreigners in Burma would shortly begin, but this undoubtedly was held up by the disturbances within the country. Both before and after the Second World War Chinese nationals were asked to register with the Chinese consulate-general in Rangoon. Pre-war registration records were all lost during the Japanese occupation, while the number who had registered with the consulate since it reopened in 1945 did not exceed 30,000 by June 1948.

Of the 194,000 Chinese enumerated in 1931, 104,000 were shown as born in Burma and 90,000 in China. There was, according to the 1921 Census Report for Burma (para. 65), a tendency among the Chinese born in Burma to give their birthplace as China. The author of the

[2] Tinker, *The Union of Burma*, pp. 371–2.

[3] By the constitution of the Union of Burma, 1946, Burmese nationality was accorded to all those of whom both parents belonged to an indigenous race of the Union, or who had at least one grandparent of such race, or who were British subjects claiming at least eight years' residence in the Union and intending to stay there.

[4] Note from the Chinese Embassy, Rangoon, quoted in a letter to the author from Mr J. S. Furnivall.

[5] G. E. Harvey in *British Rule in Burma* (London, 1946), p. 69 n., says that there were 'a couple of hundred thousand' Chinese in Burma in 1942.

report of the 1931 Census said it was impossible to estimate the error this produced in the statistics, but it was probably not large. This tendency, however (the writer understands on the best authority), did not survive the troublous times in China in the 1930s.

The following table shows the number of *immigrants* from China in the two censal years (*but nearly 25,000 were of races other than Chinese*):

Burma: Immigrants from China 1921 and 1931[6]

Natural division in which enumerated	1921	1931	Increase	
			Actual	Per cent
Total Burma (Province of)	102,344	114,270	11,926	11·7
Burman total	74,282	86,249	11,967	16·1
Delta	40,785	49,181	8,396	20·6
Coast (Arakan)	585	622	37	6·3
Coast (Tenasserim)	7,527	7,626	99	1·3
Centre	5,902	8,267	2,365	40·1
North	19,483	20,553	1,070	5·5
CHIN	23	53	30	130·4
SALWEEN	430	377	− 53	− 12·3
SHAN	27,609	27,591	− 18	− 0·1

The total population of Burma according to the 1941 Census was 16,823,798, showing an increase of approximately 12 per cent since 1931. The *Burma Handbook*[7] for 1943 in this connexion states:

Apart from the increase in areas, it is not safe to assume an increase of 12 per cent in respect of any particular group or district; it is probable that the number of Chinese has increased more than 12 per cent as a result of the opening of the Burma road in 1939. . . . The current situation in 1943 is different again from that of 1941: many of the Chinese have no doubt made their way out of the country in 1942.

The following table is abstracted from the Census of 1931:

Chinese in Burma in 1931

	Total population	Chinese
Total population of Burma		14,667,146
Total Chinese in Burma		193,594
Arakan Division . . .	*1,008,535*	*978*
Akyab	637,580	689
Arakan Hill Tracts . .	21,418	. .
Kyaukpyu . . .	220,292	140
Sandoway . . .	129,245	149

[6] *Census of India, 1931* (Rangoon, 1933), xi/1, p. 63. See p. 6 of pt. 1 regarding the non-Chinese immigrants from China.

[7] Issued by the Government of Burma (in exile) (Govt. of India Press, Simla), pp. 198–200.

	Total population	Chinese
Pegu Division . . .	*2,549,637*	*54,001*
Rangoon . . .	400,415	30,626
Pegu	489,969	7,552
Tharawaddy . . .	508,319	2,687
Hanthawaddy . . .	408,831	5,352
Insein	331,452	5,413
Prome	410,651	2,371
Irrawaddy Division . .	*2,334,774*	*25,950*
Bassein	571,043	6,280
Henzada . . .	613,280	2,624
Myaungyma . . .	444,784	7,330
Maubin	371,509	3,610
Pyapon	334,158	6,106
Tenasserim Division . .	*1,872,668*	*27,593*
Salween	53,186	166
Thaton	532,628	4,982
Amherst . . .	516,233	11,287
Tavoy	179,964	3,741
Mergui	161,987	3,835
Toungoo . . .	428,670	3,582
Magwe Division . . .	*1,722,044*	*3,196*
Thayetmyo . . .	274,177	698
Minbu	277,876	627
Magwe	499,573	1,289
Pakokku . . .	499,181	502
Chin Hills . . .	171,237	80
Mandalay Division . .	*1,696,332*	*6,050*
Mandalay . . .	371,636	3,153
Kyaukse . . .	151,320	347
Meiktila . . .	309,999	384
Myingyan . . .	472,557	727
Yamethin . . .	390,820	1,439
Sagaing Division . .	*1,918,058*	*11,123*
Bhamo	121,193	2,545
Myitkyina . . .	171,524	4,112
Shwebo	446,790	811
Sagaing	335,965	229
Katha	254,170	2,715
L. Chindwin . . .	383,434	475
U. Chindwin . . .	204,982	236
Eastern States . . .	*1,565,098*	*64,703*
N. Shan States . .	636,107	60,550
S. Shan States . .	870,230	3,899
Karenni . . .	58,761	254[8]

According to the Census of 1911, there were then 122,000 Chinese in Burma, 1,200 of these being Yunnanese Muslims. During the decade

[8] Details by race for the Naga Hills and the Wa States were not available.

1921–31 the number of Chinese residents increased by 30 per cent, from 149,000 to 194,000, whereas the Indians increased by only 15 per cent. There were in 1931, however, 1,018,000 Indians, five times the number of Chinese in Burma.

Of the total of 193,594 for 1931, 86,361 were Fukienese or Cantonese, 40,688 Yunnanese (including 685 Panthays), and the remaining 66,445 were from elsewhere in China south of the Yangtze. In 1931, 68 per cent of the Chinese other than Yunnanese were enumerated in the Delta; most of the remainder were found in the Tenasserim part of the coast area (15 per cent), and in the centre (9 per cent). The numbers of Cantonese and the Fukienese recorded were 33,990 and 50,038 respectively, but it was probable that most of the 'other and unspecified' Chinese amounting to 41,875 were also Cantonese and Fukienese.

The Chinese fanned out from Rangoon along the railway and steamer lines. Nearly half of the Chinese in Burma were to be found within a hundred miles of the capital city. In 1921 the Irrawaddy delta had 64,276 Chinese residents; in 1931 the number had increased to 86,144. Moulmein had 5,603 Chinese in 1911; in 1935 more than 12,000.[9]

In Burma the overseas Chinese did not occupy the predominant position that they do in Malaya, Siam, Indochina, Indonesia, and the Philippines, and they were decidedly second to the Indians in the commercial life of the country. In 1931 they were classified by occupation as follows: traders and merchants, 41 per cent; carpenters and workers in metal and leather, 38 per cent; semi-skilled workers, 9 per cent; clerical workers, 5 per cent; miscellaneous, 7 per cent. Only 21,436 (18,802 males; 2,634 females) were shown as engaged in the exploitation of animals and vegetation. (Apart from a few market gardeners, there were no real Chinese employed on the land itself.) Chinese general merchandise shops were found in nearly all cities and towns in Burma, and in many towns the Chinese were the sole agents for the sale of petroleum products. Since the Second World War they had taken the place of many Indian shopkeepers, the number of Indians having greatly diminished. But they did not have a grip of the rice trade as they had in Siam, Indochina, and the Philippines, this being very largely in the hands of Indians—mostly Marwaris, Maimanis, &c. The Chinese were active bidders for fishery and ferry rights in many streams.

In Rangoon Chinese business men promoted their common interests through a chamber of commerce which before the war elected a member (who had to be a British subject—though the members voting were not necessarily so) to the Burma legislature. The Chinese Overseas Bank, the Bank of China, and Chinese insurance, shipping, rice, and mercantile firms maintained five branches along the Burma Road and the payment

---

[9] J. L. Christian, *Modern Burma* (Berkeley, 1942), p. 270.

of Chinese customs could be made through these branches. No Chinese registered steamers were engaged in the Burma trade.[10]

Chinese labour was principally employed in the Shan States and it was largely Yunnanese who came to work here in the dry season.[11] The one occupation in which the Chinese contributed a substantial portion of the labour force and worked for members of another race was mining. In the case of Chinese employed by the Consolidated Tin Company at Hermingyi, Tavoy District, many worked on a piece-work system with a minimum of supervision. The Chinese mining labourers preferred the tribute system by which was paid to the owner of the mine so much for every picul of tin mined by themselves.[12] Agricultural and forest labour accounted for only 6 per cent of all Chinese employed in Burma at the Census of 1931. Chinese and Indian immigrants had a considerable share in certain trades, such as carpentry, furniture-making, and the slipper industry. However, the Burmese craftsman was in the majority and worked also as a cart-maker, goldsmith, worker in lacquer, and—in the Delta—as boat-maker.[13]

'Literacy', said the 1931 Census, 'implies being able to write a letter to a friend and to read the answer to it', and by this standard there were 52,000 literate and 75,000 illiterate Chinese males in Burma; for females the figures were 10,000 literate and 57,000 illiterate. As regards literacy in English, 5,000 Chinese males and 936 females satisfied the census test.

There were in 1931 slightly more than two males to every female among the Chinese in Burma proper, and this led to a considerable amount of intermarriage between surplus Chinese men and women of the indigenous races. The fact that the custom was (as stated elsewhere) for the male offspring of such unions to assume Chinese race and for the females to assume the race of the mother would account for the number of Chinese males born in Burma being stated as more than the number of females.

Chinese immigration into Burma may conveniently be divided into those who come overland, who may be called Mountain Chinese, and those who come by sea, who may be designated Maritime Chinese. Of the 194,000 total in 1931, more than 60,000 lived in the Shan and Wa States along the Chinese border. Of the total of 114,000 'immigrants from China' in 1931 (as has been noted above), nearly 25,000 represented immigrants from China other than those of Chinese race. Presumably all those immigrants came overland from China, and were mainly Shan-Tayoks and Shans, but a few Maingthas were included. Many of them would be caravan traders who would return to China after

[10] Christian, *Modern Burma*, pp. 271, 273.
[11] Virginia Thompson, *Labor in Southeast Asia*, p. 1.
[12] J. Russell Andrus, *Burmese Economic Life* (Stamford UP, 1947), p. 275.
[13] Thompson, p. 34.

the Census. In Bhamo district, of the 10,161 immigrants from China, only 1,523 were Chinese, the remainder being mainly Shan-Tayoks.[14] The Yunnanese are mostly found in the northern Shan States. Between 1921 and 1931 they increased by 14 per cent while speakers of Yunnanese increased by 21 per cent. In 1921 there were 4,382 Yunnanese, or 77 per cent of the total number, who spoke languages other than Yunnanese; in 1931 there were only 577, or 1 per cent of the total number.[15] Chinese other than Yunnanese increased by 40 per cent, while speakers of Chinese languages other than Yunnanese by 67 per cent. Taking the Chinese in Burma as a whole, they increased in number by 30 per cent between the two censuses, while speakers of the Chinese *language* increased by 46 per cent. The big increase in Chinese speakers was due to the reduction of the number of Chinese who spoke other languages from 27,548 in 1921 to 15,957 in 1931. These facts are of some cultural and political interest.

The illicit infiltration that took place before 1940-1 was not regarded as a menace in the sense that it would lead to problems such as exist in Malaya. The administration kept a wary eye on the Chinese because they ran the illicit opium and gambling dens, tea-shops, liquor-shops, &c. The common folk did not resent them at all. They offered dissipations and they were not so parsimonious as the Indians. It was only in 1940-1, when the deputy ministers and other officials of the KMT came into Burma and 'behaved as if they owned the place', that public opinion (including that of the resident Chinese) was aroused. The fear commonly expressed was that, under pressure from the United States, the British Government would force the Burma Government to give virtually independent control of the line of communication through Burma to various Sino-American bodies, and that under cover of this the Chinese would establish permanent control over Burma. One high authority has stated to the writer: 'Nothing made the moderate Burma politician so keen on independence as the way the British and United States Governments compelled Burma to give facilities to a Chinese regime that everyone in Burma knew was rotten.'

When the Chinese armies came into Burma in 1945 there can be no doubt that they behaved as if they were in a conquered country, and throughout the later campaigns their commanders frequently issued proclamations implying, and sometimes saying openly, that the British were gone for good and that the Chinese were now in control. Without

---

[14] *Census of India, 1931*, xi/1, 63.

[15] Yunnanese Muslims were usually called Panthays. They showed a reduction in number at the 1931 census. Most of them were enumerated in the southern Shan States (438), northern Shan States (125), Katha (241), Myitkyina (53), and Rangoon (51); the remainder were scattered. Yunnanese other than Panthays increased by 15 per cent. In the northern Shan States 87 per cent were enumerated; most of the remainder were in the southern Shan States (1,026); and in the districts of Myitkyina (2,270), Bhamo (2,116), Katha (1,431), Mandalay (549), Shwebo (213), and Rangoon (136).

any sanction from the Burma authorities they erected on the recreation ground at Lashio an enormous monument commemorating Chinese victories. Later, in January 1946, after all Chinese troops had been withdrawn, a battalion suddenly appeared at Waingmaw, just across the Irrawaddy from Myitkyina, and it was reported that the rest of the division was marching down from Paoshan. A British brigade, however, was available to counter this move and, after some tense days, the intervention of General Chiang Kai-shek resulted in the Chinese troops being ordered back.

This incident considerably alarmed Burma politicians regarding Chinese intentions. The fear was less of infiltration than of exploitation and conquest. It is noteworthy that schools and training centres in Chungking used maps showing all northern Burma and parts of Assam as *China Irredenta*.[16] If China should disintegrate, as most educated Burmans have expected during the previous eight years, then what they feared was an irruption by large fragments of defeated armies, well enough armed and organized to devastate much of the country. Which was, to some extent, what happened after the Communist victory of 1949.

6

THE CHINESE IN BURMA PRIOR TO 1850

THE story of the Chinese in Burma stands apart from that of their fellows in other territories in Southeast Asia. It resembles that of the Chinese in Indochina, or rather in Annam, in so far as the contact with these countries goes back a very long way and, until fairly recent times, the main approach to both of them was overland. But the similarity should not be exaggerated. For one thing intercourse between China and Annam was nearly a thousand years earlier than that between China and Burma; there were no trade routes between China and Annam of anything like as great consequence as those between China and Burma, and while Annam was successfully conquered and occupied for a great part of the first millennium of the Christian era, the invasions of Burma were on the whole a failure. The greater differences in the nature of the Chinese intercourse with Burma and that with the Philippines, Siam, Malaya, and Indonesia will appear in the course of this chapter.

[16] The writer, while on a visit to Chungking during the Second World War, saw a map issued by the Chinese Military Academy at Chengtu showing *China Irredenta* and including Malaya with the date of its loss by China given as 1896! (Why 1896 it is not possible to say. On 1 Jan. that year the Federated Malay States came into being. but that had nothing to do with China. The claim, if tenable, must date from the voyages of Cheng Ho in the early fifteenth century.)

Because of the difficulty of communication between China and Burma their connexion has never been close, despite the racial affinity of their inhabitants. It has been far easier for Burma to communicate by sea with India than by land with China, as is shown by the powerful influence which India has had over Burmese culture over a period of many centuries in contrast to the feeble effect of Chinese culture; thus, although the two countries have a basically common religion, yet the (Theravada) Buddhism of Burma is distinct from the Mahayana Buddhism of China, and has been derived from the west and not from the east. Politically and economically Burma has long been more intimately linked with India than with China, and the political relationship between Burma and China has never been satisfactorily defined.

For the sake of descriptive convenience, the Chinese in Burma can (as has been said in the preceding chapter) be divided into Mountain and Maritime Chinese. The former, sometimes reinforced by military expeditions, made up a greater part of the total for many centuries, and even now there are over 40,000 Yunnanese residing on the Burmese side of the border and these must nearly all have come by land. The earlier immigration, however, was very impermanent and largely seasonal, and, numerically speaking, could at no time compare with the later movement of the Maritime Chinese, whose era begins with the extension to Burma of British power in the nineteenth century and the opening up of the country to trade on a scale hitherto unknown. The history of the Mountain Chinese is to a great extent the history of the caravans; that of the Maritime Chinese belongs more to the general development of Southeast Asia.

Burma was the natural bridge for racial migrations and the temporary home of most of the peoples who inhabit the great Indochinese peninsula. The Burmese themselves are believed to have come down from the hills of the northern Shan States into the plains of Burma from A.D. 839 onwards.[1] Even at the present day the Chinese (mostly Shan-Tayoks, Chinese Kachins, and Lishus) are moving southwards into the hill country of north Hsenwi State, though on a small scale as race migrations go. It is recorded that during the T'ang dynasty a Burmese embassy, accompanied by a representative of the Shan kingdom of Nanchao in what is now Yunnan, visited China. Christian supposes that the presence of the kingdom of Nanchao as a barrier State, combined with China's remoteness, accounts for the paucity of China's influence on Burma before the time of Kublai Khan. Burma's racial affinities were with China, but its cultural ties were with India.[2]

[1] G. H. Luce, 'Burma's Debt to Pagan', *JBRS*, xxii (1932), pp. 120–7, cited by Christian, *Modern Burma*, p. 22.
[2] Christian says (p. 22, n. 20): 'The entire problem of Burma's contacts with China is dealt with, in E. H. Parker, *Burma with Special Reference to Her Relations with China*, Rangoon, 1893. See also G. H. Luce, "The Ancient Pyu", *JBRS*, xxvii (1937), pp. 239–53, for sources

C.S.E.A.— C

For many centuries the bulk of Burma's trade with China had passed along the Taiping river, in earlier days through Kaungsin, until the influence of that place was overshadowed by Bhamo from the fifteenth century onwards.[3] The caravans which passed over this route were essentially the same in the fifteenth as in the nineteenth century.

In 1284 an army of Kublai Khan marched against Pagan to enforce the payment of tribute refused by the Burmese three years before, when they had put to death the embassy sent by the Emperor of China. In 1287 Pagan was destroyed, and for a time Burma was under Chinese suzerainty. In 1298 there was another invasion, but the Chinese were expelled in that same year.[4] Burmese authorities seem generally to take the view that after 1298 Burma was independent, but a British historian, Mr B. R. Pearn, remarks: 'I do not think that the successor states to the Pagan Kingdom were tributary to China till about 1600; tribute appears to have ceased in the declining days of the Ming dynasty.' A Chinese embassy visited Burma in 1405.[5] In 1449 the Chinese attempted the conquest of Mogaung, but were successfully resisted.[6]

After the Ming dynasty was overthrown in 1644, China became the prey of freebooting armies which ravaged her outlying provinces and made periodic incursions into Burmese territory. Early in the reign of Pindale (1648–61), a Burmese army had been defeated by the Chinese at Wetwun, near the modern hill-station of Maymo, and the invaders had laid waste the country almost up to Ava itself. In 1650, however, the factors of the East India Company at Fort St George received news that the Burmese had 'defeated their plundering neighbours and that the country was likely to be settled and in a peaceful condition'.[7] Yun Li, 'the last of the Mings', proclaimed Emperor of China at Canton, was attacked by the Manchus, but escaped to Burma. Here he met 20,000 men under

on Burma's relations with China to the fall of Pagan, 1287. In Kuo Tsung-fei, "A Brief History of the Trade Routes Between Burma, Indochina and Yunnan", *T'ien Hsia Monthly*, xii (1941), pp. 9–32, the major emphasis, with reference to Chinese sources, is on Sino-Burmese overland contacts before 1600. A Japanese account of the period before the Manchu dynasty is Jinichi Yano, "Biruma no Shina ni Taisuro Chōkō Kankei ni Tsuite", *Tōyō Gakuho*, xvii (1928), pp. 1–39.

It is outside the purpose of this study to describe Sino-Burmese contacts except in so far as they bear on the economic and social life of the Chinese community in Burma, but the above note is inserted in deference to those whose interests lie in the field of the historical investigation of the trade routes.

[3] D. G. E. Hall, *Early English Intercourse with Burma* (London, 1928), p. 121.

[4] Khin Maung Gale, *New Times of Burma* (30 Nov. 1947), says: 'In that year Burma went her own way and was after that as little dependent on China as she will be dependent on the United Kingdom after 4 January 1948.'

[5] Henry Yule, *A Narrative of the Mission sent by the Governor-General of India to the Court of Ava in 1855* (London, 1858), p. 53, says that 'the army sent by the Great Khan to subdue the city of Mien (the Chinese name for Burma) was commanded by a valiant captain, and consisted principally of jesters, with whom the court was always furnished'. The invasions were along the Chinese trade route.

[6] Édouard Huber, 'Une Ambassade des Chinois en Birmanie en 1406', *BEFEO*, iv/142 (Jan.–Feb. 1904).

[7] D. G. E. Hall, p. 60, citing Foster, *English Factories*.

the Governor of Yunnan, was defeated in 1662, surrendered, and was taken to Peking and strangled.[8]

After the surrender of Yunhli, the Burmese and the Chinese appear to have remained at peace for more than a century, and no sooner was war at an end than the highways from China to Bhamo were frequented by traders and travellers. The Dutch factors in Ava developed a large clandestine trade with the Chinese merchants from Yunnan. It was not long before they came to realize the immense possibilities of opening up trade with western China through Bhamo (in later days to be a focal point on one arm of the famous 'Burma Road'). Out of this project a quarrel arose between the Dutch and the Court of Ava which brought a final breach in 1679 and the closing down of the factories. The Burmese Government prohibited their direct trade with Chinese merchants.[9]

Immediately before the next war of 1765 the trade seems to have been of considerable importance. We read of large caravans of 300 and 400 oxen, and others of 2,000 ponies, carrying silk and other merchandise between China and Bhamo.[10] About 1750 a large colony was mining silver at Mao-lung (probably Bawdwin) and the chief merchant, visiting Ava, persuaded the King to send to Peking one of those complimentary embassies which the Chinese regarded as tribute bearers. Two hairpins of silver and a gilt pagoda mounted on an elephant were sent as presents. The Emperor Ch'ien Lung entertained their envoy at a banquet and at his departure gave him a gold slab inscribed in the imperial hand, 'Happy Pacification of the Western Jewel'. But the 'Western Jewel' was far from being pacified; the Mao-lung colony was dispersed, the merchants were executed, and the envoy returned to find his King a captive in Pegu and Ava a smoking ruin.[11]

Misunderstanding now arose between certain Chinese traders and the Burmese officials at Bhamo. An enterprising trader, Loli by name, requested permission to throw a bridge across the Taiping at the village of Namba. The Burmese officials refused to grant the request on their own responsibilities and referred it to the Court of Ava. Loli was annoyed at this and became impertinent, whereupon the Burmese officials seized him on suspicion of being a Chinese officer in disguise. He was taken to Ava as a prisoner, but was later released. He was then told that he could carry on with his trading and build the bridge. On returning to Bhamo, however, he found that his goods had been tampered with. He demanded compensation, which was refused. About this time another Chinese trader at the head of a Shan caravan of 2,000 ponies had sold

[8] John Anderson, *A report of an Expedition into Western Yunnan via Bhamo* (Calcutta, 1871), p. 23.   [9] D. G. E. Hall, *Europe and Burma* (London, 1945), p. 34.
[10] Anderson, citing Burney, 'Translations of the Burmese Chronicles', *Asiatic Society J.* vi. 121 ff.
[11] G. H. Luce, 'Chinese Invasions of Burma in the Eighteenth Century', *JBRS*, xv, pt. 2 (Aug. 1925).

goods on credit to a Burmese who had refused to pay. These incidents coming together stirred up Chinese feeling which was further inflamed by the intrigues of Burmese refugees in China. A Chinese army thereupon marched into Burma and besieged Kaungton in 1767, but the campaign ended in a Burmese triumph. Another Chinese army dispatched in 1769 suffered a similar fate.[12]

The utter failure of Ch'ien Lung's Burma campaigns cost him a great deal of treasure and the flower of his generals. We find the Emperor, too, bewailing the cowardice of his Chinese troops.[13]

The history of the intercourse between Burma and China after 1770 is one of peace, in spite of minor incidents and friction such as when, soon after this date, a party of Shan Sawbwas, sent to Peking in an embassy, were seized and detained until 1778. Another embassy was, however, sent in 1787. In 1790 a Chinese embassy arrived in Burma by the Bhamo and Muangswa (Muse?) route, bringing three Chinese so-called princesses as concubines for the King of Ava. The 'princesses', it turned out, were natives of the town of Malong in Yunnan, and from the circumstance that their feet were not bound after the custom in vogue among Chinese ladies, it was evident that they were ladies of low rank and that the Chinese had 'imposed on the amorous propensities' of the sun-descended King of Ava.[14]

Father Sangermano, who lived in Ava from 1783 to 1806, speaks of the trade conducted between China and Burma in these terms:

The Chinese Junan [Yunnan] coming down by Kuangtaung and along the great river Ava, bring to the Burmese capital in great boats, several of the commodities of their country, as wrought silks, paper, tea, various kinds of fruit, and other trifles, and they return laden with cotton, raw silk, salt, birds' feathers, and that black varnish which, as we have said, is distilled from a tree: this prepared and perfumed, is the celebrated commodity known as Chinese varnish.[15]

The Chinese (said Captain Cox) thought kindly of the Burma brand of cotton from which they made nankeens. The city of Sagaing was the staple from which the boats carrying cotton started from China. Each boat carried a hundred baskets of a hundred *viss*[16] weight a piece, and late in the eighteenth century the journey took from thirty to forty days.[17]

[12] Incidents of the war were the arrogant order of the Emperor Ch'ien Lung for disposing of the Burmese and the taking of Bhamo by Colonel Hung Pang in a surprise attack. See *Ch'ien Lung Cheng Mien Tien Chi*, trans. as 'Histoire de la conquête de la Birmanie par les Chinois', by M. Camille Imbault-Huart, *J. Asiatique*, sér. vi, xi (Feb., Mar. 1878). See also Harvey, *Hist. of Burma*, p. 253. Harvey says that such instances were trivial and could have been adjusted had the two Governments been in communication with each other; but they had no embassy system.
[13] Parker, *Burma*, p. 31.   [14] Anderson, *Expedition into W. Yunnan*, p. 32.
[15] *The Burmese Empire a Hundred Years Ago as Described by Father (Vincentius) Sangermano, with Notes and Introduction by John Jardine* (London, 1893), p. 217.
[16] A *viss* was a hundred ticals in weight, or 3·65 lb avoirdupois.
[17] D. G. E. Hall, *Europe and Burma*, p. 82, citing Captain Hiram Cox, *Journal of a Residence in the Burmhan Empire* (London, 1821) (relates to the year 1797).

We are now approaching the period of awakened British interest in China when Burma seemed to offer a short cut to that remote country. Burma at this time was glorying in her defeat of the Chinese in 1765–9, and in her later conquest of Siam, for her era of expansion coincided with the growth of British power in India. Consequently, the stage was set for a clash which came over the ill-defined frontier between Arakan and Bengal and Burmese aggression in Assam.[18] Burma was a medieval State brought up against the modern world; 'failing reformation from within (says Furnivall), foreign intervention was inevitable'.[19] Continual friction led to a series of wars. The first ended in 1826 with the cession of two maritime provinces—Arakan, bordering on Bengal, and Tenasserim reaching down to the Malay Peninsula. The second war in 1852 linked up the earlier possessions through the occupation of Pegu and brought the whole of Lower Burma under British rule. In 1886, after a third war, the absorption of the country within the Indian Empire was completed by the annexation of Upper Burma. Until 1937 Burma remained a province of the Indian Empire. On 4 January 1948 it became completely independent.

Before these wars of annexation Britain's prestige in Burma was not remarkably high. Colonel Michael Symes, who was sent as an envoy to Burma in 1795 and again in 1802, was accompanied on his missions by a splendid suite, but at a function at a Burmese court a Chinese mission which happened to be in Burma at the time were given the front seats while the English were relegated to the back.[20] (One of the objects of Symes's missions was to look into the possibilities of the overland trade.)

The celebrated John Crawfurd, who was sent on a mission to the Court of Ava in 1826, provides us with a wealth of information regarding the Chinese in Burma at this period, but when he deals with the region of the Burma–Chinese frontier he is relying on hearsay evidence and his remarks must be examined with caution. Dr Anderson, for example, refers to Crawfurd's statement that 'the Irrawaddy, the largest river in Ava, is navigable only for canoes at the town of Bhamo', and points out that, on the contrary, the largest river steamers could in the seventies reach that place with ease, and it was probable that the channel of that magnificent river would be found deep enough for them for 150 miles farther. Anderson remarks that Crawfurd unfortunately fell into another error in stating that the goods from Bhamo to the capital were carried overland, and (says Anderson) it is difficult to say whether this mistake which he unwittingly fell into, or the explanation of it, is more opposed to the fact. All the trade from Bhamo to the capital appears to have been conducted by boats from time immemorial.

[18] Christian, *Modern Burma*, p. 26.
[19] J. S. Furnivall, *Educational Progress in Southeast Asia* (N.Y., 1943).
[20] D. G. E. Hall, *Europe and Burma*, p. 82.

Crawfurd says that the articles imported from China in his time were copper, orpiment (yellow arsenic), quicksilver, vermilion, iron pans, brassware, tin, lead, alum, silver, gold, silk, velvets and other wrought silks, spirits, verdigris, dried fruits, paper, fans, umbrellas, shoes, wearing apparel, and a few wrought metals—which last, according to the Chinese laws, were contraband. The orpiment from the Yunnan mines was of a very fine quality. A portion of the merchandise exported from Rangoon went to western Asia and Europe via Calcutta. The largest import to Ava, however, was raw silk. From this primarily was manufactured the cloth which was in general use among all classes of the Burmese. Its quality was coarse and it suffered damage due to its long carriage overland.

Articles imported into China via the Burma trade route included cotton, ornamental fabrics, esculent swallows' nests, deers' horns, sapphires and noble serpentine, *with a small quantity of British woollens*.[21] Raw cotton, however, was by far the most considerable article of import. The feathers, chiefly of the blue jay, were intended to ornament the ceremonial dresses of the Chinese mandarins:[22] Burmese hunters went all the way to India in search of them. The sapphires were intended for mandarins' buttons of rank.

No coin was in use in the Burma trade, gold and silver were the medium of intercourse and had to be weighed, which was a great hindrance to the negotiations.[23]

So far our interest has been exclusively directed towards the Mountain Chinese of Burma, largely because for many centuries they were practically the only Chinese to enter the country, but as information becomes available regarding Maritime Chinese we shall more and more be able to bring them into the picture.

At the end of the eighteenth century, 'the Parsees, the Armenians and a small proportion of Musselmen, engrossed the largest share of the trade of Rangoon'.[24] 'Malabars, Moguls, Persians, Parsees, Armenians, Portuguese, French, English all mingle there', says the same informant. Most of them were merchants. There is, we note, no mention of Chinese among them, which surely would have been the case had they been at all important. But later on he mentions a deputation of Chinese and the fact that that race was addicted to swine's flesh.

On Crawfurd's arrival at Ava in 1826, two Chinese, natives of Canton, came on board the ship, offering their services as provisioners and

---

[21] Commodities whose quantity or nature changed in the period under review are italicized for easy back-reference.

[22] The demand for blue feathers in China was age-old. The principal export from the vanished kingdom of Angkor to China was kingfishers' feathers for bridal coronals (and no doubt for mandarins' coats too).

[23] Crawfurd, *Journal of an Embassy to the Court of Ava* (London, 1834), ii. 187.

[24] Michael Symes, 'Embassy to Ava in 1795', in John Pinkerton, ed., *A General Collection of the Best and Most Interesting Voyages* (London, 1811), ix. 426–572.

brokers. They spoke English and had made several voyages to England, to the principal British settlements in India, and to the European ports in Malaya. 'These industrious people [says Crawfurd] are to be found in every port of the East, where there is room for the exercise of their useful industry, and wherever they are found, are always superior to the inhabitants of the countries in which they sojourn.'[25]

There were a great many residing in the Burmese capital, and some were natives of parts of China never seen in the European settlements of India. Crawfurd and his companions accepted the service of their visitors but were soon told by the Burmese that they were infringing the laws of the country and the two Chinese were ordered, at their peril, to discontinue their visits until after the English envoys had been presented at court. This was in October 1826.[26]

Howard Malcom, an American missionary (whose book of travels was published in 1839), mentions that in 1823 there had been a dreadful fire at Umerapura (Amarapura), seven miles above Ava, and the town, in which lived many Chinese who carried on trade with their own country by the annual caravans, was almost destroyed. Malcom thought that American missionaries should study Chinese and be prepared at a future date to accompany these caravans to Yunnan. He also mentions that at a few miles from Ava the Chinese had some plantations of sugar-cane and manufactured a large quantity of excellent brown and yellow sugar, 'as good as our best Havanna', at about 4 cents a pound. At Sagaing lived some Chinese who could read tracts and the Bible in their own language.[27]

A peep at the Maritime Chinese in Moulmein is given in March 1836 (as ever, the European reaction to Chinese music is hostile):

> The Chinese have just had their annual ceremonies in memory of deceased ancestors. Hearing, a few mornings since, an uncommon din of gongs and their discordant musical instruments, I went to the veranda, and saw the procession pass to the ceremony. It was a meagre affair as to pomp, but quite as absurd as if it had been in their own country. A succession of tables borne like biers on men's shoulders, were spread with hogs, goats, and poultry, roasted whole, and various other eatables; the horrid music followed; and the procession with streamers, terminated by a man or two with muskets, firing at intervals. A priest, in proper costume, walked on each side of the tables.[28]

The Mountain and the Maritime Chinese were, of course, mixed up together in parts of the country, and not all Chinese who lived in southern Burma necessarily arrived by sea. Christian says that there is no record of Chinese coming in large numbers to Burma by sea before 1800, except occasionally in coasting vessels along the Tenasserim peninsula. The first Cantonese merchant in Mandalay did not arrive until 1861.[29]

[25] Crawfurd, *Embassy to Ava*, i. 160.
[26] Ibid.   [27] Howard Malcom, *Travels in South-East Asia* (London, 1839), i. 125.
[28] Ibid. p. 58.   [29] Christian, *Modern Burma*, p. 269.

With these fragmentary observations on the Maritime Chinese we will leave them again for a while and return to their relatives on the northern confines of Burma.

The Burmese Government exercised very little authority over the Singhpos (Jingpaws or Kachins), Theinbuns, and other wild tribes who occupied the country between Assam, Yunnan, and Ava. Even the numerous Chinese caravans were sometimes attacked by the mountaineers, and the Burmese said that the Theinbun always preferred killing a man to cutting down a tree since the possession of a mere common waist-cloth or tinder-box from the man he might kill was wealth to a Theinbun.[30]

In May 1836 Burney heard that the Emperor of China had written to the King of Burma 'remonstrating with the Court of Ava for having allowed an English officer to proceed northward to ascertain the route to China'. Burney questioned the Burmese ministers, who, while admitting that a letter had been received from China, denied that its contents were more than a complimentary communication relative to a new title conferred by the Emperor on his mother. None the less, Burney was inclined to believe the report he had heard earlier, because he was aware that shortly after Captain Hannay had left Ava the previous December, a deputation of Chinese merchants from Ava had waited on Prince Minthagyi to remonstrate against Hannay's mission. They were fearful lest they might lose the monopoly they had so long held in the trade to the north of Ava and that of the produce of the amber and serpentine mines.[31]

The economist will note with interest the varieties of merchandise carried over the trade routes at different periods. In 1839 the imports from China were copper, iron vessels, silk (raw and manufactured), precious and semi-precious stones, gold and silver thread and lace, musk, walnuts, carpets, and vermilion. The exports to China from the Shan country were cotton, ivory, skins, and horns.[32]

At this period the caravans assembled at Moung-koo. In 1839 Dr Richardson saw at Zimmay (i.e. Chiengmai in Siam) a caravan of Chinese

[30] Captain Burney, *India Political Consultations*, lxix (unpubl. India Office records), letter from Calcutta of 14 Feb. 1835, cited by Walter Sadgun Desai, *History of the British Residency in Burma* (Rangoon, 1939), p. 240.

[31] Desai, citing a letter of Burney of 9 May 1836, *India Political Consultations*, India Office Range 194, vol. xv. Burney later secured through a secret agent a Burmese version of the Chinese letter in which it said that the British were accustomed to behave like the Pepal (peepul- or Bo-tree) tree (wherever this plant takes root, and particularly in old temples and buildings, it spreads and takes such a firm hold that it is scarcely possible for it to be removed or eradicated). (Burney's own explanation.)

[32] G. B., House of Commons, *Papers Relating to the Route of Captain W. C. M'Leod from Moulmein to the Frontiers of China, and the Route of Dr Richardson on his Fourth Mission to the Shan Province of Burma* (1869), cited by J. Coryton, in 'Trade Routes between British Burma and Western China', *JRGS* (1875). Deer's horn was used medicinally by Chinese, often as an aphrodisiac.

traders consisting of 200 mules and horses, and 300 more were said to be at Moung-nan where cotton abounded. The two heads of the expedition seemed to be intelligent, enterprising characters. They said they had long entertained the idea of visiting Moulmein, and, now that they were invited and were assured of protection, they would undoubtedly do so the following season, the present one being too far advanced to allow of their increasing their distance from home. They requested that an interpreter should then meet them at Zimmay.

The chiefs of the native tribes (says Richardson) were favourable to the passage of caravans through the territory, but even allowing that the members of the trading expeditions ran no danger of attacks from the people of the country, they still had to face the perils of the climate and of accident. If a man fell sick, or was disabled, he was simply left behind. The laws of the trail were ruthless. Boats used by the Chinese traders on the Irrawaddy below Bhamo were of the Burmese flat-bottomed kind and were of tolerable size, each accommodating twenty persons. They were particularly well adapted to the navigation of the river, since they did not draw more than eighteen inches.[33]

The bazaar at Katha in 1835 was well supplied with good native vegetables of various sorts, and fresh and salt fish was sold by a Chinese. Dried coconuts, sugar, and rice ranging from the coarsest quality to the finest, were also procurable.

The best quality rice was sold at 15 ticals a hundred baskets. Stic-lac, however, was very dear. *Even at this remote spot there was a tolerable display of British piece-goods, but not nearly to the extent noticed at Kyundoung.*

Bhamo at this period had (says Hannay) about 1,500 houses; but including the several villages that were joined on to it, it contained altogether 2,000 houses of which at least 200 were inhabited by Chinese. Besides the permanent population of Burmese, there was always a number of strangers there—Chinese, Shans, and Kachins, who either came to make purchases or to be hired as workmen.[34]

The route taken by the Chinese caravans started from modern Bhamo whence the merchandise was taken to old Bhamo, or Manmo, by water, and it then proceeded overland to the *choki* or *ken* of Loahlong near Mowan, which was reached in three days; thence it went to Moung-yen or Tenggyechew in the province of Yunnan, which place was reached in eight to nine days. The principle article of trade, namely cotton, was entirely in the hands of the Chinese, who arrived in Bhamo in the months of December and January. The greater part of the imports was taken to Ava, since the natives of neither Mogaung nor of Bhamo could

[33] R. B. Pemberton, 'Abstract of a Journal of a Route travelled by Captain S. F. Hannay from the Capital of Ava to the Amber Mines of the Hukong Valley in the South-east Frontier of Assam', *JRAS*, lxiv (Apr. 1835).   [34] Ibid.

afford to purchase them. What were disposed of in these places were copper pots, carpets, and warm jackets which were also in demand all over Burma. Several cotton godowns in Bhamo belonged to the Chinese, 500 of whom were in constant residence in the town, which fact, added to the numerous arrivals from other parts of the country, gave the place a very businesslike air. There was a neat Chinese temple with carvings and where tea was served to visitors. The Chinese of Burma (says Hannay), although differing from the Maritime Chinese in language and features, had the same idea of neatness and comfort, and their manners and their mode of living appeared to be much the same. The temple and the houses were not of a temporary nature but were of brick stained blue.[35]

In the 1830s the only traffic of any consequence in the Hukawng valley was in amber which was sold to a few Chinese, Chinese Shans, and Chinese Singphos (Simphos) who found their way there annually.[36]

Although it is stated above that the tribes of this area were generally well disposed towards the caravans, there was talk in previous periods of the waylaying of the traders, and in 1836 another British traveller mentions the obstructions due to the jungle and to hostile tribes. This same authority says that many of the Chinese made two trips a year—on the second occasion they brought down rock salt from the neighbourhood of Esnuk (the Muangla of the Shans). There was a great demand for English goods.[37]

From the serpentine mines of Mogaung came boats laden with masses of stone so large that it required three men to lift them.

Hannay learnt that although the greater number of Chinese came to the mines via Santa and Tali, they were only the poorer classes that did so; the wealthier came by way of Bhamo, which was the safest and best route. The total number of Chinese who visited the mines in 1836 was 480. The Chinese paid $1\frac{1}{2}$–$2\frac{1}{2}$ ticals for permission to proceed to the mines, in addition to a boat tax of 10 per cent and 10 per cent of the appraised value of the minerals they took away.

The principal features of the history of the Chinese in Burma in the first half of the nineteenth century are the flourishing caravan routes between Burma and Yunnan, and the beginnings of large-scale immigration by sea which accompanied the establishment of British power. In the year 1826 14 million lb of cotton, worth £228,000,[38] was transported

[35] Pemberton, ibid., p. 258.
[36] The price of amber was $2\frac{1}{4}$ ticals a *viss*, or $4\frac{1}{2}$ rupees for $1\frac{1}{2}$ *seer*, but the best kind, for ornaments, was more expensive. The Chinese sometimes paid in silver for amber, but also in warm jackets, carpets, straw hats, copper pots, and opium. They also bartered their merchandise for ivory and gold dust, but only in small quantities.
[37] Lieut. T. E. MacLeod, Assistant Commissioner of Tenasserim province, 'Abstract Journal of an Expedition to Kiang Hung on the Chinese Frontier Starting from Moulmein on 13 December 1836', *JRAS* (1837).
[38] Christian, *Modern Burma*, p. 213, citing Crawfurd, *Embassy to Ava*, pp. 436–8.

to China via Burmese land routes. But by mid-century great changes were impending. One of these was the decline of the overland trade, due in part to the fact that cotton was to be declared a royal monopoly in 1854; another was the Panthay rebellion, which, combined with the vagaries of Burmese policy, brought the trade to almost a complete standstill until the rebellion was suppressed in 1873. A third feature of the period was the substitution of many British-made articles for those traditionally manufactured in China, since Britain, having completed her industrial revolution, was expanding her markets throughout the world.[39]

Yule estimated the value of the trade in 1854 at: exports, £235,000, and imports, £187,000, which was somewhat less than the figures given by Anderson for the same year.

7

CIRCA 1850–1900

IN the nineteenth century, when China as a Power was in decline, and Burma was being annexed in stages by the British, the history of diplomacy in these regions is mainly one of Anglo-Chinese or Anglo-French relations. But the change in the superstructure made very little difference to the Chinese traders, miners, and labourers in Burma who persevered, as circumstances allowed, in their time-honoured routine and tactics. The British, however, dazzled by the legend of the untapped riches of Cathay, conceived an exaggerated idea of the value of the Burma–Yunnan route as a short cut to China. This route, it was argued, would by-pass the Straits of Malacca and shorten the journey by many hundreds of miles. Experience was to prove to them that the central mass of southern China was barring the way and that the Irrawaddy did not rise, as had been thought, in Tibet. But whilst the illusion was maintained it had almost the hypnotic attraction of the Northwest Passage, and a wealth of enterprise and talent was lavished on finding and unlocking the magic door. The story of the quest of a route to China by the Shan States, by the Salween, by way of Indochina, and of the rivalry of the British and French to be the first to pave the way by road and railway, is told in the voluminous literature of the times: our business here is to repeat so much of it as will reveal and explain the vicissitudes of the Chinese in Burma.

After the Anglo-Burmese war of 1824 numerous surveys were made from India and Moulmein towards the Chinese frontier. During the

---

[39] The opening of the Suez Canal in 1869 greatly stimulated this process.

interval between the first and second Anglo-Burmese wars comparatively little, however, was done towards promoting the trade by the Bhamo route; the British concentrated their endeavours on reaching China overland from Moulmein. Burma, having lost its sole remaining maritime province to the British in 1852, became an inland State and was opposed to all British efforts to cross its territory to Yunnan.[1] The mission of Sir Arthur Phayre to Ava in 1855 to persuade the King to change his mind and to permit trans-Burma trade with China, was, in this one respect, unsuccessful, though it was brilliantly successful in others.

In 1854 the cotton trade of Burma became a royal monopoly. Previously to this the Chinese merchants used often to make advances to the native cultivators, taking the produce of the cotton harvest in return. After 1854 advances were made exclusively by the King. The rate at which he paid the cultivators was 20 ticals a 100 *viss*, and the rate at which he disposed of the cotton in the capital was from 40 to 50 ticals for the same quantity. (What terms the Chinese merchants had given are not on record, but they are not likely to have been more profiteering than those of the Burma sovereign.) The cotton, cleaned from seed, was transported by boat up the Irrawaddy to Bhamo. This royal monopoly naturally restricted the share of the Chinese in the cotton trade, though they picked up about 150,000 *viss* of this product in the Shan States to which the monopoly did not extend.[2]

The Chinese who suffered most from this royal nationalization of the cotton industry lived mostly in the suburbs of Amarapura. They were, in spite of their character of middlemen, instinctively recognized by the Burmese as of close kindred in blood, and were not classified by them with the *Kalas* or other foreigners, though that term included every race of India proper, of western Asia, and of Europe. The Chinese ward (says Yule) occupied a large portion of the main street of the suburb where 'every shop and house exhibited the unmistakable countenance and [pig] tail'. 'Thinking of the Eastern people in the mass [continues the distinguished rediscoverer of Marco Polo] one was apt to class the Burmese and other kindred races with the Chinese, but when one saw the latter in the streets of Amarapura his individuality was just as recognizable as it would have been in Hyde Park.'

A large proportion of the dwellings in the quarter inhabited by the Chinese was built of brick.[3] The colony probably amounted to nearly 2,000 families in the capital and neighbouring villages. They had a temple

---

[1] Christian, *Modern Burma*, p. 214.
[2] Yule, *Mission to Ava*, p. 144.
[3] Raffles (*History of Java* (London, 1830), i. 81) noticed that the Chinese invariably constructed a house of brick and mortar when they possessed the means, and that the Chinese kampongs and wards in the Javanese cities might always be distinguished thus from those of the natives. (Cited by Yule, p. 142.)

of their own, 'the nationality of which in its bizarre character would be recognized by an English child'.[4]

While Phayre and Yule were still at Ava, there occurred a happening of even greater gravity for the overland trade than the King's declaration of a cotton monopoly. This was the outbreak of the Panthay (Mohammedan Chinese) rebellion in Yunnan. Yunnan remained under Mohammedan government until 1873. During this rule bands of marauders under petty chiefs desolated the country on the frontier and harried the few unfortunate traders to such an extent that they threatened to annihilate all trade.[5] So the success of Sir Arthur Phayre in 1862 in negotiating a treaty with the King of Ava, restricting the duty on imports from China to 1 per cent and prohibiting the levy of any tax or transit dues on goods destined for the China overland, was not as effective as it might otherwise have been.

The struggle that now ensued was between the orthodox Chinese on one side and the Mohammedans on the other. It had the most devastating effect on trade. Large tracts of cotton-growing land to the south of the capital of Burma, and to a still greater extent to the north, were now left uncultivated. Previous to these troubles the Chinese of Bhamo had had large godowns and had dealt in nothing but Chinese goods and those for export to China, but when the route had been for long closed they were forced to become general storekeepers. Whereas in the old days the shopkeepers used to wear cloth jackets which came from Canton overland, now all came by river from Lower Burma. Even the 'lasting' of their jackets (*which were of Leeds manufacture*) now came by ship from Canton. They told Clement Williams that, were the road open, they could sell in Yunnan, in preference to Chinese goods, everything that Birmingham, Leeds, Sheffield, Lancashire, and Yorkshire could produce. Mines in the Burmese Shan territory, formerly worked by Chinese who paid royalties to the Burmese, were for some time left unworked—in consequence, however, of the oppression of the Burmese superintendents rather than of the closing of the trade route.[6]

But, in spite of the closing of the trade routes, there was a considerable local trade in 1863. *The bulk of the stores consisted of British piece-goods*, cloth, coarse blanketing, long-cloth, muslins, and cotton clothes, cotton velvets, silk and cotton handkerchiefs, figured and coloured muslins, the lastings of bombazines of which Chinese jackets were made, twists,

---

[4] Yule, p. 143. In paying a visit to the temple with some other officers of the mission, Yule was very courteously received by some of the Chinese merchants who were passing their evening leisure there. For the temple served not merely as a place of worship but also as a house of resort or club for its frequenters. The temple was paid for by a voluntary tax on imports.

[5] J. Coryton, 'Trade Routes between British Burma and Western China', *JRGS* (1875), p. 231.

[6] Clement Williams, *Through Burma to Western China; Being Notes of a Journey in 1863* (Edinburgh, 1868), p. 82 ff.

sewing goods, needles, buttons, &c. *No Chinese goods were seen except for a few medicines.* Some of the Chinese were well dressed; others seemed very poor.

No Chinese goods were to be seen! What a revolution had taken place since 1793 when the Emperor Ch'ien Lung told Lord Macartney that China lacked no product within her borders and had no need to import the manufactures of outside barbarians.[7]

A Sino-Burmese was appointed by the Burmese Government as a kind of mayor.[8]

Failing to crush the Mohammedan movement, the Chinese encouraged freebooters to prey on the Panthay kingdom. These freebooters allowed trade to pass only on the payment of heavy blackmail. The intermediate region between Burma and China consisted of hills and valleys occupied by the semi-civilized Kachins and by the Shans. They were 'as credulous as children, but were fully alive to the profits of the carrying trade which had now been brought to an end'.[9]

After the suppression of the long-drawn-out rebellion and the pacification of the province, one of the first acts of the Viceroy of Yunnan was to send a letter to the King of Burma announcing the fact and requesting him to assist in re-establishing the trade between the two countries. In response to this letter the King dispatched an embassy to Peking carrying tribute; but so disturbed was the borderland that the ambassador was detained in the hills for a month by the hillmen, who had barricaded the road for the purpose of exacting blackmail. However, he eventually arrived in China and was able to lay before the Emperor a letter which has the merit of affording this study an extra touch of light relief:

> Your vassal would, with all humility, set forth that under the universal sway of His Holiness the streams and hills are all objects of his loving care, the kingdoms of the distant ocean become converted to his civilizing rule and as the sunflower bows before the sun, so does all mankind turn with adoration towards the Imperial person. . . .

The King goes on to state that since he has succeeded to the Emperor's 'barren and far-off dependency of Burma', he offers tribute, and remarks that recently, owing to war and rapine on the borders, communication has been interrupted, the horrors of strife are now over, and the universe has returned to tranquillity.[10]

[7] Sir John Pratt, *The Expansion of Europe into the Far East* (London, 1947), p. 34.

[8] Williams (*Through Burma*), remarks: 'the likeness of one Burmese to another is striking, but the absolute sameness of one Chinese shop to another is truly wonderful. Not only are they all of one shape and size, but the various goods seem to be arranged after one set pattern —the money-box, the tobacco-bottle, and all the different articles for sale, occupying the same relative position in every narrow warehouse'.

[9] Albert Fytche, *Burma Past and Present; with Personal Reminiscences of the Country* (London, 1878), ii. 97.

[10] R. K. Douglas, 'China and Burma', *Asiatic Quarterly R.*, i (Jan.–Apr. 1886), citing trans. into Chinese of the King of Burma's letter in the *Peking Gazette* for 1875.

The tribute included five tame elephants.

So say the Chinese accounts of the affair. But listen now to what an authority on Burma's history, Mr B. R. Pearn, has to say:

There is a complete clash of evidence between Chinese and Burmese accounts. The Burmese deny that in modern times they have ever been tributary to China; they sent friendly gifts at intervals to Peking, but only in response to the prior receipts of gifts from China. Also, their version of the letter which is here quoted is altogether different from the Chinese version: far from being the letter of a vassal to his lord, it uses the language of one independent sovereign to another. . . .

Certainly, in view of the Chinese practice of numbering all foreign countries among tribute-paying countries (e.g. Great Britain), the Chinese account cannot lightly be accepted. Indeed, taking everything into consideration, especially China's weak state as a Power at this time, the Burmese version is much the more plausible.

There is evidence that missions were sent to China in 1787, 1795, 1811, 1820, 1830, 1833, and 1843, and whereas the Chinese claim that these missions were tributary, the Burmese assert that on the contrary they were merely expressive of friendship between independent States and were normally sent only in response to prior missions bearing presents from China to Burma. The truth probably is that 'in nearly every instance the Burmese embassies were preceded by bogus embassies purporting to be from the Emperor of China to the King of Burma but in reality got up to deceive both the Emperor and the King by the Yunnan officials'.[11]

Writing in the period immediately following the suppression of the Panthay rebellion, a close observer and authority on the border region speaks of the Chinese in these terms:[12]

Mingled with the motley population of Shans, in the belt of the country southwest of Yunnan, is one element of which we may regard the increase in the neighbourhood of Bhamo and Mandalay with great satisfaction. I refer to the Chinese who, having left their country as immigrants from the Eastern ports, have gradually established themselves as coolies, cultivators, and traders all along the coast of the Malay Peninsula from Singapore to Rangoon, and so up the Irrawaddy to the very spot to which we are hoping their brethren will come overland to meet and trade with them.

It will be noted that Coryton regards the Chinese in Bhamo as an extension of the Maritime Chinese rather than as Mountain Chinese who had arrived overland. To what extent this was true we have no means of checking, but it seems probable that nearly all Cantonese and Hokkiens came by sea, whilst nearly all Yunnanese came by the land route.

The trade was restarted, and during the year ending October 1874

[11] E. H. Parker, *Burma, with Special Reference to her Relations with China* (Rangoon, 1893), p. 94. [12] Coryton, *JRGS* (1875), p. 230.

British steamers carried cargo valued at £200,000 to and from Bhamo. But the following year there was a disappointing lull. As late as 1882 the provinces of Kwangtung and Kwangsi were still in a state of turmoil from the recent insurrections; brigandage was rampant, transport was bad, and there were epidemics of plague, malaria, and dysentery.[13]

With the accession of King Thibaw in 1878, conditions in what remained of independent Burma became more and more chaotic. Trade declined and in 1879 the British Resident was withdrawn from Mandalay and the British Agent from Bhamo. In 1885 the ultimatum from Britain ending Burmese independence demanded, among other things, the provision of facilities for opening up British trade with China through Burma. Bhamo was occupied in December 1885. For several years after the annexation of 1886 trade decreased owing to the raids of dacoits on both sides of the frontier. Raw cotton was the only considerable export to China but the cost of transport limited its destination to points not more than 250 miles beyond the Chinese frontier. From 1890 there was a British consul stationed at Tengyueh and, for a time, at Szumao, at which places there were also offices of the Chinese Maritime Customs. The Sino-Japanese war of 1894–5 gave the overland trade a temporary impetus, the total for that year reaching Rs. 32 lakhs as compared with 22 lakhs the following year.[14]

During the negotiations which preceded the Convention of 24 July 1886 between Great Britain and China, the former seems to have been labouring under an exaggerated impression of the power of China. The result was that the two following Articles were included in the Convention:

I. Insomuch as it has been the practice of Burmah to send decennial missions to present articles of local produce, England agrees that the highest authority in Burmah shall send the customary decennial missions, the members of the missions to be of the Burmese race.

---

[13] A. R. Colquhoun, 'Exploration in South-Western China', *Proc. RGS* (1885). Colquhoun took with him a Mr Hong Beng-kaw, a Chinese gentleman educated in Scotland, and a Cantonese interpreter. Malaria has been suggested as the main reason for the eventual defeat of Kublai Khan's troops in the thirteenth century.

The British surveys and expeditions of the Burma–Chinese routes are noticed by Christian (*Modern Burma*, p. 212 ff.), and in the article in the *New Times of Burma* of 30 November by Khin Maung Gale, before cited. Notable among the expeditions of the British was that of Margary who reached Bhamo from Shanghai on 17 January 1875—the first white man to make the trip. Margary, however, was murdered at Manwyne, approximately midway between Bhamo and Tengyueh. (For the repercussions of the murder, see S. T. Wang, *The Margary Affair and the Chefoo Convention* (N.Y., 1939)). In contrast with this tragedy is the experience of J. McArthy, who travelled on foot from Hankow to Bhamo, arriving there on 26 August 1877. Throughout his journey, extending over eight months, he did not meet with a single act of incivility, was never asked for his passport, and was never refused any assistance or courtesy he desired. McArthy's success was due in great measure to his having travelled in native costume, and to his ability to converse with the people in their own language (see J. McArthy, 'Across China from Chin-Kiang to Bhamo', *Proc. RGS* (1879)).

[14] Christian, *Modern Burma*, p. 221, citing *Upper Burma Gazetteer*, pt. 1, p. 108.

II. China agrees that, in all matters whatsoever appertaining to the authority and rule which England is now exercising in Burmah, England shall be free to do whatever she deems fit and proper.

The decennial mission, however, was never sent. It was pointed out that the dispatch of such a mission would be construed in China, and perhaps in Burma, as placing the British Government in a position of inferiority. The Chinese pressed on several occasions for the sending of the mission, but finally in 1896 the obligation to send it was repudiated on the ground of 'altered circumstances'.

On 1 March 1894 a treaty was signed between Britain and China regulating the Sino-Burmese trade. Free overland trade was granted for a term of six years, after which the general tariff of the Chinese Maritime Customs would apply. Chinese vessels were permitted to ply the Irrawaddy on the same terms as British vessels. By the same treaty it was agreed that China might appoint a consul to reside at Rangoon, that Chinese subjects wishing to enter Burma might receive passports from a British consular officer, and that the subjects of the two Powers should each within the territory of the other enjoy all the privileges, immunities, and advantages that may have been, or might thereafter be, accorded to the subjects of any other nation.[15] But the trade was a disappointment to the British and Chinese alike. From 1900 until the opening of the Sino-Japanese hostilities of 1937 onwards, the trade with China was of minor importance. The railway stopped at Lashio and was not extended to the Chinese frontier.

Sir Charles Crosthwaite, who visited Bhamo in 1887, found it a disappointing place. It was nothing but a very dirty, miserable kind of village, arranged in two streets parallel to the river. Conservancy there was none, and the stench from the streets, the lagoon, and even the bank of the river was sickening. The Chinese were the most prominent of the population. They were, it was said, opium smokers almost to a man and seldom moved until midday. They managed, notwithstanding, to make money and retired to China after a few years with fortunes. Crosthwaite anticipated a large increase in the trade with China but doubted whether the town of Bhamo could grow much on its existing site.[16]

The trade, however, could not make much progress on account of the cost of transport between Bhamo and Tengyueh, the risk of attack by Kachins, and the exactions and oppressions by the Chinese officials who at one time had maintained a *likin* (octroi) station within the British boundary, not far from Bhamo. There was, however, another route used

[15] Sir E. Hertslet and Ed. Parkes, *China Treaties* (London, 1908), p. 99 ff.
[16] Sir Charles Crosthwaite, *The Pacification of Burma* (London, 1912), p. 74. The population of Bhamo in 1891 was 8,048, in 1901, 10,734, and in 1911, 9,762, of whom 3,000 were natives of India. These figures include the garrison. The figures for 1921 and 1931 were, respectively, 7,741 and 7,827 (in 1921 and 1931 the garrison was not included). These totals are sufficiently indicative of the static nature of the trade.

by traders which went by way of Mansi and Namkhan (Namhkam), a
Shan town on the Shweli. After the Kachins in the country south of
Bhamo had been subjugated, the Chinese preferred the Namkhan route,
and though the Kachins had ceased to raid, and much had been done
to improve the route to Tengyueh, the trade had not returned to that
channel.

The depressing picture given of Bhamo by Crosthwaite refers obviously to the 'off-season', and it is counterbalanced by another belonging
to a few years later (*c.* 1895), this time written by an observer with perhaps a more buoyant temperament. It gives a very striking impression of
the Chinese caravans and of the races of that border town at the period
when the trade was in full swing:

> During the rains Bhamo relapses into a small and unimportant town. . . . But the
> approach of winter heralds a great change. Over the wild borderland through which
> winds the Ambassador's Road, roughest of international highways, come the big
> caravans from China—thousands of hardy mules, hundreds of blue-clad labourers
> and portly merchants, filled out to abnormal size by dint of satin coats and furs,
> upon small ponies which amble sturdily along. . . . From the Shan States, north and
> east, come picturesque crowds of varied nationality, a permutation of Chinese,
> Burmese and many-tribed Shan, and from the border highways descend the
> cateran Kachin, to whom the Government now pays a fixed toll in lieu of the
> income they formerly derived, by robbery and blackmail, from the traders who
> made their way along this dubious highway. Bhamo now breaks into new life and
> colour, exchanging its moribund isolation for the concourse of many visitors, like
> any tourist resort in the season. . . .[17]

Our authority then describes with Celtic enthusiasm the poly-
chromatic visitors—Burmans in silken kilts and flaming headgear, Shans
in loose trousers and big straw hats, Kachins with naked swords, real
Chinamen in felt boots and black satin caps, hybrid Chinamen in
English hats, came and went in an incessant leisurely stream. And out on
the white highroad a British soldier swung by, his shoulders square,
his boots creaking, the silver head of his regimental cane gleaming
in the light. Along the same highway the trader from Yunnan rode by
at a fast amble on his shaggy steed. An almond-eyed porter, a man
of thews and sinews, struggled slowly behind with a heavy load on
his back.

Outside the market-place the view was across the white and grey walls
and distinctive roofs of the Chinese houses. In the space between, in
hollows where the river, at its rising, rushed in, Chinese market gardeners
were toiling over rows of cabbages and beans. They wore blue clothes
and large sun-hats, and carried, slung from poles over their shoulders,
cans of water from which the ingenious bamboo spout made the water
splash in large silvery jets. 'In all that the Chinese does [says O'Connor]

---

[17] V. C. Scott O'Connor, *The Silken East* (London, 1904), i. 183 ff.

there is something distinctive, from the decoration of his house, to the pattern of his pipe and the spray of his water-can.'

As for the traders themselves, their dress and trappings had altered scarce a tittle through the centuries—loose coat, trousers bound tightly round the ankles, black silk cap, and white felt shoes. As ever the Chinese trader was 'portly, affable and clean'. His means of transport, like a Canterbury pilgrim, was a stout nag with tasselled trappings and short high stirrups, but now here in Bhamo in the first decade of the century our informant observes a revolution—*the bicycle had come in!*

If we pay yet another visit to Bhamo thirty years or so later through the intermediary of a woman traveller, we shall find ourselves bewailing with nostalgia the passing of the picturesque in the present humdrum age. She is speaking of the yearly frontier meeting between British and Chinese officials:

> How drab, how un-Oriental, the Chinese officials look, dressed as they are in ordinary Chinese robes of black or dark blue silk topped with a bowler or soft felt hat! How different it must have been twenty years ago when China was still an empire and her officials came to call dressed in gorgeous dragon robes with plumes of peacock's feathers nodding in their 'button' hats.[18]

The wealth of literature at our disposal regarding the Burma–Yunnan trade routes and the characteristics of the Mountain Chinese must not distract our attention altogether from their brothers who came into Burma by more peaceful and less romantic routes by way of Canton, Amoy, Swatow, Singapore, and the Burma ports. In 1891 a total of 37,000 Chinese were counted in Burma, more than half of whom had come in by sea routes. These Maritime Chinese did not attract the attention of foreigners to anything like the same extent as did their co-nationals from over the mountain frontier,[19] but there were nevertheless some notes made by foreign observers. To one such account we are indebted for information regarding the Chinese community as a whole and its influence on the social and economic life of the Burmese which goes much deeper than the impressions of the ordinary traveller, however vivid they may be.[20]

The offspring of unions between Chinese men and Burmese women were thought (say our authors) to have a great future. The sons were brought up as Chinese; the daughters as Burmese. But the men were not suffered to wear the plaited queue of the Chinese; they merely coiled their hair round the unshaven part. These half-breeds were not addicted to smoking opium.

[18] Beatrix Metford, *Where China Meets Burma* (London, 1935), p. 60.

[19] But it should be mentioned that before the great influx of Indians began, there were fears expressed in some quarters that Burma would eventually be overrun by the Chinese. See, for example, Sir J. G. (George) Scott, *Burma as it was, as it is, and as it will be* (London, 1886), pp. 142–3.

[20] Max and Bertha Ferrers, *Burma* (London, 1900), p. 61 and *passim*.

It is interesting to observe the influence of China and Europe on Burmese trades and handicrafts, and vice versa.

The Burmese umbrella (*hti*) was on the Chinese model—a bamboo frame with a paper cover. The Chinese umbrella, however, had a thin paper cover, whereas the Burmese had a cover of *bast*-paper which outlasted several of the others. But the Chinese umbrellas were cheaper and better waterproofed. The Chinese blacksmith had already adopted the European anvil and heavy sledge-hammer for forging axles and tyres, anchors and grapnels. The bench-vice was also universal. At the same time, the Chinese adhered to his horizontal wooden box-blast fitted with valves like a double-acting pump, whereas the Burmese copied the leather double-bellows from the steam-mill workshops. Needles used to be brought to Burma from China, as well as scissors, though the latter were also fashioned in Burma. *In the 1890s both were imported from Europe.*[21] The bulk of the tailoring was in the hands of immigrants from China,[22] but their prejudice against the sewing-machine was helping to transfer the business to Burmese women. Nearly every well-to-do family in the towns, however, had its sewing-machine.

For teak-cutting, the indigenous carpenter's tools were the small adze (*pegot*), chisels and gouges (*sauk*), awls (*lun*), and a rough saw (*hlwa*), besides an axe (*pauksein*). The Burmese adopted the Chinese plane with the Chinese straddle bench. When the impulse to cheap house building was given by the presence of cheap planks, the immigrants from China got the whole work.[23] But by the end of the century the Burmese had begun to oust them from the heavy carpentering and from joinery as well.[24] Ordinary Burmese carpenters earned three-quarters of a rupee a day, the better workmen earned from one to one and a quarter rupees, compared with the one and a half rupees earned by the Chinese carpenter.

European vehicles built by Chinese were used by the better-off Burmese in the towns.

[21] Ferrers, *Burma*, p. 61.

[22] A Burma official of many years' experience comments: 'I doubt if the Ferrers are right in saying that the bulk of the tailoring was in the hands of Chinese immigrants. Chinese tailors were rare, very rare, when I crossed from India in the spring of 1915, and I never heard that they had been numerous in the recent past. The Indian *Durzi* was ubiquitous. But the advent of the sewing-machine certainly encouraged Burmese women dressmakers, and every bazaar had its quota of sewing girls with machines.'

[23] The same official also thinks that this must be an exaggeration. It was doubtless true of European-type building in the large towns, but Burmese carpenters and joiners must have done most of the work in the jungle. 'It is fair to say, however,' he adds, 'that where a Chinese carpenter or cabinet-maker did set up in business, he was always heavily patronized.'

[24] A controversy between two of my expert advisers arose over this passage. All I can do is to quote what they say. The first expert remarks, 'Even if (though I doubt it) at the end of the nineteenth century the Burmese had begun to oust the Chinese from the heavy carpentry and joinery industry, this was only a passing phase. By the early 1920s the Chinese had something approaching a monopoly of all forms of such work and their competition had almost destroyed the indigenous craft.' When the second expert replies in the terms of n. 23 above, the first expert retorts by quoting Christian, p. 170, that Chinese and Indian immigrants 'do most of the carpenter work and furniture making'.

Such was the state of the Chinese in Burma and their influence on the indigenous people at the end of the nineteenth century. Some observers saw in the Chinese 'a welcome assistant to the British administrator', though they were, unhappily, those who flocked across the frontier and went marauding through the loosely-settled districts. But even these disturbers of the peace eventually married native girls, treating them much better than did either Shan or Burmese husbands, and they remained to multiply and to implant the characteristically Chinese institutions. As a result of Thibaw's misrule the region of the frontier had long been harried by roving dacoits and this afforded to Chinese filibusters a tempting opportunity that they were not slow to exploit.[25]

These were days long before the rise of Chinese nationalism and the Chinese was still largely judged on his merits or demerits as a colonist. But already there was (at least in the minds of some Europeans) a feeling of apprehension as to the eventual meaning of the intensified immigration of Chinese. The authors whose work has been quoted above inserted a warning regarding the future:

> The influx of races whose religion it is to multiply, without regard to the prospect of subsistence, must speedily result in lowering the scale of life for everyone in Burma, a country of which now it may be said that 'a large share of the happiness of each individual is derived from the consciousness of the well-being of other individuals'.[26]

8

THE TWENTIETH CENTURY

To a greater extent than in Siam, Malaya, or Indochina, the Chinese in Burma came to regard the country as their home. They learnt Burmese more readily than the Indians,[1] and all Chinese in the country, except in large towns like Rangoon, and the very recent arrivals and the Yunnanese who lived on the land in the Shan States, spoke Burmese fairly fluently. At the same time they used their native Chinese for communication among themselves, even when they belonged to families who had been in Burma for more than a century.[2]

Despite the anti-Chinese riots of 1931 (in which the Chinese signally

---

[25] F. Wells Williams, 'The Chinese Immigration in Further Asia', *American Hist. R.* (Apr. 1900).

[26] Max and Bertha Ferrers, *Burma*, quoting Herbert Spencer, *Principles of Ethics*, i. 297.

[1] Christian, *Modern Burma*, p. 270. Burmese was the lingua franca of the country, spoken even by Chinese ignorant of one another's dialects.

[2] Harvey, *British Rule in Burma*, p. 69 n., says that the Chinese 'got on well with the people and intermarriages were frequent, yet they too were sometimes killed in anti-foreign outbreaks'.

defeated their assailants) and the 'middleman' nature of many of their occupations, the Burmese generally had a friendly feeling for the Chinese living amongst them, whom they called *pauk paw* or 'next of kin'.[3] Some villages in Lower Burma had Chinese headmen. In the towns they had a large hold on the catering trade. The opening of the Burma Road in 1939 did something to impair the good feeling towards the race, for it entailed the infiltration into Burma of Chinese contractors and hangers-on of indifferent character, and the behaviour of some of the Chinese soldiers in Burma during the Pacific War and afterwards did not improve relations between the two peoples. (The conduct of the Chinese troops in Burma in 1942 was good and discipline, in regard to relations with civilians, was really severe—until defeat came and demoralization set in.)

Some sections of the Chinese in Burma interested themselves in local politics. For instance, for many years Sir Lee Ah Yain and numerous well-to-do Chinese supported the 'Golden Valley' Party sponsored by Sir J. A. Maung Gyi and Oscar de Glanville. Chinese Nationalist politics, which so interested them in other Southeast Asian countries, seemed to the Chinese in Burma to make comparatively little appeal.

As was generally the case, the centre of Chinese business relations was the chamber of commerce, which performed similar functions to those described in the case of the equivalent body in the Philippines.[4]

All members of the chamber, including those who were not British subjects, could, under the British regime, vote for the chamber's representative in the Burma legislature. The candidate, however, had to be a British subject.

A number of Chinese attained positions of prominence under British rule in Burma.[5]

Since the Chinese in Burma are an unobtrusive community taking definitely a second place to the Indians, they have not invited to themselves the same criticism that they have in Siam, Malaya, Indonesia,

[3] John F. Cady, *The Development of Self-Rule and Independence in Burma, Malaya, and the Philippines* (N.Y., mimeo, 1948), pt. 1, p. 11, says that the Chinese in Burma generally kept clear of local politics, though they were disposed to carry on intrigues with rival Burmese parties; but this perhaps understates the case. Two Rangoon Chinese, Aw Yu-wa and Hoke Sein—the latter known as 'king of Chinatown' in Rangoon—were popularly credited with having caused the disintegration of the United Party, once the most powerful Burmese political group (Christian, p. 271). It is pointed out, however, by an authority on Burma, that Aw Yu-wa was not interested in politics, but in more dubious matters, that he was due for deportation after conviction, and interested one set of ministers in his fate. The Cabinet split on the question of his deportation, but in any case was already widely split on other issues. [4] See p. 544.

[5] Sir Lee Ah Yain, for instance, the first Chinese to hold high office in the country, served the Government of Burma for several years as Minister of Forests during the governorships of Sir Harcourt Butler and Sir Charles Innes (see Christian, *Modern Burma*, p. 273). Another Burma Chinese who deserves mention is Taw Sein-ko (b. 1864), son of a Chinese merchant, educated at Cambridge, who was Government archaeologist and adviser on Chinese affairs in 1899–1900. In 1899 he was instrumental in keeping the Burma–Chinese frontier quiet during the Boxer rebellion.

Indochina, or in the Philippines. There is, indeed, remarkably little attention paid to them in the standard works on Burma (some contriving to omit reference to them at all), but one leading authority on the country refers incidentally to their record of development in a review of Burmese economics. The Indian and Chinese money-lenders and traders (says Furnivall) were not only middlemen; they were potential rivals of the rice-millers since they bought rice for India and the Straits Settlements. Sometimes, through sympathy for the cultivators, the Chinese were pictured as villains. In 1886 some wealthy Chinese combined to purchase all the paddy coming in and to hold it up against the millers. Again (as an example of Chinese obstruction of reform), when the British annexed Upper Burma, the Government contemplated retaining the Burmese prohibitions of trade in opium and alcohol, but this was impossible because the demands by Chinese and Indians had to be met. The wiles of Indian and Chinese money-lenders were denounced in Burma as far back as the eighties.[6]

It was estimated from one source that before the Pacific War the Chinese in Burma controlled one-fifth of the country's economy,[7] but this is an exaggeration. Out of the 12 million acres cultivated, 5 million acres were in Indian hands. Over 70 per cent of the foreign trade was with India, and conducted mainly by Indians. The railways were State-owned. Shipping was mainly British or Indian. The Rangoon Electric Tramway and Supply Company, and the Upper Burma Electric Company were British-owned. Banking was mainly British, with Indian, American, Dutch, and Japanese participating. The Chinese came into the banking business late. The rice crop was financed by Indian chettiars mainly on money borrowed from the banks. Plantations and mines were British-owned, but were inconsiderable. The oil business was British except for one small Indian company. The timber business was mainly British and the chief rice-mills, sawmills, cotton-mills, and oil-mills were British, though a few were owned by Indians and Chinese. Retail trade in Rangoon and other *large* towns was mainly Indian, with some Chinese participation. Nevertheless, the Chinese had a considerable holding in rice, timber, salt manufacture, and the retail trade.

It was not to be supposed that the Chinese in Burma would have been overlooked in the Chinese Nationalist movement which was fostered by the Chinese Revolution of 1911, and intensified into a campaign after the Kuomintang successes of 1927. For years before the war with Japan the Kuomintang had its branches in Burma, and the Chinese consul in Rangoon (promoted to be consul-general in 1940) held elections among overseas Chinese of Burma to select two representatives in the National

[6] J. S. Furnivall, *Colonial Policy and Practice in the Far East* (London, 1948), p. 96.

[7] *Christian Science Monitor* (18 Dec. 1947). The estimate of the Chinese one-fifth share in Burma's economy (given by the writer in this newspaper) is considered much exaggerated by at least one Burmese economist.

Assembly of China. Voting was restricted to Chinese nationals registered at the consulate.

Education, as elsewhere, was regarded by Chinese Nationalists as an important instrument of policy. In 1935 there were 12,707 Chinese children of ages between five and ten years. Of these, 837 were in the four Chinese Anglo-vernacular schools and 2,965 were in sixty-five unrecognized Chinese schools. In 1937 the number of pupils in the latter type of school had risen slightly to 3,308. 'The Chinese do not desire government recognition of the private schools [ran the official Government Report]; they prefer to run them on independent national lines.' The Report continues:

> Some of the schools receive financial aid from the Educational Association in China, and all are supported by Chinese clubs and associations. . . . *The bulk of the Chinese schools constitute an independent school system in Burma—a system controlled, inspected, staffed, and financed by a Chinese educational body with a curriculum unrelated to the public service of education.* Approaches have been made to one Local Education Authority for the inclusion of a number of Chinese vernacular schools in the public system.[8]

(The result of the approach to the Local Education Authority does not appear to have been recorded, but we can be sure that nothing came of it. The Chinese vernacular school system was *sui generis* and based on the Three Principles of Sun Yat-sen; it would not lend itself to inclusion in any foreign system of public instruction.)

The Sino-Japanese War

Not until the Japanese had attacked Shanghai and then extended their blockade to the southern ports of China did the Chinese Central Government turn its attention to the possibility of an alternative gateway through Yunnan. The Burma Road was begun late in 1937. It followed the line Lashio–Kyukok–Kunming. A later diversion swung it north from the Chinese frontier through Bhamo to Myitkyina, and thence to join the road from Assam through the Hukawng.[9]

In spite of natural obstacles and the alternation of the wet and dry seasons (part of the road received as much as 200 inches of rain annually), by the use of the *corvée* the Chinese completed the work of opening up nearly 750 miles from Kunming to Lashio. The Chinese people of Yunnan province, with their will, their hands, the *tzow tau* (mattock-like shovel), and the bamboo basket, literally scratched out and filled in the Burma Road, crossing the Kaoli mountains, a 12,000-foot-high span of the Himalayas.[10] The highway was officially opened on 10 January 1939.

[8] *Annual Report on Public Instruction in Burma* (Rangoon, 1935–6). The italics are mine. V.P.
[9] See Tan Pei-ying, *The Building of the Burma Road* (N.Y., 1945).
[10] Public Relations Officer, Y-Force Operations Staff, *Reconstruction of the Burma Road: Operational, Logistical, and Historical Data* (N.Y., 1944).

Side by side with the Burma Road, the Chinese began the construction of a railway from Kunming to Talifu. The British authorities also began building a railway from the Lashio end.

In 1940, after the fall of France had transformed the political situation in the East, the British Government, temporarily to placate Japan, closed the Burma Road to the transit of war materials for three months from 18 July. The Japanese occupation of Burma closed the road in 1942, but in 1943, when the military situation permitted, reconstruction of the road was begun by the Chinese Government with the advice and instruction of United States engineers.

Only a small proportion of the Chinese population of Burma was able to get out of the country in time when the Japanese invaded it. In April 1947 the new Chinese consul-general to Burma, Mr Shau Chang-hau, said that 14,000 Chinese who had left Burma when the Japanese entered it in 1942 were awaiting repatriation. In 1946, he said, 2,000 had been repatriated.[11]

After the Japanese occupation of Burma in May 1942, the Chinese residents seem to have kept their political opinions to themselves and to have stayed out of harm's way as much as possible. Their relations with the Burmese continued to be fairly satisfactory, and they gave no positive support to the Japanese war effort. The Japanese-sponsored Overseas Chinese Association aroused little response from local Chinese. A military Publicity Corps, recruited by the Nanking 'puppet Government' in China, came to Burma in February 1944 for the avowed purpose of promoting more genuine support for Japan's ends on the part of the local Chinese. As the result of the increased pressure, the Chinese business men of Burma contributed 200,000 rupees for the purchase of Japanese planes, and the Chinese farmers subscribed half that sum a few weeks later. The President of the United Chinese Associations explained that it was only right for the Chinese to help at a time when they were 'enjoying normal business while thousands of Japanese, Indian, and Burmese soldiers are shedding their blood not far away'.

The conclusion of the Pacific War brought to the fore again the question of Chinese immigration. In 1939 the opening of the Burma Road had been viewed with some apprehension by a number of Burmese politicians. The fear was that by opening the road through Rangoon the British exposed the city sooner or later to bombing attack by the Japanese. It was realized that although Japan was not then at war with Britain it was quite capable of bombing Rangoon to bits, and apologizing with compensation afterwards. Fears of an influx of Chinese by this route were not great until a later stage, though they were, of course, present in the minds of some. The political mind was not at that time anti-Chinese so much as apprehensive lest Burma should get mixed up

[11] *New Times of Burma* (6 Apr. 1947).

in a Sino-Japanese quarrel. Everybody knew that, owing to their other commitments, the British would reinforce Burma only in the last resort.

A customs wrangle also developed. Goods bought by the Chinese with American credits passing through Burma were charged customs duty, but were given a drawback of seven-eighths when re-exported. The general view in Burma was that the Kuomintang officials objected to the double scrutiny of the consignments that this entailed: 'they had too much to hide'. The Burmese view also was that Burma was being driven into heavy defence expenditure by the opening of the road—expenditure which might otherwise be avoided—and was in any case entitled to some payment under international law for the permanent services used by the goods in transit and the personnel engaged. (China had not then signed the international agreement on these matters.) A vitriolic press campaign against the duties was started in the United States, and the British Government, for diplomatic reasons, then agreed to pay to the Burma revenues the amount of these dues.[12]

In November 1947, on the eve of Burma's independence, the Burma *Daily Herald* gave editorial prominence to repeated reports that, because of illegal infiltration through Lashio, Bhamo, and other routes, the Chinese population of Upper Burma was increasing at an alarming rate. It must be admitted (the paper pointed out) that such a situation had arisen partly because of the inefficiency or shortsightedness of the immigration officers, and that there were rumours that admission permits were being issued at 10 rupees a permit. There was also disconcerting news that Shan merchants were being kidnapped by Chinese bandits on the frontiers. The paper urged the authorities to take action.[13]

This immigration question now became involved with a fifty-four-year-old Chinese-Burma border issue pivoting on the triangular northern tip of Burma which at this juncture was reopened by the Chinese Government. The Chinese claim covered roughly 75,000 square miles of territory bordering on Yunnan out of Burma's total area of 262,000 square miles. The disputed area (according to a spokesman of the Chinese Foreign Office) had belonged to China as part of a tributary State during the T'ang dynasty in the seventh century. (The spokesman mentioned, in passing, that both Indochina and Siam had once been among China's tributaries.)

The frontier had never been marked on the ground north of 23° 35'. The Wa States, never fully explored, have an area of about 2,000 square miles, and it is along their northern border that Burma's boundary with China was surveyed by the Iselin Commission.

It may be mentioned that American-trained Chinese forces operated in 1944–5 in just the areas to which the Chinese asserted a claim and that

---

[12] See *Burma Handbook* (Delhi, 1943), p. 112.
[13] Cited in *The Burman* (12 Nov. 1947).

they departed thence late in 1945 with evident reluctance; also that in 1946 a Chinese force invaded Burma and camped for over a month on the Irrawaddy below Myitkyina, claiming to be looking for deserters, and left only when threatened with air action.

This claim was answered immediately by an announcement from Rangoon stating emphatically that Burma did not intend to surrender any portion of its territory and would 'defend its integrity without any hesitation'. A suggestion of possible action by the United Nations was declared by the Burmese to be out of the question since Burma's frontiers had been clearly marked on the official maps, and these could not become a subject for dispute.[14]

Though, on the face of it, it was somewhat surprising that the Chinese Government should revive this claim when it was meeting an increasingly grave internal crisis, the political reasons for such action are clear enough. The Nanking Government wished to distract attention from its own internal weakness, and at the same time to give moral support to the Chinese scattered throughout Southeast Asia, and even a remote frontier dispute was grist to their mill. At the same time it was not likely that China would push these claims too far, for by so doing it would lend support to the fear (repeated in soft tones from British, French, and Dutch sources) that China might tend to supplant the white Powers in Southeast Asia. The fear, in view of China's then situation, might seem a little unrealistic, but it might have very real cause if a strong united China were to arise in the future.

Burma became independent on 4 January 1948.

1949–63

After independence, Burma was newly subdivided politically. Its territories now comprised (1) Burma proper, consisting essentially of the Irrawaddy valley and the delta, where a wide measure of self-government prevailed, (2) the hill areas where there had been indirect rule under the Governor in the British period, and (3) the small Kayah or Karenni States which were properly not British territory but which in practice were assimilated to (2).

Almost immediately on gaining its independence the new Union of Burma was plunged into civil war. A succession of enemies of the Anti-Fascist People's Freedom League (AFPFL) appeared in the field one after another. Already the Red Flag Communists and the *Mujahids*, bands of Muslim marauders from North Arakan, were in arms against the Government. More serious, the People's Volunteer Organization (PVO), the huge private army raised by Aung San, was living off the country by extortion and refused to be disbanded. Then the White Flag Communists, who hitherto had acquiesced, at least nominally, in the

---

[14] *Christian Science Monitor* (18 Dec. 1947).

acceptance of the new constitution, now declared that the AFPFL had
become the tool of British imperialism and started a campaign to overthrow the Government by force. U Nu attempted to placate the
Leftists by plans of compromise, but without success. Within the
Government, the Socialists made a bid for power, but when U Nu
resigned the premiership, they found themselves opposed by all the independents, by the leader of the frontier peoples, and by the Karens.
The Karen rising in 1949 constituted as great a threat as that of the
Communists. U Nu then agreed to stay in office as the only person who
could hope to secure even a semblance of Government unity. But some
60 per cent of the PVOs were under arms and in a state of insurgence.
On top of this came the mutiny of two units of the regular forces. Had it
not been for the support of the minorities, especially of the Kachin
and Chin units, U Nu and the AFPFL would certainly have been
overwhelmed.

Meanwhile the economy was suffering a creeping paralysis, and the
Government's financial problem was approaching a crisis. Yet as if by a
miracle Nu was able to restore some sort of order, and in July 1950
many of the troublesome PVO surrendered but the organization remained in being. Disorder continued, trains and lorries were pillaged
and destroyed, Government troops and police were ambushed, and
peasants and rice-millers were subjected to extortion. The effective control of the Government extended only to the towns and a few miles
radius of them (and this only before sunset). The marvel was that the
economy of Burma held together and that the State could continue to
function as a political and diplomatic unity.

Burma, in spite of this turmoil, even adopted a socio-economic plan
for advancement of its own, known as *Pyidawtha*, in 1952. This has been
translated as 'Welfare State', but it also had a more specific application
as 'local self-help' or 'community co-operation'. On the organizational
side, the intention was to allot the big development schemes to the
Government agencies, but to leave the improvement in subsidiary
spheres to local offers. In the social and religious sphere, reliance was
placed on the Buddhist belief in the 'acquisition of merit' (*parivarta*)
through acts of charity and public benefit, for contributions of labour,
materials, and money towards community-development projects. The
Pyidawtha policy, however, did not seem to have survived the military
coup of 1962, the new regime preferring its own more radical type of
socialism.

On 29 October 1958 General Ne Win, the Army Chief of Staff,
assumed control of the Government. In February 1960, however, when
the elections to the lower houses of parliament gave U Nu's party a
large majority, U Nu again resumed the Prime Ministership. On 2
March 1962 Ne Win again seized power and U Nu and five of his

ministers were reported under arrest. Ne Win dissolved parliament and formed a revolutionary council with himself as chairman. No fundamental change in domestic or foreign policy, however, seemed to have been involved, though Burmese nationalism was apparently to take priority over minority interests.

Meanwhile Burma, while torn internally, had to adapt its international politics to suit a new situation, one in which it had a new and powerful neighbour, namely the People's China, whose rise had coincided with its own achievement of independence. The course it chose was neutrality, refusing to join any alliance such as SEATO (ostensibly aimed at China) and, after 1953, even rejecting American aid on the ground that it had invisible 'strings' attached to it. The occasion for the breach was alleged United States support for Taiwan in its policy of encouraging the refugee KMT troops in Burma to create bases in Burma as a springboard for attacking Communist China.

The passing of the British Raj had left Burma with an inheritance of frontier disputes with China, for during the British period there had been a number of encroachments by Burma on what the Chinese Emperors had regarded as their sphere. It was not until 1960 that these disputes came to an end with the treaty between Burma and the People's Republic. The treaty provided for the return to China of the area of Hpimaw, Gawlum, and Kangfang ('forcibly seized by Britain') and the confirmation of Burmese sovereignty over the Namwan Triangle, and was signed by U Nu, Prime Minister of Burma, and Chou En-lai, the Chinese Premier, at Peking in September 1960. Its ratification was attended by much pomp and circumstance and about 1,200,000 Burmese inhabitants living in close proximity to the Sino-Burmese boundary were presented with 2·4 million metres of printed cloth and 600,000 porcelain plates by the Chinese Government. In January 1961 Mr Chou En-lai went to Rangoon to return U Nu's visit to Peking.

Since the Government of Burma had suffered in 1950 from a Communist rebellion, and after that from local Communist insurrections, this might well have jeopardized harmonious relations between Burma and China. But the Chinese Communists were careful not to identify themselves with the Communists of Burma (whatever their secret sympathies with them), and this decision was justified by the unimpressive record of the latter in the next ten years, when they offered no prospect of succeeding in overthrowing the Government. Nor did the People's Government give any support to the Burmese 'constitutional Communist' party, the BWPP.

The rise of Communist China was bound to affect the position of the small Chinese minority in Burma. Whatever the political sympathies of the various elements of that community, past or present, the People's Government spared no pains in cultivating its good graces and winning its support. In every possible way it ensured that those persons of Chinese origin were kept in touch with the homeland. Every variety of Chinese overseas organization—Chambers of Commerce and other trade associations, trade unions, schools, temples, even Christian churches (says Tinker) all had their quota of Communist *rapporteurs*. The prestige of the New China was constantly impressed on the Chinese of Burma.

An example of this was the full-dress cultural mission which visited Burma in 1955, comprising sixty-seven members and led by Cheng Chen-to, a notable scholar in the field of literary history and Vice-Minister for Cultural Affairs.

The mission gave a season of Chinese opera, dancing, and orchestral music at Rangoon which was almost overwhelming in its splendour of colour, richness of sound, gaiety, beauty, superb artistry, and professional verve. Every night an audience of 2,000 or more watched these dazzling performances: and 95 per cent of the audience was composed of Chinese residents of Rangoon, made proud to the point of arrogance by this Chinese cavalcade, discreetly presented to combine qualities both pro-letarian and classical—but always Chinese.

And yet the two items—and the only two—which stirred the crowded Chinese audience to rise to their feet, cheering and clapping and demand-ing an encore, were a rather feeble Burmese dance and a Burmese song, which the group had learned as a compliment to their hosts.[15]

Whatever the mixture of motives in the minds of the Vice-Minister of Culture directing the troupe or of the audience applauding them, the above incident gives one a very clear insight into the position of the Chinese in Burma. There was never a 'Chinese Problem' in the past and there is not one now. Although, as we have seen in our demographical introduction, the number of Chinese in Burma is on the increase (though not in significant proportion to the total population), the newcomers continue as in the past to become entirely assimilated into the general population after two generations of residence, and regard Burma as their homeland.[16] Since Burma became independent the fortunes of the Indians have been on the wane (and unlike the People's China in the case of its overseas relatives, the Government of India does nothing to cultivate or encourage the Indians of Burma), but those of the Chinese have been rising. The pre-war economic pattern continued to be much the same. Most of the Chinese were engaged in commerce or the pro-fessions: few were poor and some were very rich. The rich Chinese (including the proprietors of garages and car-marts) contrived to en-joy the best of two worlds—keeping in the good books of the Chinese

[15] Tinker, *Union of Burma*, p. 89.
[16] Mr B. Ward-Perkins, who served in the I.C.S. in Burma from 1906 to 1923 and who has visited the country since, says in a letter to the writer regarding the Chinese in Burma, 'There was nothing in Burma like what I saw in Siam—the second or even the third genera-tion unassimilated.'

Communists in China and making money as capitalists in Burma. This capacity for adaptation to circumstances was typically Chinese.

But if the People's China to date had been successful in keeping Burma as a friendly neighbour, the Nationalist Government in Formosa had been unlucky enough to incur the resentment and hostility of the Burmese Government. This arose from the fact that a considerable number of KMT troops, cut off by the Communist advance in 1949, crossed the frontier into Burmese territory and for years lived off the countryside, extorting food and other supplies from the people. Suspicion that these KMT troops were kept in being as formations supplied and directed from Formosa, with the intention of using Burma as a potential springboard for a counter-revolution against the Chinese Communists, led to protests to Formosa by the Burmese Government. Successive military drives were made to mop up the KMT troops and the Nationalists eventually undertook to transport them in successive airlifts to Formosa. But whatever the *bona fides* of this attempt, a considerable number of the troops remained in Burma, plundering the countryside, with forays into Laos and northern Thailand.

PART III

THE CHINESE IN SIAM[1]

9

DEMOGRAPHY

THE Thai Census of 1960[2] included all persons residing in Thailand at the time of the Census except for the following—nomadic hill tribes, foreign diplomatic personnel and their families, foreign military personnel and their families, and foreign visitors. The total population for the country as a whole was returned at 26,257,916—8,271,302 in the Central Region, 8,991,543 in the Northeast Region, 3,271,965 in the Southern Region, and 5,723,106 in the Northern Region. The total number of Chinese nationals was given at 409,508.

These 409,508 Chinese nationals were subdivided as follows according to sex and age-group (Table 8):

Country of Citizenship

Chinese		409,508		
	Male	270,292	Female	139,216
Under 10	.	6,854		3,568
10–14	.	2,805		1,498
15–19	.	5,896		2,833
20–24	.	9,671		4,675
25–29	.	14,537		5,224
30–34	.	25,122		7,857
35–39	.	24,578		12,974
40–44	.	32,953		19,439
45–49	.	35,061		21,561
50–54	.	32,823		18,125
55–59	.	27,188		13,670
60–64	.	20,813		10,127
65–69	.	13,779		7,243
70 and over	.	17,136		10,145
Unknown	.	1,076		277

[1] Siam and Thailand are used in this work interchangeably.
[2] *Thailand Population Census, 1960.*

Table 5, Place of Birth, gave 384,408 persons as having been born in China (290,899 living in the Central Region, 19,821 in the Northeast Region, 29,523 in the North Region, and 44,165 in the South Region). 409,508 persons claimed Chinese citizenship.

The sex ratio of Chinese nationals was 1·9 males to 1 female.

But since the Census is again silent as to the number of *ethnic* or *cultural* Chinese in Siam, we are compelled to estimate their number from other evidence.

About half the Chinese in Thailand live in Bangkok or near-by in the Chao Phraya delta of the Central Plains. A second major concentration occurs in the Kra Isthmus in the south of the country upon which the tin and rubber industries are centred. Every town and village has Chinese residents, and while no province is without some Chinese, those in the extreme west, north, and northeast are very lightly settled. Coughlin points out that being a highly concentrated minority the Chinese are conspicuous and seem to form an even larger group than they actually do.[3] They do not form a homogeneous group, although the basis for unity is developing steadily.

Skinner has gone into the question of the probable number and distribution of ethnic Chinese in Siam in some detail[4] and arrives at a total of 2,315,000 for 1955, distributed as under:

Speech group	Proportion of total Chinese population	Number
	Per cent	
Teochiu	56	1,297,000
Hakka	16	370,000
Hainanese	12	278,000
Cantonese	7	162,000
Hokkien	7	162,000
Other	2	46,000
Total	100	2,315,000

This is probably as near as we are likely to get in the existing state of statistics, so this figure of 2,315,000 can be accepted for 1955, and additions made to allow for subsequent natural increase.

We may now treat earlier estimates of the number of ethnic or cultural Chinese in Siam as historical phenomena, with a definite political content.

A notable concentration of Chinese in southern Siam was made up principally of more recent immigrants. Here the Chinese worked in the tin and tungsten mines, in the rubber plantations, and as shopkeepers and

[3] R. J. Coughlin, *Double Identity: the Chinese in Modern Thailand* (1960), p. 6.
[4] S. W. Skinner, *Chinese Society in Thailand* (1957), chap. vi, p. 212.

merchants in the towns and villages.[5] Disregarding distribution by political
boundaries, the Chinese miners of southern Siam and of Tavoy constituted
an extension of the group in the Malay States and in Bangka and Billiton.

The distribution of Chinese was by no means equal over the country.
Already by the 1880s they formed half the population of the delta of the
Menam,[6] with a heavy concentration round Bangkok; they were settled
along the coasts in southern Siam, as above-mentioned, but in most other
parts they were extremely sparse. In 1932 there were only 14,933 Chinese
(11,340 males and 3,593 females) in the two circles of Nakon Rajasima
and Udon (composing northeast Siam), amounting to an insignificant
proportion of little more than one-third of 1 per cent of the total population (total population 3,887,000 for northeast Siam).[7] (Reginald le May
in his authoritative book on northern Siam, *An Asian Arcady* (1928), does
not mention the Chinese at all.)

The Chinese in Siam were closely associated with the rice industry.
Before the war of 1942–5 they were reputed to own 80–90 per cent of the
country's rice-mills:[8] they had brokers and buyers all over the rice-
growing areas, and their larger buying centres were at the focus of water
transport in the Menam delta. Almost without exception, the labour in
the mills was also Chinese. There was a regular traffic in coolies between
Bangkok and the Chinese port of Swatow, thousands coming and going
in a single voyage.[9]

The Chinese had been visiting and dwelling in Siam for centuries, but
their immigration in large numbers is a matter of only the last century.
In the time of King Phra Narai (1656–88) there were only about 3,000
Chinese permanently settled in the country. They had been coming
mostly overland from southern China, but in the late nineteenth and
early twentieth centuries they arrived more and more by sea from
Hainan and other adjacent mainland ports. From 1840 to 1850 Chinese
immigration averaged 15,000 annually.[10] The increased flow in more
recent years may be attributed to the expansion of Siam's export trade,

---

[5] 'This group, like its Chinese neighbours to the south, has been little assimilated by the
indigenous peoples, perhaps as much because of the relatively primitive state of these people
as of the recentness of the arrival of the Chinese' (Unger, *Geographical R.*, xxxiv/2 (1944),
p. 205). The improvement of communications, the frequent passing to and from China, the lack
of intermarriage, and the growth of nationalism are, perhaps, the more important causes.

[6] Holt S. Hallett, *A Thousand Miles on an Elephant in the Shan States* (London, 1890),
p. 460 (refers to 1884).

[7] *The Economic Conditions of North-Eastern Siam* (Bangkok, June 1932), p. 3. (North-
eastern Siam covered nearly one-third of the country.)

[8] Unger, *Geographical R.*, xxxiv/2 (1944), p. 204. A list of the principal rice-mills in Bangkok
and their owners on p. 90 of the *Commercial Directory for Siam*, 3rd ed. (Bangkok, 1929),
shows that the 71 mills all had Chinese names, but 14 appeared to have been owned by non-
Chinese, including 6 owned by the Privy Purse Department. Those having a large capacity
were practically all Chinese-owned. [9] *Commercial Directory*, p. 38.

[10] Virginia Thompson, *Thailand: the New Siam* (N.Y., 1941), p. 103. Crawfurd (*Journal
of an Embassy from the Governor-General of India to the Courts of Siam and Cochinchina*,
2nd ed. (London, 1830) says that the French writers of the period nowhere estimate the
numbers at more than four or five thousand.

to the Revolution of 1911 and the disordered state of China that ensued from it, and also to the barriers raised against the Chinese in French Indochina. The surplus of Chinese immigrants over emigrants in Siam from 1918 to 1929 was 400,000 and it is believed to have been even larger before the First World War.[11]

Let us now go back again for a century or so and note the estimates (necessarily guesses for the most part) made by foreign observers at various times. Crawfurd in 1821[12] estimated that of a total population of 2·79 million for Siam, 1·26 million were Siamese, 840,000 Laos, 195,000 Malays, 440,000 Chinese, and the remainder Cambodians, Peguans, Indians, and Portuguese. In 1828 Tomlin[13] puts the total population of Bangkok alone at 401,300, made up of 310,000 Chinese (paying tax),[14] 50,000 descendants of Chinese, 9,000 Burmans, 8,000 Siamese, 7,000 Laos, and various other races in smaller numbers.

Gützlaff says that the natives of China in his time came in great numbers from Chaou-chow-foo, the most eastern part of the Canton province (i.e. Teochius). These were mostly agriculturists; members of another tribe, the Kih or Ka (i.e. Khehs or Hakkas) consisted chiefly of artisans. Emigrants from the Tungan district of Fukien province were few and were mostly sailors or merchants. The Hainanese (Hailams) were chiefly pedlars or fishermen and formed 'perhaps the poorest, yet the most cheerful class'.[15]

According to K. P. Landon,[16] in 1890 it was roughly estimated that the total population of Siam was about 10 million, composed of over 3 million Siamese, 3 million Chinese, 1 million Malays, 1 million Cambodians, 1·3 million Laos, and about 400,000 Peguans, Karens, and other tribes. However, these estimates are undoubtedly much exaggerated. The total population of the country is given at a million more than it was by the census twenty years afterwards, and the number of Chinese, given at 3 million, even including every person who had the smallest drop of Chinese blood, must be much in excess of what it was in reality. But the

[11] Thompson, *Thailand: the New Siam*, pp. 103–4.

[12] Crawfurd, *Embassy to Siam and Cochinchina*, i. 224.

[13] Cited in Karl Gützlaff, *Journal of Three Voyages along the Coast of China in 1831, 1832, and 1833, with notices of Siam etc.*, 3rd ed. (1840), p. 23, from p. 21 of Tomlin's *Journal of a Visit to Siam* (1828).

[14] The tax of about $3 'levied on every Chinaman on first entering the country and re-collected triennially exempts them from the half-yearly servitude required by the King from every other oriental stranger resident in Siam' (Gützlaff, p. 23).

[15] Ibid. p. 71. Speaking of more recent times, Mr Lin Yu, in 'Twin Loyalties in Siam', *Pacific Affairs*, vol. ix, no. 2 (June 1936), says: 'While an accurate estimate is not possible, it is commonly accepted in Bangkok that 60 per cent. of these families are partly of Fukien stock which provided the earliest Chinese settlers in Siam, while another 10 per cent. trace back in part to the second group of Chinese settlers, the Cantonese. These groups are to be distinguished from the Swatow Chinese who now form the bulk of the Chinese community in Siam.' See also Crawfurd, *Embassy to Siam and Cochinchina*, i. 221, 222.

[16] *The Chinese in Thailand* (1941), p. 21. Dr Landon derives this from M. Gaston Rautier in an article in the *Revue Française*, quoted by Hallett, *A Thousand Miles on an Elephant*, p. 461.

estimate is worth including as a warning of the conjectural nature of most statistics regarding Siam, even in recent times.

Much more reasonable is Léon de Rosny's estimate for about 1884. He puts the total population of Siam at 5·9 million, including 1·6 million Siamese, 1·5 million Chinese, 1 million Malays, and 1 million Laos.[17] To Bangkok he gives a total of 404,000, with 200,000 Chinese and 120,000 Siamese.

MacNair quotes the estimate of more than 7 million total for Siam for 1909, of which 10 per cent were Chinese. Of these, 200,000 Chinese were believed to have been resident in Bangkok.[18] The same author also gives some immigration figures which are less conjectural. From 1912 to 1914 the inflow from Swatow to Bangkok was 143,957 and the outflow from Bangkok was 110,525; from Kiungchow (Hainan) the inflow was 27,809 and the figure for the reverse direction was 21,970. From Swatow the great majority of immigrants were almost certainly Teochius, and from Kiungchow it is probable that they were mostly Hailams, though there may have been some transhipment from mainland ports.

The whole nature of the Chinese element in Siam was changed by the immigration of Chinese women in large numbers. Up to about 1914 the Chinese male immigrants could not afford to bring their wives and they intermarried largely with the people of the country. In 1910 a Chinese woman was a rare sight in the streets of Bangkok; twenty years later there were hundreds of them to be seen.[19] By 1937 the number of (China-born) Chinese females was, according to the Census, 189,000 as compared with 336,000 (China-born) males. Thus in about seventeen years the females of pure Chinese race had risen in number from being an insignificant proportion of the community to more than half that of the males of the same category.

It is interesting to compare the Census figure of China-born females in 1937 with the number of Chinese born in Siam in 1929, namely 113,000.

IO

HISTORY PRIOR TO 1800

THE early history of the Burmese, the Siamese, and the Annamites is, briefly, that under the pressure of the Chinese they forsook the territory of west and south China and made their way southwards. Eventually the Burmese came to rest (perhaps because they could get no farther) in the

---

[17] Léon de Rosny, *Le Peuple siamois ou thai* (Paris, 1885), p. 116.
[18] H. F. MacNair, *The Chinese Abroad* (Shanghai, 1924), p. 47.
[19] Landon, *Chinese in Thailand*, p. 20, citing Reginald le May, *Siamese Tales Old and New* (London, 1930), p. 165.

valley of the Irrawaddy, the Siamese in the valley of the Chao Phya river, and the Annamites moved along the coast of the China Sea, some settling in present-day Tongking and Annam and others moving on to Cochinchina. By the twelfth and thirteenth centuries of the Christian era the founders of the Thai or Siamese nation had settled in the northern areas of what is now Siam. They found their new home inhabited by the negritos, whom they displaced. Other races they ejected or subjugated were the Khmer, Yuan, Lawa, and the Mon. By the time the Portuguese arrived Siamese influence extended to Singapore. Whether or not the Siamese and Chinese had a common origin is a speculation that does not belong to these pages; but their brothers, or cousins (if such they were), the Chinese, followed in the footsteps of the Siamese 'like their own shadows'.[1] For the 700 years of Siam's history the Chinese have been bound up with the life and trade of the country.

When Europeans penetrated the hinterland of Siam north of Ayuthia in the 1830s they found the Chinese overland trade well established there. This was in spite of the formidable natural obstacles—the mountains and the gorges of the Lantsan, the Lu Kiang, and the Lung Kong, which as we approach Shan territory assume the better-known names of the Mekong, Salween, and Shweli. 'With their characteristic churlishness', says Warington Smyth,[2] 'and with that deliberate attempt to hamper trade which these unmannerly rivers betray in all their movements, they stretch their deep valleys athwart the lines of communication. . . . It is curious what an effectual barrier this great river region has proved to communication between the Chinese and the Indian Empires.'[3] Yet there were Chinese caravan routes of ancient origin over which the caravans came yearly into what we now know as the Shan States and into Siam. Other routes led to Nan and Lampang in Siam and to Luang Prabang in what was to become French Indochina. The Chinese brought copper pots, silks, rock salt, tinsel, and lace, and took back to China copper, ivory, horns, and tea.

Of much less antiquity than the overland route, but dating back, nevertheless, for some centuries, was the seaborne trade. King Phra Narai (1656–88) in his day established a fleet to carry on commerce with China. His junks at one time numbered more than 400, but when treaties began to be made with the European Powers in the nineteenth century, the number was reduced to less than 100 by the competition of European-owned steamers.[4]

[1] Landon, *Chinese in Thailand*, p. 1.
[2] H. Warington Smyth, Director of the Dept. of Mines, Siam, *Five Years in Siam* (London, 1898), ii. 139.
[3] See p. 106 regarding the failure of de Lagrée's mission of exploration of the upper Mekong in 1866.
[4] Cited by Landon (*Chinese in Thailand*) at p. 9 from *Siam*, by W. A. Graham (London, 1924), ii. 98–99.

Except for retrospective flashes in the Chinese dynastic histories, the history of the Chinese in Southeast Asia is, generally speaking, unrecorded until the arrival of the Europeans, and it seems to have lacked incident and even energy until the greedy and rowdy traders and adventurers of the West had arrived to cause a commotion in the languid pool of native life. The Portuguese, as usual in the East, were the first, arriving in 1518; the Dutch followed at a respectful interval in 1598, and the English came a few years after them, in 1612. As Portuguese enterprise and power dwindled, that of Holland waxed great. The Dutch blockaded the mouth of the Menam river to force a favourable treaty from the reluctant Siam. In 1664 the treaty was signed with the Dutch East India Company, but as the century went on the Siamese were alienated by the truculence of the Dutch merchants and after 1706 the Dutch-Siamese trade lapsed.

In the second half of the seventeenth century the Siamese capital, Ayuthia, was regarded as one of the most important trading centres in the Far East. King Phra Narai was himself the principal merchant in the kingdom. The French arrived in 1662, in the shape of a Roman Catholic mission sent with the support of Louis XIV to convert the whole of eastern Asia. Later there was an exchange of embassies between France and Siam. Meanwhile the French cause was aided by the active support of the Minister of Finance and agent in all foreign relations, Constantine Phaulcon, a Greek by birth, who belonged to that order of adventurer-statesmen of alien race of which Marco Polo, John Law, and Disraeli were fellow members. Phaulcon was pro-French and discouraged the Dutch and English trade. This led to trouble and war seemed imminent. To protect Siam from the Dutch and English, the French in 1687 sent six warships and 1,400 soldiers to act as mercenaries in the service of Siam. At the crucial moment, in 1688, the Roman Catholic priests chose to seek the King's conversion by intensive tactics, but Phra Narai had no urge to save his soul. Fearing that the foreigners meant to subjugate their country, some Siamese nobles formed a plot against both the French and their own King. They killed Phaulcon and three possible successors to the throne, but Phra Narai, being on his death-bed, was allowed to die naturally. The *coup* ended in the departure of the French and the closing of the doors to foreign trade. Although individual Europeans continued to reside in Siam, diplomatic relations were not reopened with the European nations until the nineteenth century.[5]

Our knowledge of Siam from the seventeenth century onwards is derived from the accounts of seamen, merchants, diplomats, and missionaries. The first to give any consecutive account of the country is Joost (or Jobst) Schouten, Director of the Dutch East India Company

---

[5] Luang Chun Kasikan and others, *Prawat Sat Syam*, 3rd ed. (Bangkok, 1935), pp. 172–4, cited by Landon, *Siam in Transition* (London, 1939), p. 5.

from its establishment at Ayuthia in 1633.[6] On the way thither he passed
the site of the future capital city of Bangkok which was to be founded
in 1782. Schouten does not specifically mention the Chinese, but their
existence in Ayuthia is to be inferred from the context and his description is a useful background to our extracts from other visitors later in
the century. He says:

The city of Indica (Ayuthia); the Metropolis of the Kingdom, and seat of the
King and the chief nobles, is situate upon the River Menam, in a little round island,
encompassed with a thick stone wall, about six English miles round; the Suburbs
are on the other side of the river, closely builded, and full of Temples and Cloysters,
lying in a flat and fruitful country . . . there are all manner of China wares, Jewels,
Gold, Benjamin, Wax, Sappang, Agerwood, Tin, and Lead, etc., and also a vast
number of Hart-skins, one hundred and fifty thousand of these being caught
yearly in this countrey, and sold with much profit to the Jappaners. They drive a
great trade with all eating provisions, especially Rice, many thousand Tuns being
transported yearly by Forrainers. The city by reason of its great traffick, is frequented by several Nations, as the Indians, the more Western Asiaticks, European
Moors, and Christian Merchants. The King himself is also a merchant, and hath
his own Ships and Factories trading to Choromandel and China, being for that
cause more favoured and priviledged than any other Prince; he likewise trafficks to
Pegue, Ava, Jogoma, Lans-Jang, and other places, besides his negotiations at home,
all of which brings him in incredible profit, and no small disturbance to private
Merchants, all of which do manifest the great trade that is carried on in this
Countrey.[7]

'We may assume', says Credner, 'that the Bangkok mentioned by
Schouten already had Chinese residents.'[8] In support of this he mentions
that Engelbert Kaempfer in his map of the Menam of 1690 showed a
special settlement of Chinese.[9] Certainly they must have been resident
at Ayuthia, for not only does Kaempfer show their settlement in his plan
but he also says specifically: 'It must be observed here that the several
spots of ground, on which the Malayans, Chinese, Japanese, Portuguese,
Dutch and other nations live in Siam, and which are more particularly
expressed in the annexed Plan of the King's Residence, are called
Camps.' The Chinese Camp is in the plan located outside the city to the
northeast.

[6] *A true description of the Mighty Kingdoms of Japan and Siam, written originally in Dutch
by Francis Caron and Joost Schouten; and now rendered into English by Roger Manley* (London,
1671). (The account of Japan is by Caron and that of Siam (p. 121) is by Schouten.) This
same Joost Schouten was also at Malacca after its capture from the Portuguese in 1641 and
has left an account (see Purcell, *The Chinese in Malaya* (London, 1948), p. 30). Schouten's
account of Ayuthia is at p. 124 of his work above.
[7] Cf. Sir Maurice Powicke, *Medieval England* (London, 1948), p. 120. '. . . the King [of
England] tried to raise money by creating a monopoly for himself in the sale of English wool
abroad, and from 1337 onwards he summoned assemblies of merchants to arrange in co-
operation with them the methods by which the difficult operation could be carried out'.
[8] Wilhelm Credner, *Siam, Das Land der Thai* (Stuttgart, 1935), p. 193.
[9] Engelbert Kaempfer, *The History of Japan; together with a Description of the Kingdom of
Siam, 1690–92* (Glasgow, 1906).

In the last decade but one of the seventeenth century there were probably not more than 3,000 Chinese permanently settled in Siam.[10] (The French observers never put them above 4,000–5,000.)

In 1685 and 1686 an embassy from Louis XIV of France came to Siam. The ambassador, the Chevalier de Chaumont, and two others accompanying him, the Abbé de Choisy and the Comte de Forbin, have left accounts of their visit. De Chaumont[11] enumerates the races inhabiting the country—the Laos, eight or nine true Portuguese families but more than 100 *mesties* (Portuguese-Siamese Eurasians); the Dutch had one factory, the English the same, the Cochinchinese had about 100 families for the most part Christian, the Tongkingese seven or eight Christian families; the Malays were there in great numbers but were mostly slaves; there were Macassars, Javanese, Moors, Turks, Mogols, Golcondas, Bengalis, and Armenians. But, in this list, no Chinese! However, in another place the Chevalier says: 'It is only some Moors, Chinese, French, and English who live in the city; all the other nations are lodged in the suburbs by "Camps", that is to say all of one nation together.' The Abbé has nothing to say regarding the Chinese community as such, nor has the Comte de Forbin, the most lively and impressionable of the party, who, however, records a matter of great interest. On his return to France he had an audience of Louis XIV who asked him whether the French missionaries had converted many Siamese, and he had replied, 'Not a soul, sir'. Louis remarked that this did not agree with what Père Tachard had told Père Lachaise. Forbin, having narrated this, continues:

While I stayed in Siam several Chinese of great wit and learning confessed to me that they could not comprehend how people of one and the same faith, who had left their native country and made long sea voyages through such vast seas, could propose to convert pagans, while they themselves were not agreed in their conduct, some living with great modesty and charity, and others abandoning themselves to malice and strife, to call it by no worse name. This was the language of all Chinese with whom I talked.[12]

The embassy was received with elaborate entertainment concluding with a Chinese play. (Chaumont says it was a comedy; Choisy says it was a tragedy!) There were actors from Canton and others from Fukien: the Fukienese were the most magnificent and the most ceremonious. The Chinese started their posturing; there were some Siamese also, but the Frenchmen could not understand a word they or the Chinese said. After the comedy there was a play by Chinese marionettes, but they 'did not approach those of Europe'. Regarding the music the Abbé was affected

---

[10] Cited by Thompson, *Thailand*, p. 104, from O. Frankfurter, *Siam Society J.* (1904).

[11] *Relation de l'ambassade de Monsieur le chevalier de Chaumont à la cour du roy de Siam*, Archives curieuses de l'histoire de France, sér. 2.

[12] *Memoirs of the Count de Forbin, Commodore of the Navy of France* (trans. from the French) (London, 1731), pp. 215, 227, 229, 231.

C.S.E.A.—D 2

by it very much as Europeans visiting the East have been before and since—'La symphonie détestable, ce sont des chaudrons qu'on bat en cadence'.[13]

De la Loubère who was in Ayuthia about three years afterwards, in 1687 and 1688, during the troubles, also speaks in amusing terms of a theatrical performance:

The one was a Chinese comedy, which I would willingly have seen to the end, but it was adjourned after some scenes to go to dinner. The Chinese comedians, whom the Siamese do love without understanding them, do speak in the throat. All their words are monosyllables, and I heard them not pronounce one single one, but with a new breath: some would say that it throttles them. One of the actors who represented a Magistrate walked so gravely that he trod first upon his heel, and then successively and slowly upon his heels and toes. . . .[14]

Father Tachard, mentioned above, whose impressions of the Chinese at Batavia are quoted in Part VII of this work, was in Siam with the embassy and has recorded his experiences. In his *Journal* he says:

Since all the Nations are well received in Siam, and each is allowed to live in the free exercise of their religion, there is scarcely a single Nation that is not found there. The Chinese are the ones who do the most trade; besides that of China they also engage in that of Japan. . . . He [the Siamese King] hath also several Jonkos which are Chinese vessels, and are manned by Chinese. But though that nation brag that they have had the use of the compass for above two thousand years; yet they come very far short of the European in the art of navigation. They have no other instruments for sailing than the Lead or Sound. They keep reckoning as we do, and run some time upon such a point of wind, the currents, mountains, which they discover on Land, the colour, fineness, and mixture of the sand, with other experiences are the rules they go by.[15]

According to de la Loubère, the population at this epoch was counted every year, and an exact account was kept of men, women, and children. The population of 1687 is given at 900,000 for all races. 'From which I question not', says de la Loubère, 'that some retrenchment is to be made for Vanity and Lyes; characters essential to the Eastern people; but on the other hand, thereunto must be added the Fugitives, which do seek a sanctuary in the woods against the Government.'[16]

Engelbert Kaempfer's description of Siam refers to the years 1690–2. Between the embassy of the Chevalier de Chaumont and this period there had been, in 1688, a court revolution in Siam with a change of dynasty. Faulcon or Phaulcon (or as he signed himself, Phaulkon), the Greek who had controlled the finances of the kingdom, fell from power

[13] *Journal du Voyage de Siam fait par M. l'abbé de Choisy, en 1685 et 1686* (Trévoux, 1741), p. 286.
[14] *A New Historical Relation of the Kingdom of Siam*, trans. from the French of de la Loubère, by A. Gen (London, 1693), p. 11.
[15] *Voyages de Siam des Pères Jésuites, envoyés par le roy, aux Indes et à la Chine* (Amsterdam, 1687), p. 177. Above translation from an Eng. ed. (London, 1688).
[16] *Kingdom of Siam*, p. 47.

and was imprisoned. Having been tortured and starved for fourteen days until he was reduced to a skeleton, he was beheaded. The French, who had under General des Fargues been placed in command of the fortress of Bangkok, were ejected from Siam. King Petracha who succeeded Phra Narai was strongly anti-foreign. About the same time Japan closed her doors to foreign trade, and the Japanese settlement at Ayuthia declined. But these happenings had little influence upon the fortunes of the Chinese resident in Siam.

The prestige of the Chinese civilization had for long been high in Siam, and a number of natives of China had reached important positions. Kaempfer in a list of the 'chief mandarins' mentions Peja Jummeraad, 'a learned Chinese', who was Chief Justice of Siam.[17] (Incidentally, two diverse institutions the Siamese had already adopted from the Chinese were the cangue (a movable pillory) and the cycle of sixty years.)[18]

Siam's history in the first half of the eighteenth century included a succession of plots and counter-plots in the court entourage, the mass elimination of pretenders to the throne and all their relatives, and revolts in the provinces, but at the same time the period was free from serious wars with the country's neighbours. The reign of King Boromakot (1730–1758) was called the golden age of Siam. Then war with Burma broke out in 1759 and continued, between monsoon seasons, until 1767 when Ayuthia fell to the Burmese. The city was burned and the written records of Siamese history were lost. Whilst various aspirants for power struggled for ascendancy Siam remained in a state of disorder. Five years after the sack of Ayuthia, Phya Tak[19] shook off the Burmese yoke and set up his capital at Dhonburi, now a part of Bangkok.

Tak Sin, the first King (1767–82) to unite the Siamese kingdom under his rule after the Burmese had destroyed the ancient capital, was of mixed Chinese-Siamese ancestry, his father having been a Chinese tax-farmer named Hai Hong. Indeed his Chinese blood was one of the factors (said his enemies) that made him unsuitable as a sovereign. A conspiracy was formed against him, he was dethroned, and afterwards put to death. The new King, Chao Phya Chakri (1782–1809), founded the Chakri dynasty, which was still reigning in 1950, and established the city of Bangkok on the site of a Chinese settlement which was removed to Sampeng. He was a son-in-law of Phya Tak and had been given a Chinese name in addition to his Siamese name. It is said that the Chakri family has itself an admixture of Chinese blood, and certainly there were Chinese women in the harems of the later Kings.[20]

In 1733 a Chinese rising had taken place and 300 Chinese had attacked

---

[17] Kaempfer, *Hist. of Japan*, p. 38.   [18] Ibid. p. 70.
[19] He is variously called Pin Tat, Tia Sin Tat, Tay Cheow, or Tak Cheo. His personal name was Sin. He was later called Lord of Tak (a town). (Landon, *Chinese in Thailand*, p. 7.)
[20] Ibid. p. 8.

the palace. They were, however, dispersed and forty of their ringleaders were captured and executed.[21] But in spite of this departure from the good manners expected of guests, the Chinese retained their position in Siamese society, so that the French historian Turpin could refer to them in the third quarter of the century in these words: 'The Chinese colony is the most numerous and flourishing by the extent of its commerce, and by the privileges which it enjoys. Its compliance with received customs, a certain conformity of character and manners, seem to ensure it a continuance of its privileges and prosperity.'[22]

Turpin's anticipation was justified for at least another century and a half, after which the irony of circumstances arising from the birth of nationalism caused the Chinese to be regarded as a foreign and schismatic element in the Siamese nation.

II

THE NINETEENTH CENTURY: FIRST HALF

As in the other countries of Southeast Asia, the Chinese immigrants into Siam until the beginning of the twentieth century, and even during its first two decades, were mostly males. The majority of them were small traders, and of these a number had been sailors, fishermen, and peasants before their coming to Siam. They owned no land on their arrival—but land or no land they would have found trade more profitable. They were readily assimilated for they married Siamese women and their children were brought up as Siamese. The children of these marriages were called *Lukchin*, and were proud of their Chinese blood. Supplying the energy and the initiative that the Siamese lacked, they were welcomed and received favoured treatment from the Government, especially in the days of intense anti-European feeling among the Siamese.[1] Assimilation, too, was made easier by the racial similarity of the Chinese and Siamese which was greater than that of the Chinese and any other race in Southeast Asia. In the second or third generation the immigrants were completely

[21] W. A. R. Wood, *A History of Siam* (London, 1926), p. 232.

[22] M. Turpin, *Histoire civile et naturelle du Royaume de Siam* (Paris, 1771), p. 9. A translation of the above is in Pinkerton's *General Collection of the best and most interesting voyages and travels* (1808–14), xi. 426–572.

Rice was for very long a staple article of commerce between China and Siam. In 1722 the Emperor ordered 300,000 piculs (18,000 tons) of rice to be imported from Siam. Although the relaxations of the restrictions on the export of copper from China to Siam could not be obtained, the rice trade continued. In 1751 any Chinese bringing 2,000 piculs of rice to China from Siam was rewarded with a mandarin's button. William Nunn, 'Some Notes upon the Development of the Commerce of Siam', *Siam Society J.*, xv, pt. 2, p. 82.

[1] Landon, *Chinese in Thailand*, p. 11; Thompson, *Thailand*, p. 104.

absorbed and considered themselves as Siamese. Indeed they would have been insulted to have been called Chinese, since the Siamese were the ruling race and the Chinese were their social inferiors.

The typical merchant of Siam [says Kumut Chandruang] usually had Chinese blood, and his grandfather was very likely a pure Chinese. He may still worship his ancestors by burning gold paper, but his sons have gone to Siamese schools and learned to write on their slates in both languages. The third generation do not remember Chinese; many of them have changed their family names and forgotten their family origin.[2]

In the nineteenth century Siam, 'under a debasing tyranny, destitute of arts and commerce, alike, offered a fair field for the development of their superiority', says Finlayson[3] writing in the 1820s.

From the early 1820s onwards a number of alert European observers began to penetrate the seclusion of remote Siam and several have bequeathed us their impressions. One of these is Captain Burney who carried out a series of missions to Siam mostly in connexion with the problems of relationship between that country and Britain, arising from the latter's occupation of the island of Penang in 1786 and Singapore in 1819. He was naturally more concerned with southern Siam with its predominantly Malay population than with the north. He found that the Chinese in this region were engaging in the same sort of nefarious traffic that they were carrying on at the same time, or a little later, in the islands and the coastal region of western Sumatra.[4] There were in 1826 in almost every part of the Siamese dominions hundreds of Malays and natives of India who were most anxious, but unable, to return to their countries. Burney found that it was a common practice for the Chinese to seize Malays who happened to be on board their junks at Penang or Malacca, Java, and other places and to bring them to Siam as slaves.[5] He was also concerned with the apprehension of criminals who had fled from Penang to Kedah. One of them, Tucang Chu-koor, the Chinese monopoly farmer at Kuala Muda, against whom the Governor of Penang had preferred a charge, was arrested by the Siamese and confined in a cangue for several months.[6]

There is also included among the Burney papers an appreciation of the Chinese character written by Major James Low. Major Low was closely associated with Malaya and his writings are more than once referred to in Part V of this study, but it will be convenient to insert the character sketch here since it applies as much to the Chinese he met in the Siamese

---

[2] Quoted by Landon at p. 11 from 'Young Siam in the New World', by Kumut Chandruang, *Asia* (May 1939).
[3] G. Finlayson, *The Mission to Siam and Hué* (London, 1826), p. 167.
[4] See p. 425ff.
[5] *The Burney Papers* (Bangkok, 1910), i. 95. (Originals in the India Office, London.)
[6] Ibid. ii. 7.

territory of Kedah, &c, as it does to the Chinese in the Straits Settlements.
Low's considered opinion of the Chinese is this:

They are a time-serving people, and unlike the Indo-Chinese tribes around them,
they seem to be very deficient in imagination, and therefore less disposed than these
to give way to theoretical impulses. Their understandings are pretty sure guides to
their interests, and they perceive at a glance that the latter and any assumption of
political power in the countries they have settled in are things at complete variance
with each other. But unwilling as they may be to turn Rulers, where nothing
could be obtained or be put in competition with their mercantile gains, they do not
seem to be at all averse to intrigue with one or even with both, so that whatever be
the result their interests may continue unaffected. It need not be added that the real
leaning in such a case will be to the stronger party, although the weaker will be
cajoled by promises and aided by supplies and arms, the sale of which at high
profits they can easily effect. I have had personal opportunities of knowing this to
be true. Keeping these traits in view as checks to an over confidence in Chinese
political fidelity, it may safely be pronounced that as settlers they are eminently
valuable in new countries on account of their unceasing and well directed industry,
their enterprise as traders, their luxurious habits which swell the revenue by the
consumption of taxable commodities, and lastly perhaps because their physical
powers of endurance exceed those possessed by the Malays and the other Indo-
Chinese people.[7]

A shrewd appraisal if ever there was one, and deficient only in the
respect that it is purely an objective one from the point of view of the
usefulness or otherwise of the Chinese to the ruling Power, in this case
Britain, and takes no account of what the Chinese felt about it all or why
they felt it. This limitation we shall find everywhere in perusal of European opinion of the Chinese in Southeast Asia through the course of
three and a half centuries.

John Crawfurd, the associate of Raffles, appears a number of times in
these pages and whatever his merits as an administrator or diplomat, he
was certainly a keen and, usually, accurate observer. The following is his
impression of the Chinese in Siam in the early 1820s:

The Chinese settlers in the Siamese territory are chiefly immigrants from the
provinces of Canton and Fukien; but there is also a considerable number from the
island of Hainan and some from Chekiang and Kiangnan. The few immigrants from
Yunnan are confined to the northern parts of Laos. . . . The Chinese resort to Siam
and other foreign countries, unaccompanied by their families. They soon intermarry with the Siamese, there being no scruple on either side. They even adopt,
whatever may have been their religion before, or whether they had any or not, the
Buddhist form of worship, visiting the Siamese temples, and giving the usual alms
to the priests. A few even enter the priesthood, although the mode of life is by no
means congenial to their industrious and active character. What is probably more
remarkable, they forego their partiality for costly sepulchral monuments, burying

_____

[7] *A Retrospect of British Policy in the Straits of Malacca from the period of the First Establishment of Penang on 17 July 1786 up to April 1842*, by Major James Low, 46th Regt. Madras
Native Infantry, printed in the *Burney Papers* (1914), i/1. 105.

their dead like the Siamese. . . . They invariably dress, however, in the costume of their own country. Every male amongst them above the age of twenty, pays a capitation tax. The number assessed to this tax at Bangkok and its vicinity, was stated to me at 21,000. Indeed it is commonly computed that half the population of the capital is composed of Chinese. . . .[8]

As is usual with foreign observers, Crawfurd is keenly interested in the statistics of the matter. He was informed that the total number of Chinese in Siamese territory, Malay States excluded, was 100,000. The Chinese settlers within the territory of the Malay States, 'engaged in traffic or in working in gold or tin' were estimated at 20,000. 'An intelligent Chinese' told him that 'pestilence was necessary for keeping down population now that wars had ceased'. 'No other Asiatic but a Chinese', remarks Crawfurd, 'would have thought of expressing himself in such language.' (This early Chinese Malthusian was a trifle optimistic regarding the cessation of wars!) Pestilence certainly was very active in Siam, and in 1849, for example, 1,500 deaths a day occurred at Bangkok during the cholera epidemic, the river being thick with floating bodies. Siam was in any case a sparsely populated country and what with the ravages of ill-nourishment and disease it would have been more sparsely populated still had it not been for the Chinese. Referring to the number of Chinese, Crawfurd says: 'This shows an extraordinary increase since the close of the seventeenth century, for I find that the French writers nowhere estimate the numbers at more than four or five thousand.'

Crawfurd also affords us a minute on the subject of Siamese-Chinese relationships in the eighteenth and early nineteenth centuries which throws considerable light on the questions (disputed as late as 1917) of imperial suzerainty and a vassal's tribute. The matter was so arranged then that the vanity of the Chinese Emperors gave them the nominal overlordship over the kingdom of the Southern Ocean, whilst the cupidity of the Siamese sovereign was simultaneously assuaged:

The connection of the Siamese with the Chinese nation, although ostensibly political, is in fact purely of a commercial nature. The territories, indeed, border upon each other, but in remote and thinly populated parts of both. These are the Kingdom of Lao on the one side, and the Chinese province of Yunnan on the other. Here some traffic is carried on between them, and a considerable number of Chinese of Yunnan have settled at Lanchang, the capital of Lao, and the other towns in the country. But the great intercourse is generally maritime and such as I have already described. The King of Siam, although the circumstances be not generally known, acknowledged himself a tributary of the Emperor of China. His doing so does not arise from any particular necessity or consideration, or out of any actual dependence of Siam upon China, but altogether from this mercenary motive, that the vessels which carry the ambassadors may, under pretext of doing so, be exempted from the payment of all imposts. With this view two of the largest descriptions of junks, amounting to nearly one thousand tons each, sail annually from Bangkok to Canton

---

[8] *Embassy to Siam and Cochin-China*, p. 450. [I have modernized Crawfurd's spelling of place-names to avoid confusion. V.P.]

loaded with merchandize. They carry ambassadors annually to the Vice Roy of
Canton and, once in three years, these ambassadors go to Pekin, an honour, however, of which they are not considered worthy until they receive a title of Chinese
nobility from the Vice Roy and assume the costume of the Chinese. They carry the
Chinese Emperor a golden flower in token of tribute, but receive in return gifts to a
far greater value. The vanity of the one court and the rapacity of the other have long
rendered this course a permanent one.[9]

Our next report on the Chinese is from Karl Friedrich August
Gützlaff, the first Protestant missionary in Siam, of whose observations
we have already had occasion to make use. Mr Gützlaff, we feel, is not
of a particularly tolerant disposition and regards the Oriental races
generally with the same distaste as did his notable contemporary, Dr
Morrison, in China and Malaya.

The Chinese, Mr Gützlaff informs us,

delight to live in wretchedness and filth, and are very anxious to conform to the
servile habits of the Siamese. In some cases when they enter into matrimonial
alliance with the latter, they even throw away their jackets and trousers, and become
Siamese in every respect. As the lax, indifferent religious principles of the Chinese
do not differ from those of the Siamese, the former are very prone to conform to
the religious rites of the latter. And if they have children, they frequently cut off
their queues and become for a certain time priests. Within two or three generations,
all the distinguishing marks of the Chinese dwindle entirely away; and a nation
which adheres to its national customs so obstinately becomes wholly changed to
Siamese.

These descendants of Chinese, Gützlaff tells us, usually neglect the
literature of their paternal country and apply themselves to that of Siam.
To them nothing is so welcome as being presented by the King with an
honorary title, 'and this generally takes place when they have acquired
great riches or betrayed some of their own countrymen'. From this
moment they become slaves of the King, the more so if they are made his
officers. No service to them is so menial, so expensive, so difficult but
that they are forced to perform it. And in the case of disobedience they
are severely punished and perhaps put in chains for the rest of their lives.
'With the exception of the *Hwuy Hwuy*, or Triad Society, implicit
obedience is paid to their most exorbitant demands [those of the Siamese]
by every Chinese settler.'

In spite of the deliberate refusal of the Chinese to involve themselves
in any political responsibility, as Low has described, their policy of subservience and obsequiousness to the ruling race or party, and their
passivity under ill usage, there was occasionally a time when they were
driven to revolt. There had been one rising, as we have seen, in 1733; in
1824 the Chinese at Chantaburi rebelled, and this was followed by other
risings of their countrymen at Nakon Chaisri in 1842 and 1847, at

---

[9] *The Crawfurd Papers: a Collection of Official Records relating to the Mission of Dr John
Crawfurd sent to Siam by the Government of India in the year 1821* (Bangkok, 1915), p. 147.

Langsuen, and at Chengsao in 1848;[10] we shall read of another rebellion in 1847 later on. In the 1820s or early 1830s (the date is uncertain) a conspiracy was formed by the Triad Society. Some Chinese of this society seized some native craft at Blampasoi near the mouth of the Menam and 'began to avenge themselves upon their tyrants', but, falling short of provisions, they were chased by a small Siamese squadron, and beset by contrary winds and lacking the necessities of life, they had to surrender. The ringleader escaped to Cochinchina, but his followers were either massacred or sent to prison for life. A great many individuals (says Gützlaff) 'hope that the English (according to their own expression) will extend their benevolent government as far as Siam. Every arrival of a ship enlivens their expectations: every departure damps their joy.'[11]

Our next notable informant is George Windsor Earl who sailed the seas as a merchant from 1832 to 1834. His impressions of the Chinese in Borneo and Java are mentioned in the appropriate place in this survey.[12] When Earl arrived at Bangkok about an hour before daybreak on 10 March 1833, he found in the lower part of the port that, notwithstanding the earliness of the hour, vast numbers of Chinese blacksmiths were busily employed forging ironwork, probably for the junks that were being built on the banks of the river. He tells us that there were then about half a million Chinese in Siam, and that they 'possess all the mechanical employments' (a locution, by the way, which is often found in books of the period and is enough to date them). They were engaged in junk-building, making *quallies*, or iron pans, which latter were exported in large quantities all over Asia. Chinese junks used in foreign trade were usually built in countries where wood was plentiful. Earl supposed that a junk could be built more cheaply at Bangkok than at any other place in 'India' (in which term he undoubtedly included the whole of Southeast Asia).

He remarks, however, that the Siamese empire was 'apparently in a decline', an observation which agrees with that of other visitors to the country.[13]

In any anthology of character sketches of the Chinese the vignette of Captain Sherard Osborn would deserve a place. It refers to a visit to Kangar, Perlis, in the late 1830s:[14]

A few Chinese, the Jews of the Eastern Archipelago, were there also. They were so obsequious, so anxious to attract the attention of a British midshipman, that he, with all the dignity of that proud caste, allowed them to change a dollar for him. The Chinese were mostly money-changers. The insolent contumely they endured

---

[10] Thompson, *Thailand*, p. 32.
[11] Gützlaff, *Three Voyages along Coast of China*, p. 73.   [12] See pp. 424f., 432f.
[13] G. W. Earl, *The Eastern Seas, or Voyages and Discoveries in the Indian Archipelago in 1832–33–34* (London, 1837), p. 159.
[14] S. Osborn, *Quedah, or Stray Leaves from a Journal in Malayan Waters* (London, 1855, new ed. 1865), p. 216 ff.

at the hands of the Malays struck me very much. The natives when ill-treated, chattered like a nest of rooks. Not so the Chinese: they bore it with cringing and shrinking; one could see, by the twinkle of their little glittering eyes that they only abided their time to bite the heel that bruised them.

But he gives the other side of the medal in a footnote in the shape of the time-honoured tribute to the industry of the Chinese race: 'It is but justice to these industrious emigrants to say that they are invaluable as labourers, agriculturists, artisans, and merchants throughout our colonies; and better conducted subjects Her Majesty Queen Victoria nowhere possesses'.

Most of the Chinese who rendered exceptional service to Siam before the middle of the nineteenth century are anonymous, but one exception is Lim Hoi, a Cantonese merchant resident at Thalang in Junk Ceylon. He was returning from Penang where he had been on business when he caught sight of a Burmese sailing vessel. Something about it aroused his suspicion and he attacked and captured it. Whilst examining its contents he came across a Burmese official letter addressed to the Raja of Kedah. He therefore brought the boat and the crew to Thalang and made them over to the Governor. The official forwarded the letter and prisoners, together with Lim Hoi, to Bangkok. Here the letter was translated and proved to be an instigation by the Burmese of the Raja of Kedah to rebel against the King of Siam. The King suitably rewarded Lim Hoi and appointed him Luang Raja, 'Capitan' of the Chinese, and chief collector of the royalty on tin mines on Junk Ceylon Island. This appointment evidently included not only the tin-smelting monopoly already in existence from the last quarter of the eighteenth century, but also the collection of crown dues on the net produce.[15]

Diplomatic missions to Siam and Burma were fairly frequent during the century, and Crawfurd, Finlayson, Bowring, and Roberts have left their impressions in their reports or memoirs. Mr Edmund Roberts was the American envoy who visited a number of countries on behalf of his Government in 1835, 1836, and 1837. Dr Ruschenberger, his medical officer and historian, gives us a number of interesting facts about the Siam of the period. He notes, as Earl had done, the Chinese junks in the river at Bangkok; a row of these vessels of from 200 to 600 tons burden each were at anchor in the middle of the stream, and the line extended for more than two miles. Here they often remained for months, retailing their cargoes. They were kept, he says, 'in a most filthy condition'. In 1836, Ruschenberger estimates, there were over 400,000 Chinese in Bangkok out of a total population of 500,000. They were chiefly Teochius, but there were also Cantonese and Hailams (Hainanese) and some from Shanghai. About 30 to 80 junks annually visited the port.

Ruschenberger, too, gives us our first glimpse of the education of

[15] *Siam Society J.*, i, pt. 2 (1904), pp. 202–3.

Chinese children in Siam, though we can safely assume that the better-off families, at least, gave their boys a grounding in the Four Books, the Trimetrical Classic, &c, just as we know they did in Batavia in the sixteenth century. The schools referred to were almost certainly missionary schools, and Mr Gützlaff no doubt took a leading share in their establishment:

Two or three schools have been begun here for Chinese children, and are now in operation, but there is much difficulty in organizing and sustaining them, for the reason that Chinamen here have Siamese, Burman, Laos, and even other country women for mothers, whose prejudices are even stronger than that [*sic*] of the Chinese themselves.[16]

The same authority describes the Chinese in Siam as easily distinguishable by their complexion, being more yellow than the Siamese, 'but they have generally *docked* the *entail* to their heads, and dress à la Siamese, with a circle of hair on the *roof*. But few of the "long Tails", the distinguishing appanage to a Chinaman's head, are to be seen.' Sandals were worn by the Chinese only.

The Bangkok Chinese imported brassware and silk stuffs from China and Surat, and their cotton and woollen goods were principally from Singapore. Even the Talapoys'[17] (Buddhist priests') razors for shaving their heads were imported from Canton. They were made of thin brass of curved shape, two inches wide throughout, and six inches long, fitted with a coarse wooden handle.

Except in the case of debt, the Chinese were exempted from labour on the public works by paying the triennial tax of 4½ ticals. Some say (Ruschenberger records) that this tax was collected annually.

As at all times in their history, the Blackhaired Race were observed in Siam in the 1830s to gamble to excess.

Dr Ruschenberger adds his contribution to the long arraignment of the Chinese abroad for their lack of honesty. The Chinese, says he, 'who are noted everywhere for their villanous tricks', import large quantities of ordinary goods here, as well as good quality goods, including tea. The tea was bought up again after use and 'fired anew'. It was coloured green by the use of smalts and exported.[18]

About 1840 we have another set of statistics of the population of Bangkok offered us, and it seems to have little relation to those of Crawfurd, Gützlaff, &c. The total is put at 350,000 by Mr Neale, with 240,000 Siamese, 70,000 Chinese, 20,000 Burmans, and 20,000 Arabs and Indians. Ruschenberger and Neale must have had a very different eye for counting heads, and a very different notion of what a Chinese was

---

[16] W. S. W. Ruschenberger, *Narrative of a Voyage Round the World, during the years 1835, 36, and 37, including a narrative of an Embassy to the Sultan of Muscat and the King of Siam* (London, 1838), p. 280 ff.   [17] Sometimes spelt 'Talapoin.
[18] p. 287.

since their estimates of 400,000 and 70,000 refer to periods little re-moved one from the other.[19]

According to Neale, many Chinese who had settled and married in Siam had reaped immense wealth from sugar plantations they possessed in the interior; others were occupied in the cultivation of tobacco and several kinds of cotton, and a few made a living by collecting a gum used as incense. Gamboge, sapan wood, and other valuable products were all brought from the interior to Bangkok where, being weighed and taxed, they were retailed to the more opulent merchants established in the city, and by the latter shipped to Singapore, Bombay, and England.[20]

These impressions of the Chinese in the several countries have a great sameness, but a trend of development is observable through them as the years go on. The diversions and ritual of the Chinese, too, have a strangely static quality; the gambling, the burning of gold paper, the weddings, the funerals, vary scarcely a tittle from country to country and from century to century. Chinese theatricals and music are, of course, uniformly unpleasing to the European ear. As the Abbé de Choisy was affected by these in 1685, and the German, A. Bastian, in 1863,[21] so was Frederick Arthur Neale affected in about 1840. 'The first Chinese play I ever witnessed', he records, 'and certainly the last I should ever wish to see, for methinks a continuation of such noises for a succession of nights would render me unfit for anything but Hanwell, Bedlam always excepted.'[22]

Siam, although on the eve of the penetration by the West, was still an isolated State ruled by an absolute monarchy. The Chinese had already got their hands on to a great deal of economic power, but in an absolute State political power prevails over economic in a way that it cannot do in a democratic society. In the latter case, however harshly the Govern-ment bears on private enterprise and however great the taxation, the capitalist can nearly always recoup himself, at least in part, for his losses: in an absolute State like Siam, with the monarch not only a ruler but also a monopolist and competitor, the Chinese merchant and middleman was very much at the mercy of the despot's greed or caprice. Thus 'The Chinese cringed before their oppressors, paid a heavy tax for being exempted from military and *corvée* services, and laboured from morning to night to feed their insolent and haughty tyrants, who thought it beneath their dignity to earn their bread by their own efforts'.[23]

The Chinese, as we have so frequently seen, are a long-suffering race but are liable when driven to extremity by an affront to their pride, or (more easily) by an injury to their interests, to riot or even to rebel. We

[19] F. A. Neale, *Narrative of a Residence in Siam* (London, 1852), p. 30 (refers to period c. 1840).   [20] Ibid. p. 69.
[21] Dr Adolf Bastian, *Der Völker der Östlichen Asien: Reisen im Siam im Jahre 1863* (Jena, 1867), iv. 354.
[22] p. 95.   [23] Gützlaff, *Three Voyages along Coast of China*, pp. 29, 30.

have heard of the insurrection of 1733 and of several other smaller risings, and the Triad disturbances of the early 1830s, and now in 1847 they rose once again against their Siamese oppressors.

The occasion for the rising was the levying of a new tax on sugar refineries (or 'boilers'). The Chinese had created and had come to control a now-flourishing sugar industry. The insurgents seized the Governor of Petriu and decapitated him. Siamese troops sent to subjugate them exhibited great poltroonery against the enemy who were now besieged in a fort at Leukonchesi. The besieged garrisons were wholly ignorant of the art of war and the only ammunition they had to fire at the Siamese troops was *beans*! But notwithstanding the fact that the hardy regulars were for a while demoralized by the shower of vegetables, the gates of the city were finally destroyed. Elephants were sent out, and a general massacre of unresisting men, women, and children took place. 'It is supposed that a general rising was intended; and it is very doubtful whether the Siamese Government could have maintained itself against any very extensive combination.'[24]

The insurrection had failed and soon all was quiet again. The Chinese resumed their wonted air of submission—or at least of bland acquiescence or noncommittal blankness. There were still many compensations left to them for their lack of political power or ability to redress the grievances inflicted by an arbitrary authority. A minority identified themselves so successfully with their masters that they achieved noble rank and positions of profit, and a majority were so well off that it could be said of them a few years later that 'they were still the most privileged class in the country, *as was shown by the number of Siamese who had cultivated a queue in order to pass for Chinese*'![25]

12

THE NINETEENTH CENTURY: SECOND HALF

OWING to the weakness of China as a Power, its self-centredness and ignorance of the world beyond its frontiers, and its indifference to the fate of its traders and vagrant children beyond the mountains or the seas, the diplomatic history of Burma, Siam, Indochina, and the other countries of Southeast Asia belongs in the nineteenth century to the European nations. All the while that great events were happening, and revolutions taking place in trade and politics, the Chinese in these countries were

[24] Sir John Bowring, *The Kingdom and People of Siam* (London, 1857), i. 86.
[25] M. L. Cort, *Siam, or The Heart of Further India* (N.Y., 1866), p. 33, quoted by Thompson, *Thailand*, p. 106.

never making innovations but were ever adapting their behaviour to the
changing circumstances of living and trade. So whilst the course of international relations contains scarcely a mention of them, it is necessary to
consult the record of the diplomatic weather to understand why and how
the Chinese spread or trimmed their sails, dropped anchor, or ran for
shelter in the alternations of fair wind, calm, or storm.

The history of modern Siam may be said to begin with the treaty of
friendship and commerce concluded with Great Britain in 1855. There
had been previous treaties, but this one, negotiated by Sir John Bowring,
was of key importance and was followed by similar treaties with other
Powers. The treaty provided for extraterritorial consular jurisdiction for
British subjects and it included commercial regulations that were to
transform Siamese trade. Some of these were to affect the Chinese
merchants and revenue farmers directly. Previous to the treaty, duties
were paid on all imports with the exception of opium, the import of
which was forbidden. Opium was now put on the free list, with bullion
and personal effects, and a limit of dues of 3 per cent *ad valorem* was
placed on all imports. Monopolies were abolished by the treaty, but that
of opium for some reason still remained, as Bowring himself tells us, and
this to the great profit of the Chinese who possessed it. Presumably
foreign merchants, including British, imported opium and sold it to the
monopolist. The effect of the abolition of the other monopolies upon the
Chinese is not clear, but they, including the holder of the ninety-odd
monopolies mentioned by Bowring, had to find new channels for their
energies. Whether these new channels were advantageous or otherwise
for the people of Siam would depend on the enlightenment of Government policy rather than upon the Chinese, who, having no executive
power, felt no political responsibilities and were opportunists. In 1900
the abolition of the revenue farms in the Netherlands Indies led to
Chinese capital being employed in constructive rather than parasitic
undertakings, but in Siam in 1855 the net result would appear to have
been that the import business, previously the monopoly of the King or
his farmers, became shared and eventually controlled by British and
other European merchants. The Chinese would thus to a further extent
be thrown back on their role of middlemen, but they retained the monopoly of rice and, later on, had large holdings in tin and rubber. After the
making of the treaties with the European Powers, the China trade did not
thrive, and as has been remarked, the competition of European-owned
steamers reduced the fleet of over 400 junks to fewer than 100.[1]

In 1828 Robert Hunter, the first British merchant in Siam—the first,
at least, for a century or so—arrived in Bangkok. A timely gift to the
King of 1,000 muskets earned him the right to remain and trade. For

---

[1] Graham, *Siam* i. 209. Graham says that before 1890 the junks had entirely disappeared,
but this is an exaggeration. They survive in small numbers to this day.

long he was the only European merchant. The native commerce was at that time so completely in the hands of the Chinese that the only profitable business to be done, Hunter found, was with the court. He had sidelines, however, one of which was importing opium for sale to the Chinese.

The historian of the Chinese in Southeast Asia has constantly to be on the look out for contradictions and inconsistencies, apparent or real, in the accounts of contemporary European observers. In describing the character, the virtues, and vices of this race it has been justly remarked that no two writers agree. We can detect discrepancies of a less emphatic sort in the accounts given of the degree and speed of assimilation of the Chinese in Siam to the natives of the country. Sir John Bowring, for instance, remarks that the children of Chinese men and Siamese women are 'invariably educated to the Chinese type', and again 'the father alone seems to model the child's nature and education'.[2] How are we to reconcile this with Gützlaff's assertion (see p. 96 above) that 'within two or three generations, all the distinguishing marks of the Chinese dwindle entirely away; and a nation which adheres to its national customs so obstinately becomes wholly changed to Siamese'?

In attaching a value to the two pieces of evidence, we must remember in the first place that Sir John Bowring (1792–1859), although a polyglot, was fifty-seven before he went to the East and sixty-three when he first visited Siam, whereas Gützlaff (1803–51) went to Siam when he was twenty-five,[3] so his observations were over a longer space of time. Both Bowring and Gützlaff possessed, it appears, a knowledge of the Chinese and Siamese languages. Allowing for this, it would seem that both observers are, according to their perspectives, right. Bowring is quite correct when he notes the dominance of the father's culture over that of the mother, and Gützlaff himself (p. 99 of this survey) admits the difficulty of establishing schools for the Chinese because of the Siamese, Burmese, or Lao wives of Chinese whose prejudices (presumably in favour of their husband's civilization) are 'stronger than that of the Chinese themselves'. It would seem, then, that what we are witnessing is *in the first generation* the obstinate refusal of the Chinese system to yield to the native one, but fighting nevertheless a losing battle: the struggle continues in the second generation, though with diminishing intensity, and finally in the third generation the battle is lost and the native culture prevails.[4]

[2] *Kingdom and People of Siam*, p. 85.
[3] *Dictionary of National Biography* (1891).
[4] A woman of character would be able to influence her husband in either direction. Dr Landon cites *An English Governess at the Siamese Court*, by Anna H. Leonowens (Boston, 1870), p. 247, regarding a Chinese girl of the harem of the fourth king of the Chakri dynasty who was the only woman who ever managed him, 'She was hardly pretty, but well-formed, and of versatile tact, totally uneducated, of barely respectable birth,—being Chinese on her father's side, yet withal endowed with a naïve intuitive appreciation of character'.

In Malaya and Indonesia we do not witness a similar process. The Babas of Malacca, descendants of Chinese who intermarried with Malays and other Malaysians, retained their Chinese customs and religion whilst losing their language.[5] In Indonesia the Dutch policy of segregation of the races helped the Indonesian-born Chinese to retain their own culture in spite of intermarriage. In Annam the culture was already essentially Chinese in nature so that miscegenation had little effect on the customs and religion of the offspring.

The whole question is of paramount importance to our study and discussion of it will be resumed at a later stage, but as we follow the career of the colonial Chinese in Siam in something approaching chronological sequence it is necessary to be aware of the processes that are in train.

The changes in store for Siam as a country as the result of European encroachment were to affect the Chinese as greatly as, and in some respects more immediately than, the Siamese. A treaty with Britain abolished the whole system of monopolies and established free trade from the month of April 1856. Bowring witnessed the demeanour of a Chinese of enormous wealth among prostrate Siamese nobles when the article in question was read out to the court. He owned the opium and ninety other monopolies. 'He bowed his head in silence, but looked as if a hundred thunderstorms were concentrated in that proud, scornful, yet resigned expression. But as the opium monopoly, the most precious and profitable of them all, was preserved to him, he had the sagacity to feign a willing resignation.'[6]

A foremost quality of the Chinese overseas is adaptability—when their swings are taken away, they are quick to discover some roundabouts.

In the year 1857 it was estimated that the kingdom of Siam had 1·5 million Chinese settlers, 200,000 of whom were in Bangkok and environs. This estimate is Bowring's and is probably much nearer the truth than Ruschenberger's of a generation earlier or Gaston Rautier's of a generation later.[7] Nine out of ten of the floating bazaars which lined for miles the banks of the Menam were owned by the Chinese.[8] 'The Siamese keep the Chinese in absolute subjection; and while I was in Bangkok', says Bowring, 'I saw no instance of resistance to the native authority.'[9]

Most of the European visitors to Siam from the sixteenth to the twentieth century confined their observations to Bangkok and neighbourhood and few went any farther afield. Now, however, comes the famous French naturalist and traveller, Henri Mouhot, the discoverer of

---

[5] But see Purcell, *Chinese in Malaya*, pp. 37, 61, &c, and App., 'The Baba Language', pp. 293–5.   [6] *Kingdom & People of Siam*, i. 86 ff.
[7] For examples of estimates of population inspired by hope and faith rather than informed by cold scrutiny see Francis Light's estimate of the Penang population (Purcell, *Chinese in Malaya*, p. 40) and Stamford Raffles's regarding Singapore (ibid. p. 71).
[8] Bowring, p. 85. The estimate given above is on the same page.
[9] Ibid. p. 86. He knew of the rebellion of 1847, but maybe not of the others.

the ruins of Angkor, who explored both the upper waters of the Mekong, the gem districts of Chantabun (or Chantaburi), and the wilds of Cambodia, some provinces of the last-named being then in Siamese territory. He gives the population of Siam at 2 million Siamese, 1 million Laos, 1 million Malays, 1·5 million Chinese, 350,000 Cambodians, and 50,000 Peguans.[10]

Mouhot remarks that Siamese annals relate that in the seventh century Chinese junks used to ascend the Menam as far as Sang Khalak, a distance of 120 leagues from the sea, whereas they now navigate it for 30 leagues at most. He says that Saraburi was a place of some extent, the population consisting of Siamese, Chinese, and Lao agriculturists.

Having decided to visit Cambodia, and finding his little river-boat of no use, Mouhot discovered that the only way of going to Chantabun was by Chinese junk or fishing vessel. On 4 January 1859 he arrived at Chantabun. Christian Annamites formed nearly a third of the population, the remainder being Chinese merchants and some heathen Annamites and Siamese. In spite of its scanty population the province managed to export to Bangkok a great quantity of pepper cultivated by the Chinese chiefly at the foot of the mountains.

Every Siamese subject in Battambang on attaining a certain height had to pay the Government an impost or annual tribute equal to 6 ticals (18 francs). The Annamites paid this in eagle-wood, the Siamese in gamboge, and the Chinese paid in gum lac every four years, their tribute amounting annually to 4 ticals.

Most of the Chinese were addicted to gambling and opium-smoking. To record this is to be guilty of monotonous repetition, but it is well to note that however far from their fellows the Chinese remained true to type.

Henri Mouhot found himself installed in the house of a good Chinese, a pepper planter in the hill country of Chantabun, whose name was Taié-ou or, in Siamese, Apait. His son proved a real treasure to Mouhot. The two brothers of Apait were Catholics. Near the mountains 'were scattered the modest dwellings of the laborious Chinese'.[11] At the Chinese New Year Mouhot sat with Apait while his son played some airs on the bamboo flute.[12]

Miscellaneous information recorded by Mouhot includes the fact that the gall of apes was sold to Chinese doctors in Chantabun; that Siamese and Chinese performed together in theatricals at a funeral; that a magnificent tree called by the Siamese *Mai Jakienne* was much prized by the Chinese for junk masts; and that Chinese and European junks were constantly going up and down the Komput river. At Komput the

[10] Henri Mouhot, *Travels in the Central Parts of Indo-China (Siam), Cambodia, and Laos* (London, 1864), i. 61. [11] Ibid. p. 142.
[12] Ibid. p. 155. The Chinese flute is in a class by itself and, unlike the other instruments of the Chinese orchestra, is acceptable to the European ear.

Chinese shopkeepers sold glass, china, hatchets, knives, and Chinese parasols. The beautiful cardamon of Poursat (an aromatic, pungent spice) was much sought after by the Chinese who paid the best prices for it. Its sale was entirely monopolized by the King and his ministers.

Mouhot did not think that 'the country' (presumably Cambodia) contained above a million inhabitants, and, according to the most recent census, the number of free men fit to carry arms was returned at 30,000, besides a number of Chinese 'relatively great'.[13]

The greater part of the trade of Upper Siam was with Burma and China, the transport to Bangkok being too costly. It was carried in caravans composed of mules, pack-bullocks, and carrying-coolies. The trade with China and Burma in the 1890s was much of the same nature as it had been for many decades or even centuries; the imports from China were brassware, ponies, and silk; walnuts were also largely imported, but rather as ballast than as paying freight as the caravans were usually thirty days *en route*. The imports from Burma were chiefly piece-goods, opium, and ponies. Exports were Chinese sticklac, horns, hides, beeswax, and imported goods.[14]

The French undoubtedly had Chinese trade as their objective when they sent their expedition of exploration, under de Lagrée, up the Mekong in 1866. This expedition proved a failure, the Mekong being found to be of little use for navigation north of the 14th, or at most the 18th, parallel, owing to the presence of rapids. The Menam, however, was vastly superior to the Mekong in this respect, and, with the completion of the railway which already in the 1890s the Siamese were building to the north through central Siam, important commercial developments were expected to follow.[15]

The literature of foreign observers of Siam in the nineteenth century is considerable, and in sifting it in search of significant information we light on two books which have the merit of making actual the life of the people they describe. Both of these relate to experiences in the 1890s: one is by a transient;[16] the other by a travelling official.[17]

There are [says Ernest Young] nearly as many Chinese in the country as there are Siamese. They marry Siamese women and their children make excellent subjects, as they possess both the natural brightness of the mother and the industry of the father. Unless they renounce their nationality they are subject to a poll-tax of about 5 or 6 shillings, payable every four years. At a date made known by proclamation each Chinaman must present himself at the police station and pay the tax. The receipt given is a small piece of beeswax about the size of a threepenny piece. This bears a seal, and is worn on the wrist for a certain time, fastened by a

---

[13] Mouhot, *Travels in the Central Parts of Indo-China (Siam), Cambodia, and Laos*, p. 275.
[14] A. Cecil Carter, *The Kingdom of Siam* (N.Y., 1904), p. 33.
[15] *Encyclopaedia Britannica*, 10th ed. (1902), xxxii. 612.
[16] Ernest Young, *The Kingdom of the Yellow Robe* (London, 1898).
[17] Smyth, *Five Years in Siam* (refers to 1891-6).

piece of string. The police are very busy at this time, and there is nothing that a Siamese policeman so much enjoys as leading some unfortunate Chinaman to pay the tax. Should the seal be lost, the alien is bound to buy another as soon as he is requested by some officer of the law.[18]

First to rise in the morning in Bangkok were the Chinese inhabitants, and on rising they exploded crackers. They were carpenters, blacksmiths, butchers, bakers; they watered, swept, mended, and scavenged the roads; they were wharf coolies, servants, and rickshaw-pullers. No Siamese were to be found among these last. The rickshaws were mostly discarded ones from Singapore and were in a very dilapidated condition. The Chinese rickshaw-men never resented being cut by a driver's whip if caught on the wrong side of the road.

Blue, as ever, was the colour of the Chinese workaday clothes. Other colours were worn only at the New Year when gorgeous heliotropes, lavenders, pale blues, green, and yellow silks made their appearance, having been deposited in the interim in the pawnshops.

The only truly native quarter was a long bazaar known as Sampeng. It was about a quarter of a mile in length and contained a mixed population of Indians, Siamese, and Chinese. It somewhat resembled a street in Canton but lacked the wealth of elaborately carved and gilded sign-boards which give such a distinctive and local atmosphere to a purely Chinese street. Stretched overhead from side to side were pieces of torn cloth and sacking which acted quite as effectively in keeping out the sun as imprisoning the awful combination of foul odours that seems to be the possession of all Oriental thoroughfares. Everywhere were stagnant water and domestic rubbish. The gambling houses, opium dens, and brothels in this quarter were thronged by the lowest of the low. Electric light had already arrived in the city, but in the outskirts the lamp-lighter was still to be seen wending his way on his evening round, carrying the small ladder, boxes of matches, and bottles of oil that marked the nature of the operation. In some places in the city and in Sampeng little cholera lamps swung aloft at the end of slender poles, swaying backwards and forwards and telling where death had entered on his work of destruction.

At the end of the bazaar was the chief idol manufactory in the country, supplying all the temples of Siam.[19]

The Chinese are seen through the eyes of another contemporary observer of Bangkok thus:

Bangkok port has no rules but one:—Thou shalt not rebuke or in anyway inconvenience a Chinese coolie whatever he may do! He is the master of the port. He may grapple on to a steamer with his cargo boat when she comes up the river to seek her moorings. He may refuse to cast off when the captain has to change his berth; he may, and probably will, refuse to load the ship in any way but his own, even to the

---

[18] *Kingdom of the Yellow Robe*, p. 9: cf. p. 418 of this survey regarding a similar proceeding in Java in about 1798.   [19] Young, pp. 19, 22.

peril of ship and cargo; he may spit and smoke in the poop, and may generally lord it. But he must be allowed his sweet will; and if any officer cuts his rope away, or a quartermaster kicks him over the side, there is a general strike, and the captain is dropped by the agents. For the Chinaman is a privileged person, and the port is run for his private edification and enjoyment.[20]

Warington Smyth is not highly appreciative of the Chinese of Bangkok, but he has humour and buoyancy which atone in some measure for the malice of his abuse, as when he says, comparing the luck of other races who chance to fall or be pushed into the Menam: 'Chinese are different; a tiger will take a Chinaman without provocation, as will a shark; for he is fat and porky, and as unpopular with animals as with men'. Summing up he says: 'This is Chinese Bangkok, malodorous and ill-mannered'.

The widely operating secret societies of the Heaven and Earth or Triad we have encountered before in this part of our survey: we shall read of them again more than once in Malaya, Sarawak, and the other countries of Southeast Asia. They were responsible for riots in 1889 and six years later for fighting with fire-arms from behind street barricades. In the latter year rival factions of the Yee Heng and the Su Lee societies held one Bangkok district in a state of siege for a few days and the battle was stopped only through the intervention of Danish officers. Yet the Siamese Government went so far as to cultivate these secret societies as they were thought to offset the association of native Christians fostered by the French missionaries. The movement was regarded as particularly alarming after a Buddhist priest, who had been chaplain to the late Regent, turned Christian.[21]

With Mouhot we escaped from Bangkok for a spell and visited the confines of the northwest; with Warington Smyth we are able to take another excursion, this time to peninsular Siam of the south and at a period about forty years after the French naturalist.

There was long-standing controversy among British officials of Penang as to whether or not Kedah was subject to Siam at the time of the cession by the Sultan of Kedah of the island of Penang to the British in 1786. On this turned the question whether the British had undertaken to defend Kedah against the Siamese. In any case they did nothing to defend it when it was overrun by the Siamese in 1818. At the time when it was ceded to the British by the Treaty of Bangkok in 1909 Kedah was a border province of Siam. In the 1830s the Chinese were mining tin in Negri Sembilan and Selangor; in the 1850s they were active in the tin-fields of Perak; they had already, it seems, penetrated to the rich mining lands of southern Siam. The Chinese tin-mining community of Siam was in effect an extension of that of Bangka and Billiton. Racially and

[20] Smyth, *Five Years in Siam*, p. 10.
[21] Thompson, *Thailand*, p. 107. Dr Thompson cites the *Bangkok Times* of 8 Oct. 1901 regarding the riots.

economically the settlements were connected, though the political jurisdiction over them was divided. As has been said, in Siam the Chinese,
usually of mixed blood, sometimes attained to high office under
the Siamese with titles of honour attached. More than one of these
families retired to Penang and, keeping connexions with the source
of their wealth, formed part of the bridge linking the two Chinese
communities.

In the 1890s, at the time of Warington Smyth's visit, the Raja of the
west coast of the peninsula was a Chinese named Praya Rasada (Phya
Ratsdain in Dr Landon's spelling), known familiarly as Simbi (Sim Bee).
His two brothers were Rajas of Renawng (Renong) and Langsuan (Lang
Suan), 'but neither can equal him in energy, popularity, or good nature'.
Of his own initiative he introduced the Burmese village system into his
province. In 1892 he moved his capital bodily down the river to be
nearer the sea. The old capital, the Khoantani of Major Low, was now
being connected with the new one, Kantun, and also with the pepper-
planting district of Taptieng, by new roads. Other improvements and
reforms were in progress. Dacoity had practically disappeared; even the
secret societies, who generally were unmolested in Siam, had received a
warning in the form of the suppression of one of their number to whom
a murder had been traced. There was a police force of Sikhs and Siamese.
Cleanliness was one of the Raja's hobbies.

This Chinese, Phya Ratsdain, or Kaw Sim Bee, was a member of a
family which achieved outstanding success in Siam. Dr Landon gives an
extended account of its history and the present writer was for years
personally acquainted with some of its members and can confirm that its
standing was high both in Siam and in Penang.[22] The founder of the
family was a coolie, named Kaw Su Chiang, a native of Ch'angchow-fu
in Fukien province, about thirty-five miles from Amoy. He arrived in
Penang about 1810 when he was about twenty-five years of age with
nothing but his clothes and a carrying-pole. He soon entered the coastal
trade in which—subject to the avoidance of pirates—cloth, muskets, &c,
were bartered for tin, areca nut, birds' nests, copra, and pepper. Kaw Su
Chiang prospered as a trader and extended his interests to tin. This he
found in great quantity in the Renong district and he imported Chinese
coolies to mine it. He ruled with a patriarchal hand the community he
had created. Later he was given the title of Phra (the third highest of the
titles awarded to commoners) and made the Raja of Renong. The carrying-pole he had brought to the country he now had gilded and he showed
it to visitors with pride. He had both a Chinese and a Thai wife and of his
sons one, Kaw Sim Kong, succeeded his ageing father as Raja of Renong,

[22] The surname is usually spelt Khaw in Penang. Khaw Su Chiang's name occurs among
the subscribers to the reconstruction of the temple of the Goddess of Mercy in the 1860s
(originally built in 1800).

another became Raja of Lang Suan, a third, Raja of Kra, and 'the youngest and greatest', Kaw Sim Bee, Raja of Trang. In 1892 Sim Bee was appointed High Commissioner of the Western Provinces on the Indian Ocean with a capital at Phuket.

In the 1890s the policy of the Siamese Government was to displace the Rajas by Governors and to curtail the powers of the Rajas who remained, to rule directly, and to collect the taxes through their own officers instead of farming them. In spite of the administrative re-organization, Sim Bee retained the substance of his power to the end of his days. He was completely loyal to Bangkok. Although he spoke Thai and Chinese fluently he never learned to read Thai. 'Arrogant, choleric, and ambitious, he was so feared by the people that they prostrated them-selves when he passed.'[23]

Speaking of Taptieng, the centre of the pepper-planting district in the midst of lateritic soil approved by the Chinese planter, Warington Smyth says that it was a filthy place 'as all Chinese towns are'. There were 10,000 Chinese in the district. The Raja took the Director of the Department of Mines to one of the principal secret societies in the town where he was on good terms with the Chinese officers. The Director was elaborately introduced to the latter, and he confessed that he was favour-ably impressed by the style and appearance of their hosts as well as by the cleanliness of the place. Referring to the building occupied by the society, Warington Smyth remarks that there is 'something strong and imposing in Chinese architecture and ornament which is certainly attractive'.

Topographical information such as this, imparted by a lively writer and a keen observer, amounts to more than a catalogue of impressions, for from it can be gleaned facts that connect up the economic and social history of the Chinese of these parts. For instance, the fall in the price of pepper had halved the population of Taptieng.[24] The roads hitherto maintained by the Chinese had now become obliterated or impassable. At Palean, which was also under the Raja of Trang, there were a few Chinese and a little pepper. Tin mines were scattered through the southern part of the province from the sea to the boundaries of Lakawn. In Takuapa, where the Government was bad, the mines were set deep in the jungle, reached by rough-and-tumble forest paths. The royalties exacted by the Government were high: the communications were poor. Nevertheless, Takuapa exported 600–700 tons of tin yearly. Here the

---

[23] Landon, *Chinese in Thailand*, pp. 13–15. Abjectness was encouraged by the absolute despotism of Siam. Two ambassadors arrived in England from Siam in October 1857 and had an audience with Queen Victoria; 'they brought with them magnificent presents, which they *delivered crawling*, on 16 November' (*Haydn's Dictionary of Dates* (London, 1906), p. 1208. My italics. V.P.).

[24] In Penang, when in 1810 the bottom fell out of the pepper market, there had also been a great misfortune; but here cloves were a second crop which was a mainstay till the blight fell on them in the 1860s. See Purcell, *Chinese in Malaya*, p. 44.

arrival of the party was inopportune. Rice and opium were the chief articles of import, but the stock of these two commodities was now very low, the failure of the former being due to the loss of a rice-laden junk. The coolies were clamorous: the *towkays*[25] were anxious.[26]

Their itinerary punctuated by the gongs and crackers of Chinese funerals and weddings, the party passed to the east coast. Here there was no place of equal importance to those of the west coast for a long way south. Pran, Kuwi, Bangtaphan, and Patiyu were insignificant villages at the mouths of their streams with a population of fishermen, chiefly Chinese. The population of Champawn was said to have been 30,000 all told, but only the fishing villages on the coast had any large population of Chinese. Paknam, a fishing village, had lately been visited by cholera. 'Its male inhabitants were chiefly Chinamen: everything was consequently filthy.'

Langsuan had a population of 11,000 including 2,000 Chinese. The Raja was a Chinese who was by no means sensible of his responsibilities and exercised practically no control over the Chinese who carried on the government under him. His son was a Penang Chinese 'who needed a good licking'. The mines lay principally in the valleys along the granite outcrops of the main range dividing the Raja of Langsuan's territory from that of his brother of Renong. Some 200 Chinese coolies were employed in the mines at wages ranging from $4½ to $8 a month. The methods of mining were primitive.

In Bandon (or Kanchanadit in Siamese) the population was about 22,000, of which a large part was Chinese. These were Hainanese, Hokkiens, and Cantonese engaged in the export of timber, rattans, skins, and other jungle produce. Quite a large fleet of Chinese junks was engaged in the trade. The steamers from Bangkok on the whole were successfully boycotted by the Chinese who kept the trade as much as possible in their own hands.[27]

Singora (Songkla in Siamese), on the east coast, south of the Isthmus of Kra, was inhabited by a large number of Chinese traders who had a practical monopoly of the local trade and owned many junks. It was seized at the beginning of the nineteenth century by Chinese from Amoy led by the great-grandfather of the present Governor (c. 1890), and for a long time they were little meddled with by Bangkok, under which they had placed themselves. There was now a Siamese commissary from the capital in several of the provinces. Bribery played a large part in the Chinese methods of keeping influence.[28]

[25] *Towkay*, meaning head of a business, is a common term among the Chinese of Southeast Asia. Though a Hokkien expression, it is used by all tribes, though the Cantonese also use *Sⱬt'au*, which has the same meaning.

[26] Smyth, *Five Years in Siam*, ii. 20.

[27] Ibid. p. 84. Smyth mentions that in the 1870s piratical Chinese junks were still not uncommon along this coast.   [28] Ibid. p. 106.

Labour was needed for Singora, for example for the coffee plantations, but the lack of coolie regulations made it impossible to import either Tamil or Chinese labour. The Siamese officials considered that the existing arrangements were good enough and they did not want any more foreign labour in the country.

The Lakawn mines were worked by the Siamese before the Chinese arrived some time around 1840, and now in the 1890s there were 350 Chinese men working them, divided into five kongsis, or associations. The blast furnaces were of the Chinese pattern. The output was 800 cwt per annum with a value of $24,000.[29] The tin was bought by a Government buyer at $30 a picul. The Chinese miners 'were the wildest Chinamen we had ever met, and had mostly been imported direct by junks from the interior of Kwangtung, Kwangsi, and Hainan'. They were in the habit of holding folks up to ransom. As a contrast to these ruffians Warington Smyth met a 'charming old Chinaman', a boat-builder.

It would seem from what has been recorded above that the Chinese in southern Siam fifty years ago were living in a state of semi-independence. Not only were some of the Governors Chinese, but also the secret societies and the kongsis (which probably were to a large extent identical) were allowed fairly complete charge of their own affairs. The Siamese officials were interested principally in tribute and taxation. They were quite content for the hard-working Chinese to produce for them the profit that would not have been forthcoming from their less energetic countrymen.

13

LUKCHIN AND NEWCOMER[1]

In 1900 the civilization of China was in decay. How long it had been so is hard to decide; but if the arts and crafts are any indication of a healthy society, then the reign of Chia Ch'ing which began in 1796 is as definite a mark as any between a condition of static comeliness at the least and one in which inventiveness and skill were noticeably in decline. The decline of art may well have been an early symptom of political and social senility, of the former more certainly, for within a generation or so China was offering but the feeblest opposition to the onslaught of the West. Yet, convinced of its self-sufficiency and the adequacy of its institutions, it refused for many decades to consider political or educational reform. Arsenals, indeed, were set up in China under foreign engineers and

---

[29] The Mexican silver dollar is probably intended in these values. Smyth speaks of the 'currency nightmare'.

[1] *Lukchin* = child of a Chinese, and means the Sino-Thais.

mechanics between the First and Second China Wars, but it was not until after a new defeat by France in 1885 that for the first time history, mathematics, and science were introduced into the public examinations. Up to 1860 China had no Foreign Office, and one was created only at the behest of foreigners by a clause in the Tientsin Treaty. Japan's story was a very different one. Adapting its institutions to receive the sources of Western strength, it administered a crushing defeat to its former teacher, China, who had taught it nearly all it knew. Finally, in 1898, the mandarin Chang Chih-tung, in his *Exhortation to Learning*, issued a warning that China must adopt Western learning at once or be destroyed.[2]

The ferment belatedly generated, as by a kind of yeast which would magically rejuvenate very old and insipid wine, resulted in the rise of nationalism and the Revolution of 1911 and its chequered aftermath.

In 1900 all of this was only dimly foreseen even by the most divining Chinese: to the *Lukchin*, or 'child of a Chinese' in Siam, and to the immigrant coolie on the deck of a ship *en route* from Swatow or Hong Kong to Bangkok it had no meaning at all. They may have heard of the Boxer risings and of the anti-foreign decrees of the Empress-dowager and Prince Tuan, but almost certainly not of K'ang Yu-wei and Liang Ch'i-chao, the prophets of educational reform, or, possibly, not even of the exiled Sun Yat-sen.

China's claim to suzerainty over Siam was very shadowy (as indeed was the case with its other claims of this sort. Britain was included as a vassal in Chinese records) and had not been asserted for a long time. Tribute, or merchandise masquerading as tribute, had indeed been extremely intermittent for the last century or so, and latterly had ceased altogether, but this was a thing China was used to from its many supposed 'vassals'. After an interval of eighteen years the tribute had been renewed in 1869, but its bearers had been compelled by 'the Chinese to use the route via Canton and were not allowed to come by the Tientsin route which the foreigners used'.[3] China refused to make a treaty with Siam, although at this time its influence in that country was at its height, for the simple reason that China did not want diplomatic relations with anyone. Later on, when China itself desired such a treaty, the Siamese were reluctant to conclude one, and it was not until 1946 that one was signed.[4]

The absence of ambassadors and consuls to whom the Chinese could appeal for protection when their rights or privileges were assailed was now regarded by the Siamese with favour. Immigration from China had greatly increased after the First China War which was concluded in 1842. In the 1840s it was estimated to be at the rate of about 15,000 a year; by the turn of the century about 1,200 a month were arriving at the

[2] Purcell, *Problems of Chinese Education* (London, 1936), p. 1 and *passim*.
[3] Thompson, *Thailand*, p. 103.   [4] See p. 148.

C.S.E.A.——E

port of Bangkok in addition to an even larger number in the peninsular States. The great flood of immigrants had not yet begun, but already in the 1880s there was talk in Siam of restriction of Chinese immigration, and in 1888 the establishment of a Chinese Protectorate on the Straits Settlements model was mooted, and abandoned only on the ground of expense.[5] But so long as China had no diplomatic or consular officers in Siam there was no danger of the aliens rallying round them and forming a dangerous opposition to the authority of the Siamese Government.

It was estimated that about 40 per cent of the newcomers remained in the country, and that of these about half married Siamese women. With improved communications between Siam and China, the proportion of transients was increasing and these were disposed to look upon Siam as a place in which to make money and from which to depart as early as possible. This fact did not escape the notice of the Siamese and they remarked openly upon it. At the same time the peculiarities of Chinese social organization overseas were impressing themselves more and more on the Siamese authorities. The secret societies had long before this brought themselves to the very unfavourable notice of the Government of the Straits Settlements and there had been serious battles between rival factions in Singapore in 1854 and in Penang in 1867; but in Siam in the 1880s the Government, as we have seen,[6] encouraged their activities as an offset to the influence of the native Christians. The riots of 1889 and the conflict between the Yee Heng and the Su-lee Ku societies in the streets of Bangkok in 1895 must have convinced the Siamese that these associations were a pest and far more to be feared than were a few docile Christians. In more modern terms, the official cultivation of the Thian Ti Hui had upset the entomological balance and this must now be redressed. Of illicit organizations the Ang Yee secret societies were the most important. About 1905 Siam was seriously troubled by Ang Yee wars. Legal cases were not taken to the courts but were tried before Ang Yee tribunals. 'Competition and jealousy set group against group, and the Chinese killed one another without regard to the laws of the land.'[7]

A law was passed in 1897 requiring the registration of every society. After two years only two had registered and the Siamese authorities, owing to the lack of the machinery of investigation, were unable to prosecute those societies which had neglected to do so. Without a Chinese Protectorate like the one in Malaya, the police were completely unable to lift the cloak of mystery in which the operations of these societies were wrapped. The Chinese, for their part, were most suspicious of the designs of the Government, imagining the law to be a preliminary

[5] Thompson, *Thailand*, p. 107.
[6] See p. 108 and Purcell, *Chinese in Malaya*, chap. viii.
[7] Landon, *Chinese in Thailand*, p. 149.

to requiring them to do military service, and even the truly philanthropic societies, which had nothing to fear from revealing their existence, neglected to register.[8]

We must not, however, exaggerate the causes of friction between the Siamese and the Chinese at this period, for, compared with the situation which developed in the 1930s, complete harmony between the peoples now prevailed. Sir Josiah Crosby, who spent most of his long official career in contact with the Siamese, says of the period:

> In 1904, the Chinese question, although it was already attracting notice, was not a very urgent one, chiefly because in those days a Chinese immigrant usually took to himself a wife from among the women of the country. Children of mixed races born of such unions were brought up as Siamese, regarding Siam as their home and merging themselves readily with the population around them.[9]

Before the rise of nationalism in China and Siam there seems to have been no problem of assimilation. In three generations, as we have seen, the newcomers were completely absorbed into the Siamese people. During the process of assimilation these people performed a necessary function in Siamese society. They were a source of new energy to a people who suffered from the usual tropical lethargy, and as Siam had been under-populated throughout its history, there was no threat that the natives would be swamped in the flood of immigration.

A combination of factors was to change the situation completely within the next decade or so. The first was the growth of a feeling on the part of the two peoples that they had separate entities, that these entities were threatened by foreign encroachment, and that they must be defended by the encouragement of a sense of apartness, by aggressive activity on the political and diplomatic planes, and by protective legal measures. China was large, unwieldy, and split by tribal and clan divisions: Siam was smaller and compact, and though it had its racial minorities it was able more easily to consolidate itself into a conscious nation. The other important factor was that with an increasing immigration Chinese women were, after 1910, accompanying their men in large numbers and thus creating a wall against assimilation. The feeling of separation on the part of the Chinese was more and more fostered by the policy of the Chinese Government.

The new-found concern of the moribund Manchu Government for the wandering sons of Han—or rather of T'ang[10]—was manifested in Siam

---

[8] Thompson, *Thailand*, p. 108.
[9] Crosby, *Siam: the Crossroads* (London, 1945), p. 71.
[10] The people of north China called themselves the 'Sons of Han' (i.e. of the dynasty which ruled from 200 B.C. to A.D. 220) while the people of the south called themselves the 'Sons of T'ang' (i.e. of the dynasty which ruled from A.D. 618 to 907). The Manchus were far more identified with the north than with the south so that their concern for the immigrants from Fukien and Kwangtung had a less genuine and disinterested ring than that of the followers of the Cantonese Sun Yat-sen.

about the same time that it was in the Netherlands Indies. Apart from their increased international awareness encouraged by a succession of defeats, the Government felt, no doubt, that they should show the flag abroad and thus counteract the influence of the revolutionaries who were now plotting against the Ch'ing dynasty with the financial help of Overseas Chinese. In 1907 a Chinese commercial commissioner paid a visit to Bangkok accompanied by an imposing suite and escorted by two cruisers.[11] He did not discuss political questions, and acted solely as the head of what came to be called a goodwill mission. There were, indeed, no grievances to redress or protests to be made. At that time the Chinese were enjoying something like an equality of treatment together with privileged facilities for making a good living. That same year King Chulalongkorn made a public pronouncement in which he stated his attitude towards his Chinese subjects: 'It has always been my policy that the Chinese in Siam should have the same opportunities for labour and profit as are possessed by my own countrymen. I regard them not as foreigners but as one of the component parts of the kingdom and sharing its prosperity and advancement.'[12]

The sentiment here expressed was reciprocated in the attitude of the Chinese, especially of the second and third generations, until complete merging took place. Dr Landon gives an example of a prominent Chinese merchant whose face was unmistakably Chinese and whose father was a Chinese although his mother was Thai, who took immediate offence when he was playfully charged with being Chinese—'in spite of the fact that his shop signs were in Chinese, that he spoke two Chinese dialects, that he kept his accounts in Chinese, and sent his children to a Chinese school'. He also spoke Thai perfectly in two dialects, regarded himself as a Thai, and patriotically supported the modern Siamese nationalistic movement with large contributions to the defence forces. 'He was typical of an unnumbered host who are', as Kumut Chandruang says, 'our flesh and blood, because they keep alive our national economy.'[13] This is recounted of a generation later when all sorts of incidents had happened to disturb the harmonious relationships between the races: it must have been doubly true of the earlier period.

Mr Lin Yu stresses the great proportion of Chinese blood that must flow in the veins of the more influential classes of Siamese. He tells us that on one occasion when King Vajiravudh (1910–25) commanded those of his courtiers who had Chinese blood in their veins to stand to the right of the room, 90 per cent of them did so.[14] It was, therefore, one of the

[11] Thompson, *Thailand*, p. 108.
[12] Cited by Thompson, p. 108 from the *Bangkok Times* of 21 Feb. 1935.
[13] Landon, *Chinese in Thailand*, pp. 18, 19.
[14] Lin Yu, 'Twin Loyalties in Siam', *Pacific Affairs*, ix/2 (June 1936).

ironies of history that the officials who were to pass the immigration, educational, and labour laws which were to operate so to the disadvantage of the Overseas Chinese should be Siamese with a large admixture of Chinese.

Legal Status of the Chinese in Siam

Until 1946 there were no treaty relations between Siam and China. We have seen something of the reason for this. In the first years of the century the Chinese several times approached Siam through Tokyo with a view to establishing diplomatic relations. At one moment a treaty was actually drafted but owing to an anachronistic pride or a clumsy gaffe on the part of the Chinese draftsmen, by which Siam was referred to as China's vassal, the Siamese were enabled to withdraw from the negotiations with an injured look. Similarly at Versailles, overtures on the part of China came to nothing. Later on it will be recorded how the treaty was eventually signed and ratified, but a throng of events demand attention before such a record is timely.

Immigrants from China who were not the subjects of a European Power were regarded by the Siamese as being under their jurisdiction and were subject to the laws of the realm. After three years' residence, and at the close of every three years from that date, they had to pay a tax of $4\frac{1}{2}$ ticals, equivalent to 8s. 6d. in the 1880s and 1890s and to somewhat less in the first decade of the twentieth century. They were exempted from *corvée* labour, and all other Government requisitions, except ordinary taxes. Their children, who as there were no Chinese consuls could not be registered as Chinese, had the option of submitting to the triennial tax or of selecting a Government master and becoming Siamese. The grandchildren of Chinese immigrants were classed and registered as Siamese, and were liable to *corvée* labour as soon as they measured $2\frac{1}{2}$ sok, or 50 inches, to the shoulder, and were marked to one or other Government master. The mark was tattooed on the back of the right or left wrist, and all persons thus marked were liable to be called out in their master's department.[15]

Then, in the spring of 1909, the Chinese promulgated a nationality law whereby the *jus sanguinis* was adopted and all persons with Chinese fathers were regarded as Chinese, irrespective of where they were born. Thus there arose from this moment a problem of dual nationality. The new Chinese law, moreover, foreshadowed interference in the affairs of persons of Chinese race born abroad whom China now regarded as her nationals. The actual interference was signalized by the laws and regulations governing the composition and election of the National Assembly

[15] Hallett, *Thousand Miles on an Elephant*, p. 460, cited by Landon, *Chinese in Thailand*, p. 10.

on 10 August 1912, by which 6 out of 274 senators were to be elected by 'the electoral college of Chinese abroad'.[16]

Not having any consuls of their own to whom they could appeal, those Chinese who could claim the nationality of countries more favourably placed did so in large numbers. In 1936 there were 55,000 Asiatic subjects of Great Britain residing in Siam, most of whom were Chinese.[17] The status of Chinese born in the Netherlands was uncertain owing to the state of the Dutch law.[18]

These problems, however, belong to a later period and the purpose of this section is to make clear the situation existing on the eve of the Siamese-Chinese friction of 1910. In this year, in spite of the civil disabilities due to the lack of a treaty between the two countries, the Chinese enjoyed a favoured position. The China-born could not, indeed, vote or hold any civil office other than that of clerk or interpreter, but that was a small matter compared with the freedom to monopolize the retail and the rice trades and to levy toll through their influence on nearly every business transaction. They were permitted to travel and to live wherever they wished; they had access to the courts and police protection. They might own and lease property and settle in undeveloped areas. On the whole the Chinese would have agreed with King Chulalongkorn's statement that they had the same opportunities for labour and profit as were possessed by his own countrymen.[19]

14

THE GENESIS OF DISCORD

THERE is a process known to geographers as 'river capture'. The beds of rivers are continually extending backwards towards the hills or mountains; this is due to soil and rock from the higher slopes at the head of the valley being washed into the river and carried away. In this manner the

[16] MacNair, *Chinese Abroad*, p. 25. The principle here introduced of holding elections for membership of bodies in China among overseas Chinese was to give trouble in the future, particularly in Indonesia, Malaya, and Siam.   [17] Landon, *Chinese in Thailand*, p. 27.
[18] Amry Vandenbosch, *The Dutch East Indies* (Berkeley, 1942), p. 193.
[19] Dr Thompson at p. 114 of her *Thailand* states that 'When a Chinese married a Siamese woman, the wife—not the husband—became head of the family and controlled its property and cash'. This gives, I feel, a misleading idea of the situation. The fact is that a Siamese woman married to a Chinese did not take his nationality but remained Siamese. The children, too, were Siamese in the eyes of Siamese law. Since under the new laws of *c.* 1939–40 an alien was restricted in his right to hold land or to acquire it, a Chinese husband would often hold land in his wife's name. This both secured him in his property and protected his wife and children. A Siamese wife practically never accompanied her husband to China where, incidentally, he probably had a wife already. But there was no matriarchal system as suggested by the above statement, and the transfer of any property was entirely at the husband's discretion.

watershed may be lowered until streams from the other side may find an easier route down the channel of the river which has cut back. Without stretching the metaphor too far, we can say that something like this happened forty years ago to the stream of Chinese immigrants into Siam. Hitherto the stream had flowed into the main river of the Siamese nation, but at this epoch the river of Chinese nationalism cut back and captured the stream. Although this comparison is over-dramatic and incomplete, it should serve to suggest the striking change which took place about this time.

Whereas in 1900 the alien Chinese were living side by side with their Siamese hosts without great consciousness of difference on either side, and were being absorbed into the body of the nation by a leisurely and seemly process, in 1920 the two communities were deeply conscious of their apartness, and assimilation had to a great extent been arrested. This we know was due partly to the growth of nationalism in the two countries, especially in China, to greatly increased immigration, and the improvement in transport which facilitated frequent passing to and fro, and if we wish to fix a date, or rather an epoch for this cleavage, we may choose either the Chinese nationality law of 1909 adopting the *jus sanguinis*, or the Chinese Revolution of 1911. In point of fact, however, there is an intermediate date which it would be more fitting to select since it marked a moment when it was brought home to the Siamese that the Chinese among them formed an unassimilated element—or, to resume the metaphor, a stream which had forsaken its bed in their midst to join an alien waterway. Our reference is to the Chinese strike and riots in Bangkok in 1910.

We have seen in the preceding chapter that the Chinese in Siam had been paying a poll-tax at the rate of about 1½ baht a year for many years.[1] The Siamese, on the other hand, had for the past twenty years been paying about 50 baht a year. A new law now called for the collection of a capitation tax on all persons resident in Siam irrespective of race. The tax applied to Europeans as well as Asiatics, and the only exceptions were priests and ordained ministers. Immediately, serious riots broke out among the Chinese as a protest against the application of the tax to them, and all Chinese shops were closed in sympathy, causing a complete stoppage of trade. The riots were soon suppressed and the shops reopened, but the damage was done. The Chinese stood convicted by the Siamese as devoid of a sense of fair-play since the new law was merely intended to place all persons living in Siam on an equality as regards taxation, and the people realized for the first time the extent of the Chinese economic grip

[1] A baht was worth about one-eleventh of an English pound. Its value dropped after 1939, and after the Second World War the Siamese currency, in common with other Far Eastern currencies, suffered great inflation. Dr Landon's account in ch. ii of his *The Chinese in Thailand* has been closely followed in the present chapter.

on the country, and the ability of the settlers to paralyse at will the life of the nation. From this time forward the dislike and fear of the Chinese long felt by many Siamese of influence were reinforced by popular sentiment.

A prejudice, however, cannot derive permanent sustenance from a single incident and, to survive, it must be fed with further grievances. Also it must be demonstrated to the people that such incidents form part of a policy. It happened, then, that a long and circumstantial indictment of the Chinese was forthcoming from the hand of no less a person than the reigning monarch. There seems to be no doubt that the series of articles which appeared in the vernacular newspapers in Siam under the pen-name of 'Asavabahu' (Pegasus), and which were reprinted in the form of a pamphlet entitled *The Jews of the East* were written by His Majesty King Vajiravudh, otherwise Rama VI.

'Asavabahu's' thesis, in condensed form, was this:[2] in Siam and in Eastern territories under British and American jurisdiction there exists a situation analogous to the Jewish question in countries of the West. This is 'The Yellow Peril'. The danger arises solely from the Chinese from whom the Siamese are even more different than Europeans are from the Jews. The first similarity between the Chinese and the Jews is in the matter of 'racial loyalty'. No matter where they live, what nationality they assume, Chinese remain essentially Chinese. But theirs is race loyalty, not love of country, and, for the sake of convenience, they will register themselves as nationals of foreign countries, even when they are living in China itself. But such registration does not mean that they cease to act like Chinese. They will be loyal to their adopted country only so long as it suits their interests. What makes them undesirable is their racial consciousness; they regard their residence in the country as temporary and are unwilling to become its citizens. The purpose of every Chinese immigrant is to amass as much money as possible and then to depart—the fact that not all of them manage to do this does not alter their common motive.

It is argued that Chinese intermarry with the people of the country: so do the Jews. But when a Chinese man marries a Thai woman, the woman becomes a Chinese and adopts Chinese customs in every detail. Their children become Chinese also. But if a Thai man marries a Chinese woman she continues to be Chinese. The man finds himself adopting Chinese ways and conforming to the Chinese pattern of life. As for the children, even though they are Thai in name they are psychologically Chinese. There are exceptions, of course, but they are few. Our hope was that the Chinese would put down roots in this country: the opposite has occurred.

---

[2] The complete translation of the two chapters in the pamphlet dealing with the Chinese, by Margaret D. M. Landon, is given ibid. pp. 34–43.

The Chinese are unwilling to recognize any obligation to the country in which they reside. If there are privileges to which the native inhabitants are entitled, they demand them: if an occasion arises in which they are required to undertake the duties of citizens they evade these duties if possible. No doubt you will all remember the time four or five years ago when the Chinese suspended work. Their object was to protest against paying *the same poll-tax that all pay!*

The second characteristic of the Jews is found developed in the Chinese also. That is, the Chinese, like the Jews, are an ancient race, whose high civilization was developed at a time when our ancestors had not emerged from savagery. They divide the world into two classes—the Chinese and the barbarians (*Huan* [i.e. *Fan*]). Europeans are as much barbarians to them as are other Asiatics or blacks. They are likely to think that we exist only to be robbed or cheated. In their contact with the barbarians the Chinese recognize no right or wrong; nor do the Jews in dealing with the Gentiles.

Chinese are willing to undergo any sort of privation for the sake of money. Anyone who has watched Chinese coolies eat cannot help but feel a sense of revulsion, since it seems that the food they eat would hardly attract the curs which roam the streets. And if one speaks of places where they live, it is amazing that so many persons can squeeze themselves into a space so small that no other race on earth could manage to breathe in it. This being the case, it is not surprising that the Chinese can manage to corner all the available work for themselves.

The above are the main arguments of the pamphlet but they are greatly elaborated and illustrated by incidents. Mention is made of bogus insurance companies run by Chinese and of bankruptcy which is no shame to a Chinese. It is a smart practice to be used by the clever and knowing. They drain off the money of the Siamese and remit it to China. Friction in the future will almost certainly develop between the Chinese and the natives of Eastern countries. Even though the Jews prosper enormously in the countries in which they reside, they must use their wealth in those countries because they have no homeland to which they can remit it. But the absence of a Jewish national home is something of a liability as well. This arises from the fact that the Jews try to acquire political power as well as wealth in the countries in which they live. The Chinese, having a national home, are not unduly interested in the politics of other countries. Should they lose their national home through some calamity they will become the occasion of serious disorders. 'Therefore it is my profound and earnest desire that China shall continue to exist as a free nation in the midst of the nations forever.'

This pamphlet, *The Jews of the East*, and the articles in the Siamese language from which it is a reprint have an interest quite apart from their royal authorship. They set forth in very cogent form the Siamese case

against the Chinese, and they belong to an early period in the history of
the Siamese-Chinese friction. It is probable that they had an important,
if imponderable, part in shaping public opinion if only for an interval.
The question for us is whether they state the facts correctly or not.

We can leave aside for the moment the question, so often repeated in
Siam and other countries of Southeast Asia, whether the Chinese disposition was an anti-social element in the community or not. The important question here is whether it is true to say that the Chinese are
unassimilable. This takes us back to the discussion in Chapter 12 as to
the comparative merits of Bowring's and Gützlaff's observations on the
point in the preceding century. Bowring, we may remember, asserted
that the children of Chinese men and Siamese women were 'invariably
educated to the Chinese type', and Gützlaff asserted that 'within two or
three generations all the distinguishing marks dwindle entirely away'.[3]
We decided that Gützlaff's contention represented the true situation after
two or three generations, but that Bowring had accurately described the
situation as it appeared to be in the first generation, and that the process
of assimilation proceeded in a subtle, unseen way. When 'Asavabahu'
wrote, the composition of the Chinese in Siam was beginning to change
owing to the arrival of large numbers of Chinese women, though the sex
ratio was still less than one woman to four men,[4] and immigration of
Chinese was on the increase. But he was not referring to the barriers
raised against assimilation by the existence of purely Chinese families
within the country but to the resistance to assimilation of the Chinese
who married Siamese women. The arrival of these Chinese women was
a fact of which he does not seem to have been aware, for otherwise he
certainly would have included it as an even more powerful argument
against the Chinese race. But taking his case on this one point as it
stands, the weight of opinion is against him.

Prince Damrong had stated in conversation with an Italian newspaper
correspondent in 1911 that one-quarter of the population of Bangkok
was composed of Chinese and, unlike those of British Malaya or Java,
they conceived an affection for the country in which they lived.[5] Marrying Siamese women, they became subjects after the third generation and
served in the Siamese Army.[5] Later, in 1927, a European authority, F. H.
Giles, speaking when the situation had greatly changed, said:

The number of Chinese in this country is considerable, and it might have been
expected that they would have exerted a strong influence on the manners, customs,
and culture of the Siamese, but in the main essentials of life, the Siamese have not
been affected, they still retain in a marked degree their own customs as well as their

---

[3] See p. 103.
[4] See Skinner, *Chinese Society in Thailand*, pp. 190–5.
[5] Salvatore Besso, *Siam and China* (London, 1913), p. 45. Landon, *Chinese in Thailand*,
p. 43.

own culture which is of Indian origin. In fact, the Siamese have absorbed the Chinese, but there are signs that Chinese in the future will remain a distinct entity within the body politic of this country.[6]

The conclusion to be drawn, then, seems to be this: The Chinese immigrants into Siam were being readily assimilated until greatly increased immigration and the introduction of Chinese women created an enclave the existence of which was fostered by the Chinese Government partly for political reasons and partly for the sake of the remittances from overseas which were to be an important part of its financial strength. This enclave extended its membership from among the *Lukchin*, because many of them sent their children to schools where Chinese was the medium of instruction and they thus absorbed the nationalism taught therein, and because the increasing anti-Chinese feeling among the Siamese forced them more and more into the alien camp.

We now come back to the knotty question of whether the presence or otherwise of Chinese in the community was advantageous or detrimental to it. Those who argue that the Chinese 'drew off wealth' ignore the fact that without the Chinese there would have been no wealth to draw off. They seem to regard the country as a kind of bag containing a fixed number of coins which were never counted but always existed, and once having been removed could never be replaced, like Ricardo's Wages Fund. This notion may be true of mineral industries, such as tin-mining, but it is certainly not true of other forms of wealth. To be wealth at all, Siamese products had to be given a shape, to be gathered, and distributed and sold, and in doing all this the Chinese had the principal role. Sir Frank Swettenham, writing of the Chinese in Malaya, says: 'The reader should understand at once what is due to Chinese labour and enterprise is the evolution of the Federated Malay States.'[7] In endorsing this and other statements of the kind from the same source, Dr Landon remarks: 'What Sir Frank wrote of the contribution of the Chinese to the evolution of Malaya could be written, almost line for line, of Thailand's economic progress. There would have been no progress without the Chinese.'[8]

[6] *Siam Society J.*, xx, pt. 3 (1927), p. 239. Landon, *Chinese in Thailand*, p. 43.
[7] *British Malaya* (London, 1907), pp. 231–3.
[8] *Chinese in Thailand*, p. 44. One of the experts to whom this Part was submitted before publication comments: 'This seems to me grossly exaggerated: has there been no progress in Ceylon, Burma, Sumatra, the Philippines? Kelantan has roads, bridges, buildings, etc., all made with local labour; the rubber plantations were largely opened with Indian labour, and in Malaya the public works are maintained by them.' This comment refers to the Chinese solely as labour; it is the combination of *enterprise* and labour that Sir Frank Swettenham and Dr Landon have in mind.

15

CHINESE SOCIAL AND BUSINESS LIFE
IN SIAM

THIS chapter is in the nature of an interlude. While the forces described in the preceding pages are working subtly and inevitably to bring the Chinese question to a head in Siam in the 1930s, we will attempt to take a closer view of the life of this alien community, bearing in mind what we know of the life of the Chinese in adjacent countries so that when the time comes we may compare the similarities or contrast the differences between the two.[1]

The factor dominating the nature of the Chinese organism overseas is the sex ratio. The proportion of women to men had been rising steadily in the 1920s, and in the 1930s this process was accelerated. In 1921–2 females formed 15 per cent of total arrivals and in 1925–6 21 per cent. In 1936–7 the figure rose to 27 per cent.[2] But, even in the late 1930s, there was a considerable excess of men over women among the China-born Chinese in Siam. Taking into consideration not only the number of available Chinese women but also other factors such as expense, only about one ethnic Chinese in five could establish a purely Chinese home. Chinese of all descriptions preferred, if possible, to marry pure Chinese females and those of their own tribe—Cantonese, Hokkien, Hailam, &c—when it could be done, but the cost of these was much greater than of other women, and consequently this was out of the question for the greater number of Siam-born Chinese, or 'Sino-Thai'. The price of the bride, or 'milk-money' as it was called, was from 50 to 200 baht for a Thai peasant girl, from 100 to 300 for a Sino-Thai girl, and from 300 to 500 for a Chinese girl.[3] The effect of all this was that whatever the force of Chinese nationalism in separating the two races within Siam, most of the homes were open to native influences. At the same time immigrant Chinese adopted insensibly many Thai attitudes and a selection of Siamese words crept into their vocabulary. Such words were *knanom*,

---

[1] Chaps. iii, iv, v, and vi of Dr Landon's *Chinese in Thailand* have provided the substance of this chapter, but the selection and compression for the purposes here stated are from the angle of one who has had many years' experience of the kindred Chinese community on the Malayan side of the border.

[2] The official migration statistics did not distinguish between the races of the migrants, but Chinese formed about 95 per cent of all arrivals and departures, so that the overall percentages may be reasonably taken to apply to the Chinese alone (cf. Landon, p. 53 ff.).

[3] Landon, p. 55.

meaning cake, as used by the Thai to refer to the little snacks they
bought during the day from hawkers, *snuk*, meaning fun or pleasure,
'which is descriptive of every situation pleasing to a Thai, whether it be
related to football or a religious ceremony',[4] or *thiau*, meaning to take a
trip, but as used by the Thai meaning everything from a stroll down the
street in the cool of the day to a trip to Bangkok or England, and *mai pen
arai*—it is of no importance, it does not matter. The last expression is
obviously the counterpart of the Malay *tid'apa*, and the two convey that
feeling of tropical nonchalance or languid indifference, which must
eventually capture Chinese, Siamese, and Malay alike as they succumb
to the influence of the heat. The women, too, were invariably affected by
local ideas of cooking, health, education, religion, and so on.

What we observe here among the Sino-Thai is a process analogous to
that which created the *Baba* Chinese of Malacca and Penang. This community was the product of the intermarriage of Chinese men with Malay
and other Indonesian females, and in Penang there was also an Indian
element, and of the intermarriage of the offspring of the mixed blood.
The Chinese culture being the dominant, it prevailed in essence, in spite
of the fact that the Chinese language itself was lost and a kind of Malay
containing Chinese words and locutions was substituted for it.[5] But in the
case of the *Babas* the process of racial admixture was complete, while
with the *Sino-Thai* it was only partial. The twentieth-century forces
would in all probability prevent the repetition of the *Baba* history from
the sixteenth to the nineteenth centuries, and these forces were also
battling with the process of complete assimilation which had gone on in
Siam for so long.

From 1 October 1935 all marriages contracted in Siam had to be
registered to be legal. People were very indifferent to this marriage law
and preferred to do as they had always done. The Chinese were even
more apathetic than the Siamese towards registration, although it gave
the wife and her offspring a legal claim on a deceased husband's estate.

Customs among the Chinese in Siam have been modified partly by
native influence and partly by the changes which are going on in China
itself. There is also the effect of intercourse with Europeans, which is
probably much stronger in the neighbouring British colony and protectorate of Malaya than in Siam, and the Chinese of Siam would copy
their brethren over the border with whom they have frequent contact,
especially in the south, and some of their children attend schools in
Penang and Singapore. This process of adaptation is most noticeable in
the change in the nature of wedding ceremonies. Old-Style marriages
with the wedding chair, the bride dressed in the traditional red with a
veil of beads obscuring her face, and the day after day of ritual, have for

---

[4] Landon, *Chinese in Thailand*, p. 54.
[5] See Purcell, *Chinese in Malaya*, p. 293, App. I, 'The Baba Language'.

many years been giving way to the New Style which ranges from a modification of the old ceremony to an out-and-out occidental wedding. In the case of families long resident in Siam, Thai usage is sometimes followed to some extent. In such a case a chapter of Buddhist monks might be invited to the home, and a ceremony would take place in which the bride and bridegroom prostrated themselves while the guests poured ceremonial water over their hands.

A Chinese teacher who had lived for years in many provincial towns as well as in Bangkok answered a questionnaire put to him by Dr Landon and from his answers a fair summary of the changes going on in Siam in the 1930s and still continuing can be obtained. He said that the greatest numbers of Chinese women arrived in Thailand between 1924 and 1926. About 70 per cent of the two million-odd Chinese in Siam still adhered to Chinese custom; the unit of kinship was still definitely the clan.[6] Asked whether the clan existed as a 'dynamic social unit', the respondent answered 'Absolutely!' A man was the head of the clan, but should he die a woman might sometimes become the head. Questions relating to marriage, occupation, business transactions, education, &c, were decided by the head of the clan in consultation with the heads of the large or small families involved. Young men and women now exercised a great deal of freedom in their choice of a partner, but their profession was usually chosen for them by their fathers. Siamese was spoken only in a few Chinese homes in Siam; in homes where both parents are Chinese they prefer Chinese even though the Education Act was compelling them to use Siamese. The Chinese family, the respondent thought, would, in spite of everything, tend to maintain itself as a Chinese cultural unit for ever.

The person here interrogated, we must bear in mind, was a member of a profession pledged to hand on the torch of Chinese nationalism as well as of Chinese learning, and the chances are that he was himself born in China. His replies would represent his own sentiment rather than the precise facts, for, if he is to be believed in every particular, assimilation of the Chinese into the Siamese community must have entirely stopped. Moreover, the clan which he regards as likely to maintain itself eternally is undergoing disintegration. In China the clan, or the family, is

[6] By 'clan', *hsing* is presumably intended, that is to say, persons of the same surname, Tan, Ch'an, Wong, Ong, &c. In English the divisions into Cantonese, Teochius, Hailams, Hakkas, &c, are usually called 'tribes'. Families were subdivisions of the clan. But I am not quite sure how Dr Landon defines 'clan'. He speaks (p. 63) in his questionnaire of the clan, and the 'large family' and the 'small family'. I assume this is from Ta Chen's use of the terms, but Ta Chen does not himself define their meanings (*Emigrant Communities*, p. 127 ff.). On p. 65 Dr Landon speaks of 'clan halls'. In Malaya the centres of community life are the *wui kwuns* (*hui kwans*) which are named after the districts, &c, in China from which the given group of Chinese originates, e.g. the *Hokkien Hui Kwan* (provincial) or the *Teochiu Hui Kwan* (prefectural), or the *Mui Yüen Hui Kwan* (district). In Penang there are halls or *kongsis* based on the clan surnames of five principal families, Lim's, Chias, Tans, &c, and there is at least one hall, the Chia Hall, in Singapore.

rooted in the soil. Even there its hold is weakened when many of its members take to living in villages and towns. In Siam, as in Malaya, Indonesia, and the other ǫ̃ untries of Southeast Asia, this association with the soil is broken; the only link between members of the same clan is common sentiment. As an organization the clan can only maintain itself when there are a sufficient number of its members living in close proximity. At the same time, the pressure from the outside in the form of a campaign by the Siamese authorities to speed up assimilation had the effect of tightening up the Chinese family structure as a measure of resistance.

However, compared with education, all the factors referred to above are of minor effect in shaping the Chinese social organism, and of education we shall speak fully when we come to recite the sequence of events after the *coup d'état* of 1932.

The Chinese in Business

The Chinese were the middlemen, the exporters, and the financiers of Siam, but no one knew the exact extent or the value in money of their holdings. Even in countries like the Netherlands Indies and Malaya, where statistics of various kinds had been kept for many years, only a rough estimate of Chinese wealth was possible. Mr Callis estimated that in 1938 Chinese investment in Siam amounted to U.S. $100 million as compared with other foreign investment of U.S. $124 million.[7] In Siam not only did the authorities refuse to distinguish between Chinese born in the country and others they regarded as Siamese, but statistics in the modern sense of the term were a matter of only the last few decades, and there was not even an attempt at a complete census of the country until 1909–10. However, there was detailed information on rice, the principal product and the chief export of the country, on teak and forestry products, on maize, tobacco, cotton, peas, sesame, pepper, and coconuts, but nothing, for instance, on rubber, certainly one of the chief crops of the country and the third in export value.[8] These details gave some assistance in deciding the nature, if not the extent, of Chinese participation in the economic life of the country.

To begin with agriculture, the occupation of 80 per cent of the people. The rice grower had always remained Siamese, and the Chinese had not by 1930 made any attempt to usurp that position.[9] But as stated in

---

[7] H. G. Callis, *Foreign Capital in Southeast Asia* (N.Y., mimeo., 1942), p. 69. Mr Callis regarded this as a conservative estimate.

[8] Landon, *Chinese in Thailand*, p. 119.

[9] R. le May, *Siamese Tales*, p. 165. Soon after this was written, however, a firm of Chinese merchants from Malaya started the cultivation of rice on a large scale by mechanical means in south Siam. The experiment was successful. Thirty men were able to till an area of 600 acres of paddy whereas by ordinary methods about 300 men would be required. Instead of dividing the land into small plots, as was the Siamese method, they worked several hundred thousand

Chapter 9, the Chinese owned and operated 80–90 per cent of the rice-mills, the biggest undertaking in Siam, and their industry was not confined to the milling of rice. More often than not the Siamese farmer had to borrow from a Chinese in order to live between sowing time and the harvest, and after the harvest it was the Chinese dealer who bought the paddy and transported it to the mills in Bangkok. After milling again it was the Chinese import and export trader in Singapore, Penang, or Hong Kong who handled three-quarters of the rice exported from Siam.[10]

Fishing was the second item contributing to the Siamese income, most of it being done in inland waters, and the fish were consumed locally. The Siamese were independent of the Chinese in such cases, but where there was coastal fishing carried on by the Siamese the Chinese were the buyers and exporters, and handled the local sales. Most of the pig breeding was done by Chinese. They sold young pigs to Siamese farmers who fed them for a year or two and then sold them back to the Chinese. Being a Buddhist, the average Siamese did not want to do the slaughtering, and so had to buy his pork from the Chinese butcher.

Chinese also figured among the landowners of central Siam. They were usually merchants, and did not farm themselves. As is the case elsewhere when there were absentee landlords, the system had given rise to a great deal of discontent and abuse, but here the Siamese landlords were more heavily interested than the Chinese. The lack of building materials in central Siam also increased the dependence of the Siamese on the Chinese for such materials and for assisting in the construction of houses.

At this point it may be timely to consider the Chinese in Siam as money-lenders and middlemen. An impartial survey by Mr James M. Andrews did not bear out the widespread belief that they were unconscionable usurers.[11] The Thai farmer, and especially his wife, says Mr Andrews, was much more given to money-lending with the hope of high profits than the Chinese. Chinese lent money seldom, but they did advance commodities on credit. When he did lend money, the Chinese insisted on a written contract, security, and interest, but he did not ask for illegal rates of interest as did the Thai. Both Chinese and Siamese often lent money to friends and relatives without asking interest.

It is interesting in this connexion to remark that, whereas in Siam and Indochina the Chinese were prominent as money-lenders (subject to the above considerations), they were not so in Malaya. In Malaya it was the Tamil chetty (chettiar) who did most of the money-lending and second

acres as a unit. By the end of 1937 two large Chinese rice-owning companies had demonstrated what scientific farming and co-operative effort could accomplish (see *Report of the Rice Cultivation Committee* (Kuala Lumpur, 1931). Cf. Landon, *Chinese in Thailand*, p. 124.

[10] Lin Yu, *Pacific Affairs*, June 1936.

[11] J. M. Andrews, *Siam, Second Economic Survey* (Bangkok, 1935), p. 314. This survey was of 41 'sample' villages—10 in northeast Siam, 7 in south Siam, 11 in north Siam, 11 in central Siam, and 2 in southeast Siam. Mr Andrews considered the 'sampling' satisfactory. The printed report covers 396 pages.

came the Sikh, whose reputation for being a harsh and unfeeling creditor was universal in these parts. The chetty was considered an honest man in comparison with him. The Chinese part in local finance was more in the nature of banking or the advance of goods on credit, as apparently it was in Malaya.

Handicrafts were cultivated by Siamese women, but neglected by Siamese men. Siamese weaving could not, however, compete with Chinese-made textiles. Poor-quality *phanungs* (native costumes) were made in Bangkok by Chinese weavers, while good silk *phanungs* were imported from China.[12] Pottery manufacture was largely in the hands of the Mon people who lived not far from Bangkok, and who sold their product to Chinese traders. Most of the tiles used in the larger towns were made by the Chinese. When construction on a large scale was undertaken, Chinese carpenters were called in, and the largest part of the wooden building and fitting in the cities and towns was done by them. Iron-working, too, was done by Chinese in the market centres. The same race had a practical monopoly of the preparation and sale of rice, vegetable, and meat dishes, but the cooking and the sale of fruits, cakes, and various sweet dishes was, on the other hand, almost entirely undertaken by Thai women. In rail and road transport the Siamese held their own, but heavy transport of rice on the rivers (entailing very hard labour) had been taken over by the Chinese.

As has been remarked above, the Chinese did not, except for the recent experiment in scientific farming in south Siam, plant rice, but they went in largely for the growing and marketing of vegetables which was more profitable. But labour other than agricultural was performed by Chinese since they had no objection to long hours and hard work, and it is estimated that they made up roughly 70 per cent of the non-agricultural labouring population.

Much of the small trade in Siam was carried on by Siamese women who took to the markets fish, fruit, vegetables, spices, and cooked food for sale or barter. But trade on a larger scale developed in the rice-collecting centres, and since the Chinese were the boatmen this trade was in their hands. Having no effective competition, they were able to charge as much as they could persuade the Siamese to pay.

The extent of the Chinese participation in wholesale business was, as has been remarked before, impossible to assess with any accuracy. In the *Directory for Bangkok and Siam* for 1933, in which the larger firms were listed, 112 were shown as European, 16 as Chinese, 38 as Siamese, 16 as Indian, and 8 as Japanese. Many of the businesses with Thai names, however, were owned by Chinese. For 1940 the same authority gave the

---

[12] This statement is questioned by an expert on Siam who read the passage in manuscript. He says, 'The Siamese make beautiful *phanungs* with gold and silver thread or silk in Korat and Chiengmai. Their finest *phanungs* are almost always made in Siam.'

comparative figures as 103, 98, 56, 35, and 7 respectively. This, of course, did not give any idea of the amount of the capital investment in the firms or of the value of their turnover or profits, but the European Financial Adviser to the Siamese Government, Mr W. A. M. Doll, in 1937–8 remarked that 90 per cent of all commerce and trade was in Chinese hands alone.[13]

The Chinese banks who before the war with Japan were prepared to grant credit for private enterprise were the Oversea-Chinese Banking Corporation (capital SS $10 million), the Sze Hai Tong Banking and Insurance Company Ltd, and the Wang Lee Chan Bank Ltd.

But information as to the aggregate of Chinese wealth would not convey much of value to the sociologist unless it were accompanied by figures of distribution. The Chinese formed the middle class of the nation, but there were also Chinese workmen who received in real wages only slightly more than did the Siamese peasant. The peasant did not handle as much money (a good part of his income being in the shape of crops), but the 20–30 baht a month received by the Chinese coolie who had to purchase his food and pay for shelter did not make him substantially better off. The Chinese petty tradesmen, rubber-cutters, and skilled workers, and most pedlars and street hawkers got about 50–100 baht a month. These rates compare with the 100 baht received by the majority of Siamese officials. Better-off Chinese, not very numerous, would receive 750 baht a month and upwards, and the income of a tiny minority might reach 3,000 or more baht a month.

Whether or not the Chinese enjoyed more than their fair share of the national income, or whether or not they created more wealth than they consumed, the fact is that their position in the community lent itself to the manufacture of political capital. The Siamese generally felt that the

[13] W. A. M. Doll, *Report of the Financial Adviser in Connection with the Budget of the Kingdom of Siam, 1938–9* (Bangkok, 1939), pp. 9, 10. Landon, *Chinese in Thailand*, p. 144.
The following figures for Sino-Siamese trade may contribute some light on the subject to those who are in a position to allow for all factors:

Sino-Siamese Trade

	Imports from Siam		Exports to Siam		Total trade	
	Haikwan taels	Index no.	Haikwan taels	Index no.	Haikwan taels	Index no.
1868	615,089	100·0	69,115	100·0	684,204	100·0
1878	314,347	51·1	193,880	280·6	508,227	74·3
1888	54,003	8·8	357,654	517·5	411,657	60·2
1898	206,394	33·6	698,866	1,011·2	905,260	132·3
1908	46,802	7·6	1,938,489	2,804·7	1,985,291	290·2
1918	395,360	64·3	1,972,030	2,853·3	2,367,390	346·0
1928	6,127,987	996·3	6,622,530	9,581·9	12,750,511	1,863·6
1933	39,836,970	6,476·2	3,739,409	5,410·4	43,576,379	6,368·9

From Ho Ping-yin, *The Foreign Trade of China* (Shanghai, 1935), p. 490.

poverty of the peasants was to be blamed in large part on the Chinese money-lender.[14] A Siamese remarked with feeling in a Bangkok newspaper, commenting on some new Government regulations: '. . . the poor peasants are liberated from the bonds of the blood-sucking "shylocks" who used to lend money on exorbitant interests and sell-your-rice-at-our-offer contracts'.[15]

If this chapter has successfully compressed the facts it should help to make actual the position of the Chinese in Siam on the eve of the events of 1932 and onwards. There was nothing particularly glamorous about the lives of the majority of the sons of T"ang. In the country they lived in an *attap* (palm leaf) hut with an earth floor, lit at night by a kerosene or coconut-oil lamp, with the animals in an adjoining room; in the mining villages their home would be the cheerless coolie lines; in a town their residence would be over, or part of, the place of business. The urban 'toilet' would be a bucket which was emptied in the canal twice a day. The mansions of the rich Chinese merchant were more obvious and elegant, but less typical. However this might be, even the most humble and 'under-privileged' Chinese was classed by the strong current of Siamese opinion as one of the Jews of Asia!

16

THE REVOLUTION OF 1932

AT five o'clock on the morning of 24 June 1932 tanks, machine-guns, and troops were on the move in Bangkok. Prince Nagor Svarga, half-brother to the King and Minister of the Interior, was the first to be visited. By one o'clock in the afternoon forty important persons were held prisoners in the Throne Hall. An ultimatum had been dispatched to the King at his summer palace at Hua Hin. The revolution had begun.

The leaders of the revolution wished, if possible, to retain the reigning King as a constitutional monarch. If he were not amenable, then they would proceed towards their objectives without him. The ultimatum called upon King Prajadhipok to return to the capital again as king under the constitutional monarchy as established by the People's Party. The King accordingly returned to Bangkok on 26 June, and by 1 July the party was able to announce that His Majesty had consented to their terms. No blood had been shed.[1]

The new dispensation which had thus been ushered in was not the

---

[14] Landon, *Chinese in Thailand*, p. 130.
[15] Ibid. quoted from *Siam Chronicle* of 8 Apr. 1939.
[1] The principal authority followed in this chapter is Landon, *Siam in Transition*, chap. i.

product of a mass movement among the people; it arose in the first place
from discontent among that class of commoner which in the previous
reign had held most of the important offices of the Government, but
which under King Prajadhipok administered only eight of the twelve
ministries. A commoner, no matter how high his rank, might be tried by
the law courts: royalty, the only other class, were a set apart, and could
not be brought to trial without the consent of the King. The shift in the
balance of power made commoners feel that they were being ruled without adequate representation. A second reason for the discontent was the
secrecy with which the government of the country was conducted, and
the lavish, and apparently useless, expenditure of public funds. A third
cause, probably as important in its influence, was the dismissal of many
officials of the lower rank and the levying of a new salary tax while the
royalty remained exempt. A fourth reason was discontent among officers
of the army.

Compared with the violent political upheavals of French and Russian
history, the course and the occasion of this transition may seem un-
dramatically mild. But Siam gained much more by its painlessness than
it suffered through its lack of drama. The leading figure in the movement
was Luang Pradist Manudharm,[2] a young lawyer who had studied in
France. His were the brains and the ideas that gave it meaning and
direction.[3]

Since our concern is to follow the fortunes of the Chinese in Siam,
and since they were not involved in any way in the *coup* (save that the
blood of their race flowed in the veins of most of its leaders), we need not
describe in detail the phases of the situation as it developed. We must
watch closely, however, for any of the consequences of the revolution
which bear on the interests of our subject.

The new constitutional monarchy experienced no great difficulty
until March 1933, when Luang Pradist Manudharm introduced his
economic plan. It was discussed in both the People's Assembly and the
State Council. Of the changes that it proposed, one of the most important
was the purchase of farming land for the nation. The farmers would then
become Government employees and would receive salary and pension.
The growing and selling of rice, the principal industry of the nation,
would thus be nationalized. This would automatically eliminate the

[2] His name is also given in English as Nai Pridi Panomyong. There are two ways of
expressing the Siamese name and title in English: both forms have always been used.

[3] Dr Landon's interpretation of the course of events in Siam is here followed, but one
person who has read the text is a little dubious about the statement of the causes of the 1932
revolution and the implied denunciation of the old regime. The reduction in official establishments (he points out) and the imposition of the salary-tax were necessitated by the economic
depression (cf. the cut in the pay of public servants in Great Britain in the same period). The
old regime had its defects but it also had its merits: there has been far more corruption in high
circles in Siam since the exercise of power passed from members of the royal House to the
middle class—if only because the members of the former were so wealthy that there was no
inducement to indulge in corruption, 'Even the devil should have his due', remarks the critic.

middleman, both as buyer and wholesaler, and this middleman was usually a Chinese.

When the plan was referred to a special Committee of Fourteen the burden of opinion was in favour of giving it a trial. But opposition developed under the leadership of the Premier, Phya Mano, who suggested that the Government should attempt to better the economic situation in a more conservative way. Luang Pradist's proposal was to encourage the co-operative society idea, thus making more capital available to the peasants, to enlarge the credit stores where the peasants could buy their supplies at cost price, to establish granaries at local points and to buy up rice for shipment to Bangkok in order to eliminate the middleman, to establish co-operative rice-mills for the sale of rice direct to foreign countries, and finally to establish a settlement scheme for people who had no land. In the People's Assembly, however, many members agreed with Phya Mano in thinking that the plan was communistic. Difference of opinion became bitter, without hope of reconciliation. Finally, when it was certain that his plan would not be accepted, Luang Pradist left for Europe. After his departure an Act was passed against Communism and was also aimed against the nationalization of land, industry, capital, and labour.

A second *coup* of 20 June 1933, when tanks again rolled through the streets of Bangkok, resulted in the arrest of Phya Mano and the resignation of his Government. The charge against the regime was that it had nullified the gains of the revolution, for when Phya Mano had prorogued the People's Assembly, as a result of the differences of opinion over Luang Pradist's plan, it meant that all the powers of the Assembly had been entrusted to the King until such time as the Assembly should be reconvened—which it was thought on all sides would be never! But with a few important exceptions the new *coup* put the same elements in power again. The new Premier, Phya Bahol, the friend of Luang Pradist, made it clear that whilst he was in power the Government would never follow Communist ideas. Says Dr Landon:

Phya Mano, shrewd and experienced politician that he was, knew that a peasant's dearest possession is his land. In many districts it is considered shameful to sell a section of rice land; since that land, in peasant thought, is the rightful inheritance of the children, whose very bread and butter it is. Government ownership of rice lands cut across the very fibre of the people's thinking. It could hardly have done anything else than pauperize the country.[4]

The way was now clear for Luang Pradist's recall. He arrived quietly in Bangkok on 29 September 1933, and a commission appointed to investigate his standing with regard to Communism reported early the following year that he, personally, was cleared of suspicion on this

Landon, *Siam in Transition*, p. 34.

count. Luang Pradist had previously persuaded the commission that the consideration of his plan was irrelevant to any discussion of his personal position. The plan, however, was shelved indefinitely.

A royalist rebellion of 12 October 1933 led by Prince Bavoradej was a failure: in March 1935 King Prajadhipok abdicated. These events, however, belong to the political history of Siam, and they had no direct bearing on economic policy or on the fate of the Chinese.

The People's Party, while it was still a secret society, had drawn up a policy of Six Principles which were promulgated by radio, newspaper, and handbill on the day of the revolution in June 1932. These principles were those of equality, liberty, education, maintenance of internal order, independence, and economics. Most of these were implemented one by one, but that of economics was never promulgated though parts of it were gradually adopted.

The principle of independence involved the denunciation of the old treaties with foreign Powers, and paved the way for the negotiation of new ones on a basis of perfect equality of the signatories. When eventually a treaty with China was completed in 1946, it was naturally of this same order. In the field of economics the Chinese were to feel the force of modern nationalism, even though Luang Pradist's National Economic Policy was, in the main, shelved; in the field of education the measures of the Government were to bear fruit sooner. Let us consider economics first.

Post-revolutionary Economic Measures and the Chinese

Luang Pradist's plan, though it was not published and the two Bills based on it were dropped, nevertheless embodied the ideas behind the measures which were actually to be brought into effect. In essence it aimed to raise the economic status of the Thai as distinguished from the other peoples in Siam, to complete their adaptation to the modern technological world, to provide them with a higher degree of education, and to put them in control of industry, commerce, and agriculture. Commerce, hitherto left to the immigrants from China, was now to be opened up to the Siamese themselves. This meant that the non-citizens controlling so much of the commercial life of the nation would have to be ousted, and since 95 per cent of these aliens were Chinese it was obvious that they were going to feel the operation.

The question of remittances to their home country called additional attention to the Chinese. The European Financial Adviser, Mr W. A. M. Doll, in 1937 quoted a Chinese banker as congratulating his countrymen in 1932 on the fact that all through the depression Chinese immigrants in Siam had not diminished the scale of their remittances home, which he placed at an aggregate of $50 million (Chinese) per annum, a sum equal at the then exchange to 37 million baht. Although this sum, said Mr Doll, might be an over-estimation, careful attention should be devoted to any measure or series of measures aiming at the retention of a larger share of the country's earnings, for attainment of this object would result in building up resources of national wealth available for capital development, which in 1937 were strikingly non-existent.[5] Mr Doll, however, surprised perhaps by the ardent and radical reaction to his remarks, soon reconsidered his figures and decided that the calculation of the Chinese banker was an over-estimate and that the figure of Chinese remittances was really less than 20 million baht.[6] At the same time he issued a warning to the Siamese nation against attempting too fast to gain its economic objectives.

One way of altering the existing state of affairs was to encourage the Siamese to engage in trade and commerce; the other was to exercise discrimination against the Chinese. Both methods were tried in turn, or simultaneously. By the beginning of 1939 the trend of events had made the moment propitious for a series of definitive measures and these were guided into law by the versatile and thorough-going Minister of Finance, the brains of the revolution, Luang Pradist Manudharm.

The first of the series of Government Acts concerned a matter which on the face of it was comparatively trivial, namely the forbidding of Chinese food hawkers to sell their wares in the vicinity of the Ministry of Education. Hawking, as we have seen, was largely in the hands of the smaller Chinese tradesmen. This was followed by measures which probed deeper into the economic system of Siam. From 1936 onwards the Government had entered increasingly into business on its own account—it had established paper-mills, a sugar factory at Lampang, a silk factory at Nagara Rajasima, a tobacco factory at Bangkok, an oil refinery at Klong Toi, a cannery at Pak Chang, a textile-mill, and a soya-bean-oil distillery, and it was planning to engage in the manufacture of cigarettes, leather, and cement, to build rice-mills and a tin-smelter, and to operate tin-mines and co-operative stores. To feed these undertakings with staff it had set up vocational schools and had re-shaped the education system generally to encourage industry as an outlet for Thai energy. Further to guarantee the success of these ventures, the Government in 1939 announced that patriotic Siamese should observe five points—namely, eat food derived only from Siamese produce or Siamese manufacture, wear clothing manufactured by the Siamese, assist one another to enter into commerce, trade, and industry, help all public works and other ventures devised by the Government for the good of the nation, and finally, the supporters of the Government should show themselves worthy of public trust by

---

[5] Cited in 'The Chinese in Thailand', *The Record*, xvii/1 (July, 1937), p. 165. (Bangkok Dept. of Commerce.)

[6] *Report of Financial Adviser*, pp. 39–40; Landon, *Chinese in Thailand*, pp. 166, 167.

conducting their businesses in an honest and honourable way. The proclamation was known as *Ratha Niyom*.[7]

Response to this exhortation by the easy-going Siamese not being what had been hoped, a campaign was started in 1940 for the encouragement of Thai merchants and Thai industry.

All this activity was obviously directed towards competing with the Chinese: now in 1940 the Government sought to reinforce its campaign by regulating them more severely. On 21 February the Minister of Finance introduced a new system of taxation. On imports of food, alcohol, and cloth the tariff was to be increased: on farm implements, draught animals, and farm machinery it was to be reduced. The total taxes remitted amounted to over $12\frac{1}{2}$ million baht, but it was intended notwithstanding to raise the Government revenue from 109 to 155 million baht to pay for new social services, including 30 million baht for local improvement and primary schools. This would be done by an income tax, a shop tax, a bank tax, a stamp tax, and an amusement tax. There would also be an increase in the amounts charged for various permits such as for gamblers, prostitutes, opium smokers, &c. By the new code of taxation passed by the National Assembly on 29 March the burden was to be borne by the merchant class, which was, of course, largely Chinese.

In addition to these measures, a new amendment to the Aliens' Registration Act was passed, whereby all aliens were required to pay a yearly registration fee not exceeding 10 baht in addition to the original immigration and certificate of residence fees. For the first year the fee was set at 4 baht and dependants of aliens were not required to pay it. The Chinese being the principal alien immigrants, the fee would amount to a further tax on them.

'As law followed law, dislodging foreign business men from fields of commercial enterprise which they had held, in some cases for centuries,' says Dr Landon, 'the natural tendency among the Chinese was to seek Thai citizenship in larger numbers than previously.' This was a development not entirely welcome to the Siamese, and they met it by raising bars to such naturalization. Amendments to the law now required applicants for naturalization to possess one or other of a number of qualifications— service in the army or navy, or in other Government service, an age exceeding fifty years, employment in agriculture, ownership of immovable property for a period exceeding two years at the time when the application for naturalization is made. (In the case of landed property it must be over two rais[8] in cities, or twenty rais up-country.) In all cases where the applicant was over thirty years of age, he had to possess a good knowledge of colloquial Siamese; in cases where the applicant was under thirty he must also know how to read and write Siamese. Even then a

---

[7] *Chinese in Thailand*, p. 181.   [8] A *rai* = 1,600 square metres.

majority of the applications for naturalization were rejected for various reasons.

The Chinese complaint was that not only were they, a helpless minority, discriminated against in a breath-taking series of regulations and decrees, but also that they were allowed no decent interval to adapt themselves to the new situation. Other aliens, too, were being squeezed out of their occupations, but whereas the Shipping Act directed against Europeans gave a respite of 180 days before it came into effect, the Salt Act affecting the Chinese came into operation immediately, and no time was given to the Chinese in the industry to wind up their businesses, and the regulations against food vendors were also of immediate application.

As the fervour for nationalism grew and highly placed Siamese vied with one another in showing their enthusiasm for the newly proclaimed *Ratha Niyom*,[9] agitation against the Chinese, reinforced by active governmental measures, rapidly approached hysteria:

> By the middle of August more than thirty Chinese schools and ten of the eleven Chinese newspapers had been closed, numbers of Chinese had been deported, hundreds were being called in the tong probes, raids on Chinese schools, newspaper plants, and homes were becoming a daily occurrence; several prominent Chinese were in jail for remitting money to China, and the entire Chinese community was in an uproar.[10]

Meanwhile the Siamese and their Government, though they must have expected strong reaction to their policy, were satisfied that they were acting within their rights. Indeed it was the Chinese community that seemed to be provocative, and its secret organizations were responsible for a series of murders and other crimes. A newspaper correspondent urged the Chinese to welcome the police drive then in progress against secret societies as a measure towards cleansing the Chinese community of disruptive elements.[11] He argued that the Chinese had been given the same freedom and right to live as the Thais and they even had the right to send good Thai gold out of the country. Let them in return keep the peace and co-operate in making the land a safe and prosperous one. The Government itself felt the situation had become so tense that an official communiqué was issued denying rumours current abroad that Thailand (the new official name of the country) had changed her policy of equal friendship for all foreign nations, and that the recent police campaign

9 The principles of *Ratha Niyom* were announced by the Premier, Luang Pibul Songkram, on 24 June 1939. It was rather like the mixture of the First Principle, nationality, of Sun Yat-sen, with the New Life Movement in China. A first measure was the changing of the name of Siam to Thailand (it was changed back to Siam in September 1945 and back again to Thailand in May 1949.) The word Thai was extended to all sections of the people. There were regulations, too, for dress and deportment, and insistence on a national moral code which forbade Thais to act in the interests of foreigners as, for instance, by being their agents in the sale or purchase of land, or disclosing any information to them detrimental to the interests of the country.   10 Landon, *Chinese in Thailand*, p. 189.

11 *Thai Chronicle* (16 Aug. 1939) cited by Landon, p. 192.

against secret-society activities constituted an anti-Chinese move. Thailand's foreign policy (it stated) remained the same as before—offering equal friendship to all—and the recent action against certain Chinese residents had been necessitated by the Government's task of maintaining public safety, peace, and order. Simultaneously the Government broadcast in the Chinese language to the Chinese in Siam, Malaya, and Hong Kong justifying its actions.

On 29 November Generalissimo Chiang Kai-shek, thinking the time opportune for him to take a hand in the affair, sent a telegram to Luang Pibul Songkram, President of the Council and Minister of Foreign Affairs. He had watched with admiration (he said) the recent accomplishments in Siam which had filled the hearts of all Asiatic peoples with pride, and, having stressed that the Chinese people were by nature peace-loving and law-abiding and the Chinese residents of Thailand hard-working and conscientious, and had long lived on the best of terms with the Siamese, he requested the Government of Thailand to give full protection to the lives and property of Chinese citizens residing in Thailand and permit them to engage in their lawful pursuits without molestation as heretofore.

What was happening within the Chinese community in Siam at this period can be divined by analogy from the simultaneous developments in Malaya. The war with Japan was now in full swing and the Chinese generally regarded themselves as being participants. But the Government of Siam, in the same way as the Government of Malaya, was at peace with Japan and desired nothing to happen within its territory which would prejudice its status. Within the community there was a difference of opinion amounting to a split between the Chinese Nationalists, organized by the Kuomintang, who wished to bring about a complete boycott of Japanese goods, and the non-politically-minded merchants who wished to conduct business as usual, even, in the ordinary way, dealing in Japanese goods. Many of these merchants were otherwise supporters of the Kuomintang and were generous contributors to the funds for relief (*anglice*, the maintenance of the war) in China, but some of them drew the line at sacrificing their businesses in competition with traders of other nationalities who had no scruples regarding trading with the Japanese. Organizations of youths and girls who wished to make the boycott a total one resorted to direct action to enforce it and this, in Malaya, brought them into collision with the police. Pressure amounting to blackmail was at the same time applied in some cases to secure contributions to China relief and for the private needs of these organizations. In Malaya the organizations were known as the Anti-Enemy-Backing-Up Societies and they had close associations with the Communist Party. All this activity, whether of the Kuomintang or of other political societies, was to be distinguished from that of the 'secret societies' who were acting purely for their own profit. In both Siam and Malaya all these organizations were in one sense 'secret societies' since legally they were not permitted to exist, but by long usage the term has become associated with the Heaven and Earth or Triad societies.[12]

Discrimination against the Chinese has been analysed by Dr Landon u de r 'minor industries' and 'major industries'. The former included, for instance, birds'-nests concessions (in which the Chinese were to be completely squeezed out of a business which was one of their traditional occupations), food vending, salt and tobacco, the Signboard Act (taxing signboards in Chinese), the butchering and retailing of meat (also to be taken from the Chinese), domestic shipping, and the Liquid Fuel Act, which threatened the existence of the foreign oil companies and, indirectly, that of their Chinese agents and sub-agents. Under 'major industries' Dr Landon lists rice, tin, rubber, and teak forests. In each case the object was to eliminate the Chinese from the industry.

Backdoor immigration became a serious problem almost as soon as the law went into effect. One way was to be landed from a junk in some quiet spot; another was to land in Malaya, paying the landing fee which was only SS $5 (11s. 8d.), and then to enter Siam secretly by one of the numerous jungle paths over the frontier. The Siamese Government's answer to this was the Registration of Aliens Act of B.E. 2479 (1936–7). No charge was made for the certificates, but each applicant had to supply photographs of himself which were good likenesses and which had to be changed every five years. A widespread check-up was begun with the object of discouraging illicit immigration. A fine of 200 bahts was imposed for failure to produce a certificate on demand.[13]

Even this was not enough to stem the tide of immigration, and the Immigration Act of 1937–8 empowered the authorities to charge the immigrant a fee of 200 bahts. The new law also placed on the carrier a responsibility for the alien, and heavy penalties were provided for a shipping firm or other carrier who, knowingly or unknowingly, brought an illicit immigrant into the country. This last measure had effect, and after the introduction of the 200 baht fee in October 1938 the number of

[12] Dr Landon refers to the 'tong probes'. *Tong* (properly 'T'ong') is a Cantonese word meaning 'hall', 'court', and in mandarin 'T'ang'—not to be confused (as it often is) with 'Tang', a society, as in Kuomin*tang*. It is not used in this sense in Malaya and apparently describes what is known there as a *hui*. Its association, it seems, is with the ancestral hall of a clan. This is its meaning in the United States. The whole question of the connexion between huis, tongs, and political organizations needs much more clarifying and I personally feel that there is a closer connexion between the Heaven and Earth Society and modern political societies than is usually thought. Certainly the type of 'hoodlum' who naturally turned to secret societies and extortion finds a modern outlet for his talents in the Communist Party in Malaya and elsewhere (V.P.).

[13] For further details regarding the discrimination against Chinese in immigration and labour see Thompson, *Thailand*, p. 115. A law of 1935–6 forcing rice-mills to employ a 50 per cent minimum of Siamese workers failed, since it was found impossible to carry on owing to the shortage of labour.

Chinese entering Siam was usually less than the number leaving it. Had
it not been for the war in China, which was reducing the power of the
country to support its still-increasing population, it seems almost certain
that Chinese immigration would have come to a standstill.

We have left to the next chapter an account of the efforts of the
Siamese Government to counteract the propaganda of the Chinese Revolution and to force assimilation at an increased rate. As always in
Southeast Asia, the field of education is where the most decisive battles
are fought. But the evidence above collected and summarized would
amount to a complete dossier by itself. Can it be said on the facts set out
that the Siamese were justified? One witness, at least, thinks they were,
and this is Sir Josiah Crosby, who was British Minister in Bangkok from
1934 to 1941. In a book published in 1945 he says: 'It has been alleged
against the Siamese that what they were doing at this time amounted to a
persecution of the Chinese community. To this view I am unable to sub-
scribe and I consider such an accusation to be altogether too sweeping.'[14]

Later he states thus his opinion regarding the future relation of the
two countries: 'I see no reason why Siam and China should not get on
quite well in future, provided that the Chinese will extend to Siamese
national rights and susceptibilities the same recognition which they are
so insistently and so understandably demanding for their own.'[15]

A contrary opinion is that of Dr Landon who, writing of the same
period but at an earlier date, says:

Thailand has a right to autonomy. The fact that she is using this right to
discriminate against a helpless minority is, however, a sad commentary on the
Government. The Government has an honourable record of solid achievement
in many fields of endeavour, but a record that is stained now by its treatment of the
Chinese.

However, Dr Landon's criticism of the Siamese Government is not so
much of what they were doing but of how they were doing it: 'If the
Chinese in the salt industry had been given a year in which to wind up
their businesses, if the food vendors as well as the Chinese in other industries affected by the new laws had been given the same period, there
would have been little if any room for criticism.' The last two passages
must be read in juxtaposition. The fault, it seems, lay in *suddenly* depriving thousands of unfortunate human beings of their means of livelihood;
not in reserving an industry to the native people.

[14] Crosby, *Siam*, p. 75.   [15] Ibid. p. 76.

17

EDUCATION AND THE CHINESE IN SIAM

THE paucity, or absence, of information regarding the instruction of youth within the Chinese community of Siam up to the twentieth century need not deter us from asserting that such instruction existed in every family where there was at least one literate member, and that it bore almost exactly the same form and character as in China itself or in countries of the Nanyang. This assurance derives from the knowledge that there had been no radical change in Chinese elementary education for centuries. If a school existed, it was almost certainly in a temple or matting shed, often ill ventilated and ill lighted. In one corner would be the tablets to Confucius, the 'Teacher and Pattern for all Ages', and to the god of letters. Incense sticks would be burning in front of both. On entering the room the boy would bow to the tablet of Confucius, salute his teacher, and take his seat. The school course would consist in the first stage of committing to memory the canonical books and of writing an infinity of diversely formed characters as a mental exercise. In the second stage, the pupil would translate books into the colloquial language (i.e. 'reading') and he would have lessons in composition. In the third stage, there would be belles-lettres and the composition of essays. Pupils learnt their lessons aloud (a feat of concentration when all the other pupils were doing the same thing with another book or a different part of the same book), and recited them when learnt with their backs to the teacher. There were no graduated classes; in fact, there were as many classes as there were pupils. The books would be the *San Tzŭ Ching*, or Trimetrical Classic (a work of A.D. 1050), then the *Ch'ien Tzŭ Wen*, or Millenary Classic, the Odes for Children, the Canons of Filial Piety (*Hsiao Ching*), &c, and in due course the pupil would pass on to the Four Books, which, from the Sung dynasty, comprised the Great Learning, the Doctrine of the Mean, the Analects, and Mencius.

There would, of course, be a good deal of variety even within these circumscribed limits, and in a mercantile community such as that of the Chinese in Siam the use of the abacus would certainly be added to the curriculum.[1]

That, generally speaking, the existence of instruction among the Chinese in the Nanyang attracted such little notice from the authorities

[1] For an account of the old-style Chinese schools see Purcell, *Problems of Chinese Education*, p. 18 ff.

of the country in which they dwelt was due to the fact that the instruction was by no means universal, that it was largely domestic, and that
when Chinese schools did exist (and the uproar created by pupils 'backing' their lessons or yelling out their tasks would certainly not conduce
to secrecy) they were always few and small.[2] Chinese who could afford it
(and there were not many) sent their children back to China for instruction.[3] What effect this kind of education had in sharpening or dulling the
pupil's intellect is a question with which we are not immediately concerned, but it is certain that it left an indelible mark or *cachet* on its
recipient which was as unmistakable as that of Eton or Harrow. In the
old days the instruction was not politically suspect for it enjoined obedience to authority and was otherwise ultra-conservative in tone.

However this might be, the education of the Chinese by themselves
had indubitably the effect of confirming the Chinese in his sense of being
one of the Black-haired Race, in his apartness from the native peoples
and belief that they were all 'outside Barbarians', and when the spirit of
nationalism began to arise in Siam and China it was soon regarded as
the essence and the symbol of segregation. But as the age-old Chinese
system began at last to meet the modern demands upon it, and to transform itself and cease to be conservative, the suspicion and hostility of the
authorities were increasingly directed towards it.

As for Siamese boys, there had also been education of a sort for them,
but in the modern sense it came in with the American missionaries in
about the 1830s.[4] Progress was extremely slow in the face of the *vis
inertiae* of native apathy, so much so that when Prince Damrong was
appointed Minister of Public Instruction in 1908, it was still necessary to
pay families to send their children to school. The priests, too, resisted
the modern ideas of education with great determination. Little by little,
with much effort, they were converted, and they now conformed to the
desire of the sovereign, so that in many *wats* (temples) the teaching was
equal to that in the best schools.[5] In 1914–15 there were only 119,000
pupils, with 4,500 teachers: by 1936–7 there were 1,227,000 pupils, with
27,000 teachers.[6]

Since 1898 there had been in existence a scheme for national education.
In 1919 a law was promulgated making primary education compulsory
for all boys and girls between the ages of seven and fourteen. By this
private schools and law schools were formally brought under the supervision of the Ministry of Public Instruction, and their heads had to be
registered with the Government. The first Primary Education Act was
passed in 1921. With the passage of these laws the Government began to
undertake the regulation of all schools. All children of compulsory school

[2] In Batavia the Chinese school in the eighteenth century had only about 400 pupils.
[3] Thompson, *Thailand*, p. 109.   [4] Landon, *Chinese in Thailand*, p. 261.
[5] *Statistical Year Book—Siam*, chap. viii, quoted by Landon, *Chinese in Thailand*, p. 263.
[6] Ibid.

age had to attend schools run by the Government or private schools which had permits from the Government.[7]

So far what has been recounted is the creation of the *machinery* for the control of these private schools: the application of this control had, however, begun to be applied before the Acts of 1919 and 1921, albeit with a gentle hand. In 1918 the law had required that in every Chinese school the principal must have completed at least two years of Siamese schooling, that the teachers must have passed two Government examinations within one year, and that three hours a week should be devoted to the study of the Siamese language. This ruling, which was a shock to Chinese conservatism, provoked protests in Chinese newspapers, and the opposition of the Chinese together with the impracticability of the laws resulted in lax enforcement for a number of years.[8]

Meanwhile a great increase in the number of Chinese schools in Siam had resulted from the zeal for education, which had received a new impulse from the Chinese revolution of 1911, and which was given further momentum by the success of the Kuomintang drive in 1926–7 and the adoption of the Three Principles of Sun Yat-sen as the foundation of Chinese education the following year.[9] Of 1,581 private schools listed for 1935–6, 206 were Chinese, and of the 1,541 listed in 1936–7, 259 were Chinese.[10]

Before 1928 the rise of these schools had excited a very general attention to them on the part of the Siamese, and obviously the administration were expecting in due course to find them a cause of embroilment. Writing in 1924 Graham says:

. . . These schools, which date from shortly after the Chinese revolution, were at first looked upon by the Siamese with suspicion, as it was thought that they inculcated revolutionary principles, and checked the free mixing of Chinese with Siamese blood which had been so much to the advantage of Siam. The suspicion which seemed at one time likely to lead to interference and suppression, though not unreasonable, had apparently faded away, a measure of purely nominal control had been accepted, and the schools in question flourish and increase. They are certainly creating a class with aspirations and ideals largely foreign to, and seemingly incompatible with, those of Siam.[11]

The change of attitude can be traced to the visit of King Prajadhipok to the southern provinces in 1928. His Majesty learned then that many schools were flagrantly ignoring the orders of the inspectors, and his visit was quickly followed by that of the Minister of Public Instruction with the aim of devising a more adequate control of these schools.

[7] Ibid. p. 265.
[8] Lin Yu, *Pacific Affairs*, June 1936; cf. Thompson, *Thailand*, p. 109.
[9] Purcell, *Problems of Chinese Education*, p. 161.
[10] Landon, *Chinese in Thailand*, p. 267. Schools with secondary classes as well as primary were counted as two schools.
[11] Graham, *Siam*, i. 256–7, cited by Landon, p. 265.

This was the beginning of a campaign which was to last for many years.

The promotion of education was an essential plank in the platform of the party which accomplished the revolution of 1932. The aim was to create a population that was 50 per cent literate within the ten years it had fixed as the limit of its own party control of the country's affairs. The existence of a system of Chinese schools side by side with the native Siamese schools was a grave impediment to this programme. In the words of Dr Landon:[12] ' . . . the schools were alien in character and purpose. From the beginning they were founded to preserve the foreign culture of a minority population, to perpetuate the Chinese language and Chinese nationalism. Whenever the law conflicted with their purpose, they got round it if they could—and disobeyed it if they could not.'

To check this process, and at the same time as a measure towards eradication of Communist propaganda in the schools, the law of 1919 was for the first time applied seriously in Bangkok, and affected Chinese schools in particular because of their heavy concentration in the capital.[13] In the past it had been the practice for Chinese to be taught in the Chinese schools in the morning and Siamese in the afternoon. In many cases children did not bother to attend the afternoon session. Government inspectors found that children who had been attending school for three years could not read Siamese. The conclusion to be drawn was that the Siamese language was not being taught.

The response of the Government to this defiance of its decrees took the form of a requirement that in a 28-hour school week, 21 hours were to be devoted to studies in the Siamese language, and one hour was to be given to physical education. Mathematics, science, geography, history, &c, were to be taught in the Siamese language. Foreign languages might be taught in the afternoon only and Chinese might be taught only as a foreign language. If these regulations had been strictly obeyed it would have meant the practical elimination of the teaching of Chinese, since this language was much more difficult than Siamese to learn and the time left for its study was quite inadequate.[14]

Added to this was the insistence that stiff examinations in Siamese must be passed by teachers in Chinese schools. This measure dated from four years before the Siamese revolution of 1932. Before that it had been possible for teachers from abroad to start teaching in schools in Siam immediately after arrival by obtaining permission from the inspectors to defer their examination in Siamese for six months, which period might in some cases be extended up to four years. The order following on the royal

---

[12] *Chinese in Thailand*, p. 269.   [13] Thompson, *Thailand*, p. 110.
[14] The writer when Assistant Director of Education in charge of Chinese schools in the Straits Settlements, 1930–2, found that the 5–7 hours a week devoted in most Chinese schools to the learning of English was quite inadequate and the results were, in effect, nil; and Chinese is more difficult to learn than English.

tour in 1928 had made it impossible for anyone to teach who had not passed the fourth primary examination in the Thai language.

The new regulations and the strictness with which they were enforced roused the Chinese community of Bangkok to present a petition to the Government asking for more time to be allowed for teaching the Chinese language, and that teachers from China be absolved from passing the stiff examination prescribed. But the Government refused to make any concessions on this score. They insisted, however, that other foreign schools should comply with the regulations in exactly the same way as the Chinese were required to do.

If there is one technique in which the Chinese surpass all other races it is that of obstruction, and they now called out their shock troops of passive resistance (if one may so put it) to render the regulations inoperative. Local Chinese qualified to do so passed the examination in Siamese and a stock of certificates to teach was created for the use of newly arrived teachers from China; another plan was to clip ten minutes or so off each hour allotted to the Siamese language, using the gain for teaching Chinese.[15] The Siamese inspectors, though exasperated, maintained their courtesy and calm, and the result was that seventy-nine Chinese schools out of a total of over a hundred were closed.

One more shot, at least, the Chinese had in their locker in this new cultural battle, and that was to pack off their children to school in China or Malaya; this they did with thousands above the age of five.[16]

In view of the indignation aroused and the commotion caused in the Chinese community (and for all their reputation for resigned endurance they are an extremely excitable race), it is a little surprising that the crisis passed off without a boycott, strike, or some incidents of violence. It happened, however, that at this juncture a party led by the Minister of Commerce of the Chinese Government made a tour of Siam and on their return to China they reported that the Chinese enjoyed more freedom under the Siamese Government than under any other foreign Government in the world—in fact that they were in a most favoured position in the country. This, no doubt, had a sobering influence on the Chinese community, though there was nothing in the attitude of the Siamese

[15] Landon, *Chinese in Thailand*, pp. 272–3. 'One school in Bangkok used a burglar alarm when inspectors were sighted and teachers without permits would then hide in cupboards while qualified teachers took over their classes.'

[16] Dr Landon says (p. 273): 'One of the wildest rumours was that the Government was planning to pass a law prohibiting the return of Chinese children to China for study. Another version of this rumour claimed that the Government was going to collect a tax of two to five hundred baht on every child sent out of the country to study.'

Mr Lin Yu (*Pacific Affairs*, June 1936, p. 196) states this rumour as a *fact*—and says that when the Chinese talked of establishing Chinese schools in Malaya, the Siamese Government immediately decreed that any child of school age leaving Siam would be liable to a tax of 500 bahts! Dr Landon's account is undoubtedly the correct one and Mr Lin Yu's acceptance of the rumour lends support to Luang Pradist's complaints against Chinese newspapers and other manufacturers of rumour.

educational authorities to suggest that they were to be treated more leniently or that they had nothing to fear in the future from even more stringent regulations.

The following year, 1934, the conflict was reopened by the publication of a list of fifty banned books. This list was merely a recapitulation at the end of the year of books of a strongly anti-foreign or nationalist nature which had been banned one or two at a time over the years (some of them dated from 1925 onwards when anti-foreignism was deliberately introduced into textbooks);[17] but the effect on the Chinese was as if the fifty had been suddenly banned all at once. In 1938 a further forty-three books were banned as containing Communist or other objectionable doctrine (an act, incidentally, that was likely to secure the support of at least the anti-communistic Chinese).

Meanwhile spokesmen for the Chinese stated the Chinese case in foreign periodicals, and the Bangkok newspapers were by no means silent on the subject. One of the latter, the *Bangkok Daily Mail*, owned by Prince Svasti, the father-in-law of King Prajadhipok, and with (usually) an American editor, commented in an editorial,[18] 'it is indeed strange that some kind of compromise measure could not have been arrived at (regarding the time allotted for teaching Chinese) after the Chinese residents here presented their petition'. Nothing happened and shortly afterwards the newspaper ceased publication for good.

Luang Pradist (Pridi) himself in July 1936 announced the firm intention of the new regime to persist in the course it had undertaken, and there was increasing evidence that it was having a great measure of success in securing its aims. More and more Siamese teachers were employed in place of Chinese in Chinese private schools. There was little point in having Chinese teachers now that the time for teaching the Chinese language was so restricted, and, incidentally, the Siamese cost less, a matter of importance now that the Chinese merchants were less disposed than before to contribute to the funds of the schools. In April 1939 there was a new tightening-up of the regulations. Children between seven and fourteen, who hitherto had been allowed to study Chinese five hours a week, were in future to be allowed to study it for only two hours a week, with concessions in favour of the Chinese language for those above that age. At the same time the regulation that in all subjects other than language study Siamese must be used as the medium of instruction was insisted upon anew. In the meantime the amount of Chinese taught in the Government schools had decreased during the years of the constitutional regime until it was on the point of disappearing altogether.

Under the ultra-nationalistic regime of Luang Pibul, action to enforce Siamese education at the expense of Chinese was intensified. From April

[17] See Purcell, *Problems of Chinese Education*, p. 165 ff.
[18] 1 July 1933, Landon, *Chinese in Thailand*, p. 272.

to July 1939 twenty-five private Chinese schools were closed; in August seven more were closed. The reason given in the latter instances was that the action was in the course of a campaign against Chinese 'secret societies', including the Kuomintang, and in order to forestall plans for organizing sedition and unrest. During the rest of 1939, and throughout 1940 and 1941, the offensive went on and was being vigorously maintained, along with other measures to control the Chinese, at the moment when the Japanese troops landed at Singora.

18

BEFORE AND AFTER THE SIAMESE-CHINESE TREATY OF AMITY OF 1946

CONSIDERATION for the feelings of a friendly nation had, even before 1942, been of secondary importance to the requirements of Siamese domestic policy; but when, on 25 January of that year, Siam threw in its lot with the Japanese and declared war on Britain and the United States, this factor was altogether removed. China, although not technically at war with Siam, was an ally of the two Western Powers and its nationals were now to all intents and purposes enemy nationals. It cannot be said, however, that the new discriminatory measures introduced were anything more than a continuation of a course already embarked upon.

By a decree of 10 June 1942, twenty-seven trades and professions were reserved exclusively for Siamese. Aliens were to be allowed a period varying between ninety days and one year to leave the reserved occupations, which were as diverse as hairdressing and brick manufacture. The impediment to making the decree effective proved to be the lack of Siamese competent or willing to fill the vacancies left by the Chinese, and as was the case with earlier similar measures it brought no revolutionary change.[1] Concurrently, however, the pro-Japanese dictator, Luang Pibul Songkram, took other strong measures to keep the Chinese 'in their place', and Chinese of non-Siamese citizenship were excluded from residence in certain Siamese cities.[2]

As in other countries of Southeast Asia, the 'iron curtain' descended with the Japanese occupation and cut off Siam from outside view. What came through was mainly sparse intelligence, and long after the liberation, very little supplementary evidence was available. It seems,

---

[1] P. P. Pillai, ed., *Labour in South-East Asia; a Symposium* (Delhi, 1947), p. 209. The *New York Herald Tribune* of 14 Nov. 1945 says twenty-one occupations, but the principle is not affected.   [2] *New York Herald Tribune* (14 Nov. 1945).

however, that the main action against the Chinese was as described above. The more dramatic developments were to come only after the Japanese surrender.[3]

During the period following Phibun's overthrow in 1944 the Siamese Government which came into power withdrew a number of anti-Chinese regulations, including the one prohibiting the Chinese from following any of twenty-seven stated professions.

In September 1945, when after the Japanese surrender Allied troops had entered Siam, the Chinese in Bangkok assembled to celebrate the Allied victory. This led to a clash and Bangkok officials had to intervene to end sharp fighting between Chinese civilians and Siamese troops and police.[4] A number of Chinese were reported killed.[5]

However, against this unsatisfactory background, a Siamese-Chinese Treaty of Amity, so long delayed, was eventually negotiated and signed on 23 January 1946. It provided for the exchange of diplomatic representatives and laid down a number of reciprocal rights to be enjoyed by the nationals of each contracting party in the territory of the other in matters of travel, trade, and education. This was the first time that Siam and China had been in treaty relationship.

In spite of all the measures devised to prize the rice monopoly out of the grip of the Chinese merchants, the latter in 1946 still managed to retain control of the marketing of that essential commodity. In the postwar Far Eastern world the food position was critical, verging on the disastrous. The eyes of the deficiency countries were directed towards the only two with any considerable export surplus, namely Burma and Siam. The exporting ability of both these countries had been greatly reduced by the war. The Siamese Government was under an obligation imposed by the peace treaty with Britain to export to Malaya and other countries a given quantity of rice free and a further quantity at a given price, but it found all attempts to meet its obligations frustrated by the enormous scale of the smuggling then in progress. It was said that for every two tons produced by the middlemen for Government export at least one ton was smuggled over the frontier or by ship, at a price many times the official one. Moreover, the Siamese Government was unable to obtain revenue on a reasonable scale through the tax on the country's main export, rice, at a time when the trade was the most profitable. In

---

[3] There is evidence that the Allied cause had support among the Siamese population. For instance, the *Straits Times* of 9 Apr. 1948 reported that Wong Seng Wun (apparently a Cantonese), the leader of the White Star guerrillas, an outlaw band along the Siam-Malaya border, had offered to suppress any agitation which might be 'provoked from outside' in the four Malay-speaking provinces of Pattani, Narathiwat, Yala, and Setun as a mark of gratitude to the Siamese Government for supplying rice to the guerrillas when they were in the field against the Japanese. This at the same time was a gesture of anti-Malay feeling, for there was at this time agitation among the Malays against Siamese rule. It seems, too, that the White Star guerrillas were Communists who were pro-Ally only during the war with Japan.
[4] *New York Times* (25 Sept. 1945).   [5] Ibid. (29 Sept. 1945).

these circumstances resentment of the Chinese stranglehold on rice was naturally provoked anew.

The Minister of Commerce, in pursuance of his determination to end the stoppage in the flow of rice to the Government market, made plans for the entire reorganization of the rice industry. A committee was appointed to consider the appointment of wholesale and retail agents of the Ministry of Commerce under the rice-rationing system planned for the following year. The committee decided that the number of wholesale agents for Bangkok and Dhonburi should be thirty, each catering for the needs of about 4,000 families. Many dealers had also applied for appointment as retail agents, and it was reported that all the retail agents would be appointed from Siamese applicants. The Prime Minister, however, turned down a suggestion that only Siamese dealers should be appointed both as wholesale and retail agents under a rationing system, while Chinese merchants should be allowed to carry on with their existing rice business so long as they did not sell above the controlled prices. This, said the Prime Minister, would be contrary to a promise given to the Chinese ambassador (who had now arrived) that Chinese merchants would be welcome to help in the rationing plan.[6]

Strong protests from the Chinese merchants were received by the chairman of the committee on the appointment of rice-selling agents, and on one occasion he received a fuseless bomb accompanied by a letter threatening that if he did nothing to assist the Chinese rice merchants he would receive another bomb, this time 'complete with fuse'![6]

The progress in the rice war is described in the vernacular press of January 1948. First of all we learn that of the eighty or so mills in Bangkok, most had had to stop as a result of the new system of rice trading introduced by the Ministry of Commerce. By this system only the Thai Rice Company and affiliated mills were entrusted with the milling and grading of rice. About 10,000 labourers were unemployed as a result of the new measures. But the affected rice-mills had already appointed representatives to negotiate with the Minister of Commerce. Khaung Aphaiwong explained that the new system was introduced to ensure sufficient rice for internal consumption, and to improve the quality through carefully supervised grading.[7]

On 18 January, however, a communiqué of the Rice Office of the Ministry of Commerce stated that the Ministry had now accumulated appreciable reserves and that paddy was coming to Bangkok in an even flow. Rice godown and rice-mill owners had promised to improve the quality of the rice, and the Minister had therefore lifted the order to

---

[6] *Siam Nikorn* (16 Dec. 1946).

[7] Ibid. (5 Jan. 1948). These developments all belong to the period subsequent to Marshal Pibul Songkram's new *coup d'état*, but are included here to take the rice story as far forward as possible. That the quality of rice exported had greatly deteriorated since before the war was the subject of constant complaint in Malaya during 1946–7.

intercept rice and paddy boats along the waterways, in order that rice-mills and merchants might be able to make their usual purchases.

It does not seem that the war against the Chinese rice merchant and mill owner had been won by the nationalization of the industry, but temporarily, at least, a working compromise had been reached.

Immigration

In the second half of August 1946 some concern over the influx of Chinese immigrants into Siam had been revealed in the Bangkok press as a result of the entry of an additional shipload of over 2,000 Chinese. In a press interview the Minister of the Interior stated that he was informed that there were from 40,000 to 50,000 Chinese in Swatow awaiting transportation to Siam. In June a report had mentioned that there was a rush of bookings in Swatow because of the rumour that the Government would shortly raise the immigration tax. Both the Prime Minister and the Minister of the Interior assured the public that there was no cause for alarm, that the Chinese were a law-abiding people, that the Government would maintain a policy of magnanimity, and that sympathy was due from the Siamese to the Chinese since the latter were suffering from famine conditions in their own country. At the same time the Ministers assured the public that the Government would repatriate Chinese who were without employment or the means of support. Mention was made of the fact, however, that the Siamese were entitled under a clause of the Sino-Siamese Treaty of Amity to enforce an immigration quota and it was stated that the subject was now under consideration and would be placed before Parliament in due course.

Statistics published by the Minister of the Interior showed that 70 per cent of recent immigrants were women and children, that 10 per cent had been in Siam before, and that immigration exceeded emigration by only 10 per cent. About 3,000 arrived in June 1946, 4,000 in July, and August expectations were even greater. The pre-war average had been about 30,000 a year, so that, if the Swatow figures were accurate, twice as many Chinese desired to enter Siam as in 1939.[8]

Early in 1947 the immigration question became involved with that of the outbursts of violence, amounting to some hundreds, laid at the door of the San Min Chu I Youth and other secret societies, and arrests

[8] About this time a group of Chinese leaders approached the Government with a proposal to establish a Chinese immigrant city along the banks of the Chao Phya river, but Government support for such a scheme was not likely to be forthcoming. Because there had been several cases of cholera on a ship that had recently arrived, the entire shipload was quarantined in a rice-mill and the Government announced that the necessary inoculation must be secured by the Chinese at the port of embarkation twelve days before sailing. To the group under quarantine the Minister of the Interior made a speech on 27 August advising them as to the friendly relations existing between Siamese and Chinese nationals, and of the laws they were expected to abide by, and concluding with a presentation of powdered milk to the children and expectant mothers.

accounted for the 400 Chinese awaiting deportation in February of that
year. It was at this time officially announced that the details of the proposed new immigration regulations had been completed, and that shortly
a communiqué could be expected fixing an immigration quota of 10,000
a year for Chinese and 200 for other nationals. The introduction of the
new measure coincided with a fresh crop of rumours, including one that
Chinese officers as well as Chinese civilians were infiltrating from the
famine areas of China.[9]

Finally, in 1948, the immigration quota for Chinese, as well as for
other nationals, was fixed at 200. This, of course, was a much more
drastic measure of immigration control of the Chinese than any that
had been enforced hitherto.

Education

The eternal dispute as to whether the children of Chinese immigrants
should be educated in Chinese or Siamese continued as before, but
between the liberation and the *coup d'état* of November 1947 there was
no very important development. In November 1946 it was learned that
the Ministry of Education would in future include the Chinese language
in the curricula of the (Government) schools, but at the existing stage it
would be taught only in the commercial schools and language courses.
Later, however, the teaching of this language might be extended to other
faculties.[10] The following week it was reported that some Chinese schools
had been opened in Bangkok without proper permission from the
Ministry of Education and this breach of the law had been brought to the
attention of the Chinese ambassador.[11] The new Chinese ambassador, for
his part, as might have been expected, had already been agitating for concessions to Chinese schools, but it appears that the Ministry of Foreign
Affairs had replied that none of his requests could be complied with,
as the regulations applied to American, British, and French schools
equally.[12]

If, however, the Chinese daily, *Hua Ch'iao Pao*, is to be trusted, the
ambassador's persistency was not altogether without result. The newspaper said that some of the six demands had been agreed to, including
the one that Chinese teachers should be exempted from Siamese examinations. Following up this reported success, the paper in an editorial
referred to the Compulsory Education Act of 1935 and the Private
Schools Act of 1946, insisting that Chinese schools in Siam were greatly
affected by these Acts. Freedom of education had been taken away from
the Chinese. Chinese children under fifteen years of age were forced to
receive Siamese education. Only a few hours were left for Chinese study.

[9] The *Satcha* (14 Jan. 1947).
[11] *Suparb Burus* (23 Nov. 1946).
[10] *Prachakorn* (19 Nov. 1946).
[12] *Siam Radsra* (4 Dec. 1946).

In the past Chinese teachers who did not pass the examination in Siamese were not allowed to teach.[13]

Diplomatic and Other Relations

Mr Li Tieh-tseng, the first Chinese ambassador to Siam, arrived in Bangkok on 6 September 1946, and was most enthusiastically received by the Chinese community. But his position was by no means an enviable one. Unlike most ambassadors to a foreign country, he could not in the first place rely on the undivided support of his nationals within the country. The Chinese community was sharply divided into factions, and the ambassador, as representative of the Kuomintang Government of China, would be the natural object of hostility from the Chinese Communists within Siam. Two attempts on his life were reported soon after his arrival. Furthermore, he was beleaguered by hundreds of Chinese pressure groups. In consequence he was harassed and uncomfortable. Several incidents between Siamese and Chinese a few days before his arrival, possibly due to the heightened sense of national importance felt by the Chinese, caused him to emphasize in a speech during the flag-raising ceremony that he would be of aid and protection only to the law-abiding.

The new claims on the ambassador's attention were myriad. He had to preside over the inauguration of a number of new Chinese consulates in Siam; he had apparently received instructions to press for a settlement in regard to the death and injury of Chinese in the victory celebrations of September 1945; he was soon to submit memoranda to the Foreign Ministry demanding action regarding the teak commandeered from Chinese nationals; he had to request a softening of the conditions of the control of Chinese schools and teachers; he would before long be confronted by a Bill which, if passed, would affect the right of residence and vocation of the Chinese in Siam.[14] These and a hundred other things he had to attend to, and in his spare time he would be expected to travel the length and breadth of the country to the numerous centres to which his countrymen had penetrated. Apart also from his duty to pursue the interests of his country with the Siamese Government, he would have to be ready with replies to the complaints which the Siamese themselves would certainly prefer in return against his Government and the Chinese community within Siam.

One such complaint concerned the taking of votes among Chinese nationals in Siam for the elections which were to be held in China the

[13] *Hua Ch'iao Pao* (30 Jan. 1947).
[14] A Bill for reservation of certain areas for economic and agricultural purposes sponsored by Luang Arthaphorn Phisan, M.P. for Trat, was introduced in the National Assembly in July 1947. The ambassador's contention was that the Bill, if passed, would violate Article VI of the Treaty of Amity. (The *Kiatisak* (13 July 1947).)

coming October. This procedure, which had been the cause of friction in other countries in Southeast Asia in the past, was said to be regarded by the Siamese Ministry of Foreign Affairs as a 'direct violation of Siamese sovereignty'. It was recalled by the Siamese press that when the German residents had voted for the elections in Germany they had gone over three miles from the Siamese coast to do it.[15] The reply by the secretary of the embassy to a press inquiry was that by the rules of the election the embassy had no right to concern itself with the matter.[16]

On 15 October the Chinese ambassador officially informed the Foreign Ministry that his Government had dropped the plan to authorize the consuls to supervise the voting of Chinese nationals in Siam in the forthcoming general election. In announcing this, the Siamese Premier, Mr Dhamrong Nawasawat, said that this officially closed the issue. At the same time it was officially stated by a spokesman of the Chinese consulate-general that plans were under way for the registration of all Chinese citizens in Siam.[17]

It must have been a matter of the greatest difficulty for the Chinese ambassador to decide the order of priority for addressing himself to the manifold problems. The Chinese press and the 'pressure-groups' were agitating for action in a hundred different directions at once. At the same time the new diplomatic and consular representatives did not wish to appear to lack initiative on their own account. For example, it was stated on 19 August 1947 that, following the inauguration of the Chinese consulate at Singora, all Chinese consulates would hold a meeting to discuss the conditions of livelihood in Siam and promote a policy for action.[18] Negotiations for the trade agreement foreshadowed in the Treaty of Amity would also come within the sphere of the ambassador.[19] Other questions competing for attention were the border troubles, in which Chinese outlaw bands claiming KMT affiliations were reported to be fleeing into south Siam from Malaya, and the increasing Chinese secret society and mob disturbance in Bangkok and towns in the vicinity.[20]

In reviewing the first year of diplomatic relationship between Siam and China it could not be fairly said that the innovation had eased the tension between the peoples within Siam. It had indeed intensified the

---

[15] *Nakorn Sarn* (22 Aug. 1947).   [16] *Heung Yian Pao* (16 Sept. 1947).
[17] *Straits Times* (17 Oct. 1947).   [18] *Hua Ch'iao Pao* (19 Aug. 1947).
[19] It had already been announced that the Chinese Government had successfully negotiated with the Ministry of Foreign Affairs for permission for Chinese cargo boats to anchor in Siamese waters and trade with Siam, in the absence of mutual agreements to this effect (the *Satcha* (23 Aug. 1946)).
[20] When Mr Li Tieh-tseng returned to Bangkok on 26 September from a visit to the south he stated that during his trips from Singora (Songkla) to Penang he had found peace and quiet, ness. There had been no murder of five Siamese police by Chinese bandits as had been reported.

C.S.E.A.——F 2

existing feeling. Soon after the arrival of the Chinese ambassador one Siamese newspaper had commented:

Although there is some degree of truth in the old saying about Sino-Siamese relationships, it is not the less a fact that, due to some reason or other, natural or even blood relationships seemingly have failed to become a guarantee for the good conduct of either party.... The establishment of diplomatic relations between Siam and China has become all the more necessary now in order to ensure this natural relationship against unfair play on the part of either the Chinese or the Siamese....[21]

Nor did some sections of the press, especially the Chinese press, tend to unruffle feelings or to allay suspicions. The *Suparb Burus*, for example, on 1 December 1946 complained of an article in the *Hua Ch'iao Pao* calling upon the Chinese community to unite against the Siamese so that 'the influence of China may dominate the whole of the Chao Phya river'. 'No Chinese will believe', comments the Siamese editor, 'that any Chinese newspaper would be permitted to behave in this way in any country other than Siam.'

The happenings above described, though not by any means constituting a detailed history, are enough to indicate the trend between the Japanese surrender and the *coup d'état* of November 1947. The deterioration of the military situation in China to the disadvantage of the National Government, and the increase of Communist activity in Malaya and other adjacent countries, together with the return to power of Marshal Pibul Songkram who had been identified with the anti-Chinese policy of before and during the war, were factors that were bound to influence the fortunes of the Chinese in Siam.

19

POST-WAR DEVELOPMENTS

EARLY on the morning of 9 November 1947 Siamese Army units under the leadership of Field-Marshal Pibul Songkram[1] seized control of the Government by a *coup d'état* in Bangkok. The Premier Luang Dhamrong Nawasawat was reported missing and Nai Pridi Panomyong (i.e. Luang Pradist Manudharm) was said to be sheltering in Singapore.

Faithful to the historic policy of the Chinese in positions of dependence, important members of the KMT in Bangkok lost no time in calling on the Marshal. They brought with them baskets of flowers. Pibul asked the Overseas Chinese to be calm and to adhere firmly to peace, not

---

[21] *Naeo Na* (11 Sept. 1946).
[1] Luang Pibul Songkram was placed under house arrest in September 1945, but released the following March, the Bangkok High Court having decreed that the War Crimes Act could not operate retrospectively.

giving way to fearful expectations. Both sides, it was reported, had a 'sincere talk'. The Marshal assured the deputation that there would not be any anti-Chinese action. In return the Chinese spokesman, Mr Lee Li-yow, promised the Marshal that China and the KMT would support his work until its successful fruition. In conclusion he expressed a hope that 'the sentiments of the Chinese and Siamese would remain for ever as fresh and as beautiful as the garlands of flowers in this basket', and he hoped that the mutual friendship would be eternal.[2]

Marshal Songkram followed up his assurance to the KMT deputation by a declaration on 12 December in which he said, 'it should be clearly understood that I am in no way involved in politics since I have handed the powers of administration over to the Government, retaining only my military post'. He insisted that the restriction of the areas in which aliens could reside, the reservations of certain trades for Siamese nationals, and other measures he had introduced were merely a part of his war-time policy to prevent the Japanese from getting full control of the country. He solemnly asserted that the acts of the past would not be repeated. It was his firm belief, he said, that the Khuang Aphaiwong Government, now in power, composed of discreet and far-sighted gentlemen, would be instrumental in safeguarding and in enhancing Sino-Siamese relations. 'I will give them all the support in my power.'[3]

The Chinese, both diplomats and ordinary civilians, watched the fortunes of the new regime with a strong personal interest. After the bloodless November *coup*, the monarchists gained the upper hand and in the January elections Aphaiwong's Democratic Party won a majority in parliament over Pibul Songkram's own Tharmatipat Party. In February Aphaiwong (Khuang Abhaiwongse) accepted the post of Prime Minister, but, like his predecessors, he found the influence of the fighting forces too strong for him, and early in April, when Marshal Pibul again headed a combination against the Cabinet, Aphaiwong was forced to resign in spite of his parliamentary majority. The Regency Council then asked the Marshal to form his new Government, which was thereupon made up of nine soldiers and seventeen civilians of his own choosing.[4]

The United States, Britain, China, and India recognized the Government of Khuang Aphaiwong in March 1948 following popular elections which had returned the Democratic Party to power with a large majority. Pibul (Phibun) came to power in April by theoretically constitutional means. There was, therefore, no question of recognizing him, since theoretically there had been no *coup d'état* but continuity in the Siamese Government. (The United States and the other Powers had for a short time considered a policy of non-recognition [i.e. withdrawing recognition] but did not pursue the idea.)

[2] *Chong Yuan Pao* (12 Nov. 1947).   [3] *Straits Times* (12 Dec. 1947).
[4] *The Times* (1 May 1948); *New York Times* (7 Apr. 1948).

Before China had recognized the Marshal's regime the flag question had once more come to the fore. Following protests from the Chinese in Siam against the law prohibiting the flying of the Chinese flag over Chinese private schools except on 'special occasions', the Chinese ambassador had referred the matter to Nanking. The Chinese consul at Paknampok about this time ordered all Chinese schools within the consulate area to hoist the Chinese flag alongside the Siamese flag. This led to an incident which a Siamese education officer reported to his superiors. Chinese schools were then instructed that they could fly only the Siamese flag daily, and the Chinese flag in addition to that of Siam only on special occasions under the Flag Act of 1936. When some Chinese schools stopped putting up the Siamese flag they were informed that they were committing an offence. If they persisted in their action they were warned that strong measures would be taken against them.[5]

Although the press in China and the Chinese press in Siam made a great deal of incidents such as these, it seemed that Marshal Pibul intended to adhere closely to his promise that the old days of repression would not be repeated. 'They were very angry with me once', he repeated in April: 'I shall take careful steps', he added.[6] It was therefore with some dismay that the Chinese residents of Siam heard on 13 May that the Siamese Government had forbidden new Chinese schools to open, ordering that the number must now be reduced from 490 to 148. This was hailed as the first anti-Chinese action since the Marshal had returned to power.[7]

When the Chinese in Siam realized the full import of this new decree they were filled with consternation. It was much more thorough-going than anything that had been decreed before. For weeks the papers were flooded with arguments pro and con. Meanwhile there was a rumour that the schools had refused to comply with the regulations and were closed, and that all teaching in the Chinese schools had come to a standstill. Actually, as it turned out, only a few schools had closed and these shortly were reopened. Then the Ministry of Education intervened with counsels of moderation. Let the schools reopen, it said, and comply with the Government regulations. Chinese educationists could then seek for changes in the regulations. Only parliament could alter the regulations, insisted a spokesman of the Ministry. Subsequently more liberal teaching hours were granted to the Chinese schools.

[5] Bangkok United Press message to *North China Daily News* (4 Feb. 1948). On 14 February 1948 Mr Sahas Mahakhun, President of the Chinese Chamber of Commerce, and representative of other Chinese associations, called at the Ministry of the Interior and the Foreign Office to present a petition that Chinese schools in Siam be permitted to fly the Chinese flag (*The Standard*, Bangkok (14 Feb. 1948)).   [6] *North China News* (12 Apr. 1948).
[7] *New York Times* (15 May 1948). General Mankorn Promyodhi, Minister of Education, at a press conference the same day said that the number of Chinese schools in Bangkok would be reduced gradually from 100 to 8 and in the rest of Siam from 390 to 140. Any school which was closed for an infringement of Siamese rules would not be allowed to reopen (ibid.).

By the beginning of 1949 agreement between the Siamese and the Chinese Governments had been reached on the daily ceremony of hoisting the Siamese flag and the use of Siamese as the chief medium of instruction: on the other points at issue negotiations were proceeding.

All this on the face of it looks like a renewal of the old campaign to insist on the assimilation into the Siamese people of all who made Siam their home. In one sense it was, but a new factor had come to the surface in Chinese affairs in Southeast Asia generally which was to mean a re-ranging of forces, and this we must investigate if we are to make a fair appraisal of the Siamese Government's policy.

When the rise of nationalism effected a dichotomy in the Siamese organism, the pull was either towards Siam and its traditions or towards Chinese racialism in its new bourgeois-socialist guise. After the purging of the KMT of its leftist elements in 1927 the Communists had split off and gone underground. Both in Siam, where no political parties were allowed, and in Malaya, where neither the KMT nor the Communist Party were registered societies permitted to operate, the activities of both the parties were illegal. But they were nevertheless in operation and in clandestine conflict with one another. The Chinese Communists, however, in spite of their universal doctrines, were Chinese first and Communist afterwards when it came to an issue where a third party was involved. Although a large proportion of the poorly-paid Chinese teachers who came to the Nanyang were sympathetic to Communism and disseminated its doctrines clandestinely to their charges, when it came to a contest with the Siamese authorities they were whole-heartedly on the side of the KMT even though the Communist Party denounced its members as bourgeois traitors and betrayers of the revolution.

One does not need to have crossed the border into Siam to understand the dilemma in which the Chinese *towkays*, the merchant leaders and members of the committees controlling Chinese schools, found themselves in this long-developing situation. Many of the older ones had had little education themselves, and though they wished their children and grandchildren to share in its blessings they had no desire to have them brought up as Communists. The KMT with many younger and active leaders did its best to ensure that the teachers engaged were orthodox in the faith of Sun Yat-sen, but it was beyond their powers to ensure that even a majority of the 3,000 teachers, paid so little and subjected to all the vexations imposed by Siamese educational policy, were inculcating the doctrines approved by Nanking and nothing else. So it was that many Chinese, though ardent nationalists, had mixed up with their feelings a secret sympathy for the Siamese Government in its campaign against subversive action.[8]

[8] *Straits Times* (7 May 1948).

Since all political organizations were illegal, the Government was correct in refusing in its campaign to distinguish between Chinese Communists and Nationalists. At the same time it was somewhat ironic that a popular underground movement among the Siamese in furtherance of the Government's aims should also have taken the form of secret societies. Early in May the existence on a large scale of these societies, variously describing themselves as 'Black Siamese', 'Black Elephants', 'Black Tusks', and 'Buddha's Disciples', was disclosed when they splashed the city of Bangkok with posters and leaflets demanding an immediate cessation of Chinese immigration into Siam, and calling on the Government to set up 'China-towns' in Bangkok and other major cities in the kingdom. The police were said to be trying to track down these secret societies.[8]

Early in June the Chinese Communist terror began in Malaya. Overt war to the death was declared against the Government and capitalists and KMT members alike, without distinction of race. Since the Communist guerrillas in Malaya were Chinese almost to a man, the tendency among Europeans in Malaya was to identify with them the Chinese race as a whole, even though Chinese merchants, shopkeepers, and employees on mines and estates as well as Europeans were being struck down with strict impartiality. In the Siamese parliament an allegation was made that the Chinese were trying to 'colonize' Siam, and had offered huge bribes to the police authorities in pursuance of this aim. The Deputy Minister of the Interior, replying to a question on the subject, stated that an investigation had been ordered by the Government. At the same time the Siamese authorities ordered a vigorous campaign against all secret societies, and the illegal carrying of arms. They meant to 'crush the Chinese menace', but simultaneously they meant to eradicate all secret societies of whatever colour. 'Black Elephants' or 'Buddha's Disciples' might propagate correct sentiments: in the long run they might prove a double-edged weapon.[9]

At the beginning of 1949 informed opinion inclined to place the number of Chinese Communists in Bangkok at 30,000, this being the estimated number of adult male demonstrators in the May Day procession of 1948. There was a strong branch of the Communist Party with close affiliations with the movement in China, but it was doubtful whether the active members numbered more than a few hundred. Communist influence had been apparent in three spheres—labour, education, and commerce. Shortly after the war the Communists took the lead in forming a Central Labour Union, really a federation of trade unions, but it attained nothing like the same scale as the Malayan General Labour Union, and there was little industrial unrest in Bangkok. There were, however, it was reported, some powerful business interests in Siam

[8] *Straits Times* (7 May 1948).   [9] Ibid. (7, 10 May 1948).

which, if not wholly Communist in sympathy, were so hostile to the KMT that they were proving useful allies of the Communists.

1949–63

The history of the Chinese in Thailand (as we will now call Siam since this title was officially adopted in 1950), as of other countries in the region, must be seen in the changed political setting consequent on the rise of Communist China.[10] The alignment of Thailand in international politics, culminating in its membership of SEATO in 1954, and the defence commitments consequent thereon were duly reflected in the Thai attitude towards the local Chinese.[11]

Since 1946 the Chinese Communist Party of Thailand had been operating more or less in the open though checked by the police, but with the Communist victories in China the strength of the party within the Chinese community greatly increased. Already, by 1948, the Central Labour Union (Saha Achiwa Kamakon) had come under Communist control, and in November 1949 it was affiliated to the World Federation of Trade Unions and sent delegates to the Federation's conference in Peking. The other union, sponsored by the KMT, was unable to attract any comparable support.

The Chinese schools had for many years been a focus of Chinese political activity, and this was now intensified by the Communists, and there was also a noticeable shift towards the Communist viewpoint in the press. The newspapers controlled by the Singapore millionaire, Mr Aw Boon Haw, also took a pro-Peking line in keeping with the policy of their proprietor at that time (though he changed his views when the Communists confiscated his Tiger Balm factory in Canton in 1951).

It was, however, the Chinese community as a whole and not exclusively the Communists who were a source of anxiety to the Thai Government. Both the Communist- and KMT-controlled schools were to a great extent ignoring the Private Schools' Act, encouraged both by the Chinese Embassy and the Chinese Communist Party of Thailand, and the police raids, arrests, and closures of schools were made irrespective of the political colour of the offenders. It was natural, of course, that Phibun should be more kindly disposed towards the KMT since they were weaker than the Communists, but the closing of the Nationalist Ch'ing-hua school in Chiengmai in 1949 and the arrest of some sixty of the town's most prominent KMT members for illegal solicitation of funds showed that the Government intended to be impartial in applying the law.

[10] Account of the early stages of this change has already been taken in the Postscript to the first edition of the present work.
[11] See Skinner, *Chinese Society in Thailand* and Coughlin, *Double Identity*, to which the author is indebted for many of the facts in this addendum.

To begin with, Phibun had tended to minimize the new threat presented by the rise of the People's China, and it was only when the latter began to show an active interest in the fortunes of Chinese minority in Thailand that he intensified his measures against the Communists. In January 1950 Peking Radio accused the Thai Government of oppressing the local Chinese, alleging ill-treatment of individuals by the police and unjust deportations, and demanded assurances against the recurrence of these abuses. In a bid to compete with the People's Government for the good will of the Chinese of Thailand, the Revolutionary Committee of the KMT thereupon offered their condolences to 'the hundreds of thousands of local Chinese who had lost their livelihood' through the action of 'the Phibun clique' against Chinese commerce and industry. Phibun, therefore, found himself opposed by both the Chinese factions, but the Communists obviously constituted the more serious problem.

In 1950 Thailand was drawn more closely into the orbit of American Far Eastern policy. After the war, the United States had taken special pains to cultivate Thai friendship, and had entered into agreements with the Thai Government for American military aid and technical and educational assistance. The first fruits of this policy were Thai intervention on the side of the United Nations in the Korean War, backed by the dispatch of troops and supplies of rice to help feed the combatants and for relief purposes. As an auxiliary means to assist financing of those measures, contributions were obtained by the Government (under pressure) from Chinese business men. These contributions were represented as part of the fight against Communism.

Other Government measures of this time were directed against the Chinese, Thailand-born Chinese, for example, over 18 years of age being allowed to proceed to China only under a bond in 5,000 baht (tikuls) guaranteeing their return on reaching 21 (conscription age), and remittances to China were controlled by the Bank of Thailand from December 1951 to prevent their being used for the purchase of arms to fight the U.N. troops in Korea.

The following year (1952) saw the Thailand Chinese split openly into two factions, KMT and Communist, using the Chinese Chamber of Commerce as a main battleground and extending the feud to every other Chinese organization. Each faction possessed a newspaper and these added fuel to the flames of hatred. It was at this juncture that the Thai Government reverted to a full-scale policy of 'containment' (as Mr Skinner terms it) towards the Chinese.

The first measure of this more stringent policy was the increase in the fees for Aliens Registration Certificates (to be distinguished from the immigration fees). At first these certificates were issued without charge; in 1939 a fee of 4 baht (U.S. $1·60) a year was charged; and was subsequently increased to 20 baht (U.S. $8) a year. In January 1952 the cost of an Aliens Registration Certificate was jumped up to 400 baht (U.S. $20) a year.[12]

The announcement of this increase aroused the Chinese to a paroxysm of protest. They demonstrated in large numbers and were kept in check only by the Thai police, armed with fire-hoses and tear-bombs. Few of the Chinese aliens paid the 400 baht—indeed most of them could not afford to. Within the year it was reduced to 200 baht and certain classes (those under 15 and over 60, widows, the infirm, and those with sons in the Thai armed forces) were exempted altogether.

A disastrous fire in Bangkok at this time rendered many thousands of Chinese homeless, and though the Chinese benevolent societies collected some 3 million baht for relief, the disputes within the Provisional Relief Committee rendered its distribution a matter of politics. The amounts collected by the Chinese newspapers for relief provided an index of political sentiment at this time at 30 per cent pro-Communist; 7 per cent pro-KMT; and the remainder 'neutralist'.[13]

With the growing ascendancy of the Communists within the Chinese community, the energies of the Thai Government were now concentrated on dealing with what they regarded as a Communist plot. Coinciding with a series of raids on Chinese associations and mass arrests, an anti-Communist Bill was rushed through the Assembly by General Phao and became the Un-Thai Activities Act. It prescribed imprisonment of from five to ten years for propagating Communism and it was clear that it was aimed primarily at those Communists who were Chinese.

During the period of their anti-Communist drive, which resulted in mass arrests and deportations, the Thai police showed themselves disposed to accept the KMT Chinese as their allies and depended upon them for much of their information. In March 1953 a plan was announced to form a Chinese anti-Communist volunteer corps to be dispatched under police command to border regions to assist in the campaign to suppress Communism, but this corps did not eventuate. The following year, the British operations against the Chinese Communist guerrillas in Malaya compelled a group of the latter to seek refuge on the Thai side of the frontier, and, to deny aid to them, the Thai Government gave orders for all aliens to vacate certain areas in September 1954, but when tin-mining and rubber-tapping virtually ceased owing to the lack of Chinese labour the Government rescinded the order.

The close identification of the Thai Government with the anti-Communist policy of the West favoured a revival of KMT influence within the local Chinese community. The KMT supporters took full advantage of the improved situation and organized propaganda on a considerable

[12] Coughlin, *Double Identity*, p. 27.
[13] Skinner, *Chinese Society in Thailand*, p. 333.

scale. One form this propaganda took was the organization of public
sacrifices to honour the relatives of Thailand Chinese said to have been
done to death by the Communists in China, and in the performance of
these sacrifices they attempted to enlist the co-operation of Thai Buddhism throughout the country. Another promising means of appealing to
Thai sentiment was through sport; and basketball and tennis teams were
brought over from Taiwan to play the local Chinese and Thai champions.
Simultaneously the KMT were able to purge the Chinese Chamber of
Commerce of Communist elements, and, now that the Chinese Communist newspapers had been closed down by the Government, the KMT
organs had the field of Chinese journalism to themselves.

When SEATO came into being as a consequence of the Manila Treaty
of September 1954, Thailand was a member country. All along Thailand
had opposed recognition of the Peking regime, and had accepted the
restrictions imposed by the United States on trade with the Chinese
mainland. However, when the Asian-African conference was convened
at Bandung in April 1955, the Thai Government felt it expedient to
participate and sent its Foreign Minister, Prince Wan, who thus became
a colleague of Mr Chou En-lai. The agreement reached at Bandung
between the People's China and Indonesia regarding the nationality of
Overseas Chinese opened the eyes of the Thais as to the consequences
that might ensue should Thailand ever recognize the alien Chinese in
Thailand as citizens of the People's Republic, for, as in Indonesia, those
Chinese who elected for Chinese nationality would be subject to the
protection of the People's China whose consuls would have to be accepted by Thailand. At the same time, Thailand's realization of the
growing influence of the People's China in the Far East was reinforced
by the latter's trade offensive, when large quantities of Chinese goods
were imported into Thailand indirectly via Hong Kong and Singapore,
and at prices which gave the Chinese importers an advantage in the
local markets. The supply of cheap Chinese goods, however, tended to
lower the cost of living in Thailand. In 1959 the Thai Government issued
a decree prohibiting the importation of goods from China, but smuggling
continued. The policy of Thailand towards the People's China continued to be determined by fear of the Chinese minority within its
frontiers and by its membership of SEATO; and the successive crises
in Laos, when the Communist Pathet Lao seemed on occasions to be
about to control the whole country, raised an alarm in Thailand that its
frontiers were threatened by a Communist (and ultimately Chinese)
advance.

Although the system of government in Thailand was in no real sense
democratic, the fact that half the National Assembly were elected provided scope for the expression of public opinion at the elections. No less
than twenty-three political parties had come into existence before the

1957 elections, and when Phibun's own party, the Seri Manangasila Party, obtained a majority there was a popular cry of 'ballot-rigging'. Public indignation was extremely strong and culminated in a large-scale student demonstration. Sarit saw his opportunity and by his tactful handling of the situation, while serving under Phibun as Minister of Defence, prepared the way for his own rise to power. Directly he felt strong enough he carried out a military *coup*, and Phibun and Phao left the country. Sarit was now the latest 'charismatic' leader, basing his support on the cultivation of his personal popularity with the Thai masses.

Under Sarit's regime there was substantial economic progress in Thailand, but the Government's preoccupations were mainly strategic. 'Anti-Communism' was the key-note of Sarit's policy, and the support he gave to United States strategic schemes was to prove financially very advantageous to Thailand. But it was fear of China and the Chinese minority which the regime most carefully nourished with unceasing propaganda.

Such was the setting into which the Chinese of Thailand had somehow to continue to fit. They had been submitted to discriminatory restrictions for many years, and account has already been taken of some of the principal pre-war measures designed to this end (although those measures applied technically to *all* aliens and not merely to those of Chinese race). The royal decree of 2 June 1942, reserving 27 occupations to Thai nationals, was superseded by another of 1949 reducing the number of reserved occupations to 7, but in 1952 two more occupations—female hairdressing and dressmaking—were added to the reserved list. After 1952 there was no further *legislative* curtailment of Chinese economic activities, but the Government continued to effect this through ministerial regulations and directives (a method which attracted less publicity), and the 'anti-Chinese' bias of the Government was now reflected by individual Thai officials in their administrative acts. The consequence was that Chinese found it impossible to obtain licences as retailers of tobacco, wine, sugar, &c, or as butchers or holders of market stalls, and were unable to run coffee-shops, to retail pork, or to sell cloth for use by Buddhist monks or as religious offerings. In pursuance of this extreme nationalist policy, the discharge was ordered from the civil service not only of aliens (a small number being employed as specialists or menials) but of all persons of alien parentage (i.e. locally-born Chinese). And restrictions of a similar sort were extended to the railways, docks, &c. After Marshal Sarit's seizure of power in 1957 the 'anti-Chinese' campaign was intensified.[14]

How was it, then, that in face of this long-continuing campaign against them, the Thailand Chinese were able, not only to survive, but to continue to dominate in commerce and trade? The first part of the

[14] See Coughlin, *Double Identity*, pp. 132–3.

answer must certainly be that the Chinese were much more efficient and skilful in business than was the average Thai, and they were furthermore more industrious. (The Government, however, hoped to encourage Thais to seek their livelihood in commerce and handicrafts by affording them special protection, and with some measure of success.) The restrictive measures taken against them had drawn the Chinese community closer together with increased reliance on their Chamber of Commerce, trade guilds, and district (dialect) associations. Added to this was another important reason for Chinese commercial survival, namely the fact that the larger Chinese business men, in order to protect their interests from economic controls and eventual nationalization, had formed alliances with Thai politicians and soldiers, appointing them directors of their companies at a handsome remuneration. These Thai, however, were usually no more than nominal directors, and were retained only so long as they were able to be useful to their Chinese friends. Thus at the higher levels the Chinese were able to effect 'co-operation' of a kind with the more influential Thais (often half-Chinese themselves), though at the lower levels there was a conflict of economic interests between native and foreigner.

It cannot be argued that the relations between the native and foreign communities in Thailand represented a healthy state of society. As one observer remarks, 'De-alienization policies, which some Thai governments have followed, involved the imposition of restrictions on the economic activities of the Chinese, and these often contradict the requirements of economic growth', and he concludes that 'Thailand cannot afford to forego the contribution of these aliens, particularly the resident Chinese, for a considerable time to come'.[15]

What meanwhile were the prospects for assimilation of ethnic Chinese into the Thai nation?

Since 1949 the quota for immigration from China had been reduced to a nominal figure so that the situation as it existed before is not reproduced. No longer was there a constant reinforcement of the unassimilated Chinese who were oriented to China. Thus the continuance of the large minority which looked to the ancestral homeland for guidance and inspiration depended on the success or otherwise of the Thai Government's policy to convert them to a Thai outlook. The policy of repression worked in two opposite directions—to consolidate the Chinese community for common protection and at the same time to drive many of its individual members to identify themselves with the Thai for the same motive. But the key to victory either of China or Thailand lay in education. The Thai Government had never relinquished its efforts to restrict the learning of Chinese and to encourage the learning of Thai. Skinner

---

[15]   Eliezer B. Ayal, 'Some Crucial Issues in Thailand's Economic Development', *Pacific Affairs*, xxxiv/2 (Summer 1961).

says that the policy strengthened the 'in-group' solidarity of first- and second-generation Chinese, but in the case of the third generation, they were encouraged to hasten the assimilation process in order to escape the odium attaching to those who were not yet entirely Thai. The only third-generation Chinese who still looked upon themselves as Chinese were those educated in Chinese schools.[16] In the meantime, so long as Thailand refused to recognize the People's China, the latter could station no consuls in Thailand, and could exercise only a remote influence in restraint of the assimilation of ethnic Chinese to Thais. In the meantime, however, the *modus vivendi* between the Thai Government and the Chinese minority served the interests of both parties.

[16] Skinner, *Chinese Society in Thailand*, p. 381.

PART IV

THE CHINESE IN VIETNAM
(NORTH AND SOUTH),
CAMBODIA, AND LAOS

20

DEMOGRAPHY

IN the first edition of this work the countries of this region were col-
lectively considered as 'Indochina'. At this time the whole region was
nominally under French control, but since then the several countries
inside it have gained their independence and 'Indochina' has ceased to
be a political description. Cochinchina, Annam, and Tongking have resumed their historical identity as Vietnam, though it is split into two
parts under hostile political systems roughly along the 17th parallel of
latitude by the Geneva agreement of 1954. (This, in fact, is the second
time that Vietnam has been arbitrarily partitioned in recent times, the
first being in 1945 when the 16th parallel was fixed as the boundary line
between the north and south regions to be surrendered respectively by
the Japanese to the Chinese forces and the Southeast Asia Command.)
But although there was in 1960 a political partition of Vietnam (into the
Democratic Republic of Vietnam to the north and the Republic of Viet-
Nam to the south), and Cambodia and Laos were now independent, and
while the distribution of the Chinese is here considered according to the
new political divisions, it is convenient to retain the historical account
which follows as relating to the whole region of ex-French dominion.

Under the French (c. 1937) over four-fifths of the Chinese of Cochinchina, Annam, and Tongking were resident in what today is South
Vietnam and the remainder in what today is North Vietnam, and in spite
of the 1954 influx from North to South, it does not appear that the proportions have since materially altered. But in estimating the numbers of
ethnic Chinese in Vietnam in 1960 the writer was confronted by the
same difficulties as in 1949 and the statistical information available was
even more sparse. In the circumstances, therefore, the best procedure

seemed to be to give the estimates for 1960 first and to leave the figures for the previous period as part of the historical narrative for 'Indochina' as a whole.

Dr Phan-Van-Thinh,[1] chargé d'affaires for the Republic of Viet-Nam, has supplied the writer with a firm estimate of the *present* (1962) number of Chinese in South Vietnam. He says, under the date of 19 September 1962:

> I have made enquiries about the matter with the authorities concerned in which you requested my services, relating to a reliable estimate of the number of *ethnic* Chinese now living in South Vietnam. I am not positive about the accuracy of my interpretation but I thought it somewhat convenient to assume that apart from the Chinese Nationals (holding Chinese nationality) the Chinese-born Vietnamese nationals (either holding this quality now for some time or having acquired it quite recently) might be regarded as ethnic Chinese as well, in a practical and temporary way of thinking. Given this, the present figure of *ethnic* Chinese is approximately 802,500 in South Vietnam.

The *Statistical Yearbook of Viet-Nam, No. 8, 1958–9* (1960, p. 43), gave the total population of South Vietnam as 13,789,300—8,908,400 in the Southern Division, 4,296,500 in the Lowlands of Central Vietnam, and 584,400 in the Highlands of Central Vietnam. Most of this population was in the country districts, but 2,331,600 were in the larger towns (1,823,000 in the Southern Division, 408,100 in the Lowlands, and 100,100 in the Highlands).

In a table of 'nationalities other than Vietnamese' (p. 44 of the same *Yearbook*) there was stated to be (1958–9) a total of 128,498 Chinese *nationals* (64,824 males and 63,674 females). 123,638 of these were in the Southern Division, 4,110 in the Lowlands, and only 750 in the Highlands. The Saigon-Cholon complex, it was clear, still accounted for the majority of Chinese, both 'ethnic' and 'national'. The deaths recorded by the registry office Saigon in 1958 were, 1,228 Chinese (nationals) in a total of 5,304, and in 1959, 1,069 in a total of 6,116. Of the 856 marriages registered by the same office in 1958, 5 were between Chinese and Chinese nationals (man and wife) and 9 between Chinese national husbands and Vietnamese wives, or vice versa.

Since the war, the immigration of aliens had been strictly controlled. In 1958 (p. 53) the entries of Chinese nationals totalled 1,384 (1,057 men, 321 women, and 6 children), 1,354 of the total into the Southern Division. The departures were 1,711 Chinese nationals (1,194 men, 480 women, and 37 children), 1,693 of those being from the Southern Division. The figures for 1959 (p. 54) were, arrivals 1,403 total (785 men, 401 women, and 217 children), and departures 1,718 (1,050 men,

[1] Author of a doctoral thesis, *Les Chinois au Vietnam* (unpubl., 1954). He has stated, in a letter to me: 'South Vietnam (Viêt-Nam) is divided into South Viêt-Nam (here called the Southern Division to save confusion), the Lowlands of Central Viêt-Nam and the Highlands of Central Viêt-Nam'.

422 women, and 246 children). It will be seen that the departures exceeded the arrivals by about 300—a great contrast to the pre-war migration flow. (See table, p. 178 below.)

Apart from the above official figures, all that we have to guide us in estimating the number of Chinese in North and South Vietnam in 1962 are a few odd (and often conflicting) calculations. For example: 'In 1951, Saigon-Cholon had a population of 1,603,831 which represented an increase of nearly one million in a space of ten years . . . in 1951 the Chinese community in Saigon-Cholon numbered 583,000'.[2]

Again, the Saigon correspondent of *The Times*, in a report published in that newspaper on 2 October 1956, spoke of 'the 800,000 strong Chinese minority' in South Vietnam; but a United Nations commission stated in 1959 that 'it is currently estimated that there are 600,000 Chinese in South Vietnam'.[3]

In making our estimates we had to bear in mind the fact that after the Geneva agreement there was a great exodus of some 800,000 refugees from the north to the south, including some thousands of Chinese, and also (more importantly) that the Diem Government intensified the drive for compulsorily assimilating the Chinese into the Vietnamese community by compulsory naturalization at birth and other measures. On account of this drive we should be prepared to find that the proportion of Chinese nationals to total ethnic Chinese was much less than in 1937.

But, even assuming that our estimates on average annual increase basis are correct, this estimate takes no account of the displacements caused by the civil war, or of any large-scale illicit immigration (which is credible in the light of the million increase in the population of Saigon-Cholon between 1941–51, above cited, and of the 'constant stream of Chinese immigrants into Viet-Nam' mentioned by the UN/ILO/FAO report).

Looking for a check in recent independent estimates we do not find much to assist us. There is a certain agreement as to the *order* of magnitude of the Chinese community in South Vietnam, but very little as to that of the corresponding communities in North Vietnam, Cambodia, and Laos (as the footnote below indicates).[4]

---

[2] *Annuaire des États Associés, 1953*, cited by D. Lancaster, *The Emancipation of French Indo-China* (1961), p. 250.

[3] UN/ILO/FAO, *Technical Assistance Programme Toward the Economic Development of the Republic of Viet-Nam* (1959).

[4] Estimates of the number of Chinese in the successor States to French Indochina include:
South Vietnam, 700,000 (*Statesman's Year-Book, 1956*); 126,000 Chinese (not including those who have adopted Vietnamese citizenship) (do. *1961*); 600,000 (UN/ILO/FAO *Technical Assistance Programme*, 1959); 800,000 ('A Guide to Overseas Chinese', *The Times*, 8 May 1956).
North Vietnam, 60,000 (*Statesman's Year-Book, 1956*); 30,000 (do. *1961*); 100,000 ('A Guide to Overseas Chinese', *The Times*, 8 May 1956).
Cambodia, 250,000 (*Statesman's Year-Book, 1956*); 250,000 (do. *1961*); 180,000 ('A Guide to Overseas Chinese', *The Times*, 8 May 1956); 300,000, *The Hindu*, 31 Oct. 1961.
Laos, 12,000 (*Statesman's Year-Book, 1956*); 40,000 (do. *1961*); 15,000 ('A Guide to Overseas Chinese', *The Times*, 8 May 1956).

In the light of the above, I have thought it safe to adopt 800,000 as an estimate of the number of Chinese in South Vietnam in 1960.

Cambodia

No proper census of population had ever been taken in Cambodia.[5] Estimates of total population for 1955 varied from approximately 4,800,000 (U.S. Department of Commerce) to 5,125,000 (Canadian Department of Mines and Technical Surveys, based on a sharp increase since 1946 of 2·6 per cent per annum). The official Cambodian estimate was 4,740,000 for 1948.[6] The *Statesman's Year-Book, 1962*, however, gives an estimated total population of 5,040,000 for 1958 including 300,000 Chinese, 85,000 Chams, and 5,000 Europeans.

With such wide variations in population estimates we are driven back once more on a consideration of probabilities.

We know that in recent years Chinese and Vietnamese have migrated in substantial numbers to Cambodia and have intermarried with the Khmer to some extent. We know also that *legal* Vietnamese migration has been at a virtual standstill since 1940 and that since 1949 the Chinese have no longer come directly from China but by way of Vietnam until 1951, and from Hong Kong. Illegal entries have regularly occurred. Added to this we must take into consideration the exit of all races (including Chinese) from North Vietnam between 1952 and 1953 owing to the civil war.

If 218,000 represented the correct order of magnitude of the ethnic Chinese minority in Cambodia in 1950, then at a 3 per cent annual rate of natural increase the 1960 figure would be 293,000. But there is also the half-caste fringe to be taken into our calculation. D. J. Steinberg and others in *Cambodia* say that the 'number of *pure* [my italics] Chinese was conservatively estimated at 275,000 in 1955'. A 3 per cent rate of natural increase would make this 329,000 for 1960. In the light of this, the figure of 350,000 ethnic Chinese in Cambodia for 1960 is adopted for 1960 (allowing a margin for *métis*).

Laos

The UN *Demographic Yearbook, 1961* (p. 111), gives an estimated total population of Laos for mid-1960 of 1,805,000. The *Statesman's Year-Book, 1961*, gives an estimated total of Chinese in Laos at 40,000, but the issue of the *Year-Book* for 1962 drops the figure to 35,000. The *Bulletin Statistique de Laos, 1958*, gives an estimate of a total number of Asians in Laos of 40,000, including 30,000 Chinese—an increase from

---

[5] A census was reported to be in progress in mid-1963.
[6] D. J. Steinberg and others, *Cambodia: Its People, Its Society, Its Culture* (New Haven, 1959), p. 28.

Cambodia

Estimate of Population and Percentage Distribution of Ethnic Groups between Provinces, 1950*

Province	Khmer		Vietnamese		Chinese		Europeans		Total	
	No.	Per cent	No.	Per cent	No.	Per cent	No.	Per cent	Population	Per cent
Battambang	339,354	9·6	15,923	5·1	15,626	7·2	97	2·2	371,000	9·1
Kampot	222,617	6·3	8,659	2·7	21,673	9·9	19	0·4	252,968	6·2
Kandal	460,128	13·0	52,318	16·5	15,542	7·1	5	—	527,993	13·0
Kampong Cham	522,880	14·8	31,564	10·0	16,010	7·3	257	5·8	570,711	14·0
Kampong Chhnang	175,111	4·9	16,773	5·3	4,113	1·9	3	—	196,000	4·8
Kampong Speu	171,861	4·9	252	0·1	4,341	2·0	15	0·4	176,469	4·3
Kampong Thom	203,717	5·8	5,310	1·7	2,471	1·1	2	—	211,500	5·2
Kratie	72,585	2·1	4,403	1·4	2,431	1·1	20	0·5	79,439	2·0
Preyveng	307,668	8·7	45,958	14·5	7,403	3·4	—	—	361,029	8·9
Pursat	115,253	3·3	9,649	3·1	4,732	2·2	20	0·5	129,653	3·2
Siemreap	211,108	6·0	2,278	0·7	1,672	0·8	2	—	215,060	5·3
Stungtreng	42,000	1·2	2,636	0·8	2,360	1·1	4	—	47,000	1·1
Saairieng	193,983	5·5	8,993	2·9	3,954	1·8	120	2·7	207,050	5·1
Takeo	343,714	9·7	14,880	3·8	5,601	2·6	100	2·4	364,295	8·9
City of Pnompenh	150,000	4·2	100,000	31·4	110,000	50·5	3,800	85·1	363,800	8·9
Total	3,531,979	100·0	319,596	100·0	217,929	100·0	4,464	100·0	4,073,967	100·0

* Abridged from Table 1, p. 291, of Steinberg and others, *Cambodia* (1959). Adapted from working papers prepared under contract with Human Relations Area Files.

the 10,000 reported in 1953. This figure is accepted by Frank M. Le Bar and Adrienne Suddard in *Laos; its People, Society and Culture* (1960, p. 33).

North Vietnam

We have now come to the region which presents the greatest difficulties of all. Reliable information regarding the Chinese in North Vietnam was in 1963 virtually unobtainable. In the Census of 1960 racial groupings are ignored. The reason for this reticence was no doubt political. The theory was that with the introduction of Communism the Chinese, who had been middlemen, money-lenders, &c, under the old entrepreneurial system, were now being deprived of this function and merged into the general community. By the end of 1960 the bulk of former private enterprise and commerce had been transformed into joint-stock companies run for the State by its former owners. The public sector owned nine-tenths of all industry and commerce and four-fifths of all transport. Approximately three-quarters of all petty traders and artisans had been organized in state-controlled co-operatives. From these facts alone it could be gathered that the position of the Chinese as middlemen in North Vietnam had been radically transformed under the new regime.[7] *The Statesman's Year-Book, 1962*, states (p. 1587): 'There were also about 30,000 Chinese, chiefly in Hanoi and Haiphong' (55,000 is the figure adopted in the table, p. 3).

One of the few pieces of information released by the Hanoi Government about the Chinese in North Vietnam is that there is still a sizeable community of Chinese farmers in the district of Tay Ninh (Moncay). This is apparently the settlement of Hakkas engaged in rice-growing and fishing which is referred to later on in this chapter under the heading of 'Occupations'.

In this situation, the writer appealed to Mr P. J. Honey, Lecturer in Vietnamese at the School of Oriental and African Studies at London University, who replied:

... Basing myself upon such references to Chinese residents which have appeared in the press over the last three years or so, I estimate the resident Chinese population of North Vietnam as between 50,000 and 60,000 and probably closer to the latter figure. I have come across one press reference to 20,000 Chinese living in Hanoi alone, and I think this can be accepted as accurate.

In addition to the resident Chinese, there were the visiting Chinese technicians. On 15 May 1963, in a speech given during the visit of Liu Shao-ch'i, Ho Chi Minh referred to the 'more than 5,000 Chinese experts in Vietnam . . . helping to build up scores of enterprises'.

---

[7] See William Kaye, 'A Bowl of Rice Divided: the Economy of North Vietnam', *China Q.*, Jan.–Mar. 1962.

The writer has adopted 55,000 as the number of Chinese in North Vietnam for 1960.

Having given the population figures for 1960, I will now go back to those for 1937 since they still have historical significance and, moreover, in some respects give the most recent 'break-down' available.

Number of Chinese in each of the Countries of French Indochina and their percentages to the Total Population in 1937[8]

Country	Total population	Density of total population per square km.	Number of Chinese	Percentage of Chinese to total
Cochinchina	4,616,000	71	171,000	3·7
Cambodia	3,046,000	17	106,000	3·48
Tongking	8,700,000	75	35,000	0·4
Annam	5,656,000	38	11,000	0·19
Laos	1,012,000	4	3,000	0·3
Total	23,030,000	31	326,000	1·42

Population pressure developed in the northern plains at an early date. Not only had the entire area there been under cultivation for a long time, but also the people, especially the Tongkingese, had had a gradual admixture of Chinese blood 'and had acquired considerable skill, if not real mastery, of trade and industry'.[9] These facts limited the opportunities for new immigrants such as the Chinese. The Chinese were also restricted in scope by the fact that the over-population of the Tongking and Annam deltas had meant that there was only a small agricultural surplus for export, and consequent limitation of the natives' buying power had restricted foreign trade, one of the greatest interests of the Chinese. Moreover, Europeans had appropriated most of the control of modern industry, especially mining. In southern Indochina colonization was quite recent and was still going on in the middle of the twentieth century. Here the Chinese managed to establish themselves in Cochinchina by exploiting the Annamite-Cambodian conflict, and they had not to meet the same competition as they had in Annam and Tongking from the less numerous and less industrious native peoples. The coming of the French with their improved techniques, such as dredging, added to the opportunities of the Chinese by extending the cultivation of rice in central and western Cochinchina, in the sale of which the Chinese obtained the leading position.[10]

[8] Charles Robequain, *The Economic Development of French Indo-China* (Oxford, 1944), p. 34; *Statesman's Year-Book, 1948*, p. 948.　　　　[9] Robequain, p. 35.
[10] Ibid.

Let us now look rather more closely into the distribution of Chinese in 1936, province by province.[11]

Cochinchina (171,000)

Among the five provinces of the Union of Indochina, Cochinchina, with the smallest area, received more Chinese immigrants proportionately than the others, and accounted for more than half the Chinese total for the whole of Indochina. Between the Gulf of Siam and the China Sea, Cochinchina occupied the best situation in the line of international maritime communications and this favoured the reception of the Chinese who came almost entirely from the southern provinces of China, namely Kwangtung and Fukien. The economic conditions here —with rich alluvial rice cultivation, convenient river communications, and a much more developed domestic and foreign commerce—were also more favourable for the Chinese, who were mostly merchants.

Cochinchina was colonized from the seventeenth century onwards by the Annamites, who form the mass of the population today; but at almost the same time the Chinese flowed in, and to them the Annamites were prepared to relinquish trade since they were so much more experienced in it than they.

Cambodia (106,000)

Fourth in population among the provinces of the Union, Cambodia had about one-third of the total number of Chinese. The situation of Cambodia on the Gulf of Siam, near to Cochinchina, explained the important size of the Chinese community, and here again the easy communications and the small aptitude of the natives for commerce have favoured the immigrants, opening to them an opportunity in the highly-developed trade in rice and pepper. A number of Chinese in Cambodia also lived by the actual cultivation of pepper.

Tongking (35,000)

Even though Tongking borders on south China and the climate consequently resembles that of China and the other provinces of the Union, and although communication between the two countries by the sea routes is easy, the Chinese in this area are weak in numbers as compared with Cochinchina and Cambodia. Only one-eleventh of the total was to be found here. To the reasons for the sparseness of the Chinese population indicated above must be added a number of others—(a) the countries bordering on Tongking were inhabited by little-evolved tribes (Meo, Yao, Lolo) and they supplied therefore few Chinese immigrants to Tongking;

[11] Wang Wen-yuan, *Les Relations entre l'Indochine française et la Chine* (Paris, 1937), p. 25 ff. is here followed.

moreover these half-civilized peoples had been pushed back towards Upper Tongking by Chinese who occupied the conquered territory and had no reason to emigrate; (*b*) the foreign commerce of Tongking was less important than that of other provinces of Indochina; (*c*) in Tongking the retail trade was more in native hands than it was in Cochinchina; (*d*) owing to the frequency of typhoons off the coast it was less accessible than Cochinchina; and finally, (*e*) the over-population of the delta of the Song-Ko (namely, 430 inhabitants to the square kilometre, excluding the big towns) deprived the Chinese of room for settlement.

Annam (11,000)

From the situation of Annam on the borders of the China Sea, its history, its civilization, and its social customs for a long time derived from China, with which it has lived in close association, one would have imagined that the number of Chinese immigrants in the country would be considerable, whereas it was relatively small. Indeed, it was less important than in Tongking, Cambodia, or Cochinchina. The Annamite chain of mountains stretches from north to south; interior communications are difficult and commerce in consequence is much restricted. Besides, the rice which is cultivated for the most part in the coastal plains, far from producing an important export trade for a middleman, is not enough to support the population, maize being grown to help make up the deficiency. To these considerations Annam owed its small population of Chinese.

Laos (3,000)

Laos had the greatest area of the provinces of the Union, but the smallest population of Chinese. The reasons for this were a very broken surface, lack of seaboard, the inconvenience of internal communications, and lastly, only small commerce was practicable. Laos was a country backward in economic evolution. Hence the Chinese were few.

The following figures for 1921 and 1931 will be useful for comparison:

Number of Chinese in each of the Countries of Indochina

Country	1921	1931	Increase
Cochinchina	156,000	205,000	49,000
Cambodia	91,000	148,000	57,000
Tongking	32,000	52,000	20,000
Annam	7,000	10,000	3,000
Laos	7,000	3,000	− 4,000
Total	293,000	418,000	125,000

Places of Origin in China of Immigrants into Indochina

From 1891 for Cambodia, and from 1906 for Cochinchina, the French Government, in order to facilitate its administration, divided the immigrants from China into five groups according to their place of origin or their dialect.[12]

1. Canton group. This group comprised the Chinese originating from the northwest of Kwangtung province, and above all from the delta of the West river. It was principally composed of the commercial element; many among them, however, were equally workmen, artisans, or boatmen.

2. Fukien (Hokkien) group. This comprised the natives of the southern districts, and above all those of the Amoy region. Although less numerous than the Canton group, they had also a great commercial influence.

3. Hainan (Hailam) group. The majority of these came from one of the centres of the west district of Wenching in the island of Hainan. They embarked from Hoihow to become pepper planters and domestic servants in Indochina.

4. Teochiu group. This district in Kwangtung province (called Trieu-chau in Sino-Annamite) was one of the cradles of Chinese immigrants. These embarked at the port of Swatow, and were notably agriculturists, boatmen, and coolies. They were generally called Hoklos (in Chinese this means 'men of Fukien').

5. Hakka (Kheh) group. The Hakkas, probably in the fourteenth century,[13] emigrated from north China to the northeast of Kwangtung and particularly to the sub-prefecture of Mei-Hsien. They were mostly cultivators and workmen, though some were artisans and even business men (above all tea merchants). They, too, came via Swatow.[14]

A large proportion of the Chinese were urban and their numbers in the larger cities in 1931 are given below:[15]

City	Total population	Chinese
Cholon	134,000	66,000
Saigon	122,000	34,000
Phnom Penh	96,000	29,000
Haiphong	124,000	19,000
Hanoi	128,000	5,000
Namdinh	?	1,500
Tourane	27,000	600

[12] Wang Wen-yuan, *L'Indochine française et la Chine*, p. 12 ff.
[13] Mr Wang Wen-yuan says 'in the fourth century B.C.'
[14] Mr Wang Wen-yuan does not give the numbers for the several groups and they do not appear to be available from other sources.
[15] Wang Wen-yuan, p. 35. An expert, commenting on these figures, says: 'It seems to me that Cholon is closer to ninety per cent Chinese. Even in 1931 this was probably the

Owing to the world trade depression the number of Chinese in Indochina declined between 1931 and 1936. By 1934 the number of Chinese in Saigon and Cholon had dropped to 28,000 and 49,000 respectively. There was, as we shall see, an excess of departures over arrivals for several years, but by 1936 there was once more a net gain.

The Chinese were very unevenly distributed throughout the country and were much more numerous in the two southern provinces of Cochinchina and Cambodia than anywhere else. Eighty-five per cent of the total were to be found here. In the six cities, Cholon, Saigon, Phnom Penh, Hanoi, Haiphong, and Namdinh, there were 126,000 Chinese (38 per cent of the immigrant Chinese), which figure was about 29,000 less than in 1931 (see table above). In 1936, 106,000 were in the three southern settlements, but only 20,000 were in the Tongking delta.

Estimates for 1940 showed a total of 380,000 Chinese in Cochinchina, 127,000 of these being in the Cholon area. In 1939 there were reported to be only 15,000 Chinese in Annam.

Immigration and Sex Ratio

In 1889, 57,000 immigrant Chinese were counted in Cochinchina, of whom nearly 16,000 were in Cholon and district, 7,000 in Saigon, 5,000 in Soctrang, 4,000 in Travinh, and approaching 3,000 in Giadinh, Cantho, Baclieu, and Mytho, and in the neighbourhood of 1,500 in both Sadec and Chaudoc.[16] By 1906 the total Chinese population in Indochina had reached 120,000,[17] an increase of 63,000 in the intervening seventeen years. The mean annual immigration was, from the official figures, 3,720. Between 1906 and 1921 there was a further increase of Chinese immigrants in Cochinchina to a total of 156,000.

It will be remarked that the increase of Chinese in Indochina was greater in the first period than in the second. This was due to the fact that the French colonization of the country attracted a large number of Chinese merchants who benefited from their exemption from taxation. But after 1906 a decree severely restricted the immigration of Chinese into the country, and French policy was subsequently opposed to their

case.' Cholon, when I visited it in 1935, certainly appeared to be virtually a Chinese city, but the above figures from Wang Wen-yuan are confirmed by Robequain, *French Indo-China*, pp. 34–35 (V.P.).

The following figures of total population were supplied to me by M. Roger Lévy:

	Saigon		Cholon	
	Chinese	*Total*	*Chinese*	*Total*
1932	32,000	104,506	66,000	122,818
1934	28,031	114,945	49,355	106,476

[16] *Annuaire de l'Indochine française . . . 1889*, p. 530 (cited by Wang Wen-yuan, *L'Indochine . . . et la Chine*, p. 16).

[17] Lucien Haudebert, *L'Indochine française* (1909), p. 66 (cited ibid. p. 17).

C.S.E.A.—G

entry. The First World War, moreover, slowed up the progress of French colonization and threw the whole system of world commerce out of gear. In the period 1906–21 the Chinese entering the country consisted almost entirely of persons who came to join their friends or families, and no large element without connexions was entering in the hope of bettering their lot.

From 1921 to 1931 there was a great increase in the Chinese population of the Union, from 293,000 (156,000 in Cochinchina and 91,000 in Cambodia) to 418,000. The main reasons for this were the expansion of trade, the construction of railways and roads, and the opening up of land hitherto uncultivated, all resulting in much more rapid progress than before. This time it was Cambodia that received the largest contingent of Chinese immigrants, making an increase of 57,000 (from 91,000 to 148,000), though Cochinchina with an increase of 49,000 (from 156,000 to 205,000) was not far behind. Tongking received an accession of 20,000 and Annam of 3,000. In Laos alone was there a decrease in numbers of the immigrant Chinese, for here the numbers fell from 7,000 to 3,000.

The Decrease in Chinese Immigration after 1931. In the peak years of Chinese migration between China and Indochina there was a tremendous passing to and fro. From January 1923 to December 1927, 381,000 Chinese entered and left Indochina (a mean of 76,000 annually); in the four years 1928–31 the total reached almost 495,000 (at an annual mean in precise figures of 123,750). Thereafter there was a decrease in both arrivals and departures. In 1927 there was a net gain of Chinese immigrants of 31,000; in both 1928 and 1929 of 30,000; in 1930 of 18,000: but in 1931, 1932, and 1933 these gains became losses of 8,000, 16,000, and 8,000 respectively. The world economic crisis had set in and trade depression was making itself felt among the Chinese in the Indochinese Union.[18]

Recovery in Chinese Immigration after 1933. After the trade depression the number of Chinese passing to and fro between China and Indochina again increased with once more a net excess of arrivals over departures, as shown by the following figures for 1936:

Migration of Chinese to and from China in 1936[19]

Country	Entries				Departures			
	Males	Females	Children	Total	Males	Females	Children	Total
Annam	682	176	203	1,061	619	213	228	1,060
Cochinchina	14,237	11,822	9,668	35,727	8,233	7,129	5,206	20,568
Tongking	11,108	2,696	2,833	16,637	11,033	2,610	2,300	15,943
Total Indochina	26,027	14,694	12,704	53,425	19,885	9,952	7,734	37,571

[18] Abstracted from Wang Wen-yuan, *L'Indochine . . . et la Chine*, table on p. 21 (source: *Annuaire statistique de l'Indo-Chine*, ii, p. 67; iii, p. 57; v, p. 54).

[19] *Annuaire statistique de l'Indo-Chine, 1936–37* (1938), vii. 33.

That is to say, there was a net gain of Chinese of 15,854 in the year, but even then the gross figures were much less than they had been for the peak years.

Sex Ratio. In 1921, of the 285,710 Chinese in Indochina (excepting Annam), 184,320, or 65 per cent, were males, and 101,390, or 35 per cent, were females. In 1929, the peak year of Chinese immigration into the country, the proportion of women to men was its smallest, namely 33 per cent, whereas, in the years 1923 and 1932, when the immigration was at its lowest, the proportion was up to 63 per cent. All this goes to prove that the object of the great majority of the Chinese was not to establish themselves permanently in Indochina but to return to their own country when they had achieved a competence. The adverse sex ratios, however, meant a considerable amount of intermarriage with the Annamite or Cambodian women, a feature, *mutatis mutandis*, common to all countries in Southeast Asia except Malaya.

Sino-Indochinese or Métis

The offspring of Chinese-Annamite marriages were known as *Minh-huong*, but those of Chinese-Cambodian marriages had no distinctive name. When mixed with Chinese the Muongs and the Thōs of northern Tongking were known as *Hung-dans*, *Māns*, and *Miens*.[20]

Since the Chinese male immigrants arrived in Indochina unmarried, they usually took wives among the native population, being influenced, no doubt, not only by the natural desire for a mate but also by the advantage such an alliance would have in trading with the people of the country. Such marriages were very well looked upon by the Annamites and Cambodians, for the Chinese man had the reputation of being sober, industrious, and economical, and he was also esteemed in native circles as being of incontestably superior intelligence.

It was obviously in Cambodia and Cochinchina that the number of *métis* would be greatest, for it was in these countries that the immigration of the Chinese was most intense. The Minh-huong were strongest in Cochinchina. In 1921 about 64,500 were enumerated, and in 1931, 73,000. (The largest numbers were to be found in six provinces— Soctrang, 13,000, Baclieu, 11,000, Travinh, 8,500, Cantho, 4,000, Rachgia, 4,000, and Hatien, 3,000. In the first three and the fifth of these provinces the number of *métis* was greater than that of the pure Chinese.)

As for Sino-Cambodians, most of these were to be found (as would be expected) in Cambodia. In 1921, 68,430 were counted. Half of these were in the two provinces of Kampong-Cham (19,000) and Kamdal (18,000), and two-fifths in the following—Takeo (7,500), Preyveng (7,000), Kampong-Thom (7,000), and Battambang (6,000). Only a tenth

---

[20] *Encyclopaedia Britannica*, 11th ed. (1910), xiv. 491.

were located in the provinces Kampot, Pursat, Soairieng, Stungtreng, and Kratie.

The total of these two kinds of half-castes (figures for 1921 for Sino-Cambodians and of 1931 for Minh-huong) came to 141,430; that is to say, six *métis* as against nineteen pure Chinese per thousand inhabitants.[21]

Occupations

Until at least the partition of 1954, trade and kindred occupations absorbed the majority of Chinese of the region. The Chinese was seldom a rice grower here, though a single group, the Hakkas, were an exception to this rule. A tribe apart from the other Chinese, they crossed the land frontier, pushed back the Annamites and Thai, and settled in the alluvial plains and low hills bordering China between Moncay and Tienyen. They lived in little villages scattered all over the country and subsisted on carefully irrigated farms and on fishing.[22] The Chinese had also specialized in certain highly-skilled cultivation, for example, the market gardens adjoining large cities, especially in the south. They retained, too, the almost complete monopoly of pepper growing, which was already in their hands when the French came, and, with the exception of one French pepper company, all the pepper farms near Tien and Kampot on the Gulf of Siam were owned by Chinese. Here the Chinese were Hailams (Hainanese). A Chinese labourer was rarely found on European plantations in Indochina, Annamite labourers from the delta of the north being preferred as being cheaper and more manageable.

Chinese labour was used in the construction of the Yunnan railway, but was subsequently found less necessary as native labourers were trained. The Chinese were also to some extent employed as skilled workers in modern industry (e.g. as timbermen, carpenters, blacksmiths, mechanics, &c). The law did not permit them to participate in mining as it did in Malaya. They operated most of the saw-mills in Indochina, however, and owned sugar refineries on the plains of Cochinchina and one at Tayninh. Chinese owned most of the rice-mills in Indochina, as they did in Siam. In urban centres, where it was permitted to be such, they were large landowners.[23]

It was in trade that the Chinese excelled. They had developed a comprehensive system of rice purchasing which covered the whole of Cochin-

---

[21] Wang Wen-yuan adds together figures separated by a decade. All I can do is to point out the fact (V. P.).

[22] Robequain, *French Indo-China*, p. 36. The author warns that these Chinese in Tongking should not be confused with those who sail every year from the ports of south China to fish in the waters of the Gulf as far south as Vinh.

[23] It was estimated that in 1936 the Chinese owned 62,000 hectares of land (155,000 acres), 46,000 of which (114,000 acres) were in Cochinchina (T. E. Ennis, *French Policy and Developments in Indochina* (Chicago, 1936), p. 125). Robequain (*French Indo-China*, p. 37) says that one of the richest Chinese in Indochina was reputed to own half the land in Saigon.

china and Cambodia. They were also prominent in the export trade, such as in fish and hides. By and large, the Chinese were confined to the plains, and were *par excellence* the middlemen of the country. They were not to be found, as was once hoped, clearing the uncultivated lands in the back country.

21

THE CHINESE IN INDOCHINA FROM
EARLY TIMES

AN outline account of Chinese contacts with Indochina in the earliest times has already been given in Chapter 2 and the story is here resumed and carried down to the twentieth century.

Several Emperors of the Western Han dynasty deported criminals to the territory of Giaochi, and in the following centuries Indochina became a common place of refuge for the fugitive supporters of fallen dynasties. In A.D. 877 the descent of the pirates under Hoang-chao upon the capital of Kwangtung province forced a large number of Chinese to seek safety in these southern regions, in the train of 100,000 Arabs and Persians who were also fleeing from the peril of the invasion.[1]

Indochina forms a geographical barrier between India and China, its lands offering no natural or easy road between the two. Nevertheless, it was to be the meeting-place of the two civilizations. Early in the Christian era priests, merchants, and adventurers came over from India, apparently from Bengal and the Coromandel coast, and sowed the seed of the Hindu culture in southeast Indochina. Meanwhile, in the Indochinese peninsula, favoured by the north-south direction of the river valleys, the Chinese pressed down in a spasmodic but unending emigration. With them they brought the essential elements of their own culture, and, although in the tenth century the Annamites threw off the Chinese political dominion, the impress of the Middle Flowery Kingdom on the people of Annam was indelible.

Until about the year 1000 Tongking and the major part of Annam were considered to be part of 'colonial' China.[2] Many centuries later, in 1680, Chinese officers and several thousand men, supporters of the overthrown Ming dynasty, arrived in Indochina and settled in the Mytho

---

[1] Wong Shion-fi, *General History of Southeast Asia* (in Chinese) (Shanghai, 1920). Cited by Wang Wen-yuan, *L'Indochine . . . et la Chine*, p. 11. These round numbers must be treated with reserve, being rhetorical rather than statistical.

[2] H. F. MacNair, *The Chinese Abroad* (1924), p. 49, says that these territories were under the direct rule of China from 36 B.C. to A.D. 968 and that Tongking was regarded by China as a vassal State until 1884.

area of Cochinchina. Later, in the eighteenth century, other important groups arrived and settled in the Hatien region of that country. Since that time there has been a steady flow of newcomers, mainly men.[3] Chinese infiltration into the sparsely populated lands of Indochina was by sea as well as by land, but the French occupation of the country promoted the entry of Chinese merchants and artisans by the sea routes.

A second period of Chinese immigration into Indochina is marked by the arrival of the partisans of the Sung dynasty, when the latter were overwhelmed by the Mongol invasion of the thirteenth century. These partisans were composed of soldiers and civilians who spread out into the regions of Giaochi (in Tongking), Tenchen (in south Annam), and in Tchenla (in Cambodia).[4] A third period of large-scale immigration into Indochina was dictated by a similar set of circumstances when, in 1680, about 3,000 Chinese owing allegiance to the Ming dynasty, which had now been replaced by the Ch'ing (Manchu) dynasty, landed at Tourane and proceeded to the Court of Hué to ask for a grant of land which they might cultivate in return for the payment of taxes in force. The Court granted this request and established them in the provinces of Lower Cochinchina on the plain of Donnai, which had recently been acquired, namely, at Bienhoa and Mytho.[5]

Finally it should be recorded that in 1715 a Chinese named Mac Cuu, originating from Lei-Tchou (Lichow), took possession by surprise of Hatien belonging to Cambodia, and, as was then the custom, paid homage for this province to the Court of Hué, on the express condition of being nominated chief mandarin of this country. In consequence of this, a thousand or so of his partisans established themselves in Cambodia.[6]

At the outset the children of Chinese and Annamite mixed marriages were considered as Chinese, but from 1829 onwards they were treated as Annamites and grouped in separate communities in each province. They were given the same protection rights as the Annamites and were allowed to hold office in the kingdom, a right never conferred on their forebears.[7]

Commercial Relations

Commercial relations between China and Indochina go back to remote antiquity. As early as 183 B.C. the Empress of China published an edict forbidding the Chinese people to export iron or metal goods to Nam-Viet and limiting the export of horses, cattle, and sheep to the males of the species. In the T'ang dynasty (618–905) the maritime commerce of

---

[3] Olov R. T. Janse, *The Peoples of French Indo-China* (Washington, 1944), p. 18.
[4] Wong Shion-fi, *Gen. Hist. of Southeast Asia*, p. 43 (cited by Wang Wen-yuan, p. 11).
[5] Charles B. Maybon, *Histoire moderne du pays d'Annam, 1592–1820* (Paris, 1920), p. 119.
[6] Ibid. p. 122 (Wang Wen-yuan, p. 11).
[7] *Labour Conditions in Indo-China*, p. 244.

southern China became the most important. In the Sung dynasty (960–1226) Chao Ju-kua, the author of *Chou-Fen-Chi* (*History of the Vassals of China*), speaks admiringly of the importance of Chinese trade at Jen-Tchen, Pin-Tung-Lung (in the south of the present Annam), and at Tchen-La in Cambodia.

In the second half of the sixteenth century, at the time when European merchants arrived in Indochina, the King of Cochinchina (now in South Veitnam) gave permission to the Chinese to choose a convenient site in their territory for building a town where they could hold their fair. This town was called Faifo and was in the centre of present South Vietnam. It was divided into two separate quarters—one Chinese and the other Japanese—each ruled by a governor. The opening of the period of trade in this town coincided approximately with the new year. The natives adopted the practice of bringing there the produce of the country—raw and processed silk, ebony wood, eagle wood (much employed as an aromatic in the Far East), sugar, musk, cinnamon, pepper, and rice. The Chinese vessels arrived loaded with porcelain, paper, tea, silver bars, arms, sulphur, saltpetre, lead, and lead oxide. When the trading transactions, which lasted about seven months, were over, the foreign merchants left with their return cargoes.

In the seventeenth and eighteenth centuries Faifo remained the commercial centre of Indochina. There were in 1768 nearly 6,000 Chinese there who were the most important merchants. The merchandise imported from China consisted of brass, tea, porcelain, raw silk, drugs and medicines of all sorts, paper, paintings, cloth, &c. It came from Amoy and Ningpo and sometimes from Japan.[8]

For long the Chinese in Indochina were content with the foreign imports which their compatriots brought. They, for their part, purchased for export to China gold, ivory, areca nuts, woods for dyeing, gamboge, pepper, salt fish, birds' nests, rhinoceros horns, and all other Indochinese products cited above. The rivalry of Chinese and European merchants then made itself felt in the Indochinese market, but it could not arrest the progress of the Indochinese commerce. Towards the end of the nineteenth century, when France became established in Indochina, the principal Indochinese commercial centre began to grow up in Saigon-Cholon. France from that time strove to develop the production and the commerce of her colonies, and in 1883 demanded that China should open the towns of Yunnan (Montseu, Tsemao, and Lungchau) to commerce. She undertook the improvement of interior and exterior communications, the exploitation of mines, and the equipment of ports.[9] The city of

---

[8] Maybon, *Hist. . . . du pays d'Annam*, p. 51 ff.; Wang Wen-yuan, *L'Indochine . . . et la Chine*, p. 115.

[9] According to Chinese (foreign-directed) customs statistics, the Sino-Indochinese commerce reached 1,469,000 taels in 1893, 6,670,000 in 1913. In 1868, before the French occupation, the commerce between Annam and the Chinese empire was valued at only 383,000

Cholon, five kilometres from Saigon on the Chinese Arroyo, was founded about 1778 by a group of Chinese immigrants who, having been established at Bienhoa to the northeast of Saigon, by order of the Court of Hué moved to Cholon in order to escape the ravages caused by the revolt of the Tay-Son. Cholon began as a group of villages. To their new residence the Chinese gave the name of Taignon or Tingan. A map of the Saigon citadel of 1795, by M. le Brun, called this agglomeration the Chinese Bazaar. But, in spite of the foresight of the Court of Hué, the Chinese who had fled to Cholon were overtaken by the rebels and massacred. In 1782 the Tay-Son killed 10,000–11,000 Chinese in this town and in Saigon, burning and looting the Chinese shops.[10] Taignon, however, recovered its impulse under the Emperor Gia Long (1775–1820) who, having suppressed the revolt of the Tay-Son in Cochinchina, lived in Saigon from 1789 to 1793.[11]

The Annamite name of Cholon, which signifies 'great market', was given to this town in the time of Le-Van-duyet, the Grand Eunuch of the palace of Gia Long, who was appointed Governor of Giadinh in 1801.

Chinese Communal Organization in pre-French Indochina

In both Annam and Cambodia the Chinese organized themselves into communities called *bangs*, according to their dialect or province of origin. Officers, called *bang truong*, corresponding to the Chinese captains in other Southeast Asian countries, were selected for them by the native authority, and these were responsible to the Government for the good behaviour of their fellows and for the payment of taxes. They enjoyed the same civil rights as Annamites and were exempted from military service and *corvée*. The laws of Annam, which were applied to them on an equality with the Annamites, being derived from Chinese sources, were congenial to their spirit. From time to time the Emperors of Annam, however, entertained doubts as to their bona fides and reminded them of their position as aliens by banishing individuals concerned in commercial fraud or clandestine trade in opium.[12]

A very favourable picture is given of the Chinese in Saigon by a British visitor in about 1822:

We were absolute strangers who had come to pass a few hours only in the town; yet in almost every street we were invited by the more wealthy Chinese to enter their houses and partake of refreshments. They could not have known beforehand that we were to visit the place, yet some of the entertainments laid out for us were in a style

taels; in 1913 the exports were valued at 4,780,000 taels (13 times the 1868 figures) and the imports at 1,880,000 taels (45 times the 1868 figures) (Wang Wen-yuan citing Chao Zoobiang, *Étude sur le commerce extérieur de la Chine*; thesis for a doctorate of the University of Paris (1936), p. 143).

[10] J. Bouchot, 'Notes historiques sur Cholon', *Extrême Asie* (May 1948).
[11] Maybon, *Hist. . . . du pays d'Annam*, pp. 99–200 (Wang Wen-yuan, p. 59).
[12] Virginia Thompson, *French Indo-China* (London, 1937), p. 165.

of elegance and abundance that bespoke of affluence, as well as of the hospitality of our hosts. Amongst others, we were invited by three brothers who had been settled in the country for some time. They wore Cochin-Chinese dress, and in appearance differed little from the native inhabitants. Their manners were engaging, perfectly easy and polite; their house was both handsome and spacious, nor did anything appear wanting to render it a very superior mansion, even in the opinion of a European. They received us in a large, well-furnished ante-room; a table was soon covered with a profusion of fruit, the most delicate sweet-meats, and a variety of cakes and jellies. They insisted upon attending us at table themselves, nor could they be induced to seat themselves while we were present.[13]

The Chinese under the French Regime

Christian missionaries were the first Frenchmen to come to Indochina, the most famous of them being Father Alexandre de Rhodes, of the Society of Jesus, who arrived in Tongking in 1627. Traders arrived later. In the eighteenth century the French East India Company, wishing to extend its field of action in the Far East, sent representatives to Indochina to survey the country's resources and to devise plans for their development. But although these representatives duly submitted their report, no action was taken. Then, in 1787, Pigneau de Behaine, Apostolic Vicar of Indochina, secured the conclusion of the Treaty of Versailles between France and Annam, which provided that, in return for support given the prince against the rebels, France was to obtain the port of Tourane and the island of Poulo Condore off the Cochinchina coast. Owing to the French Revolution this came to nothing, and it was not until 1840 onwards, when the British were smashing open the doors of China, already ajar, that the attention of the French Government was again drawn to Indochina. The persecution of white missionaries by the Annamite Emperors was the occasion of intervention by France and Spain.

After a fruitless attack on Hué, the Franco-Spanish expedition turned south and captured Saigon in February 1859. By the treaty of 5 June 1862, the Emperor Tu Duc ceded the three eastern provinces of Cochinchina, Bienhoa, Giadinh, and Mytho, and the island of Poulo Condore to France. Vinhlong, Chaudoc, and Hatien, in western Cochinchina, came under French tutelage in 1867. In the meantime, menaced by the competitive expansion of both Annam and Siam, Cambodia accepted French protection in 1863, but it was not until 1884 that an agreement was reached which defined the general principles of law and administration for governing the country.[14] There were said to be 56,000 Chinese in Cochinchina in 1886 out of a total population of 1,745,000.[15]

Having consolidated their position in Cochinchina, the French turned

[13] George Finlayson, *The Mission to Siam and Hué in the Years 1821-2* (London, 1826), p. 168. Finlayson mentions that the principal articles sold in the bazaars of Saigon were coarse china, Tongking crapes, silks, and satins, Chinese fans, and porcelain.
[14] Robequain, *French Indo-China*, p. 3 ff.
[15] Paul Bonnetin, *L'Extrême Orient* (Paris, 1887), p. 109.

C.S.E.A.— G 2

their eyes towards the northern plain of Tongking. It was chiefly the desire to open a good road to China that prompted them to extend their power in this direction, but the existence of mines of coal, zinc, tin, lead, &c, was also a strong inducement.[16] Lagrée's expedition of 1867–8 had shown that the route to Yunnan through the Mekong valley was not practicable, and the Red river valley seemed to offer the easiest gateway to the province. The French influence was rapidly expanded by individuals, but French official opinion lagged behind them. A treaty of 1874 acknowledged France's right of protectorate over all the Annamite countries, but its terms were ambiguous and in 1882 the Emperor Tu Duc, in alliance with China, began to make trouble for the French. This time the French responded with action backed by adequate military force and imposed the treaties of 1884 and 1885 which made definite the French control over Annam and Tongking.

Laos was added to the French sphere last, and by the gradual extension of French influence first from Tongking and Annam. Clashes ensued with Siam which claimed suzerainty over all countries where Thai dialects were spoken, and the French protectorate over Laos was not established until the Franco-Siamese treaty of October 1893, under which Siam renounced all claims to territory to the left of the Mekong. Further treaties and agreements finally established the western frontiers of French Indochina, the most important being the Franco-Siamese treaty of 1904, by which Siam renounced all the sovereignty it still retained over Laos and Bassac, and that part of the kingdom of Luangprabang located on the right bank of the Mekong, and a further treaty between the two countries in 1907, by which Siam ceded to France the Cambodian regions of Battambang, Siemreap, and Sisophon. The last-named regions were to be a source of dispute culminating in Siamese action after the fall of France in 1940, and ending with their return to Indochina in 1945.

By 1866 the Chinese centre of Cholon had already 500 tiled houses, two canals made by excavation, and five bridges under construction, including one of iron. The quay along the Arroyo Chinois was covered with warehouses and shipyards. In the centre of the town was placed a fountain of Chinese design, and the streets were lit by reflecting lamps fed with coconut oil. In 1870 the town was extended in size. By 1879 there were said to be 44,000 Chinese in all Cochinchina.[17] Cholon in 1889 had a population of nearly 16,000 Chinese and Saigon of over 7,000 in a total of 56,000 Chinese residents for the whole of Cochinchina.

[16] After the capture of Hanoi, the French came across some books in Chinese about these mines. Studies were made of these and other extensive material from which it appeared that the Court of Hué had received revenue from 123 mines, of which all but six were located in Tongking. At the time of the conquest the Chinese were still working the coastal mines (Thompson, French Indo-China, pp. 114–15).

[17] ILO, Labour Conditions in Indochina, no. 26 (Geneva, 1938), p. 245 (quoting Dubreuil).

Fear of Chinese machinations among the more docile Annamites, and of being overwhelmed in this region by their numbers, prompted the French to impose a heavy poll-tax on the Chinese resident in Indochina. The Chinese Government protested against an invidious distinction being placed upon its subjects and appealed to the treaty stipulations. The French responded by placing a tax on *all* Asiatics, and inasmuch as the Chinese alone travelled frequently or far, a Service de l'Immigration was established at Saigon to watch them, and, if possible, to control their immigration. The regulations for this were contained in decrees of 1874 and 1876.[18] A Chinese reaching Saigon by sea, unless a contract labourer, had to be registered and receive a card. If he came overland, he had to buy a pass from the administration and exchange this subsequently for a *permis de circulation*, good for one month. For breaking these regulations the penalty was expulsion from Indochina, and if the expelled Chinese was found returning he was sentenced to three years' imprisonment. Exception was made for women and children *who almost never immigrated and whose presence was much desired by the administration*.

Decrees regulating, taxing, and punishing (and, of course, always irritating) the Chinese in the colony followed thick and fast upon one another during a period of twenty years (says F. Wells Williams). The legislation was ever a matter of checks and hindrances, an artificial system which looked splendid in Paris but worked badly in Saigon. An example was the Government order in November 1880 that every Asiatic not a French citizen, unless he be a landowner or an indentured labourer, be required to provide himself with a workman's book containing his name, first names, birthplace, occupation, the names and domicile of his parents if belonging to the colony, his signature, photograph, and number, and the date of issue of the book, with sundry remarks if any room remained for them. For such a book the fee was 2.50 francs and replacement if it were lost cost 2 more francs. The population of this region was roughly estimated at 2 million souls, and if every adult male there got his book it was not strange (says Wells Williams) that the French *fonctionnaires*, though numerous, should complain of being overworked in tropical Asia! Moreover, these attempts at prevention and control were not in the least effective in hindering the influx of Chinese into the colony. By January 1885 the notion of this little book was allowed to drop so far as immigrant Chinese were concerned, but they were required to buy a personal identity card at the beginning of every year.

For purposes of taxation the Chinese were divided into three groups—first, indentured labourers of the first and second class; second, landlords paying between 60 and 200 piastres in taxes; third, all others—women and

---

[18] F. W. Williams, 'Chinese Immigration in Further Asia', *American Hist. R.*, v/3 (Apr. 1901).

those under fifteen and over sixty being exempted. To leave the colony every Asiatic was made to pay 2 francs for a permit.

In spite of the completeness of these arrangements the Chinese were not kept well in hand and the expected prosperity was still somewhat painfully awaited (Wells Williams continues). But the French would not give up their centralized system, their cards of identity, and their classification by category. Regulations at the end of the century (dating from a decree of 19 February 1890) were slightly less severe than of old, but they compelled the incoming Asiatic to go to the capital, register at the Bureau of Immigration, accept a place in one or other of the groups recognized by the Government, obtain a travelling certificate, have his *permis de séjour* renewed each year, and when he departed to receive a passport. The three groups covering all Chinese were now paying respectively 80, 60, and 7 piastres annually in taxes. Anyone found to be associated with a secret society not authorized by law was heavily punished by fine and imprisonment and then expelled.[19]

In Tongking the situation was complicated not only by the existence of a long conterminous Chinese frontier but also by a deep disgust of Frenchmen towards a country which had cost so much blood and treasure and yet had apparently proved of so little worth. Legislation applying to this region was of a rather haphazard sort. Immediately after the conquest the poll-tax already referred to was ordered (in 1885) to be levied on all Chinese alike. In December 1886, after a protest from Peking, the distinction was made less invidious by applying the tax to all Asiatics whether resident or immigrant.[20] The *carte de séjour* and regulation into categories were also adopted as administrative measures, but here six groups were constituted—those paying 300 francs and more in taxes, those paying 60–300, those owning land, licensed labourers, employees, &c, and lastly, the common workman. The yearly cost of the card was fixed at 300, 100, 25, and 10 francs respectively, according to category. But these terms merely had the effect of stopping the Chinese coming at all! In the 1880s so many restrictions were placed on trade in Haiphong that the Chinese left this prosperous region in order to avoid the excessive taxes.[21]

Here as elsewhere (remarks Wells Williams) the European found him-

[19] The system described by Wells Williams certainly does seem exceedingly cumbersome, but a system of landing permits (exchanged afterwards for certificates of admission) worked very well in Malaya.

[20] The writer has followed Wells Williams for this period without greatly questioning his conclusions, but it has been pointed out that the registration of all Asiatics does not on the face of it seem necessarily anti-Chinese, that there seems to be confusion between registration of population, revenue measures, and immigration controls, and that the poll-tax may have been solely a revenue device. Without more precise information the writer cannot give an opinion on Wells Williams's case; the important question seems, however, to be whether French policy was hostile to the Chinese or not. The answer undoubtedly is that they were rather grudgingly tolerated, and that their immigration was subject to strict control.

[21] Ennis, *French Policy*, p. 119.

self helpless without the assistance of Chinese in his plantations and mines, his boats and wagons, his ships and houses. The laws were again tinkered with, the categories extended and amended through a long series of changes, the result of which was to let down the barriers almost entirely and to allow the Chinese to enter on his own terms.

By applying for a permit from French consuls in the south China treaty ports, the Chinese could, by a decree of May 1890, travel and trade for two months in Tongking and Annam without any payment at all, while for those who chose to remain the categories were so reduced as to rest very lightly upon the artisan and trading classes.

At the end of the nineteenth century there was still a great wall of prejudice between the French colonials and the Chinese immigrants, but the latter carried on their trade and work, showing little concern: they were able to survive by their supreme adaptability. It is even said that during the first trying years of occupation, when the French had only very uncertain and irregular means of communication between Cochinchina and the world beyond, the Chinese of Saigon maintained and profited by a regular courier service direct to Canton, where they learned the latest market quotations and easily outdistanced all their European commercial rivals.

In Cochinchina the Emperor Minh Mang had introduced strict regulations governing the immigration of Chinese. Before being allowed to land, immigrants had to be accepted by the chief of a village or tribal organization and their names were then entered in a register. This system the French retained and extended. The *congrégations*, as the French called them (they should be distinguished from commercial syndicates of the same name), appear to have been the same in origin as the *bangs* mentioned earlier in this chapter and as the *huis* and *kongsis*[22] in other Southeast Asian countries; but here in Cochinchina they had a special position because the French, who found them useful instruments in imposing corporate responsibility, gave their headmen wide police and fiscal powers over their members. The *congrégations*, five in number,[23] assisted the French in the assessment of taxes and their collection from the Chinese, and they also assisted the immigration officials. In addition, they carried out the functions of district or clan associations elsewhere, and they managed Chinese schools, temples, cemeteries, hospitals, &c.

The Chinese themselves in course of time found the powers of the headmen oppressive and protested against the insistence on *congrégations* as being discriminatory against their race. In the Franco-Chinese negotiations of 1930 and 1935 their protests were unavailing, but by the 1946 treaty important modifications of the system were obtained. The name *congrégations* (to which the Chinese objected because of its associations

[22] See p. 272.　　　　[23] See p. 213, n. 1.

in the past) was replaced by *Groupements Administratifs Chinois Régionaux,* and the Chinese consuls were given the right of vetoing candidates for the position of headmen of these bodies.

The Chinese had the right of free movement, or trading freely, of acquiring property, or submitting tenders for public contracts, of fishing in territorial waters, and of taking part in the coastal trade in the navigable waters. Their personal and family status were maintained according to Chinese custom. They were subject to the jurisdiction of French tribunals and enjoyed the right of possessing property in common. On the other hand, however, they were subject to certain special restrictions in accordance with the regulations for the *congrégations. They were further subject to a special personal capital tax in proportion to profits gained.* In Cochinchina this tax consisted of (*a*) a fixed tax of 15 piastres and (*b*) a graduated tax equal to the amount accumulated from the principal of patents, and of credits paid in the different localities where they owned establishments. The effect of this fixed tax was to prevent all but a certain economic élite of the Chinese from re-entering Indochina.[24]

22

THE ECONOMIC ROLE OF THE CHINESE
IN INDOCHINA

BY neither the French rulers nor the people of Indochina generally can the Chinese immigrants be said to have been made welcome. Phrases such as 'the Chinese stranglehold on Indochina',[1] 'the Chinese cyst', and 'the Chinese excrescence' were heard on every side. Regulations imposed upon the Chinese accounted for the comparatively small numbers of immigrants. At one time the Chinese merchants complained of the Government restrictions prohibiting the export of any commodity other than rice. Later they protested against the harsh treatment to which importers of goods had to submit and, above all, against the heavy taxes. Taxes, they claimed, were actually seven times as heavy for a Chinese coolie as for an Annamite. Thus it was impossible for the poor Chinese to get into the country, and life was difficult even for the well-to-do business man. Most of the Chinese entering Indochina in the 1920s were sent for by their families or by Chinese firms who preferred Chinese employees.

---

[24] Étienne Dennery, *Economic Relations of French Indochina* (1933), I.P.R., Banff Conference Papers, Misc. Papers, vol. xv.
[1] Dennery, *Asia's Teeming Millions (Foules d'Asie)* (London, 1931), p. 130.

The extent of the demand for their services was the main check upon the stream of immigrants. There was little of the impulsive or casual in the motives that brought the new settlers. The immigration was conducted on a prearranged system, filling up vacancies in the groups of Chinese, and adding to the communities only as prudence or resources dictated. In the admission of Chinese to Indochina there was nothing of peaceful penetration, no suggestion of a 'Yellow Peril'. The influx was by no means miscellaneous as it had been, for example, in Malaya, but was an immigration very representative of the differing social classes of China.[2]

The Chinese in Agriculture

The French Government had constantly endeavoured to employ Chinese coolies in the fields. From the earliest days of conquest, the first Admiral-Governors of Indochina had decided that cultivation would benefit from the services of Chinese immigrants, but all to no purpose. Subsequent attempts to induce the Chinese to take to agriculture were equally fruitless. One reason was the fact that no concessions of rice-growing land were made to Chinese immigrants. However, one group, the Hakkas, had managed to establish themselves as rice growers. Dwelling in little villages bordering China between Moncay and Tienyen, and living on rice growing and fishing, they appeared to be firmly-rooted peasants.[3] As has already been stated, the Chinese in other places had specialized in highly skilled cultivations such as market gardens adjoining large cities, and before the arrival of the French they had made a monopoly of pepper planting on the Gulf of Siam. They had also planted mulberry trees. Government regulations practically excluded Chinese from 'red land'[4] grants so that they took small part in rubber cultivation. A Chinese coolie was rare too; on European plantations in Indochina Annamite labourers were preferred.

Chinese pepper and mulberry trees were tended with the same exact care as the market gardens. The time-honoured methods of their tillage might be observed on the banks of the Gulf of Siam. Each tendril of the pepper vine was the product of extraordinary patience—burning end-lessly repeated, with the ashes regularly sprinkled round each tree, the soil absolutely levelled, the daily spraying against insects, trenches and ridges constructed so that the seed could be planted at mathematically correct intervals, a tiny stone ledge built under each row, yearly cuttings

[2] Ibid.
[3] Robequain, *French Indo-China*, p. 36 ff.
[4] In southern Indochina there are extensive basalts which, as they decompose, produce a rich soil called 'red lands'. Rubber is the leading crop on these lands which also produce coffee and tea. There were seventy small holdings of rubber in Chinese hands in the neighbourhood of Saigon which held a place of only small importance in the total output of the country.

and harrowings, the frequent renewal of props—'a labour that like some religious rite becomes ever more complicated with the passage of time'.[5]

The reasons for Chinese agriculturists not being in demand in Indochina (which, however, had need of them) were said by Mr Dennery to be four in number: (1) planters of Cochinchina found that Chinese labour was too expensive compared with native labour; (2) the conditions of life conceded to Chinese in Indochina were hardly favourable (severe immigration restrictions, heavy taxes); (3) in Indochina concessions on the 'red lands' were not made to foreigners; and (4) (finally and above all) Indochina had in recent years been more a country of rice planters than of plantations, and though a Chinese might have been attached to a rice-field in his own country he was rarely so attached when he quitted his native soil.[6]

Early in the century an article comparing Javanese labour favourably with Chinese had awakened the interest of the Cochinchina planters.[7] The Javanese were good and steady workers, although less robust than the Chinese. Though their labour output was smaller, they readily attached themselves to the soil, were more easily disciplined, and were totally without that commercial aptitude which made the Chinese a problem. The Dutch Government naturally opposed their wholesale migration, but in 1906 Indochina was successful in obtaining the right to import Javanese labour under certain conditions. This experiment proved largely successful; 45 per cent of the first group and 85 per cent of the second group renewed their contracts. The First World War, however, changed the willingness of the Dutch to permit labourers to leave Java. The conditions became stricter. Moreover, it was observed that the Javanese were more expensive than Annamites and the fact that they were Mohammedans complicated the problem of feeding them. In 1928 a census of foreign labourers in Indochina showed that of the 12,000 total, the vast majority were Chinese.[8]

Fishing

In fishing the Chinese enjoyed an appreciable role. The inhabitants of the region of Haininh (Moncay) practised not only agriculture but (and as actively) fishing as well. Twenty-one Chinese fishing villages were counted. The produce of their deep-sea fishing was estimated at 5,800 tons of fish in 1929. More productive than this was the fishing carried on in the Gulf of Tongking by the junks coming annually from China to fish

[5] Aug. Chevalier, *Le Poivrier et sa culture en Indochine* (Paris, 1925; cited by Dennery, p. 136). Indochinese pepper was exported almost exclusively to France. It reached from 1927 to 1934 an average output of 4,000 tons (worth 40 million francs) (Wang Wen-yuan, *L'Indochine . . . et la Chine*, p. 48).   [6] *Asia's Teeming Millions*, p. 131.
[7] *Quinzaine Coloniale* (July 1903) (cited by Virginia Thompson, *French Indo-China*, p. 151).
[8] Thompson, *French Indo-China*, p. 151.

from the south China ports. At the customs station at Catba, near Haip-hong, figures were kept from 1924 onwards for these junks. In 1924–5 there were 407 junks; in 1925–6, 483; in 1926–7, 442; in 1927–8, 246; in 1928–9, 362; in 1929–30, 300.[9]

The junks engaged in the fisheries were based on Pakhoi and Hoihow and were constructed with solidity to stand up to the worst weather. They ranged between 30 and 100 tons' burden and had two or three masts, and a crew of about fifteen each. They were for the most part armed against pirates who might attack them. The Chinese from south China who had the right to come down as far as the latitude of Vinh were able, on an average, to lift up to 6,000 tons of fish from the Tongkingese and Annamite waters.[10]

These Chinese fishermen from their home ports, be it noted, always ventured into the high seas, and were not in competition with the Annamite fishermen who contented themselves with harvesting the coastal waters, and even then in only a half-hearted fashion.

Another fishing-ground, this time within the territorial confines of Indochina, in which the Chinese enjoyed the lion's share, was the lakes of Cambodia. Before the establishment of the French protectorate the King often granted the fishing rights to Chinese who in their turn sub-let them, and the sub-lessees retained the right of negotiating with the actual fishermen. Thus it happened that between the State as the granter of the concession and the real fishermen the old native regime allowed five, and sometimes six or seven intermediaries to reap, without work and without risks, profits that were quite substantial for each of them.[11]

Under the French regime these fisheries were leased every four years by public auction which was the occasion for keen competition among the Chinese or the Sino-Cambodians who kept in their hands the local and export trade in dried fish. The net catch was on an average about forty tons of fresh fish per square kilometre in the southern, middle, and western parts of the Great Lake. In the northwest the exhaustion of certain sills of the lake rendered the fishing less easy. It was estimated that about 100,000 tons of fresh fish were obtained annually from this one lake.

The Chinese in Trade and Industry

The boat traffic on the rivers and streams of Cambodia and Cochin-china (especially the latter) offered the Chinese many opportunities for profit. Their junks and sampans were used in the transport of rice

[9] Wang Wen-yuan, *L'Indochine . . . et la Chine*, p. 50.

[10] Pierre Gourou, *Le Tonkin*, published on the occasion of the French International Colonial Exhibition (Paris, 1931), p. 144; Wang Wen-yuan, p. 50. This apparently refers to fish caught under licence in Indochinese territorial waters.

[11] Loys Petillot, *Une Richesse de Cambodge: la pêche et les poissons* (Paris, 1911), p. 112; (cited by Wang Wen-yuan, p. 51).

brought by the Chinese rice merchants. These boats, moored along the rivers, served them as dwelling-places. According to the 1921 Census, of the 156,300 Chinese in Cochinchina and 91,000 in Cambodia, 5,500 and 2,690 persons respectively were enumerated on board these crafts (that is to say, 35 per thousand in Cochinchina and 28 per thousand in Cambodia). This was itself an indication of the importance of the boat traffic in the economic activity of the country, especially in Cochinchina where the Chinese possessed nearly all the junks, totalling 3,000.[12]

The agricultural and other pursuits mentioned above are ones in which the Chinese are actively engaged for the most part with their hands, though even here they have tended towards the role of entrepreneur; but they employed their skill also as artisans and in the handicrafts. Many were in business for themselves as artisans, in some cases employing others as workers and apprentices. In the cities they were tailors, shoemakers, and joiners.

Particularly in Cholon [says Robequain] the variety of Chinese manufactures is extraordinary. There are buildings divided into seemingly identical compartments which shelter the most diverse manufactures—food pastes, basketry, boots, paper boxes, brushes, candles, &c. Here is a duck-raising establishment where the eggs are put into incubators filled with paddy chaff; when ready to hatch they are set out on a piece of screen where hundreds of ducklings emerge cheeping from their broken shells. In an old shed glass makers are blowing paste through a long tube to make bowls, bottles, and lamps. Elsewhere looms placed side by side operate in crowded rooms.[13]

The influx of immigrants in the last year or two before the Second World War, especially of women, had greatly helped the development of these workshops. Around Moncay the Chinese had set up shops for ceramic making; at Haiphong they were engaged in machine and ship construction. Chinese also owned most of the sawmills in southern Indochina and they had a practical monopoly of the mills preparing rice for export. They had sugar refineries on the plains of Cochinchina and at Tayninh. In mining, however (as has already been remarked), the law did not permit them to participate as it did, for example, in Malaya.

As insecurity in China increased, Chinese immigration into Indochina was intensified. It was of a type not of special interest to French colonization as regards labour, nor as regards commerce (for which the French looked largely to France), nor as regards agriculture. Because, generally speaking, the Chinese who came to Indochina did so to engage in commerce or to hire their services to their compatriots already established in the country, it was not considered necessary to create in this colony a department on similar lines to the Chinese protectorate in Malaya, where

---

[12] Dennery, p. 142; Wang Wen-yuan, p. 51.
[13] Thompson, *French Indo-China*, p. 37.

there were numerous Chinese agricultural and mining labourers in need of protection.[14]

But in trade, and in all its forms and ramifications as distinguished from industry, the Chinese found himself in his element. To begin with, he had at his disposal the network of guild and co-operative organizations which enabled him to work with his eyes and ears open and with the mutual assistance of his fellows and competitors. Secondly, he had opposed to him the Annamites and Cambodians who almost entirely lacked his qualities of economy and perseverance. At the same time no cultural gulf yawned between him and the Indochinese: they were (barring the the qualities just mentioned) very similar to him in temperament and attitude of mind. It was this (says M. Robequain) which gave the Chinese a big advantage over the European merchant. He could live as the native did, or on a slightly higher level; he was entirely acclimatized in the country which adjoined his own, and he did not require the standards of hygiene and comfort indispensable to the European: he learnt languages readily and gained an understanding of local psychology which, although less refined and developed than his own, was nevertheless similar in character; he never experienced the feeling of misunderstanding or basic incompatibility which so often overwhelmed the European in dealing with native behaviour and reactions. Because the Chinese understood the native, he was better able to gain the latter's confidence and, for the same reason, could deceive him more readily. He also knew how to make himself indispensable between the European and the Indochinese.[15]

Chinese Rice Merchants

The Chinese rice merchants had rice-mills or husking-mills where the paddy was processed—husked, blended, packed—on behalf of the exporters. Often they themselves combined both functions, in which case they were called miller-exporters of rice. The greater part of the rice of Indochina was exported from Saigon, and the miller-exporters were concentrated particularly at Cholon, the industrial and commercial centre adjacent to Saigon. With the exception of three French firms, all the rice-millers at Cholon were Chinese: they owned in 1932 nearly all the seventy-five rice-mills in this city. At Haiphong in Tongking there were two Chinese rice-mills, one capable of dealing with twenty tons of paddy a day, and at Haly, near Haiphong, there were three other mills of, however, much less capacity. This group of rice-mills was the principal one in Indochina.[16]

Purchase of paddy to feed the rice-mills was not, except to a very

[14] E. Delamarre, Inspector General of Labour in Indochina, *L'Émigration et l'immigration ouvrières en Indochine* (Hanoi, 1931), p. 45 ff.   [15] *French Indo-China*, p. 38.
[16] Henri Yves, *Économie agricole de l'Indochine* (Hanoi, 1932), p. 343; Wang Wen-yuan, *L'Indochine . . . et la Chine*, p. 38.

limited extent, in the hands of the miller-exporters of rice. The great majority of them bought their paddy from merchants specializing in this trade, of whom in Cholon alone there were about a hundred. In general, these merchants worked with their personal capital and had considerable funds at their disposal. They created buying pools through the inter-mediary of agents (*ramasseurs*) and they had large fleets of junks available to them, the number of which in Cochinchina alone, as we have seen, was estimated at 3,000.

Accessory to the rice trade was that in jute rice-sacks brought from British India, from which again the Chinese drew the greatest profits. The Chinese paddy merchants were organized into syndicates, which made it impossible for the rice-miller to obtain his paddy direct; he could obtain it from the producer only through the intermediary of the syndicates. At the same time it was difficult for the native proprietor of a rice-field to attempt to carry his grain to the miller at Cholon or any other big town.[17]

The whole of this intricate organization was a matter of agency. The Chinese paddy merchants in the great centres of Cholon, Haiphong, Phnom Penh, and Hanoi did not effect their own purchases of paddy on the spot; they had, as we have said, agents placed at the points of con-centration of paddy growing and in the river ports whose role was ordinarily to direct the activities of the *ramasseurs* who were, in turn, under their orders. The functions of the first intermediaries were also nearly always carried out by Chinese. The agents were often simultane-ously wholesale or semi-wholesale grocers. The money necessary for the trade was furnished by the employer and distributed to the *ramasseur* by the agent. There were also, however, especially in Tongking, big grocers who bought paddy on their own account, transported it in their junks to the large towns, and there re-sold it to the merchants specializing in paddy buying.

In Cochinchina the agents for paddy buying had warehouses in which they stored the paddy which the *ramasseurs* had bought, or which the great landed proprietors had consigned there on the condition that the paddy should be stored without charge and should be sold at once through the intermediacy of the agent. In Cambodia, where few of these entrepôts existed, the agents took the paddy more often than not by bullock-cart or lorry to a point of embarkation in the river system whence it was transported to Cholon in junks.

The custom was for the agents to trouble themselves only with trans-actions of 10,000 gia[18] and above. Their accountants handled consign-ments of 5,000 to 10,000 gia, their sub-accountants amounts of 500 to 5,000 gia; quantities below 500 gia were handled by the *ramasseurs*.

We finally come down to those *ramasseurs* of paddy (called *Hang-Sao*

[17] Yves, pp. 346, 348; Wang Wen-yuan, p. 39.
[18] A gia is an Annamite measure equal to 40 litres.

in Tongking) whose business it was to buy the paddy in the village markets, either by searching for it among the small farmers (*ta diens*) or the small or medium landowners from whom it had already been bespoken in advance by loans on account of the expected harvest. The *ramasseurs* were usually Chinese who, assisted by their native wives, kept general stores. This was more generally the case in Cambodia than in Cochinchina, there being indeed scarcely a hamlet in the former which had not a trader of this kind. The *ramasseurs* did not work with their own capital but received the requisite money from their superior agents or from the big merchants who carried on the trade in rice in the larger cities as a side-line. These village stores served as banks and their proprietors generally made advances or loans to the peasants.

The credit system (as Mr Wang Wen-yuan puts it) 'descended in a cascade'. The wholesale merchants extended credit to the semi-wholesale merchant of the centre of an area, who in turn delivered merchandise to the retailer, and he in turn gave credit to his customers, the peasants and the small proprietors, all the year round and was repaid only at the harvest, and then usually not in money but in kind.

The role assumed by the Chinese in Cochinchina was to bring together the great native landowners, the chetties (Indian money-lenders)[19] and the European undertakings. The same system as in the rice industry was in force in the cotton and sugar-cane industries.[20]

M. Robequain says that the Chinese trader speculated on the peasants' improvidence rather than on the crop yield, and the interest rate he charged was so high and the borrower so indolent that the debt was never fully repaid, and every year the larger part of the crop went to the Chinese as interest payment.[21] Nor did his gain end here. Simultaneously the Chinese trader was making big profits on imported goods; he was also the broker or 'news chronicler' who visited the smallest hamlets; he was the collector who peddled or loaded sacks on carts and junks; he was the owner of the bulging junks.

Other Trades

Other trades in which the Chinese were engaged in Indochina were those in cotton, sugar, condiments, silk, and tea. The export of the Mekong cotton-mills was small. Three Chinese cotton undertakings (*trusters*) at Krauchmar (Cambodia), Chiné (Tongking), and Kampong-Cham (Cambodia) carried on business in association with a Chinese

---

[19] In addition to the Chinese there were in 1937 6,000 'Asiatic foreigners' in Indochina. They were mostly Indians who were British subjects, almost all of them residing in Cochinchina and Cambodia where they were brokers or money-lenders. Most came from around Madras, others from the Sind. The chetties specialized in financing the rice harvest, thus competing with the Chinese (see Robequain, *French Indo-China*, p. 168).

[20] Wang Wen-yuan, *L'Indochine . . . et la Chine*, pp. 40, 41.

[21] *French Indo-China*, pp. 38, 39.

factory in Cambodia which was in direct contact with the Chinese and Japanese markets, but while by 1932 the Chinese association still existed, two French factories had taken the place of the Chinese one. The sugar trade was very prosperous in Annam but was also distributed in some small measure throughout Indochina. The Chinese again monopolized this trade. They gave loans which were repayable in molasses processed at their central refineries. Their principal refineries were at Thuxa (Quangngai) where about twenty Chinese firms were concentrated and treated the molasses of the region. Also important were Chinese refineries in the Saigon area. In the condiment trade, which was almost entirely in Chinese hands, cinnamon bark and cardamon held an important place in the exports of the country. At Phnom Penh, Saigon, and, above all, at Hanoi there were many Chinese merchants dealing in silk and silk textiles. It was they who introduced Chinese silk culture into Indochina and reanimated the native industry. Finally, a considerable number of Chinese were engaged in the tea trade in the Union, especially in Annam. In Laos some Chinese harvested wild tea in the mountain region of Phousang and prepared it for sale. This was known as Tranninh tea.[22]

Following the example of the Dutch in Indonesia, the French established People's Banks or 'Funds'. Their main purpose was to supply the funds needed by individuals, small farmers, and craftsmen, who, were it not for the People's Banks, would have to borrow from money-lenders at very high rates, and further to enable communities or hamlets to obtain quickly and on favourable terms the necessary funds to carry out certain undertakings in the public interest. In Cochinchina the People's Banks had another purpose, which was to facilitate redemption or re-purchase of property mortgaged or sold under pressure of circumstances and thus to secure a better distribution of land.[23]

Before 1945 there were:

In Tongking	.	.	16 Provincial Funds and 13 branches	
„ Annam	.	.	10 „ „ „ 6 „
„ Cochinchina .	.	19 „ „	
„ Cambodia	.	.	7 „ „	

These 'Funds' and their branches advanced money on a short-, medium-, or long-term basis, according to the borrower's needs, the amount of the advance, and the value of the collateral security. They likewise financed the operations of agricultural, craftsmen's, and marine co-operative societies. The numbers of these societies in Indochina before 1945 were respectively thirty-two, seventeen, and nine.

The People's Banks and the co-operative societies were controlled by the Office for People's Banks, an autonomous body under Government

[22] Wang Wen-yuan, *L'Indochine . . . et la Chine*, pp. 42–43.
[23] Office of the Special Commissioner in Southeast Asia Social Welfare Conference, 18–23 Aug. 1947, *People's Banks; Measures affecting the Indigenous Population*. Paper no. 9b.

supervision. But, at any rate in Annam, Tongking, and Cochinchina, these institutions could not hope to be effective in providing credit to peasants on an adequate scale so long as conditions remained as disturbed as they were. Nor is there any evidence to show the effect of these People's Banks on the Chinese or Indian money-lending business. If experience of similar institutions in Indonesia and of co-operative societies in Malaya is any guide, the banks met only a small proportion of the credit needs of the people and the money-lenders had almost as much business as before. One reason for this is that the money-lender did not demand the same security as did the banks, and another is that the money-lender would advance money for purposes which the banks would refuse to recognize, considering them 'unproductive'.

The Trade Depression of 1929–33

The above description of the Chinese economic activities in Indochina refers for the most part to the period just previous to the great world trade depression of 1929–33. In 1931, 1932, and 1933, as we have seen, the number of Chinese returning to China always exceeded the number of new arrivals in the colony. One of the closest observers of Indochinese economy (says M. Robequain) writing in 1933, remarks,

> In so far as it was in the hands of the Chinese, the whole commercial structure of Cambodia has crashed. There is practically nothing left of it, and the same thing has happened in Cochinchina, although in a lesser degree. . . . With one or two exceptions, the Chinese, who had a virtual monopoly of rice distilling, have disappeared; only one of every four of those who monopolized the sale and purchase of paddy are still in the colony, and nine out of every ten of those engaged in the sale of hardware and fabrics have gone. The fact must be faced that a whole generation of Asiatic merchants is on the way to replacing those who have disappeared.[24]

When the trade depression had ended and the new order was established, the Chinese did not regain all the influence they had lost. In the rice-milling trade they now had competition from the French and even from the Annamites who operated a few husking-mills, especially in Cochinchina. Another factor tending to the dislocation and decline of Chinese business was the big increase in trade between Indochina and the metropolitan country, France. Moreover, the training the native was now receiving in public schools and private institutions was making it possible for him to take the place of the Chinese in occupations for which he had hitherto been considered unsuitable. The Chinese 'comprador' in banks and large business firms had declined from his position as a 'universal informer and touter, responsible for his client's solvency' (Robequain) and had become a mere middleman.

[24] Dennery, p. 157; Robequain, *French Indo-China*, p. 43. See also Thompson, *French Indo-China*, p. 127.

Extent of Chinese Holdings in Indochina and of Remittances to China

As is the case elsewhere in Southeast Asia, the information under this heading is very scanty. Remer, cited by Callis, placed the value of Chinese remittances from Indochina to China in 1930 at H.K. $5 million. An estimate of the total value of Chinese investments in Indochina has never been attempted, but Mr Callis in 1941 considered that it was safe to place it at U.S. $80 million as compared with a foreign investment of U.S. $384 million.[25]

23

SINO-INDOCHINESE RELATIONS

In view of the contiguity of Annam and China and the intercourse between the two countries extending over more than two millennia, the general reader may be tempted to conclude that Annam was to all intents and purposes an extension of China, sharing its culture in a modified form and with the blood of its peoples inextricably commingled. The truth is, however, that for a number of reasons the two countries have retained individualities which are quite distinct. The temperaments of the Chinese and the Annamites are of a different order in spite of their strong racial affinities. To take one example: 'The Chinese (says Mr Brodrick) have never been able to communicate to the Annamese their cheerful good humour. In his fears, in his hates, in his complicated and baffled spiritual unrest, the Annamese is as unlike the Chinese as it is possible to imagine.'[1] Again, the Annamite culture, though owing so much to the Chinese in every way, had retained its own roots and its own identity.[2]

Apart from these temperamental, cultural, and linguistic considera-

---

[25] H. G. Callis, *Foreign Capital in Southeast Asia* (N.Y., mimeo, 1942), p. 84, citing C. F. Remer, *Foreign Investments in China* (N.Y., 1931), p. 185. (Remer gives the following remittances to Hong Kong in millions of Hong Kong dollars for 1930: Straits Settlements 42·0, Dutch East Indies 29·0, Siam 20·0, Philippines 12·5, Indochina 5·0.)

[1] A. H. Brodrick, *Little China, the Annamese Lands* (London, 1942), p. 45.

[2] The writing of the Annamite language is one indication of this relationship, and a note on this subject (based on a section of Mr Brodrick's work above cited) may be illuminating. Annamite, now mostly written in Latin letters with diacritical marks, called *quoc-ngũ*, was invented in the seventeenth century by Portuguese missionaries. Traditionally, however, it was written in Chinese characters, and was still so written in all formal documents of the Court of Annam. The language today consists of four layers: (1) of pure Annamite origin, owing nothing to Chinese. This does not account for half the whole. It consists of the terms needed by a primitive people. (2) Words derived long ago from Chinese and considerably deformed as compared with modern Chinese pronunciation. (3) Words of Chinese origin which differ in pronunciation or in sense from their Chinese prototypes. (4) Sino-Annamite proper, i.e. Chinese characters read aloud in Annamite. Very often in the olden days Annamite mandarins from all over the country exchanged letters in pure Chinese, intelligible both to Chinese and Annamites, written in Chinese ideograms intermixed with other ideograms made up of Chinese elements but peculiar to Annam. This is the so-called *chũ-nõm*, or Southern

tions, the nature of modern Chinese immigration into Indochina has decided the quality of the Chinese influence. The vast majority of immigrants (as we have seen in the preceding chapters) came by sea and settled in Cochinchina and Cambodia: they did not filter down over the border into Tongking and Annam. These last two provinces, indeed, have a comparatively small number of Chinese residents. The bulk of the immigrants, too, did not come from the official or scholar classes who had been the main means of cultural transfusion in former periods, but they were, so to speak, an entirely new infusion. Thus it is that although we must look into history for an explanation of the similarities of Annamite and Chinese, we must not attribute more than is justified to their common cultural heritage.

Opinions on the Role of the Chinese

Cultural influence is at the best hard to describe with exactness; blood admixture of the first generation is a much more definite quantity and can be expressed in statistical terms.

In the first chapter of this Part the number of Chinese *métis*, or mixed Chinese and Indochinese, was estimated at about 140,000 compared with 326,000-odd immigrant Chinese (*c.* 1936). The number of Minh-huong and Sino-Cambodians here given does not, of course, account for all the persons in Indochina having some admixture of Chinese blood but only for those with Chinese fathers and Annamite or Cambodian mothers. After two or three generations the half-breeds become amalgamated with the native population, and the process has been going on in varying degrees of intensity for the last 2,000 years. The Chinese heritage is quite obvious in the new provinces of Trans-Bassac and Baclieu in Cochinchina. Many of the half-breeds have taken to agriculture. Such admixture has always been regarded as advantageous to the country, especially where it produces the Sino-Cambodian.

This new race [says René Morizon], for it is truly a new race, which is being created, is very robust. It has been observed in the course of the last few years that the annual medical statistics published in Cambodia by race, reveal a mortality that is infinitely less with Sino-Cambodian *métis* than it is with the Chinese and pure Cambodians. The mixed blood offers, in fact, a greater resistance to cholera and to smallpox than does that of their parents. Their coefficient of health would be analogous to that of Europeans. It is, indeed, superior, for that of the latter must be attributed less to any particular robustness than to the minute hygienic care which is lacking to the people of the country.[3]

Writing. Annamite literature is scanty and its development has been hampered by the existence of the vast majestic body of Chinese classics.

(Mr Brodrick uses 'Annamese' instead of 'Annamite' throughout. The former is apparently formed on the analogy of 'Chinese' and may eventually replace 'Annamite', but I have used Annamite for the sake of consistency. At the present time 'Vietnamese' is replacing both 'Annamite' and 'Annamese'. V. P.)

[3] R. Morizon, *Monographie du Cambodge* (Hanoi, 1931).

Up to the reign of Minh Mang (1820–41) these half-breeds were re-garded as Chinese, but a need to increase the population caused that Emperor to turn them into Annamites.

This infusion of their blood into the native population must therefore be counted as a heavy item on the credit side of the Chinese balance-sheet with Indochina, especially as the descendants of the union usually became farmers—an occupation that no one denounced as parasitic or unproductive. Certainly the Sino-Cambodians were regarded as welcome in Cambodia, for as M. Morizon says: 'It is for them (the Chinese) that the Cambodian reserves his sympathy. It is them that they admire and in whom in particular they sense superiority. The Chinese enjoy among the Cambodians the same prestige as the Greeks and Romans did among the barbarians.'[3] Which is prestige indeed!

The fact of this prestige is reconcilable with the functions of entre-preneur and usurer which the Chinese simultaneously discharged only because of the very tactful way he went about his business. Says M. Dennery:

The Chinese (who is known as 'uncle') prefers to remain on good terms with his debtor. After each of his visits he takes something away with him—a measure of paddy, the daughter of the house for concubine, or a new contract. The native is still in his debt, and the Chinese finds the delay convenient. He prefers goods to money down; he is a money-lender because he is a merchant.[4]

It is worthy of remark that it is in the part of Indochina where culture has an Indian, not a Chinese, background that the Chinese is more acceptable than he is in Annam which has a Chinese culture. But in spite of the advantage which the admixture of his blood is admitted to be for the native peoples, it cannot be denied that the Chinese in Indochina, as in Siam, Malaya, and the Philippines, constitutes a 'problem'. This has not escaped the notice of the many observant Frenchmen who have been associated with the colony and some of them have expressed their views with great directness. If the Chinese had (let us imagine) been com-mitted for trial, for example, the case for the prosecution could not be more vehemently put than it is by M. Gourou:[5]

The Chinese are masters of the Cochinchinese copra market, and fix prices practically as they wish. Their harmful influence is not limited to displacing the producers. As the Chinese take no interest in the copra's quality, they exert no influence on the producers with a view to leading them to improve their product's appearance, and to this the Cochinchinese copra owes its poor reputation. . . . The role of the Chinese is no less harmful in the fisheries, so important to Cambodia. The owner-captains of the fishing boats are in debt for life to the Chinese money-lenders and these, in fact, extract the largest part of the entire returns from the fisheries. When the time comes to purchase equipment for the fishing season

---

[3] *Monographie du Cambodge.*   [4] Dennery, p. 143.
[5] Pierre Gourou, *L'Utilisation du sol en Indochine française* (Paris, 1940; unpubl.; trans. by S. H. Guest and E. A. Clark), p. 561 of MS.

(bamboo, boats, screens, nets, &c) the owner-captains ask the moneylenders for advances.[6] And the latter multiply their opportunities for profit by getting themselves reimbursed very abundantly in kind for the advances they have made in money—for the market price for fish for export is fixed by a Chinese syndicate—by obliging the owner to equip himself with rice, lines, and sundry materials from the middleman-moneylender's own stock. The fisherman is helpless against this exploitation, because the Chinese assigns a clerk to go with him, to watch that he sells his fish to no other buyer than his creditor, and makes no purchases from the shop of another tradesman, and because the only wholesalers are Chinese, who back one another up. The master fishermen are generally Annamese. They sublet from the Chinese lessees, who have secured their fishing lots from auction (*vide* Chevey and Le Poulain, *Bulletin économique de l'Indochine*, pp. 278 et seq., 1939). The Government has regulated the sub-leases in order to prevent the exploitation of the worker by the creditor, but in practice, the Chinese get round the rules. The contracts for the sub-leases are correct but, for example, the sub-lessee will agree that the Chinese lessee will be his partner for half-shares, which gives the capitalist half the gross profits. . . . The useless and excessively greedy middleman, whose profits do not remain in the country and constitute heavy invisible exports (we are thinking as much of the chetty as of the Chinese) must be eliminated without violence, without specifically hostile measures, but by the mere progress of rural credit organization and of improvement of the general economy.

M. Robequain, for his part, sets out the charge as he sees it—indeed with a heavy entry on the debit side, but nevertheless with some extenuating items for the Chinese immigrant. He says that the Chinese are often criticized, and frequently with good reason, for their unscrupulousness and their harsh treatment of the natives: their practice of taking advantage of the shortcomings and poverty of the peasants is quite rightly termed hateful, as is their shrewdness in evading the laws and regulations imposed on them, in avoiding all official control, and in working under the cover of unstable and irresponsible associations. They are denounced as parasites who do not create wealth but fatten on the riches created by Indochinese labour, benefiting the while from the security established by Europeans, and the roads and railways which European technical skill and capital have built. The Chinese are branded as speculators shrewdly taking advantage of monetary instability. They send large sums of money annually to China and the Chinese returns shamelessly to his native country as soon as he has made a fortune, or, in the event of bankruptcy, he suddenly disappears.[7]

But (says M. Robequain) these criticisms, exaggerated at times, should be somewhat tempered. While the shrewdness of the Chinese must be admitted, it cannot be justly claimed that his activities are harmful. In many of their material and spiritual characteristics the native civilizations testify to the age-old influence of the Chinese. Unlike the Westerner,

---

[6] The rate of interest paid by the Cambodian peasant to the Chinese trader is usually 100 per cent for 6 or 8 months (Gourou, p. 386).

[7] Robequain, *French Indo-China*, pp. 39, 40.

he has not ruthlessly imported the revelations of a new world. His activity, no less influential, has been undertaken gradually. His colonization of Indochina is, therefore, not wholly to be condemned.

Although the Government of Indochina took a neutral stand on the Chinese question (the Chinese, after all, paid a considerable portion of the taxes), French unofficial opinion was divided. Some recognized the ability of the Chinese as workers but were alarmed because they discouraged French business and business men. Others considered them a dangerous element because they introduced into Indochina the political controversies of the Kuomintang and other parties. A third group held that they were a counterbalance to the indolence of the Annamites. They would, it was said, cultivate every inch of cultivable land if they were allowed to do so. Those who favoured the Chinese were opposed to their mass immigration but were anxious that the French might benefit from the steady labours of the Chinese on land unused by the Annamites. They wished, however, that only the 'coolie' class should be admitted. Many colonial experts took this view, recognizing that Indochina was large enough to hold all Chinese moving into it for years to come. Furthermore, it was expected that, once established, they would eventually consume the products of French manufacture.[8]

In the regions opened up by the French Government the Chinese were said to be obtaining a foothold by dint of clever propaganda against all rivals. In the French-leased territory of Kwongchowwan, for example, where the harvests were poor owing to the lack of fertilizers, a German firm had, in 1930, established an installation in order to engage in soil chemistry and it offered easy credit to the farmers. The Chinese (it was alleged), in order to undermine the German influence, spread reports that their methods were destroying the plants, ruining the soil, and poisoning all who ate the foodstuffs produced therefrom. Such stories were believed, with the result that the Chinese gained in prestige and the Germans (presumably) lost their trade.[9]

Chinese knowledge of the natives, and their willingness to travel into parts of the interior where the French had never penetrated, were more than a match for the superior French organization of trade. High tariffs protected imports from France (58 per cent of the import trade was reserved for the metropolitan Power in this way), but as against this the Chinese sold articles such as swallows' nests, Chinese medicines, or joss-sticks which only Chinese manufactured. They even encroached on the French clientèle, being willing to take less profit than their foreign trading rivals. Before the depression of the 1930s, a fair balance had been struck, and while the Chinese handled native imports and exports the French did the same for the Europeans.[10]

[8] The arguments in this paragraph are from Ennis, *French Policy*, p. 119.
[9] Ibid. p. 126.   [10] Thompson, *French Indo-China*, p. 174 ff.

Another great asset of the Chinese trader was his intimate knowledge of the market and the fact that his accounts were kept in Chinese, a language which no French official could read. In 1927 an edict was published requiring the keeping of commercial books in roman letters and arabic numerals. This edict was criticized by the French as not being strong enough to be effectual and by the Chinese as being highly prejudicial to their business, and in 1930 a compromise made the regulation apply only to big businesses which had to be officially registered. By means of this regulation the Government attempted to ascertain the names of the persons who were behind the leading Chinese firms.[11]

Commercial Relations between China and Indochina

From 1913 to 1935 inclusive the mean annual Sino-Indochinese trade was valued at 99 million piastres (64 million for exports; 35 million for imports) in a total of 285 million, the mean annual value of the total exterior commerce of Indochina. Averages over the years 1919–35 show that 34·6 per cent of Indochina's special trade was with China:[12] 34·5 per cent was with France.

Of the merchandise exported to China (1931–5) 68 per cent was for foodstuffs, 29 per cent for raw materials, and 3 per cent for manufactured articles. Of the merchandise imported from China 44 per cent were raw materials, 4 per cent manufactured articles, and 16 per cent foodstuffs. Rice and its derivatives accounted for 62·1 per cent of the total exports from Indochina to China direct, oil for 22 per cent (1931–5), and for 1935 alone the rice figure had risen to 86·8 per cent of the total. Merchandise imported from China into Indochina included tin (24 per cent for 1931–1935) and raw and manufactured silk (20·3 per cent for 1931–5).[13]

These figures are taken from Mr Wang Wen-yuan's detailed exposition of the subject, but it has been pointed out that being *average* figures

[11] For an account of a similar controversy in the Philippines see pp. 543–5 regarding the Book-keeping Laws. Dr Thompson (*French Indo-China*, p. 178) says: 'The steps were designed to eliminate the Chinese trick of using names like "Eternal Happiness" and "Springtime of Youth" to prevent the prosecution of the real directors of a bankrupt enterprise who could melt away under suchlike joyous nomenclature. . . . Chinese merchants were henceforth to report their business balance after six months and if they planned to leave the colony, they must announce their departure a month in advance.' The business signs, or 'chops', under which the Chinese traded undoubtedly facilitated the secrecy they required either for legitimate or other reasons, but they were not invented expressly for the purpose of deceiving foreigners. They were names of firms in the same way as are, say, the Savoy Tailors' Guild or Ardath Cigarettes. In Malaya, opposition to the compulsory registration of the names of Chinese partnerships came not only from the Chinese traders themselves, but also from British import firms who argued that it had taken many years for them to build up their systems of trade information, and they did not see why rivals should profit by the enforced divulgence of trade secrets.
[12] The 'special' import trade comprised merchandise from abroad declared to be for the supply of ships having their base in Indochina, or placed in the category of temporary admission, &c.
[13] Wang Wen-yuan, *L'Indochine . . . et la Chine*, p. 117 ff.

conceal big annual differences, especially for 1934 and 1935. For 1934–7 the actual figures were:

	1934		1935		1936		1937	
	Export	Import	Export	Import	Export	Import	Export	Import
France	49·0	57·0	33·3	55·0	55·0	53·0	56·0	53·0
China	5·4	4·0	15·1	7·8	2·9	9·2	5·4	7·2

France's trade policy for Indochina was frankly protectionist; but even as far back as 1892, when the principle was being applied in all its rigour, it was found expedient to make an exception in the case of much of the merchandise imported from China which was necessary to the Indochinese population.

In 1922 recognition by the Washington Conference of tariff autonomy necessitated a new treaty with Indochina. But there were obstacles. First of all the French demanded a *quid pro quo* for the acceptance of Chinese consuls in Indochina and for a diminishing tax on Chinese goods, in the shape of indemnification for the loss of French lives and damage to property in China and a cessation of political agitation among the Chinese in Indochina itself. The delay in ratifying the treaty that had been arranged allowed China to raise her tariffs and to devalue her currency. Eventually the treaty was agreed in principle in 1930,[14] but this fact did not noticeably ease trade relations. Indochina's trade with China fell off perceptibly after 1930, and trade restrictions between the two countries were later intensified by protective measures. The central or provincial Governments replied to increased Indochinese tariffs by raising their duties on coal and (especially) on rice. The Nanking agreement of 1935, however, lowered the rates which had proved the worst trade barriers.[15] These agreements provided for migration between the two countries on reasonable terms, and for the establishment of Chinese consulates in Hanoi or Haiphong and Saigon. (The French agreed to receive Chinese consuls solely to obtain concessions for coal exported to China from Tongking.) Most Chinese goods originating in the provinces bordering on Indochina could be exported through the latter country duty free. Munitions might be shipped across Tongking at the wish of the Chinese Government free of transit duty. This last provision naturally led to conflict between Japan and Indochina when, in 1937, the blockade of Chinese ports by the Japanese caused the Haiphong–Kunming and Hanoi–Langson railway lines to carry an ever-increasing portion of China's military supplies. As a consequence of Japanese protests, Japan and France agreed in the course of 1938 that the frontier

[14] Thompson, *French Indo-China*, p. 178 ff.
[15] Robequain, *French Indo-China*, p. 327.

should be open only to goods contracted for before July 1937. The closing of the frontier, subject to this exception, was modified in some cases, but the traffic suffered much interruption and on the whole the railway was grossly inadequate for Chinese requirements. In December 1938, after further Japanese protests, the Indochinese authorities stopped all transit to China over the Yunnan Railway. Following this success, early in February 1938 the Japanese occupied Hainan Island, commanding not only the Shanghai–Hong Kong–Singapore shipping lanes but also large areas of the Gulf of Tongking and the port of Haiphong. In reply the French reopened the Yunnan Railway to Chinese war materials on 20 March.[16] In April 1939 the Japanese occupied the Spratly Islands about half-way between Saigon and North Borneo. In 1940, when the fall of France made it virtually impossible for the colony of Indochina to resist Japan when the latter country renewed its old complaint regarding the shipments of war supplies to Kunming, the French acceded to the Japanese demands.

All these events were bound to affect the fortunes of the bulk of Indochina's Chinese population—the traders. So far as they identified themselves with China they suffered with her in this period of misfortune and their communications with and remittances to their families there were interrupted and diminished, but in a purely material way they had compensations for their hardship. The rice market, in which they were so greatly interested, was saved because conditions in Japan and Japanese-occupied China created a greatly increased demand for the Indochinese product just at the time when the market from Europe and North Africa collapsed. Much of the rice sent to Hong Kong and 'other Chinese ports' was probably shipped to Japan or used to feed Japanese troops in China.[17] In default of restrictions imposed by national authority, patriotism has small modifying influence on the simple business law of profit making.

[16] Suppl. to Robequain, by John R. Andrus and Katrine R. C. Greene, p. 353.

[17] Saigon's rice export totalled 1,681,000 tons in 1939 of which 162,000 tons went to Hong Kong, 78,000 to other Chinese ports, 461,000 tons to France, 147,000 to other European countries, and only 8,000 tons to Japan; in 1940 Japan took 476,000 tons, Hong Kong 244,000 tons, other Chinese ports 235,000 tons, French colonies 104,000 tons, France 91,000 tons, and other European countries 49,000 tons.

24

VIETNAMESE NATIONALISM AND CHINESE POLITICS

IF we were to display the pieces of political fabric representing each country in Southeast Asia one by one there would be a great deal of warp and woof irrelevant to our survey of the Chinese. At the same time it is not always possible to isolate the Chinese theme when it is a mere thread, even a concealed one, without snapping it. In Indochina the nationalist movement was largely independent of that in China itself, though having contacts with it and in some respects being inspired by it, and with some of its leaders educated in the school at Whampoa or the Chinese political arena. We must therefore aim at sketching in only so much of the nationalist pattern in Indochina as will serve as background to the Chinese story.

Although the Annamite people were thoroughly sinicized in their beliefs, their habits, and their general cultural patterns, they did not surrender to the invader their sense of being a people distinct and apart. Annam is full of pagodas and temples erected in honour of national heroes who had resisted the Chinese invaders or the Chinese pirates from the south.[1]

After the French invasion of Annam, intermittent fighting between the conquerors and the Annamites continued while the imperial Court of Hué became the scene of anti-French intrigue and palace revolution. But as the nationalist forces arose and took shape in the first and second decades of the twentieth century there was little co-operation among them and they were united only by their common dislike of French rule.

The early nationalist associations in Indochina put forward a moderate programme. It was only when lack of any marked success in promoting their aims had discredited them with the bulk of their followers that the more leftist associations or groups robbed them of popular support. Belonging to the category of moderates was the Tongkingese Party of the Pham Quynh and the Constitutional Party of Bui quang Chieu. Their failure led to the rise of parties which concentrated upon direct action. In 1927 the New Annam Revolutionary Association (*Tan-Viet-Cach-Menh-Dang*) was established, drawing its membership both from the nationalist-minded *petite bourgeoisie* and the Communists. It organized a

---

[1] Dang-Chân-Liêu, 'Annamite Nationalism', *Pacific Affairs*, xx/1 (Mar. 1947).

series of strikes in consequence of which it was subjected to severe repression by the Government, and in 1929 was dissolved. The Communist
elements of the old Cach-Menh-Dang then joined with the New Annam
Revolutionary Youth Association (*Viet-Nam-Cach-Menh-Thanh-Nien-
Hoi*) to form the Indochinese Communist Party under Nguyen Ai-quoc[2]
—a party whose ancestry derived from the revolutionary Association for
the Restoration of Vietnam which had existed earlier in the century. In
1931, two years after its founding, the Communist Party claimed 1,500
members and some 100,000 peasant adherents.[3]

The *Viet-Nam-Quoc-Dan-Dang*, founded about 1927 in Tongking, was
modelled on the Chinese KMT founded by Dr Sun Yat-sen. It appealed
to youth, and from the outset it was a terrorist association. It issued
propaganda addressed to students, employees, and the army, and endeavoured to secure feminist support. The year of its foundation is
significant, for it was in the same year that Chiang Kai-shek, now on his
victorious march to the north, purged the KMT of its Communist
elements which had hitherto formed the left wing of the party but which
now split off into their own organizations. The attempts of the Quoc-
Dan-Dang to link forces with similar groups in Siam came to nothing,
but it had succeeded in establishing relations with the KMT and with
the Yunnan branches of the same society. Since it did not change its
name and continued to exploit its KMT connexion, it seemed that it
ignored the purge of 1927. In January 1929 it attempted unsuccessfully
to assassinate Pasquier, the Governor-General of French Indochina, and
a month afterwards succeeded in murdering Bazin, head of the Labour
Recruiting Bureau.

Finding the police hot on the trail, the Quoc-Dan-Dang decided pre-
maturely to launch the next stage of its revolutionary programme—the
phase of overt action—and a series of acts of violence resulted. A mutiny
took place at Yenbay, at Hanoi bombs were thrown at the Commissariat,
and the sub-prefect of Vinhbao was assassinated. An abortive attempt to
set up a revolutionary regime in the three Annamite provinces and to
initiate a drive in concert with the Yunnanese supporters of the association ended in the execution of thousands in 1930–1. By 1933 the party
was officially reported dead as an organized group.[4]

We have observed so far the alliance of sympathy between the Vietnamese nationalists, proceeding early from moderate to violent pro-
grammes, and the Chinese Nationalists, especially in Canton and Yunnan.
But the movements were quite separate from one another and were
developing along different lines. The difference is underlined by the

---

[2] Who was later to be known as Ho Chi Minh.
[3] The exact origins of these parties (says Mr Dang-Chân-Liêu) are as hard to determine as
the sources of rivers, but this is not very important since it is the rivers and not the springs
with which political history has to deal.   [4] Thompson, *French Indo-China*, p. 489.

contrasting personalities and careers of the two leaders. Those of Chiang Kai-shek are well enough known: those of Nguyen Ai-quoc are less so.

Nguyen Ai-quoc (the personal name, Ai-quoc, is apparently a self-adopted one and means 'lover of his country')[5] was born in 1892 in Annam. He went to France and in Paris in 1920 he founded the Inter-colonial Union of Coloured Peoples: in 1923 he was studying in Moscow and in due course he passed on to Canton. Borodin was now associated with Dr Sun during one of his periods of control in the southern capital, and Nguyen Ai-quoc and he are said to have arranged to work in co-operation from both sides of the Sino-Indochinese border, distributing anti-colonial tracts in both China and France. Young Annamites then received instruction at the politico-military school at Whampoa, founded to train leaders for the KMT. Nguyen Ai-quoc's interests were more nationalistic than communistic at this stage. When Chiang Kai-shek's purge got under way, both Borodin and Nguyen Ai-quoc sought refuge in Russia. The Annamite students who had received training in Canton and Whampoa returned to their own country to make use of their new-found political knowledge.

With the Communists made temporarily impotent by vigorous French action, the more moderate Annamite nationalists were hopeful when the Front Populaire came into power in France in 1936 that this would mean a less repressive policy towards themselves, and the replacement of the illiberal Governor-General René Robin, and the declaration of an amnesty encouraged this hope. But when the nationalists in Indochina staged strikes with the idea of forcing even larger concessions, the new regime stiffened up against them. When the Popular Front fell, the Anti-Imperialist Democratic Front which had formed itself in Annam in the optimism of the hour went underground with the rest of the nationalist parties.[6]

After the acceptance of the Japanese demands on Indochina in 1941 Vichy officials remained in nominal control of the colony. In concert with the Japanese they put down nationalist risings and pro-Allied sabotage. The Vichy regime suited Japanese purposes until March 1945 when the increasing nearness of the Allies decided the Japanese to take a more direct control of Indochina. On 10 March they announced that 'the colonial status of French Indochina' had ended, and the following day the Annamite Emperor was reported to have declared the indepen-

---

[5] Nguyen is apparently the surname. Later on, in 1933, Nguyen Ai-quoc changed his name to Ho Chi Minh—*Ho* characterizes the Annamites just as Han does the Chinese; *Chi* means 'intelligence'; *Minh* means 'bright, brilliant', and in Sino-Annamite is the same as the Chinese *Ming* in Ming dynasty.

[6] For this period Ellen J. Hammer, 'Blueprinting a New Indochina', *Pacific Affairs* (Sept. 1948), and *The Emergence of Viet Nam* (N.Y., mimeo., 1947) by the same author are mainly followed.

dence of the kingdom of Annam. In August he made a declaration uniting Annam, Tongking, and Cochinchina (the three *ky*, which were separate provinces under the French). Later he gave the name of Vietnam to the kingdom in an attempt, no doubt, to suggest that the battle for Annamite independence which had so long been fought under the banner of that name had at last been won. On 18 March the protectorate of Cambodia announced its independence, and on 10 April Laos followed suit.

Meanwhile during the years of Japanese dominance the Vietnamese had not been altogether passive. At Dongdang in Tongking, and at Coalankh in Annam in 1941 they had risen against both Vichy and the Japanese. In 1942 members of the Annamite and anti-fascist groups had escaped to China to form the Viet Minh[7] (League for Vietnam Independence) which was pledged to fight both Vichy and Japan for the independence of a democratic Vietnam. After the Japanese collapse, the Japanese radio quoted Premier Tran Trong Kim as declaring the determination of the people of Vietnam to 'defend their independence'. But his regime came to an end on 22 August when the Viet Minh established a provisional Government under Ho Chi Minh for the Annamite provinces. Bao Dai abdicated, but preferring, as he said, to be a citizen of a free country rather than the king of an enslaved one, he joined the Viet Minh Government as political adviser. On 2 September the new Government issued its declaration of independence based on that of the United States.

The wartime agreements between the British and the Chinese fixed the sixteenth parallel as the line of demarcation between the British and Chinese troops where they were to be allotted the task of disarming the Japanese—the British to the south of the line and the Chinese to the north. The two forces now duly entered Indochina to carry out their tasks. The British had already announced their intention of before long handing over control of Saigon and of southern Indochina to the French. The intentions of the Chinese, however, remained for the time being obscure.

Before the account of events is resumed in the ensuing chapter, it would be well to summarize and explain developments that have been described.

In the tangle of events and policies a distinction must be made between China as a Power and Chinese nationals in Indochina. The first was a political entity playing of necessity the international game of power politics whilst conducting simultaneously a war of resistance against the Japanese and against the Communists in its midst; the second were a community, very largely bourgeois in composition and interest, which was striving to maintain its existence in the tussle between the conflicting

---

[7] Viet Minh, the abridged title of a group of several Annamite parties, in full the Vietnam Doc Lap Dong Minh Hoi (League for the Independence of Vietnam), Roger Lévy, *L'Indochine et ses traités* (Paris, 1947), p. 10.

elements in Indochina. For reasons of political prestige the Chinese Nationalist Government did its best to protect the interests of its children in Indochina, but at the same time it had to keep its eye on international and internal developments. With the defeat of the Japanese the game became more complex than ever.

We have seen, so far, no fewer than four separate forces of Chinese origin operating simultaneously in Indochina. The first was the ancient conquest and colonization of Annam which had stamped its ineffaceable imprint on the culture of Annam; the second was the influx of immigrants, mostly by sea, which the economic expansion of Indochina under the French regime had made possible; the third was the influence of Chinese nationalism on Annamite nationalism bifurcating into left and right; the fourth was China as a Power fighting the Communists in her midst and at the same time struggling to maintain her international position. In the fourth category of action China had to take into account the two forces striving to fill the vacuum left by the Japanese surrender, namely the new-born France reasserting her old claims in Indochina, and the new republic of Vietnam. At the juncture to which we have so far brought the narrative, the Indochinese territory, north of the sixteenth parallel of latitude, including the whole of Tongking, most of Laos, and part of Annam, was still under the control of Chinese troops.

After the Japanese Surrender

Between September 1945 and January 1946 the French Government was preoccupied with obtaining the evacuation of Tongking by Chinese troops.[8] The negotiations for the evacuation were conducted at Chungking, and the Franco-Chinese agreements were signed on 28 February 1946. The first agreement was concerned with the abandonment by France of the privileges and concessions accorded to her in the past by the 'unequal treaties' (this was following on the renunciation by Britain and America of similar privileges and concessions in 1943). By another agreement the Chinese Government accepted that French troops should relieve the Chinese troops north of the sixteenth parallel and take over their mission of disarming the Japanese. The agreement assured to the Chinese resident in Indochina the maintenance of the territorial advantages of their organization by *congrégations*. It established a customs zone at Haiphong, outlined a future commercial treaty, and fixed the conditions for the re-purchase of the French section of the Yunnan Railway.[9]

The Franco-Chinese agreement on Sino-Indochinese relations contained articles which provided that Chinese should continue to enjoy

---

[8] 'Come to disarm the Japanese troops (says Lévy, p. 17), the Chinese lived on the country and emptied it of its substance.'
[9] The text of the agreements is to be found in Lévy, p. 75 ff.

the rights, privileges, and exemptions that they had traditionally possessed in Indochina, notably those in respect of travel, taxation, education and property-ownership.[10]

Meanwhile, in the northern half of Indochina, despite Chiang Kai-shek's declaration that China had no territorial ambitions, and despite the French gesture in returning Kwongchowwan to China, the influence of the Chinese occupation was in effect in favour of the Vietnam nationalists. The French in Indochina found that General Lu Han, commanding the Chinese troops in the northern half of the country, was consistently unco-operative. The Chinese had refused repeated requests from the French to be allowed to bring in soldiers and administrators, but the Vietnamese, on the other hand, were allowed to keep their weapons. The control remained virtually in their hands, and their flag, a yellow star in a red field, flew from many buildings. The Chinese, too, brought in Annamite nationalist groups favourable to China. Moreover, from Tongking and Annam the Chinese had invaded Laos.

By the agreement of 28 February the Chinese were under obligation to withdraw all their troops by 31 March, but there was delay in their evacuating Indochina. There were several clashes between Chinese and French troops, and there was an incident on 6 March 1946 when the French cruiser, the *Émile Bertin*, and auxiliary ships carrying 20,000 troops waiting outside Haiphong for permission to disembark were fired on by shore batteries manned by Chinese. Eighteen men were killed and nearly forty injured in the warships by the firing. It was not until 9 March that the first French contingents landed. There were still 1,200 Chinese troops left in northern Indochina in July 1946. On 4 March the Southeast Asia Command had relinquished authority over south Indochina to the French.

1949–63

The civil war which broke out in Indochina in December 1946 lasted for eight years. During this period a number of political changes took place. On 8 March 1949 an agreement signed between France and the Emperor Bao Dai on behalf of Vietnam recognized the independence of Vietnam within the French Union, and certain sovereign powers were

[10] The *Journal Officiel de l'Indochine* of 7 Oct. 1948 contained Decree No. 272/3416 of 28 Sept. 1948, arising from an exchange of notes in Paris between the French Foreign Minister and the Chinese ambassador. The main provisions of the decree were that the groups known as Chinese *congrégations* should be called Chinese regional administrative groups, that the election of chiefs and sub-chiefs of regional administrative groups should be held and the candidates approved by the Chinese consular authorities, that the term of office of the chiefs and sub-chiefs should be fixed at four years, that chiefs and sub-chiefs might be removed if convicted by the French authorities or Chinese consular representatives of abuse of power, administrative irregularity, insolvency, activities contrary to the interests or security of the French Union, the national Governments, or the Government of the Chinese Republic, and that the chiefs and sub-chiefs were to be the intermediaries for receiving administrative orders addressed to the group.

transferred to Vietnam. Others remained partly in French hands until September 1954. The remainder, connected with services in which Cambodia, France, Laos, and Vietnam had a common interest, were regulated by the Pau conventions of December 1950. Those conventions were finally abrogated by the Paris agreements of 29 December 1954 which completed the transfer of sovereignty to Vietnam.

The civil war finally ended in the costly defeat of the French and nationalist troops at Dien Bien Phu in 1954, and a cease-fire agreement was reached on 20 July, at the Geneva conference. The agreement was signed on behalf of the Commander-in-Chief of the French Union Forces in Indochina and on behalf of the Commander-in-Chief of the People's Army of Vietnam. The Government of the Republic of Viet-Nam (S. Vietnam) did not sign the agreement.

The final declaration of the Geneva conference (21 July 1954) was that general elections for the whole of Vietnam should take place in 1956, but, for reasons that will in a moment be plain, these elections were not held and Vietnam remained divided into two halves. The cease-fire line became the frontier between them. This line, with certain modifications, followed the 17th N. parallel. An international commission composed of representatives of Canada, India, and Poland was appointed to control and to supervise the provisions of the agreement.

In South Vietnam a referendum held on 23 October 1955 showed a majority of 98 per cent in favour of the deposition of Bao Dai and the elevation of Ngo dinh Diem to be Chief of State. On 29 October, accordingly, M. Diem (as he was generally known by foreigners) was proclaimed Chief of State and his first act was to declare Vietnam (by which the whole country was intended) a Republic of which he became the President. On the grounds that neither he nor the Republic had been signatories of the Geneva agreement, he later declined to carry out its provisions regarding the holding of elections for Vietnam as a whole.

On 26 October 1956 a new constitution was promulgated under which executive power was vested in the President and legislative power in a single-chamber assembly. Both were to be elected by universal suffrage and secret ballot.

But the new Government had to face the continuation of the civil war within its own boundaries. North Vietnam, as was to be expected, was encouraging and helping the insurrection,[11] but the internal insurgents, the 'Viet Cong', and their civilian associates, were undoubtedly the hard core of the rebellion. The nocturnal guerrilla activity of the latter was in time succeeded by daytime action in battalion force, and the United States, which had virtually succeeded France as the 'protecting' power, though in the form of a military and economic treaty, was compelled to

[11] Evidence to this effect is contained in *The Special Report* signed by the Indian and Canadian members of the International Supervisory Commission, June 1962 (Cmd. 1955).

step up its military and economic aid (amounting to a large percentage of the local budget) to keep the Diem Government in being.

Meanwhile Cambodia had in 1949 been granted independence as an Associate State of the French Union, but the transfer of the French military powers to the Cambodian Government on 9 November 1953 was considered there as marking the attainment of sovereign independence. In January 1955 Cambodia became financially and economically independent, both of France and the other former Associate States of Indochina, Vietnam and Laos.

Under a treaty of 19 July 1949 between the President of the French Republic and the King of Laos, Laos became an independent sovereign State within the French Union. Before the return of the French, the Chinese forces accepting the Japanese surrender had recognized a Laotian independence movement known as Lao-issarak. With the withdrawal of the Chinese, the Lao-issarak were forced by the French and Laotian forces to flee the country, but the movement was revived and extended as the Pathet Lao under Prince Souphannouvong, and in April 1953 the Viet Minh aided by the Pathet Lao invaded Laos. Under the Geneva agreement the Viet Minh forces withdrew and the forces of Pathet Lao moved into the northeastern provinces of Phong Saly and Sam Neua.

Some 890,000 refugees, many thousands of them Roman Catholics, fled southwards from North Vietnam at the time of the partition and also among the refugees were some thousands of Chinese.

Since the occupations of the Chinese in Vietnam were mainly commercial or entrepreneurial, the pressures exerted on them consequently differed in the Communist society of the north and the capitalist society of the south.

South Vietnam (*Viet Nam Cong Hoa*—Republic of Vietnam)

Under the French regime, all Chinese in Vietnam were, as we have already seen, members of the *congrégations*. They had no contact with the local authorities except through their elected leaders. They thus developed no loyalties other than to their *congrégation*. On the achievement of independence the Government of South Vietnam sought to extend its direct control over all foreigners residing in Vietnam, including not only the French but the Chinese, who constituted 99 per cent of the total. At the same time it sought by means of thorough-going legislation to integrate the Chinese into the Vietnamese community, relying no longer on the more gradual process of assimilation which had always been going on. Simultaneously the Government aimed to break what it considered to be Chinese economic stranglehold on Vietnam.

Ordinance No. 48, conferring Vietnam citizenship automatically on all Chinese born in Vietnam, was promulgated on 21 August 1956. All

Chinese born in Vietnam were henceforth to be considered as Vietnamese nationals and must take Vietnamese names. The legislation was retrospective and all Chinese born in Vietnam at any time were now Vietnamese. This measure was generally regarded as the most drastic action yet taken by any Asian country to absorb an alien minority.

Following close on this Ordinance, a Decree (No. 53) was promulgated on 6 September prohibiting non-Vietnamese nationals to engage in eleven occupations. These were mostly in the retail trade (fishmonger, butcher, general storeman, coal and firewood merchant, dealer in petroleum products, second-hand goods, scrap metal, the transport of persons and merchandise) and also including, significantly, the entire intermediary trade in rice. Those aliens engaged in the first seven of these occupations had to liquidate their businesses within six months; in the last four categories within one year.

The Chinese reaction to those measures was a general move towards civil disobedience. Although the original deadline had been set at 9 May 1957, by 17 June only 3,500 Chinese had come forward for their identification cards out of an estimated total of 500,000–600,000 Chinese and some 300,000 *Min-huong*. The Government of Taiwan then intervened as protectors of the Chinese of Vietnam, offering them repatriation to Taiwan, but negotiations between it and the Diem Government resulted in deadlock. The matter had now become one of 'face' and the South Vietnam Government was determined to bring the new measures fully into force.[12]

Taken together, the effect of those two pieces of legislation were contradictory—the Government seemed to push the Chinese out with one hand and to take them in with the other. While 'alien' Chinese would not be allowed to participate in the eleven reserved occupations, all 'nationalized' Chinese, by virtue of the fiction of being Vietnamese, would be able to pursue the trades from which the other law had excluded them. As it turned out, this ingenious expedient did not please anybody. The Chinese refused to believe that they would be treated on an equal footing with the Vietnamese in trade, and they were furious at having what they considered an inferior national status thrust upon them without option. Those Chinese who were compulsorily nationalized, moreover, would now be liable for 18 months' military service, from which they had hitherto been exempt, and this would entail actual fighting in the civil war under the most arduous and dangerous conditions. The Vietnamese business men, on the other hand, grumbled that the Chinese stranglehold was being confirmed instead of exorcised.[13]

---

[12] See Bernard Fall, 'Vietnam's Chinese Problem', *Far Eastern Survey*, May 1958, and Wesley R. Fishel, *Problems of Freedom: South Vietnam since Independence* (Michigan, 1957[?]).
[13] Saigon correspondent of *The Times*, 28 Sept. 1956.

North Vietnam

Regarding the Chinese in North Vietnam it is not possible to add any-thing of importance to what has already been said under the heading of 'Demography' for the reasons there stated. The constitution of the Democratic Republic of Vietnam, which came into force on 1 January 1960, was comparable in many respects to that of the People's Republic of China. North Vietnam remained firmly within the Communist bloc and virtually cut off from the remainder of the country.

Laos

In 1945, under the inter-Allied arrangement, the surrender of the Japanese troops north of the 16th parallel of latitude was accepted by the Chinese army of the KMT and the latter established a Government in the north of Laos under Prince Petsavath, the founder of the Lao-tian independence movement known as Lao-issarak, but when the French took over the region from the Chinese in 1946 he was com-pelled by a united force of French and Laotians to abdicate and flee the country.

A King of Laos had been recognized under the pre-war French pro-tectorate, and by the Convention of July 1949 between the French Republic and Laos, Laos became an independent sovereign kingdom within the French Union. In 1949 the bulk of the Lao-issarak adherents returned to Laos but a few remained in exile.

The dissolution of French Indochina was marked by the successive removal of the existing bonds between its units. In December 1954 certain services which the four States had held in common were trans-ferred to the Government of the three Associate States and at the same time the customs union, to which Laos had belonged since 1950, was dissolved.

Lao-issarak was the survivor of the wartime 'underground' and patriotic movements and it had Communist associations. In 1949 the Free Lao leaders in exile in Thailand divided into two groups: one accepted the recent agreement of King Sasavong Vang with the French as a satisfactory solution and so returned home; others did not accept it and so did not return home. Of the latter, Prince Souphannouvong, who belonged to a junior branch of the royal family, made his way to North Vietnam and linked up with the Viet Minh. In April 1953 North Vietnam forces, aided by those of the Pathet Lao, invaded Laos.

The French failure to maintain their military position in Indochina resulted in the Geneva conference which reached an agreement on 20 July 1954 whereby all North Vietnam forces and all French forces, except a certain number for training and the maintenance of the French military bases, were to be withdrawn from Laos, no fresh troops or armaments were to be introduced, and, pending a political settlement, the forces of the Pathet Lao were to move into the northeastern provinces of Phong Saly and Sam Neua. The cease-fire was to be supervised by an International Control Commission.

No political settlement was in fact obtained for another eight years. The intervening period is characterized as one during which the United States (which had virtually taken over France's supervisory function) aimed to secure a *friendly* Laos, while the Neo Lao Hak Sat, the political party representing the Pathet Lao under Prince Souphannouvong, aimed to create a *Communist* Laos. The United States, as a means for furthering its policy, supported the conservative elements under Prince Boun Oum. The elements in Laos which favoured a *neutral* Laos were led by Prince Souvanna Phouma.

At times there seemed to be a decided danger that the conflict between the factions might lead to a war between the Communist and Western blocs. However, in April 1961 a joint appeal by the British and Soviet Foreign Secretaries (as co-Chairmen of the 1954 Geneva conference) led to a cease-fire which became effective early in May. But it was not for more than a year after this (during which the propaganda of China and the United States vigorously impugned the other's sincerity) that a political settlement was reached. The three princes, after a four days' meeting on the Plaine de Jarres, reached a full agreement for the formation of a national union.

Such was the setting in which the 35,000 or so Chinese shopkeepers, millers, money-lenders, &c. resident in Laos had to operate. They led their own lives apart from the Laotians, but in the early 1950s had only 3 schools of their own (as compared with 16 Catholic schools, 7 French schools, 4 privately owned schools, and 1 school for children of American Government personnel in Vientiane)[14]—which does not suggest that their children were all educated through the medium of the Chinese language. The total enrolment of *all* the schools in 1950 was only about 5,000. Yet, of the few persons outside the governing Lao élite who were able to read the Laotian newspapers and other publications, the Chinese were the most numerous. As for radio sets (long-wave since the cost of short-wave sets was generally prohibitive) the ownership of these was, besides those of the Laotian army, confined to Government officials in the larger towns, the more prosperous Chinese shopkeepers, and a few wealthier village headmen.

Until the advent of American aid to Laos, Chinese business men dominated the markets, but thenceforth until 1958 the United States commodity-import programme, coupled with a patronage-ridden import

---

[14] F. le Bar and A. Suddard, eds., *Laos; its People, Society and Culture* (1960), p. 84. But Prof. Joel Halpern (*The Role of the Chinese in Lao Society* (1961)) has noted that in 1957–9 there were some 3,200 Chinese in private schools. And in 1961 it was reliably reported that there was a total of fifteen Chinese schools in Laos.

system and an unrealistic exchange rate, vastly increased the number of importers and the quantity of imports into Laos. As a result Lao traders emerged in sufficient numbers to offer a challenge to the position of the foreign business men. In 1958, however, monetary reforms were introduced which cut down quick profits but at the same time stabilized the trade and accelerated the formation of Lao-financed commercial enterprises by attracting some foreign capital into Laos. In running these enterprises the Chinese (as well as some Thais) combined with Lao investors.

The first commercial bank in Laos was opened in 1953 when the Bank of Indochina (now the Banque Française d'Asie) opened a branch in Vientiane. Since then other banks have appeared, among them the Lao-Thai Bank, financed mainly by capital from Thailand, including some Chinese capital. The commercial banks, however, were primarily used by business firms since those Laotians who used money (almost exclusively urban dwellers) either stored their cash at home or invested it in jewellery, gold belts, religious objects, or other portables of value. When in need of credit, the individual Laotian would turn to the uncontrolled money-lender, usually Chinese, though sometimes Indian or Vietnamese. The interest they charged was seldom less than 2·5 per cent per month and might exceed 100 per cent per annum. If the money-lender were Chinese, he was most likely to be also a middleman who bought whatever rice the villager had available for market and sold him supplies. So far, the rural credit facilities established by the Government to weaken the money-lender's grip had not been on such terms as could compete successfully with the money-lender's greater flexibility and the fact that he was also the known 'middleman' who would buy the borrower's produce and had the goods he wanted ready at hand gave him the position of advantage.[15]

It should be added, however, that in July 1959 a Royal Ordinance became law which was designed to restrict the following occupations to Lao nationals—customs (officials), land and water transport, immigration, trade in arms and ammunition, trade in radios and radio parts, printing, taxi-, lorry-, and samlor-driving, forestry (for grant of concessions), trade in firewood and charcoal, pawnbroking, butchery and fish-mongering, and hairdressing. The Vietnamese were exempted from the provisions of this Ordinance by two existing Conventions. Consequently it fell wholly upon the Chinese, and was severely enforced. The Chinese even had difficulty in finding Laotian dummies to help them evade it. The result was that they lost quite a bit of ground to the Vietnamese in Laos, who were, for example, able to take over the butchery business—hitherto a Chinese preserve.

[15] Le Bar and Suddard, *Laos*, pp. 194-5.

Cambodia

It would seem that the distribution of the Chinese of Cambodia has not greatly changed since 1949. Approximately 130,000 Chinese (30 per cent of the city's population) were located in Phnom Penh in 1955. Elsewhere they lived principally in the cities of Oudong, Kampot, Battambang, and Kampong Chhnang. The Teochius were the most numerous (about 60 per cent), the Cantonese next (about 20 per cent), then the Hokkiens (7 per cent), and the Hakkas and Hailams 4 per cent each.

The Cambodian Government persisted in refusing equal civil rights to the Chinese. They remained second-class residents. Since independence, moreover, the Cambodian Government had actively encouraged native business men to replace the Chinese. But on a personal as distinguished from a policy basis, the Cambodians seemed favourably disposed towards the Chinese as a whole—which is remarkable in the light of the fact that to many Cambodians the Chinese seem 'the stereotype of the crafty and greedy merchant'.[16] In spite of the compulsory 'apartness' of the Chinese it was likely that the process of cultural assimilation would move steadily forward.

But notwithstanding the care which the Chinese commercial community took to dissociate itself from politics, they could not fail to be associated in the Cambodian mind with the policies of the great country of their origin, so near to little Cambodia, namely the People's China. In recent years Cambodia had been dominated by the personality of Prince Sihanouk. As King Sihanouk, he had succeeded to the throne in 1941, but in 1955 he abdicated in order to form a political movement, the Popular Socialist Community. The objects of this community were to 'realize the unity of the children of the Khmer fatherland', with a view to 'the birth in Cambodia of a true socialist and egalitarian Democracy, and, finally, to the restoration of the fatherland to its past grandeur'. Prince Sihanouk's Socialism was emphatically not Communism, but it was nevertheless very thorough-going of its peculiar kind.

In the cold war, Sihanouk's policy was actively neutral (or 'neutralist' as it was pejoratively termed by his critics). This attitude was publicly endorsed by the Governments of the People's China and of North Vietnam, who both declared their intention to respect Cambodia's neutrality. On the occasion of Sihanouk's state visit to Peking in December 1960, a joint statement was issued by himself and Liu Shao-chi, Chairman of the People's Republic, which referred to the signing of the Sino-Cambodian treaty of friendship and mutual non-aggression which (said the joint statement) had 'not only ushered in a new stage in the friendly relations between China and Cambodia, but also con-

---

[16] Steinberg, *Cambodia*, p. 45.

stitutes an important contribution to the safeguarding of peace in Indo-China and Asia'.[17] Sihanouk's intention, however, was to keep on good terms if possible with both world blocs—but China was nearer to him than the United States. Cambodia, moreover, had continual clashes and friction regarding minority problems with its traditional enemies, Thailand and South Vietnam—both of whom were allies of the United States.

Cambodia's anxiety to keep on good terms with Communist China did not prevent it from taking action to restrict the activities of the local Chinese as well as Vietnamese, &c. In April 1957 a law was passed which forbade foreign nationals from engaging in eighteen specified trades. The consequence was widespread unemployment. A Workers' Relief Committee was set up with the Cambodian Labour Minister as Chairman to distribute funds donated by the People's Relief Administration of the People's Republic of China to the unemployed and to collect contributions for the same purpose from Overseas Chinese resident in Cambodia. Prince Sihanouk also contributed 100,000 reals for the relief of unemployed foreign workers affected by the new law.[18]

[17] Press Release, Office of Chargé d'Affaires, People's Republic of China, London.
[18] *New China News Agency*, 10 Sept. 1957.

25

DEMOGRAPHY

1. FEDERATION OF MALAYA

THE following statistics are abstracted from the 1957 Census:[1]

Racial Composition, 1921–57

Race	Population in thousands Census Year				Percentages Census Year			
	1921	*1931*	*1947*	*1957*	*1921*	*1931*	*1947*	*1957*
Total	2,907	3,788	4,908	6,279	100·0	100·0	100·0	100·0
Malaysians*	1,569	1,864	2,428	3,125	54·0	49·2	49·5	49·8
Chinese	856	1,285	1,885	2,334	29·4	33·9	38·4	37·2
Indians†	439	571	531	707	15·1	15·1	10·8	11·3
Others	43	68	65	112	1·5	1·8	1·3	1·8

Note: all figures are rounded

* Includes nomadic aborigines.   † Includes Pakistanis.

Number of Females per 1,000 Males

	1911	*1921*	*1931*	*1947*	*1957*
Malaysians	..	..	973	1,010	1,013
Chinese	215	371	486	815	926
Indians	320	424	514	687	746
Total population	592	648	703	891	937

[1] *Federation of Malaya Official Year Book 1961* (Kuala Lumpur, 1961).

Percentage of the Population, by Race, enumerated in the Federation & born in the Federation or Singapore

	1921	1931	1947	1957
All races	56·4	58·9	78·3	84·8
Malaysians	..	..	96·0	97·4
Chinese	20·9	29·9	63·5	75·5
Indians	12·1	21·4	51·6	65·0

Federation of Malaya
Population by Country of Birth, 1957
(in thousands)

Country of birth	Malaysians		Chinese		Indians		All races	
	No.	%	No.	%	No.	%	No.	%
Federation of Malaya	3,035	97·1	1,735	74·3	450	64·7	5,283	84·2
Singapore	9	0·3	27	1·2	3	0·4	40	0·6
China	..	..	557	23·9	1	0·1	559	8·9
India	1	..	..	..	239	34·3	244	3·9
Indonesia	72	2·3	3	0·1	..	..	76	1·2
Other	8	0·3	12	0·5	3	0·4	76	1·2
Total	3,125	100·0	2,334	100·0	696	100·0	6,278	100·0

Chinese by Specific Community, 1947 & 1957

Specific community	1947		1957		Increase %
	No. thousands	%	No. thousands	%	
Hokkien	538·2	28·6	740·6	31·7	37·6
Hakka (Kheh)	397·4	21·1	508·8	21·8	28·0
Cantonese	484·0	25·7	505·2	21·7	4·4
Teochiu	207·0	11·0	283·1	12·1	36·7
Hainanese	105·5	5·6	123·0	5·3	16·6
Kwongsai	71·1	3·8	69·1	3·0	2·8
Hokchiu	38·6	2·0	46·1	2·0	19·4
Henghua	9·6	0·5	11·9	0·5	23·8
Hokchia	6·4	0·3	9·8	0·4	52·1
Other	26·7	1·4	34·3	1·5	28·6
Total	1,884·5	100·0	2,333·9	100·0	23·8

Federation of Malaya: Migrational Statistics

(in thousands)

Year	Malaysians			Chinese			Indians			Others		
	Arrivals	Departures	Net	Arrivals	Departures	Net	Arrivals	Departures	Net	Arrivals	Departures	Net
1947		2·2		26·2	29·9	−3·7	19·0	27·4	−8·4	7·8	7·4	0·4
1948		5·8		38·4	40·8	−2·4	24·2	25·1	−0·9	9·4	8·8	0·6
1949		31·0		32·8	42·0	−9·2	20·9	21·5	−0·6	17·9	14·4	3·5
1950		84·5		32·7	34·1	−1·4	29·3	21·9	7·4	35·8	29·3	6·5
1951		134·6		37·4	48·3	−10·9	32·0	25·7	6·3	25·5	23·7	1·8
1952		127·2		34·4	39·9	−5·5	37·8	24·8	13·0	25·3	22·4	2·9
1953		101·9		31·9	33·5	−1·6	39·2	19·9	19·3	24·5	21·4	3·1
1954		135·2		30·9	29·7	1·2	24·0	24·3	−0·3	21·3	18·6	2·7
1955		169·3		36·5	33·7	2·8	31·0	27·9	3·1	24·5	21·6	2·9
1956		158·7		44·8	39·5	5·3	35·8	29·8	6·0	31·1	26·1	4·9
1957		168·8		49·2	46·7	2·5	37·8	32·1	5·7	33·6	28·4	5·2
1958		152·1		47·9	44·7	3·2	38·5	35·5	3·2	35·1	28·9	6·2

Federation of Malaya: Racial Composition of Each State

State	Malaysians			Chinese			Indians		
	1931	*1947*	*1957*	*1931*	*1947*	*1957*	*1931*	*1947*	*1957*
Federation of Malaya	49·2	49·5	49·8	33·9	38·4	37·2	15·1	10·8	11·3
Johore	46·4	43·8	48·0	41·4	48·1	42·4	10·1	7·5	7·7
Kedah	66·6	68·0	67·7	18·2	20·9	20·5	12·0	9·3	9·7
Kelantan	91·2	92·1	91·6	4·9	5·1	5·7	1·9	1·1	1·2
Malacca	51·0	50·3	49·1	34·9	40·2	41·5	12·4	8·2	8·1
Negri Sembilan	37·3	41·3	41·5	39·5	42·7	41·2	21·4	14·2	15·1
Pahang	61·7	54·3	57·2	29·0	38·9	34·6	8·0	5·9	7·0
Penang	32·7	30·5	28·8	49·8	55·4	57·2	15·6	12·8	12·2
Perak	35·7	37·8	39·7	42·3	46·6	44·2	20·7	14·7	14·9
Perlis	80·9	78·3	78·4	13·2	16·7	17·4	2·0	2·4	1·8
Selangor	23·1	26·4	28·8	45·3	51·0	48·2	29·2	20·4	20·1
Trengganu	91·5	92·0	92·1	7·4	7·0	6·6	0·8	0·8	1·1

Mr. Fell, the Superintendent of Census says:

Striking changes have occurred in the racial composition of the population. In 1921 the Malaysians comprised 54% of the total population but ten years later in 1931, the figure had fallen to 49%, and even though the immigration of other races into the Federation had been severely restricted between 1947 and 1957 and the rate of natural increase since 1952 has been as high as that of the Chinese the Malaysian community has still not achieved a figure of 50%. Without doubt the pre-war increase in the proportion of Chinese in the community is accounted for by the heavy net immigration, which reached its peak in 1937.

Federation of Malaya: Census 1957
Population Projections by Race, 1962–82
(in millions)

Year (30 June)	Malaysian	Chinese	Indian	All races	% increase of 1957
1957	3·130	2·238	0·698	6·289	..
MEDIUM					
1962	3·709	2·771	0·843	7·463	18·7
1967	4·381	3·282	1·014	8·831	40·4
1972	5·158	3·888	1·230	10·450	66·2
1977	6·081	4·616	1·510	12·404	97·2
1982	7·130	5·502	1·851	14·703	133·8
HIGH					
1977	6·255	4·875	1·560	12·887	104·9
1982	7·545	6·028	1·974	15·767	150·7
LOW					
1977	5·722	4·442	1·411	11·773	87·2
1982	6·503	5·152	1·664	13·539	115·3

1957 Population of the Federation of Malaya, by Race

Administrative district	Total all communities	Malaysians	Chinese	Indians	Others
FEDERATION OF MALAYA	6,278,763	3,126,706	2,332,936	695,985	123,136
JOHORE	927,565	444,907	392,425	71,002	19,231
Johore Bahru	158,343	54,642	76,556	20,591	6,554
Kluang	91,884	23,495	48,708	14,862	4,819
Muar	221,003	118,649	90,735	10,159	1,460
Batu Pahat	196,976	124,193	65,109	5,153	2,521
Segamat	93,944	30,618	46,090	14,423	2,813
Kota Tinggi	40,397	19,663	16,536	3,529	669
Pontian	99,087	57,683	39,886	1,357	161
Mersing	25,931	15,964	8,805	928	234
KEDAH	701,643	475,747	143,833	66,986	15,077
Kota Star	221,907	159,342	49,126	9,196	4,243
Kubang Pasu	89,221	73,875	11,366	2,596	1,384
Padang Terap	14,531	12,458	498	99	1,476
Yen	49,166	41,448	7,136	448	94
Kuala Muda	121,242	58,467	34,931	23,782	4,002
Sik	19,578	16,699	906	112	1,861
Baling	67,683	48,539	9,183	8,673	1,288
Kulim	72,429	31,525	22,115	18,286	503
Bandar Bahru	29,351	19,054	7,007	3,218	72
Langkawi	16,535	14,340	1,565	536	94
KELANTAN	505,585	463,292	28,816	5,642	7,835
Kota Bharu	150,884	135,150	13,393	1,423	918
Pasir Mas	82,847	78,807	2,855	199	986
Ulu Kelantan	34,564	28,340	4,028	1,968	228
Pasir Puteh	53,866	52,171	1,046	88	561
Bachok	51,520	50,152	964	32	372
Machang	39,440	36,315	2,662	336	127
Tumpat	60,365	53,173	2,425	459	4,308
Tanah Merah	32,099	29,184	1,443	1,137	335
MALACCA	291,246	143,252	120,690	23,248	4,056
Malacca Municipality	69,851	9,350	53,149	4,883	2,469
Malacca Central	80,322	47,727	28,012	3,544	1,039
Alor Gajah	80,534	50,328	22,265	7,637	304
Jasin	60,539	35,847	17,264	7,184	244
NEGRI SEMBILAN	364,331	151,426	149,911	54,428	8,566
Seremban	129,206	31,622	68,415	23,918	5,251
Kuala Pilah	96,255	55,513	31,751	8,455	536
Rembau	34,328	25,577	5,772	2,851	128
Tampin	27,733	10,743	10,622	5,046	1,322
Port Dickson	53,484	15,401	23,979	12,840	1,264
Jelebu	23,325	12,570	9,372	1,318	65

Administrative district	Total all communities	Malaysians	Chinese	Indians	Others
PAHANG	312,949	179,113	108,140	21,832	3,864
Kuantan	52,117	25,857	22,320	3,069	871
Bentong	37,235	7,587	26,101	3,182	365
Raub	37,613	16,884	17,484	2,762	483
Cameron Highlands	12,107	2,445	5,116	3,410	1,136
Pekan	42,688	39,079	3,126	418	65
Lipis	58,317	40,241	14,186	3,455	435
Temerloh	72,872	47,020	19,807	5,536	509
PENANG	572,132	165,081	327,287	69,031	10,733
City of Georgetown	234,930	26,759	171,272	32,023	4,876
Penang N.E.	56,961	10,666	36,857	6,574	2,864
Penang S.W.	47,007	25,267	21,584	2,049	107
Butterworth	110,841	54,246	41,088	13,269	2,238
Bukit Mertajam	75,330	31,798	36,813	6,214	505
Nibong Tebal	47,063	18,345	19,673	8,902	143
PERAK	1,221,390	484,878	539,368	178,480	18,664
Upper Perak	43,599	25,537	15,434	1,637	991
Krian	117,530	72,635	27,419	17,020	456
Larut and Matang	174,357	77,015	67,417	26,154	3,771
Kuala Kangsar	151,200	89,267	43,392	17,037	1,504
Dindings	95,170	26,899	51,529	16,323	419
Kinta	367,139	65,890	244,074	48,140	9,035
Batang Padang	98,796	37,353	41,164	18,932	1,347
Lower Perak	173,599	90,282	48,939	33,237	1,141
PERLIS	90,866	71,268	15,763	1,547	2,288
Perlis	90,866	71,268	15,763	1,547	2,288
SELANGOR	1,021,891	291,393	488,634	201,047	31,817
Kuala Lumpur	477,224	75,662	299,813	76,106	25,643
Ulu Selangor	82,934	20,515	38,655	22,560	1,204
Kuala Langat	79,754	35,713	24,277	19,378	386
Klang	149,957	37,005	65,454	44,393	3,105
Ulu Langat	68,214	27,072	29,043	11,229	870
Kuala Selangor	154,808	95,426	31,392	27,381	609
TRENGGANU	278,165	256,349	18,069	2,742	1,005
Besut	53,326	51,691	1,210	118	307
Kuala Trengganu	124,333	116,065	7,090	875	303
Ulu Trengganu	22,682	22,242	389	36	15
Marang	14,550	14,164	356	24	6
Dungun	30,694	25,772	3,667	970	285
Kemanan	32,580	26,415	5,357	719	89

Source: H. Fell, *1957 Population Census of the Federation of Malaya* (Kuala Lumpur), vol. i. Figures corrected in final report to total 6,278,758—Malaysians 3,125,474, Chinese 2,333,756, Indians 696,186, others 123,342.

2. SINGAPORE

A Census of Singapore was taken on the night of 17–18 June 1957.[2] The population as enumerated was 1,445,929 (excluding (a) 27,299 non-locally domiciled Services personnel and transients afloat, and (b) 2,619 persons enumerated in Christmas Island, which was transferred to Australia on 1 January 1958) as compared with (1947) 938,144 (excluding 25,860 Service personnel, 2,530 transients afloat, and 7,517 Japanese surrendered personnel). Thus between 1947 and 1957 it increased by 54·1 per cent as against an increase of 68 per cent over the sixteen-year period 1931–47. The prime factors contributing to this rapid increase were a high and stable birth-rate, a very low and declining death-rate, and some movement of people into Singapore from the Federation. This was in contrast to the decades before the Second World War when a majority of the increase in population could be attributed to immigration rather than to the natural increase.

Population Increase, 1947–57

Racial group	1947	1957	1947–57 Increase	%
Malaysians	113,803	197,059	83,256	73·2
Chinese	729,473	1,090,596	361,123	49·5
Indians and Pakistanis	68,967	124,084	55,117	79·9
Eurasians	9,110	11,382	2,272	24·9
Europeans	9,279	10,826	1,547	16·7
Others	7,512	11,982	4,470	59·5
Total	938,144	1,445,929	507,785	54·1

Of the total, 75·4 per cent were Chinese, 13·6 per cent Malaysians, 8·6 per cent Indians and Pakistanis, and 2·4 per cent were other races.

Population by Sex & Sex Ratio

	1947 Male	1947 Female	1957 Male	1957 Female	Males per 1,000 females 1947	Males per 1,000 females 1957
Malaysians	62,264	51,539	103,249	93,810	1,208	1,101
Chinese	387,373	342,100	555,663	534,933	1,132	1,039
Indians and Pakistanis	51,715	17,252	85,988	38,096	2,998	2,257
Eurasians	4,445	4,665	5,676	5,706	953	995
Europeans	5,136	4,143	5,767	5,059	1,240	1,140
Others	4,030	3,482	6,417	5,565	1,157	1,153
Total	514,963	423,181	762,760	683,169	1,217	1,117

[2] *State of Singapore Annual Report 1959*, p. 48.

An estimate of the mid-1959 population by racial group and sex, based on the 1957 Census figures plus excess of births over deaths plus net migration was (in thousands), Malaysians 217·3, Chinese 1,190·1, Indians and Pakistanis 134·6, Eurasians 12·0, Europeans 12·2, others 13·3.
The following table gives the comparative natural increase of the several racial groups:

Natural-Increase & Crude-Natural-Increase Rates

	1947		1957		1958		1959	
	Natural increase	Natural increase rates	Natural increase	Natural increase rates	Natural increase	Natural increase rates	Natural increase	Natural increase rates
Malaysians	3,444	30·3	7,350	37·3	8,074	38·9	8,673	39·9
Chinese	24,261	33·3	38,567	35·4	38,576	33·8	38,368	32·2
Indians & Pakistanis	2,209	32·1	4,229	34·1	4,324	33·4	4,316	32·1
Eurasians	275	30·2	285	25·0	275	23·4	270	22·4
Europeans	238	6·8	317	29·3	273	24·0	244	20·0
Others	107	14·2	362	30·2	397	32·3	418	31·3
Total	30,534	32·6	51,110	35·3	51,919	34·3	52,289	33·1
Male	14,723	..	25,584	..	25,923	..	26,061	..
Female	15,811	..	25,526	..	25,996	..	26,228	..
Both sexes	30,534	..	51,110	..	51,919	..	52,289	..

The estimate for Dec. 1960 (*Statesman's Year-Book, 1962,* p. 219) was 1,253,400 Chinese, 232,400 Malaysians, 140,400 Indians and Pakistanis, 13,000 Europeans, 12,500 Eurasians, and 13,700 others; total 1,665,400.

Singapore and the Federation of Malaya formed a single unit for the purpose of immigration control. The quota system was never effective in permitting selective immigration by which only those immigrants beneficial to the country were admitted. To remedy this, as from 1 August 1953 amendments were made to the Immigration Ordinance by which all newcomers were prohibited from permanent entry unless they fell within one or more of the categories specified in the schedule. In 1959 further amendments were introduced. The main change was to limit the classes of persons entitled to entry into Singapore without a permit or pass to citizens of Singapore only, but reserving a qualified right to Federal citizens. The other classes of persons who, prior to the amendment, had enjoyed a right of entry—such as British subjects born in Malaya, British subjects ordinarily resident in Malaya, British subjects naturalized in Singapore—had their right abrogated. A further restriction on the entry of persons for permanent residence was made by the

Immigration Prohibition Order effective from 1 December 1959 by which the wife of a resident who was not a citizen of Singapore (not herself a citizen) was not eligible for entry if she had been separated from her husband for more than five years, and the entry of the children of citizens, who until 1 December 1959 had been allowed to enter if they were under 15 years of age, was limited to those under 6 years old.

The Singapore Citizenship Ordinance 1957 introduced a Singapore citizenship which could be acquired by birth, descent, registration, or naturalization. Until the coming into operation of the State of Singapore Act (UK), 1958, all persons born in Singapore were British subjects and citizens of the United Kingdom and Colonies. During 1959, 70,083 persons applied for Singapore citizenship by descent or registration— 12,006 applications were approved, 1,700 refused, 10,045 abandoned or withdrawn, while 46,332 were under consideration at the end of the year. Since the introduction of Singapore citizenship, 339,214 persons were registered by 31 December 1959. Singapore citizens by birth were not required to register.

A noticeable feature of the year 1959 was the increased number of prosecutions for illegal entry into Singapore, 136 persons being prosecuted for offences against the Immigration Ordinance, as compared with 39 in 1958. With the action taken by the Indonesian Government against alien retailers in villages, the majority of whom were of Chinese racial origin, there had been a bigger number of illegal immigrants from Indonesia entering Singapore.

Figures at the 1957 Census showed that 64·3 per cent of the total population were born in Singapore, 8·6 per cent in the Federation of Malaya, and the remaining 27·1 per cent in other countries.

Of the 6,073 persons permitted to enter Singapore for residence in 1959, 5,014 were wives and children of persons lawfully resident as compared with 4,625 in 1958. Similarly, there was an increase in the number of persons admitted under special compassionate grounds. The majority of the latter were aged parents of local residents. The figure was 1,023 (including 243 fathers, 730 mothers) as compared with 868 in 1958. The majority of immigrants issued with entry permits were from China and India.

The figures that follow relate to an earlier period.

Chinese compared with Total Population at Various Periods
(From 1947 Census Report)

PENANG

Year	Total population			Chinese		
	Male	Female	Total	Male	Female	Total
1812	..	..	26,107	..	..	7,558
1820b	..	..	35,035	..	..	8,595
1820c	..	..	6,185	..	..	325
1833	..	..	86,275	..	..	11,010
1842b	..	..	40,499	..	..	9,715
1844c	..	..	51,479	..	..	4,107
1851	65,755	42,159	107,914	19,750	4,438	24,188
1860	76,339	48,433	124,772	27,050	9,172	36,222
1871	84,149	49,081	133,230	30,347	6,214	36,561
1881d	122,656	65,589	188,245	54,851	12,503	67,354
1891	150,445	81,558	232,003	68,672	18,316	86,988
1901	154,190	89,904	244,094	72,926	24,545	97,471
1911	167,535	103,821	271,376	77,401	32,805	110,206
1921	176,942	117,273	294,215	86,113	47,121	133,234
1931	197,487	143,888	341,375	101,429	68,556	169,985

b figures for Penang Island only.
c   „   „   Province Wellesley only.
d excluding Pulau Pangkor and the Dindings from 1881 onwards.

Note: The Census table from which this was taken also gives authorities for the counts.

MALACCA

Year	Total population			Chinese		
	Male	Female	Total	Male	Female	Total
1750	..	..	9,635	..	..	2,161
1766	..	..	7,216	..	..	1,390
1817	..	..	19,647	..	..	1,006
1827	..	..	33,162	..	..	5,006
1829	..	..	30,164	..	..	4,797
1834	..	..	29,260	..	..	4,143
1842	..	..	46,096	..	..	6,882
1852	35,170	27,344	62,514	7,735	2,873	10,608
1860	36,023	31,244	67,267	7,037	3,002	10,039
1871	41,936	35,820	77,756	9,876	3,606	13,482
1881	52,059	41,520	93,579	15,721	4,020	19,741
1891	50,337	41,833	92,170	14,226	3,935	18,161
1901	51,469	44,018	95,487	15,061	4,407	19,468
1911	75,676	49,276	124,952	29,974	6,120	36,094
1921	90,934	62,757	153,691	33,563	12,290	45,853
1931	105,245	81,632	186,877	42,573	22,729	65,302

PAHANG

Year	Total population			Chinese		
	Male	Female	Total	Male	Female	Total
1891	..	..	57,444*	..	..	3,241
1901	46,746	35,970	84,113	8,225	470	8,695
1911	72,234	46,474	118,708	21,827	2,460	24,287
1921	88,068	58,199	146,267	27,830	6,424	34,254
1931	105,514	74,603	180,117	37,662	14,629	52,291

* An unreliable census.

JOHORE

1911	122,324	58,308	180,632	56,914	6,633	63,547
1921	186,556	96,038	282,594	79,209	18,188	97,397
1931	323,660	181,929	505,589	158,488	56,769	215,257

KEDAH

1911	137,139	108,847	245,986	28,750	4,996	33,746
1921	194,917	143,790	338,707	47,492	11,984	59,476
1931	237,831	191,860	429,691	53,787	24,628	78,415

KELANTAN

1911	144,319	142,432	286,751	7,225	2,619	9,844
1921	157,723	151,851	309,574	9,497	3,378	12,875
1931	184,705	177,812	362,517	12,029	5,583	17,612

TRENGGANU

1911	76,153	77,920	154,073	3,259	910	4,169
1921	77,309	76,670	153,979	6,167	1,158	7,325
1931	92,631	87,443	180,074	10,468	2,892	13,360

PERLIS

1911	16,808	15,938	32,746	1,319	308	1,627
1921	21,236	18,851	40,087	2,701	901	3,602
1931	26,027	23,269	49,296	4,564	1,936	6,500

PERAK

Year	Total population			Chinese		
	Male	Female	Total	Male	Female	Total
1879	50,658	30,326	80,984	19,114	1,259	20,373
1889	179,590	..	..	107,274	..	..
1891	158,847	59,022	217,869	89,337	5,940	95,277
1901	242,173	91,605	333,778	137,362	13,530	151,192
1911b	349,821	152,538	502,359	183,621	35,814	219,435
1921	386,610	224,559	611,169	165,089	62,513	227,602
1931	476,697	308,963	785,660	221,495	111,089	332,584

SELANGOR

1884	..	..	46,568	..	..	28,236
1887	..	..	97,106	..	..	73,155
1891	67,051	14,541	81,592	47,610	3,234	50,844
1901	136,823	31,966	168,789	98,212	11,386	109,598
1911b	221,360	73,106	294,466	124,638	26,534	151,172
1921	267,256	133,847	401,103	122,001	48,725	170,726
1931	327,721	205,814	533,535	154,456	87,040	241,496

b, including an estimated proportion of the shipping population.

NEGRI SEMBILAN

1891	40,561	24,658	65,219	14,845	546	15,391
1901	64,565	31,463	96,028	31,330	1,601	32,931
1911	87,651	42,548	130,199	36,965	3,878	40,843
1921	119,635	59,193	178,828	53,694	11,525	65,219
1931	148,381	85,418	233,799	68,360	24,011	92,371

SINGAPORE

1821	..	..	4,727	..	..	1,159
1823	7,106	3,577	10,683	2,956	361	3,317
1833	15,181	5,797	20,978	7,650	867	8,517
1836	22,755	7,229	29,984	12,870	879	13,749
1840	..	..	35,389	..	..	17,704
1850	42,107	10,784	52,891	25,749	2,239	27,988
1860	70,122	11,612	81,734	46,795	3,248	50,043
1871	74,348	22,763	97,111	47,104	7,468	54,572
1881	105,423	33,785	139,208	72,571	14,195	86,766
1891a	141,619	43,498	185,117	100,446	21,462	121,908
1901	171,874	58,030	229,904	131,007	33,674	164,681
1911b	222,760	88,543	311,303	166,057	58,173	224,230
1921	292,353	138,992	431,345	220,307	101,268	321,575
1931	362,882	207,246	570,128	265,618	158,175	423,793

a, including Christmas Island and Cocos-Keeling Islands from 1891 onwards.
b, excluding Labuan from 1911 onwards.

26

TUMASIK AND MALACCA, 1349–1795

OUR first undoubted landfall in the history of the Chinese in Malaya is in 1349 when Wang Ta-yuan, a Chinese trader, writes of Tumasik, or old Singapore, the 'Sea Town'. He says that when Chinese junks went to the western sea the people of Tumasik let them go unmolested, but when, on the way back, they reached the Carimon Islands, the crews of the junks got out their armour and padded screens to protect themselves against arrow fire, for it was certain that two or three hundred pirate ships would attack them. Tumasik was besieged in this year by Siamese ships, and according to Wang Ta-yuan, the arrival of the Chinese fleet effected the relief of the city. He further states that 'the people live mixed up with the Chinese' in Tumasik. So here, it seems, we have a more or less permanent settlement of Chinese in fourteenth-century Malaya.

Wang Ta-yuan also visited Trengganu in the same year, but he does not mention any Chinese settlement there.

By 1365 Majapahit, the last Hindu empire of Java, claimed Tumasik as a dependency, but within a few years that medieval haunt of pirates fell under the domination of Siam. It was the murder of Siam's governor of Singapore that drove his guest, a Palembang prince married to a Majapahit princess, to flee up-country where about 1400 he founded Malacca.[1] From the beginning the kingdom was a tributary of Siam to which it sent 40 taels of gold annually.

At the beginning of the fifteenth century Malacca began to have close contacts with China. In 1403, says the Ming History,[2] the Emperor of China sent the eunuch Yin Ching to Malacca with presents of silk brocade. The King, Parameswara, 'was very glad' and in 1405 sent a return mission to China. The Emperor spoke in laudatory terms of his master, appointed him the King of the country of Malacca, and gave him a commission, a seal, a suit of silk clothes, and a yellow umbrella. The

[1] Sir Richard Winstedt, *Malaya and its History* (London, 1948), p. 32. Sir Richard says 'about 1403', but in view of the fact that Yin Ching visited Malacca in that year (though he points out that the Chinese histories can in some cases be wrong) he proposes changing this to the more indefinite 1400 in the next edition of his book. Godinho de Eredia gives the date of the foundation of Malacca as 1398 in *Meridional India and Cathay* (dedicated from Goa, 1613), trans. from the Portuguese with notes by J. V. Mills, *JRASMB*, viii, pt. 1 (1930), pp. 1–288. See also Winstedt, 'The Malay Founder of Mediaeval Malacca', *Bull. of Oriental and African Studies* (1948), xii, pts. 3 and 4.

[2] *Chinese Dynastic Histories*, Book 325.

King, through his representatives, then 'requested that his mountains might be made guardians of the country, to which request the emperor gave his consent; he prepared an inscription with a piece of verse at the end and ordered a tablet to be erected in these mountains'. In 1407 Parameswara again sent envoys to China.

The dates of Cheng Ho's voyages have been discussed in Chapter 2.[3] Whether or not he visited the Malayan kingdom in his earlier voyages of 1405–7 when his fleet passed through these waters, it seems certain that he did go there in the voyage of 1414–15, for he brought back with him the King of Malacca, his wife, and his son to present tribute. Cheng Ho took with him on this third voyage the Chinese Mohammedan Ma Huan, who later wrote a book describing the voyages called the *Ying yai sheng lan* or 'General Account of the Shores of the Ocean'.

Ma Huan tells us that at the time of Cheng Ho's visit the soil of Malacca was barren and saline, the crops were poor, and agriculture was not in favour. He states that it was Cheng Ho who in 1409 gave Parameswara 'a silver seal, a cap, and official robes and declared him king, on which', he remarks, 'Malacca ceased to be a dependency of Siam'. But the Siamese, to judge by their subsequent conduct, did not seem to be aware of this fact!

Ma Huan tells us that Malacca 'is visited by Chinese merchant vessels; whenever these come a barrier is made' and to this Groeneveldt adds a note, 'for the purposes of collecting tolls', which seems the most likely explanation. But it does not appear that there was at this time any permanent Chinese settlement in Malacca.

The *Hai Yü*, or 'Report from the Ocean', published in 1537, but like so many Chinese books referring probably to a much earlier period, tells us that the cost of living in Malacca was high, about five times what it was in China, that fowls, dogs, geese, and ducks were imported, and that pork, a forbidden article of food to the native Mohammedans, was eaten by the Chinese 'who live here'. This suggests that some time previous to the writing of the *Hai Yü* the Chinese began to reside in Malacca, but a further reference to the 'merchants of ships who live in an hotel' would seem to point to these, at least, being but temporary sojourners.[4] Book 325 of the Ming History states of Malacca that the men and women wear

---

[3] See pp. 17–18.

[4] A footnote to the present writer's *The Chinese in Malaya* (London, 1948), p. 19, examines the Chinese text of this passage. According to the *Hai Yü* (cited by Groeneveldt) the King lived in a house of which the fore-part was covered with tiles left here by Cheng Ho. The Rev. W. G. Shellabear says that Chinese contacts with Malacca were very early, but that when the Portuguese and the Dutch were fighting for possession of Malacca, there appear to have been few, if any, Chinese remaining there, for Valentijn says that in 1641 the Dutch imported Chinese from Batavia to work in the fields and gardens, and that up to that time the trade seems to have been monopolized by Indian merchants. Up to the end of the sixteenth century (says Shellabear) Chinese immigration into the Malay Archipelago was confined almost exclusively to the island of Java, where they enjoyed the greatest security, and freedom to carry on trade under the protection of the Dutch.

their hair in a knot, but some are of lighter colour, being descendants of the Chinese.[5]

Now we come to the Portuguese authorities on Malacca, most of whom refer to the Malay period. Among them are d'Albuquerque,[6] the natural son of the conqueror of Malacca, Osorio,[7] Barros,[8] and Eredia,[9] and in 1944 their number was added to by the publication of the *Suma Oriental* of Tomé Pires[10] from a manuscript recently discovered.

D'Albuquerque says that before the coming of the Malays, Malacca's site was occupied by twenty or thirty persons who lived by fishing and piracy. The place, after the founding of the Malay kingdom, depended on passing Chinese junks for trade. A King named Xaquendarsa,[11] after begetting many sons, went to China for three years. 'Sri Maharaja' of Malacca went to China in 1424 and sent envoys in 1431 in a Sumatran vessel. These envoys returned with Cheng Ho in that year and were instructed to convey the usual injunctions to the Siamese that they should cease interfering with Malacca. Tribute was sent to China in 1433 and 1435, and in 1445 Malacca sent envoys asking for recognition. There are in these works a number of references to Malacca's Chinese contacts during this century. The second King of Malacca is said to have married a daughter of the King of China's captain (this suggests a more or less settled Chinese community to justify a 'Captain China'). But the impression we receive, nevertheless, is that during this century the merchants of Arab and Indian merchants were more important, at least in the aggregate, than were the Chinese—ships of Cambaya, Chaul, Dabul, Calicut, Aden, Mecca, Shehr, Juda, Coromandel, Bengal, Gores (Liu Chiu Isles), Java, and Pegu are mentioned as coming to Malacca.

There were four court officials at Malacca during the Malay period, called Shahbandars—one a Chinese, another a Javanese, a third a Cambayan, and a fourth a Bengali. The Malay Temenggong, who was judge of the custom house, was over all these. Malacca (according to d'Albuquerque) was the 'most extensive place in the world for trade'.

This information is amplified by Osorio and the others. The former remarks that Malacca was about four miles in length, but its breadth was inconsiderable; it abounded with trees which produced excellent fruits,

[5] But it is to be remembered that the Chinese dynastic histories were written after the close of the dynasty and by stay-at-home scholars, so that there is little guarantee that facts relating to more recent affairs have not crept in.

[6] *The Commentaries of the Great Afonso Dalboquerque* (compiled by the son), trans. from the Portuguese ed. of 1774 by W. Gray Birch (London, Hakluyt Soc., 1880), vol. iii.

[7] Jeronimo Osorio da Fonseca, *The History of the Portuguese during the Reign of Emmanuel*, trans. by James Gibbs (London, 1752).   [8] João de Barros, *Da Asia* (Lisbon, 1778–88).

[9] Emanuel Godinho de Eredia, *Meridional India and Cathay* (dedicated from Goa, 1613), trans. from the Portuguese with notes by J. V. Mills, *JRASMB*, viii, pt. i (1930), pp. 1–288.

[10] Tomé Pires, *The Suma Oriental of Tomé Pires* (London, Hakluyt Soc., 1944) (written in Malacca and India from 1512 to 1515), trans. by Armando Cortesão.

[11] Xaquendarsa (says Winstedt), the Parameswara (Paramjçura of Pires), was Muhammad Iskandar Shah. *JRASMB*, xiii, pt. i (Mar. 1935), p. 25.

but most of the staple foods were imported. The walls and buildings of the town were exceedingly elegant and magnificent.

Captain Begbie[12] says that according to the *Malay Annals* one of the five excellent wells at Bukit China was dug by Chinese in the reign of Mansur Shah. Sultan Mansur Shah was (see Winstedt's *History of Malaya*) a young man and reigning in 1459. If this is so, it suggests that there was a Chinese community in Malacca at the time.

In Malacca there is a tablet stating that Captain Li Chi-t'uan was a native of Lu Kiang (Fukien) who left home at the beginning of the Ming dynasty and settled in Malacca. The tablet purports to have been erected in the I Ch'ou year of the Lung Fei reign. There was no such reign in the Ming or Ch'ing dynasties and the invention possibly marks the refusal of the Malaccan Chinese to recognize the new Manchu dynasty.[13] But this tablet is evidence that the early settlers in Malacca came from Fukien province.

Some of the oldest Chinese relics now extant in Malacca (or indeed in Malaya) are to be found at Bukit China, which, together with Bukit Gudong and Bukit Tempurong, forms an enormous burial ground, said to be one of the largest outside China. A very few old graves with coral tombstones, the inscriptions of which are no longer legible, are still discernible at Bukit China. Some of these probably date back to the sixteenth century, if not earlier. There are about a dozen Chinese graves of the second order of antiquity dating from the last decades of the Ming and the first decades of the Ch'ing dynasty. One or two of them have the words 'Imperial Ming' clearly inscribed on them. The Bukit China cemetery is said to have been bought and donated by Li Kap (i.e. Kapitan Li) in the middle of the seventeenth century.[14]

The Rev. Father Cardon, the outstanding modern authority on the history of Malacca, says that, in spite of the fragments of evidence suggesting the contrary, he is driven to the conclusion that the Chinese began to establish themselves in Malacca only at the beginning of the Portuguese occupation.[15] The traditions of the Chinese of Malacca themselves do not encourage setting a very early date to their settlements. The records of no family go back farther than the first half of the seventeenth century. The Li traditions go back farthest, though those of the Tans and the Tays are not much less ancient.

In the year 1509 Diogo Lopes de Sequiera, a Portuguese commander, arrived at Malacca with the intention of attacking it. When he came to anchor in the port he found there four Chinese ships, the captains of

---

[12] Begbie, *The Malayan Peninsula* (Madras, 1834).

[13] A similar device was adopted at the beginning of the present century, when 'Patriotic Debentures' were sold by Sun Yat-sen, for they were inscribed with the name of the T'ien Yun period which had no existence.

[14] Rev. Yeh Fen's article on the Chinese in Malacca in *Historical Guide of Malacca* (Singapore, 1936).   [15] In an unpublished article communicated to the author.

which immediately waited on him. Sequiera was much taken by their polite, friendly behaviour and agreeable manners and was at once at home with them. He paid visits to their junks and was well entertained. Noticing that the Portuguese, thinking themselves secure, walked about the city without fear, the Chinese warned him against trusting to the good intentions of the natives who were, they said, a deceitful, wicked, and perfidious people who would fall on them as soon as they thought it safe. Sequiera disregarded their advice, with the result that a number of his men were seized and imprisoned. He held a council of war at which he said that all ships, except those of the Chinese, ought to be burnt and the city battered down by cannon, but he had not sufficient force to carry out his plans.

Among the instructions given to Sequiera by his superior was one particularly concerning the Chinese. He was to ascertain a whole catalogue of facts concerning them—where they lived and how far away, how often they came to Malacca, whether they were weak men or warriors, whether they were Christians or pagans, and, if the latter, what they worshipped, and many other matters of a similar sort. The answers that Sequiera gave to these questions do not appear to be extant, but it is possible that they may be hidden away in the archives of Portugal.

We now come to the year 1511 when the great Alfonso d'Albuquerque[16] conquered Malacca, professedly in revenge for the treatment of Sequiera, but actually to carry out the project which Sequiera had been unable to accomplish. When the Portuguese fleet announced its arrival with a fanfare of trumpets the Chinese merchants who were at Malacca made their way to present their respects to the commander. There were five Chinese junks in the port and they had been detained there for some days by the King of Malacca who had intended to use them against the King of Daru with whom he was at war. The Chinese were indignant at their treatment and wished to help the Portuguese commander in any way they could, giving him information and placing their junks at his disposal.

The story of the assault on Malacca belongs to the general history of that place, and all that we need do here is to record the fact of the conquest, and to mention that after the city had fallen d'Albuquerque massacred most of the inhabitants without quarter to man, woman, or child. One of the Chinese junks was dispatched with a Portuguese, Duarte Fernandes, to bring the King of Siam news of the event.

Sultan Mahmud fled to Pahang when driven out of Malacca by the Portuguese. He then sent an embassy headed by his uncle, Nacem Mudaliar, to the Chinese Emperor to appeal to him for help. The embassy was well received, but whether or not the Emperor was sympathetic

[16] More properly Afonso Dalboquerque, but the above form is more common.

to the request for help he had his hands full at the time repelling Mongol invaders.

Tomé Pires (whom Sir Richard Winstedt regards as the principal Portuguese authority for the Malay kingdom of Malacca), who was in Malacca very soon after the Portuguese conquest, says of the Chinese as he saw them:

All the Chinese eat pigs, cows, and all other animals. They drink a fair amount of all sorts of beverages. They praise their wine greatly. They get pretty drunk. They are weak people, of small account. Those who are to be seen in Malacca are not very truthful, and steal—that is the common people. They eat with two sticks, and the earthenware or china bowl in their left hand close to their mouth with the two sticks to suck in. This is the Chinese way.[17]

The Portuguese followed a policy of exclusive monopoly and as far as possible compelled all passing ships to call at Malacca. In 1546 the duty was 10 per cent on all Chinese goods and 8 per cent on all Bengal goods, but this did not include the miscellaneous exactions of officials and others. This policy brought the Portuguese into collision with other nations and for the 129 years of the occupation of Malacca they were almost constantly at war, first with the neighbouring Asian countries, and latterly with their European rivals, the Dutch. Malacca was besieged several times, but was not captured until after the Dutch siege of 1640–1.

In Portuguese Malacca the Chinese quarter was known as Campon China (Campon, or *Kampong*, being the Malay for village). There is no record of the number of its inhabitants (the Portuguese in their enumerations lumped together all non-Christian Asiatics as 'infidels'), but, to judge from the size of Kampong China as shown in Eredia's map, the population cannot have been very extensive, and we know that there were only 300–400 Chinese in Malacca after the Dutch conquest in 1641.

When d'Albuquerque left Malacca he did not appoint a separate headman for the Chinese, but it would seem that a captain of the Chinese was recognized soon after.

Malacca was a ruined city directly after the Dutch conquest. War and disease had taken their toll. The suburbs were entirely ruined. There was hardly a house standing. The gardens and orchards on both sides of the city had been destroyed and the beautiful fruit-trees had been hacked down. The total population of Dutch, Portuguese, and slaves and Chinese was counted at 2,150. The contemporary Dutch official, Commissary Justus Schouten, compares this poor total ruefully with the 20,000 he estimated to be the population of the city and environs before the siege.[18] No separate enumeration of the Chinese was made, but Schouten estimates their numbers at 300–400.

[17] *Suma Oriental*, p. 116. Prof. A. C. Moule says that this is the earliest European description of chopsticks.

[18] P. A. Leupe, *The Siege and Capture of Malacca from the Portuguese*, trans. by Mac Hacobian, *JRASMB*, xiv, pt. 1 (1936).

The 300 to 400 Chinese shopkeepers, craftsmen, and farmers should be allowed to settle down at their own convenience, provided that they cultivate the gardens within their territory. They can hire or occupy those empty houses which can be saved from collapse or destruction. As it is dangerous to allow a great number of foreigners to crowd in a weakly garrisoned place, admission within the city walls should be refused to all inhabitants and foreigners.

Schouten expected the Chinese to figure in the reconstruction of Malacca. He said that to assist in the cultivation of the ruined gardens in the southern suburbs (which later the Dutch East India Company would resume and lease out at a profit) 'some 800 to 1,000 Chinese would be very useful'. But, in spite of the temporary remission of poll-tax to encourage the Chinese to come to the settlement, the Dutch terms for trade were not such as would encourage Chinese or other traders to come in any great numbers.

Governor Balthasar Bort in 1678 made a very exact survey of Malacca.[19] There were then 137 brick and 583 atap houses with a population of 4,884 persons. In the city itself the Chinese had 81 brick and 51 atap houses with 127 men, 140 women, 159 children, 93 male slaves, 137 female slaves, and 60 children of slaves; outside the north suburb there were 324 Chinese; outside the north suburb on the seashore, 24; on the way to Bukit China, 78; together with other small communities. The total was 852 Chinese for all the Malacca territory outside the fortress—not a large number, especially considering that the women were natives, mostly Batak and Balinese slaves. In addition there were 40 Chinese within the fortress.

As a means of securing their monopoly the Dutch from Malacca patrolled the Straits as far as Singapore. The instructions given to the captains of patrol ships in 1667 concerned junks and other vessels manned by Koxinga Chinese.[20] All such vessels were to be regarded as enemies since Koxinga had wiped out the Dutch factory in Formosa, and when sighted were to be overtaken and overpowered. After the capture of such a vessel no more than 'common plundering' was to be allowed to the Dutch crew, the hatches were at once to be sealed, and the complete cargo was to be brought to Malacca and handed over. As regards the Chinese who did not belong to Koxinga's faction, they were to be 'amicably persuaded' to come to Malacca. But if they persisted in going to Johore (with which the Dutch were on terms of hostility) they were not to be obstructed.

The captains were told how to distinguish between the two kinds of Chinese by their mode of doing their hair—the Chinese who had submitted to Tartar rule had their hair shaved or cut to the crown of their head, while the remainder was worn in a long plait or an unplaited tress;

[19] Balthasar Bort, *Report on Malacca*, trans. by M. J. Bremner, ibid. v, pt. 1 (1927).
[20] Koxinga himself had died in 1662. (See A. W. Hummel, *Eminent Chinese of the Ch'ing Period* (Washington, 1943) under Cheng Ch'eng-Kung.)

very often they wore Tartar (Manchu) caps of plaited rush or straw adorned at the top with a tail of red horse-hair or silk. The Koxinga Chinese wore their hair long fastened up at the back, though, to escape recognition, they sometimes dressed their hair in the Manchu fashion— but only at the moment when the Dutch caught up with their ships.

The Chinese of both Dutch and Portuguese Malacca were not prominent in local affairs. Baretto de Resende's 'Account of Malacca' (still in manuscript) written in 1646, but referring to the period c. 1638,[21] and Valentijn's *Account of Malacca* published in 1726[22] make practically no mention of the Chinese. Father Cardon says: 'At first sight one is astonished that the Portuguese historians make practically no mention of the Chinese in Malacca, but, on reflection, this silence explains itself. The Chinese, being merchants, were more adept at handling the abacus than the musket.' Even in 1606, 1629, and 1641 there is no mention of any Chinese element in the defence of the city. 'With them Mars yielded to Mercury.' Ruy de Brito says that they are 'a people who exert themselves effectively in commerce; you will get nothing out of their hands without paying the proper price'.[23] Nor had the Chinese yet begun to supply the artisans for the Peninsula, for after the capture of Malacca in 1641 the Governor is found asking the Laksamana of Acheen to send him 200 Malay carpenters and timber to repair the bridge.

Throughout the eighteenth century the Dutch East India Company declined, and the process was accelerated during the latter decades. The English East India Company took advantage of this and built up a flourishing smuggling trade in the archipelago. Gradually the Dutch abandoned their conquests—one group of islands after another. The occupation of Penang in 1786 was a deadly blow to Malacca. By 1795 all that was left of the Dutch East Indian Empire was Java, the Moluccas, Malacca, and a few forts elsewhere. In 1795 England captured Malacca and then the Moluccas. That same year a commission appointed by the States General reported that the Company was bankrupt and its commerce nearly annihilated. In 1798 the charter was annulled by the newly-founded Batavian republic and the Government took over the administration of what was left of the Company's possessions.

The conditions in Malacca, as we have seen, were not encouraging to Chinese settlement, but the Chinese population had increased to 2,161 by 1750. How far this increase was due to immigration and how far to natural increase through intermarriage with local women and slaves is not certain. In 1750 the total population of Malacca was 9,635, but by 1760 the Chinese had dropped to 1,390 out of a total population of 7,216.

---

[21] MS. no. 197 Sloane Collection, British Museum. See also G. Maxwell, 'Baretto de Resende's Account of Malacca', *JRASMB*, xx (1911), pp. 1–24.

[22] Trans. by Muller, ibid. nos. xiii (1884) and xxii (1890).

[23] Letter to King Dom Manoel of Portugal, dated 6 Jan. 1514 (*Alguns Documentos do Archivo Nacional da Torre de Tombo*) (Lisbon, 1892).

As a footnote to this chapter we may record that under the more en-lightened[24] British administration, immigration revived somewhat, and in the present century rubber has brought a new prosperity. One important fact that hindered Malacca's progress was that its harbour was too shallow for modern ships.

In 1827 the Chinese accounted for 3,989 of the free population and for 521 of the slaves and slave debtors; in 1834 there were 4,143 Chinese in a total population of 29,260; in 1842 the figures were 6,882 in 46,097; in 1860 10,039 in 67,267. In the last year there were only 3,002 females to 7,037 males.

27

PENANG AND SINGAPORE, 1786–1900

THE British had had a dozen factories in the Malay Archipelago in the early seventeenth century, but, unable to withstand competition backed by the Dutch Government, or, alternatively, to share the cost of Dutch forts, they decided in 1623, after the massacre of their nationals at Amboyna, 'to abandon Malayan spices for the calicoes of India'.[1] They did not, however, withdraw entirely from the Archipelago, holding on at Bantam till about 1683, and at Bencoolen on the west coast of Sumatra until 1824, and they continued to drive a large private trade with Kedah. During the eighteenth century, when the British were frequently at war with the French, the East India Company found the need for a station where its ships could careen and refit during the northeast monsoon. Eventually in 1785 the Company obtained through a young trading captain, Francis Light, a lease from the Sultan of Kedah of the practically uninhabited island of Penang. The British flag was hoisted there on 17 July 1786 and it was soon afterwards named Prince of Wales Island (a name which, however, did not stick). A strip on the mainland named Province Wellesley was added in 1800.

After the foundation of Penang the immigration of the Chinese to Malaya greatly increased.[2] In a letter dated 1 October 1786 Light wrote:

[24] 'More enlightened' because it had learnt by experience. In the matter of corruption (as we now understand it) and nepotism there was little to choose between the Dutch and English East India Companies. The difference was that the English knew, just in time, when reform was due.   [1] Winstedt, *Malaya*, p. 53.

[2] The day after Light had hoisted the flag some Chinese, headed by a 'Captain China', arrived bringing with them a present of some fishing nets. They may have been from Kedah, but Mr W. L. Blythe, formerly Secretary for Chinese Affairs, Malayan Union, thinks that they may have been inhabitants of the island itself—a few tens only, he suggests. According to Norman Macalister, *Historical Memoir relative to Prince of Wales' Island* (London, 1803), when the island was first occupied there were only two or three individuals there, 'natives of the island, who subsisted on fishing, and extracting from the trees, dammar and wood oil'. Thomas Forrest, senior captain of the H.E.I.C.'s Marine, who visited Kedah and Perak in

'Our inhabitants increase very fast,—Chooliahs (Tamils), Chinese, and Christians; they are already disputing about the ground, everyone building as fast as he can.' In a letter of 1 February of the following year, he says:

Did not the Dutch keep a strict watch over the Chinese, most of them would leave Malacca: 40 of them were prepared to come in the *Drake*, but were stopped by the order of the Dutch Government, and not a man allowed to leave Malacca without giving security that he will not go to Peenang [*sic*]—a Macau [Cantonese] ship intended to come here, but the Shabandar called the Captain aside, when he was about to depart, and told him by no means to stop at Peenang for there were 34 prows gone to cut off the Settlement; the contempt and derision with which they treat this place, and the mean dirty art they use to prevent People coming here, would dishonour any but a Dutchman. . . .

In December 1788 he reports, however, 'Our town increases very fast, with some very creditable families of Chinese, Malabars, and Malays'. That year more than 400 acres had been cultivated.

Francis Light was eight years in Penang and died there in October 1794. On 25 January of the year of his death he wrote to his superiors in Calcutta an official report giving his considered opinion of the Chinese settlers in which he said:

The Chinese constitute the most valuable part of our inhabitants; they are men, women, and children, about 3,000, they possess the different trades of carpenters, masons, and smiths, are traders, shopkeepers and planters, they employ small vessels and prows and send adventures to the surrounding countries. They are the only people of the east from whom a revenue may be raised without expense and extraordinary efforts of government. They are a valuable acquisition, but speaking a language which no other people understand, they are able to form parties and combinations in the most secret manner against any regulations of government which they disapprove, and were they brave as intelligent they would be dangerous subjects, but their want of courage will make them bear many impositions before they rebel. They are indefatigable in the pursuit of money, and like the Europeans, they spend it in purchasing those articles which gratify their appetites. They don't wait until they have acquired a large fortune to return to their native country, but send annually a part of their profits to their families. This is so general that a poor labourer will work with double labour to acquire two or three dollars to remit to China. As soon as they acquire a little money they obtain a wife and go on in regular domestic mode to the end of their existence. They have everywhere people to teach their children, and sometimes they send males to China to complete their education. The females are always kept at home with the greatest strictness until they are married; then they enjoy greater liberty. They are excessively fond of gaming, there is no restraining them from it. This leads them into many distresses and frequently ends in ruin.[3]

1783 states: 'Pulo Pinang has plains and gently rising hills with a good soil, and was formerly inhabited, as we may judge by the names of places said to exist in those days; but of which no vestige now remains, except perhaps some fruit trees, Batoo fringey, Tellu batang [bahang?], Sungy pinang, Tellu Kumbock, Tellu be lappas, and Sungy karuang. . . .' (*A Voyage from Calcutta to the Mergui Archipelago* (London, 1792), p. 24.) The names given by Forrest are those of places existing today. Batu fringey (Ferringhi) means the 'rock of the Franks', i.e. the Portuguese.   [3] 'Notices of Pinang', *J. of Indian Archipelago*, v (1850), p. 9.

But in spite of the numbers of immigrants that flocked to Penang the settlement's tenure of existence was precarious for many years. The Directors of the East India Company were not entirely satisfied that this was the place they wanted as a naval and trading station and in which to grow spices. Besides, the expense of the settlement made them inclined to abandon it on more than one occasion.[4] The tide of opinion turned at the beginning of the century and by 1805 the Directors' hopes had risen so high that Penang was made the Fourth Presidency of India and given a governor and an expensive staff. The optimism was not justified. The timber of Penang proved unsuitable for shipbuilding; the trade, while giving promise, became stationary about 1810, and in the 1820s the settlement was entirely outclassed by Singapore. The bottom, too, fell out of the pepper market at the end of the first decade of the century, and in 1860, after a chequered success of the crop, blight practically destroyed the nutmegs. But later Penang attained prosperity through sugar planting, and when the mainland was opened up, and the tin and rubber industries were developed, Penang, like Malacca, shared in the general prosperity.

But this is greatly to anticipate. In the early years the clearing and planting of the island gradually progressed. The Malays cut down the larger trees, and the remainder of the operations necessary for putting the land into a fit state for cultivation was performed by the Chinese at the rate of 20 dollars an *orlong*.[5] But the lack of any systematic encouragement of agriculture by the Government was a great handicap to the progress of the settlement. Among other crops the Chinese were partial to gambier, but this rapidly exhausted the soil. Rice, however, was not a popular crop with them. In the 1830s the Malays outnumbered the other cultivators of paddy in Penang and Province Wellesley by 41 to 4. In the latter class were the Indians, Burmese, Siamese, and Chinese. The Chinese, with the exception of the Cantonese, looked down on the paddy planters—a curious fact, 'for what', asks James Low, 'but lack of a paddie-field forced them from their country?'[6]

Other products of the Penang soil were coconuts, tobacco (in small quantities, never exported), *sireh* (a leaf with which betel-nut is mixed for chewing), the nipah palm, and indigo. The Chinese were the only real cultivators of indigo, which was not of any importance until after 1822. In the early days, too, they kept orange gardens, but they soon found it more profitable to grow other things instead.

But the crop *par excellence* for the Chinese cultivator proved to be sugar. The Chinese had the monopoly of sugar-planting from about 1800

---

[4] For a detailed discussion of the reasons of this and the land muddle, see Purcell, *Chinese in Malaya*, p. 41 ff.

[5] The *orlong* varied in different parts of Malaya. In Penang it was an acre and a third.

[6] J. Low, *A Dissertation on the Soil and Agriculture of the British Settlement of Penang* (Singapore, 1836), pp. 82–83.

up to about 1846 when the Imperial Government decided to admit the sugar and rum of Province Wellesley at the reduced colonial duties, while at the same time the same products of Singapore were charged foreign duties. The reason for this was that Singapore was already a great entrepôt for the collection of sugar from China, Java, and Manila, and it would have been very difficult to have distinguished between locally grown and imported sugar. The Government action was a death-blow to Singapore sugar planting and at the same time gave a great impulse to sugar planting in the Province. European speculators were not slow to take advantage of the situation. They copied the methods of the Chinese so far as the planting was concerned, but did not imitate their primitive apparatus for manufacturing the product. To their crude methods of extracting the sugar from the canes was due the Chinese failure to build up a big industry.

Penang's agriculture was a disappointment to the Directors and so in the end was its trade. This increased rapidly from 1786 to 1810; it then remained practically stationary, and the establishment of Singapore led to a great falling off in its volume. But by 1840 it had recovered its 1825 figure and there was a steady advance thereafter.

In spite of struggles and setbacks (a big fire had consumed most of the town in 1789), the wealth of the inhabitants, especially the Chinese, increased. This is indicated by the fact that when in 1802 the Lieutenant-Governor proposed to acquire a piece of land for a fort he had to buy it back from a Chinese baker and twenty-five others for $40,885! This was land on an island which fourteen years before had been uninhabited. When Amie, a Chinese baker (probably the same one just mentioned), lost his shop through fire in 1808 and property within a sweep of 250 yards of the port was consumed, a committee estimated the loss at $534,750.

In the early days the Chinese were left very much to themselves. They were governed through their headmen appointed by the authorities. Until the first Charter of Law of 1808 there was no proper legal system and Light had been instructed to act according to 'universal and natural justice' (whatever that may have been).[7] A magistrate, Mr George Caunter, gave his own interpretation of this in 1797 when he sentenced a Chinese man and woman to have their heads shaved and to stand twice in the pillory from four to six in the evening and the man to be imprisoned and then sent off the island. Headmen were appointed in 1792 for each community to administer justice for petty offences.

The subject of Chinese associations is dealt with in a later chapter in this section, and all that we need remark here is that in 1799, a few years after the foundation of Penang, the existence of secret societies was manifested in riots, and thereafter at intervals of a few years these riots broke

[7] See R. Braddell, *The Law of the Straits Settlements; a Commentary* (Singapore, 1915), p. 7.

out again. How far these societies were at work and how far the Chinese were exercising their natural aptitude for organizing obstruction as a community is not certain, but it was a common thing for the inhabitants of a district to turn out *en masse* at the sound of a buffalo horn to resist the police who were trying to effect an arrest or perform some other duty. In 1825 the secret societies even conspired with the Siamese to overthrow the Government of Penang. From 1846 to 1885 there were riots in Penang, Malacca, and Singapore of exceptional violence in which many hundreds of Chinese were killed. The Government was slow to deal with this disease of the community—no doubt partly for the cynical reason that the riots affected only the Chinese themselves, but mostly because it was entirely ignorant of the proper way to attack the problem.

It will be understood, then, that the police of these early days had a heavy task entrusted to them. The police of Penang were principally drawn from the immigrants from Bengal and Madras, but there were a few Chinese and Jawi Pekan (Malay-Indian half-castes) among them. The police of Province Wellesley were somewhat differently recruited (in the 1830s at any rate). They were mostly ex-sepoys armed with muskets and swords. A third of their total of about seventy were employed in guarding the frontier with Siam.

The staple article of local commerce was the *sinkheh* (Hokkien) or *sanhāk* (Cantonese), the new recruit from China. Every year the Chinese merchants engaged in the traffic would charter a vessel leaving in April or May with the southwesterly monsoon for Macao. The charterer usually sailed as supercargo in the vessel. When the vessel got to Macao or Amoy the charterer set his agents to work to cajole unsuspecting people by alluring promises of quick fortunes to be made overseas. The bounty money varied according to the respectability of the victims. The agents received a flat rate of a dollar a head. The recruits were herded together on the junk and many had to undergo appalling hardships. In a storm the passengers were nailed down under hatches.

In January or February the vessels were back again in Penang. The anchor had scarcely dropped when the prospective buyers flocked on board to buy the *sinkhehs*. The price paid for a master workman—a tailor, goldsmith, carpenter—was 10–15 dollars; a coolie fetched 6–10 dollars; a sickly coolie 3–4 dollars or less. The *sinkheh* then agreed to work for twelve months, receiving food, clothing, and a few dollars for services. If a coolie was not bought and paid for, he was kept on board the junk or in a godown until a purchaser turned up. The *sinkheh* was not well treated. Complaints were on occasion lodged before a sitting magistrate and at his order the *sinkheh* was released on signing a bond to pay his passage money, an agreement which he usually faithfully honoured.

The annual arrivals of *sinkhehs* in Penang in the third and fourth decades of the nineteenth century were about 2,000–3,000 a year. The natives of Kwangtung were considered to be more robust than the Hokkiens and Teochius. They made the best squatters and pioneers in opening up the land for the Hokkiens and Teochius. Unfortunately they had no capital and had to get advances from their friends. The usual purchasers of the land were Hokkiens or Teochius. Most of the plantations which came into the hands of shopkeepers of these tribes, through the default of debtors who owed them money, had been started by Cantonese. All the carpenters, blacksmiths, and shoemakers were Cantonese, and so were most of them in the first half of the twentieth century.

But whilst conceding to the Chinese the credit they deserve as pioneers, we must not be guilty of injustice to the other races who in some directions played as important a part in the development of Penang. For instance, most of the public works, bridges, buildings, roads, and the aqueduct were built by Bengal convicts who had been brought to Penang before 1800. The Malays, too, did most of the heavy work of tree-felling.

Before the gates of immigration had been opened up by the modern expansion of industry and by quicker transport, and they had been swamped in numbers by the China-born, the Straits-born Chinese constituted a sort of local aristocracy. Their blood was not pure Chinese, but although they would have Malay, or Malay-Indian or other half-caste mothers, children of the *Babas* (as they were called) were almost all brought up in the ways of their fathers. It is remarkable the tenacity with which the Straits Settlements *Baba*, who did not speak anything but Malay, adhered to the Chinese way of life in Penang and Malacca, modified though it was by Malay and other influences. They had a language of their own, and still have, known as Baba Malay. But it differs from Malay in many important respects and is practically a separate language.[8]

Strict adherence to chronological sequence would have brought Singapore into our narrative much earlier than this, for it had been founded in 1819 by Raffles. When he had arrived there on 28 January 1819 the only inhabitants were about 120 Malays and 30 Chinese.[9]

The histories of Penang and Singapore merge into one another officially with the placing of Singapore and Malacca under the control of the former in 1826; in 1830 the three, together forming the Straits Settlements, were made a Residency subject to Bengal. But the immediate success of the younger settlement had almost from the first deprived Penang of its position.

Although it does not seem to be clearly stated anywhere, it is likely that the first Chinese in Singapore came from Malacca and Riau (Rhio),

[8] For a detailed description of Baba Malay see Purcell, *Chinese in Malaya*, p. 293 ff.

[9] T. J. Newbold, *Political and Statistical Account of the British Settlements in the Straits of Malacca* (London, 1839), i. 279. See also W. Bartley, 'Population of Singapore in 1819', *JRASMB*, xi, pt. 1 (1933), p. 177.

the island nearby which had been occupied by the Dutch shortly before this time. Certainly the most prominent Chinese in the early years were Malaccans. Very soon, however, the news of the establishment of a British settlement in a position so favourable for tapping the trade of the archipelago attracted immigration from China direct. The first junk from Amoy arrived in February 1821.

On 11 June 1819 Raffles wrote to the Duchess of Somerset: 'My new colony thrives most rapidly. We have not been established four months, and it has received an accession of population exceeding 5,000—principally Chinese, and their number is daily increasing.' By August 1820, according to the same authority, it numbered between 10,000 and 12,000, the majority being Chinese. But it is likely that the enthusiasm of the pioneer and his wish to impress the Directors with the rapid success of his settlement led him into exaggeration, for T. Braddell, who went carefully into the matter at a later date, gives the total population for 1821 as 4,727 with the Chinese at 1,159. For 1823 he shows an increase to a total of 10,683 with the Chinese at 3,317.[10]

At the beginning the various races of immigrants settled where they liked, but very soon we find Raffles planning his town and allotting areas to Chinese, Klings, Bugis, Malays, &c. He directed that all Chinese should leave the northern side of the river where they had located themselves and form a new village from the bridge down to the river on the site of the present Boat Quay. By 1821 there were 3,374 yards of road 15 yards wide in Chinatown. Raffles considered that the first in importance among the immigrant peoples was 'beyond doubt the Chinese'. 'From the number of Chinese already settled, and the peculiar attractions of the place for that industrious race, it may be presumed that they will always form by far the largest part of the community.'[11] Raffles continued: '. . . in establishing the Chinese campong on a proper footing, it will be necessary to advert to the provincial and other distinctions among this curious people'.[12]

He said that it was notorious that the people of one province were known to be more quarrelsome than those of another and that the peoples of the various provinces were liable to quarrel among themselves. A different area should be allotted to resident merchants from that occupied by itinerant traders. The 'Amoi' (Hokkiens from Amoy) claimed particular attention and the committee appointed by Raffles was invited to consider whether it would not be desirable to allot them a separate division 'even to the westward of the Cantonments, beyond the European town and the Sultan'.

---

[10] T. Braddell, *Statistics of the British Possessions in the Straits of Malacca* (Penang, 1861).

[11] Raffles's prediction has certainly not been falsified to date. In 1960 the Chinese accounted for 1,230,700 out of a total population of 1,634,000.

[12] 'Notices of Singapore', *J. Ind. Archipelago*, viii (1854), p. 106.

The intention of the founder of Singapore was to place the Chinese population in a great measure under the immediate control of their own chiefs, and the committee was instructed to 'fix up such centrical and commanding sites for these authorities and appropriate to them such larger extent of ground, as may tend to render them efficient instruments of police, and at the same time raise them in the consideration of the lower classes'.

As time went on the system of indirect rule which had been adopted in all three settlements was modified and at length virtually replaced by direct rule.

Raffles paid great attention to social distinctions in the communities under his control, though in regarding the merchants as 'the higher and more respectable class', he was ignoring the Confucian teaching which placed the scholar first, the farmer second, the artisan third, and the merchant fourth (not to mention the soldier, whom it did not classify). In Singapore there were no Chinese scholars. Farmers were (says Raffles) a third and interesting class, particularly of the Chinese population, 'but as no part of the ground intended to be occupied as the town can be spared for agricultural purposes they will not fall under your consideration, except in as far as it may be necessary to exclude them'. The first two classes mentioned by Raffles were those engaged in mercantile speculation and those gaining their livelihood by handicrafts and personal labour.

The main concern of Raffles and his successors up to the middle of the nineteenth century was to increase the importance of Singapore as a trading settlement. In this they were singularly successful and the annual value of the trade increased in a phenomenal way. The various communities were therefore principally of interest as bringers of wealth to Singapore, and so long as they did not disturb the peace they were left very much to themselves. Thus for a long time no attention was paid to the activities of the *hui*, or secret societies, which often operated to the detriment of the Chinese community but did not interfere with other communities. Gambling, another characteristic institution, if it may be so called, that the Chinese had brought with them, created more noticeable disturbances of the communal life and was therefore a matter in which the Government showed an early interest. Raffles had strictly forbidden gambling farms, but Farquhar, his Resident, who had no great moral objection to gambling and saw the advantage of the farms to the revenue, disobeyed Raffles's instructions during his absence and this led to frequent and serious collisions between the two.[13]

A big problem in the early days of Singapore, as in the early days of Penang, was that of law and order. The Chinese, and the same is true of

[13] See Song Ong Siang, *One Hundred Years History of the Chinese in Singapore* (London, 1923), pp. 17–18.

other Asiatic immigrants, were not exclusively composed of enterprising merchants and industrious artisans and peasants: they had brought with them some of the worst characters for whom China itself had no room. There were frequent robberies and murders, even in broad daylight, and most of them went unpunished. Moreover, there was only a handful of police and as yet no code of laws under which criminals could be punished.

The rudimentary police force was augmented in September 1821. A number of European merchants met at the request of the Resident to raise funds by voluntary subscriptions to increase the strength of the existing police force. The meeting decided to suggest to the inhabitants of Kampong Glam and China Town the desirability of subscribing to the fund for the purpose of extending the police systems of their areas, but there was no immediate response. Only when robberies increased did the Chinese begin to realize the necessity of contributing to the Night Watch Fund.[14]

The first riots occurred in 1824, but, according to Song Ong Siang and Buckley, there is no reason to believe that they had any connexion with the operation of secret societies.[15] It was not until 1831 that there was any mention of the existence of these societies. Then Buckley tells us that Singapore was in a very lawless state, several murders being reported in a week, and no proper measures being available to trace the criminals or to secure life and property in the outlying parts of the town. While a gang of convicts were working in a road, a number of other Chinese ran out of the jungle and rescued ten of the convicts by carrying them off and knocking off their irons. The whole (local?) police force, *eighteen strong*, was mustered and recovered five of the convicts. There was said at the time to be a secret society of over a thousand men established in the jungle where they actually had an armed fort. Twenty more years elapsed before the next Chinese riot broke out. Then from 1851 to 1854 occurred a series of events which culminated in the great riot of the latter year.

The secret societies found that the conversion of the Chinese in the interior of Singapore Island to Roman Catholicism had the effect of creating throughout the island groups of men independent of their protection. They resented this, and in 1851 there was a general attack on the Christian Chinese in the country districts. The disturbances lasted for a week, and when the Indian convicts who had been sent out in gangs to follow the rioters and disperse them failed to do so the soldiers were called out. Over 500 Chinese were killed by the secret societies, including many well-to-do converts who had become planters. The grand jury in 1851 complained against the societies 'whose power was dreaded by the

[14] Ibid. p. 25. C. B. Buckley, *An Anecdotal History of Old Times in Singapore* (London, 1903), pp. 165, 212–13.   [15] Ibid.

Chinese of all classes and which by their recent destruction of numerous *bangsal* (coolie lines) belonging to the Christian Chinese and by their outrageous attack on the police in the vicinity of Bukit Timah had exhibited a dangerous combination against public security and peace'. In August 1853 the grand jury again drew attention to the necessity for adopting stringent measures to detain witnesses in particularly grave cases until the trial of the prisoners came on (to safeguard the witnesses from intimidation). The Government, however, did not take the situation very seriously. Then suddenly in May 1854 occurred the biggest riots that had ever been known in Singapore. These were *kongsi* riots and for ten days the whole island was the scene of pitched battles between the rival factions. Four hundred Chinese were killed.[16]

In a later chapter of this section[17] the nature of Chinese secret societies in Malaya receives attention and it is sufficient in this summarized history of the Chinese in Singapore and Penang to make mention of the successive outbreaks without attempting to go deeply into their causes. Certain it is that the Thian Ti Hui, or Heaven and Earth Society, was the most powerful and dangerous of these subversive societies, and even allowing that the distinction between the beneficent *kongsis*, or district and clan associations, and the malevolent *huis* is largely an arbitrary one we may take it the latter were mainly responsible for the riot outbreaks of 1854.

As early as 1799 secret-society activity caused disturbances in Penang. There was a long period of apparent acquiescence, when the system of extortion worked without obvious friction, but from 1846 to 1885 there was a series of outbreaks in Penang and Malacca, as well as in Singapore. The Government found no effective means of dealing with the menace until 1889, and until then the societies continued their depredations without serious hindrance. That their activities were not entirely anti-social must, however, be admitted in mitigation of their offence. The eventual solution of the problem belongs to a later period. At this time the obstacle to any really effective measures was the lack of any official with a knowledge of the Chinese language and customs.[18]

Even more serious to the Straits Settlements from the point of view of interference with trade was piracy. Pirates swarmed in the waters of the Straits and about the neighbouring islands. They were Malays, Lanuns, and others. Their usual prey were the junks which plied between China and the Straits and the native craft trading between the

---

[16] The number has been given in several works as 4,000 and the writer copied this figure in his *Malaya: Outline of a Colony* (London, 1946). He is satisfied now, however, that 400 is very much nearer the truth.   [17] Chapter 29.

[18] The ingenious device of Colonel Cavenagh, the Governor of the Straits from 1859 to 1867, may here be mentioned. When trouble started the Governor had the known lodge masters of the *hui* patrol the streets under the surveillance of special constables to restore order (see Sir Orfeur Cavenagh, *Reminiscences of an Indian Official* (London, 1884)).

islands. As late as 1835 attacks were actually made in daylight on boats plying between the shore and ships lying at anchor at the mouth of the harbour. Many vessels were captured when barely out of sight of Singapore town. The Government had only a few armed ships at its disposal and occasional raids by these were powerless to quell the evil. Criticism in the press and representations by the merchants produced no results and in 1832 the Chinese merchants in Singapore obtained the sanction of the Government to equip at their own expense four large trading vessels, each manned by thirty Chinese, well armed and carrying several guns, to go out and attack the pirates lurking just outside Singapore harbour. The vessels went out, attacked two *prahus* and sank one while the other made off. One or two Chinese were killed. The Chinese merchants agreed to pay $200 for every pirate boat attacked, and also $200 to the relatives of any man killed in the expedition. The Government was shamed by this into building two special ships at Malacca for anti-piracy purposes. But measures were still inadequate until in 1836 H.M.S. *Wolf* arrived in response to petitions to the home authorities and the campaign for suppression began in earnest. It was the advent of the steamship which made suppression possible. Between 1835 and 1860 Malay piracy was almost ended and the depredation of Balanini and Lanuns greatly curtailed.

The Chinese in Singapore were drawn from the various parts of the southern provinces of China, and though they had in common the same traditional culture and similar customs, this was not enough to fuse them into a whole. Tribes speaking different dialects regarded one another almost as foreigners, as indeed they do sometimes to this day. There was no hint of Chinese nationalism in its modern sense. In May 1840 British troops intended for use in the First China War arrived and camped on the Esplanade, arousing no manifestation of hostility on the part of the local Chinese. In 1857, at the beginning of the Second China War, some ill will towards the British was shown by a section of the poorer classes, but when Lord Elgin arrived in Singapore on 6 June of that year, on his way to China as British High Commissioner and Plenipotentiary, he was presented with an address by the Chinese merchants in which they referred to the great advantage the Chinese population was enjoying under British rule. Chinese tribes were brought into a proximity un-exampled in their native country, and even when they were of the same tribe from the same village they had not the restraining organization of their village headmen.

In retrospect it seems clear that many of the difficulties of govern-ment of the Chinese in Singapore arose from the fact that the governing officials had little knowledge of the usages of the people whom they had to control. Progress towards harmonious combination had therefore to be made in two different directions—the first was by the Chinese getting

used to the laws, the habits, and the prejudices of the ruling race, and
the second by the ruling race getting to understand the nature of the
people they had to govern. It must be admitted that the Chinese made
much greater headway in their task than the British, for long, did in
theirs. Until the Chinese Protectorate was established in 1877 there was
practically no British official who had any knowledge of the Chinese
language. Governor Fullerton at one time gave orders that all European
officers were to make themselves acquainted with the Chinese and the
Siamese languages, but there is no evidence that he was obeyed. Until
the transfer in 1867 of the Straits Settlements to Colonial Office jurisdiction the civil servants were from India and were India-minded; after
British intervention in the Malay States in 1874 they became Malay-
minded (which they still mostly are although the majority race had
remained till the end Chinese).[19]

The ambition of nearly every Chinese was to return to China as soon
as he had amassed a competence, but only a proportion realized this
ambition and the rest remained to settle, making only periodical visits to
China. As communications with China improved and passage-rates fell,
the tendency to pass to and fro increased. The immigrants did not for
long bring their women with them. This was partly because they preferred to keep their wives and children in their native land, partly because
most of them could not afford to take their families overseas, and partly
because the authorities in China, so lax in preventing the emigration of
males, took great precautions to prevent women being taken overseas.
Later the prohibition was relaxed and eventually ceased, but up to the
1920s the women of Hainan were not allowed to leave their island.

The result of this attitude was that a large number of Chinese took
local wives. This intermixture of races was therefore a factor tending
towards settlement, but it was interrupted when emigration of Chinese
took place in great numbers and the barriers of race rose up. Many did
not go back to China because, as has been said, they were too poor, but
some did not return because they were too rich and dared not leave their
property and their interests. There were 13 women to 100 males at an
early period and as time went on the richer China-born tended to have
two wives, one in China and one in Malaya, and concubines in addition;
but for the majority the sex ratio remained disproportionate.

The ill-balanced sex ratio of the Straits Chinese had a great effect on
their social life. For a section it tended to produce miscegenation which
might eventually, had it not been for improved communications and the
influx of more Chinese caused by the development of the country, have

[19] So ignorant were the authorities of Chinese matters that in the early years of Singapore,
after the abolition of the gambling farms, the Chinese were allowed unrestricted gambling
for fifteen days at Chinese New Year under the impression that gambling formed part of their
religion!

resulted in the creation of a race with interests identified with Malaya rather than with China. For another, and a larger section, it meant celibacy and with this came the problem of prostitution and the traffic in women and girls.[20]

The class of Chinese most encouraged in the early years of Singapore was the merchant. There was, however, an influx of industrious agriculturists as well. The Europeans were interested exclusively in cloves, nutmegs, and sugar, and, so far as Singapore was concerned, the cultivation of these turned out to be a complete failure. Gambier and pepper planting was left almost entirely to the Chinese who owned large plantations of these crops. There were also numbers of squatters, many of whom had worked off the debt for their passage money in the first year or so and who took to agriculture on their own.

It is certain that Chinese gambier and pepper plantations were in the long run an evil for Singapore. Gambier had an exceptional power of denuding the soil, so that it destroyed the cultivable land as the Chinese moved on from plot to plot. There were generally three acres of pepper to thirty acres of gambier and when one of these crops died the other soon followed. The wasteful cultivation had begun to exhaust the richness of the island by 1840 and more and more Chinese deserted it for the mainland of Johore where they restarted the same system.

Of vegetable gardening in Singapore the Chinese had the monopoly, but of pineapples the principal cultivators were the Bugis. There were minor crops, such as *sireh*, and a single acre of indigo cultivated by Chinese. Singapore Island was unfavourable to the growth of rice, which succeeded quite well at Malacca and Penang. But human agency had as much to do with the failure of the rice crop as had nature. By 1831 (says the *Singapore Chronicle*) rice planting had become a thing of the past. The Governor, Mr Fullerton, had put on a tax or quit rent of one dollar an acre per month, which completely prohibited the coolies from China taking up any agricultural employment as they found it impossible to make the jungle produce sufficient to meet such a heavy impost, and the gardens which were prospering were neglected.[21]

Chinese squatters and labourers in Singapore Island in the 1830s had to contend with many dangers and hardships. There was malaria, for instance, and in the gambier plantations the coolies clearing the ground often got splinters in their legs which formed ulcers. Besides disease and the hard life they led they suffered greatly from robbery and from the marauding of tigers.

---

[20] For a more detailed discussion of the subject of the sex ratio, &c, see Purcell, *Chinese in Malaya*, p. 86 ff. The women and girls problem receives attention in Chapter 29 of this section. An astonishing improvement in the sex ratio of Chinese was shown by the 1947 Census.

[21] The wages of Chinese agricultural labourers of the period are given in an article by F. L. Baumgarten, 'Agriculture in Malacca', *J. Ind. Archipelago*, iii (1849).

As in Penang, it was rarely the original pioneers who profited from their toil. They were encumbered by advances carrying a crippling rate of interest.

The principal types of Singapore Chinese were, however, the merchant and the artisan. The Chinese were besides everything from actors, acrobats, and musicians to druggists and school masters, from fishmongers to pawnbrokers, and from cartwrights, fortune-tellers, down to *samsengs*, or rascals and thieves.[22] In a community which was exclusively commercial or agricultural there was not much scope for the expression of personality. The important business of life was getting a living or, if possible, amassing a fortune, making regular remittances to the family in China, eating and drinking, placating an unseen world of spirits, and, perhaps above all, getting buried decently. There was no cultivated leisured or academic class. The typical successful Chinese is described by the famous naturalist, Russel Wallace, as he saw him in Singapore between 1854 and 1862:

> The Chinese merchant is generally a fat round-faced man with an important and business-like look. He wears the same style of clothing (loose white smock, and blue or black trousers) as the meanest coolie, but of finer materials, and is always clean and neat; and his long tail tipped with red hangs down to his heels. He has a handsome warehouse or shop in town and a good house in the country. He keeps a fine horse and gig, and every evening may be seen taking a drive bareheaded to enjoy the cool breeze. He is rich, he owns several retail shops and trading schooners, he lends money at high interest and on good security, he makes hard bargains and gets fatter and richer every year.[23]

Yet there were outstanding characters among the Chinese—Tan Che Sang (*c.* 1763–1836), a wealthy Cantonese, who vainly tried to conquer his weakness for gambling by cutting off the first joint of his little finger with an oath never to play any more; Tan Tock Seng who founded the hospital of that name; Dato Toh Ah Boon of Johore, who created the Toh Ah Boon scholarship, and in more recent times Dr Lim Boon Keng, one-time Principal of the University of Amoy, Sir Song Ong Siang (or Sir Ong-siang Song), Tan Cheng-lock, and a number of others. As wealth became consolidated and leisure more common, better-off Chinese found an outlet for their released energies in philanthropy, social service, and, later and in less degree, in politics.

[22] J. D. Vaughan in *Manners and Customs of the Chinese of the Straits Settlements* (Singapore, 1879), p. 16, gives about 200 occupations followed by Straits Chinese.

[23] *The Malayan Archipelago* (London, 1869), i. 32–33.

28

THE MALAY STATES

THE Ming History says that in 1378 the King of Pahang, Maharaja Tajau, sent envoys with a letter on a gold leaf to China, and these brought as tribute foreign slaves and the produce of the country. Cheng Ho or his associates visited Pahang on his fourth voyage (probably in 1414)[1] and in that year we hear of tribute being sent to China again. In 1436 Fei Hsin, a Chinese Muslim and Arabic scholar, mentions another early visit to Pahang.

This is practically all we hear of the Chinese in these eastern parts of the peninsula until the visit of an Englishman named Gray in 1827.[2] Gray's journal of 21 January 1827 says: 'I am informed by the merchants that they have discovered a tin mine, near the river Leppa (Lepar), at the distance of two days' pulling from the settlement of Pahang; it is expected to turn out favourably and to be opened to the dry season by about 800 Malays, besides a number of Chinese.' In 1838 Abdullah,[3] on his way to Kelantan, landed at Kuala Pahang for provisions. He sailed up the Pahang river to Kampong China (Pekan Baharu). There he found hundreds of Malays and Chinese, armed to the teeth, awaiting him on the bank. The Bendahara, with the Chinese headman, was away at the gold-mines at Jelai. The Chinese at Kampong China were Hakkas and they intermarried with Malays or Balinese slaves. Their children spoke Chinese rather than Malay.

The veil over Pahang is rarely lifted thereafter until Clifford's expedition in 1887. In the intervening years these Chinese were engaged in mining in Pahang, though in what numbers is uncertain. They had the monopoly of mining ingot-money, but were permitted to mint only four times a year and up to a certain value. They had mints at Kuantan, Lepar, Semantan, and Pekan Lama. This monopoly survived until 1893.

Let us now pass to the south of the Peninsula and remark the progress of the Chinese in Johore.[4]

The Dutch policy of monopoly had caused the Chinese merchants to

[1] See J. J. L. Duyvendak, 'The true dates of the Chinese Maritime Expeditions of the early fifteenth century', *T'oung Pao* (1939), xxxiv.
[2] 'Journal of a route overland from Malacca to Pahang, across the Malayan Peninsula', *J. Ind. Archipelago*, vi (1852), p. 373.
[3] The author of the *Pelayaran*, quoted by W. Linehan on p. 60 of his 'History of Pahang', *JRASMB*, xiv, pt. 2 (June 1936).
[4] Winstedt, 'A History of Johore', *JRASMB*, x, pt. 3 (Dec. 1932), p. 49.

seek a centre of operations where they were out of their reach. By 1657–61 Johore had become such a centre. By 1661 all Sumatra, Perak, Malacca, and Johore were reported to be over-stocked with English and Moorish cloth brought from Surat and Coromandel by Chinese merchants in the Malay Peninsula. Chinese coarse earthenware, tea, and tobacco are also mentioned as articles of commerce at the time. Although threatened with reprisals by the Dutch, Johore traded with and sold produce to the Chinese.

At the end of the seventeenth and beginning of the eighteenth centuries Captain Alexander Hamilton (quoted by Winstedt) says of Johore: 'The people of Industry are the *Chinese* who inhabit among them in their towns; and there may be about 1,000 families of them settled in the Johore Dominions, besides a much greater number who drive a foreign trade among them!'[5]

On 2 March 1702–3 five Englishmen from Pulo Condore were shipwrecked on the coast of Johore. At New Johore they found '6 great junks and several proes'. They also saw several Chinese who lived and traded there. At some palace revels the shipwrecked Englishmen saw 600 Chinese armed with swords and targets who 'marched with Chinese plays and then fenced'.[6]

In 1784 Johore was engaged in war with the Bugis and was helped by the Dutch. When the Bugis were defeated the Chinese in Johore who helped them were allowed to keep their property, but had to pay a fine of $20,000. An agreement was made by Johore with the Dutch whereby, among other provisions, Chinese native craft might trade at Rhio provided that they did not come from Celebes or Borneo, or carry cloves or mace, and provided also that they did not carry tin from Palembang or Bangka.

It seems clear that the Chinese did not settle in the interior in Johore until after the thirties of last century. Begbie in 1834 gives the estimated population of the towns of Johore, Pulau Tinggi, Sungai Papan, and Segamat, but does not mention any Chinese. Nor does Newbold in 1839, though he enumerates quite small villages. (Incidentally he estimates the entire population of Johore at 25,000.) But by the late thirties the Chinese squatter from Singapore, whose nature it is to move farther and farther into the interior, had begun the invasion of Johore.

At Timiong (Temiang) there were, in 1836, 35,000 Malays and a few Chinese. Newbold does not mention any other Chinese in other parts of the state including Muar and Segamat. Captain MacPherson,[7] who visited

---

[5] *A New Account of the East Indies* (Edinburgh, 1727) as quoted ibid. x, pt. 3 (1932), p. 49.
[6] W. Vaughan, *Adventures of Five Englishmen from Pulo Condore, a Factory of the New Company, of the East Indies, who were shipwrecked in the little kingdom of Johore* (London, 1714).
[7] 'Narrative of a trip to Dok in the Muar territories', *J. Ind. Archipelago*, new ser., ii (1858), pp. 299–300.

Muar in 1857, says of that territory: 'It is useless to hope for energy with the Malay. . . . It wants a strong infusion of Chinese life and skill.'

The British policy until the seventies was strictly one of non-intervention in the Malay States, but long before that the Straits Settlements Government had shown concern for the welfare of the British subjects of whatever race who were living in the Malay States. For example, Cavenagh, the Governor of the Straits Settlements, in his *Reminiscences*[8] tells us that in 1861 he received a complaint against the Temenggong of Johore. The Temenggong's eldest son, a young chief, admitted that his people were in the wrong.

> I then [says Cavenagh] referred to the case of some Chinamen who had been confined on the charge of gambling, remarking that though I did not wish to interfere with his authority, or to prevent criminals from being punished, I could not permit British subjects to be at the mercy of the caprice of any native chief, and, therefore, required them to be sentenced according to some known law. He asserted that the law in force was the Hukum-i-Sharat [Shara'] (ecclesiastical law), according to which the Chinese might have their hands cut off, and he had inflicted a more lenient punishment.

In 1865 two British men-of-war steamers were sent to Pulau Tinggi to apprehend one Che Bujang, a Malay, who had plundered and murdered a Chinese wood-cutter, a British subject, but he was not traced.

By the early seventies there were twenty-nine Johore rivers with Chinese estates on their banks. By this time the population was growing fast. In 1885 the Duke of Sutherland found at Johore a 'gay little Malay town' where there had been only a little fishing village in 1855.

It was the demand for pepper and gambier that brought the Chinese squatter to Johore. Those who could satisfy the Malay authorities as to their means were allowed to form settlements, up some named river, for the planting of pepper and gambier, and the titles they received from the ruler were called simply 'Surat Sungai' (river documents). This system was called the *kangchu* system (literally 'owner of a river').[9]

The heads of the settlements received lengthy written instructions. Among other things they were responsible for keeping up the supply of opium and spirits to their men. They had the rights of running the gambling, the monopoly of pawnbroking, and selling spirits and pork. The *kangchu* system continued until 1917 when it was abolished.[10]

We now travel up the west coast of the peninsula, going back a good few years, and find that Thomas Forrest, senior captain of the H.E.I.C.'s Marine (whom we have already encountered in a footnote in the preceding chapter and who will turn up again in our account of the Chinese in

---

[8] Cavenagh, *Reminiscences*, pp. 312–13.

[9] See A. E. Coope, 'The Kangchu System in Johore', *JRASMB*, xiv, pt. 3 (Dec. 1936), p. 249.

[10] 'Kangchu Rights Abolition Enactment', *Johore Govt. Gazette* (1 Dec. 1917). See also J. V. Cowgill, 'Chinese Place Names in Johore', *JRASMB*, ii, pt. 3 (1924), p. 221.

Indonesia and the Philippines), visited Perak in 1783. His impressions of his visit to Perak are of exceptional interest to us. He says:

> I went up in a country covered boat from Tanjang Putus, where the vessel lay, to pay my respect to the King of Pera, who received me in a large upper-room house with great state, having about 20 guards in the room, dressed in black satin garments embroidered on the breast with a golden dragon; they wore mandarin caps, and appeared altogether in the Chinese style: some were armed with halberts, some held pikes in their hands, and a few had musquets without bayonets.[11]

The dress and regalia of modern Malay royalty are fashioned on an Indian (Hindu) model. This passage from Forrest, however, makes the survival of Chinese influence quite clear. It is only the modern swing away from China which has made the Malay Sultans of the peninsula forget that they were once proud to wear the Imperial Yellow of the Ming.

Newbold's account of the Chinese in Sungai Ujong (later one of the states of Negri Sembilam) is referred to later on in this chapter. He says that the estimated population in 1832 was 3,200 Malays, principally Menangkabaus, and 400 Chinese employed in the mines.

At this time the wages of the Chinese miners were 5–8 dollars a month, as compared with 3–5 earned by Malays. From daybreak till 7 a.m. they were engaged in clearing away water that had collected in the workings during the night. They breakfasted from 7 to 8, worked from 8 to 11, dined from 11 to 1, and worked from 1 to 5 when they ceased for the day.[12]

Anderson tells us that in 1824 Lukut had recently become a great place for tin.[13] Of its 1,000 inhabitants 200 were Chinese miners. It was at Lukut in 1834 that the great massacre of the Malays by the Chinese took place. In 1874 there were about 10,000 Chinese miners there.

Selangor in the first part of the nineteenth century was much more thinly inhabited than Perak. Anderson in 1824 puts the population of the capital at 400, and says that the inhabitants of the villages on or near the Selangor river occupied 975 houses only.[14] There was an influx of Chinese miners to the state after the fifties. By 1871 there were 12,000 Chinese in Selangor (Lukut was then in Selangor) and the output of tin was 3,000 piculs a month.

There can be no doubt that the Chinese contacts with Kelantan date from a very early time, but there is no evidence of any settlement except abandoned gold workings. Anker Rentse[15] speaks of one such settlement

---

[11] Forrest, *Voyage to Mergui Archipelago*, p. 28.
[12] 'Account of Sungie Ujong, one of the States in the Interior of Malacca', *JASB*, iv (1835), pp. 538, 540.
[13] John Anderson, *Political and Commercial Considerations relative to the Malayan Peninsula and the British Settlements in the Straits of Malacca* (Prince of Wales Island, 1824), p. 202.
[14] Ibid. pp. 191–2, 196.
[15] 'History of Kelantan', *JRASMB*, xii, pt. 2 (Aug. 1934).

on the Sokor river. He then refers to the settlement at Pulai, still existing, which he considers to be of a much later date. However, it was very old. The type of plough used by the Chinese there for their rice cultivation is said to be different from the Malay type. Local Chinese tradition credits the foundation of the Pulai settlement to a Hakka chief, one Chong Pah Chai, who about 200 years ago was a notorious robber in South China and fled to Pulai.[16]

In the 1930s Pulai still had its 'Kapitan' who must have been about the last of the Chinese captains in Malaya.

Of the Chinese in Kedah we hear very little before the nineteenth century, but Thomas Forrest who visited it in 1783 gives us a glimpse of the Chinese trade with that State. This is what he says:

The government is monarchichal, under a Malay Mohammedan prince, who like many other Malay princes engrosses almost all the whole foreign trade of the port, excepting that of an annual Chinese junk, which pays *a certain sum only* as duty, and then has leave to trade freely with the inhabitants. This junk imports immense quantities of coarse China-ware, thin iron pans, and many other articles from that country, and exports *biche de mer*, called swallow, sharks fins, edible birds nests, rattans, tin, dammer, tortoise-shell, deers skins and sinews, bullocks and buffaloes hides and horns, and many other coarse articles.

The town contains about 3 or 400 houses, inhabited by Chinese, Telingas [Kalingas?] and Malays.[17]

Newbold says that in 1828 the number of Chinese miners on Sungai Ujong was nearly 1,000, divided into nine *kongsis*[18] chiefly of the Thian Ti Hui, or Heaven and Earth League (or Society). Each was under its respective *towkay*, or chief. He remarks that their mysterious oaths and secret laws appeared to be not very dissimilar from those which bound the Carbonari of the Europe of his time. Jealousy of their fast-increasing power and numbers, or some alleged offence, but more probably the treasure amassed by the brotherhood of the Thian Ti Hui (whose property was in common), led in 1828 to their massacre by the Malays. But by 1830 the mines were again worked by 400 Chinese, who continued there until the disturbances of 1833, when many returned to Malacca.

We see, then, that wherever the Chinese went they took their secret societies with them. Indeed, these supplied practically the only social organization possessed by the community. In Perak, Chinese miners appeared in Larut from Penang, whence they brought the rival secret societies, the Ghee Hin and Hai San.

It now becomes necessary to give an outline of the activities of the Chinese miners and their secret societies which in the seventies were to

[16] S. M. Middlebrook, 'Pulai: an early Chinese settlement in Kelantan', ibid. xi, pt. 2 (Dec. 1933).
[17] *Voyage to Mergui Archipelago*, p. 24.   [18] See p. 272.

lead to British intervention in the Malay States and to the transformation of the whole position in the Peninsula.

Before 1850 the district of Larut was almost uninhabited. About 1840 a Perak-born Malay named Che' Long Ja'afar had married a daughter of the Panglima Bukit Gantang, or keeper of the pass between Larut and Kuala Kangsar, and had settled near the present township of Taiping. There were said then to have been only three Chinese in the whole of Larut. Che' Long Ja'afar discovered a patch of rich mining land at Klian Pauh, the site of the present Taiping jail, and soon Chinese miners from Penang were flocking into Larut. Later new mining lands were discovered at Klian Baharu, the present-day Kamunting.

In 1850 Long Ja'afar obtained from the Sultan of Perak a title to the district of Larut as his own property. He died in 1857 and was succeeded by his son, Che' Ngah Ibrahim, who was recognized by the Sultan as the ruler of Larut in succession to his father. Swettenham, who knew him personally, says that Che' Ngah Ibrahim was not pure Malay, but partly Indian and of a shrewdness and business capacity foreign to Malays.[19] He became known as the Raja of Larut, or Mentri of Larut, or Tengku Mentri.

Meanwhile the influx of Chinese to the new mining-fields of Klian Pauh and Klian Baharu was so great that it was beyond the capacity of the Mentri to keep order, and the Chinese, free of any control from above, began faction fights among themselves.

It became customary in the records of the period to describe the cleavage as between the 'Four Districts' and the 'Five Districts'. The former were the members of the Ghee Hin and the latter of the Hai San and Toh Peh Kong organization. In fact the divisions of the Larut 'wars' of 1862–73 were precisely those of the Penang riots of 1867. The Four Districts were mostly Ghee Hins and Cantonese, and the Five Districts were mostly Hai Sans and Khehs.[20]

But while the fundamental cause of the fighting was the tribal hatred between the Cantonese and the Khehs, the division of forces was not altogether on a tribal basis. Quite often a Hakka would be a member of

[19] Sir Frank Swettenham, *British Malaya*, revised ed. (London, 1929), p. 123. See also C. Northcote Parkinson, *British Intervention in Malaya 1867–1877* (1960) and C. D. Cowan, *Nineteenth Century Malaya; the Origins of British Political Control* (1961).

[20] The term 'District' as used to refer to the places of origin in China of the rival factions is a very loose one. Skinner, who first uses the expression in an official document ('Précis of Perak Affairs', 10 Jan. 1874, published in *Perak Papers*, 1874–9), enumerates the See Kwan, or Four Districts, as the Sin Neng, Sin Whee, Seow Keng, and Whee Chew, and the Go Kwan, or Five Districts, as the Cheng Sia, Poon Say, Soon Tek, Lam Hye, and Tong Quan. Kwan is an obsolete term for prefecture or department. The first two of the Four Districts are districts in the Kwang Chau prefecture, while the last two are complete prefectures in the same province. The Five Districts appear to have been districts proper, but Poon Say is not identifiable. The Districts are differently named in another document of 1 Jan. 1847, but the exact territorial identity of the Districts in China is not important if we remember that the people of the first were mostly Cantonese and of the latter mostly Khehs (Hakkas).

the Ghee Hin and a Cantonese of the Hai San, or vice versa, and such was the hold of his society on a member's allegiance that it was more powerful than the call of the tribe. As Vaughan and others have pointed out, men of the same tribe, clan, and district of China, even of the same family, might be found ranged against one another in mortal combat through the accident of their secret-society allegiance. This fact will often explain the apparent change of an individual or group from one camp to another as the ebb and flow of power effected new combinations.

In the year 1862 trouble broke out between the Hai San men at Klian Pauh (now Taiping) and the Ghee Hin men at the Kamunting mines, a few miles away. The occasion was a gambling dispute between a party of Ghee Hins visiting Klian Pauh and some Hai Sans. Immediately the cry was raised of 'Kill these interlopers!' Fourteen of the Ghee Hins were seized and thirteen of them barbarously murdered. Only one escaped to tell the tale. Tribal war then broke out between the villages.[21]

Both sides appealed to the Malay head of the district. Ngah Ibrahim was an opportunist. As soon as he saw that the Hai San men (who had begun these disturbances) were the stronger party he threw in his lot with them, put to death the Ghee Hin leader, So Ah Chiang, and drove his followers out of Larut. The dispossessed miners appealed to the British Government.[22]

The struggle henceforth was between the Ghee Hin and the Hai San for the exclusive possession of the tin-fields of Larut.

At this time most of the Chinese in Perak were regarded as British subjects since the majority claimed to come from Penang, though many of them were professional fighting men especially imported from China. Colonel Cavenagh, the Governor, responding to the appeal of the Ghee Hin,[23] ordered a blockade of the coast, and yielding to the pressure Ngah Ibrahim paid a sum of $17,000 as damages. The dispossessed Ghee Hins returned to the occupation of the Kamunting mines and Ho Ghi Siu was appointed as headman in Larut in succession to the murdered So Ah Chiang.

So ended the first Larut 'war'.

The following years were a period of quiescence in Perak, but the battle of the factions was transferred to Penang where the upshot was the disturbance of 1867. During this period the White and Red Flag Societies, the Malay counterparts of the Ghee Hin and the Hai San, established themselves alongside their respective Chinese allies in the underground

[21] For this period see Winstedt, *History of Malaya* (London, 1935), p. 230 ff.; the same author's *Malaya and its History*, pp. 62–77; R. J. Wilkinson, *History of the Peninsular Malays*, 3rd ed. (Singapore, 1923).

[22] 'History of Perak', *JRASMB*, xii, pt. 1 (June 1934), p. 80.

[23] Winstedt and Wilkinson both say that the claim for damages was by the Go Kuan (Go Kwan) British subjects, but, as Mr W. L. Wynne of the Malayan Police remarked in an unpublished study, 'Triad and Tabut', it was the Ghee Hin (See Kwan) who were dispossessed and who appealed to the Governor for redress.

of Perak's politics. The Hai San had been defeated by the pressure brought on them by the British in the Larut troubles of 1863, but they were by no means disposed to accept this defeat as final. The Ghee Hin burnt some Hai San houses at Jelutong in Penang in 1865, but it was not until 1867 that there was a full-scale trial of strength between them.

The two factions used Penang and Perak alternately as a battle-ground. In Perak the bone of contention was the mining land, but the actual occasion for the new conflict about to take place was the alleged intrigue between Lee Ah Kun, the head of the Ghee Hin in Larut, and a woman of the Hai San camp who was said to have been a relative of Chang Keng-kwee, then head of the Hai San in Penang. Lee Ah Kun and the woman were seized by the Hai San, carried round the district in pig baskets, and finally drowned in a mining pool. This was the signal for a retaliatory outbreak of the Ghee Hin.

Meanwhile the Mentri of Larut was in a dilemma. He had, under the pressure of the British, made his peace with the Ghee Hin and restored them to their holdings, but secretly he remained the ally of the Hai San. But the Ghee Hin now took the initiative, and, though inferior in numbers to the Hai San, drove them back from Klian Pauh upon the Mentri's fort at Matang. Seeing how things were going, the Mentri evacuated the defeated Hai Sans to Penang at his own expense (the junk hire alone cost $15,000) and made overtures to the victorious Ghee Hins. At the same time he addressed the Governor of the Straits Settlements, Sir Harry Ord, explaining what had happened. The dispossessed Hai San also made a report to him just as the dispossessed Ghee Hin had done in 1862. The Governor declined to interfere.

It is at this point that the Chinese faction-fights became mixed up with the question of the succession to the throne of Perak. Rival candidates for the throne which had become vacant by the death of Sultan Ali in 1871 appealed for the support of one or the other of the Chinese factions. The disorder worked itself up to a climax. An attack by the Hai San in October 1872 at Larut on the unsuspecting and unprepared Ghee Hin was completely successful. 'Hundreds perished in the fighting', says Winstedt, 'several hundreds more died of exposure or privation in the jungle.' In this same month 2,000 Ghee Hin refugees found their way to Penang of whom more than 100 were wounded. All the Ghee Hin women fell into the hands of their enemies. A few preferred suicide to dishonour; the rest were divided up between the Hai San headmen and the Mentri's chiefs, for the Mentri had taken up once more the policy of siding with the victors.

In the third phase which followed, the Ghee Hin were for the first time the aggressors. They prepared a fleet of junks and blockaded the coast of Larut and seized Matang. The struggle lasted for a year and led to British intervention in Perak.

The history of the British intervention belongs to the general history of Malaya and has been dealt with in detail by C. Northcote Parkinson, C. D. Cowan, and others. We must content ourselves here with a relation of the main facts.

In November 1873 the new Governor, Sir Andrew Clarke, arrived in Singapore charged with the task of bringing about 'limited interference in the affairs of the Malay States for the preservation of peace and security, the suppression of piracy, and for the development of roads, schools, and police, through the appointment of a Political Agent or Resident in each State'. This represented a complete change of policy which was defined in a dispatch from the Secretary of State to the new Governor. It included the passage (since famous): '. . . Her Majesty's Government find it incumbent to employ such influence as they possess with the native princes to rescue, if possible, these fertile and productive countries from the ruin which must befall them if the present disorders continue unchecked.'

After Mr Pickering (later the first Protector of Chinese) had opened up negotiations with the Chinese headmen of Perak, the latter were summoned together with all the major Malay chiefs of Perak to meet the Governor at Pangkor on 20 January 1874. The result was two treaties, one in Malay between the British and the Perak chiefs present, being the Treaty of Pangkor proper, and one in Chinese between the British and the headmen in Penang and Larut of the Ghee Hin and Hai San. By the latter the representatives of the two contending parties agreed on the unconditional submission of their case to the decision of the British Government.

The main provision of the Pangkor Treaty proper was that Raja Muda Abdullah became Sultan and agreed to accept a British Resident 'whose advice must be asked and acted upon on all questions other than those touching Malay religion and custom'. Mr J. W. W. Birch was appointed first British Resident of Perak on 17 November 1874. He attempted to ensure that the revenues of the various districts of Perak, which were a perquisite of the individual chiefs and which they farmed out to the Chinese, were made available for public purposes. His intention was to replace these perquisites by fixed allowances. This, coupled with his interference with religion and custom (especially with regard to slaves) and his generally tactless and pig-headed behaviour, aroused resentment among the chiefs and within a year Birch was murdered. This was followed by military intervention by the British. The campaign was short and decisive. By 17 December 1875 (Birch had been murdered on 2 November) all organized resistance was at an end though guerrilla warfare followed. The British resolved on the continuance of the 'Residential' system and Mr Hugh Low was appointed Resident.

Hugh Low established a State Council for Perak which had four

Malay and two Chinese members, in addition to two British official members. One of the Chinese members was Kapitan Ah Kwee and the other was Kapitan Ah Yam. Kapitan Ah Kwee was none other than Chang Keng-kwee, who had taken a leading part in the recent disturbances and was now leader of the Hai San in Penang and Larut, while Kapitan Ah Yam had been the leader of the Ghee Hin and White Flag in Penang and Larut ever since the murder of Lee Ah Kun in 1872. Raja Dris (Idris), one of the Malay members, was in sympathy with the White Flag and in fear of the Red Flag,[24] and another Malay member, the Orang Kaya Temenggong, was (says Wynne) probably a member of the Red Flag. So that the first Perak State Council had a decidedly secret-society flavour. But it must be remembered that in those days if you were a Chinese leader at all, it had to be a Triad or Tokong leader. None the less it was clear that the British had very much to learn about the underground machinery of Chinese social life before they could competently govern their newly acquired protectorates.

Secret-society activity continued unabated during the first years of the British regime. Crimes of violence were so common that an attempt was made to secure the registration of Chinese coastal workers on the south coast of Larut—woodcutters, sawyers, and fishermen of the *kongsi*—but it was defeated by the impossibility of giving a Chinese a fixed identity; only the fingerprint system, introduced twenty-five years later, finally succeeded in doing this. On one or two occasions the murders instigated by the societies had Europeans for victims. Such was the killing of Captain Lloyd, Superintendent of the Dindings at Pangkor Island, and his wife in October 1878. The next big challenge by the Ghee Hin was an attempt to seize Taiping town, stronghold of the Hai San, in what became known as the Taiping riots in October 1879. A salvo of artillery fire from Walker, the Chief of the Perak armed police, frustrated the attempt and can be said to mark the end of the Larut wars.

Apart from the rivalry over the tin-fields, the secret societies had another rich source of profit to quarrel over. This was the monopoly of the revenue farms. The farming system was undoubtedly an unavoidable phase in the transition from the feudal exactions imposed during the Malay period to an orderly system of public finance. The farmer was invariably a Chinese, or a syndicate of Chinese, who by public tender obtained the right to collect the duty or revenue under the various heads. There was keen competition among the syndicates to obtain the farms, and the Government, once the farm was let, was relieved of further responsibility. It received a fixed sum while the farmers extracted as much as they could from the public. The system lingered on in some States well after the end of the nineteenth century, but was eventually abolished.

[24] The White Flag was composed of Malays and Tamils who, in riots, sided with the Chinese Ghee Hin; the Red Flags, also Malays and Tamils, sided with the Chinese Toh Peh Kongs.

In the years following the Perak war there was a great influx of Chinese into the State. In 1882 the Resident, then Sir Hugh Low, was becoming apprehensive of the upset of the balance of power and of the ability of the Chinese to combine against the Government. In his report for 1882 he points out that 30,000 Chinese might be assembled in a few hours at Taiping. The number of Chinese miners had increased, he said, from about 9,000 in 1877 to probably 50,000 at the time of writing.

A Secretary for Chinese Affairs was appointed at the beginning of 1884 following on the creation of the post of Protector of Chinese in Singapore in 1877, and Mr C. A. Schultz assumed this appointment. Schultz was inclined to regard the secret societies in a favourable light, believing (like Vaughan in the Straits) that they had done and were doing good among their countrymen by assisting them and adjusting minor disputes among members. However, from 1884 to 1889 a series of riots, directly traceable to Triad and Tokong rivalries, was proof of the lawless tendency of these organizations. The facts became too notorious to be ignored. In August 1889 an Order in Council was issued absolutely prohibiting all Chinese secret societies. The first measures not proving sufficiently effective, a Registration of Societies Enactment was passed on the lines of the Colony Ordinance in 1889, and provided for exemption, registration, and dissolution of societies. This eventually proved an effective piece of legislation.

Perak was the key State, so to speak, for this period, but British intervention was also taking place in the other States one by one. We will shortly review happenings in Kedah, Selangor, and Pahang in the latter part of the nineteenth century in so far as they relate directly to the Chinese.

Little is heard of the Chinese in Kedah during the centuries, but it is clear that Chinese settling in Province Wellesley must have spilled over into Kedah from an early date. The riots which took place in Kedah in February 1876 between Ghee Hins and Toh Peh Kongs, just when the Sultan of Kedah had completed arrangements for the deposed Sultan Ismail of Perak, taking refuge there, to give himself up to the British, are attributed by Wynne to the interest of the Ghee Hin in his escape. The Chinese in Province Wellesley threatened at the time to join in the disturbances.[25]

In Selangor a civil war over a disputed succession led to British intervention. Sultan Mohammed had died in 1857 and Sultan Samat succeeded to the throne on a disputed title in 1860. Civil war ensued and to the horrors of internal strife was added that of piracy. Chinese as well as Malay pirates were concerned. Raja Ya'akob, the third son of the Sultan,

---

[25] It must be remembered that Kedah did not come under British protection until 1909 when the suzerainty over the State was transferred from Siam to the British by the Treaty of Bangkok.

who had now more or less established his rule, was behind much of the piracy carried on by his followers and for his benefit. British intervention followed, and the Sultan was glad enough to accept the appointment of a British Resident. (One item in Selangor's earliest budget was $300,000 owed to a Malacca merchant for munitions of war.)

One of the headmen of the Hai San between 1864 and 1884 was the well-known Yap Tek Loy, a Hakka, who became Kapitan China of Selangor during this same period. In 1884 the acting British Resident referred to Yap Tek Loy as 'the recognized head of the Chinese in Selangor who on this, as on all other occasions, cordially co-operated with the police in maintaining order in the State'. Actually Yap Tek Loy, being a Tokong headman, was supporting the authorities to the extent of keeping out the Triad influence, which since its collapse in 1880 had been seeking fresh fields of development farther south.

With the progress towards direct government and the blows against the power of the secret societies, the captains became an anachronism. They had, we have seen, already disappeared long ago in the Straits Settlements. In 1901, with the death of the Kapitan China of Perak, Cheang (or Chang) Keng Kwee, who had been an original member of the Perak State Council in 1877, the appointment lapsed.[26]

In 1888 Pahang had a population of 50,000 Malays and a few hundred Chinese.[27] The majority of the latter were employed in the tin-mines at Bentong. The Sultan of Pahang, Ahmad, had given large tracts on the Lipis to Europeans, Arabs, Chinese, and Malays without regard to the local chiefs and the small Chinese who had spent $30,000 on prospecting and the small Malays whose gold was taken without compensation. The arbitrary and inefficient rule and prevailing anarchy made the situation ripe for British intervention. The immediate occasion for this arose in February 1888 when a Chinese British subject, Go Hin, was stabbed outside the palace, clearly by the Sultan's orders. The British Government demanded compensation or that the Sultan should accept a British Resident. The Sultan asked for a British Resident to be appointed. In October 1888 J. P. Rodger was appointed as the first British Resident and found himself confronted with the same difficulties that confronted Birch in Perak in 1875. It was years before the Residential system began to work smoothly in the State.

While the field of high politics was monopolized by dynastic wars, and the main forces behind the scenes were the secret societies, Triad and Tokong, Ghee Hin or Hai San, the mass of the Chinese, though they

[26] G.B., Colonial Office, *Annual Report for the Federated Malay States, 1901*, Cd. 1297. It appears (from information supplied to me by Mr W. L. Blythe) that the appointment was not abolished at that time, but remained without a holder until 1921 when Chung Thye Pin was appointed by the Sultan of Perak. After his death no one else was appointed (see S. M. Middlebrook, 'Yap Ah Loy, 1837–1885', *JMBRAS*, July 1951).

[27] Swettenham, *British Malaya*, p. 270.

might be members of these organizations, were peacefully occupied in their labour of development. Their progress in opening up the country is readily traceable in the annual reports of the States and of the Federation (since 1896). For example, in 1891 the *Perak Annual Report*[28] states that in Kuala Kangsar a Chinese had tried the experiment of planting rice by Chinese labour and the result was so encouraging that he was formulating a scheme for importing Chinese agriculturists on a large scale. The pepper industry was fairly established in the hands of Malays and Chinese as the result of Government encouragement. Sugar was grown for export by Chinese in Krian. Alluvial tin-mining was still practically in the hands of Chinese, though four or five European and Australian companies had done very well, principally on the 'tribute' system (i.e. their land was worked by Chinese who paid them a percentage of their output). In 1893 great developments were reported in Kinta. 'The advancement', says the *Perak Annual Report* for that year, 'was almost incredible.' Ten years before it was 'little more than a vast stretch of jungle, unapproachable except by a shallow and rapid river, and possessing not a single mile of first-class road nor a village of any importance'.[29] By 1897 the population of Perak was estimated at 215,000 of whom 100,000 were Malays and 90,000 Chinese.[30]

The record for the other States was different only in scale, not in proportion. The tin industry was expanding; the rubber industry was in process of creation. The revenues of the Federation (which had been formed in 1896 to include Perak, Selangor, Negri Sembilan, and Pahang) were increasing by leaps and bounds, and were being applied to roads and railways, public buildings, and health measures. Modern Malaya was coming into being.

[28] *Straits Settlements Annual Reports. Annual Report by the Acting British Resident of Perak* (1891), p. 367. The cultivation of rice by Chinese, however, came to nothing owing to the policy of Malay Land Reservations which meant that the good rice-growing land was largely reserved for Malays.   [29] Ibid. p. 410.

[30] J. M. Gullick in *Indigenous Political Systems of Western Malaya* (London, 1958, p. 23) has brought together much information regarding the numbers of Chinese in the Malay States in the latter part of the nineteenth century. At Larut the Chinese population was estimated at 4,000 in January 1874, 27,000 in December 1874, 15,000 in 1876 and 9,000 in 1877; a rough count in 1879 gave a total of 16,953. At Kuala Lumpur the main mining centre of Selangor, the Chinese mining population was estimated at 10,000 in 1870, 5,000 in 1873, and 20,000 in 1879; at the count of 1884 it was returned as 28,236. Lukut, once an important mining centre in Selangor had dwindled from 2,000 in 1870 to 300 in 1874. The Chinese population of Sungei Ujong was estimated at 10,000 in 1874, and 6,000 in 1878. (The estimated Malay populations were Perak 1870, 30,000; Selangor 1874 (after seven years of civil war), 5,000; 1878, 10,000; 1884 (rough Census), 17,097. Negri Sembilan, 30,000–40,000.)

29

CHINESE SOCIAL LIFE AND EDUCATION
IN MALAYA

THE British administrators of the Straits Settlements in the early days
were, by large, interested in the immigrants as traders, artisans, and
labourers and were not greatly concerned with their social behaviour so
long as they did not interfere with the authorities or with the other communities. They appointed headmen for the Chinese, Chooliahs (Tamils),
Bugis, &c, who had powers to deal with minor offences and disputes, and
they farmed out the collection of taxes to the highest bidder. The communities were only too pleased to accept this arrangement as it guaranteed
them the maximum of freedom to live their own lives with the maximum
of protection under the aegis of the British.

When Penang was founded no system of law existed, and Francis Light
and his successors were compelled to act according to the dictates of their
consciences. In 1800 Sir George Leith, the Lieutenant-Governor, was
instructed to frame regulations that were to be in principle 'the laws of
the different peoples and tribes of which the inhabitants consist, tempered
by such parts of the British law as are of universal application being
founded on the principles of natural justice'. He made no progress towards carrying out these grandiose and impracticable instructions and
it was not until 1807 that a Charter of Justice was granted to Penang
which introduced English law as it then existed, subject to certain
modifications for the native inhabitants, as will be explained below. The
law was subsequently modified or added to by statute law. When, however, the Malay States were one by one brought under British protection,
the English common law was not introduced. In these States the Indian
law was frequently copied (e.g. the Penal Code, the Contract Enactment, &c).

The establishment of the Recorder's Court in Penang in 1807 did
away with indirect rule through the native Captains, but in Singapore
from its foundation in 1819 until the Charter was extended to it in 1826,
justice was administered through the headmen (the 'Kapitan China' in
the case of the Chinese). In the Malay States the 'Captain' system was
continued into the present century, but in its later stages the title
became more and more honorary and was finally abolished.[1]

---

[1] For the legal history of the Straits Settlements see Braddell, *The Law of Straits Settlements* (Singapore, 1931), pp. 80–81 and *passim*, and C. H. Withers Payne, *The Law of Administration of Succession to Estates in the Straits Settlements* (Singapore, 1932), pp. 12–14 and *passim*.

In explaining the first Charter of law, Sir Edmund Stanley, the first Penang Recorder, stated that 'it secures to all native subjects the free exercise of their religion, indulges them in all their prejudices, and pays the most scrupulous attention to their ancient customs, usages, and habits'. The operation of the Charter was, however, soon held not to be unlimited and could not be construed as giving to all inhabitants of the Colony the full benefit of their own laws, religion, and customs. In *Regina* v. *Willans* (1858), Sir Benson Maxwell delivered a judgment of which Dr Withers Payne says:

This judgment lays down the rules that first the Charters have not in any respect modified the law of England by any exceptional adaptation of it to the religion and usages of the East; and secondly, that such native law as had up to 1858 been recognized in this Colony, had been so recognized not because any of the Charters demands an exceptionally indulgent treatment of such matters but simply because of the general principles of the Law of England.[2]

In the course of a later judgment of 1869 Sir Benson Maxwell, C.J., said:

In this Colony so much of the law of England as was in existence when it was imported here, and is of general (and not merely local) policy and adapted to the condition and wants of the inhabitants, is the law of the land: and further, that law is subject, in its application to the various alien races established here, to such modifications as are necessary to prevent it from operating unjustly and oppressively on them.[3]

In short, the law of the Straits Settlements was English law modified where necessary by native custom, not the reverse.

An instance of Chinese custom being followed and not English law occurred in 1843 when it was decided that adopted children of a Chinese were entitled to the joint administration of his estate in preference to his nephew. Polygamy was held to be a Chinese institution in a number of cases (the leading one, well known as the 'Six Widows Case', was in 1908),[4] and in 1867 it was decided that a secondary wife was entitled to a share of the intestate's property. On the other hand, Chinese custom was departed from in a number of instances. In 1868 administration was refused by the court to the adopted daughter of a Chinese, and since that year until the present time adopted children have not been recognized by the court as entitled to administration or to a share of the estate. Although (says Braddell) by Chinese law and custom adopted children are legitimate and find a most important place in the structure of Chinese

---

[2] Payne, p. 12.   [3] 1 Kyshe, 216, 221 (cf. Payne, p. 8 n. [3]).

[4] The Court of Appeal held that all the widows of a Chinese were entitled to share under the Statute of Distribution.

I am indebted to Mr J. V. Mills (formerly a judge in Malaya) for the following table of additional cases.

Chinese law and custom followed:
(a) Marriage conferred no marital rights on the husband as regards the wife's property (Withers Payne, pp. 25–27).

(b) A natural child is legitimated by a subsequent legal union of the parents (*Choo Eng Choon* (1911), 12 S.S.L.R. 120, 124).

family law, in the Colony this is entirely denied to them as the judges felt themselves bound to hold that 'child' in the Statute of Distribution can only mean a child begotten of the body.[5]

The Chinese at least would have retained a virtual *imperium in imperio* for longer had it not been for certain shortcomings of their social system which, when transported overseas, were forced on the attention of their rulers. One of the symptoms of this was the civil disturbance caused by collisions between rival secret societies which led to riot and bloodshed; another was the disorder and abuse traceable to the Chinese addiction to gambling. The latter received much earlier attention from the authorities because its evils were more obvious, and it was only at long last that any effective notice was taken of the activities of the secret societies.

The societies of Malaya are all generally believed to be offshoots of the Thian Ti Hui (the Heaven and Earth League), otherwise known as the Hung (Flood) League.[6] The Hung League was known to itself under the names given above, and also as the Sam Hup (or Three Unities League) or Triad Society.[7] In China they were originally religious or benevolent 'self help' associations, which assumed a political or anti-dynastic character at the time of the Manchu conquest, and later degenerated into organizations of criminals for exploiting and intimidating the community. Their rivalries, especially regarding control and limits of the 'protection areas' into which they parcelled towns and districts, brought them into collision.

Europeans have made a distinction between the *huis* (as the secret societies were called) and the *kongsis*, or district or clan associations, labelling the former as secret and subversive, and the latter as open and beneficial. In Chinese usage, however, *kongsi* (as Mr Blythe has pointed out) includes *hui*, and no distinction is made between good and bad.

Chinese law and custom followed (*contd.*):
(c) All widows divide equally the one-third share given by the Statute of Distribution (*Choo Eng Choon* (1911), 12 S.S.L.R. 120).
(d) Children legitimated *per subsequens matrimonium* divide equally the two-thirds share given by the Statute of Distribution (*Choo Eng Choon* (1911), 12 S.S.L.R. 120).

English law followed:
(a) The court declined jurisdiction in (polygamous) matrimonial causes (divorce, &c) (*Meyer* v. *Meyer* (1927), S.S.L.R. 14).
(b) The court refused to recognize legitimation of a natural child by recognition (*Khoo Hooi Leong* v. *Khoo Chong Yeok* (1930), A.C. 346, 356).
(c) Females held to have equal rights of succession with males (*Lee Joo Neo* v. *Lee Eng Swee* (1887), 4 Kyshe 325).

As most of the Malayan Chinese have a Chinese domicile, the law of China has frequently been applied in a determination of their rights and obligations.

[5] *Law of Straits Settlements*, p. 88.

[6] Wynne's contention that the second of the large rival groups into which the secret societies were divided in Malaya was an offshoot, not of the Thian Ti Hui, but of the Han League cannot be substantiated.

[7] For a fuller treatment of Malayan Chinese secret societies and their activities, see Purcell, *Chinese in Malaya*, chap. viii.

In fact, it is likely that the district and clan associations were as much involved in the early disturbances as the *huis*, and it was only when the society legislation towards the end of the century began to separate the sheep from the goats, allowing the registration of the 'beneficial' *kongsis*, and making the rest illegal, that this distinction was made, and even then only by Europeans.[8]

Such was the complexity and the secrecy and intricacy of Triad ritual that not enough was known about it to enable the authorities to set about curbing the League's activities until after the publication of Schlegel's epoch-making work in English at Batavia in 1866. Based on documents seized by the Dutch police, this threw a wealth of light on the Triad Society and is still the standard authority.[9]

As early as 1799 the *kongsis* or the *huis* (as the case might be) set the administration in Penang at defiance: in 1825 they actually plotted an insurrection in league with the Siamese to overthrow the Government; in 1826 Newbold notes the Triad Society in Malacca as being 4,000 strong; in Singapore the Triad was certainly established before 1825, and about 1840 the Ghee Hin was strongly suspected of executing the most daring robberies and murders, particularly at Singapore where a large body resided among the jungle and fastnesses in the interior of the island. It was, like the Triad at Malacca, composed almost entirely of Cantonese and there was bad blood between it and the Hokkien society lately established.

The list of riots and other violent interferences with the normal life of the community is a very long one, and some of the incidents have been recorded in the two preceding chapters. They culminated in a series of outbreaks at various periods. The establishment of the Chinese Protectorate in 1877 marked a stage towards an understanding of the problem, for hitherto there had been no officials with an adequate knowledge of the Chinese language.[10] After many abortive attempts to

[8] There has for a long time been a great deal of confusion over this matter—a confusion shared by the author when he wrote the chapter on secret societies in *Chinese in Malaya*. The above, however, is the opinion to which he now inclines. Certainly since the registration laws were passed the 'beneficial' societies have been encouraged to come into the open and those which have operated underground have invariably been criminal or semi-criminal in nature. All Chinese social organization was necessarily 'secret' whilst it was not recognized or was banned by the Government. The Chinese municipal organizations in Borneo, the *kongsis*, were, and are, referred to as 'secret' societies, as are all Chinese political organizations in Siam where they are illegal. The whole subject called for a thorough review and for the reconsideration of the terms used. T'ien Ju-k'ang, *The Chinese of Sarawak*, throws further light on the situation. Mr Maurice Freedman has also published his researches in the field of social anthropology in Malaya. Professor Firth calls attention to the need for continued investigation of the Chinese family and Chinese associations at pp. 28–29 of his report on *Social Science Research in Malaya* (Singapore, 1948).

[9] Gustav Schlegel, *Thian Ti Hwui or Heaven-Earth-League; a Secret Society with the Chinese in China and India* (Batavia, 1866). See also J. S. M. Ward and W. G. Stirling, *The Hung Society* (London, 1925).

[10] Schlegel, p. 11, quotes Oliphant, *Narrative of the Earl of Elgin's Mission to China and Japan*, i. 20, as saying that at this period there were 70,000 Chinese in Singapore and not a single European understood their language.

C.S.E.A.—K

legislate for the situation, the Societies Ordinance was passed in 1889 and came into force on 1 January 1890. The principal provision of this law was that a society of any sort was illegal until it had applied for and had been accepted for registration. Power was given to the Governor-in-Council to order the dissolution of any society. This law did not by any means effect the extinction of the *huis*—they continued to operate underground in a restricted way—but it did mean that powers now existed for dealing with them. China-born Chinese assisting in the management of illegal societies were banished, and deportation to their native land, curiously enough, was something they feared next to death.[11]

In the first decades of the twentieth century the *huis* languished under constant official pressure, and were overshadowed in importance by the political societies, but after the Pacific War they again revived.

Another specifically Chinese problem in Malaya was the traffic in women and girls. The preponderance of men over women among the Chinese produced a very unbalanced community and this led to the importation of women and girls to be prostitutes.

The policy pursued with regard to the problem of an incoming traffic in Chinese women may be divided into three periods. During the first period up to 1927 brothels were allowed throughout Malaya and Chinese girls were permitted to enter the ports of the Straits Settlements for the purpose of becoming inmates of these (providing that they did so of their own free will; the duty of the Chinese Protectorate was to prevent the *traffic* in women and girls); during the second period from 1927 to 1930 brothels continued to be allowed but no avowed prostitutes were allowed to enter the country; the third period began in 1930, after which brothels were not allowed in the Straits Settlements or the Malay States, nor were avowed prostitutes allowed to enter the Peninsula.

Upon the closing of the brothels the exploiters turned to various other expedients for profiting by the girls. These expedients taxed the ingenuity of the Protectorate and of the police to counter them. On the arrival of each vessel from China all women and girls on board were taken to a depot where they were examined by Protectorate officials. Those whose bona fides were established were immediately released; if there was any doubt the person into whose charge the girl was going could be required to enter into a bond that she would not be disposed of to others or trained or used for the purposes of prostitution. In cases where there was reason to believe that the girl was the victim of traffic, she was committed to an institution known as the Po Leung Kuk by the Protector. Here she would remain until provision could be made for her welfare or she reached the age of eighteen years. Many girls were placed

<hr>

[11] The Imperial authorities in China were indeed, it is said, in the habit of executing persons so deported as undesirables. If this were true then the dislike of banishment was more understandable.

in the home as the result of raids of Protectorate officers on 'sly' brothels, together with others who had been the victims of cruelty.

Many girls were married off to Chinese men who applied to the Protectorate for a wife.

Besides the girls arriving from China who were placed in the Po Leung Kuk for protection there were some cases of *mui tsai* who had been ill treated. The term *mui tsai* was applied to a girl who had been transferred from her own family, either directly or through a third party, to another family with the intention that she should be used as a domestic servant, not in receipt of regular wages, and not at liberty to leave her employer's family of her own free will or that of her parents. In effect, a 'slave girl'—though the term is too strong. The system was a by-product of conditions in China where so many families lived on the verge of starvation, where infanticide was common, and the disposal of a girl as a *mui tsai* was often the only way of saving her from death. The lot of a *mui tsai* was rarely a happy one though her employer had some definite obligations towards her, including that of marrying her off when she reached marriageable age.

In 1936 a Commission was appointed to report on *mui tsai* and in January 1937 it had submitted a Majority and a Minority Report.[12] It was the Minority Report (by Miss E. Picton Turbevill, O.B.E.) that was adopted by the British Government together with some recommendations of the Majority Report. The former included the abolition of the status of *mui tsai*.

Among the problems arising among the Chinese in Malaya should be mentioned that of opium, but since it is one common to all the Chinese communities of Southeast Asia it was made the subject of notice in Chapter 4 of the first edition of this Survey. All that need be stated here is that in 1907 a Commission on Opium was appointed which made its report the following year, that at midnight on 31 December 1909 the opium farms in Singapore, Penang, and Malacca suspended business and the Government Monopolies Department entered into possession of the premises and reopened them for business as usual the following day; that a policy of gradual suppression of opium-smoking was followed for many years, and that His Majesty's Government on 10 November 1943 adopted a policy of total prohibition of opium-smoking in British and British-protected territories in the Far East then in enemy occupation.[13]

The phenomenal growth of Chinese education during the twenty-five years previous to the First World War brought the bulk of the Malayan

---

[12] G.B., Colonial Office, *Report of the Commission on Mui Tsai in Hongkong and Malaya* (1937).

[13] See p. 3, *Report of the Opium Commission* (Singapore, 1908). Vols. i and iii were published as Cds. 4321 and 4322 (1909).

Chinese within the sphere of influence of the educational movement which started with the revolution in China, and its importance is primarily political rather than cultural.

In 1938 there was a total of 268,007 pupils of all races attending educational institutions of all kinds in the Straits Settlements and Federated Malay States alone.[14] Of these 204,040 were in institutions maintained or aided by Government funds. Of the latter, 18,522 Chinese boys and 8,452 Chinese girls were in Government and aided English schools; 34,813 boys and 14,458 girls were in aided Chinese schools. The total number of Chinese children in all Chinese schools in the Straits Settlements and Federated Malay States was 91,534 (66,645 boys and 24,889 girls). That is to say that the number of Chinese children attending schools in which Chinese was the medium of instruction far exceeded that of the Chinese children attending schools in which English was the medium.

Including vocational schools, Government and private (1,214 boys and 165 girls), it was estimated that altogether 94,619 boys and 36,347 girls of Chinese race (total 130,966) were receiving an education of some kind in 1938. This gives a percentage literacy of total population of 44 per cent male and 10·7 per cent female (based on the 1931 Census figures; the 'general literacy' rates per mille from the 1947 Census are given on p. 273 of the first edition of this work).

Raffles had in mind an enlightened and far-reaching scheme when in 1823 he set aside a piece of ground for the Singapore Institution and provided an endowment for it. He meant to found a college with 'literary and moral' departments for Chinese, Malays, and Siamese, and with a scientific department attached to the English section but common to all. His intention (so far as we can divine it) was to make Singapore a centre for scholarship in these three Eastern languages, with the idea, perhaps, that the cultural creativeness of the three departments would overflow into the others, and that they should have a common ground in English and in science for which English was the natural medium.

As it turned out, Raffles's scheme came to nothing. His grant was applied in 1827 to elementary schools, and later in 1837 a school was founded with English, Malay, and Chinese classes—the Malay and Chinese failed through the apathy of the pupils, and only the English remained. The school became known as the Raffles Institution. Not until the foundation of the King Edward VII College of Medicine in 1910 did Singapore have any institution of collegiate standing, and it was not until 1928 that Raffles College came into being.

Meanwhile the various races of Malaya, with the active help of the Christian missionaries, were doing their best to educate their children

---

[14] Figures for the Unfederated Malay States are incomplete, so those for the Straits Settlements and Federated Malay States alone are given here.

according to their own lights and resources. A select committee of the Legislative Council of the Straits Settlements, appointed in 1870 to inquire into local education, found a great variety and number of schools in the Colony, some purely educational, others combining charity with education, many under the control of the Roman Catholic clergy, but all, apparently, having a system of their own, unchecked, as a rule, by Government supervision.

The several Malay Governments took an increasing share in the provision of schools and the control of education. In the 1930s education in English was provided in a number of Government schools and schools conducted by missionary bodies which received grants-in-aid from the Government and were subject to inspection and control. Usually fees were charged, albeit small ones, and there was no approach to free universal education in English. The curriculum led through secondary education for those who could afford it and could profit by it to the Cambridge Examinations and usually to clerical employment in Government service or in private firms. The lucky few were able to proceed to the professions either through the College of Medicine or Raffles College, or through some university outside Malaya. There were numerous scholarships open to children attending English schools.

In the Malay States primary education in Malay was free for all Malay boys and girls, and compulsory for all boys living within a mile and a half of a Malay vernacular school. Estates employing over a certain number of Tamil labourers had to maintain a school and give free vernacular education to the children of Tamil labourers working on the estate. There were no such facilities for Chinese.

The popularity of education in English led to an over-emphasis on literary education and the production of more clerks than employers could absorb. The Government therefore concentrated more and more on technical and vocational training. Technical and agricultural colleges were established and also trade schools in which a boy could learn any trade from tailoring and book-keeping to plumbing and electric welding.

Meanwhile the system of English education did not touch the bulk of the Chinese. The fees, though small, and representing only a fraction of the cost to the Government of the pupil, were prohibitive to the great majority, and, quite apart from the question of expense, the migratory nature of such a great proportion of the population meant that many Chinese children arrived in Malaya too old to be received into the English schools. There was also a widespread feeling that English education led only to the 'white-collared' occupations which were already over-crowded. Independent of this was the sentiment which so many Chinese had in favour of education in their own language, a sentiment greatly reinforced by the nationalism fostered by the revolution.

By the beginning of the thirties the Malayan Governments were fully aware that the Chinese vernacular schools were claiming the great proportion of Chinese boys and girls at school, and that unless something was done to provide a counter-attraction the Chinese population of Malaya, even including many of the *Baba* families, would irrevocably be drawn within the sphere of Chinese nationalism and would tend to look, not to Malaya as their country, but to China. Such a happening would vitiate the whole declared official policy which was to create a Malayan spirit and sense of common nationality as the prerequisite for self-government within the British Commonwealth of Nations. The proposal of one Governor was to give to all races in Malaya free education in Malay which was to be made the common language of the country, but this was obviously unacceptable to the Chinese, let alone the other non-Malay communities, for Malay education would have led them no-where in this modern world. It was then proposed that there should be universal free education in English. But nothing was done, and the Chinese community was surrendered to Chinese nationalism and, in effect, to Communism, for this was more and more disseminated through the influence of poorly paid (and therefore leftist) teachers, so many of whom were employed in the Chinese vernacular schools.

The Chinese in Malaya had always done their best to educate their children, but facilities were few and teachers hard to come by. The schools were originally, of course, of the Old Style in which the Four Books were learned by rote. The teacher, as likely as not, combined his profession with that of fortune-teller, or geomantic diviner, and general learned odd man of the village, and any man who could read and write fluently was considered as fully qualified to teach. The schools themselves had to be seen to be believed. Most of them were dirty, ill-ventilated, and ill-lighted basements, out-houses, or attics: sanitation was non-existent; skin diseases were common among the pupils; the hubbub of pupils 'backing' their lessons was deafening to any European who came within range.

It was in Malaya that the Chinese Revolution of 1911 found some of its principal supporters, and it was natural that the new zeal for education which was born with the Revolution should be shared by the Malayan Chinese. After 1917 when the National Language movement started in China, *Kuo yü* was adopted as the medium of instruction in all public schools.[15] It was only in the private schools that the Old System was retained.[16]

While the Governments were preoccupied with education in English or Malay, the Chinese schools were left for some time to their own

---

[15] See p. 37 for general references to Chinese education.
[16] The number of Old System schools and pupils in the Federated Malay States and Straits Settlements in 1931 was 120 and 2,539: in 1938 the figures were 158 and 4,646 respectively.

devices, but in 1920 onwards were brought under Government supervision and inspection.

Chinese schools in Malaya fell into the three following categories:

1. Those managed by properly constituted committees. (These might be run by district or surname associations or by Chinese families in a certain town or district.)

2. Pseudo-public schools, i.e. schools organized by one or more teachers who chose their own 'committee members', i.e. shopkeepers, &c, who had been persuaded to lend their names, the principal teacher running the school to make what he could out of it.

3. Private schools run by teachers who relied on school fees, these schools being usually small and old in type. There were several *ping min* (common people) schools at which a nominal fee of 50 cents (1s. 2d.) a month was charged. The fees in the other schools were around 3 dollars (7s.) a month.

The main motive of the authorities in bringing the Chinese schools under inspection was admittedly political, but once the inspectorate staff was created and had started with their work it became clear that political control brought with it some very definite educational responsibilities. In no way were the Chinese schools abreast of the English schools: their methods of instruction, their premises, their sanitation were all inferior to those of their English-speaking contemporaries. This was scarcely to be wondered at when it is remembered that the latter benefited from a system built up in more than fifty years of experience, enforced by a trained staff and supported, or aided, from Government revenue.

When a system of Government grants-in-aid was introduced for Chinese schools it was not at first received with any great enthusiasm. The teachers felt that their liberty to teach what they liked and how they liked was being encroached on and their influence for long was enough to prevent many school committees from applying for these grants. However, the pressure of economic circumstances (including the trade depression of 1930–2) brought about a change in attitude and most schools eligible for them applied for and received grants. They soon found the advantages of so doing, for the money made it possible to carry on the schools without debt, the good offices of the medical and health authorities and the municipalities and Sanitary Boards were ensured, and the teaching staff benefited from the advice of the inspectors of schools who held qualifications equal, if not superior, to those of any of the Chinese teachers. Light, ventilation, health measures of all sorts, and precautions against fire received an attention they had never had in the past.

In 1938 $341,369 was paid in grants to Chinese schools in the Straits Settlements and Federated Malay States. The Unfederated Malay States had no system of grants-in-aid to Chinese schools. The State Governments recognized no responsibility in this regard. Thus, those Chinese who wished to have their children educated in their own language had to maintain their own schools. In Johore alone in 1938 there were 245 Chinese schools with 14,423 pupils.[17]

One problem for the authorities was the subversive teaching of the pupils orally, and another was textbooks. Some schools were not educational institutions at all, merely centres of Communist propaganda, especially the Hailam night-schools for adults, where Marx, Engels, Lenin, and other Communist authors were studied by pupils who had not enough general education to understand anything except the message of opposition to the local Government.

Textbooks were an almost insoluble problem. Those used in the Chinese schools in Malaya were all printed in China. The two principal firms publishing them were the Commercial Press and the Chung Hua Press, both of Shanghai. After 1925 a great deal of anti-foreign material was introduced into them, intended in particular to stir up hatred of the British. (For example, a drawing in a textbook intended for children of about twelve years of age showed the 'May 30th Incident' at Shanghai in 1925 with British and Sikh policemen in uniform shooting down an unarmed crowd. In the history books much play was made with the 'Opium War'.) That the Chinese schoolchildren of Malaya should have race-hatred instilled into them in this manner could not, of course, be tolerated by the Government. The use of these textbooks containing seditious matter or matter calculated to incite interracial hatred was forbidden, and the import of such books was prohibited. The outcome of this action was that the two principal Chinese publishing firms each produced a series free from objectionable matter and these were used in Malayan schools.

The solution, however, was a purely negative one. The textbooks were about China exclusively: there was no mention in them of Malaya's history, geography, trade, commerce, its mixed population, or interests. It had been found impracticable to produce a series of textbooks locally for use in Malayan Chinese schools, though there was an obvious need for one.

Concurrently with these difficulties the Malayan Governments had to meet the increasing interest of the National Government of China in the education of Overseas Chinese. Applying the Chinese law of nationality, the Chinese Government naturally regarded all Chinese overseas, including the Straits-born Chinese who were British subjects, as a proper object for their official solicitude. The Overseas Affairs Department (later Ministry) wished to bring the education of the children of Overseas Chinese into line with home policy. The Chinese Government sent

[17] But see p. 281 for the astonishing post-war increase in school population.

representatives to inspect the schools, requested that returns should be submitted to Nanking, and even instituted a system of grants-in-aid of their own for Overseas Chinese schools. Such an attitude could not be viewed by the Malayan Governments with complacency while they regarded so many Chinese attending the schools as British subjects. Nor was it purely a matter of concern to the Malayan Governments. Many of the Chinese who had been born in Malaya, or who regarded Malaya as their home, were jealous of the pretensions of a remote Government in China to concern itself with what they regarded as a purely domestic matter. In race and sympathy they might be Chinese: politically they regarded themselves as Malayans.

Altogether the Malayan educational system was not promising to those who hoped for the achievement of a 'Malayan outlook'. The experience of educationists was in favour of educating a child in its own language before allowing it to learn another, but even so it was certain that if there were ever to be any progress towards the creation of a Malayan nation there must first be a move to unify the diverse and conflicting educational systems operating in the country.

The years following the Second World War were marked by a really astonishing increase in school population. It seemed as if the Malaysian peoples, made aware by the Japanese occupation of what the absence of education really meant, had decided to make a determined drive to get their children educated. In the Federation, enrolment at the end of 1948 stood at 510,000; in December 1941 the figure had been 263,000. In Singapore the figure was 101,000 as compared with 72,000 in 1941 and the former figure did not include about 15,000 in unregistered schools. There is nothing to show what proportions of the increase were Chinese children, but the author would hazard a guess that it was largely accounted for by the increased attendance in Chinese vernacular schools paid for in the main by the Chinese community.[18, 19]

[18] G.B., Colonial Office, *British Dependencies in the Far East, 1945-9*, Cmd. 7709 (1949), p. 42.

[19] The Communities Liaison Committee (with Malay, Chinese, Indian, Ceylonese, and British representatives) on 19 September 1949 passed a resolution that 'every encouragement should be given to the establishment of a steadily increasing number of Government and Government-aided schools where children of all races attend together and the medium of instruction is Malay and English. *As such schools increase communal schools should be progressively reduced*' (*The Times*, 20 Sept. 1949). (The italics are mine. V. P.)

30

THE ECONOMIC POSITION OF THE
MALAYAN CHINESE

ONE aspect of the share of the Chinese in local industry is the value of their investment and the returns derived from it; the other is the number of Chinese in the labour force of the industry.

Regarding the former only scanty information is available. It is, for example, impossible from existing records to discover with exactness the comparative extent of British, Chinese, and other investments in the basic industries of tin and rubber. However, an attempt has been made by an economist, Mr Helmut G. Callis, to estimate the extent of Chinese holdings in all undertakings in Malaya as they were before the Japanese invasion. In 1937 he estimated that the total Chinese investments in Malaya approximated to U.S. $200 million (approximately £40 million) as compared with other foreign investments of $454·5 million (approximately £90·9 million). The other foreign investments Mr Callis divides into rentier, $82·5 million, and entrepreneur, $372 million, slightly over 70 per cent of the entrepreneur investment being British.[1]

Chinese family remittances from Singapore and the Federation in 1948 totalled SS $15,422,846. This was a decrease of SS $7,522,287 compared with SS $22,945,133 in 1947. Of the total remittances to China from Malaya in 1948 Singapore accounted for SS $10,228,101 and the Federation for SS $5,194,745.[2]

Tin was the product of the Malay Peninsula in which the Chinese were mainly interested from the time of their earliest trading contacts. It is likely that they did in some instances superintend the mining of it, and Chinese may have been employed in certain undertakings, but the labour up to the nineteenth century was principally Malay. Towards the end of the eighteenth century the annual output in Perak was estimated at 5,000 piculs (16·8 piculs = 1 ton). The bulk of this tin was mined by Malays in Kinta and Batang Padang.[3] Newbold, as we have seen in a previous chapter, gives an estimate of the number of Chinese in the various mining areas in the 1830s, but it was not until the discovery of

---

[1] *Foreign Capital in Southeast Asia* (N.Y., mimeo., 1942).
[2] *Straits Budget* (3 Mar. 1949).
[3] For an account of Chinese mining see A. G. Macdonald and E. S. Willbourn, *Mining in Malaya*, rev. ed. (London, 1940).

the rich deposits in Larut in the fifties that Chinese miners flocked to the fields in large numbers.

The gradual increase in the use of machinery, combined with an evergrowing efficiency, enabled deposits to be tackled which owing to depth, poverty of content, or wetness, could not be worked at a profit in the past. Electric power was in 1939 rapidly replacing steam and oil in mines. One result of the developing importance of technology was that the proportion of ore mined by European methods as against Chinese methods tended to increase. This rise, however, was arrested after 1931 largely owing to the incidence of the tin scheme.[4] The introduction of the dredge in the first years of this century marked a revolution in the history of the industry. The dredges were owned by European companies, though Chinese and others, of course, were free to invest in the shares of these companies, and did so.

Mining methods of the second quarter of the twentieth century in Malaya were divided into dredging, gravel-pump, hydraulicizing, open-cast, alluvial shafting, lode mining, and *dulang* or panning. Most popular with the Chinese was the gravel-pump method. In this a pressure-pump was generally used to feed monitors which gave jets of water powerful enough to cut and disintegrate the ground. The broken material was washed along a channel in the bottom clay, and water was lifted by the gravel-pump to the head of a *palong*, or flume, which might be anything from 40 to 120 feet above the sump. The heavy tin ore was held in the *palong* by wooden bars, placed one above the other at intervals across the bottom of the flume; most of the lighter sand and clay passed out of the *palong* with the stream of water to be deposited in the allotted dumping space.

In considering the part played by the Chinese in mining in Malaya we must take care to distinguish between ownership and methods, and labour. It is the Chinese who provide the bulk of all the labour. Thus the enormous excavations in open-cast mines have been made by them— the old mine at Sungai Besi in Selangor was 3,000 feet long and 1,200 feet wide, with a depth of 125 feet, representing 16 million cubic yards of earth, all cut by hand labour using the *changkol* (form of hoe). An even larger hole was at the Hong Fatt Mines near by, which was 310 feet deep and from which 30 million cubic yards of earth had been removed.

Open-cast mining by hand labour is a purely Chinese method. *Dulang* washing, or panning, is a method employed for obtaining tin ore in many

[4] Source: *Quarterly Bulletin of Statistics relating to the Mining Industry in the Federated Malay States* (1939), vol. xi, no. 4, p. 11. The following are percentages for selected years:

	European	Chinese
1920	36	64
1925	44	56
1930	63	37
1938	67	33

parts of the country. The work was done by Chinese women, usually Hakkas. A shallow wooden dish, about 30 inches in diameter and $3\frac{1}{2}$ inches deep in the centre, was dug into the sand of the sluice or stream bed and a quantity of sand and water was scooped into it. The dish was then subjected to a peculiar motion by which the waste material was washed over the edge and the ore remained. *Dulang* washers were a fairly common sight in Malaya and were a striking reminder of the toughness of the Chinese. The women were bent double for hours in the heat of the sun, often immersed to the knees in water, and often with a baby strapped to their backs!

Other kinds of mining in Malaya depended largely on Chinese labour —coal (at Batu Arang in Selangor), gold (at Raub lode mine and, in a minor way, by alluvial mining), wolfram and scheelite, and the pre-war Japanese iron mines in Trengganu and Johore used Chinese labour.

While the Chinese predominated in the tin industry the Indian labourers were much more numerous in rubber growing. Chinese were used for the heavier work of clearing and planting and in the general opening-up operations, and they were also widely employed as tappers and their women as weeders. Their industry was greater than that of the Indians, but they were more difficult to handle. They were intense individualists and would only work satisfactorily as tappers when they were paid by piece work.

There were in the Federated Malay States, 84,342 Chinese men and 16,447 Chinese women employed in the rubber industry in 1931 as compared with a total of 131,099 Indians and 27,618 Malays. In the Unfederated States the figures were 61,374 Chinese and 34,776 Malays, while Indians were not separately enumerated.[5]

A table published in 1932 gives the nationality of ownership of planted rubber estates of 100 acres and over in 1931. It shows that the Chinese in the Straits Settlements and Federated Malay States owned 12·5 per cent of the total as compared with 84 per cent owned by non-Asians (including British, French, Belgians, Americans) and 2·3 per cent owned by Indians.[6] In addition to this, Chinese owned many small-holdings. Small-holdings under rubber in the whole of Malaya accounted for 1,215,522 acres as compared with 1,855,797 acres for estates over 100 acres. The statistics do not show the extent of the Chinese ownership, but since a large proportion of the rubber holdings owned by Malays were rented by them to the Chinese to tap, 'ownership' does not convey very much. The production of the estates over 100 acres in 1931 was 239,435 tons for the whole of Malaya, and of the small-holdings, 195,422 tons.

As estate owners the Chinese had the advantage of smaller overhead

[5] Figures from the *Census Report, 1931*.
[6] Source: *Malaya Rubber Statistics Handbook* (Singapore, 1932), p. 15.

costs as compared with the European estates, but the latter were worked on more scientific lines.

After the war rubber production from small-holdings just about equalled that from estates, and in a period of falling rubber prices the Chinese rubber owner, particularly the small-holder, was in a favourable position *vis-à-vis* the European estate with its higher costs.

Malaya's important and growing secondary industries were largely in Chinese hands. The pineapple industry, a creation of the 1930s, was entirely a Chinese enterprise. Canned pineapples in 1938 accounted for 1·2 per cent of Malaya's entire export trade. In Singapore, Penang, Kuala Lumpur, Klang, Ipoh, and elsewhere the Chinese owned oil-mills, biscuit factories, rubber works for the manufacture of shoes, tyres, &c, iron foundries, sawmills, and sauce factories; there were Chinese shipping companies; they ran motor agencies and repair shops; the bulk of the retail trade everywhere was in their hands.

It is generally true to say that the Malays are the peasant proprietors and do most of the rice-growing (small though it may be compared with the consumption of the country) and the policy of Malay land reservation keeps the best rice land for the Malays. In the Federated Malay States in 1931 there were 78,009 Malays (44,421 males and 33,588 females) engaged in paddy planting; the Indian rice-growers were 1,892 (1,689 males and 203 females); the Chinese were only just over a thousand (1,038—including 77 females). In the Unfederated Malay States the proportions were: 159,861 Malays to 5,888 Chinese, while Indians were not separately enumerated. In the Straits Settlements, where the land under rice was small, there were 2,877 Malay, 84 Indian, and 322 Chinese planters.[7]

Fishing was comparatively a small industry. In the Straits Settlements there were, in 1931, 9,159 Malay fishermen, 335 Indians, and 6,092 Chinese; in the Federated Malay States, 5,717 Malays, 56 Indians, and 7,291 Chinese; in Johore, 2,552 Malays, no Indians, and 2,257 Chinese; in Kedah and Perlis, 2,185 Malays, no Indians, and 522 Chinese; in Kelantan, 6,601 Malays, no Indians, and 15 Chinese; and in Trengganu, 10,204 Malays, no Indians, and 171 Chinese.

The tendency in many regions of Malaya is for the fresh-fish trade to be in the hands of the Malays and the trade in cured and dried fish to be in the hands of the Chinese. Professor Firth says that the reason for this would seem to be that the handling of the latter commodities, particularly in large-scale export trade, demands distant business connexions, and at some stage the capacity to lay out capital and wait some time before it returns. Malays, Javanese, &c, are not necessarily lacking in these respects, but the Chinese commercial pattern is better adapted to take

---

[7] It has often been remarked in Agricultural Department reports that Chinese rice planters get a much higher yield per acre than other planters.

advantage of the situation. The Chinese *towkay* advances money, or more
often goods such as rice and cloth to the fishermen in the slack season
against the security of their coming catches, and he also lends money for
the purchase of boats and nets, or he may even lend such equipment
without charge. In return he contracts with the fishermen to take their
fish at an agreed price, or at a price of his own setting, usually rather
below the free-market price.[8] The Chinese have also in recent years
extended their participation in the actual fishing.[9]

Labour and Immigration

In the first part of this chapter labour has been considered purely in
its statistical aspect: it must now be regarded from a more human
angle.

Collecting agents for labourers were employed in China in the second
half of the nineteenth century 'whose character', says Morse, 'may be
fitly expressed by the word "crimp" '. These men were given a capitation fee for every emigrant they brought to the receiving depot, or
'baracoon', at the port of departure. This fee was at the outset 3 dollars
a head (figures of 1853) but no check on malpractices was possible, and
in addition they appropriated to themselves, on the score of defraying
expenses, the money advanced to the immigrants, which at the outset
was 8 dollars each, but might, even officially, have been much more, and,
in the competition of forwarding agents, might come to 100 dollars a
head. With such rewards dangled before their eyes, the reckless and irresponsible crimps lost no opportunity and adopted every known
method to draw their fellow countrymen as far as the entrance door of
the baracoon—there their responsibility ended. The pledged emigrant
was charged with the head-money paid to the crimp, with the advance
made (nominally) to himself, and with the cost of maintenance at the
depot. Without payment of this charge the emigrant was not free to
leave; and as a single dollar was to him a great sum, he ceased to be a
free agent from the moment he entered the doors of the depot.[10]

The coolie ships were floating hells. Even the modest space—12 square
feet (2 ft × 6 ft)—allowed by the Hong Kong Ordinance, was provided
only in a few ships, and in general the space was only 8 square feet in
slow sailing vessels. The mortality was great: suicides (the Asiatic form
of ultimate protest) were common. 'But even the timorous rat', says

---

[8] Raymond Firth, *Malay Fishermen: Their Peasant Economy* (London, 1946), pp. 13–14.
For a discussion of the economics of Malay fishermen *vis-à-vis* the Chinese see pp. 59–62,
68–69, and 333–8 of the same work. See also p. 202 of this study.

[9] The author well remembers when he was Protector of Chinese in Kedah in 1938 acting
as a referee in a dispute between the Malay and Chinese fishermen of the State. The former
resented the introduction by the latter of 'Siamese' fishing-traps which were much more
efficient than those previously in use along the coast and which reduced the catch of the
Malay fishermen.

[10] H. B. Morse, *International Relations of the Chinese Empire* (London, 1918), ii. 167–72.

Morse, 'will turn when cornered, and these timorous coolies not infrequently rose in mutiny against their oppressors.'

This is only the beginning of the recital of misery and horror which would fully describe the ordinary experience of Chinese coolies enticed or conscripted for labour in the Nanyang, from the beginning of large-scale emigration until measures undertaken by the several colonial Governments began to have some effect.

Raffles, as in many other things in advance of his time, had as early as 1823 published an ordinance in which he made provision for the protection of immigrants to Singapore,[11] but this ordinance apparently dropped out of notice and for many decades there is no mention of supervision or control of Chinese immigration. Official attention seems next to have been called to the abuses of the coolie traffic by a petition in 1871 to the Governor from a number of Chinese merchants and citizens who spoke of the cheating and deceiving of the *sinkheh* (new arrival) by vagabonds who boarded the ships and clandestinely dealt in the coolie trade, spiriting away the *sinkheh* who was never heard of afterwards. This was the start of widespread agitation in which the *Straits Times* joined, but when the Government introduced a Bill, and, in spite of considerable unofficial opposition, passed an ordinance to protect the immigrants, it did not obtain public support. A large public meeting of the same year (1873) passed a resolution 'that the proposed Chinese Coolie Immigration Act is both impolitic and unnecessary: impolitic because it never can accomplish the object that it is designed to secure'.

These were the days of militant *laissez-faire* and the ordinance became a dead letter. It was not until the appointment of Mr Pickering as Protector of Chinese in 1877 and he had made a report revealing the scandalous state of affairs—gangs of men for shipment to Sumatra and the like—that a second Chinese Immigration Ordinance was passed. It provided for the regulation of ships engaged in the immigration trade and for the establishment of depots to receive the immigrants, and it made obligatory the registration of all contracts of labour by Chinese immigrants. Further legislation followed at intervals to remedy the defects in the existing law which experience had revealed.

A Protector of Chinese was appointed for Penang in 1880 and gradually a chain of Protectorates was established through the Peninsula.[12]

In Singapore the Protectorate concentrated upon stopping abuses connected with the importation of labour. The standard of accommodation on both junks and steamers was improved. The coolie had his contract properly explained to him and he was told to whom he should

---

[11] Ordinance quoted in *Labour Commission Report* (Singapore, 1891), p. 4.

[12] Pickering interested himself in the welfare of *transit* labour as well as that coming into the Colony and thus incurred the criticism of the Deli (Sumatra) Planters' Committee whose position was stated in *The Deli Chinese Question* (1882).

apply for his legal rights. The coolie depots were licensed and super-vised and care was taken to stop the kidnapping of labourers, both those who had paid their passage and others, for work up country or even outside Malaya. The number of passengers arriving who paid their own fares steadily increased and the presence of these independent men naturally tended to improve the status of the indentured labourers. Some of the more enlightened employers, such as the Penang Sugar Estates and the contractors from the Tanjong Pagar Dock Company, paid the passages from China of men recruited by their agents and employed them as free labourers.

In the meantime an agreement regarding labour had been made between Britain and China. In addition to other matters, the treaty em-powered consuls to watch over the interests of the emigrants.

Indentured labour lasted, so far as the Chinese were concerned, until 1914, when it was abolished.[13] Thereafter the law provided that no engagement to labour for a period exceeding one month and no written contract to labour should be entered into.

The Labour Code as it stood at the time of the Japanese invasion was the product of extensive experience. Its provisions which touched the Chinese were numerous and covered everything from the truck system to health and housing regulations. With it went a body of auxiliary legislation such as the Workmen's Compensation Ordinance of 1933, based on English law. Yet compared with the elaborate provisions for Indian labour, which regarded the Tamil labourer as much in need of paternal care, those to protect the Chinese labourer were very sparse. This was due to the belief that the Chinese, as a race, were well able to look after themselves. The inspection of places of labour—estates, mines, &c—was carried out by Protectorate and health officers, but the duties of the former consisted mostly in mediation between employer and em-ployed. By the thirties the feeling was growing that more should be done for Chinese labour. To this end Mr W. L. Blythe, of the Malayan Civil Service, was appointed in 1937 to inquire into the conditions among Chinese labourers, and in due course he submitted an exhaustive report.[14]

The Blythe Report concentrated on rubber estates and tin-mines, but investigations were also conducted in other industries—sawmills, rubber and match factories, and in some of the shop industries such as carpentry, shoemaking, and polishing. The most striking general impression re-ceived was of the noticeable change in the outlook of the bulk of the labourers in the preceding few years. Progress in the emancipation of the Chinese labourer from indentured labour and widespread debt slavery

---

[13] This voluntary act on the part of the British Government killed the Penang sugar industry, and should be accounted to the British for altruism.
[14] This report was printed in Malaya, but was not published. See also W. L. Blythe, 'Historical Sketch of Chinese Labour in Malaya', *JRASMB*, xx, pt. 1 (1947), pp. 64–114.

had been greatly accelerated. Provision had been introduced into the Labour Code to deal with these abuses and much of the work of the Chinese Protectorate lay in their eradication. Difficulties occurred in the unwillingness of labourers to complain of 'old established customs' and they were more or less bound by ties to the contractor. Ten years previously the system had begun to disintegrate as labourers became increasingly aware of their rights, and the death-blow was given to it by the introduction of the Aliens Ordinance in the Straits Settlements (1 January 1933).

Under this Aliens Ordinance the Governor-in-Council was given power to limit the number of aliens landed in the colony. The immediate result of this enactment had been a big increase in the cost of recruitment of labour from China and higher shipping rates charged by the shipping companies. Consequently it became much cheaper to recruit labour in Malaya where there was already an adequate supply. During Mr Blythe's tour no insistence on the old system was encountered. Recruitment was taking place from the local lodging-houses where labourers lived when unemployed, and there were some squatters living on vegetable gardens.

Concurrently with the development of free labour in Malaya a growing labour emancipation movement had also been taking place in China. The stronghold of the movement was Kwangtung province from whence the majority of labourers on estates and mines in Malaya were drawn. Labour unions had been established in Malaya which were associated with the town industries, but they had had a 'leavening influence throughout the whole of Chinese labour'.

Amongst other developments a change was brought about in labour conditions by the introduction of cheap Japanese bicycles. Squatters rode to work on them, labourers on the mines and estates used them to ride into the villages for supplies, and there was a continuous interchange between labourers and their fellows in the vicinity. Still another development was the extraordinary increase in the employment of Chinese women on the estates. Whole shiploads of Cantonese women had been arriving during the previous few years in search of work. This spate of female immigration was probably due to the slump in the silk industry in China owing to the widespread use of rayon, and because women were exempt from the Malayan immigration quota. Most of the women employed on estates and mines were imported, and it would appear probable that Chinese labour forces were witnessing a transition from male to family labour. Marketing and cooking were being done by the female and by the contractor. Less opium was being smoked and some mines refused to employ smokers.

There appeared to be more direct contact between the management of European estates and their labour force, although this was far from being general. The proportion of the labourers who could speak Malay was increasing and the system of direct employment was being successfully put into practice to the exclusion of the contractor and to the benefit of the labourer and of these estates.

Wages varied according to local conditions from 38 cents on estates in Perak to as high as $1·27 on the Budu estate (Kuala Lipis Road). Weeders' wages varied from 55 to 80 cents per man employed on the *Kungsz-kung* (daily rates) and from 50 to 60 cents for women. The monthly budget of the average tapper, buying his own food, amounted to $11, without leaving provision for amusements, opium, or remittances to China; rice, pork, and fish came to about 45 per cent of his expenditure.

When the price of rubber fell, the Chinese labourers expected to be paid at lower rates, but they counted on having higher ones when the price rose.

In mines the rates of wages varied greatly owing to the many different classes of labour, skilled and unskilled, and wages varied from $90 to $100 per month in the case of European companies, and from 86 cents to $1 daily paid by contractors. Employees provided their own food; lodging and lighting were provided by the company. On open-cast and hydraulic mines rates were lower, but food, lodging, and lighting were, in many classes of labour, provided by the companies. Nominal wages for labourers on lode mines were 70 cents a day for Chinese men, 60 cents for Chinese women, and 40 cents for Chinese youths.

A mining coolie's average monthly budget amounted to $9·70, including the purchase of food.

In foundries and engineering shops the workers were better organized than in most industries, and matters relating to wages, conditions of labour, holidays, &c, were usually settled with the fitters' and mechanics' associations. An eight-hour day was universal, with an increased rate for overtime. Wage rates varied considerably, a no. 1 fitter receiving from $2·72 to $2·96 daily and a general labourer 80 cents.

The Blythe Report recommended a number of alterations and additions to the Labour Code, including a suggestion of making the principal contractor liable for wages in excess of fourteen days to the labourers employed on the contract. In 1936 and 1937 there had been a good deal of labour unrest. The sub-contractor system[15] lay at the root of many of these troubles.

The outbreak of war in 1939 caused a rise in the cost of living. Wages did not rise in keeping with this increase, though labourers were aware that the profits of the industry had risen too. The result was a number of serious strikes and the discontent was, as always, exploited by the agitator. There had been an excess of labour in 1938 which was em-

---

[15] By this the person who had obtained the contract let it out piecemeal to sub-contractors. Quite often sub-contractors who had failed to make a profit defaulted in the payment of wages.

ployed on relief works, but the war changed the situation. Eventually adjustments of wages were made and the labour situation was comparatively settled for the remaining period before the Japanese invasion.

Completely free immigration of all races into Malaya had been allowed up to 1929, but the following year an Immigration Ordinance was brought into force as from August. In 1929, the last year of free immigration, the number of Chinese adult male labourers entering the Colony was 195,613, but in 1930 the number dropped to 151,693, and in 1931 to 49,723. The quota for male immigrants from January to September 1931 was 5,238 a month, and from October to December, 2,500. Emigration from China direct to the Federated Malay States was stopped altogether. No restriction was placed on the immigration of women and children.

There were a number of considerations influencing the Government in its decision to restrict immigration. In 1929 the world trade depression had started and was most felt in Malaya from 1930 to 1932. There was great unemployment, especially among the Chinese, and the Government repatriated many thousands of them to China at the cost of some millions of dollars. Repatriation was entirely voluntary, but the great majority of the unemployed availed themselves of the concession. It was felt by some that it was a mistake to get rid of labour which might be required again before very long and that a scheme of relief work on a large scale should be undertaken; in 1938, before the war absorbed all surplus labour, the Federated Malay States Governments did indeed adopt a relief scheme in place of free repatriation. There were some employers who thought that there should always be a considerable surplus of labour in order to keep down wages, but the Government did not accept this view: it believed that labour should be introduced only in such quantities as could be absorbed by the labour market.

The Immigration Restriction Ordinance was administered for nearly four years and was then replaced by the Aliens Ordinance on 1 April 1933. From January to July 1932 the quota had been 2,500 a month and had been reduced to 1,000 a month from August to December. The quota was fixed at 1,000 from January to the end of March 1933, and remained at 1,000 to the end of the year. It remained at this figure when the proclamation was made under the Aliens Ordinance.

The restriction of immigrants applied to *all* aliens, but since the Chinese were most affected the measure was represented in interested quarters in China as discrimination against the Chinese race. This was not the case, and the considerations were purely economic.

Under the Aliens Ordinance newly arrived immigrants were issued with landing-permits. Certificates of admission were issued either in exchange for a landing-permit or on payment of a fee of 5 dollars. They were valid for two years and renewable for further periods of two years.

Possession of a certificate of admission meant that the holder was not counted against the quota and could therefore obtain a passage from China to Malaya at a rate far less than that payable for quota passages. With restriction the prices of quota passages had soared, and since the sale of these passages was the monopoly of lodging-houses in China it was beyond the power of the Malayan authorities to deal with the 'racket'.

Illegal landings, in particular from junks full of Hailams which landed their passengers usually on the east coast of Malaya during the northeast monsoon, were attempted, but rarely with success (those who landed illegally, when apprehended, were returned to China), and the machinery of the new Immigration Department which had been created to administer the Aliens Ordinance worked very satisfactorily. But the intention to restrict immigration on a qualitative as well as a quantitative basis turned out to be impracticable. What was wanted in Malaya were agriculturists and labourers: the persons who could afford to pay high fares were traders and shop assistants of whom Malaya had already a sufficient supply.

The improvement in the economic situation in Malaya in the latter part of 1933 was reflected in the immigration figures, when the quota of 1,000 which had not been filled during the first nine months in the year was completely taken up during the last quarter. The tide definitely turned in April 1934 and for the year the excess of arrivals over departures was 142,089, whereas the deficit in 1933 had been 38,449.

From January to April 1934 the quota remained at 1,000 a month, was raised to 2,000 for May and June, to 3,000 for July, and to 4,000 from 1 August to the end of the year. It remained at 4,000 until 1 February 1937 when it was raised to 6,000 a month. It was reduced from 6,000 to 3,000 a month as from 1 January 1938, and again to 500 a month from 1 April, at which figure it remained up to the time of the Japanese occupation of 1942.

A suitable footnote to this chapter will be a summary of the facts of the organization of Chinese labour up to the Japanese occupation.

The original associations of Chinese engaged in a trade included both master and man. They were like the medieval guilds of Europe. In the early days in Malaya the various lodges of the Triad Society were not illegal and fulfilled some of the functions elsewhere filled by trade associations. They were large mutual-benefit associations, covering between them the whole of the Chinese population. The trade guilds proper had existed in China from ancient times, and were particularly common in Malaya among old-established trades, such as tailoring, shoemaking, carpentry, &c. Each type of guild was governed by a committee composed of employers and employees. Rates of wages, hours of work, holidays, and terms of apprenticeship were decided by the guilds. In addition they frequently fulfilled the role of friendly societies, providing funeral benefits for the members and accommodation for unemployed.

Legislation providing for the registration of societies was introduced in the Colony in 1889 and in the Federated Malay States in 1895. The organization of societies specifically for employees did not, generally speaking, take place until the 1920s.

The inspiration of the modern labour movement in Malaya resulted from the development of the movement in China. The first National Labour Conference was held in Canton in 1922. In 1927, when the KMT was purged, the Central Government took action which resulted in the suspension of all labour unions and the cessation of all labour activities until the promulgation of the Labour Union Law in 1929. After that the labour movement in China was under the direct supervision of the KMT.

Political and industrial labour agitation in Malaya became more and more intermingled. After the Double Seventh (7 July 1937) when Japan attacked China, the labour organizations were connected with the Anti-Enemy-Backing-up Society, which took direct action against those dealing in Japanese goods.

The shortcoming of these labour associations, which were registered by Government, was that they had no suitable machinery for collective bargaining. The trade-union legislation, brought into force in 1941, was designed to supply this deficiency. The Japanese invasion interposed itself, and the law was never seen in operation. After the surrender, and under the iron heel of Japanese military government, the free organization of labour ceased entirely. The rule was a simple one—either one worked for the Japanese war effort or one did not eat.

31

CHINESE POLITICAL SOCIETIES IN
MALAYA, 1911–41

THE first political society with revolution in China as its object was the Hsing Chung Hui, founded by Dr Sun Yat-sen in 1894 in Honolulu, whither he had come to get assistance for his scheme to overthrow the Manchu dynasty. Dr Sun is believed to have visited Singapore first of all in 1900 (the statement that he was arrested there and deported for five years is not borne out by any official record). From 1900 to 1905 the Hsing Chung Hui was responsible for every armed rising in China. In the latter year it was combined with certain other revolutionary societies under the title of Tung Meng Hui, with Dr Sun as president.

The Singapore branch of the Tung Meng Hui was formed in February 1906. There was already in existence in Singapore a political party known as the Chung Hui Tang which had been formed by Yau Lit, an original member of the Hsing Chung Hui in Hong Kong. Dr Sun returned to Singapore in 1906 and proceeded to form another branch of the Tung Meng Hui in Kuala Lumpur. He failed, however, to do the same in Ipoh because of the opposition of the royalist party (i.e. pro-Manchu). Branches were formed later in Penang, Seremban, Malacca, and Kuala Pilah.

From 1905 to 1909 Singapore was a rendezvous for political refugees from China, prominent among whom were Sun Yat-sen, Wang Ching-wei, and Hu Han-min. In 1907 a Chinese newspaper, the *Chung Hing Yat Pao*, was started with the object of advocating revolution in China. Other revolutionary papers sprang up and these were constantly at war with papers supporting the royalist (imperial) cause, notably the *Union Times* and the *Yat Pau Press*. Dr Sun Yat-sen contributed many articles to the revolutionary papers and he received a warning from the Protector of Chinese about his attitude to the Manchu Government with which Great Britain was on friendly terms.

After an armed rebellion in China in 1908, arranged by Dr Sun, 700 rebels had to retreat to Tongking. Some of these were sent by the French to Singapore on Dr Sun's representations. They later became connected with gang robberies in Jurong. It is interesting to note that between 1909 and 1911 a Triad society in Malacca carried out a large number of gang robberies, the proceeds of which were sent to China to aid the revolutionary cause!

These years saw the birth of many societies, clubs, and reading-rooms which were a cloak for revolutionary propaganda. Prominent amongst these was the Chinese Philomathic Union in Penang which was registered under the Societies Ordinance in November 1908. In 1910 the *Kwang Wah Yat Pao* was founded in Penang by Tung Meng Hui members.

Dr Sun remained in Penang during 1910 and part of 1911, where he made appeals for funds to finance risings in Canton. His activities here led to a warning by the Protector of Chinese that he should leave the country. He left for Europe, later going to America, where he remained until the revolution had succeeded.

As a result of the revolution the KMT came into being in China on 13 August 1912, and was a fusion of five societies including the Tung Meng Hui.

After the formation of the KMT, Lu Chih was sent from China to organize a society, and in 1912 the Straits Settlements Government decided to register it under the Societies Ordinance, taking the view that the activities of the Tung Meng Hui had never been directed against the authority of the Governments of Malaya and that, the revolution having succeeded, the position of the party would be regularized. The first branch was consequently registered in Singapore on 18 December 1912, under the title of the 'Singapore Communication Lodge of the Kuomintang of Peking'. In 1913 of the eight principal office-bearers seven were British subjects, and one of these was Dr Lim Boon-keng. The lodge was closed in 1914. This was due to the discovery of a scheme by which the lodge was ostensibly to be dissolved and to be replaced by a company, the Southseas Industries Co., Ltd, and in part to pressure put on the lodge by the registrar of societies to furnish him with names and addresses of the members. Hereafter the lodge existed in secret. A secret Penang branch also continued to exist. Other branches were registered under the Societies Enactment in the Federated Malay States, all in 1913, but disappeared or went underground, and were declared non-existent by a *Gazette* Notification of 1922. Other branches registered in the Federated Malay States at one time or another were also dissolved.

Let us consider here briefly the subsequent history of the Kuomintang up to 1927, first in China and then in Malaya.

In 1913 the party came into the open again under Yuan Shih-k'ai, but an incipient revolution was suppressed and the KMT proscribed. Yuan Shih-k'ai's subsequent attempt to make himself Emperor was frustrated, however, by the KMT which roused the southern provinces to rebellion. Under Li Yuan-hung, who had a brief period of power, it aroused the opposition of the northern militarists and was dissolved in 1917. Thereupon Dr Sun Yat-sen formed a KMT faction at Canton with assistance from military leaders from Kwangsi, Yunnan, and Fukien. The history of this adventure was most chequered. Dr Sun was driven out by his lieutenant-general, Chen Chiung-ming, in 1921: he returned again in February 1923, taking with him Michael Borodin, the Bolshevik adviser: he left for Peking again in 1924, probably because Canton had become too hot to hold him, and he died there in March 1925.

Dr Sun's teaching became of political importance only when he had been dead for two years. With the coming into power of the KMT from 1927 under Chiang Kai-shek the 'Three Principles' were adopted as the basis of the policy of government. The fundamental law of citizenship, for example, was based on the first principle, 'nationalism'. This was to have a considerable implication in the politics of Malaya. It is desirable therefore that we should take account of the *San Min Chu I*, which were embodied in a series of lectures delivered by Dr Sun in 1924–5.

The following is a very brief summary of the *San Min Chu I*.

I. *Nationalism.* The Chinese belong to the yellow race because they belong to the blood-stock of the yellow race. China is the only country where 'race' and 'nation' are the same. To save China we must certainly promote nationalism. The Chinese people are of the Han or Chinese race with common blood, common language, common

religion, and common customs—a single race. China is in danger of a
'White Peril'. Not only is there a danger of China being swamped by
the superior numbers of the white race—there is a more immediate
and pressing danger in foreign political and economic domination and
oppression. 'Cosmopolitanism' is merely a camouflage for imperialism.
Nationalism must precede internationalism. We are the wronged races.
To revive China's nationalism we must awaken the people to an understanding of China's position. China must recover its ancient morality.
We must learn the strong points of the West—scientific knowledge
and methods.

II. *Democracy*. Human government has passed through three stages
—the theocratic, the autocratic, and the democratic. We are now in
the fourth period—the era within states when people are battling
against their monarchs and kings. The issue is now between good and
evil, between might and right. The essential question is this: is China
today ripe for democracy? We Chinese must now follow world tendencies; nevertheless we must avoid false theories like Rousseau's
'natural rights'. The watchword of the French Revolution was Liberty,
Equality, Fraternity. The Chinese do not yet understand what liberty
really is. The Chinese have taken personal liberty for granted always
like fresh air. The Western doctrine of liberty is out of place in China
today, and generally misapplied. The aim of the Chinese Revolution
should be unity and freedom for the nation. Equality, too, is an
artificial, not a natural, thing, and the only equality we can create is
equality of national status. Because of the nature of her civilization
China does not need personal liberty and equality as Europeans did.
We will use our Principle of the People's Sovereignty and re-make
China into a nation under complete popular rule, ahead of Europe or
America. The machinery of government can be this—the people can use
the controlling powers of suffrage, right of recall, right of referendum,
and right of initiative. The five administrative powers of the Government are the legislative, judicial, executive, examination, and censorship.

III. *Livelihood*. The principle of livelihood is Socialism; it is Communism; it is Collectivism. The problem is a recent one due to the
rapid progress of material civilization all over the world. The introduction of machinery brought unemployment. Although Socialism
has been a growing force for several decades, Western nations have not
yet found a solution for the questions involved in it. Marx was the
first Socialist to rely on the facts. Since the interests of capitalists and
workers inevitably conflict and cannot be reconciled, Marx said,
struggle ensues and this struggle within society is what makes progress. But the actual facts do not bear this out. Socialized distribution
has done much to destroy the monopoly of the tradesman; heavier
taxation has had results beneficial to the workers. When the capitalists

improve the living conditions of the workers, and the workers can produce more for the capitalists, this means both increased production and higher wages. Here surely is a reconciliation of the interests of capitalists and workers. Class war is a disease of social progress. The KMT some time ago settled on its party platform that the principles of livelihood were to be carried out by the equalization of land ownership and by the regulation of capital. If we follow those two methods we can solve the livelihood problem in China. Food is the chief problem of livelihood. China has to import food. Because of foreign economic domination China exports food it needs for itself. We must improve agriculture, use scientific methods, study afforestation. We must create native industries. China must champion native goods and boycott foreign goods . . . [here the lectures break off].[1]

Sun Yat-sen's ideas for the salvation of China were formulated in other works of earlier date than the 'Three Principle' lectures summarized above, but the latter were the most explicit expression of his thoughts. The *San Min Chu I* subsequently became the Bible of the old 'New China'. Mr O. M. Green speaks of the 'almost mystical influence on all classes of Dr Sun's "Three Principles" '.[2] He remarks that it is worth recording that almost from the outset of their career the Communists clamoured for government 'in accordance with the principles of Dr Sun Yat-sen'. In fact both sides were appealing to the same authority. The question was, 'What did Sun Yat-sen mean?'

This study is concerned with the politics of China only in so far as they are reflected among the Chinese of Malaya. The rift between the KMT and the Communists is a fact well known to the world at large: the controversies over the evolution from party to popular government belong to the history of China itself.

The local Government had suppressed the KMT in Malaya in 1925, since its activities were considered to be subversive of British rule, but it remained well established there. It was the agent for the distribution of a considerable quantity of nationalist propaganda printed in Canton which was strongly anti-British in tone. ('British imperialism feeds on blood . . .' is a quotation from it sufficiently indicating its tone.)

The activities of the KMT in Malaya at this time might be classified under the headings (1) organization, (2) collection of funds, and (3) propaganda. (2) was always an important aim.

[1] For an extended summary and detailed criticism of the *San Min Chu I* see the present writer's *Problems of Chinese Education* (1936).

[2] *The Story of China's Revolution* (London, 1945). Green says of Dr Sun: 'As a political thinker he was emotional and vacillating. At one moment he is found speaking with glowing admiration of Great Britain and the fruits of her political wisdom and integrity as displayed in Hongkong; at another he denounces her as the World's Public Enemy No. 1; while his famous "Three Principles of the People", the *San Min Chu I*, contain grains of real inspiration overlaid with childish reasoning, absurd inaccuracies and violent anti-foreignism, surrounded by a farrago of blatant untruths.'

There was at this time an endeavour to swing towards the left wing which was issuing increasingly virulent propaganda, and KMT labour organizations began to appear in the country under the name of 'mutual-benefit associations'.

The policy of the Malayan Governments was repressive of the KMT, and a flood of anti-British, anti-capitalist, and anti-imperialist literature was condemned by the censorship. The bulk of the Chinese who took the principal part in this revolutionary agitation were Hailams (Hainanese). In 1926 they organized an association to promote an anti-foreign boycott in Singapore, supported by public disorder. Later many Khehs (Hakkas) also showed a disposition to leftist politics. They were a type of Chinese distinctly apart from the remainder and with a reputation for impatience of authority and independent views.

Apart from the actual subversive part of the KMT activities, the attitude of the Malayan Governments was decided by the following consideration—that recognition would legalize the position of an *imperium in imperio* and it would legalize a rule of the KMT which provided that in any secret, official or semi-official, non-foreign institutions, such as labour unions, clubs, chambers of commerce, schools, city councils, district councils, &c, the members must conform to KMT organization in order to strengthen the power of the KMT which would give directions to them.

The triumphant progress of the KMT in China in 1926 and 1927 put the Malayan Governments in somewhat of a quandary. The recognition of the National Government of China, with the KMT in the position of dictatorship, caused the British Foreign Office to consider that non-recognition of the KMT was an anomaly. Thereafter ensued an agitation by the Chinese for the removal of the ban, which the Malayan Governments resisted. The KMT argument was that there was general sympathy among the Chinese in Malaya for the Nationalist cause, and there was no disposition by the headquarters to recognize the extremist branches under Hailam directions. The policy of these elements was to support Dr Sun Yat-sen's principle to unite Soviet Russia with the Communists and to join with the peasants and labourers. Such a policy found little support among the Chinese middle classes and among Cantonese skilled labour.

The purging of the KMT of its Communist elements by Chiang Kai-shek had its repercussions in Malaya. The situation was reviewed for the first half of 1927 by the Governor, Sir Hugh Clifford. Sir Hugh had not been long in the country and first had doubts as to the wisdom of the current policy, but his views subsequently underwent a marked change. He wished at first to draw a dividing line between the moderate and the extremist branches of the KMT. His opinion was that the moderates welcomed the ban on the KMT in spite of their strong nationalist sentiments. The Straits Settlements Government denied that they regarded Chinese nationalism as a thing to be suppressed. All that the Malayan Government asked for was that when aliens came to Malaya they should leave their domestic policies behind, particularly such manifestations thereof as conflicted with the interests and the ideals of the country in which they were temporary residents.

The purging of the KMT resulted in the extremists splitting off into organizations of their own, such as the Modern Revolutionary Committee of the Kuomintang of China, the Southseas Provisional Commission of the Communist Party of China, the Communist Youth Party, and the Nanyang Labour Union. These groups, consisting mainly of Hailams, diverted their energy to spreading Communism amongst the Malayan Chinese. The Malayan authorities were influenced greatly in their attitude towards the KMT by the following considerations. They felt that an important objective of the KMT in Malaya was the raising of money. Added to this, it was felt that the Chinese Government probably wanted on purely nationalist grounds to extend its influence over any large Chinese communities which had grown up in the countries outside its jurisdiction.[3] Also it was remembered that the Chinese secret societies had always relied upon terrorism to compel adherence to their ranks, and there seemed to be no reason to suppose that the supporters of the KMT would depart from this traditional practice. The Chinese Central Government, feeling in a strong position after its success in China itself, persisted in its endeavours to get the ban removed. It has been mentioned above that the British Foreign Office considered that it was illogical to treat the KMT as a prohibited society in view of the fact that de jure recognition had now been accorded to the National Government of China which was founded on and closely interwoven with the KMT. Nevertheless, the reluctance of the Governor, Sir Hugh Clifford, to give way continued. He pointed out that large numbers of leading members of the Chinese community viewed with apprehension the consequences of recognition, and they felt that so long as registration was refused the Chinese would have an excuse for declining to be admitted to membership. If registration were allowed the pressure that would be brought to bear on the local Chinese population by the KMT would be irresistible. He added several other arguments, but running through them was the fear of a highly organized imperium in imperio.

We need not pursue in detail the history of the struggle of the KMT for the right to organize in Malaya. The aggressive propaganda policy of the Chinese Government did not improve the atmosphere. For example, in July 1929, they published a list of 'Humiliation Days' together with the alleged facts of the events commemorated. These included the

---

[3] Up to the middle of June 1928 about $2,100 million had been received by the Central Government from the KMT in Malaya, Netherlands East Indies, and the Philippines.

Shanghai and Shameen incidents, and the list was calculated to cause bitter ill-feeling against Britain. It was suspected by the Malayan Governments that the KMT regarded Indochina, Hong Kong, and even Malaya itself as *terra irredenta*. Sun Yat-sen's first principle of nationality which adopted the theory that nationality followed the *jus sanguinis* and not *jus soli*, was always in the minds of the Governments of the countries affected. But the situation was in fact an anomalous one, since the KMT continued to organize in great detail in the Nanyang. Voluminous correspondence passed backwards and forwards between the central party and its Malayan branches. Sir Cecil Clementi, the new Governor, who had taken up his post in 1929, took a strong line with the KMT. He summoned the members of the local executive and supervisory committees and told them that their organization could no longer be permitted and must be dissolved.

In November 1930, owing to the reactions in China to Clementi's policy, it was considered that the time had come to modify it. Capital was being made out of it by Hu Han-min and others to stir up feeling against the Malayan Governments. Discussions took place between Sir Miles Lampson, British Minister in China, and Mr Wang Cheng-ting, and in consequence of this a compromise was reached whereby the Malayan Governments were to take steps to amend their local legislation, making it clear that the KMT of China was not, as such, an illegal society in Malaya, that there was no objection to any Chinese in Malaya being a member of the KMT of China, and that there would be no interference with the members of the *Tang* so long as their activities were not inimical to the interests of the local Governments and provided no attempts were made to re-establish control over branch *Tangpu* or other form of local *Tang* organization in Malaya.

The amending legislation was passed in Malaya, though it cannot be said that it made any difference to the situation. But it was only after the start of the Sino-Japanese hostilities in 1937 that the Malayan Governments had cause for serious complaint. In the meantime, in 1939, the Chinese Government had organized its Overseas Department.

The situation hereafter turns upon the conflicting policies of the Chinese Government and of the British Government. The Chinese were at war with the Japanese and naturally used every means in their power of consolidating sentiment on behalf of their country among persons of their own race, and of embarrassing the Japanese in commerce. The sums of money remitted from Malaya and elsewhere were also an important factor in their resistance to Japan. Britain, on the other hand, was at peace with Japan, and was therefore bound to suppress any activity within its territory against Japan. The Malayan Governments, none the less, were not at all unsympathetic to Chinese nationalism during this period and were as lenient as possible, allowing the remission of large sums of money to China for the China Distress Relief Fund, used to help resistance to the Japanese.

We have now approached the last phase of the relations between the Malayan Governments and the KMT before the Japanese invasion of December 1941. In June 1941 the activities of the San Min Chu I Youth Corps in Malaya in stirring up feeling against Japan (with which Britain was then at peace) were assuming such alarming proportions since the recent visit of a General Wu that the Governor resolved on action against it. The British ambassador in Chungking, Sir Archibald Clark Kerr, suggested a visit of two or three Malayan officers to make contacts with Chinese officials to discuss this and related matters. In consequence of this two officers of the Malayan civil service, and the inspector-general of police, Straits Settlements, visited Chungking. This was a short time before the Japanese invasion, which interrupted negotiations regarding the KMT.

We will now resume the history of the Communist Party in Malaya in pre-war years.

Evidence of Communist activity came to light in 1934 in the shape of directions issued by the Comintern parties in Shanghai to the Central Committee of the Malayan Communist Party. Mass activities were ordered, to include strikes, sabotage in the naval base, transport boycotts, demonstrations against increased taxation, &c. On receipt of this letter the Malayan Communist Party and the Malayan Communist Youth Corps launched a 'purification' campaign, and a 'rushing' period was started to give impetus to the party's forward march to its final goal, the Malayan revolution. During the Jubilee celebrations in May 1935 the Malayan General Labour Union demonstrated against them, anti-British slogans were posted up, and there was some incendiarism against the decorations in Penang, Kuala Lumpur, and Singapore, and a few pamphlets were thrown about in the streets. A recital of these incidents, however, gives a more serious impression than is warranted by the facts.

The Central Committee of the Malayan Communist Party this time requested a sort of secret liaison with the Third International, and asked for relationships to be established between the Malayan Communist Party and those in India and England. It also recommended that students be sent from Malaya to the U.S.S.R. for training and that an inspector be sent to Malaya to inspect party organizations. In order to co-ordinate and unite the Communist effort a unification committee was formed by the Central Committee, composed of one Indian, one Malay, and one Chinese.

The Communist Party had some limited success in fostering discontent amongst the Cantonese and Hokkien labourers at the naval base, at the new prison, and at the military barracks. During 1935 anti-Japanese and, at the same time, anti-KMT campaigns were launched and demonstrations occurred outside the Japanese Club, but by December 1935 the activities of the party slumped, though a good deal of anti-war and anti-Japanese propaganda continued to be distributed. During 1936 the party took an active share in organizing strikes.

Following the *coup d'état* in China, when Chiang Kai-shek was captured in Sian by Marshal Chang Hsüeh-liang, the National Salvation Movement, which resulted from this incident, was brought prominently before the public, and in Malaya a central committee took advantage of the situation to form branches for raising funds to assist the troops fighting the Japanese in Suiyüan.

The outbreak of war between China and Japan in July 1937 was exploited by the Communist Party, which brought new recruits of its own to the National Salvation Association, and in order to foster anti-Japanese feelings an overseas branch of the association was formed with two committees—underground and open. The former became responsible for recruiting Communists amongst its members, while the latter was designed to attract anti-Communists and members of other party organizations who would not have joined had they been aware of any Communist influence. By 1938 there was an outcry against Trotskyites and a new policy was put into practice with an anti-Japanese and anti-imperialist front for organizing strikes. The organization of the party was very complex with the central committee directing all activities, the Communist Youth Section, General Labour Union, a Picket Corps (used for intimidation purposes), a Special Branch (a sort of Communist Gestapo), and a Malayan Racial Emancipation League, to bring Malays and Indians into the Communist fold. Added to this were an Oversea Chinese National Salvation Association to play on the patriotic feelings of young Chinese, and, having brought them under its influence, to teach them the principles of Communism, and a Proletarian Writers' Association. The healing of the breach between the KMT and the Communists in China after the Sian *coup d'état* had further repercussions in Malaya. The names of the various Communist organizations in Malaya were changed to suit the general anti-Japanese policy part, e.g. the General Labour Union, now became the Labouring Classes Anti-Enemy-Backing-up Society. (The complexities of the reorganization at this period are difficult to follow and a mere recital of names would confuse the story.)

After the outbreak of war with Germany in 1939 the Malayan Communist Party began to turn its attention to a possibility of war between Great Britain and Japan, and it eventually issued pamphlets setting forth the terms on which it would be prepared to assist the local Government in such an event. These were similar to those presented by the

China Communist Party and the National Government of China, and included (a) the abandonment of reactionary policy, (b) the adoption of the democratic system, and (c) the improvement of the livelihood of the people, in addition to an official expression of willingness to co-operate with the Communists. But, receiving no response from the Malayan Governments, the Communists, notably the Anti-Enemy-Backing-up Society, continued to issue anti-British literature.[4] About the middle of September 1940 the Malayan Communist Party received instructions from the China Communist Party in Hong Kong to the following effect: that all anti-British movements and strike agitations were to cease forthwith in Malaya, and henceforth the party was to concentrate on consolidating an anti-Japanese front and to support the National Salvation Movement in Malaya, and no opposition was to be offered by the party to any campaign initiated by the Chinese community in Malaya to aid the British war effort. The Malayan Communist Party decided to accept these orders. The movement had been inspired by an agreement reached in 1940 between the Chinese National Government and the Chinese Communist Party in Chungking. But in spite of this the agitation in industry by the party continued.

It seems certain that the local Communists were in a dilemma. Between 22 June 1941, when Germany attacked Russia, and 8 December 1941, when Japan attacked Malaya, their position was anomalous. However, after the attack upon Russia by Germany the Communist Party became much less bitter in its attacks on Britain, and after the invasion of Malaya the policy entirely changed. The party now came up wholeheartedly on the side of the local Government.

It was not until the invasion had been in progress for nearly a month that an effort was made to have the Chinese political parties together in a common war front, and at the end of December 1941 the Chinese Mobilization Committee was formed under the chairmanship of Mr Tan Kah-kee. This Committee had the approval of both the Kuomintang and the Communist Party, and received the blessings of the Governor, Sir Shenton Thomas. Its members took part in resistance to the Japanese in many ways, and they acted as auxiliary police in Johore Bharu, filling in the gap between the departure of the regular police and the arrival of the enemy. On the arrival of the Japanese in the mangrove swamps of Singapore Island a contingent, part of 'Dalforce', fought with considerable bravery. But this was a last-moment development, and was too late to be really effective. The end came with the fall of Singapore on 15 February 1942.

[4] It is convenient here to mention that the Wang Ching-wei faction, which never obtained any particular hold in Malaya, issued anti-British literature, some of which found its way to Malaya.

32

THE SECOND WORLD WAR AND AFTER

WHEN the war with Germany broke out in 1939 the function allotted to Malaya in imperial strategy was that of producing rubber and tin to feed the war machine and to enable Britain to obtain the United States dollars so essential to the war effort before the days of Lend-Lease. It had never been the policy to arm the peoples of Malaya or to train them for military service. By the fall of France the whole position was altered, and it was obvious that Malaya must take urgent measures for its own defence.[1]

It has often been asked why it was that the Malays and the Chinese were not armed *en masse* in this crisis. The answer was that the supplies wherewith to arm and the personnel to train them did not exist in the country. The only course open was to extend the existing forces as far as possible.[2]

Besides adding to the volunteers and creating the local defence corps, the Government now organized the so-called passive defence services—air raid precautions, medical auxiliary service, auxiliary fire service, and rescue, burial, and demolition squads. In all these services the Chinese were the most numerous race. They were also largely represented in the miscellaneous war services—canteens, blood transfusions and employment in censorship, telephone exchanges, Government offices, and in the departments of the navy, army, and air force.

Since the outbreak of the war between China and Japan in 1937 the China Distress Relief Fund had been generously supported by the Malayan Chinese, but after the beginning of the war between Germany and Britain in 1939 a Patriotic War Fund was started in Malaya which also received liberal support from the Chinese community. Millions of dollars were raised for the comforts of British troops and British people suffering distress in any part of the world. Of this fund, to which the Chinese were the largest subscribers, £375,000 was remitted for the people of London during the German air attacks. In addition to this,

[1] For details regarding the war effort of the several communities in Malaya, see Sir George Maxwell, ed., *The Civil Defence of Malaya* (London, 1944).

[2] There was one Chinese company of volunteers each in Singapore, Penang, and Malacca with a paper strength of 120 for each company. All the Chinese members were English-educated. There were no Chinese companies in the Federated Malay States. In February 1941 the local defence corps, which until then had for all practical purposes been European, was opened to non-European British subjects and British-protected persons over eighteen.

£575,000 was raised from local subscriptions for the Malayan Bomber Fund.

During the Japanese invasion everything the Chinese community could do to assist the British cause they did. Apart from their contribution to the passive defence and other services, there are numerous stories of the assistance given by Chinese squatters and coolies to British troops at the risk of their lives; there was never a case of a European refugee asking for help in the shape of food or money or active support and being refused it.

In the last week of December 1941 (as has already been related) the Chinese Mobilization Committee was organized under the chairmanship of Mr Tan Kah-kee for the purpose of recruiting the full manpower of the Chinese community in the defence of Malaya. Many of the recruits were labourers on defence work, but a force of about 1,000, most of whom were Communists, became a part of 'Dalforce', and fought in the mangrove swamps of Singapore Island during the last phase of the campaign. Though inadequately armed, they fought with courage and suffered many casualties.[3]

Chinese gangs, on the other hand, were foremost in the looting and then in the rioting and terrorism that took place during the Japanese advance. The advanced parties of Japanese had themselves engaged in looting and rioting, but when the main body of the Japanese army arrived their treatment of the local looters and robbers was summary and exemplary. Condemned offenders were publicly executed and their heads displayed on poles in the market-places and on bridges. This had a deterrent effect, but the wastage created by the looters was colossal—rice, afterwards to be so precious, was strewn over the roadway and tins of provisions were littered everywhere.[4] Rape, too, was also a real scourge in occupied Malaya. Most atrocious, perhaps, was rape by gangs of armed robbers, Chinese, Malays, and Indians. But it was the Japanese conquerors who conducted rape on the grand scale.

The Chinese, beyond all others, the Japanese regarded as their implacable enemies, and of the Chinese the Communists stood first. Soon after the surrender of Singapore on 15 February 1942 identification parades were organized to pick out Chinese who had been active against the Japanese or who were likely to be so. Informers—men, women, and

[3] 'Not long after the outbreak of war in the Far East, the Malayan Communist Party had put up a proposal to the Government that the Chinese should be allowed to form a military force to fight the Japanese, and that it should be armed by the British. The Commander-in-Chief at first refused to allow this, but as the war situation rapidly deteriorated he eventually gave permission for the organization [one for training jungle fighters] to train and use a certain number of the Chinese selected and supplied by the Malayan Communist Party. When necessary, sanction for release from gaol for this purpose was also given (F. Spencer Chapman, *The Jungle is Neutral* (London, 1949), p. 160). The first batch of Chinese Communists was picked up for training on 20 Dec. 1941.

[4] In this account, *Malaya Upside Down*, by Chin Kee Onn (Singapore, 1946), has been followed and also a manuscript account by Chew Hock Leong.

C.S.E.A.—L

boys—hooded like members of the Ku Klux Klan, picked out victims by the hundreds or thousands.[5] There was mass execution lasting for days. The numbers that perished in the purge have been variously estimated, even into the hundred thousand, but from the evidence given at the war crimes trials in 1947 it would appear that 5,000 or more is nearer the truth.[6] Eyewitnesses of the murders, Europeans as well as Chinese, are numerous. Some victims were shot as they stood; others were tortured to death. Hundreds were put on to lighters, towed out into the harbour, and forced to jump in the water. From the launches or naval vessels which towed them Japanese machine-gunned them as they swam or struggled in the water.

Those Chinese who were particularly singled out for execution were (1) all who had had anything to do with the China Relief Fund, (2) rich men, who, presumably, had given most generously to the Relief Fund, (3) adherents of Tan Kah-kee, an indefatigable organizer of the Fund, (4) newspaper men, schoolmasters, and high-school students, (5) Hainanese (whom the Japanese regarded as Communists one and all), (6) newcomers to Malaya who presumably had left China because they disliked the Japanese, (7) men with tattoo-marks who, according to the Japanese, were all members of secret societies, (8) volunteers, volunteer reservists, and members of 'Dalforce', (9) Government servants and men such as justices of the peace, members of the Legislative Council, &c, who were likely to have pro-British sympathies.

'Many a wanted whale slipped through the meshes of the Japanese net and many a minnow caught in it were not those the Japanese really wanted', say Messrs Low and Cheng.

Next item on the programme of the 'Liberators of East Asia' and the creators of the 'Co-Prosperity Sphere' was to squeeze every cent they could out of the Chinese community. The leading Chinese were told that a 'gift' from the Chinese of $50 million had been decided upon. This was to be handed over on 20 April 1942, but when the day came the amount had not been fully subscribed. All that could be obtained in actual cash was $29 million. The rest was to be raised by loans from the

---

[5] So say N. I. Low and H. M. Cheng in their book *This Singapore* (Singapore, 1947), p. 18, from which the above analysis of wanted men is quoted. They further give the story of a survivor of the machine-gunning on the beach at Tana Merah Besar, Singapore, in March 1942. The Chinese selected for execution were tied up in bunches of 8, 10, or 12, according to the length of electric wire available. Ordered to move off towards the sea, they were machine-gunned from pill-boxes. 'When the machine-gunning stopped soldiers came running to bayonet us.'

[6] Official estimates place the number of Chinese killed in the massacres at 5,000, but this figure is believed to be conservative' (*The Times*, 11 Mar. 1947). A Japanese officer, Lt.-Col. Hishakari Takafumi, gave evidence at a war crimes trial in Singapore in March 1947 that first of all he was told that 50,000 Chinese were to be killed in Singapore soon after the Japanese entry into the town but that later he was told that it had been found impossible to kill all the 50,000 people and that after half that number had been killed an order was received 'to stop the massacre'. Two Japanese officers were sentenced to death and seven to life imprisonment for these massacres (*Straits Times*, 3 Apr. 1947).

Yokohama Specie Bank on security furnished by the contributors themselves and guaranteed by the respective Chinese associations in each State or Settlement. When the 'gift' was presented General Yamashita[7] somewhat ungraciously declared that it in no way redeemed the previous action of the Straits Chinese in having supported Britain and Chungking. 'What really matters', he said, 'is the attitude of the Malayan Chinese in the construction of the Co-Prosperity Sphere of Greater East Asia.'

To the insatiable Japanese the 'gift' was, of course, only a beginning. Within five months of the fall of Singapore the economic exploitation of Malaya had fairly begun. The Kaishas arrived; the Mitsui and Mitsubishi were the first in the field in the wake of the conquering army. Lesser Japanese civilian traders came in shoals for what was left of the spoils. They formed *Kumiai*, i.e. syndicates or guilds. They became, in effect, Government-protected compartments of the black market. They held the monopoly to fleece the public, but they were assisted by unscrupulous, get-rich-quick elements among the Chinese.

The gambling propensities of the Chinese and other Asiatics were obvious sources of profit to the conquerors, and gambling farms, long abolished by the British, were resuscitated in 1943.

It is clear from all the evidence available that the Japanese regime was marked by bribery, corruption, and incompetence. In the planning of the military campaign there was some effective thinking with streaks of brilliance: in their administration of Malaya the Japanese committed a whole series of foolish errors. Some of these were due to a shortage of trained administrators (they had to rely often on ex-barbers, packers, or photographers) and more were due to a peculiar psychological blindness.

Meanwhile the population, and the urban Chinese in particular, were suffering terrible hardship. Those who lived in the country districts and could produce a little for themselves were somewhat better off than the town-dwellers, but all over Malaya malnutrition was general. The Japanese had no shipping to spare for the importation of rice from Burma and Siam, even if they had been disposed to allow the expenditure.

Outwardly there was compliance, and Oriental acceptance of the conqueror; inwardly there was an ever-growing hatred. The Chinese have a capacity for subtle obstruction, for appearing to co-operate when they are working in the opposite direction all the time. They used their ingenuity to escape the face-slapping and other indignities which Japanese soldiers were fond of inflicting without any excuse; they kept out of the way of the Japanese as much as possible; they did nothing willingly for the conqueror, and avoided him by all sorts of devices. There was, indeed, a minority who 'co-operated' with the Japanese for what they could get out of them, but there was even among these disreputable

[7] Afterwards hanged by the Americans in the Philippines.

Chinese not a man who did not secretly hate and despise the 'barbarian dwarf'[8] for whom he was working.

A campaign was started soon after the capitulation to compel the population to learn the Japanese language. Bonuses were paid to Government and municipal servants who acquired a certain proficiency, while schools discontinued the teaching of English and included Japanese as a compulsory subject. But the campaign was barren of enduring results.

The general Japanese education policy was that vernacular schools for Malays and Indians should continue as before the occupation, with Japanese teaching added to the syllabus. No Chinese schools were permitted, but Government-managed Nippon Go (Japanese language) schools were instituted and attended by Chinese children and children of other races as well. There was little enthusiasm for a Japanese course of studies, and, although the teaching of English was theoretically prohibited, it was continued surreptitiously. 'It is interesting to record [says the report of the Malayan Union Education Department for 1946] that the oral examination conducted in Malaya as part of the 1946 Cambridge School Certificate examination, gave results that were surprisingly good in view of the years that had been lost.'[9]

Very soon after the Japanese occupation, resistance groups began to be organized in the country. The Chinese were the only ones in the field for the first two years of the occupation, but thereafter Malay groups were formed under British officers in north Perak and Kedah. The Malays also had a resistance group in Pahang from an early period, called the Wataniah.

There were two kinds of Chinese resistance groups. Firstly there were the armed military groups living hidden in the hills and jungles, and secondly there were underground organizations whose members lived openly in the towns or villages and who either assisted the guerrilla groups or resisted the Japanese in some other way. Intermingled with the underground movement was a political association first called the Anti-Japanese Union (AJU) and later the Malayan People's Anti-Japanese Union (MPAJU), an almost entirely Chinese organization controlled by the Malayan Communist Party. The MPAJU supported the guerrillas, formerly known as the AJA, but later called the Malayan People's Anti-Japanese Army (MPAJA). It was also known as the 'Three Star' Army from its badge—one star for each race—Chinese, Malay, and Indian—but it was in essence a Chinese movement. At the same time KMT branches continued to exist underground. Later on, in 1944, a guerrilla force claiming adherence to the KMT was located on the Siamese border. It was said to owe allegiance to Chungking and to be

---

[8] The term wo, a dwarf, was traditionally used for the Japanese, but in point of fact it was only in the shortness of their legs, not in the size of their bodies, that the Japanese differed from the Chinese.

[9] 'Education in the Malayan Union', Colonial Review, v/5 (Mar. 1948), p. 148.

bitterly opposed to the MPAJU. There were clashes between this and sections of the MPAJA, but Force 136, a British Force operating in the country, was able to localize it and to prevent serious fighting. The total armed KMT strength was estimated to be not more than 500.

A small group of Malay guerrillas were raised by Force 136 officers in north Perak and were given the name of Ashkar Melayu Setia (AMS) or Loyal Malay Army.

Lastly there were some small gangs who were later disowned by the MPAJA—professional bandits of pre-occupation days who donned the anti-Japanese cloak only to give cover to banditry.

The MPAJA was organized during and after the Malayan campaign of 1942 under the direction of the Malayan Communist Party. It was divided into provincial groups, each with its own group leader. The disposition of the groups was: first group, Selangor; second group, Negri Sembilan; third group, north Johore; fourth group, south Johore; fifth group, Perak; sixth group, west Pahang; seventh group, east Pahang; and eighth group, Kedah. The groups themselves were split up into a number of small camps hidden in the jungle. Their food supplies were received from outside, especially from the AJU, and augmented with the produce of their small gardens in the jungle. In some areas they were greatly assisted by the Sakai tribes (aborigines) who gave them more than they could spare from their own stock of food.

There were two or three officers who had remained behind to organize sabotage, and at least one of these, Lieut.-Colonel Spencer Chapman, D.S.O., had made contact with the MPAJA.[10] But it was not until May 1943 that reconnaissance parties of Force 136 arrived in the country by submarine or were dropped from aeroplanes. The leader of the first party was Lieut.-Colonel J. L. H. Davis.[11] He was able to establish relations with the Perak group of the MPAJA. Eventually an agreement was drawn up by which the MPAJA pledged itself to co-operate with and accept orders and instructions from the Supreme Allied Commander during the period of hostilities and in the period of military occupation thereafter, in return for arms, ammunition, and explosives, and the equivalent of 150 taels of gold per month (roughly $3,000). The MPAJA were not to be used for political purposes and no political questions were to be discussed.

The relations between Colonel Davis, Major Broome,[12] who had now

[10] For a detailed account of the MPAJA during the Japanese occupation see Chapman, *The Jungle is Neutral* (1948). This chapter was written before Colonel Spencer Chapman's book was published. The author spent over three years in close association with the MPAJA and his book provides an invaluable account of the Chinese guerrillas. Colonel Chapman, while having great admiration for the courage and other qualities of the rank and file, considers that the leaders were much more concerned with creating a Communist Republic than with fighting the Japanese.

[11] Afterwards Colonel J. L. H. Davis, D.S.O. (of the Malayan police).

[12] Afterwards Colonel R. N. Broome, M.C. (of the Malayan civil service).

joined him, and the guerrillas was excellent. In all the MPAJA camps the discipline was good. All food and material needed for the camps was bought and paid for in the free market, though the raising of funds by the AJU on behalf of the guerrillas was, it seems, by use of the methods of the old Anti-Enemy-Backing-up Societies. The men in the camps were given military training and education in Chinese mathematics. The general atmosphere was almost like that of a Boy Scout camp.

While Malaya was still in the occupation of the Japanese, the Malayan Communist Party published its programme of nine points which were (1) to drive the 'Japanese Fascists' out of Malaya and to establish a republic; (2) to establish a Government with representation from all the nationalities, improve living conditions, and develop industry, agriculture, and commerce; (3) to give freedom of speech, association, &c, and abolish the old oppressive laws; (4) increase wages, abolish high taxation, and money-lending at high interest; (5) reorganize the guerrillas into a National Defence Army; (6) establish free education in the several languages; (7) confiscate Fascist property and restore property confiscated by the Japanese; (8) practise tariff autonomy; and (9) combine with Russia and China to free the oppressed peoples of the East.

After the agreement had been made with the Supreme Allied Commander, the establishment of a Republic was placed in abeyance. The propaganda issued by the MPAJA was not at this time anti-British, but definitely anti-imperialist.

The total strength of the MPAJA proper in 1944 was about 3,000–4,000, and in 1945, before the intended invasion, it had grown to 6,000–7,000. The function allotted to the guerrillas was similar to that allotted to the Maquis in France, but the Japanese surrender changed all the plans, and instead of the invasion there was a peaceful reoccupation.

The British forces of liberation reached Malaya early in September 1945. Forces landed at Penang on the 3rd, at Singapore on the 5th, they reached Kuala Lumpur on the 12th, Ipoh on the 16th, but some outstations were not reoccupied until the end of the month. In the interval between the Japanese evacuation of centres to assemble for surrender and the arrival of the British troops the MPAJA came out of the jungle and assumed control. There was a great deal of looting by bandits and others during this same interregnum.

Malaya's welcome to the British Services was entirely spontaneous and genuine, but the welcome had been prepared by the Chinese generally on the assumption that the liberating forces would be Chinese, not British. The triumphal arches erected in the towns and villages were inscribed (in Chinese characters) to the 'Allied Armies' and in the interior they were usually inscribed to the various groups or battalions of the MPAJA alone. There is no doubt that many of the guerrillas for years had been so isolated from the world and from all information except what was contained in their own propaganda that they honestly believed that the Japanese surrender had been due to their own exclusive efforts, and this feeling was encouraged in any case by the better-informed leaders of the AJU behind the scenes.

There had been a complete alteration in the political atmosphere of Malaya since 1941. Until then, thanks to British influence, the relations between the Chinese and the Malays, in spite of the conflict of their interests, had been harmonious. The Japanese occupation had changed that. To begin with, the bulk of the Malays were, it seems, not particularly hostile to the Japanese occupation, and many indeed welcomed the change since it promised to put an end to the economic and political encroachments of the Chinese. It was only later that the clumsiness of Japanese methods alienated the Malays as a whole.

Meanwhile, the Japanese were using the Malayan police force, which was composed mostly of Malays, to suppress the Chinese resistance movement. This fact naturally led to strong resentment, and after the news of the surrender there was retaliation against the Malay police. The result was that the latter became demoralized and a complete reorganization of the force became necessary after the reoccupation before it was of any real value again. In the clashes which took place before the Japenese surrender and in November onwards the Malays were, howearv, the aggressors. In March 1946 the Chinese retaliated on a village on the Perak river and killed thirty or forty Malays. The measures taken by the authorities to suppress the trouble took the form of military patrols, including tank patrols when feasible, and the sending of propagandist parties of Chinese and Malays to affected areas to keep the peace.

At the moment of the British return to Malaya the old Chinese *towkay* (head of a business) had for the time being entirely lost his leadership of the community. Upon the liberation the leadership passed to the MPAJA leaders who were now converting their union into a 'People's Democratic Movement'. In Singapore and other large towns the Communist Party and the New Democratic Youth Corps were much to the fore. For the time being the KMT and the San Min Chu I Youth were not in evidence. It was clear from the beginning that the leftist leaders were making a determined bid for power. They made it obvious that their promise of 'co-operation' with the British Military Administration was nothing more than a pretence. Colour, however, was given to this pretence by the omission of the first point (a republic) from the now-published Communist Party aims, but it was clear that this was no more than an act of expediency and the original objects were merely in abeyance, not dropped.

Rallies of dozens of leftist organizations, from the General Labour Union (GLU) to the Coffee Shop Workers and the Barbers' Cultural Union, and several women's organizations, were held in strength in open spaces in towns and cities with speeches calculated to stir up the strongest emotion. The serious food situation, the delay in the arrival of rice for relief, and the inflation were exploited to arouse discontent. This led to rice riots in Perak in October. One device used on a number of occasions was to smear banners with the blood of victims—or alleged victims—of 'Fascist terrorism' and to carry them in rallies or in processions, and agitators did their best to work the crowds into a state of vengeful hysteria. When they succeeded there resulted a sound like the snarling of wild beasts. But at the beginning the popular feeling was so favourable towards the British that such incidents could not be developed into an insurrection.

One of the outstanding tasks of the British Military Administration was to disband the guerrillas without incident. The regular Malayan People's Anti-Japanese Army numbered now about 3,000–4,000 and to an invitation issued to the remainder of the bona-fide guerrillas to become part and parcel of the MPAJA a couple of thousand responded. Then at the beginning of December the MPAJA was disbanded, each man handing in his arms and equipment and receiving a gratuity of $350. Altogether some 6,800 men were disarmed and received gratuities.[13]

The keynote of British Military Administration policy had been the widest possible tolerance consistent with public safety; complete freedom of speech and association were allowed. Apart from the wish of the administration to give the Communists the fullest opportunity to prove the sincerity or otherwise of their offer of co-operation, it was thought expedient in the interests of the mental health of the people that they should, after their long repression, be allowed to indulge their new-found sense of liberty and to 'blow off steam'. Moreover, the BMA had, in order to conform with the policy of the British Government, to avoid any suggestion that they were interfering with the legitimate activities of organized labour. In those early days the food shortage and consequent inflation caused understandable discontent amongst labourers, and of this the Communist Party was able to make use. In its employment of this freedom the leftist press showed itself quite unconstrained by any considerations of what was either fair or sensible, and the *Voice of the People* and the *New Democracy* in Singapore (both Chinese-language papers) were telling their readers that the 'savage British Fascists were worse than the Japanese', without reference to the fact that when the Japanese were in occupation the writers of this invective had not pursued an equally active line.

Against the BMA the obvious weapon was the strike. Soon after the return of the British a series of strikes occurred which while fundamen-

[13] The official figure, however, does not seem to square with the official figures of weapons recovered—i.e. 4,715 dropped and 5,497 recovered, plus 56 recovered from KMT guerrillas. The so-called KMT guerrillas were disbanded in June 1946.

tally economic in origin were worked up by trouble makers for political ends. Concessions were made and a settlement was reached. Then in January the GLU became more ambitious in its aims. Utilizing the fact that about thirty ex-members of the MPAJA had been arrested for offences which ranged from the possession of stolen property to murder, as well as the fact that a Chinese and three Indian labourers had been arrested for voluntarily causing hurt to a public servant during the troubles in December, the GLU demanded the unconditional release of all these persons under a threat of a general strike. This challenge the BMA, of course, accepted.

The strike began on 29 January 1946, and it was officially estimated that the number of persons who stopped work in Singapore, Johore, Negri Sembilan, and Selangor was over 150,000. About 3,500 intimidators operated with lorries and bicycles and also on foot, even intimidating the servants of BMA officials at their houses or billets. But on the 30th, for some reason which is not yet quite clear, the strike was called off. It may be that the GLU saw that the stoppage was not popular, and the Chinese Chamber of Commerce in Singapore had told the Principal Adviser on Chinese Affairs that they would get their members to reopen their shops at once if they were afforded protection.

But the fact that they had succeeded in bringing about a stoppage on such a large scale had whetted the appetites of the Communists' organizers behind the scenes for even greater successes. A rumour soon began to circulate that the next move of the GLU would be to declare a public holiday on 15 February 1946, nominally as a day of 'humiliation', but quite obviously to celebrate the defeat of the British by the Japanese when Singapore had been surrendered on that date four years previously. Meetings and processions were to be held all over the country. The rumour turned into a certainty when manifestoes were issued declaring that the British in 1942 had abandoned the people of Malaya in a cowardly manner and that it was resolved to mourn this betrayal on the forthcoming anniversary.

Before the strike of January the GLU had got its bands of intimidators out early, but this time the military authorities and the BMA had taken precautions. The result was that on the morning of 15 February Singapore had every appearance of normality, the buses were running, trishaws and rickshaws were on the road, the markets were open, and all essential services were in operation. This was because cordons placed round the city had prevented the movement of intimidators who on the previous occasion had come in by lorry from Johore. One small party did indeed attempt to hold a demonstration, and participants armed with bottles, crowbars, and sticks came into collision with the police. Being assailed by the crowd, the police were forced to open fire and one Chinese was killed and another died later. Up country, however, in north Johore (a notorious centre of disturbance both before the war and during the terror of 1948) a more serious incident occurred when the police had again to open fire and fifteen persons were killed.

Once more the Communists had challenged the BMA in an endeavour to bring them into hatred and contempt, and they had completely failed. Ten Chinese who were behind the plot were later expelled to their native China.

The immediate result of the firm measures taken by the military and the BMA on 15 February was that an almost audible sigh of relief went up from all races throughout the country. Now that the authorities had taken firm action, coolies, shop assistants, vegetable gardeners, squatters in remote districts—the great body of the ordinary people—plucked up courage to resist the demands for 'subscriptions' made by the Communists and their proliferating dependent societies. The membership of the leftist organizations fell off in a spectacular way. But the revolutionary elements were by no means defeated. Henceforth they would have to work more underground than they had since the liberation of Malaya.

While the battle was in progress between the Chinese Communists and the BMA, which was supported now by both the KMT and the San Min Chu I Youth, now resuscitated, there were some significant developments among the Malays. These had never formed a political party. They were Malays and Mohammedans—nothing more. But in the postwar world when every race and nation had become politically minded, it seemed merely a matter of time before they too would enter the arena. So when on 30 November 1945 the creation of the Malay Nationalist Party was reported at Ipoh many people jumped to the conclusion that the movement had actually started. But it was soon apparent that the new party was under the auspices of the Malayan Communist Party and advocated identification of Malay and Indonesian interests. The eight resolutions passed at the inaugural meeting were very similar to the Communist Party's Eight Points.[14]

The Malay Nationalist Party after some initial success lost ground rapidly, though later on it recovered somewhat. The Malays as a whole were conservative and wanted no affiliation with the Communist Party, nor did they want any identification of the Malays of Malaya with the Indonesian movement. It was not until March of the following year that a really representative Malay party was formed under Dato Onn bin Ja'afar. This was to become the United Malay Nationalist Organization, or UMNO, whose object was the uniting of the Malays of Malaya in an effort to secure a reversal of the whole policy of the Malayan Union. (This development is discussed in the following chapter.)

The tactics of the MCP were to watch every new development in

---

[14] So it appeared at the time, but see p. 339 n. 13.

Malayan politics. Seeing that there was the beginning of a strong national feeling among the Malays it did its best to anticipate the movement and to get control of it by forming its own Malay Nationalist Party.[15] Similar tactics were employed with regard to the new Malayan Democratic Union whose formation was announced in December 1945. The sponsors were Chinese of the professional class, but the 'guest' speakers included several members of the Communist Party. Since the 'Eight Points' of the manifesto of the MDU began with the key point, Self-government for Malaya within the British Commonwealth of Nations, it was not easy to see what legitimate appeal such a party had for the Communists. Nevertheless, a Communist later joined the committee of the union. But soon after the MDU showed signs of wishing to purge itself of Communist influences and towards the end of the year it took on—at least temporarily—a more democratic colour.

The MDU aimed to be the party of the domiciled non-Malay Communities—Eurasian, local-born Chinese, local-born Indians, and others. In practice, it never became anything more than a small but vocal group in Singapore. The party exercised considerable influence for a time, by reason of the intellectual and professional standing of some of its members. It failed because of its fanatical hostility towards the British regime and its alliance with left-wing elements, neither of which was approved by the middle classes of the English-speaking Asian public.[16]

33

CONSTITUTIONAL EXPERIMENT

THE historical summary given in Chapters 26–28 shows the piecemeal fashion in which the Malay Peninsula came under British protection. With each Malay State a treaty was made whereby the ruler undertook that the advice of the British Resident or Adviser (as the case might be)[1] would be asked for, and acted upon, in all questions other than those touching the Mohammedan religion or Malay custom. Perak, Selangor, Negri Sembilan, and Pahang were federated in 1896 and decentralized in 1935. Separate treaties were made with the four northern States, the suzerainty over which was transferred from Siam to Britain in 1909. The result of all this was that at the time of the Japanese invasion a country about the size of England had no fewer than ten separate Governments.

---

[15] The MNP, however, became the nucleus of the Pan-Malayan Islamic Party (see p. 347).
[16] G. L. Peet, *Political Questions in Malaya* (London, 1949), p. 13.
[1] In Johore the official was called General Adviser, in Kedah, Perlis, Kelantan, and Trengganu, British Adviser. In each of the four Federated States there was a British Resident.

The Federation comprised the four original States that came under British protection. The hope of the British was that the States which subsequently entered into treaties with Britain would join the Federation of their own volition. But for various reasons this did not come to pass. For one thing they observed that the Federation had become very like a Union, and that the sovereignty of the ruler of each State was impaired by the strong Central Government that had developed at the federal capital, Kuala Lumpur. Measures taken towards decentralization did not achieve the desired end. In 1909 a Federal Council was created in order to give effect to a desire for the joint arrangement of all matters of common interest to the Federation or affecting more than one State. In 1927 the Federal Council was reconstituted, and the rulers withdrew from active participation in the deliberations of the Council, which was enlarged by the addition of a number of official and unofficial members. In 1936, as a further step towards decentralization, the post of Chief Secretary to the Government was abolished and that of Federal Secretary was substituted, the precedence of which was after that of the four Residents. The intention was to replace the official who had become the virtual ruler of the Federation by one whose duties were purely those of co-ordination and liaison, and though the machinery of the Federation was retained to facilitate the disposal of business common to the four States, their full sovereignty was ensured to them so that they were on an equality in this respect with the States outside the Federation. At the same time the departmental advisers were concentrated in Kuala Lumpur and Singapore and they were expected to co-ordinate policy throughout the country. But the system did not work well and the States tended more and more to be self-sufficient entities.

All these modifications in the existing shape of the Malayan constitutional 'set-up' were argued by the Colonial Office and by the Governors and high officials of Malaya itself as if the only political realities were the States, their Sultans, and the treaties with the King; the interests of the 'immigrant races' (though the immigration may have taken place a century ago or more) were a secondary consideration. The ruling caste (and through its single-minded advice, the Colonial Office) was emphatically 'Malay-minded'. Since, however, our subject is the Chinese in Malaya, let us see how they were affected by the situation.

Having no share in the administration of the country, the Chinese limited their interest in British intervention in the Malay States to security for their trade and persons if they happened to be engaged in commerce or labour within the boundaries of the Malay States. The Straits Settlements Chinese frequently petitioned the British Government to intervene to restore order in the Peninsula, which was in a state of semi-anarchy. When the States one by one came under British protection the Chinese benefited by the establishment of a system of law and by an efficient administration. Their own part in government was limited to representation on the Federal and State Councils and on various boards and committees. In the Straits Settlements the Legislative Council consisted at the outbreak of war with Japan of 27 members: 13 officials and 13 unofficials presided over by the Governor. Of the 13 unofficials, 6 were Asiatics, of whom 4 were Chinese. The Federal Council in 1940 had 28 members, of whom 12 were unofficials, including 2 Chinese. Each State had also a council which usually included, besides the ruler, 2 Malay chiefs, 2 British unofficial members, 2 Chinese unofficials, and 1 Indian.

Unity in this diversity had been maintained by the guiding hand of the British Government acting through advice given to the rulers. Economic and social rivalries had been kept from developing dangerously, and social harmony had prevailed. This was well enough so long as 'government from above'—paternal government—endured: the question was how could the country be made to stand on its own feet when the time came? How could the several elements be fused into a whole? As early as 1880 Sir Frederick Weld, the Governor of the Straits Settlements, had declared that 'nothing we have done so far has taught them [the people of the country] to govern themselves, we are merely teaching them to co-operate with us and govern under our guidance'.[2] Practically all that had been done in this direction up to the Second World War had been to carry out a policy of progressive replacement of European district officers in the Malay States by Malays, but, apart from giving them a few minor legal and other posts in the Straits Settlements, nothing had been done to give the Chinese experience of administration.

This was where the problem rested at the start of the Second World War. Britain was absorbed in her struggle for survival, and it was not until it became likely that the lost dependencies of Southeast Asia might be recovered in the not too distant future that attention was directed towards the question of post-war policy. In July 1943 the Secretary of State for the Colonies stated: 'We are pledged to guide Colonial peoples along the road to self-government within the framework of the British Empire.' The first precise declaration of the policy to be adopted in the case of Malaya came in the form of an answer by the Secretary of State to a question in Parliament made on 10 October 1945. Its gist was as follows:

Careful consideration had been given to the future of Malaya and the need to promote the sense of unity and common citizenship which would develop the country's strength and capacity, in due course, for self-government within the British Commonwealth. The policy of the British Government would therefore call for a constitutional Union of Malaya

---

[2] Dispatch of 21 Oct. 1880, cited by Rupert Emerson in *Malaysia: A Study of Direct and Indirect Rule* (London, 1937), p. 131.

and for the institution of a Malayan citizenship which would give equal citizenship rights to all who claimed Malaya as their homeland. For this purpose fresh agreements needed to be arranged with the Malay States rulers and fresh constitutional measures for the Straits Settlements. The Malayan Union would consist of the nine States in the Malay Peninsula and all of the two Settlements of Penang and Malacca. Singapore at this stage would require separate constitutional treatment and, in view of its special economic and other interests, provision would be made for it to be constituted as a separate Colony. But the ties between Singapore and the mainland might well work towards ultimate union. The peoples of Penang and Malacca would lose none of their rights as British citizens. There would also be created a Malayan Union citizenship for which the qualifications would be birth in Malaya or a suitable period of residence.[3]

Simultaneously with this declaration, Sir Harold MacMichael arrived in Malaya to arrange new treaties with the Sultans. He spent three months in the country and then issued a statement announcing that he had 'successfully concluded with each of the Malay Rulers, after consultations conducted with friendliness and good will, an agreement, which, supplementing the existing Treaties, grants full jurisdiction in each State to His Majesty the King of England'.[4]

A White Paper expanding what had been said in the House of Commons by the Secretary of State for the Colonies in October was published on 22 January 1946 when the success of Sir Harold MacMichael's mission was announced.

The White Paper[5] specifically stated the intentions of the British Government. It began by giving an account of the previous position and explained the need for reform. The British Crown (said the Paper) must provide the common link which would draw together the communities of Malaya and promote a sense of common interest and the development of common institutions. To secure jurisdiction for His Majesty in the Malay States, Sir Harold MacMichael had concluded an agreement with each of the Malay rulers, which, supplementing the existing treaties, granted jurisdiction in each State to His Majesty.[6]

After describing the proposals of the Government for the constitution of Singapore as a separate colony, and the administration of the Settlements of Penang and Malacca with the Malay States in a Malayan Union, the White Paper gave details of the new constitution to be created for governing the country. Singapore (including the Cocos-

[3] H.C. Deb., vol. 414, coll. 255–6.
[4] G.B., Colonial Office, *Report of a Mission to Malaya* by Sir Harold MacMichael (1946).
[5] Ibid.; *Malayan Union and Singapore*, Cmd. 6724 (1946).
[6] For a detailed discussion of the British proposals see Purcell, 'A Malayan Union: the Proposed New Constitution', *Pacific Affairs* (Mar. 1946); Phyllis Kaberry, *The Development of Self-Government in Malaya* (London, 1946, mimeo.); and Gerald Hawkins, 'Reactions to Malayan Union', *Pacific Affairs* (Sept. 1946).

Keeling Islands and Christmas Island) would be constituted a colony under a Governor and Legislative and Executive Councils. The constitution of the Malay Union would provide for a central authority consisting of a Governor with an Executive and Legislative Council. Subsidiary powers of administration and legislation would be exercised by a local council for each State and Settlement. These councils would consist of both official and unofficial members, 'but while it is the intention that their constitution shall be broad-based and representative, the final determination of the numbers and of the details of representation will not be decided until there has been consultation with local opinion'. In the initial phase after the termination of the Military Administration the Governor would be empowered to legislate with the help of an Advisory Council to be selected on a basis as broadly representative as conditions in this phase allowed.

In view of the special position of the Malay Rulers as traditional and spiritual leaders of the Malay people, it was intended that the Ruler in each State should preside over a Malay Advisory Council whose members he would appoint subject to the approval of the Governor. The main functions of these Malay Advisory Councils would relate to matters affecting Mohammedan religion, but they might also advise the Ruler on any other matters at the request of the Resident Commissioner acting with the Governor's approval. On matters of Mohammedan religion, excepting the collection of tithes and taxes, each ruler, with the help of his Council, would have legislative powers within his State.

Matters of pan-Malayan importance such as higher education, immigration, currency, &c, would be matters of common arrangement between the Union and the Colony.

The White Paper went on to lay down the policy for the creation of Malayan Union citizenship. The policy of His Majesty's Government was to promote a broad-based citizenship which would include, without discrimination of race or creed, all who could establish a claim, by reason of birth or a suitable period of residence, to belong to the country. It was proposed, therefore, to create by Order in Council a Malayan Union citizenship. The following persons would acquire this citizenship:

(a) persons born in the territory of the Union or of the Colony of Singapore.
(b) persons who at the date on which the Order in Council becomes operative have been ordinarily resident in those territories for ten years out of the preceding fifteen. (In calculating the fifteen years' period, the period of the Japanese occupation would be disregarded.)

It would also be possible for persons to acquire Malayan Union citizenship after five years' ordinary residence in the Malayan Union or Singapore.

Save with the consent of the Governor, no person who was not a

Malayan Union citizen could be admitted to public office or membership of central and local councils.

Those acquiring Malayan Union citizenship otherwise than by birth would be required to affirm allegiance to the Malayan Union. But citizenship was not to affect nationality.

In a second White Paper of March 1946[7] Malayan Union citizenship was somewhat differently defined, viz.:

> The Malayan Union citizenship Order in Council will provide that the following persons will become Malayan Union citizens:
>
> (a) Any person born in the Malayan Union or Singapore before the date when the Order comes into force, who is ordinarily resident in the Malayan Union or Singapore on that date.
> (b) Any person of eighteen years of age or over ordinarily resident in the Malayan Union or Singapore on the date when the Order comes into force, who has resided in the Malayan Union or Singapore for a period of ten years during the fifteen years preceding the 15 February 1942, and who swears or affirms or takes the oath of allegiance (i.e. to be faithful and loyal to the Government of the Malayan Union).
> (c) Any person born in the Malayan Union after the date when the Order comes into force whose father is a Malayan Union citizen at the time of that person's birth and either was born in the Malayan Union or Singapore or was a Malayan Union citizen under (b) above or had obtained a certificate of naturalization. The minor children (viz. children under 18) of persons in categories (a) and (b) will also be Malayan Union citizens. [Japanese nationals were debarred from becoming Malayan Union citizens.]

The Citizenship Order was, however, deferred until full consultation had taken place.

Soon after the announcement of the British Government's policy for Malaya in October 1945 there had been signs that this policy did not meet with the approval of at least a number of ex-Malayan civil servants. On 29 October Sir Frank Swettenham, a former Governor of the Straits Settlements, asked in *The Times*: 'Who has asked for these changes and a Malay Union? Certainly it is not the Malays.' There was no public indication of any opposition until after the publication of the White Paper (Cmd. 6724) in January, but there was then a demonstration of Malays in Kedah, said to be 50,000 strong and carrying banners denouncing the recent agreements. On 3 March a Pan-Malay Congress was convened in Kuala Lumpur to discuss the Malayan Union proposals and the question of sending a delegation to London to explain the Malay viewpoint. At this meeting the Sultan of Selangor urged the Malays to be united, declaring that 'many things can be achieved by unity'. At this meeting Dato Onn bin Ja'afar emphasized that the Malays must play their part

[7] G.B., Colonial Office, *Malayan Union and Singapore; Summary of Proposed Constitutional Arrangements*, Cmd. 6749 (1946). The Malayan Union was created by Order in Council of 27 Mar. 1946 (1946, No. 463) and came into being on 1 Apr. 1946.

while yet the time remained, in 'warding off the devastating ignominy of race extinction'. About this time Dato Onn organized the United Malay Nationalist Organization (UMNO) which he claimed was supported by 70 to 80 per cent of the Malay population.[8]

Meanwhile, in *The Times* of 16 April there had appeared a letter signed by seventeen prominent ex-Malayan civil servants, including two ex-Governors of the Straits Settlements and an ex-Chief Secretary, attacking the Malayan Union (which had come into being on 1 April) and characterizing the MacMichael agreement as 'an instrument for annexation'. The letter said in conclusion: '. . . We have good reason to believe that their Highnesses and the people of Malaya would consider favourably a true federation of the nine states in association with the Straits Settlements.'

The extent of the influence of this letter is a matter of opinion, but there can be no doubt that it powerfully encouraged opposition to the infant Union: it is also reasonable to suppose that it carried considerable weight with His Majesty's Government and strongly affected public opinion in England as its authors had intended that it should. But there is no reason to believe that the distinguished signatories to the letter ever expected that the agitation would lead to the complete reversal of the constitutional proposals contained in the White Paper or to the abandonment of the principle of equal citizenship. They could not have foreseen that the Government would, in effect, permit the Malays alone to frame a constitution for the country.[9]

In May two Members of Parliament visited Malaya where they were greeted by widespread mass demonstrations of Malays which were coupled with demands for the repeal of the Union and the 'MacMichael Treaties'. The allegation was that the new agreement had been obtained under duress.[10]

The Sultans had boycotted the installation ceremony of the new Governor of the Union on 1 April when the British Military Administration ceased to exist and civil government was resumed, and Malays refused to serve on any council or board. This deadlock continued until a Federation was substituted for the Union, as we shall see in due course ensued.

To understand how the Chinese in Malaya were affected by these changes we must recall what their position was before the Japanese occupation of 1942.

Chinese born in the Straits Settlements were British subjects. Since

[8] *Sunday Times* (Singapore, 26 May 1946).
[9] As one of the signatories remarked to the writer when the proposals for the Federal constitution was announced—'Now they have gone too far the other way!'
[10] The Malay anti-Union agitation focused on the agreement negotiated by Sir Harold MacMichael, but all that this agreement did was to give power to His Majesty to legislate by Order in Council to create a new constitution. The agreement said nothing about the constitution itself.

representative government was in a rudimentary state this did not confer the same privileges that it does in Britain (e.g. there was no franchise). Nevertheless, the status was highly valued by the Straits-born Chinese. They were eligible for seats on the Executive and Legislative Councils and on the municipalities, which latter had Asiatic majorities and were virtually self-governing. They could travel on a British passport. No British subject could be banished from the Straits Settlements.

The position of the Chinese born in the Malay States was, on the other hand, very ill defined in law. In practice they were given passports as British-protected persons, but it is somewhat doubtful whether they had this status in law. They were not generally regarded by the Sultans as their subjects. Since there was no franchise in the Malay States their position led to no discriminatory disability on this account, but the preference given to Malays in the Government services usually meant that the Chinese were excluded from the higher ranks, though in the Federated Malay States they held the majority of the clerkships. The Malays also had the privileges of the Land Reservations which meant that Chinese were virtually excluded from rice cultivation. But at the same time it must be admitted that the Chinese showed no special disposition to grow rice, much preferring more lucrative employment in commerce or in industry. The creation of a common Malayan Union citizenship would have given them an equal status with the Malays except that the Malay Land Reservations were to be retained.

But, although the Chinese were the race that would gain most by the creation of a common citizenship, it cannot be said that they greeted the proposals with any particular enthusiasm. It seems that they expected many more concessions than were contained in the Secretary of State's announcement. Soon after Sir Harold MacMichael's arrival the *Sin Chew Jit Pao*[11] (an old-established Singapore Chinese-language newspaper) asked why the Sultans had been chosen as the persons with whom arrangements were to be made. The Sultans (the paper said) represented only a small proportion of the Malays and had no claim at all to represent the Chinese. The paper in the same issue said that the China-born Chinese paid rates and taxes and were as much entitled to share in the Government as the locally born. Moreover, the Malaya-born Chinese had only a 'colonial education' and therefore did not understand world tendencies and could not be expected to represent Chinese interests. The leftist papers, of course, pooh-poohed the whole proceedings. The *New Democracy* (*Sin Min Chu*) remarked that the 'feudalistic Sultans should be relegated to the realm of forgotten things'.[12]

As time went on the proposals awakened no more than a lukewarm interest among the Chinese journalists of Malaya. The MCP had endorsed the idea of a unified Malaya but not in the form envisaged by the

[11] 15 Oct. 1945.   [12] 12 Oct. 1945.

White Paper; the MDU also favoured union, but was principally interested in the question of democratic representation; the KMT was not interested in local politics except in so far as they impinged on the politics of China. Altogether there was apathy among the Chinese regarding the Union. When in April 1946 the Government of the Malayan Union invited the opinion of representative bodies and individuals comment was practically confined to the Communist press.

Without encouragement from the Chinese to maintain the Malayan Union, the British Government yielded to the pressure of the Malays and their European supporters. On 25 July a Working Committee consisting of representatives of the Malayan Union Government, of the rulers, and of UMNO was appointed to submit agreed views, if possible, for both sides to examine and criticize. (There was, it will be seen, no racial representation except of the Malays on this committee.) The Malay Nationalist Party was excluded from the deliberations. The committee sat at intervals from 6 August to November 1946 and then embodied its proposals in a report containing a draft of a proposed Federation Agreement and a model State Agreement.[13]

The key consideration behind the Working Committee's proposals was the special position of the Malays, and implicated with this were the meaning of 'citizenship' and the policy to be followed for immigration. 'There was a very real fear [the Report said] on the part of the Malays that they may steadily become submerged in a country in which (except for the aborigines) they are the indigenous people unless the categories of persons admissible to citizenship are confined to those who look upon Malaya alone as their homeland.' The Malays (unlike the immigrant races and, by insinuation, the Chinese) had no alternative homeland. The acceptance of the proposals for citizenship must, moreover, be contingent on a strict control of immigration.

The Report of the Working Committee does not here call for a detailed examination since the proposals contained in it were in principle endorsed by the British Government and embodied in a White Paper published in July 1947.[14] This White Paper said:

These proposals, while substituting for the Malayan Union a new constitution in Federal form, appeared to His Majesty's Government to be calculated in general to achieve their own fundamental objects of essential cohesion and a basis for common loyalty. The proposals . . . received the conditional approval of His Majesty's Government. . . . It was made quite clear, however, that there was no question of a final decision until all the interested communities in Malaya had been given a full and free opportunity of expressing their views, *since the proposals had been formulated by the Government and Malay leaders alone*.[15] Accordingly in December the

[13] *Constitutional Proposals for Malaya: Report of the Working Committee appointed by His Excellency the Governor of the Malayan Union, their Highnesses the Rulers of the Malay States, and the Representatives of the United Malays National Organization* (Kuala Lumpur, 1947).
[14] G.B., Colonial Office, *Federation of Malaya*, Cmd. 7171 (1947).
[15] The italics are mine (V. P.).

Government of the Malayan Union had appointed a Consultative Committee composed mainly of influential representatives of the non-Malay communities, which was instructed to hold meetings throughout the Peninsula, to receive oral and written representation, to collate the evidence submitted to it and to report the substance of the evidence to the Governor with such comments and recommendations as it should think fit.

The Consultative Committee[16] consisted of eight members (two of them being Chinese, one of them a member of the Legislative Council) under the chairmanship of the Director of Education, Mr H. R. Cheeseman, C.M.G. (total nine members). The recommendations of the committee (in the words of the White Paper Cmd. 7171), endorsed the retention of the main structure of the Federation proposals recommended by the Working Committee and the greater proportion of its detailed arrangements but recommended an increase in the size of the Federal Legislative Council and an alteration in the terms of Federal citizenship.

The Working Committee had recommended that the Council should consist of the High Commissioner as President with 3 ex-officio members, 11 official members, and 34 unofficial members to be nominated partly on a direct racial basis and partly as representing various interests, but in such a manner that, excluding ex-officio and official members, Malays were to include the 9 Malay Presidents of the Councils of State and 1 representative of each of the Settlement Councils. The Consultative Committee, on the other hand, recommended the increase of the official membership to 52, including 1 representative from each Settlement Council, while in addition the 9 Malay Presidents of the Councils of State in the Malay States were to be added as official members. The Consultative Committee's net proposals gave 29 seats to the Malays and 29 to the other communities, 3 remaining unallocated. The two Chinese members of the Consultative Committee wished to include the 9 Presidents of the Councils of State as ordinary Malay members, thus reducing the total Malay membership to 20.

As regards citizenship of the Federation, the Consultative Committee recommended that the following persons should be Federal citizens:

(a) Any subject, whether born before, on, or after the appointed day, of His Highness the Sultan of any State.

(b) Any person who is a British subject or any person born in any of the Malay States, whether before, on, or after, the appointed day who is permanently resident in either of the Settlements or any Malay State.

(c) Any person whose father is, at the date of that person's birth, a Federal Citizen.[17]

The British Government decided to go 'some of the way, though not the whole way, to meet the recommendations of the Consultative Com-

[16] *Report of the Consultative Committee* (Kuala Lumpur, 1947).   [17] Ibid. p. 11.

mittee'. As regards membership of the Legislative Council it decided to increase the total membership, but it kept a considerable Malay majority. There were to be 50 unofficial seats whose allocation would be likely to give Malays 22 seats and Chinese 14 seats, while Indians and Pakistanis would have 5, Europeans 7, Ceylonese 1, and Eurasians 1. While the 9 Presidents of the State Councils would be Malays the 2 representatives of the Settlement Councils might be from any community. This meant that the total Malay unofficial representation would be about 31 as compared with 14 for the Chinese.

Malayan citizenship (it should be borne in mind) was not a nationality, and did not affect or impair the status of British or other nationals who become Federal citizens.

The Federal citizenship proposed by the British Government might be acquired either automatically or on application.

The following persons would automatically be Federal citizens:

(*a*) Any subject, wherever born, of His Highness the Ruler of any State.

(*b*) Any British subject born at any time in either of the Settlements who is permanently resident (that is to say has completed a continuous period of 15 years residence) anywhere in the territories to be comprised in the Federation.

(*c*) Any British subject born at any time in any of the territories now to be comprised in the Federation whose father either

(i) was himself born in any of these territories ; or
(ii) has resided therein for a continuous period of not less than 15 years.

(*d*) Any person born at any time in any of the territories now to be comprised in the Federation, who habitually speaks the Malay language and conforms to Malay custom.

(*e*) Any other person born in any of these territories at any time, both of whose parents were born in any of such territories and have been resident in them for a continuous period of not less than 15 years.

(*f*) Any person whose father is, at the date of the person's birth, a Federal citizen.

The expression 'subject of His Highness the Ruler' of any State means

(i) any person who belongs to an aboriginal tribe resident in any State; or
(ii) any Malay born in that State or born elsewhere of a father who was, at the time of the birth of such person, a subject of the Ruler of that State; or
(iii) any person naturalized as a subject of that Ruler.

The provisions regarding *application* for citizenship are as follows:

The High Commissioner may grant a certificate conferring the Status of a Federal citizen on any person who applies therefore and satisfies the High Commissioner—

(*a*) that either
(i) he was born in any of the territories now to be comprised in the Federation and has been resident in any one or more of such territories for not less than 8 out of the 12 years preceding his application; or
(ii) he has been resident in any one or more of those territories for not less than 15 out of the 20 years immediately preceding his application.

(*b*) The applicant must satisfy the High Commissioner that he is of good character, possesses an adequate knowledge of the Malay or English language, has made a declaration of permanent settlement in the prescribed form, and if his application is approved, that he is willing to take the citizenship oath. In accordance with the recommendation of the Working Committee on applicant for citizenship will be required to be of the age of 18 or over.[18]

In formulating this new constitution and citizenship the British Government, it was clear, was endorsing what the Working Committee had declared to be the 'Special Position of the Malays'.[19]

These provisions of the Federation of Malaya which was created by Order in Council on 1 February 1948 have taken up a lot of space, but it is necessary that they should be studied in order to receive an idea of the worlds that separated the principles behind the Union and the Federation. Instead of being relegated to being mere heads of religious councils, the Sultans were now restored to more than their pre-war prestige. Instead of the Union which envisaged proportionate representation for the different communities, the Malays were in the Federation given a large majority without any relation to their numbers. Moreover (and this deserves italics), *the Appendix A of the new White Paper gives a schedule of the subjects for the Central Legislature. The 144 subjects in this schedule do not include the all-important subject of land.*

Under the Federation citizenship rules any subject of a Sultan was automatically a Federal citizen. No definition of 'subject of the Sultan' was given, but it seemed that he or she might very well have been born in Java or Sumatra and might have arrived in Malaya only yesterday. The Malay Reservations Enactment of the Federated Malay States 1913[20] says: ' "Malay" means a person belonging to any Malayan race who speaks the Malay language or any Malayan language and professes the Mohammedan religion', and such were always accepted as subjects of the Sultans. On the other hand, the majority of the Chinese born in the Malay States were not automatically Federal citizens unless both their parents were born within the Federation.[21]

The Union citizenship proposals certainly came nearer the desideratum of justice and equality than did those of the Federation. The

---

[18] In the actual Federation of Malaya Agreement (*Malayan Union Govt. Gazette*, Kuala Lumpur, 22 Jan. 1948 and Suppl. of 31 Jan. 1948) the rules were varied from those outlined in Cmd. 7171 in some minor ways. For example, for 'wherever born' in the first (*a*) above, was substituted 'whether born before, on, or after the appointed day', and 'permanently resident' was substituted generally for the continuous period of 15 years' residence.

[19] *Working Committee Report*, p. 23.   [20] No. 15 of 1913.

[21] A Malayan Federal Citizen was a British Protected Person under the British Protectorates, Protected States, and Protected Persons Order in Council, 1949. It was officially estimated that of 1,952,682 Chinese resident in the Federation of Malaya at the end of June 1949, 375,000 were Federal citizens by operation of law. After May 1949, however, when registration of Federal citizens by application began, many Chinese applied for Federal Citizenship. During August and September 4,483 certificates of citizenship were issued to Chinese out of a total of 4,708 certificates issued to all races and it was reported that the number of applications after that date greatly increased.

error committed, it seems, was in creating the Union before an adequate opportunity had been given to the people of Malaya to consider the proposals, and, having frightened the Malays into demanding the repeal of the Union, the next error was to stampede before their demands. The Chinese were no doubt to blame to some extent for their lukewarm attitude towards the Union and their refusal to defend its principles if not the method of its introduction, and they suffered politically for the concessions which had been made to the Malays in default of their speaking for their own rights. But if their realization of what was happening was slow, they afterwards demonstrated that they regarded the new Federal constitutionwith distaste.

Chinese reaction to the constitution expressed itself in a number of ways. The action which most impressed itself on the public and the official notice was a 'hartal',[22] or stoppage of work, sponsored by Mr Tan Cheng-lock's Pan-Malayan Council of Joint Action, the Associated Chinese Chambers of Commerce, the Malayan trade unions, and (of course) the Malayan Communist Party, as a protest against the proposals for a Malayan Federation. On 20 October 1947 virtually all business and transport were at a standstill and Singapore was without buses, trams, or taxis, and no employees of the Harbour Board were at work. Obedient to the request of the organizers, the Chinese community of Singapore as a whole stayed at home.[23] The hartal, however, was not by any means country-wide, and the Government was successful in persuading Chinese to serve in the Councils, &c. There has, indeed, been considerable Chinese co-operation in the working of the Federation.

Another protest took the form of boycotting the new Singapore Legislative Council elections when in 1947 only about 20,000 out of 100,000–200,000 eligible electors registered themselves for the elections to be held in 1948. The result of this was that in a city predominantly Chinese only one Chinese was elected.[24]

Before concluding this chapter it would be informative for us to examine the evidence submitted to the Consultative Committee by the various communities.

This evidence was most miscellaneous and various, coming both from individuals and associations. It ranged from mild criticism to downright rejection of the Working Committee's Report. Although the recommendations of the Report were virtually those of the Malay rulers and of UMNO, some diehard Malay associations disapproved of them as being

[22] It is strange that the Indian word 'hartal' should have been adopted for a mainly Chinese occasion. [23] See *Straits Times* (6 Oct.) and *The Times* (21 Oct.).
[24] *British Malaya*, Apr. 1948. According to *British Dependencies in the Far East, 1945–9* (Cmd. 7709), p. 54, persons eligible to vote were those born in Singapore, the Malayan Federation, or the Borneo territories who had resided in Singapore for three years prior to polling day. Of those eligible some 22,000, or 15–20 per cent of those eligible, had their names inscribed.

too liberal. For example, the Lembaga Kesatuan Melayu of Johore
stated:

> When we look at the handing over of a Government of Islam to the Government
> of non-Islam we shall find that the action is against the wishes of Islam (holy
> Qu'rān [Koran] verse 4: 58, 2: 38, 3: 158) . . . according to Islam there is no separa-
> tion between politics and religion. It is a great sin for Islamic peoples to transfer the
> Government of the Malay States to non-Islam. . . .

On the other hand, the Singapore Chinese Chamber of Commerce
was 'greatly perturbed by these proposals because Chinese interests were
to a large extent ignored', and these views were echoed by the other
Chinese Chambers of Commerce in the country. But three Chinese
associations of Penang—the Chinese Town Hall, the Chinese Chamber
of Commerce, and the Straits Chinese British Association—in a joint
'petition' to the Secretary of State, expressed the general feelings of their
fellows most adequately. 'The proposals [the petition said] are vitiated by
an anti-Chinese bias. The provisions for the acquirement and loss of
citizenship, the immigration policy contemplated, and the ridiculously
inadequate representation of Chinese interests in the Federation Legislative Council are unmistakable indications of anti-Chinese bias.'

British policy towards the Chinese has for many years been characterized by suspicion verging often on hostility. When Chinese
nationalism began to be aggressive, instead of adopting measures to
encourage the Malayan-born Chinese to regard themselves first and
foremost as Malayans, thus raising a bulwark against the pretensions of
Chinese imperialism, the Malayan Governments chose instead to dig
themselves in on the line of the treaties with the Sultans. The result was
that all persons of Chinese race, whether they liked it or not, found
themselves classed with the Nationalists of China. This policy was
greatly reinforced after the stampede took place from the principles of
Malayan Union citizenship and after the relinquishment by the British
of much of the control to the Sultans and their Mentris Besar.

Many years before, in October 1932, Mr Tan Cheng-lock, then the
senior Chinese representative on the Legislative Council of the Straits
Settlements, had said at a meeting of the Council:

> I look in vain for any tangible sign or indication of any active interest, practical
> sympathy, and encouragement that has been shown by the Government of late
> years towards that body of worthy, staunch, and traditionally loyal British subjects,
> viz. the Straits-born Chinese who have formed a continuous Colony in this country
> for more than 500 years, and the locally-born Chinese subjects of the Protected
> Malay States who have made this country their home. On the contrary, these loyal
> citizens of Malaya are, practically speaking, not to be allowed in future to own and
> cultivate rice lands in this country of their birth though foreign Malaysians from
> Sumatra and Java are granted that privilege; nor have those of them who are unable
> to find employment as clerks and in other classes of work in the towns been given
> facilities to go back to settle on the land; their appeal to have representation on the

Executive Council of the Colony has been rejected outright; English education for them has been and is to be further restricted by the raising of school fees and the 'over-age' and other rules, while at the same time Government intends to disown, or has now actually disowned, according to this Council paper now laid on the table, all responsibility for giving them any Chinese education at the expense of the State. They are told that if they want free education they can go to the Malay vernacular schools, which it is impossible for them to do and is therefore not a practicable proposition but a useless concession. . . .[25]

It is worthy of note that this same spokesman of the Straits-born Chinese (whose family had been in Malaya since the eighteenth century) spoke at the same Council meeting of 'the hearty support which Your Excellency's recent ban against the Kuomintang has received from the majority of the Chinese population in Malaya'.

Though the opinion may smack of 'hindsight', it seems now that a great opportunity was lost in these pre-war years to encourage the Malayan-born Chinese to resist the pretensions of Chinese nationalism and to regard themselves as Malayans first and foremost.

34

BEFORE AND AFTER INDEPENDENCE[1]

AFTER the setback received in February 1946, the Malayan Communist Party found it expedient to conduct their main operations underground. They were active in tightening still further their grip on labour and in fomenting strikes. When the Associated Chinese Chambers of Commerce organized their 'hartal' as a protest against the proposals for a Federation of Malaya in October 1947, working through the trade unions and directly, the Communists joined in the movement, exploiting, as always, any popular dissatisfaction. Then, it seems, in March 1948 the party decided to stage an armed insurrection. The way for this was to be paved by widespread labour unrest during April, stimulated by the intimidation (and, if necessary, removal) of trade union leaders who were unwilling to collaborate, the use of arms, and the burning of factories. A great political demonstration was timed for 1 May. Although these preliminaries misfired, it was decided, nevertheless, to adhere to the original programme and to give the order for the outbreak of armed violence in early June.[2]

[25] Straits Settlements, *Legislative Council Proceedings* (19 Oct. 1932), cited in part by Emerson, *Malaysia*, p. 513.   [1] This chapter carries events roughly to the end of 1948.
[2] To what extent the outbreak was directed by external authority, and what connexion, if any, it had with the Communist Party conference at Calcutta in Jan. 1948 had not been established by 1963.

The intention was that a revolt should start simultaneously in various parts of the Federation. Terrorism directed against Europeans and Chinese was to prepare the way for the revolt in order to create regions which would, in due course, be declared to be independent Communist areas. These should be gradually extended until the whole country was under Communist control. The declaration of a Communist Republic of Malaya was timed for 3 August 1948.

The outbreak in June was really only an accentuation of the violence and lawlessness which were already sporadic. The Commissioner-General, Mr Malcolm MacDonald, in a broadcast from Radio Malaya on 6 June, spoke of Communist agitators making a desperate attempt to impose a rule of gun and knife, and said that the bestial campaign must be struck down. He added that there was evidence that leaders of international Communism were resolved on a political offensive in the East if they were checked in Europe. Reports began to come in of shooting, violence, and loss of life on estates in the Federation. The Commissioner of Police reported a vast increase in acts of violence; Perak planters asked for drastic action to curb the outbreak. On 12 June three KMT leaders were shot in daylight in Johore. On 13 June Sir Edward Gent, High Commissioner for the Federation, stated that a policy of banishing undesirable British subjects was under consideration, and a Bill was being rushed through giving extensive powers to the authorities in any area where a public emergency was declared. On 15 June three European planters were killed on estates in Perak, and thereafter these incidents were frequent.[3]

A state of emergency covering the entire Federation was declared on 18 June and was extended to Singapore on 24 June. The MPAJA issued a manifesto calling on all former comrades to take up arms against the British. On 20 June 4,000–5,000 guerrillas were reported to be massing in the jungle.[4] On the same day the police station at Mentakab, Pahang, was attacked.

On 23 July the Secretary of State for the Colonies stated in the House of Commons that the MCP had been banned, together with three other satellite bodies which were either involved in the current fighting or

[3] *The Malayan Bulletin*, published monthly by the Association of British Malaya (now British Ass. of Malaysia), is mainly followed in this chapter. In reply to a question in the House of Commons on 16 June 1946, Mr Rees-Williams, Parliamentary Secretary to the Secretary of State, stated that there had been at least 13 serious incidents in recent weeks, including 10 murders and 3 attacks on European managers of estates.

The *Malayan Monitor*, a Communist monthly bulletin issued by H. B. Lim from 132 Fleet Street, London, appeared at the end of 1947. It published an account of the progress of the campaign in Malaya from the Communist point of view, and included a communiqué of alleged Communist successes—e.g. 2 October, guerrillas blow up railway line near Sungei Siput; 20 October, President of Johore Planters' Association shot dead; 28 October, guerrillas shoot 28 police in Perak—and of alleged crimes against the people of Malaya, e.g. 12 October, burning of Poh Leh Sun village, Johore, by armed forces. It had, obviously, the support and assistance of the British Communist Party.   [4] *Daily Telegraph* (20 June 1948).

were recruiting or supply agencies for the terrorists. The bodies referred to were the MPAJA, the New Democratic Youth League, and a Malay organization of youth, Ikatan Pemela Tanah Ayer (PETA).[5] A large number of persons was detained for 'screening' under the Emergency Regulations, and quantities of arms were captured, including a seizure by the Singapore police and the Netherlands East Indies authorities of a large cargo of arms.

Throughout July and August the terrorism continued, action to check it being tremendously complicated by the nature of the country, four-fifths of Malaya still being under jungle and swamp. At the end of August the General Officer Commanding stated that 'things are improving, and the way in which the bandits are being hit is improving'. This view was endorsed by the *Straits Times* which said that 'the tempo of the onslaught had slowed down'. The successful campaign against the Communists in south Kelantan, where they had been well organized, was a serious defeat for them. Nevertheless, the trouble was by no means over and destructive attacks and wanton murders continued, including the murder of Dr Ong Chong-keng,[6] a Chinese member of the Legislative Council, and other Chinese and Europeans. Chinese bandit gangs on the Siamese border presented another threat to the Federation. Negotiations were in progress with Siam to facilitate action by the Federation security forces against the gangs, and it had been agreed that police and Government officers on both sides might cross the frontier using special passes and might be accompanied by a small escort of police. A British consul was appointed to Singora who had wireless facilities for communicating with the British Embassy at Bangkok and the Federal Government at Kuala Lumpur.[7]

By the end of October it was felt in circles of authority in Malaya that the situation showed distinct signs of improvement. The policy of keeping the bandits on the move (by the use of 'Ferret Force', &c) had been successful; it had interrupted their training and there had been a decline in terrorist violence. The latest police and services press conference had a note of 'cautious confidence'. In the Legislative Council at

[5] 'The PETA represents the most militant sections of Malay youth' (*Malayan Monitor* (Feb. 1949)). The Malayan Communists claimed also the Peasants' Union, and AWAS (Malay Women's Emancipation Association) as Malay 'democratic' organizations.

[6] Some mystery attaches to this murder, and from information received since the above was written it appears doubtful whether the motive for it was political or that it was committed by Communists.

[7] The Siamese frontier had always been a problem, even in pre-war days, for its thick jungle allowed bandits and others to pass freely to and fro, retreating from either the British or the Siamese authorities. After the liberation the so-called 'KMT guerrillas' were active here. The problem had been complicated since the war by the recrudescence of the Patani question. Patani is a Siamese State whose population is mainly Malay, and some of these had been conducting an agitation to take Patani out of Siam and to join with their brethren in the British-protected Federation of Malaya. This movement had made the Siamese very guarded in their commitments on frontier matters.

Kuala Lumpur the acting Chief Secretary stated on 5 October that the Federation Government intended to take steps to prevent known Communists from Australia, Siam, and Indonesia entering the country, and no exception would be made for British Communist M.P.s who might want to stay on estates and mines.

In spite of the terror, of which a leading motive was to sabotage Britain's economic recovery plan by cutting off the supplies of tin and rubber so valuable in obtaining dollar exchange, the production figures showed that up to that time these activities had had little effect on rubber production. Estate rubber production for August was 33,727 tons, the fourth largest figure since the liberation, and only slightly less than the exceptional output of July. The London *Times* of 12 October stated that the troops, which had now been reinforced by British units, including a contingent of the Guards, were adapting themselves with great facility to the form of battle in which they were engaged; wherever possible they lived off the country, thus adding to the mobility given them by supplies dropped from the air. Specialized training was in hand and the next move would be an extension of army dispositions under the direction of the police to cover the whole of Malaya.

Most of the 223 civilians who had been murdered up to the end of October were Chinese, whilst the Europeans murdered totalled 17. Of the 343 terrorists officially reported to have been killed, 6 were Malays, 3 Indians, and 2 Siamese. The rest were mainly foreign-born Chinese.[8]

At the end of November official statements and private communications from Malaya stated that the main purpose of the Communists, namely, the dislocation of the economy of Malaya and the establishment of a Communist regime, had been completely defeated. The whole position was said to be better and the morale of the people had improved. Many more troops had been trained and had been rapidly deployed. Estates were better protected and production figures had not flagged. Bungalows in some areas had become miniature fortresses. The terrorists were concentrating their attacks on communications, particularly the railway, and on planters and others on the roads. Despite this, the strain on planters and miners and others in the front line remained severe, and it was clear that, while good results were being obtained, individuals were still liable to murderous attacks, and the time had not yet come to take things easily.

As one measure for dealing with the terrorist campaign and its supporters in civilian clothes a scheme of national registration was imposed

[8] See *British Survey: Communism in South East Asia*, no. 19 (Nov. 1948), p. 16. In spite of the greater optimism of official reports, letters from rubber planters in the fighting area continued to give a gloomy impression of the situation up to the end of 1948. The total number of civilians killed at the end of July 1949 was 508, including five casualties officially listed as accidental. The figure included 318 Chinese, 75 Malays, 43 Sakais, 34 Indians, 29 Europeans, 7 Indonesians, and 2 others (*British Malaya*, Sept. 1949).

whereby every person in the Federation and the Colony was required to possess a registration card.

The great danger for the Government was that it might allow itself to be led into repressive action against sections of the population which, willingly or unwillingly, were assisting the Communists, and this would arouse enmity against itself. It was obvious that the British, a small minority, could not 'hold down' a population numbering nearly six millions, and that government must be at least with the acquiescence of the governed. Indeed, so long as the British were able to continue their administration this was proof positive that the Communists had failed to secure popular support. But ruthless or unwise action against large sections of the community might easily reverse the situation and make it impossible to hold Malaya. The greatest menace, therefore, lay in that school of thought which regarded all Chinese as Communists and therefore as enemies. Luckily in 1949 the Malays as a people were not trapped into such an attitude, and they made a distinction between bandits and ordinary Chinese.

When the Communist outbreak began the Chinese in Malaya were in a condition of political apathy. They were dissatisfied with their position under the constitution of the Federation of Malaya, even though the Associated Chambers of Commerce under the guidance of Mr K. C. Lee and Colonel H. S. Lee had withdrawn their official opposition to the constitution and had agreed to give it a trial. In Singapore the new elections, as we have seen, had been boycotted by a majority of Chinese, under MDU leadership, though the Progressive Party (Chinese) put up candidates for all districts. It was not altogether surprising, therefore, that they were first of all inclined to regard the outbreak of terrorism as a matter between the Government and the Communists. This attitude, however, afforded an opening for those who wished to regard the insurrection as a purely Chinese affair, supported openly or tacitly by the Chinese community as a whole. The reluctance of the Chinese to join the auxiliary police even though their countrymen were the major victims of the guerrilla attacks lent colour to the suggestion.

Typical of the criticism of the Chinese and their leaders was a leading article in the Kuala Lumpur *Malay Mail* of 29 October headed 'The Towkay and the Terrorist'. The writer quoted a correspondent of the London *Daily Mail* as saying that the terrorist campaign could hardly last another month unless it had the solid, if somewhat reluctant, backing the Chinese terrorists still got from their Chinese kinsmen. The paper commented that the fight against the terrorists was being carried on 'with little or no help from the Chinese', and that in addition the Chinese Communists relied on their own countrymen for the support without which they could not be kept going. That most of the support was gained by terrorization and was more or less unwillingly given did not alter the fact. One source of assistance on which the terrorists relied was, of course, the squatter community.

A study of the Chinese-language press of the period throws some light on the evolution of the Chinese attitude towards the troubles. On 21 July the Officer Administering the Government, Sir Alec Newboult, made a broadcast in which he appealed to the Chinese community for active co-operation. Prominence in the Chinese press was extended to statements from the Chinese consul-general, Penang, and of Dr Ong Chong-keng (the Chinese Member of Council afterwards murdered), who supported Sir Alec's plea, and also to a similar plea made by the veteran Mr Tan Kah-kee of Singapore. The Kuala Lumpur *China Press* published a long editorial denying the charges of non-co-operation. It drew attention to the unenviable position in which the Chinese found themselves—heading the list of arrests for terrorism on the one hand, and topping the list of arrests under the Emergency Regulations on the other. The paper explained that the slowness of response in joining the special police was due to their lack of experience in this branch of the service as well as to the language difficulty. The Chinese press, however, gave publicity to a subsequent move on the part of the Selangor Chinese Chamber of Commerce to enrol Chinese members for the auxiliary police.

During August the Chinese papers increased their support for the movement for Chinese to join auxiliary police units, and in September the appeal received even greater stress. But the number of Chinese enrolled remained small.

The reference to the squatter community calls attention to what was undoubtedly the main source of Communist strength. Chinese squatters had existed for many years; during the trade depression of 1931–3 their numbers were greatly augmented by unemployed labourers, and again they received accretions during the Japanese occupation. It is estimated that they numbered between 350,000 and 500,000 in 1948.[9] They occupied their land either on temporary occupation licences, which could be terminated by the Government at will, or (mostly) on no licences at all. In the Malay States there had since 1913 been a policy of land reservation in force for the Malays and this meant that nearly all the land suitable for rice-growing had been reserved for Malays. During the Japanese occupation Chinese squatters were allowed to encroach on these Malay Land Reservations and to open up new land for cultivation, and after the liberation, when the country was desperately short of food, the British Military Administration allowed them, for the time being, to remain in the reserved areas. The civil Government, however, resolved to move these squatters as soon as it was feasible.

It happened that the areas in which the squatters were principally

[9] This was the official reply to a question by the Hon. Mr Tan Siew-sin in the Legislative Council of the Federation, but it is thought by some authorities to be too high an estimate.

located were on the fringe of the jungle and therefore afforded a convenient shelter and source of supply for the guerrillas. Also the guerrillas made levies of men for their forces, compelling them under threat of reprisals against themselves or their families to join them in raids. After the raids the recruits were usually returned to the villages. The British troops on several occasions burnt down the huts of squatters who had collaborated with the terrorists and destroyed their crops, thus sealing the enmity between them and constituted authority.

The *Straits Times* said that public opinion was undeniably worried about the burning of squatters' huts and the destruction of their crops, 'unavoidable though this might be'. It thought that there was a very real danger of turning purely passive or forced co-operation with the terrorists into bitter resentment against the Government. The Chinese press of this period showed great concern at the drastic action being taken, and gave the fullest publicity to the burning by the police of Kachau village near Kuala Lumpur. The paper *Kin Kwok* of Ipoh published a leader headed, 'Don't drive them to the hills'.

However, in this twelfth hour of the Emergency, the Malayan authorities had to deal with the situation as it then existed with more regard to immediate expediency than to long-term policy. New measures were introduced in November for the repatriation of any alien who assisted the Communist terrorists in any way. Such repatriation was to apply to any person who paid 'protection money' to them. A number of Chinese miners and shareholders were arrested under the new regulations. By the beginning of January 1949, 500 squatters from the Kajang district had already been moved to a detention camp to await a passage to China. Compensation was being paid them for loss of stock and produce.

Another matter, equally disturbing to public opinion as the squatter question, was that of 'regrettable incidents' in which British troops were involved and in which innocent Chinese lost their lives. One of these became known as the Batang Kali shooting. Another disagreeable happening was the burning of huts at Kachau without proof that they belonged to persons guilty of collaboration with the terrorists.[10]

To revert now to the leading article of the *Malay Mail* of 29 October. This, after having mentioned the squatter question, concentrated on the alleged complicity of the wealthy Chinese *towkays* in the current disturbances. The *towkays*, it said, were not only refraining from joining the auxiliary police; many of them were submitting to intimidation and

[10] As an outcome of the unfortunate affair at Batang Kali, near Rawang, early in December, when twenty-four Chinese were shot dead by the military forces as they attempted to escape from custody, considerable hostile criticism was aroused in the press, and the army instituted an inquiry. The investigations were supervised by the Attorney-General's Department which declared itself completely satisfied that the forces had conducted themselves in a correct fashion.

contributing, admittedly under duress, both money and supplies to the support of the terrorists.

That there is some substance in these charges is very likely. Traditionally the Chinese have always followed the line of the least resistance when subjected to intimidation. 'Protection money' to secret societies and to political societies after them had for long been a heavy item in the budget of a trader and it was paid in dollars and cents by even the smallest farmer. The reply of the Chinese *towkay* was that in default of protection from the authorities he was taking the only course open to him to ensure the safety of himself and of his family. At the same time it was increasingly apparent that, while the Communists were nearly all Chinese, it was the Chinese also who were the principal victims of the attacks, and the Chinese as a community began to be stirred from apathy and to rally increasingly to the support of law and order. In September a Chinese plan had been adopted for the recruitment of volunteers for the auxiliary police from Chinese firms, estates, and mines.

In describing the background of the Communist insurrection it is easy to overlook a number of causes which, while small in themselves, were basic. Among these was the psychological state of the ex-members of the MPAJA. After the liberation of Malaya in 1945 the state of mind of the guerrillas passed through various phases. Most of them were mere youths who had been isolated in the jungle during the formative period of their lives. Their education was rudimentary and their sources of information were most limited. Then when the Japanese surrendered and concentrated according to the terms of the surrender in certain centres, the MPAJA had come out of their hiding-places and had filled the vacuum as the overlords of the country until the British forces had made a belated appearance. During this interregnum the Communists had tasted power, and it irked them to have to surrender it to the BMA. It is also a fact that a small minority of the personnel of the large force of re-occupying troops regarded the country as if it were an occupied enemy country and treated the MPAJA with scant courtesy. Once they were disbanded many of them were unemployed and had leisure to brood on their grievances. The gratuity of $350 a man did not satisfy them, and they expected to be paid for their services throughout the Japanese occupation. Many of them (and MCP headquarters too) had amassed large quantities of Japanese notes which the British had refused to honour.

These were among the specific grievances of the ex-MPAJA, but the Chinese community as a whole nursed additional resentments. For one thing the European Government and municipal servants who were interned, and also a few who were not interned but were allowed to remain out of the camps to operate public utilities or to engage in scientific work, had received full pay for the period, while Asian Government and municipal servants who had not been interned had to fight for years to obtain even a proportion of the pay they would have received if the British had not been forced out of the country. The fact was, however, that the Europeans who had been employed by the Japanese had to refund the amount received by them as payment for this employment.

Another reason for discontent was that many Chinese thought that collaborators with the Japanese had been too lightly dealt with after the liberation. The prosecution of collaborators had not been in the hands of the BMA, but of a special legal branch of the army which had conducted investigations and prosecutions on their own account without any reference to the administrative authority. A number of suspected collaborators had been arrested after the liberation, but nearly all of these were eventually released since the evidence against them was not thought to be strong enough. The military legal authorities apparently took the view that it was better to let a guilty person escape punishment than to convict an innocent one. And, indeed, during the occupation almost any individual who carried on his ordinary occupation was liable to be suspected of collaboration. The ex-MPAJA and the Communists, in particular, agitated for the wholesale arrest of persons they claimed to be collaborators, but by 'collaborator' they usually meant anyone who was opposed to their political views.

It was the policy of the post-war Governments in Malaya to encourage the growth of trade unionism; the necessary legislation had been passed before the Japanese invasion, and in 1946 English trade unionists of experience had been sent to Malaya to assist the labourers to form their unions. At least one of these English officials confessed himself as very disillusioned by what he found. In February and March 1948 two other British trade unionists, Messrs S. S. Awbery, M.P., and F. W. Dalley, visited Malaya to report on developments. Their report was issued in November 1948. It emphasized that the trade union movement in Malaya had a very different history and tradition from the British movement. It derived from associations which had social rather than industrial functions, from anti-Japanese resistance groups, and from new trade unions established after the war. The report described the clever and ruthless attempts made by Communist leaders to gain control of the movement and use it as a weapon for seizing political power. The mission approved the Government decision to encourage responsible trade unionism by collective bargaining. It said, however, that the Federation of Trade Unions, established at different levels, though disclaiming Communism, worked according to Communist directives and maintained contact with Communist associations in other countries. On the other hand, the report considered the trade union position 'as good as we had hoped and much better than we had feared'. The mission recommended improvement of the negotiating and arbitration machinery, measures to

C.R.E.A.—M

suppress intimidation, compulsory national education, and improved housing.[11]

With the outstations of the mainland in the grip of Communist terror (though the towns remained tranquil and Singapore's crime statistics were smaller than before the war), and with emergency regulations in force, the setting was not congenial in 1948 for the growth of healthy democratic politics. But there was, nevertheless, some notable development.

We have noted in a previous chapter the birth of the MDU in December 1945 and how the Communists sought to dominate a party formed with the declared object of securing representative government within the British Commonwealth. The following year the party assumed a much more genuine appearance under the leadership of Philip Hoalim and of an English-educated Eurasian, John Eber. However, in December 1946 the MDU leaders, in a move to offset the influence of UMNO, formed a federation of all parties which opposed the UMNO programme. This included, in addition to the MDU, the Malay Nationalist Party (MNP),[12] the Pan-Malayan Federation of Trade Unions, the Malayan Indian Congress, the MPAJA Old Comrades' Association, the Malayan New Democratic Youth, the Angatan Wanita Sedara (Women's Party), and the Angatan Pemuda Insaf (Youth Party). The federation called itself the All Malaya Council of Joint Action (AMCJA). Its six objectives were—the unity of Malaya including Singapore, a fully representative elected legislature, equal political rights for all who regarded Malaya as their real home and the object of their loyalty, the assumption by the Malay Sultans of the position of fully sovereign and constitutional rulers, the control of Mohammedan affairs and matters affecting Malay custom to be in the hands of the Malays, and lastly the encouragement of the advancement of the Malay community.

This collection of strange bedfellows did not last long. The MNP with the Angatan Pemuda Insaf seceded from AMCJA to form a Malay Council of Joint Action, and this was followed by the creation of yet another front, namely, the Pusat Tenaga Ra'ayat (People's United Front) or PUTERA, comprising the main body of MNP, a youth organization, a woman's organization, and many smaller bodies. The leading spirit in this new creation was Dr Burhanuddin, the founder of the MNP. PUTERA added four more points to the six-point programme of

[11] S. S. Awbery and F. W. Dalley, *Labour and Trade Union Organization in the Federation of Malaya and Singapore* (Kuala Lumpur, 1948). Inst. of Pacific Relations, *Three Reports on Malayan Problems* (N.Y., 1949, mimeo.) contains a summary of this report at p. 22 ff.

[12] On p. 315 the MNP was said to be under Communist auspices. So it seemed at the time, and certainly it has Communist blessing; but although accused of being Communist by its opponent UMNO it was permitted by the Government to continue when the MCP was banned in the summer of 1948.

AMCJA—that Malay should be the official language of the country, that foreign affairs should be jointly controlled by the Malayan and British Governments, the term *Melayu* to be applied to all citizens of Malaya, and the national flag of the country to incorporate the Malay national colours.

AMCJA was thought to be a Chinese-dominated and Chinese-financed front, while PUTERA ostensibly represented anti-UMNO Malay feeling and was guided, no doubt, by the founder. A certain amount of bargaining ensued between the two federations, the Chinese element making concessions in the shape of proposing Melayu as the name of Malayan citizenship and the retention of the Malay Sultans as constitutional sovereigns; PUTERA, for its part, dropped its Communist associates and omitted all reference to the question of immigration.[13]

The outbreak of the Communist terror temporarily at least effected a cleavage of Malaya into two sides—Communist and anti-Communist. The grave turn of events in China itself had naturally a strong influence on the Chinese politics of Malaya. The victories of the Communist armies and the breakdown of the National Government leading to the resignation of President Chiang Kai-shek gave great encouragement to the Malayan Communists to continue their campaign.

On 24 June the MDU decided to dissolve 'in the present political situation and curtailment of civil rights'. The MCP and the Singapore Federation of Trade Unions (SFTU) ceased to function at the same time. Soon afterwards the MCP, the MPAJA Old Comrades' Association, the New Democratic Youth League, and PETA were declared unlawful by the Malayan Governments. The Malayan Indian Congress, the sole survivor of the AMCJA, called a truce with the Governments during the emergency.[14]

[13] The above represents the author's information regarding the political developments in Malaya at this period, but the situation was so complex and confused that it is desirable to include here another version of what was happening. Peet (*Political Questions of Malaya*, p. 13), says:

All these opposition bodies [i.e. the MCP, MDU, MNP, Malayan Indian Congress, and Pan-Malayan Federation of Trade Unions] except the Communist Party, banded together after it was announced that the Malayan Union had been scrapped and that a new constitution was to be drafted. This coalition became known as PUTERA-AMCJA, those being the initials of the principal member bodies. PUTERA was the Malay wing, AMCJA the non-Malay wing. The following of PUTERA among the Malay population appeared to be small. AMCJA was mainly, though not entirely, based upon the trade unions which were under strong Communist influence and were mainly composed of Chinese and Indian immigrant workers.

See also the same pamphlet for an account of the 'People's Constitutional Proposals' produced by this coalition.

[14] The Societies in Singapore excluded from the provisions of the Societies Ordinance as political Associations (i.e. allowed legally to function) at the beginning of 1949 were the China Democratic League, Kuomintang, Malayan Indian Congress, Malayan Nationalist Party, Malay Union, Pusat Tenaga Ra'ayat, Progressive Party, and the Labour Party of Singapore. In May 1949 the China Democratic League and the Kuomintang were deleted from this list as foreign political organizations. The position thereafter was that these Societies now came under the provisions of the Societies Ordinance and if they wished to maintain branches in the

In an attempt to fill this large void Mr Tan Cheng-lock, in September 1948, contemplated the formation of a Malayan Chinese League with the basic idea of the combination of the Chinese, not only in the interests of racial unity, but to bring about Sino-Malay friendship. At the same time Mr Tan stated that there was much to be done before the League would become an accomplished fact.

The most hopeful development of the early months of 1949 was the formation of the Communities Liaison Committee and the Malayan Chinese Association with Mr Tan Cheng-lock as president. The first was intended to bring together the leaders of Malay, Chinese, Indian, Ceylonese, and European communities. In welcoming the new Malayan Chinese Association, Sir Henry Gurney, the High Commissioner of the Federation, said: 'The Chinese community is undoubtedly placing great hopes on the successful formation of this new body which will represent the Chinese point of view and promote and assist the maintenance of peace and good order.'

35

THE PERIOD 1949–63

1. THE FEDERATION

THE period 1950–63 was very important in the history of the Chinese in Malaya. The main influences affecting the community in those years were (a) the Emergency, (b) reaction to the success of the Communist revolution in China, (c) the rapprochement with the Malays which culminated in the achievement of independence by the Federation of Malaya in 1957, and (d) the 'Greater Malaysia' proposals.

In the last chapter the account of the Emergency has been brought down to the end of 1948.[1] It remains to summarize the course of the Communist terror from this point onwards.[2]

During 1949, 618 members of the 'Malayan Races Liberation Army' (formed by the Communists as from 1 February 1949) were officially reported killed and 337 captured. Casualties suffered by the civilian population were 334 killed, 200 wounded, and 162 missing; police, 164 killed and 170 wounded; military, 65 killed and 77 wounded. These figures give a fair impression of the *scale* of the fighting. Actually, from

---

Colony they would have to apply for exemption from registration. The move was a reflection of the developments in China and the wish of the Singapore Government to eliminate foreign political activity.

[1] Events up to October 1950 were included in the Postscript of the first edition of this work.
[2] See also the present writer's *Malaya: Communist or Free?* (1954), chaps. v–vii.

first to last, not more than 3,000–5,000 Communist guerrillas were actually engaged in combat (this representing the optimum number for jungle warfare in Malaya) though the Min Yuen, the Communist auxiliary civilian organization, was estimated to number perhaps 20,000, who collected food and money for the guerrillas and distributed propaganda. Over 99 per cent of the guerrillas were Chinese. The claim publicized, therefore, by Peking Radio that the insurrection was one of the 'Malayan Races' was without substance.

In April 1950 Lieut.-General Sir Harold Briggs was appointed Director of Operations, charged solely with the prosecution of the Emergency. It had already been realized that to kill terrorists was not enough, since replacements were always available; what was required was to break the Communists' morale and to remove or disrupt the guerrillas' sources of supply. What became known as the 'Briggs Plan' was, in fact, the implementation of the recommendation of the Squatter Committee appointed by the High Commissioner in December 1948. These involved the resettlement of some half a million Chinese squatters, distributed by the circumstances of war and the food shortage consequent on the Japanese occupation over a wide area, into what became known as the 'New Villages'. There were long-term as well as short-term objectives in those measures, but the short-term object was to control the squatters and to prevent them from supplying the Communist guerrillas in the jungle with food, arms, and man-power. A great part of this resettlement was complete by the end of 1950 but was still in progress in 1952, and was the foundation of the success of the operations against the Communists.

Although casualties continued at fluctuating rates, the pressure brought on the guerrillas by the security forces (consisting of British and Malay troops, Gurkhas, &c, and about 100,000 Malay police and Home Guard) compelled the former to change their strategy. In a 'Politburo' directive dated 1 October 1951 (a copy was later captured by the security forces) serious errors were admitted by the Communists. To win over the masses, the party (the directive said) must stop seizing identity and ration cards, stop burning villages and new coolie-lines and attacking post offices, reservoirs, power stations, &c, and stop the indiscriminate slaughter of 'running dogs' (collaborators with the Government) which often involved the death of members of the 'masses' as well. Rubber trees, tin-mines, and factories must no longer be destroyed because of the resentment of workers who thereby lost their employment.

Five days after the issue of the new Malayan Communist 'Politburo' directive, the High Commissioner, Sir Henry Gurney, was murdered in ambush by Communist guerrillas while travelling by car from Kuala Kubu to Fraser's Hill. The immediate effect of the murder was to reduce the morale of the people of Malaya to its lowest ebb, and it was some time before reaction set in with a stiffening of determination to rid Malaya once and for all of the authors of this new and greatest outrage. Mr M. V. del Tufo, Chief Secretary of the Federation, then on leave, was recalled to administer the Government.

It was at this juncture that the British Government decided to fill the vacancy caused by the murder of Sir Henry Gurney by appointing a soldier, not only to command the forces in the Federation but also as High Commissioner at the head of the civil Government. The officer chosen for this position was General Sir Gerald Templer, who had no previous experience of Malaya. To guide him in his task, General Templer was given a directive by the Colonial Secretary (Mr Oliver Lyttelton, later Lord Chandos) which laid down a policy for preparing Malaya for self-government at some unspecified time in the future.

Although military operations were thus given priority over everything else, the political evolution of Malaya did not stop on account of the Emergency. In fact, the Communist insurrection made the solution of the political problems of greater urgency than before. Among those of outstanding importance was the relationship between the Malays and the Chinese, an uneasy one during and since the Japanese occupation and which had deteriorated even more since the Emergency. Although the Communist guerrillas were a small minority and had not gained the support of the Chinese community as a whole, they were nevertheless Chinese, and the Malays were very conscious that they were confronted by a Chinese bid to take over the country.

The formation of the Malayan Chinese Association (MCA) early in 1949 has already been referred to. Most of the political parties which had sprung up since liberation had Communist affiliations and disappeared on the application, or threat of application, of the Emergency Regulations. Except for UMNO, no widely representative party had yet come into being. The Chinese community, in particular, was without representation. The new federal constitution, moreover, was strongly weighted in favour of the Malays, and, having failed to put up a fight to save the Union, the Chinese position had weakened even further. Thus Mr Tan Cheng-lock's creation of the MCA provided a representative organization for the Chinese community. The formation of the MCA coincided with that of a Communities Liaison Committee at the inspiration of Mr Malcolm MacDonald, to bring together the Malay, Chinese, Indian, Ceylonese, and European communities.

The situation was far from being stable enough at this juncture to favour the formation of a party which would represent all the communities, and the premature attempt by Dato Onn bin Ja'afar to do this resulted in failure. Having obtained promise of support both from Mr Tan Cheng-lock and the president of the Trade Union Council, Mr P. P. Narayanan, he launched the Independence of Malaya Party (IMP) in

September 1951, resigning from the presidency of UMNO for the purpose. But the new president of UMNO, Tunku Abdul Rahman, would have nothing to do with IMP and described it as a 'destructive move'. It was clear that the advent of IMP, founded on the principle of racial equality, had created profound misgivings in the minds of many Malays who feared that their 'special position' would thereby be undermined. UMNO now passed a resolution expelling members of the IMP.

One feature of the development was that Dato Onn was a Government official, the paid Member for Home Affairs. This was probably the decisive factor in his failure to maintain his position as a national leader. Reaction against 'Colonialism' had now reached Malaya, and Dato Onn's association with the existing 'Colonial' Government was sufficient to discredit him politically.

The consequence of this failure to create an interracial party was that the Malay and Chinese communities fell back on their community organizations, and the gulf between the two races widened.

Meanwhile, General Templer proceeded to step up the military operations against the Communist guerrillas with great vigour. For him, winning the jungle war was 'Priority No. 1' and he regarded his political directive to put Malaya on the road towards self-government as an ancillary weapon to his troops. To deny supplies to the guerrillas, he initiated a system of collective punishment of the inhabitants of 'New Villages' suspected of supplying them, imposing curfews and drastically reducing the rice ration. He would visit the erring village in person with an escort of eight armoured cars, and having rebuked the villagers and imposed his punishments, he would depart. It often happened, however, that directly he had gone the guerrillas would emerge from the jungle and shoot anyone who had 'collaborated' with him. The guerrillas had, in fact, the whip-hand in this respect and, moreover, the General's hands were tied by the fact that he was unable to resort to the extremes of retaliation which the guerrillas adopted without hesitation. It was thus difficult for him to defeat the Communists by making his rebukes and penalties more feared than the latter's savage retribution. Nevertheless he did raze one village to the ground in Province Wellesley as an example.

Although General Templer's energetic leadership did much to restore the morale of the Europeans, and also in a lesser degree of the Malays, on the political front his task was more complicated. Here the tangled skein of Malayan politics was even harder to unravel than the nexus of jungle warfare. On the face of things, there was an unbridgable rift betwen the Malays and the Chinese. The Communist insurrection was a Chinese one and enjoyed a large measure of support from the Chinese squatters. There were no Chinese troops on the Government's side and next to no Chinese police, though there were some Chinese in the Home

Guard. The only support on which the Government could depend, apart from the British troops, was that of the Malay police, troops, and Home Guard. It was essential, however, for the success of their operations that the Government should have the good will of the Chinese community as a whole.

The far larger section of the Chinese community in Malaya was urban and their interests being for the most part commercial and trading they were opposed to those of the Chinese Communists in the jungle and not identifiable to any extent with those of the Chinese squatters. Chinese urban labour, moreover, though it joined the new trade unions only in limited numbers, had interests nearer to those of the Chinese business men and retailers than to those of the guerrillas. If the Chinese community as a whole had been committed to the Communist rebellion the result must have been out-and-out civil war. This might well have involved the active support of the People's China for the insurgents, which, in the event, confined itself to verbal encouragement of the Communist guerrillas. The bulk of the Chinese were, in effect, 'sitting on the fence'. It was therefore of the utmost importance for the security of the regime that they should not be alienated.

It was at this juncture that an unexpected rapprochement occurred between the Malays and Chinese that took everyone outside the circles of Malay and Chinese leadership completely by surprise.

A striking feature of the Kuala Lumpur municipal elections held in February 1952 was an alliance between UMNO and MCA to defeat the IMP candidates. In this they were very successful. The MCA and UMNO candidates won 9 seats and the IMP only 2; 1 seat went to an independent. The elections were held on a very small electoral basis, but they aroused great interest throughout Malaya because of the test of party strength involved. This tactical understanding was to prove the beginnings of a wider agreement, resulting eventually in an alliance with the objective of Malayan independence.

The steps whereby the understanding between UMNO and the MCA gained strength are too intricate for full description here, but have been described elsewhere.[3] It is sufficient to record that by August 1953 the alliance had become a practical reality. During his visit to Malaya some twenty months before, Mr Lyttelton, the Colonial Secretary, had declared that Malaya would be given independence as soon as the various races of the country were united. When he said this he was most probably (and excusably) convinced that such a dispensation would come to pass only in the remote future, but the UMNO–MCA convention held on the 23rd of that month passed a resolution to work for a sovereign and independent State within the British Commonwealth and to demand that elections to the Federal Legislature should be held in 1954. It

[3] In particular in the writer's *Malaya: Communist or Free?*, chap. viii.

pledged itself to uphold the principle of full responsible democratic government. The aim was a legislature with an unofficial majority.

Faced by these developments, General Templer appointed a committee *of the Federal Legislative Council*, itself an entirely nominated body, to advise on the constitution of a new legislature. Not surprisingly, perhaps, considering its constitution, this committee advised that the new legislature should not have an unofficial but an official majority.

The remainder of the story can be told very shortly. In April 1954 an UMNO–MCA delegation came to England, headed by Tunku Abdul Rahman and Mr T. H. Tan, to request the Colonial Secretary to approve a legislature with an unofficial majority. Mr Lyttelton at first refused to meet the delegation, but when he did receive it he refused to accede to its demands. The consequence was that on the delegation's return to Malaya all those UMNO and MCA members on the Legislative Council walked out of the Council Chamber, and all UMNO and MCA members who were serving on boards and committees resigned from them. As a result the full burden of government was thrown on the officials.

In August of the same year the British Government changed its policy. All that it would agree to, however, was a legislature with 52 unofficial members. Thus a party which won *all* the seats to be filled by election would have a majority of five over the officials. This compromise the Alliance accepted and on the strength of it proceeded with its campaign for independence.

The reasons for the British Government's change of attitude are not yet clear; acceptance of the facts must have had a lot to do with it. The upshot was that under a new Colonial Secretary (Mr A. T. Lennox-Boyd) the Colonial Office and the Government of the Federation co-operated fully with the Alliance in working out a constitution for Malayan independence within the Commonwealth. At the elections held on 27 July 1955 the Alliance obtained 51 of the 52 unofficial seats.

The London conference held in January and February 1956 between the British Government, the Rulers of the Malay States, and the Alliance Party (as the Alliance was called now that it was reinforced by the inclusion of the Malayan Indian Congress (MIC)) agreed on a constitution which provided for one of the 9 Rulers of the Malay States to be elected from among themselves to be the Yang di-Pertuan Agong (Supreme Head of the Federation). It also provided for a parliament consisting of the Yang di-Pertuan Agong and two Majlis (houses of parliament), known as the Dewan Negara (Senate) and the Dewan Ra'ayat (House of Representatives). The Senate was to consist of 38 members and the House of Representatives of 100 members, but the first House of Representatives was to consist of 104 members as a transitional measure.

C.S.E.A.—M 2

On 31 August 1957 the Federation of Malaya became the eleventh sovereign member-State of the Commonwealth of Nations.

The first election to the new House of Representatives was held on 19 August 1959, with the following results—Alliance Party 73; Pan-Malayan Islamic Party (PMIP) 13; People's Progressive Party (PPP) 5; Socialist Front 8; Party Negara (PN) 1; Malayan Party 1; independents 3.[4]

It is very instructive to study the changes that had taken place in the representation of the Malayan communities since the elections of 1955.[5] But as a preliminary, note must be taken of the basis of the UMNO–MCA Alliance and later of the Alliance Party.

We have already taken account of the process whereby the Malay States came under British protection, and of the system of 'rule by advice' which was evolved. The treaties between Britain and the Malay States all recognized the 'special position' of the Malays as 'the people of the country', which was not affected legally by the great influx of immigrants since under the Protectorate system the members of the legislatures were all nominated—not elected (though some were nominated on the recommendation of special interests, such as the rubber and tin industries). The Union contemplated a common citizenship with equality of all races, but did not last long enough for this to be brought about; under the Federation of 1948 the citizenship legislation was from the beginning heavily in favour of the Malays, though an additional number of non-Malays was admitted by later legislation (account of which has been taken in Chapter 33). But up to independence the fact remained that Malaysians (whether Malayan born or Muslim immigrants from Indonesia) were 'subjects of the Rulers' and automatically Malayan citizens, whereas the Chinese, Indians, &c had to satisfy certain conditions of the law in order to become citizens. Under the treaties the Malays enjoyed a number of privileges, but citizenship became of decisive importance once elections were held.

How was it that this inequality of citizenship was accepted, even provisionally, by the Chinese when the Alliance was originally formed? The answer must, one feels, be this. The Chinese community as a whole were better off economically than the Malay community as a whole. The latter consisted largely of peasant cultivators living on a subsistence agriculture and their standard of living was lower than that of the Chinese in general. It is true, no doubt, that the majority of the latter were wage-earners and poor, but they were usually able to demand higher wages than Malay or Indian labour, and there was a large body of Chinese retailers, artisans, &c who were comparatively well off. Moreover, a small section of the Chinese community owned a considerable pro-

4 *Statesman's Year-Book, 1961*, p. 225.
5 See T. E. Smith, 'The Malayan Elections of 1959', *Pacific Affairs*, xxxiii/1 (Mar. 1960).

portion of the wealth of the country.[6] The alliance, therefore, was based on a tacit agreement to maintain the pre-independence *status quo*—the Malays retaining the political and the Chinese the economic ascendancy.

This agreement remained the tacit basis of the Alliance Party (in which the Indians took very much of a third place owing to their much smaller numbers and influence), but the question was how long the two majority races would accept the arrangement.

The electorate of just over 1,280,000 persons in 1955 was very largely Malay. It was estimated that of the registered voters 84 per cent was Malay, 11 per cent Chinese, and the remaining 5 per cent mainly Indian. In 1959 the electorate had increased from 1,280,000 to 2,177,000, and the proportion of non-Malay electors was considerably larger than in 1955. No official figures of the ethnic composition of the electors are available, but it was estimated to contain over 750,000 Chinese as compared with 150,000 in 1955, and approximately 57 per cent of the increased electorate was Malay, 36 per cent Chinese, and 7 per cent Indian.

Independence and the new constitution had made it much easier than before for non-Malays to obtain citizenship by registration or naturalization, and any person, irrespective of race, born in the Federation on or after Independence Day was automatically a Federal citizen. Nevertheless, there was not complete equality of citizenship and therefore of suffrage, and the allotment of seats by the Alliance had, in 1959 as in 1955, to be by prearrangement between UMNO, the MCA, and MIC. In 1955 the Alliance had chosen 35 Malays, 15 Chinese, 1 Indian, and 1 Ceylonese as its candidates for the 52 seats. When the time came for the allotment of the 104 seats for the 1959 parliamentary election, UMNO wanted 75 Malay, 27 Chinese, and 2 Indian candidates, whereas a large section of MCA wanted at least 35 Chinese candidates. The final compromise agreed upon was 69 candidates from UMNO, 31 from the MCA, and 4 from the MIC.

This dispute within the Alliance highlighted the discontent of many members of the MCA, especially the younger ones, with the Alliance agreement. The malcontents were impatient of the continued inequality of the races, however modified by law, and the resolution of the MCA to accept the compromise solution was agreed to only by a narrow majority. A number of members resigned from the MCA in consequence of this dispute and some of them stood as independent candidates at the elections, two of them being elected.

But the Alliance was no longer the only party in the field. The State elections which had preceded the parliamentary elections revealed the strength of the opposition. Chief among the opposition parties was the Pan-Malayan Islamic Party (PMIP), led by the Dr Burhanuddin who

---

[6] In 1951, 5,145 Chinese in the Federation paid tax on M$62 million in a total of 13,420 tax-payers, as compared with only 773 Malays paying tax on M$8 million.

had founded the Malay Nationalist Party in 1945. PMIP called for Malaya for the Malays in an Islamic theocratic State. The party promised to 'restore' Malay sovereignty by changing the constitution, and all treaties permitting the stationing of foreign troops in its territory were to be abolished under its manifesto. Dr Burhanuddin was an advocate of a 'Greater Indonesia' to include Malaya. The support for PMIP came almost exclusively from the east coast states of Kelantan and Trengganu in which there was a large Malay majority.

Another, and less formidable, opponent of the Alliance Party (at least in the coming elections) was the People's Progressive Party which denounced Malay nationalism and wooed the Chinese voters, standing for multi-lingualism and only one class of citizenship. In particular it condemned the Malay bias in the existing education policy (a policy initiated by the Alliance Government and the greatest bone of contention within the MCA). PPP also had a strong Socialist flavour and called for the nationalization of the tin and rubber industries. The Socialist Front (comprising the Labour Party and the Party Ra'ayat) also had a rather vague Socialist programme. The other parties were negligible in the number of their supporters.

The result of the elections held on 19 August 1959 was as follows— the Alliance, 73 seats (52 of its 69 Malay candidates, 19 of its 31 Chinese candidates, and 3 of its 4 Indian candidates having been successful); PMIP won 13 of the 16 seats in Kelantan and Trengganu; the PPP won 4 of the 20 seats in Perak; and Socialist Front won 8 seats (3 out of the 8 in Penang and 5 out of the 14 in Selangor). Dato Onn's Party Negara (which stood for a pro-Malay programme very different from that of IMP) won only the single seat in Trengganu contested by himself. The Malayan Party (a party of purely local significance) won a single seat in Malacca.

The trends revealed both by the State and parliamentary elections were of great significance to the future of the Federation and to that of the Chinese. Mr T. E. Smith gave his opinion that

> If the next few years see a continuation of the social and economic progress which has marked the first two years of independence, the narrow Malay communal parties may well fail to make much further headway, and the main danger to the Alliance is likely to come from the left-wing parties. It is significant that the Alliance was most unsuccessful in around the larger towns in Malaya. . . . In the course of the next five years the Malay vote, though remaining predominant, will continue to diminish slowly in importance. The extent to which the Alliance can find a real basis for Chinese and Indian support may therefore determine the outcome of Malaya's next Parliamentary election.[7]

The Communist insurrection was officially declared to be at end in 1960, though pockets of guerrillas still continued to exist in the jungle on

[7] *Pacific Affairs*, Mar. 1960. In the 1946 elections the Alliance won 89 of the 104 seats; the PMIP only 9 seats.

the Malayan–Thailand border. The British view was that the defeat of
the Communists was due to military action, especially the campaign of
General Templer. The Alliance Government, however, gave the principal
credit to the attainment of independence. The Prime Minister, Tunku
Abdul Rahman, said in December 1961: 'When we took over with independence in 1957, the Communists had been claiming to be fighting
for Malayan freedom. But once we had our freedom the argument
lost force, and by 1960 we were able to end the emergency.' The number of incidents of violence certainly diminished notably with the
coming of independence—but it must be left to history to apportion
the credit.

2. SINGAPORE

The political evolution of Singapore was faster than that of the
Federation in that the elective principle and universal suffrage were
introduced into its constitution at an earlier date, but slower in that
Singapore remained a 'colony' for some years after the Federation had
become independent. But since Singapore is politically an accidental
creation and not in any real sense a 'country' (being geographically and
economically part of Malaya) it is not realistic to compare its politics
with those of the Federation as if the two were of the same order of
magnitude. However, since Singapore was now self-governing and had
a population preponderantly Chinese containing a strong Communist
element, the part it played was of great significance.

Although on the resumption of the civil government in Singapore in
1946, it was planned to grant a certain measure of popular representation, the new constitution did not meet with local approval and the
Chinese were completely uninterested in the elections of 1948. In the
elections of 1951, the Progressives and Independents were opposed by
the Labour Party which demanded an immediate union with the
Federation. Out of the 9 seats, the Progressives won 6, Labour 2, and
the Independents 1. But out of the 300,000 qualified to vote, only about
20,000 actually went to the polls.

The British Government had in the meantime appointed a commission, headed by Sir George Rendel, to recommend a new constitution. In due course this commission recommended a legislature with 25
elected members out of a total of 32. Under the provisions of the new
constitution, which was brought into force by an Order in Council of
28 February 1955, the election of the 25 members was by universal
suffrage of resident citizens of the United Kingdom and Colonies over
21 years of age. Subject to the Governor's reserved power for foreign
affairs, defence, and internal security, the Assembly had full responsibility

for the internal affairs of the Colony. When the elections took place, more than 50 per cent of the new electorate voted.

A schism had taken place in the Labour Party in 1954 when one faction formed the Labour Front with the newly formed Socialist Party. Then in November 1954 still farther to the left there appeared the People's Action Party (PAP) under the leadership of Mr Lee Kuan-yew, who had the majority support of the trade unions at this time. The conservatives were even more divided—the Progressives having to compete with a new party of the left and with a branch of the UMNO–MCA Alliance. At the election of 2 April 1955, 10 seats went to the Labour Front, 4 to the Progressives, 3 each to the PAP and the Alliance, 2 to the Democrats, and 3 to the Independents.

There was no one party with a sufficient majority to form a Government, but the leader of the Labour Front, Mr David Marshall, was able to do so with the assistance of the Alliance. But his Chief Ministership was at once beset with difficulties, including strikes and violent agitation among the pupils of the secondary schools over the vexed subject of Chinese education. Then, in the external sphere, the question of the future relations between Singapore and the British Government were uppermost. The Federation was now proceeding rapidly towards independence with the blessing of the British Government and Singapore did not see why it should not do the same. The great obstacle to an understanding was the controversy over 'security', which hinged on the extent of the powers to be retained by the British Government to protect the Singapore base in the case of civil disturbance. This was the rock on which negotiations foundered when they were opened in London the following April. A complete deadlock ensued and Mr Marshall returned empty-handed to Singapore, and on arrival there he resigned.

Mr Marshall was then succeeded as Chief Minister by another member of the Labour Front, Mr Lim Yew-hock, a Malayan Chinese, who reopened negotiations with Britain the following year. In March 1957 a new conference was called and this time agreement was reached. Regarding the disputed composition of the Defence Committee, it was now agreed that it should consist of 3 British representatives, 3 Singapore ministers, and a representative of the Federation who should have the casting vote. The Legislative Assembly would consist of 51 members, elected by universal suffrage of all adults, male and female, on a common roll irrespective of community. The Queen's representative was to be a Malayan Yang di-Pertuan Negara, or Head of State.

A new self-governing State of Singapore was brought into being under the new constitution at midnight on 2–3 June 1959. At the first elections held in May PAP, under Mr Lee Kuan-yew, had won an overwhelming victory. Of the 51 seats, 43 were won by PAP, 4 by the Singapore People's Alliance under Lim Yew-hock, 3 by UMNO–MCA, and 1 by an Independent. PAP was committed to a programme that was 'Anti-Colonial' and decidedly to the left, but making a feature of coming to terms with the Malays of the Federation. In fact, a 'merger' of some kind with the Federation was part of PAP's election pledge. Malay was to be accepted as the official language of Singapore. Mr Lee was emphatically not a Communist in spite of the trade union support for him which included, in the beginning, that of Communist trade unionists, but the question soon arose as to whether he would be able to keep the Communist element within the PAP under control.

As time went on, it was increasingly obvious that the Communists were manœuvring for control of the PAP and that Mr Lee's leadership was consequently threatened. In August 1960 the latter declared that a collision was bound to take place between the 'adventurers of the left' and the 'colonialist imperialists' and that PAP policy was to allow them to tear one another to pieces.

More overt signs of the threat to Mr Lee's leadership of the PAP Government were the successes of two of his declared opponents at by-elections. The first success was that of Mr Ong Eng-guan at a by-election in April 1961. Mr Ong had been a PAP minister but had been compelled to resign after making a personal attack on the Prime Minister. Mr Ong had come into the limelight some years before when as Mayor of Singapore he had banned the use of the civic regalia inherited from the British period and had had the Union Jack removed from the Council Chamber. Only two months later, a second and perhaps more serious setback for Mr Lee Kuan-yew was the success at another by-election of Mr David Marshall, the ex-Chief Minister under the previous constitution, who beat the PAP candidate by a majority of 3,598 to 3,052.

At the time of this election, the question of a 'merger' with the Federation had become the leading political issue, and the Communists were opposed to it. They therefore gave their support to Mr Marshall, who also was opposed to the Prime Minister's 'Malaysia' policy, and at the same time they withdrew their supporters from the Legislative Assembly. The Barisan Socialis party of the extreme left represented this 'anti-Malaysia' line.

The indications late in 1961 were that the Communists were moving against PAP and its Malaysia policy, and that the Prime Minister retained only the firm backing of the civil servants and the University of Malaya in Singapore and its students (the English-speaking element of the population). The split between the English-educated and the Chinese-educated was an important political factor in Singapore as in Federation politics. In the second half of 1961 Mr Lee gave a long series of talks over Radio Singapore in which he revealed how the Communists were aiming increasingly to gain control of the PAP. The battle, he said, was now transferred to the industrial front and the trade unions.

In 1962 the scheme for a 'Greater Malaysia' by merging the Federation with Singapore and the British Bornean territories had come to the forefront of Malayan politics both in the Federation and Singapore, and Mr Lee favoured the scheme in pursuance, he said, of PAP's election pledge. But before the circumstances under which the 'Greater Malaysia' scheme are described, it is desirable to give an account of the relations between the Chinese of the Federation and Singapore with China subsequent to the success of the Communist Revolution in that country in 1949, since the significance of the 'Greater Malaya' scheme can be understood only against the background of these relations.

The People's China and the Malayan Chinese

When the People's Government was set up the Emergency in Malaya was some fifteen months old. It was to continue for another eleven years, for it was not until 1960 that it was officially declared at an end. The People's Government gave the Communist guerrillas in the Malayan jungle its support and encouragement as a 'people's rising', and this alone was enough to arouse the hostility of the non-Communist section of the Malayan Chinese community, that is to say the majority. Moreover, those non-Communist Chinese who were attached to China for sentimental and national reasons found in the earlier period of the Revolution that their own property and families or relatives in China were subject to the same stresses and disabilities which affected the bourgeois Chinese in general. It was only later that the People's Government, realizing the unwisdom of this policy, took measures to protect the property and remittances of the Overseas Chinese and made a bid to encourage their investment in Chinese undertakings. For some years, too, there was a rush of Chinese students from the Nanyang to China for higher education, but this flood had diminished to a trickle in recent years. The reasons were partly the hardships of life in China and the unpopularity of the 'half-time work; half-time study' system, but also the fact that the great pressure on Chinese schools and colleges led the authorities in China more and more to persuade Overseas Chinese students to stay overseas and to utilize the educational institutions of the countries they lived in. The natural disasters and economic setbacks of 1959–61 made the situation in China even less propitious for the overseas student.

Added to all this was the fact that the Malayan Chinese earned their livelihood within a capitalistic framework, and the Chinese have never been a people to quarrel unnecessarily with their 'bread and butter'. They had to come to terms with the majority races among whom they lived, and Singapore was the only State in Southeast Asia in which they constituted a majority. But even Singapore (as we have seen) was willing to adopt Malay as the official language, and to accept a Malay as Head of State. Mr Lee Kuan-yew himself took lessons in Malay.

From a 'bread-and-butter' point of view, education in English was preferable to that in any other language, and there was therefore keen competition for admission to the English schools. But while for many Chinese education in Chinese was a *pis aller*, many others of recent immigrant stock felt emotionally committed to send their children to Chinese schools. The emphasis on the Malay language in the Federation at the expense of Chinese was even more a source of discontent within the MCA with the Alliance Party than was inequality of citizenship. In Singapore the Nanyang University which taught largely in Chinese but in which, nevertheless, English was the official medium of instruction, was endeavouring to get its degrees recognized as a qualification for public employment on an equal basis with those of the University of Singapore (as the University of Malaya in Singapore became from 1 January 1962), but (at the time this was written) without success.

The tendency of the Malayan Chinese to remain culturally apart was not overlooked by the other communities, especially the Malays, and the idea of a merger between the Federation and Singapore was for long rejected by Tunku Abdul Rahman. It was only when he began to be faced with the possibility of a Communist Singapore on his doorstep that the Tunku veered round towards the idea of a merger to include the Bornean territories, which would give an opportunity for bringing Singapore under some sort of federal control. It happened that for considerations that were by no means identical with those that swayed the Prime Minister of the Federation, but which had much in common with them, the Singapore Prime Minister, Mr Lee Kuan-yew, was also in favour of the proposal.

3. A 'GREATER MALAYSIA'

In the Federation, parliament passed a motion in October 1961 agreeing in principle to the concept of Malaysia. Of the opposition parties in parliament, the Socialist Front accepted the merger in the debate, but later opposed it. PNIP opposed the idea as contrary to the interests of the Malays and suggested the inclusion of Indonesia and the Philippines in any larger unit. The PPP were also against the merger, on the ground that a full merger should not take place until after a general election in Singapore. In the Singapore Assembly, while the main opposition parties supported the principle of merger with the Federation, those with Communist sympathies took issue with the Government over the question of an early election and over the proposed control of internal security by the Central Government. The PAP Government's view was that they were committed to merger by their party's election manifesto and that the party therefore already had a mandate to reach agreement with the Federation Government on the subject. The only difference between Singapore and other States in the enlarged Federation would be that more powers would lie with the Singapore State Government. The Barisan Socialis (Socialist Front), which had been formed as a coalition against Mr Lee Kuan-yew and PAP, and which followed the Communist line, described the intention to go ahead with plans for a merger without first fighting an election on the issue as reprehensible, and they argued that the Central Government's handling of educational and labour problems in the name of internal security was an interference with freedom. The PAP Government could remain in office only until June 1963 (under the provisions of the constitution) but it was clear in 1962 that they intended to complete the negotiations over merger before they appealed to the electorate.

The merger proposals approved by both the Federal and the Singapore Governments provided that considerably greater autonomy for Singapore (to include education and labour as reserved subjects) would be balanced by a relatively small number of seats (namely 15 seats instead of the 25 or 30 it could expect on a population basis) on the Federal Parliament.[8]

In November 1961 Tunku Abdul Rahman went to London to negotiate for the Federation with the British Government. An agreement was reached, but whether or not the proposed Malayan Federation would permit the military bases to be used by Commonwealth forces for SEATO purposes depended upon conflicting interpretations of the agreement. In the event, it was a matter that would have to be decided by the new Malaysian Federal Government when it came into being. In May 1962 Mr Lee Kuan-yew went to London on a similar mission.

What of the attitude of the Bornean territories towards inclusion in the merger? In February 1962 a commission of inquiry appointed by the British Government under the chairmanship of Lord Cobbold to seek the views of Sarawak and North Borneo in this matter, met in Singapore. The report of this commission was released in June and is taken account of in Part VI of this book.

In mid-1962 the issue was by no means settled. English- and Malay-speaking Singapore people were enthusiastic about the merger, but the attitude of the Singapore Chinese remained uncertain until the referendum was held in September 1962. Mr David Marshall declared that the Chinese were not afraid of Tunku Abdul Rahman and his threats and some said they would fight for Singapore, and the Barisan Socialis attitude remained so extreme that Tunku Abdul Rahman had given warning that 'if the extremist and opposition parties want to create trouble and cause bloodshed after the merger and the creation of Malaysia, it is better that we do not have a merger at all'. In this event

---

[8] See T. E. Smith, 'Proposals for Malaysia', *The World Today*, May 1962 (p. 197), for the Singapore Government's defence of this allotment of seats.

the Federation would have to close the Johore Causeway (the gateway to the Federation) for its own safety, thereby bringing hardship to business men in Singapore and inconveniences to the people. The Federation's Finance Minister, Mr Tan Siew-sin, had pointed out that it might not even be necessary to close the Causeway, so vulnerable is Singapore, since a short and simple customs order levying an additional cess on rubber exports crossing the causeway would reduce what is today the largest rubber market in the world 'almost to the level of a tropical slum'.

Meanwhile the negotiations for the 'Greater Malaysia' were taking place. An intergovernmental committee had been appointed to work out the proposals, but by the end of 1962 it was considered unnecessary for it to hold any further plenary meetings and the work of drafting a number of points of detail was delegated to an *ad hoc* committee of specialists representing the four Governments. The motivation of the supporters of the new federation was undisguisedly 'fear of Communism', which was interpreted by the Malays at least in simpler terms as 'fear of the Chinese'. The Greater Malaysia, including the Bornean countries, would have a total population of about 10 million, of which the Chinese would account for about 4·5 million. Had it not been for the concentration of over a million Chinese in one small island—Singapore—it is unlikely that this fear would have received such an urgent expression.

But whilst the negotiations for the merger between the British and Federation Governments continued smoothly, and 31 August 1963 was fixed as the date for the Federation of Greater Malaysia to come into being, Mr Lee Kuan-yew was in difficulties in Singapore. The PAP majority in the legislature was falling away under pressure from the Communist-inspired opposition. On 3 July 1962 the PAP lost its absolute majority of one over all other parties when a woman member, Mrs Hoe Puay-choo, resigned from the PAP. The Prime Minister, however, persevered in his intention to submit the Greater Malaysia question to a referendum. This was held on 1 September. Three alternative forms of merger were offered to the Singapore electors on their ballot paper. Of the 624,000 citizens automatically registered as electors, 561,559, or 90 per cent, voted under the system of compulsory voting first introduced for the 1959 general election. Of those voting, 396,626, or 71 per cent, voted for Alternative A, the Government's proposal which allowed Malaysian citizenship to all Singapore citizens, and reserved autonomy to Singapore on matter of education and labour; 9,422, or 1·7 per cent, voted for Alternative B, of merger like any other State of the Federation; and 7,911, or 1·4 per cent, for Alternative C which offered merger on terms no less favourable than those offered to the Borneo territories. 144,077 blank votes, or 25 per cent, were cast under the influence of the joint campaign of the Barisan Socialis, the United

People's Party, the Workers' Party, the Liberal Socialist Party, and the United Democratic Party (the first three having 16 members in the Assembly, and the latter two none).

The result constituted a great victory for Mr Lee Kuan-yew's policy in the face of intense Communist opposition. But as the Singapore correspondent of the magazine *Malaya* remarked, 'The achievement of the referendum does not solve the basic problems of Singapore; it merely sets the constitution and ideological framework within which it must—and can—be satisfactorily found'.

On 2 February 1963 the Singapore police, acting on a decision taken by the Malayan Internal Security Council (on which Britain, the Federation, and Singapore were represented) arrested 111 left-wing politicians and trade unionists, including 10 women, and held them under orders of detention. Many of them had been detained by the previous Labour Front Government and had been actively associated with PAP. An official statement said that since the formation of the Barisan Socialis in July 1961, it had been increasingly evident that the party and United Front organizations were under the control of the Communists. The latter, working through the Barisan and United Front organizations, had done their utmost to sabotage the formation of Malaysia. By 8 February the number arrested had risen to 115. On 21 April, after a riot following a protest against the arrests outside the Prime Minister's office, five left-wing leaders were arrested including the Barisan Socialis leader, Dr Lee Siew-choh.

PART VI

THE CHINESE IN BRITISH BORNEO

36

DEMOGRAPHY

THE term 'British Borneo' (which was purely one of convenience and had no constitutional sanction) comprised the Crown Colonies of Sarawak (area 50,000 square miles) and North Borneo (area 29,387 including the island of Labuan (35 square miles) which was previously one of the Straits Settlements but which has been part of North Borneo since 1946), and the protected State of Brunei (area 2,226 square miles) making a total area of about 82,000 square miles.

Sarawak

Sarawak's total population at the Census taken at midnight on 15–16 June 1960 was 744,529, spread somewhat unevenly through the five administrative divisions. The estimated population at the end of June 1961 was 760,099, made up as follows:

Cultural group	Population	Percentage of total
Sea Dayak	239,409	31·5
Chinese	236,473	31·1
Malay	132,903	17·5
Land Dayak	59,267	7·8
Melanau	45,155	5·9
Other indigenous	38,562	5·1
Other non-indigenous	6,691	0·9
European	1,679	0·2

These figures ignore the balance of immigration-emigration, but the number of immigrants and emigrants in recent years has been negligible.[1] Nearly 60 per cent of the Chinese lived in or around the towns of

[1] *Sarawak, Annual Report 1961* (1962), pp. 7, 8.

Kuching, Sibu, and Miri. The majority of them were present-century immigrants and their descendants.

Rubber and pepper continued to be the main sources of income for Chinese agriculturalists.

Sarawak: Chinese Population

Year	Chinese population	Increase	
		Number	Percentage
1939	123,626	..	..
1947	145,158	21,532	17·4
1960	229,154²	83,996	57·9

Of the 229,154² total Chinese population (1960), 182,785 were born in Sarawak, 696 in Brunei, 621 in North Borneo, 1,365 in Singapore and Malaya, 1 in India, Pakistan, or Ceylon, 357 in Indonesia, 726 in Hong Kong, 42,893 in China, 57 in Taiwan, and 72 in other countries.

Easily the biggest tribal groups were the Hakkas and the Foochows, each of which (1960) numbered more than 70,000 persons; they were followed by Hokkiens (28,000), Teochius (22,000), and Cantonese (17,000). The remaining two groups were much smaller, the Henghuas (8,000) and the Hainanese (5,000). The Hakkas predominated in the First and Second Divisions, the Foochows in the Second Division, and the Cantonese in the Third Division.

Sarawak 1960: Total Population by Sex, District, and Community

(Abstracted from 1960 Census, Table 1)

District	All Communities			Chinese		
	Persons	Male	Female	Persons	Male	Female
Sarawak	744,529	375,846	368,683	229,154	120,369	108,785
First Division	247,954	125,847	122,107	97,297	51,228	46,069
Lundu	13,408	6,952	6,456	3,009	1,702	1,307
Bau	23,119	11,928	11,191	8,196	4,500	3,696
Kuching Municipal	50,579	25,360	25,219	36,721	18,627	18,094
Kuching Rural	98,877	50,339	48,538	39,433	20,952	18,481
Serian	37,378	18,783	18,595	6,627	3,658	2,969
Sadong	24,593	12,485	12,108	3,311	1,789	1,522
Second Division	109,422	54,489	54,933	12,081	6,914	5,167
Simanggang	40,389	20,513	19,876	5,139	3,005	2,134
Lubok Antu	16,129	7,643	8,486	1,896	1,035	841
Saribas	28,292	14,047	14,245	2,832	1,626	1,206
Kalaka	24,612	12,286	12,326	2,234	1,248	986

² The corrected total was 236,473.

Sarawak 1960

Total Population by Sex, District, and Community (continued)

(Abstracted from 1960 Census, Table 1.)

District	All Communities			Chinese		
	Persons	Male	Female	Persons	Male	Female
Third Division	261,487	130,436	131,051	92,712	47,677	45,035
Sariket	28,154	14,483	13,671	14,780	7,795	6,985
Binatang	34,693	17,517	17,176	12,520	6,379	6,141
Sibu Urban	29,630	15,114	14,516	22,698	11,771	10,927
Sibu Rural	47,652	23,840	23,812	29,349	14,516	14,833
Kanowit	41,588	20,617	20,971	6,304	3,313	2,991
Kapit	41,046	20,024	21,022	2,713	1,506	1,207
Mukah	38,724	18,841	19,883	4,348	2,397	1,951
Fourth Division	96,666	50,447	46,219	24,086	12,965	11,121
Bintulu	27,436	14,183	13,253	3,418	1,906	1,512
Miri Urban	13,350	7,092	6,258	8,012	4,259	3,753
Miri Rural	25,984	13,613	12,371	8,420	4,503	3,917
Baran	29,896	15,559	14,337	4,236	2,297	1,939
Fifth Division	29,000	14,627	14,373	2,978	1,585	1,393
Limbang	15,438	7,785	7,653	1,450	784	666
Lawas	13,562	6,842	6,720	1,528	801	727

Sarawak: Chinese Communities by Sex, 1947 & 1960

Community	1947			1960			Sex ratio	
	Total	Male	Female	Total	Male	Female	1947	1960
Cantonese	14,622	7,944	6,678	17,432	9,005	8,427	841	936
Foochow	41,946	23,655	18,291	70,125	36,715	33,410	773	910
Hakka	45,409	25,423	19,986	70,221	37,443	32,778	786	875
Hokkien	20,289	10,928	9,361	28,304	14,499	13,805	857	952
Teochiu	12,892	7,468	5,424	21,952	11,506	10,446	726	908
Other Chinese	10,000	5,974	4,026	21,120	11,201	9,919	674	886
All Chinese	145,158	81,392	63,766	229,154	120,369	108,785	783	904

Between 1948 and 1960 the net immigration of Chinese into Sarawak totalled only 7,779 persons.

As in the past, the Hokkiens, Cantonese, and Teochius were generally speaking the business men and traders, while the Hakkas and Foochows were the agriculturalists, and the Hainanose were the restaurant and coffee-shop keepers. Two groups not separately enumerated above were the Hinghuas (8,000) and the Hainanese (5,000).

Sarawak: Chinese Population in Districts, 1939–60

Census district	Total Chinese population			Increase or decrease	
	1939	1947	1960	1939–47	1947–60
Kuching Rural	18,450	23,695	39,433	+5,245	+15,738
Kuching Municipal	19,109	21,699	36,721	+2,590	+15,022
Sibu Urban ⎫	25,486	6,201	22,698	+6,280	+16,497
Sibu Rural ⎭		25,565	29,349		+3,784
Sarekei ⎫	15,136	18,723	14,780	+3,587	+8,577
Binatang ⎭		6,879	12,520		
Miri Urban ⎫	9,846	2,586	8,012	−381	+1,133
Miri Rural ⎭			8,420		+5,834
Bau	9,630	7,222	8,196	−2,408	+974
Serian ⎫	4,272	7,602	6,627	+3,330	+2,336
Sadong ⎭			3,311		
Kanowit	3,023	3,652	6,304	+629	+2,652
Simanggang	3,036	2,939	5,139	−97	+2,200
Mukah	2,514	3,366	4,348	+852	+982
Baram	2,341	2,682	4,236	+341	+1,554
Bintulu	1,879	2,056	3,418	+177	+1,362
Lundu	1,815	1,903	3,009	+88	+1,106
Saribas	1,934	2,047	2,832	+113	+785
Kapit	1,159	1,392	2,713	+233	+1,321
Kalaka	1,188	1,725	2,234	+537	+509
Lubok Antu	1,156	1,384	1,876	+228	+492
Lawas	789	940	1,528	+151	+588
Limbang	863	900	1,450	+37	+550
SARAWAK	123,626	145,158	229,154	+21,532	+83,996

North Borneo

The total population at the 1960 Census was 454,421—European 1,896, Dusun 145,229, Murut 22,138, Bajau 59,710, other indigenous 79,421, Chinese 104,542, and others 41,485.

The Chinese Population, 1911–60[3]

Census of	Number	Increase	
		Number	Percentage
1911	27,801	..	..
1921	39,256	11,455	41·2
1931	50,056	10,800	27·5
1951	74,374	24,318	48·6
1960	104,542	30,168	40·6

[3] L. W. Jones, *North Borneo, Report on the Census of Population taken on 10th August, 1960* (Kuching, Mar. 1962).

The tribal breakdown of Chinese (1960) was as under:

	Male	Female	Total
Hakka	11,895	6,168	18,153
Cantonese	9,855	2,413	12,268
Hokkien	2,809	1,213	4,022
Teochiu	2,056	424	2,480
Hailam (Hainanese)	1,170	124	1,294
Other Chinese	837	202	1,039

The population Census held on 10 August 1960 was the seventh to be taken in North Borneo, the decennial series having begun in 1891 and continued regularly with the exception of 1941. The *preliminary* population figures of the 1960 Census compared with 1951 were as under:

Population by Community compared with Census of 1951[4]

Community	1960	1951	Percentage increase
Dusun	145,650	117,867	24
Murut	22,343	18,724	19
Bajau	61,838	44,728	38
Other indigenous	80,002	61,690	30
Chinese	104,855	74,374	41
European	1,807	1,213	not significant
Others	37,833	15,545	143
All communities	454,328[5]	334,141	36

The following is a summary of arrivals and departures through the parts of the Colony during the period 1 January to 31 December 1960:

	Arrivals	Departures
Indigenous	2,406	2,349
Chinese	9,130	8,705
European (including Eurasian)	3,226	2,966
Others	15,252	9,758
Total	30,014	23,778

[4] *Colony of North Borneo Annual Report, 1960.*
[5] Corrected total, 454,421.

The *final* Census contained (Table 1) the total population by sex, census, and community, from which the following, giving totals and figures for Chinese only, are abstracted.[6]

North Borneo: The Chinese Population in Districts, 1921–60

Census District	Number			
	1921	*1931*	*1951*	*1960*
Sandakan Town	9,052	10,962	11,518	21,315
Tawau	4,368	6,177	11,118	14,881
Jesselton Town	2,150	2,696	7,539	14,529
Kudat	3,980	3,992	7,265	8,570
Tenom	1,352	1,491	4,055	6,131
Papar	3,968	3,562	4,311	5,370
Sandakan Rural	1,211	3,882	6,314	5,327
Jesselton Rural	2,547	4,080	5,511	5,171
Lahad Datu⎫				⎧ 4,808
⎬	2,755	3,952	4,168	⎨
Semporna ⎭				⎩ 985
Beaufort	3,476	2,945	4,011	4,618
Labuan	1,614	2,257	3,005	4,574
Tuaran	494	1,050	2,651	3,774
Kennigau	165	481	588	1,582
Sipitang	159	405	654	756
Kota Belud	167	418	410	676
Labuk	540	332	547	643
Kinabatangan	765	704	260	380
Kuala Penyu (Mempakul)	409	495	295	163
Ranau ⎫				⎧ 147
⎬	72	156	86	⎨
Tambunan ⎭				⎩ 110
Pensiangan	12	19	40	32
NORTH BORNEO	39,256	50,056	74,374	104,542

Although North Borneo is only a small country, it is one of the very few in Southeast Asia in which a reliable Census has been taken in recent years, and of the still fewer in which account has been taken of the Chinese. For this reason we should take special note of the information it gives.

The activities of the Chinese in North Borneo at the 1960 Census had about the same scope as at previous censuses. Much of the total area of small-holdings, particularly those growing rubber, and nearly all the smaller-scale businesses in the Colony were in the hands of the Chinese. In 1960 they numbered 104,542 or 23 per cent of the population. In the whole country they had increased by 41 per cent since 1951. More than

[6] Jones, *North Borneo, Report on Census.*

two-thirds of the increase had taken place in the five districts of Labuan, Jesselton, Tenom, Sandakan, and Tuaran.

North Borneo: Percentage of Locally Born, 1951, 1960

	1951		1960	
	Total	*Percentage*	*Total*	*Percentage*
European	1,213	34·8	1,896	35·9
Indigenous	243,009	99·0	306,448	99·4
Chinese	74,374	65·7	104,542	76·8
Others	15,545	51·2	41,485	36·1
All communities	334,141	89·1	454,421	88·1

Chinese lived in the towns or near them, and in this they form a contrast to the indigenous people who were in general not attracted to town life.

The increase in the number of Chinese was by no means all 'natural', but just how much was due to immigration was not known because even if accurate records were kept in the early days of the country almost all of them were destroyed during the Pacific War.

Of the total number of Chinese of 10 years of age and over 38,158 were literate and 30,691 were illiterate; 11,914 were literate in English, 2,224 were literate in English only, 1,264 were literate in Malay, 111 were literate in Malay only, 34,801 were literate in another language, 26,002 were literate in another language only, 1,022 were literate in English and Malay, 8,668 were literate in English and another language, and 131 were literate in Malay and another language. The 'other language' was presumably Chinese, and the figures indicate the popularity of Chinese education.

Brunei

A Census of the population of Brunei was taken on 10 August 1960.[7] The estimated population at mid-year, based on the Census figure and births and deaths registered and migration recorded up to the date of the Census, was 83,877, an increase of 6,204 since mid-1959. The Census figure for 1960 was an increase of 43,207 persons over the 1947 Census figure. The Malays formed the predominant race in the State, there being 45,135 Malays and 21,795 Chinese registered. The balance of the population 16,947 comprised indigenous groups including Kedayans, Dusuns, Dayaks, Muruts, Europeans, Indians, and Eurasians.[7]

[7] *State of Brunei Annual Report 1960* (Kuala Belait, 1962).

37

HISTORY

SOME account of early Chinese contacts with Borneo has already been given in Chapter 2 of this Survey, and the story is now resumed with the arrival of the Europeans.

Brunei

Early in the sixteenth century the Sultan of Brunei was overlord of the territories which are now occupied by Brunei, Sarawak, and North Borneo (including Labuan), as well as of Sulu and some parts of the Philippine Islands. In the sixteenth and seventeenth centuries 'European intrusion of an unenlightened character' reduced the power of Brunei. Lawlessness ensued, and by the middle of the nineteenth century piracy had become such a scourge that the official charts warned merchants against trading in these waters. In 1841 James Brooke obtained the cession of a large area of the Sultan of Brunei's territories, and subsequent areas were ceded to Sarawak at various dates up to 1905. Labuan was ceded to Britain in 1846. In North Borneo British and American traders endeavoured at an early period to get a footing, but it was not until 1877 that Alfred Dent and his associates obtained a large area in return for annual payments. Brunei now became the smallest of the four territories over whose total area it had once held at least nominal sway.

In 1888 an agreement was concluded with the Sultan under which the control of foreign relations was placed in the hands of the British Government, and in 1905, by a further agreement, Brunei received a British Resident.[1]

We have seen that Pigafetta did not find any Chinese in Brunei (or 'Borneo Proper', as it was afterwards called) when he visited it in 1521, but it is nevertheless certain that both before and after his visit a large trade was carried on direct with China in pepper, gambier, birds' nests, tripang, dried fish, rubber, wax, sago, and jungle produce.[2] The hills around Brunei town are terraced with the gardens of former cultivators. Treacher puts the total population of Brunei in 1889 at about 12,000–15,000, with about 80 Chinese and a few Tamil shopkeepers. He also tells us that in the old days, when 'it enjoyed a numerous Chinese

---

[1] See G.B., *Colonial Office List* (1948), pp. 196–7.
[2] Peter Blundell, *The City of Many Waters* (London, 1923), p. 126.

population', the surrounding hills were covered with pepper plantations, and there was a large junk trade with China.[3] 'But Brunei' (says Peter Blundell) 'gave up pepper and grew pirates and naturally the trade languished.' There is no pepper grown in Brunei now; there are few Chinese plantations, indeed, of any sort. 'Wise through experience, the Chinese let others sow and tried themselves to reap.'[4] (This observation holds good for all Southeastern Asia: the Chinese forsook agriculture for trade because the latter was more profitable.) 'The Malay cuts down the sago palms in the swamps, brings the trunks up to Brunei, rasps them into powder, and treads and washes out the raw sago for shipment to Singapore. The Chinese advances the money while he is doing his work, takes over the sago in exchange, and reaps the profits on the sale. This is also the case with jelutong. The Chinese is thus the "hated capitalist".'

There were few places in Brunei where the Chinese was not to be found:

. . . He goes out singly or in pairs in his clumsy row-boat far up to rivers where savage chiefs reign undisturbed over tribes of naked brown men . . . and seemingly regardless of the fact that he might pay forfeit for his temerity with his head, proceeds to swindle every man jack of the blood-thirsty tribesmen of their stores of gum, wax, rubber, rattans and other articles of value. He weighs the articles in his own scales, which all present are aware are doctored in his favour, and pays them with tobacco, knives, cotton cloth, looking-glasses, and beads of hardly any value at all.[5]

(The writer of this unsentimental account of the Chinese trader in Brunei concludes by wondering that the latter isn't murdered!)

The main history of the Chinese in British Borneo belongs, however, to the vastly greater territories on Brunei's borders and not to this small rump of a once considerable empire.

Sarawak

Within the last century or so political accident has drawn a line through the Chinese of Borneo, placing some of them on the Dutch side of it and some on the British, but the history of each section must be considered as complementary to the other. That of the Dutch section begins much earlier than that of the British—even before the Dutch had established their effective rule the Chinese *kongsis* were flourishing—and will be told in Part VII of this Survey. Both are continuations of the story of the Chinese in pre-European Borneo which began hundreds of years ago.

Both the Dutch and the British colonies have so far (and despite a three and a half year interruption by the Japanese) defied the gloomy prophecy of John Crawfurd that 'all attempts on the part of European nations to establish a permanent territorial dominion over Borneo, we

---

[3] W. H. Treacher, 'British Borneo; Sketches of Brunei, Sarawak, Labuan, and North Borneo', *JRASSB* (1889), p. 27.
[4] Blundell, *City of Many Waters*, p. 126.   [5] Ibid.

may rest assured, will, in the long run, be baffled by the insuperable obstacles of an uncongenial climate, a stubborn soil, a rude and intractable population, and the absence of all adequate financial resources'.[6]

It is not too much to say, however, that these European nations might not have been as successful as they were without the help of the Chinese.

In 1839–40 Sarawak (which comprised the districts now constituting the first and second divisions) was in rebellion against the tyranny of the Malay officials, insufficiently controlled by the Raja Muda Hassim, and the insurgents held out at Blidah fort in Siniawan district. The insurrection was suppressed through the instrumentality of James (afterwards Sir James) Brooke, who in September 1841 became Raja of Sarawak.[7]

It seems that before Sir James Brooke arrived in Borneo the scattered population of the extensive district which afterwards came under his control as Raja of Sarawak may have amounted to about 20,000.[8] Brooke himself relates that when he visited the River Lanou in 1839 he found about two and a half miles from the south of the river mouth a settlement which had been recently established by Chinese. It was on the same side of the river as Tumgong, and consisted of thirty men ('real Chinese') with five women of the mixed breed of Sambas. 'Nothing [said the future Raja] could be more flourishing than this infant settlement, and I could hardly credit their statement that this had been formed for only four or five months. The soil they represented as the most excellent, and none are better judges.' Many acres were cleared and under cultivation. Rice, sireh, sweet potatoes, Indian corn, &c, were growing abundantly and they were able to supply Brooke's party with seven piculs of sweet potatoes without noticeably diminishing their crop. They also showed their visitors some birds' nests, bees-wax, lignum aloes, and ebony collected in the vicinity.[9]

Brooke considered the mixed breed of Chinese and Malays to be a good-looking and industrious race, partaking much more of the Chinese character than that of the natives of the country. This mainly arose from education and early formed habits which were both altogether Chinese, and in religion and customs they likewise followed in great measure the paternal stock. '*They are a race worthy of attention* [he said] *as the future possessors of Borneo.*'

---

[6] John Crawfurd, *A Descriptive Dictionary of the Indian Islands and the Adjacent Countries* (London, 1856), p. 66. Commenting on the passage 'uncongenial climate, a stubborn soil, a rude and intractable population', an ex-North Borneo official of many years' experience says: 'Did ten words ever contrive to convey so many gross libels as these amount to? . . .' He points out that North Borneo is particularly healthy, the soil of prolific fertility, the Chinese of North Borneo was, generally speaking, the salt of the earth, the natives, also generally speaking, most tractable.   [7] *Encyclopaedia Britannica*, 11th ed. (1910–11), xxiv, 208.

[8] Anonymous article in *China Review* (1878–9), pp. 1–11. (The writer adds that this was thought to be an exaggerated estimate.)

[9] Capt. the Hon. Henry Keppel, *The Expedition of H.M.S. Dido for the suppression of piracy, with extracts from the Journal of James Brooke, Esq., of Sarawak* (N.Y., 1846), i. 67.

The numbers of this people could not be estimated, but they must have run to thousands—3,000 of them were said to be on their way to 'The Bornean territory'. The head of the settlement, which was near the town of Tumgong, was a Cantonese who had long resided in the vicinity of Sambas.

It was clear that James Brooke already had his eyes on the Chinese as future settlers in his territory, for he says, 'I shall be strengthened by incomers, especially Chinese'.[10] He also adumbrated his policy—'divide and rule is a good motto in my case'.[11] He thought that in attracting them to Sarawak their dissatisfaction with the territory where the *kongsis* still held sway, especially at Montrado, would stand him in good stead. He mentions a report received the day before which stated that a man sent by the Sultan to demand gold from the Chinese *kongsis* had been killed and that the letter from the Sultan, after being defiled, had been publicly burnt. The Chinese of Sarawak, Brooke added, were undoubtedly intriguing with those of Sambas.

Although the future Raja of Sarawak had formed a favourable impression of the Chinese as colonists for his territory, he was undoubtedly put on his guard against them by the reputation of the *kongsis*, even though he sympathized with their resistance to the tyranny of the Bornean native chiefs. In another place in his journal the Raja concedes that the Chinese have many good points—'they are active, industrious, and commercial', and he adds that considering the badness of the Government under which they have lived, deprived of trade and subject to all the evils of extortion and monopoly, one should give them much credit for the qualities they display.[12]

An early description of Kuching (1843) says that the *Julia*, a ship belonging to Mr Brooke, sailed every month for Singapore laden with antimony ore, and, at the same time, she acted as a mail-packet between Singapore and Kuching. At the point near the bend of the river was the fort. It was a strong building of large timbers and mounted 24-pounder iron guns in excellent condition. This was a very necessary defence, as the European Raja had many enemies. Another building, of which the top just appeared over the trees, was the Chinese 'joss-house' or temple, for there were many Chinese settlers in Kuching who were most useful as carpenters, blacksmiths, and agriculturists.[13]

On his return to Sarawak after an absence in October 1850, Brooke was pleased to hear that some thousands of Chinese had passed over from Sambas into Sarawak and thus had begun the long-wished-for migration.

In the Dutch-protected State, Sambas, southwest of Sarawak, there

[10] Ibid. p. 172.   [11] Ibid. p. 179.
[12] Capt. Rodney Mundy, *Narrative of Events in Borneo and the Celebes down to the occupation of Labuan, from the Journals of James Brooke Esq., together with the operations of H.M.S. Iris* (1848), i. 286.
[13] Frank S. Marryat, *Borneo and the Indian Archipelago* (London, 1848), p. 98.

were two distinct parties among the Chinese—those who sided with the gold-workers of Montrado, and those who, on account of their position, were under the influence of the Dutch. The latter were the agriculturists of Pamangkat and a few small companies of gold-workers. At the beginning of 1850 there had been trouble between the factions. The Chinese of Montrado had gained the upper hand and had driven the few Dutch soldiers into the town of Sambas, and then set upon their allies. The Pamangkats had fled for their lives into Sarawak, where they had settled down as agriculturists or among the established gold-workers. This movement was encouraged by the British officers, who did their utmost to aid them, and more than a thousand of them were supported by the Government at one time. They well repaid this attention (says St John) as in a few months they had tripled the revenue.[14] The Chinese immigrants attempted for years to form secret societies in Sarawak, but the Raja's vigorous hand had crushed every attempt. On the surface this policy appeared to have been successful—indeed, it was so far as the Chinese of the capital were concerned, but in the interior, among the gold-workers, the *kongsi* stood in the place of the secret society, and its chiefs carried on an exclusive intercourse with their fellow-countrymen in Sambas and Pontianak and with the T'ien-tei Wui (Cantonese Heaven and Earth Society) of Singapore.

Smuggling was one of their main activities, and some Chinese who were convicted of being connected with it were fined, and others were punished for gross assault on other Chinese. But these trivial cases were not the cause of the Chinese insurrection which took place in 1857. One of the real causes was that the second war between China and Britain was now in progress, and all the Chinese in Southeast Asia had been greatly excited by the rumour that the British had retired from Canton and that the Viceroy had offered £25 a head for every Englishman slain. Everywhere in Southeast Asia the secret societies were extremely active, seeing in this news an opportunity to stir up a rebellion against the British and to seize power for themselves. The Heaven and Earth Society sent an emissary from Malacca and Singapore to incite the gold-workers to rebel. The arguments used were not only that the British were crushed at Canton but also that the British Government was discontented with the Raja, Sir James Brooke, and that it would therefore not interfere if the Kongsi destroyed only him and his officers, and did not meddle with other Europeans or obstruct the trade.[15]

This alleged discontent with Brooke on the part of the British Government referred to the long campaign against him by his enemies in England and elsewhere. These for the most part belonged to that stay-at-home school of British humanitarianism which systematically at-

[14] Sir Spenser St John, *The Life of Sir James Brooke, Rajah of Sarawak, from his personal papers and correspondence* (London, 1879), p. 225 ff.   [15] Ibid. p. 293.

tributed the basest motives to the proconsuls of the empire, and it was alleged that the Raja had been guilty of brutality towards the Dyak pirates and head-hunters, who in reality were not pirates or head-hunters at all. Eventually a commission of inquiry was appointed to sit in Singapore and this exonerated Brooke, though it caused him great annoyance 'and introduced some embarrassment into his relations with the natives under his rule who not unnaturally conceived that he had forfeited the favour of his own government'.[16] This misguided opinion was shared by the Chinese secret societies.

Already in 1856, before the Raja's return, the Chinese *kongsi*, or 'Gold Company', had been behaving with so much violence that Mr Crookshank, who was in charge of the Government, thought it advisable to man the stockades in Kuching and to bring up a force from Sekrang. This action temporarily overawed the Chinese, but in the following year, after the Raja's return, they attacked the Government House and other British residences and murdered several of the British. Brooke escaped in the darkness by jumping into the river, diving under the bow of a Chinese barge, and swimming to the other side. After having occupied the capital for a few days and destroying a good deal of property, including the Raja's house and his valuable library, the Chinese retired, followed by a large body of Malays and Dyaks who had stood by the Raja all through, and who, intercepting the Chinese in their retreat, destroyed a considerable number of them.

Thus terminated [says Sir Spenser St John] the most absurd and causeless rebellion that ever occurred, which, during its continuance, displayed every phase of the Chinese character—arrogance, secrecy, combination, an utter incapacity of looking to the consequences of events or actions, and a belief in their own power and courage which every event belied. The Chinese have never fought even decently, and yet, till the very moment of trial, they act as if they were invincible.[17]

One thing the rebellion proved without a shadow of doubt was how firmly the Brooke regime was based on the support of the Malays and Dyaks, for at no moment was there any sign of wavering. Though more than 3,500 Chinese were killed or driven out of the country, the revenues from the Chinese soon rose, instead of falling, which was proof that smuggling had been carried on. The breaking of the 'Gold Company' was felt by the Chinese community as a whole as a great relief.[18]

The Chinese of Sarawak with whom the Raja had to deal were of an

[16] *Dictionary of National Biography* (1886), vi. 429.
[17] St John, *Sir James Brooke*, p. 312.
[18] Ibid. p. 314. The above account follows St John and other observers. However, an anonymous writer in the *China R.* (vii, 1877–9), criticizes Brooke's policy towards the Chinese in Sarawak, contrasting it unfavourably with that of the Dutch in their part of Borneo. The latter (says the writer) in modern times had adopted a policy of treating the Chinese with confidence, inviting them to take part in the administration of justice and regulating their taxation according to their own traditional arrangements and customs of the natives, whereas the writer quotes from Brooke's journal to show that he had early in his career acquired a

especially stubborn and lawless kind. Speaking at the end of the century
F. Wells Williams says:

> In North Borneo the protectorate may be passing through certain phases that
> marked the early years of Penang and Singapore. Here, and in Raja Brooke's
> dominion of Sarawak, the Chinese are for the most part either pirates or the descen-
> dants of pirates and the old hostility between them and the truculent Malays is apt to
> break out at any time in bloody frays.[19]

In the light of these happenings it is important to note the development of the point of view *vis-à-vis* the Chinese of the second white Raja
of Sarawak, Sir Charles Vyner Brooke, the nephew of the first Raja. He
is writing in 1866, nine years after the insurrection, and his memories of
the treachery of the *kongsis* had had time to soften. He says:

> John Chinaman as a race are an excellent set of fellows, and a poor show the
> Eastern countries make without their energetic presence. They combine many good,
> many dangerous, and it must be admitted, many bad, qualities. They are given to
> being overbearing and insolent (unless severely kept down) nearly to as great a
> degree as Europeans of the rougher classes. They will cheat their neighbours and
> resort to all manner of deception *on principle*. But their redeeming qualities are
> charitableness and liberality; a fondness for improvements; and, except in small
> mercantile affairs or minor trading transactions, they are honest. . . . The Chinaman
> would be equal to the master, or white man, if both worked fairly by the sweat of
> his brow. . . . Upon my first arrival I was strongly possessed by the opinion that the
> Chinamen were all rascals and thieves—the character so generally attached to the
> whole race at home. But to be candid, and looking at both sides, I would as soon
> deal with a Chinese merchant in the East as with one who is a European, and I
> believe the respectable class of Chinese to be equal in honesty and integrity to the
> white man.[20]

In spite of the tolerance of Sarawak's rulers towards them the number
of Chinese in that State did not grow with any great celerity. There were
about 5,000 of them at the time of the Census in 1871.[21] and in the later

---

distrust of the Chinese which did not allow him to treat them with understanding. This
isolated article, though it is written with skill and restraint, conceding to Brooke many fine
qualities, is not sufficient, of itself, to prove a case; but it nevertheless merits the attention of
the historian making a close study of the period. It must be borne in mind, however, that at
the time when the article appeared feeling was still high, and the party in England which had
persecuted Brooke may have had some influence on this anonymous writer's views.

[19] 'The Chinese Immigration in Far Eastern Asia', *American Hist. R.* (Apr. 1900).

[20] S. Baring-Gould and C. A. Bampfylde, *A History of Sarawak under its Two White
Rajahs 1839–1908* (London, 1909), p. 31.

[21] The Census of 1871 was, according to Baring-Gould and Bampfylde (p. 32), 'made in a
very imperfect manner', and from the allowance made by the report for its error we can well
believe it. These are the figures:

Malays	52,519
Dyaks	70,849
Chinese	4,947
Indians	364
	128,679
Allowance for evasion and omission 10%	12,867
	141,546

seventies the anonymous article above quoted does not place them above
7,000. After their display of turbulence in 1857 they seem to have sought
a quiet life. A visitor to Sarawak in 1890 notes that 'the Chinese are not a
communicative race', and states that he was naturally, therefore, unable
to obtain any information as to the average yield per ton of gold ore. The
women workers, he found, earned 40 to 50 cents a day (a good rate for
that period). At Lundu he saw a Government tobacco and coffee estate
which had been abandoned by the Chinese in order to grow pepper elsewhere. At Sibu there was a large population, mostly of traders, who exchanged European goods for jungle produce. It was noticeable that the
Chinese alone traded direct with Singapore; the remainder, both here
and at the other outstations, being merely agents for the business houses
at Kuching. At Kapit there was a good Chinese bazaar. In 1890 the
revenue farms produced: opium $144,240; gambling $34,096; arrack
$20,780; pawnshops $3,196—the Chinese, as usual, being the farmers.[22]

The year 1899 saw the establishment of the Foochow Chinese colony
at Sibu.

The second Raja Brooke (the first had died in 1868) had had the great
idea of bringing to Sarawak some experienced farmers who would settle
on the jungle land and show the Dyaks what might be done with energy
and perseverance. He said that the idea came to him during the years
when he was developing his garden at the *astana* (palace) at Kuching. He
and his Ranee had almost to stand over the Malay and Dyak workers in
order to get the lawns, flowers, and vegetables into shape. 'These brown
men simply could not probably would not work properly.' As he tried to
direct the gardeners in the difficult job of making the jungle take on
order he wondered if he could not find farmers in some overcrowded
land whose misery would make them listen to the appeal of a new home.[23]

The Chinese pioneer who was persuaded to come from China to form
the colony at Sibu or 'New Foochow' (as it was to be known) was a
Christian named Hwang Nai-siang from Mintsing in Foochow province.
He and his fellow converts belonged to the American Methodist
Episcopal Church. The party started off in a junk and at Hong Kong
they were joined by an American bishop named Warne.

The estimates from the Consular Reports,* 1877 (presented to both Houses of Parliament by
Royal Command in February 1878) are much more probable, viz:

Malays	60,000
Chinese	7,000
Milanuas	30,000
Sea Dyaks of the Batang, Lupar, and other reserves .	90,000
Land Dyaks	35,000
	222,000

* Cited by St John, *Sir James Brooke*, p. 379.
[22] G.B., Foreign Office, *Notes of a visit to Sarawak and its Trade*, by N. P. Trevenen (1891).
[23] This account of the Chinese Foochow colony at Sibu is taken from Frank T. Cartwright,
Tuan Hoover of Borneo; an Odyssey of Chinese Pilgrim Fathers (N.Y., 1938), p. 54 ff. and
passim.

On arrival at Sibu the immigrants were assigned plots of jungle land which, however, belonged to a private owner. 'By some erratic reasoning [says Mr Cartwright] the proprietor had prophesied that the people would be self-supporting in six months, but the strain of clearing and planting the land quickly disproved the prophecy.'

Dyaks were hired to fell the trees and to slash away the jungle vines and undergrowth. Slowly and painfully, with sickness and accident claiming their toll, small clearings were made. Rice was planted, but the crop utterly failed. Whereas in China the rice lands had been cultivated for many generations and all the stones had been removed, here, on the contrary, the earth was full not only of stones but also of widespreading jungle roots: the soil was porous and irrigation was therefore next to impossible. Crude heavy axes, made by local blacksmiths, and saws, equally simple, were all the tools at command. Torrential rains came on in their season and washed out the rice that was approaching maturity.

The second year there was a slightly better success, but heavier rains than usual back in the mountains drove out the wood rats, which swarmed down towards the plain and played havoc with the swelling heads of rice.

That the settlement eventually made headway was largely due to the American missionary, Mr Hoover, who, when the private ownership of the land was abolished, became an unpaid Government official and nursed the settlement into vigour. In 1912 the aged Raja wrote in the *Sarawak Gazette*: 'We have much to thank the Americans for, for their missionary work is quite promising, and they have introduced Chinese for cultivation of different kinds.' Another settlement of the same kind was made at Baram.

A Chinese, writing in 1940 of the Chinese settlement at Sibu, says that 99 per cent of the inhabitants were from Fukien province with a small percentage from Kwangtung.

This same Chinese writer tells us a number of other things of interest.[24] He says that the education of the Chinese in Sarawak had made progress entirely under their own efforts. The majority of all classes could read and write their own language. Of late years (pre-1940), fifty primary schools and ten middle schools with complete courses were established in Kuching and Sibu. The best known of them were the Fukien school, the Ming Teck public school, and in Sibu the Kwang Hua middle school and the Tung Hua middle school. All these followed the Chinese system of education.

After the 'Double Seventh' (7 July 1937) when the Japanese attacked China, the people of Sarawak (says Mr Hwang) were inspired with a spirit of patriotism; some returned to China to fight, others raised money or collected clothes for relief in the ancestral country. The funds collected

[24] James P. Hwang, 'The Chinese in Sarawak', *China Critic*, xxxix/6 (9 May 1940).

from voluntary contributions amounted to some $5,000 a week. Mr Hwang regrets that a Chinese consulate had not been established in Sarawak up to that time, and complains of the restrictions on trade imposed by the British after the outbreak of the war with Germany in 1939.

After the liberation of Sarawak from the Japanese, the Chinese resumed their active interest in the education of their children. Wherever they are concentrated in any numbers, their own schools, organized and financed almost entirely by the local Chinese communities, are to be found. At Kuching the Chinese Chamber of Commerce was found in 1949 to be levying a tax of its own on all incoming and outgoing Chinese cargo in order to obtain funds for the Chinese schools (a common practice with Chinese Chambers of Commerce in southeast Asia). When arrangements were being made for the establishment of a local authority at Limbang in the fifth Division (whose population includes 6,802 Malays and 742 Chinese), it was discovered that, whereas the Malays would be contributing only Malayan $220 in school fees towards the maintenance of the Malay school and its teachers (the rest of the money coming from Government grants), the Chinese would be contributing M $7,080 to the Chinese school, which, with four teachers, was completely independent of Government assistance.[25]

'Not only is much of the wealth of the Colony in their hands [says Mr Ian Morrison, writing in 1949], but they [the Chinese] are at a far higher stage of political consciousness and educational advancement than their neighbours.'

In Sarawak the British policy of preparing colonial peoples to govern themselves is being advanced mainly by the development of local government institutions. The 'plural' nature of Sarawak society is proving an obstacle to the establishment of local authorities. In only one Authority, at Limbang, has it been possible so far (1949) to bring in the Chinese. There the school fees paid by the Chinese, far higher *per capita* than those of the non-Chinese, are paid into the Treasury and paid out again to the Chinese school. The non-Chinese in Limbang have accepted the fact that the Chinese are accustomed to a far more expenisve type of education than the non-Chinese have had hitherto and that they are entitled to enjoy it if they are prepared to pay for it.

It is hoped that Limbang will provide a precedent for all other authorities where there are Chinese.[26]

Much more remains to be discovered regarding the Chinese in Sarawak, but there is enough in the available records to provide a complement to the histories of the race in other countries of Southeast Asia.[27]

[25] Ian Morrison, 'Local Self-Government in Sarawak', *Pacific Affairs*, xxii/2 (June 1949).
[26] Ibid.
[27] The investigations of Dr T'ien Ju-K'ang, who from 1949 onwards was in Sarawak studying Chinese associations in Kuching, have added much to our knowledge of the subject besides throwing light on Chinese social organization in general.

North Borneo

On 29 December 1877 a treaty with the Sultan of Brunei gave the title of three adjoining territories to Alfred Dent and his associates in return for a payment of $12,000 per annum. The Sultan appointed Dent and his associates and successors as Maharaja of Sabah and Raja of Gaya and Sandakan, with power of life and death over the inhabitants, and with all the absolute rights of property vested in the Sultan over the soil of the country, with the rights of making laws, coining money, creating an army and navy, levying customs, &c. The same day another treaty with the Pangeran Temenggong (Chief Minister of Brunei) was executed for the transfer of two additional provinces which were his private property. The Sultan of Sulu received $5,000 for his claims over North Borneo.[28]

In November 1881 the British Government granted a charter to the company which had taken over the concessions from Dent and his associates, and it assumed charge of the territory under the title of the British North Borneo Company.

When the company took over from the provisional association on 1 July 1882 the stations of Sandakan, Penangan (eighteen days' journey up the Kinabatangan River), Silam, Papar, Kudat, and Gaya had already been established, and every effort was being made to attract Chinese to the country. William Medhurst, who was appointed immigration commissioner, organized a system of obtaining immigrants from southern China which at first met with success. Streams of Chinese began to pour into North Borneo—whole families, often including grandparents—mostly of the labourer or farmer class, with a sprinkling of traders and shopkeepers; all were under advances from the company, and these advances were sometimes supplemented by grants of land with the produce of which the settlers were to repay their loans. This experiment was only too successful, for the inflow of immigrants was not properly controlled. The result was an overwhelming inrush which the young country could not stand. The labour market became over-stocked; the Government had to retrench, finding it impossible to give out unlimited loans; the traders who had come down direct from China found themselves at a disadvantage with the Straits-born Chinese, who were versed in trading with the natives and could speak their language; and many of the farmers, dismayed at the sight of the Borneo jungle, absolutely declined to squat upon the land allotted to them and took to picking up a living as best they could.[29] A reaction set in and a return current began which by 1883 had carried hundreds back to their native shores.

Nevertheless numbers of Straits-born Chinese continued to flock to

[28] George McT. Kahin, 'The State of North Borneo 1881–1946', *FEQ*, vii/1 (Nov. 1947), *passim*.
[29] Owen Rutter, *British North Borneo* (London, 1922), p. 131 and *passim*. See also Treacher, *JRASSB* (1889 & 1890).

the country, and the two leading Chinese firms in Singapore put on the North Borneo run steamers of their own which competed successfully with the European lines even though the latter were subsidized by the Government. When Mr Pryer took over Sandakan in 1878 there were only two Chinese there, and in 1883, notwithstanding the fact that many had returned to China, the number had risen to 3,000. A large number of Hakka Christians had settled happily at Kudat, where their descendants were living and thriving when the Second World War interrupted their prosperity.

The country soon attracted notice among capitalists in China too, and the first two companies to start operations were both Chinese—the Chinese Sabah Land Farming Company and the Yaen Yew North Borneo Cultivation Trading Company, with concessions of 40,000 acres and 10,000 acres respectively. A large sum was laid out also in a new Chinese immigration scheme which, however, failed, as did others in 1883 and 1902.

The failure of these schemes did not deter the authorities in North Borneo from initiating others. Mr W. H. Treacher, the first British Governor of British North Borneo, had declared in 1891:

Experience in the Straits Settlements, the Malay Peninsula and Sarawak has shown that the people to cause rapid financial progress in Malayan countries are the hard-working, money-loving Chinese and these are the peoples whom the Company should lay themselves out to attract to Borneo. . . . Once get them to voluntarily migrate and the financial success of the Company would, in my opinion, be secured.

Treacher's views have dominated the country's labour and immigration policy ever since.[30]

From 1924 to 1930 inclusive an average of 6,928 Chinese, 6,810 Javanese, and 3,866 natives were employed annually in North Borneo out of an average of 17,606 labourers in enterprises employing 20 or more persons. The Superintendent of the 1931 Census was able to declare with jubilation: 'The one bright spot in spite of all these adverse conditions [i.e. those arising from the trade depression] is the increase that is still shown in the number of Chinese who can fairly be regarded as the mainstay of the commercial and agricultural population.'[31]

The increase shown by the Census report was just over 27 per cent in

[30] Similar views had earlier been expressed by Joseph Hatton in *The New Ceylon, being a sketch of British North Borneo* (London, 1881), p. 124, who said: 'It would seem, then, that the principal hope of civilizing and making prosperous the islands in the Indian Archipelago lies in the power to attract the very class of labourer which America has obtained from China, with power to control and economise it.'

[31] To escape the charge of being destitute, each adult European or American was required to possess $500 and $200 for each dependant; for Eurasians the sums were $150 and $50; for Asiatics $70 and $10. Since naturalization was open only to persons who had lived for five years or more in North Borneo, a large portion of the Chinese population was subject to this law. Indentured labour was abolished in North Borneo in 1933; probably, as in the Netherlands Indies, it was no longer necessary to maintain an adequate labour supply by this means (Kahin, *FEQ*, vii/1).

the inter-censal decade, while the increase in Chinese females was over 72 per cent, 'thus justifying to the full the policy of state-aided immigration that had been barely started when the 1921 census was taken and which has been still further encouraged and developed in the last ten years'.

But the satisfaction felt by the authorities with the success that had attended their policy of attracting Chinese to North Borneo was followed later in the thirties by a mounting apprehension. In 1937 a total of 7,912 Chinese arrived, mostly labourers, which was a number much more than labour requirements necessitated. Therefore in 1938 a regulation was introduced raising the minimum sum required to be in the possession of Asiatic immigrants from SS $10 to $70 for each adult and from $3 to $10 for each dependent minor. Even so the number of immigrants for that year was 3,342. Already in 1936 powers had been granted to the Protector of Labour and other Government labour officers to deport Chinese on grounds of health, unsuitability for the work for which they had been engaged, unjust treatment by an employer, unemployment, &c.[32]

The general economic structure of North Borneo was not different from that of other Southeast Asian countries. Enterprises requiring relatively large outlays of capital (estates and timber undertakings in particular) were chiefly in the hands of Europeans, with a few wealthy Chinese participating. Some of the labour was indigenous, but the greater part of it was Chinese, Javanese, &c, imported for the work. The Chinese constituted by far the majority of the commercial and artisan sections of the community, while most of the natives pursued a subsistence agriculture.

To encourage the immigration of Chinese agriculturists, especially with the object of increasing rice production, the Government granted a free passage from Hong Kong to the relatives or friends of any Chinese freeholder within the State. The result of the policy for the encouragement of rice production was that by 1938 the area planted with paddy was 90,195 acres, second only to rubber, which occupied 126,640 acres.

In North Borneo the Chinese money-lender was adversely criticized. Laws were introduced by the Government to control his activities, but their effectiveness was not likely to have been greater than in other Southeast Asian countries; even so the maximum legal interest was 10 per cent per mensem on loans of $1 or less, 7 per cent on loans of $10 or less, and was not reduced until 1939, when the maximum legal rate was made 4 per cent per mensem.[33]

---

[32] Census, p. 1.
[33] Kahin. My experience as a magistrate in Malaya was that it was extremely difficult to ascertain what sum had actually been advanced as the money-lender (in Malaya usually a chetty and not a Chinese) made the borrower sign a promissory note for a sum much greater

As in Sarawak, a considerable proportion of the Government revenues in North Borneo was obtained from gambling and opium farms which were leased to Chinese. The policy followed, however, was much on the lines of that in Malaya. The chandu monopoly was taken over by the Government about 1911, and the farms were finally abolished in 1930.

As in the other countries of Southeast Asia, the Chinese in North Borneo concerned themselves with organizing and supporting their own schools, in which the Chinese language was the medium of instruction and the textbooks were, generally speaking, those approved by the Chinese Ministry of Education. Certainly in North Borneo there was little counter-attraction offered to Chinese parents for their children, for in 1938 only $33,000, a mere 2 per cent of all Government expenditure, was spent in education. This went to maintain or to assist 18 Malay vernacular schools and 1 Chinese school (96 pupils out of a total of 1,347 pupils for all the registered schools). To mission schools was allotted $7,800. There were also 72 unaided schools with 3,776 pupils, most of which were Chinese, supported by the Chinese community. The total enrolment for all schools was 8,912. No secondary education existed outside Chinese schools.

The Government did its best to control the instruction in Chinese schools, and in 1935 100 Chinese textbooks were blacklisted.

When the Japanese occupied British Borneo in 1941–2 the Chinese from the first adopted a policy of passive resistance.[34] There was a tendency for them to move from their usual centres of commerce on the coast or the main rivers and to establish themselves as peasant farmers in less accessible and conspicuous places. This meant a considerable curtailment of trading activity which in turn had a detrimental effect on the Japanese war economy as the occupation continued.

1949–63

While the Federation of Malaya obtained full independence in 1957 and Singapore was in 1957 given full internal self-government, the British territories in Borneo still remained under British rule (the Colonies of Sarawak and North Borneo) or British protection (Brunei).

A new constitution was granted to Sarawak by the Queen in August 1956. The Council Negri was to consist of 24 elected members, 14 ex-officio members, 4 nominated members, and 2 standing members appointed for life prior to the session; the Supreme Council of 10 members,

---

than he actually received. The remedy for usurious practices lay, it seemed, not in the reform of the law to any extent but in the extension of Government and co-operative society credit facilities. (V. P.)

[34] These facts concerning the Chinese during the Japanese occupation are taken from Tom Harrisson, 'The Chinese in Borneo, 1942–46', *International Affairs*, xxvi/3 (July 1950).

including 5 elected by the elected members of the Council Negri. The introduction of the elective principle with an unofficial majority meant that Sarawak was now on the way towards a democratic Government. North Borneo, however, remained for the time being a 'paternalism', ruled by a Governor aided by an Executive Council of 4 *ex-officio*, 1 official, and 5 nominated members. In Brunei the Sultan, in September 1959, promulgated a constitution under which there was to be a Privy Council, an Executive Council, and a Legislative Council.[35] The Legislative Council was to be presided over by the Mentri Besar and had an unofficial majority, having 8 *ex-officio* members, 6 official members appointed by the Sultan, and 3 members nominated by him. To those there were to be added 16 members elected by district councils.

The introduction of the elective principle into the Sarawak constitution was to give an outlet for democratic opinion and stimulated the formation of a number of political parties organized on a racial basis, a Chinese-led party being the first in the field. (Attention was given to this development in the Cobbold Report, as will be noted in a moment.)

But while the Borneo territories were proceeding by slow stages towards self-government, the proposals for incorporating the territories of Sarawak, North Borneo, and Brunei, with the Federation of Malaya and Singapore, into a federation of 'Greater Malaysia' promised to bring about changes of great political and economic importance for the Borneo territories. As the *Sarawak Annual Report 1961* stated in its General Review of the Year, 'The year 1961 may well prove to have been a turning point in Sarawak's history, not because of any cataclysmic change but because it saw the promulgation of an idea which has since dominated political thinking in the Borneo Territories'. This was Tunku Abdul Rahman's concept of a 'Greater Malaysia'.[36]

In June 1962 the Report of the Cobbold Commission, appointed to ascertain the view of the peoples of North Borneo and Sarawak on the proposed merger, was submitted to the British Prime Minister, Mr Macmillan. The Commission consisted of three British members (one being the Chairman, Lord Cobbold) and two members nominated by the Government of the Federation of Malaya, one a Chinese and the other a Malay.[37]

The Commission reached a considerable measure of agreement on the appropriate basis for entry of the Borneo territories into a Federation of Malaysia, but there was a fundamental divergence on the question of phasing. Many of the proposals were seen by the British members of the Commission as objectives that should be progressively worked towards, and where possible introduced during a transitional period, whereas they

[35] *Brunei Annual Report 1960.*   [36] See pp. 354–6, 381.
[37] *Report of the Commission of Enquiry, North Borneo and Sarawak 1962*, Cmnd. 1794, Aug. 1962.

were seen by the Malayan members as recommendations which should start to take effect immediately on the creation of Malaysia. The Report recommended that a decision of principle about the future of the territories should be taken by the two Governments as soon as possible and that the existing constitution of the Federation of Malaya should be taken as the basis of the constitution of the new Federation. The Commission encountered some opposition to the name 'Malaysia', particularly from a number of non-Muslim elements of the population of Sarawak, stemming from the same cause as anxieties regarding religion, language, and the Head of the Federation. The Commission, however, did not see how any other name would be appropriate in view of the geographical-historical relevance of the name of Malaysia and its current usage. There was a difference of opinion between the British and the Malayan members of the Commission regarding the position of religion in the constitution, the British members recommending that the Malayan Federal provision that Islam is the national religion should not be extended to the Borneo territories, and the Malayan members recommending that it should be so extended.

As regards the 'national language', this should be left to the peoples of the Borneo territories to decide for themselves, but a majority opinion favoured Malay and English as the official languages in the Borneo States. Recommendations were also made regarding citizenship of the proposed Federation. On this latter point there was a great deal of feeling on the part of the Chinese (which will in a moment be explained).

Uneasiness was first felt among the other races at the time of the first elections when the first political party, the Sarawak United Peoples Party (SUPP), was formed with predominantly Chinese leadership. Taken as a signal for the beginning of the bid for power of the non-natives at the time when the natives felt themselves not yet in a position to compete, this set in motion a strain in race relations springing from an unbalance in economic power. For this reason the Party Negara (Panas) and later the Sarawak National Party (SNP) with native leadership came into being followed by the formation of the Barisan Anak Jati Sarawak (Barjasa) and its proposal to enter into an alliance with SNP. The proposals for a Malaysian Federation and the prospect of independence within the Federation had served to accentuate these developments. The Commission, therefore (says the Report), fully understood the reasons for the alignment of political forces along racial lines. Nevertheless, it was a matter of the gravest concern. In the absence of some project like Malaysia, the Chinese, with their rapidly increasing population and their long start over other races in education, could expect, when independence came, to be in an unassailable position in Sarawak. This, in turn, could put the Communists, with their highly developed organization, to work on the fears and frustrations of the great body of non-Communist Chinese, in an equally unassailable position. The Malaysia proposals would interfere with this development. Communist elements had therefore worked ceaselessly to exaggerate the fears which the Chinese community as a whole and members of other communities had of Malay domination and to make capital out of every possible issue, e.g. a special position for the natives, citizenship, national language, and religion. They had also worked on the emotions of a large body of younger Chinese who had been educated in Chinese schools, who were strongly nationalistic, and who had feelings of frustration and anxiety about their prospects.

As regards citizenship, the Chinese felt acutely about this. Their anxieties derived above all from a fear that, even if their forebears had been born in Sarawak, they would under 'Malaysia' become second-class citizens with a status inferior to that of the indigenous races. They were anxious that the future citizenship law should make no change in the current arrangement under which all persons born in Sarawak were automatically citizens without any residential qualifications, and persons who had resided in Sarawak for a total of 5 years (including the last 12 months continuously) out of the 8 years immediately preceding the date of application were eligible to apply for nationalization.

The Commission recommended that a citizen of the United Kingdom and Colonies born in Sarawak or North Borneo should by operation of law be a citizen of Malaysia, that a person should be eligible for registration as a citizen if he or she had resided in Malaysian territory for eight years out of the preceding twelve and that a person born in Malaysia after its creation should be a Malaysian citizen by operation of law, provided that one of his or her parents was a citizen or a permanent resident of the Federation.

The Chinese witnesses whom the Commission interviewed also insisted that English should be retained as an official language indefinitely, and that if Malay or Iban or both were made official languages, Chinese (Mandarin) should be added too, and that the present British officers should be retained.

The general attitude of the Chinese in North Borneo towards the proposals for a Greater Malaysia were similar to those of the Chinese in Sarawak, with the important difference that there was no sign in North Borneo of the extreme views which were expressed to the Commission in Sarawak in opposition to the scheme by some of the delegations of the SUPP which were undoubtedly influenced by Communists.

Late in April 1963 the Sarawak Government tightened security measures to prevent any harmful action by a minority of Chinese Communists. A Government order called on non-native holders of gun licences residing in certain areas to hand over their weapons and ammunition immediately to the police. A Government spokesman said:

'This group is entirely of Chinese make-up and its members owe loyalties not to Sarawak but to the cause of international Communism. Their aim is to establish a Chinese Communist State right here in Sarawak.' The same spokesman also stated that groups of young Chinese in the First, Second, and Third Divisions of Sarawak had been disappearing from their homes to undergo military training in the jungle.

Malaysia

While this edition of the work was in the press, the following developments took place.

In the first half of 1963 President Sukarno declared his opposition to the creation of Malaysia on the grounds that the willingness of the peoples of Sarawak and Sabah (North Borneo) to be included in the proposed Federation had not been correctly ascertained. As a concession to President Sukarno, the establishment of Malaysia was postponed for sixteen days in order to allow a United Nations commission time to report on their visit to the Borneo territories. In due course the United Nations Commission confirmed the report of the Cobbold Commission, and the Federation of Malaysia (comprising Malaya, Singapore, Sarawak, and Sabah — but not Brunei) was proclaimed on 16 September 1963. President Sukarno, however, continued his opposition to the Federation, and announced a policy of 'confrontation', which apparently included every form of hostile operation short of an actual declaration of war.

PART VII

THE CHINESE IN INDONESIA

38

DEMOGRAPHY

MR DONALD E. WILLMOTT, who has made a special study of the Chinese in Indonesia, says:

Taking into account actual and probable immigration figures and birth and death rates, the writer estimates that there were some 2,100,000 Chinese in Indonesia in 1950, of whom about 1,500,000, or over 70%, were born there. The foreign-born Chinese population, according to the same estimate, was about 600,000. Since 1950 no significant amount of Chinese immigration into Indonesia has been permitted, and the percentage of Totoks [*Sinkhehs*], as compared with that of Peranakans [Indonesia-born Chinese], has been decreasing at the rate of about one per cent per year.[1]

In 1962 no census had been held in Indonesia since 1930, but a report from Jakarta of 22 December 1961 gave the total population of Indonesia as 95,889,000, and stated that the annual rate of increase was 2·3 per cent.[2]

The *Statistical Yearbook of Indonesia, 1959*, gives tables of arrivals and departures by nationality from which the following is abstracted:

Indonesia: Migration

	Arrivals (Chinese)	Total (all races)		Departures (Chinese)	Total (all races)
1938	66,705	119,818	1938	44,804	102,961
1939	46,654	95,573	1939	38,875	87,899
1940	36,190	69,693	1940	49,616	81,372
..	..	..	..	..	..
1951	20,701	57,165	1951	21,141	71,095
1957	10,658	74,782	1957	14,870	81,414
1958	7,432	57,776	1958	9,532	7,995

[1] *The National Status of the Chinese in Indonesia, 1900–58*, 2nd ed. (N.Y., 1961), p. 68.
[2] *The Times*, 22 Dec. 1961.

After Indonesian independence the number of departures tended to exceed the number of arrivals, and this tendency had been greatly accentuated since the application of the new laws in 1959 onwards prohibiting aliens to engage in certain occupations. (This movement is described in Chapter 48, but we are here concerned only with its demographic effects.) Some 300,000 Chinese nationals were estimated to have been displaced by the new laws, and a large proportion of them were awaiting repatriation to China and some thousands had by 1962 already departed.

The effect of the nationality laws and the dual citizenship agreement with China[3] was to increase the number of Chinese who were Indonesian nationals and to decrease the number of Chinese who were Chinese nationals. Writing of an earlier period, Mr Willmott says:

If our estimates are correct, from 40% to 45% of the Chinese living in Indonesia in 1955 were considered Chinese subjects. Whether the new round of options called for in the Dual Citizenship Treaty will substantially change this picture is a matter for speculation. But it appears that, under any circumstances except mass deportation, there will soon be at least one million alien Chinese in Indonesia.[4]

What is a 'Chinese' in this Indonesian setting. Mr Willmott considers that

There is virtually no ambiguity about who is to be considered Chinese. Although a great many Chinese men have taken Indonesian wives, especially before World War I, the children of those marriages have almost always been raised as Chinese. Even the most assimilated and acculturated Chinese families have usually retained their Chinese names.[5]

To arrive at the number of Chinese in Indonesia in 1960 fitting into this definition, the reasonable course would be to take Mr Willmott's 1950 figure of 2,100,000, to add a national increase of (say) 2·5 per cent per annum (see Mr T. E. Smith's remarks at p. 2), and to deduct an estimate of the loss through excess of departures over arrivals. On this basis, 2·1 million at 2½ per cent increase per annum would be 2,688,210. The net loss from 1950–8 was about 2,000–4,000 per annum, but from 1959 onwards when mass repatriation was in progress the net loss would be far greater. Therefore if we adopt a round figure of 2·5 million Chinese in Indonesia in 1960, this will be about as near as we can get until new census figures are available.[6]

3 See above, pp. xv–xvi and below, pp. 481–6.
4 *Chinese in Indonesia*, p. 69.
5 *The Chinese of Semarang* (N.Y., 1960), p 15.
6 I am indebted to Mr R. E. H. Waring for the following information regarding Portuguese Timor: 'There are about 5,000 Chinese in Timor, and they retain an entirely Chinese way of life mixing in to only a very minor extent with the local Timorese. They marry local Chinese

Having committed ourselves to this estimate, let us now review the demographic picture historically in the light of the more satisfactory figures that were available during the Dutch period.

The Chinese community of Indonesia was made up of a number of heterogeneous components differing from one another by reason of the period of time they had resided in Indonesia—which might range from over three centuries to a single day—by reason of the different tribes in China from which they had been drawn, and by reason of the difference in their occupations, not to mention their politics.

At the beginning of the nineteenth century there were estimated to be about 100,000 Chinese in Java and Madura. In the year 1815 they were enumerated at 94,441.[7] The figures for the Outer Islands are conjectural, but will be given as is appropriate in the historical synopsis to come. The rate of increase of the community is indicated by the figures for Java and Madura for 1860—namely: Indonesians 12,514,000; Chinese 149,000.

It will be seen from these figures that the number of Chinese in Indonesia had more than doubled since the beginning of the century. The increase was greatest during the decade 1920–30 and amounted in that period to an average of 4·3 per cent per annum. This figure, compared with the normal increase of a people under settled conditions which is from 1 to 2 per cent, is indeed high.

Although no exact figures were adduced by the Census, it is safe to say that in 1930 the Chinese community was divided roughly into 750,000 born in Indonesia and about 450,000 immigrants. (The

---

girls and only a very few ever marry Europeans or Timorese. They do not send their bodies back to China for burial nor do they maintain much in the way of relations with other Chinese in Continental China. There is some little correspondence with Chinese in Continental China but this is almost entirely of a commercial nature. They do not go to Continental China on holiday or save up to go there "to die" or anything of that sort. They do maintain relations with other Chinese both in Macao and in Hong Kong, but here again these are almost entirely business relations. They are for the most part engaged in clerical jobs or in commerce where again they keep themselves very much to themselves. There is a Chinese (Formosan) Consulate in Timor but they have little or no relations either commercial or otherwise with the Formosan Chinese. For the most part they have retained their Chinese nationality and have not integrated with the local population. A few, however, have become Portuguese and send their children to study in Portugal. They are of the Cantonese linguistic group and they are a growing community. Politically they are indifferent to the Indonesians and to Indonesian pressure against Portuguese Timor. As far as an outsider can know, they do not maintain any particular relations with Chinese or others in Indonesia and are completely content with the status quo. They are not regarded as a "security risk" by the Portuguese but they are a closely knit community who mind their own business and who do not want war, an Indonesian invasion or anything which would upset their businesses or way of life.'

[7] Sir Thomas Stamford Raffles, *History of Java* (London, 1817), table facing p. 70 (51,332 males: 43,109 females in a total population of 4,615,270). Dr Vlekke remarks: 'I am inclined to be rather doubtful about Raffles' statistics. He had little means of *exact* information regarding the number of Chinese or of any other population group.'

Indonesia: Population in Various Years[8]
(in thousands)

Year	Indonesians	Europeans	Chinese	Arabs	Other Asiatics	Total
			Java and Madura			
1860	12,514	..	149	6	..	..
1870	16,233	37	175	8	..	..
1880	19,541	44	207	11	..	..
1890	23,609	55	242	14	..	..
1900	28,386	72	277	18	..	..
1905	29,979	73	295	19	..	..
1920	34,429	134	384	28	3	34,978
1930	40,981	193	582	42	11	41,719
			Total Indonesia			
1860	..	44	221	9	..	..
1870	..	49	260	13	..	..
1880	..	60	344	16	..	..
1890	..	74	461	22	..	..
1900	..	91	537	27	..	..
1905	37,348:	95	563	30	..	..
1920	48,300:	168	809	45	22	49,344
1930	59,138:	240	1,233	71	45	60,727

Indonesian-born were known as *Peranakans*, and the China-born as *Sink-hehs*.) Of the group of Indonesian-born 500,000 had fathers who were also born in the country, and belonged therefore to families who had been in the Indies for more than one generation. The immigrant group divides itself into those who are only temporarily resident in the country and who pass frequently to and fro, and those who definitely settle, marry, and beget children. The growth in size of the Chinese community was thought to be due mainly to the increase in the number of the class who settle permanently and to the natural increase among those who have been in the country for more than one generation. Other factors such as the fecundity of marriages and the death-rate (though improved hygiene has undoubtedly affected both infant mortality and the expectation of life) are considered to have been of much smaller importance than the increase in the number of newcomers who become permanently domiciled and the rise in the birth-rate due to this cause. Nor is concubinage thought to have contributed significantly to the increase in the Chinese population.

In Java and Madura the majority of the Chinese adults were born in Indonesia and only about 30 per cent were born elsewhere; the Western

[8] *Statistical Pocket Book of Indonesia, 1941* (Batavia), p. 5.

Division of Borneo also had a large proportion of native-born Chinese. But in the other parts of Indonesia, especially in Sumatra, the foreign-born Chinese were in the majority. In Sumatra, of 100 adults of 20 years of age and over 80 were born outside Indonesia.[9]

It was only within the decade or so before 1930 that the immigration of Chinese women attained dimensions worth mentioning. There were fewer women than men amongst the Chinese inhabitants because few women were included among the immigrants, but amongst those born in Indonesia women were in the majority. The distribution of women was very unequal, but the overall ratio was 642 women to every thousand men: in Sumatra there were only 450 women to every thousand men. Many of the Chinese coolies in Sumatra's East Coast were unmarried.[10]

Now as to the tribes from which these Indonesian Chinese are drawn. Those who came first of all to the country in large numbers were Hokkiens, that is to say natives from Fukien Province in the neighbourhood of Amoy and not the Hokchius from the same province of China. The numbers of other tribes of Chinese do not appear to have been considerable until the nineteenth century. The Hakkas (Khehs), however, first settled in West Borneo about 1740–5. They and the Teochius, greatly in demand as estate coolies, began to be numerous in east Sumatra, Bangka, and Billiton in the second half of the nineteenth century, when Western agriculture and mining began to develop. By 1930 there were about 550,000 Hokkiens in Indonesia. In Java and Madura they formed the great majority, and in the east of the Archipelago accounted for more than half of the Chinese inhabitants. In Sumatra, with the exception of the Division of Sumatra's West Coast and Bengkalis (in the latter of these divisions many of them were occupied in fisheries) and also in the Western Division of Borneo, they were less numerous than the Hakkas and the Teochius.

Since in some parts of Indonesia (e.g. a few remote parts of the Outer Islands, the interior of Borneo, and some parts of the Moluccas) it was possible only to carry out a simple enumeration, no distinction was here made between the various tribes of Chinese, but it is probable that the great majority of the race residing in West Borneo were Hakkas; 200,000 of this tribe were enumerated in the area of the complete census—some 45,000 in Bangka and Billiton, nearly 14,000 in the estate area of

---

[9] The proportion of Indonesian-born to foreign-born Chinese varied very much indeed with the tribe. Only 22 per cent of Hokkiens, for example, were born outside Indonesia as compared with 66 per cent for Cantonese and 62 per cent for Teochius (*Census of the Netherlands Indies* (1930), p. 294). For many other interesting demographical details, especially regarding the sex ratios, the reader is referred to the reprint of *Chinese and Other Non-Indigenous Orientals in the Netherlands Indies* here cited. It is mentioned, for instance, that among the young women born in the Indies there were many who were later divorced.

[10] Ibid. p. 6.

Sumatra's East Coast, and some 65,000 in East Java. There were also small communities of them elsewhere.

In numerical position next after the Hakkas, the Cantonese (Kwong Fus) aggregated about 135,000 in the Indies, fairly distributed over the entire Archipelago, but were slightly more numerous in the estate area of the East Coast of Sumatra, in South Sumatra, East Borneo, and Celebes.

Less numerous than the Cantonese (Kwong Fus) were the Teochius. The great majority of their total of 90,000 were to be found in the large circle round Singapore; about 32,000 in the estate area of Sumatra's East Coast, also in Rhio (Riouw), Inderagiri, and Djambi, and almost 22,000 of them in the northwest part of Borneo.

From the large percentage of them born in Indonesia, the more normal sex ratio, and their fairly regular age-groups, it was to be assumed that the majority of the Hokkien community were domiciled in the country. This was also true of the Hakkas in western Borneo. The other groups of Chinese consisted of migrants. 'If these other Chinese races [i.e. tribes] are becoming domiciled, the movement must still be young', says the census report.

Occupation

Of all the Chinese working in Indonesia the merchants in 1930 formed the largest group (172,000, or nearly 37 per cent of the total). More than half of the working Hokkiens were merchants, but in West Java in the neighbourhood of Batavia and in the West Coast of Sumatra the larger number had taken to agriculture and market-gardening, while in Bagan Si Api Api in Sumatra the Hokkiens were generally fishermen. The Hakkas of Java and Madura also included many merchants, but the tribe was also interested in industry. In Sumatra they were engaged in mining and in West Borneo in agriculture. The Teochius were also mostly engaged in agriculture and market-gardening, but in the estate area of the East Coast of Sumatra the majority of them were coolies on tobacco estates, for which work they appeared to be especially adapted. In West Borneo business claimed this tribe as well as agriculture. In the other parts of the Indies the majority of them were merchants, while a few engaged in industrial enterprises.

The Cantonese were rather sharply differentiated from the other Chinese tribes by the fact that two-fifths of them were employed in industry in contradistinction to trade or the production of raw materials. In Sumatra, however, many Cantonese were also agriculturists, market-gardeners, or miners. In Bangka they formed an important group among the mine workers, while in Palembang numbers of Cantonese artisans were employed in the petroleum industry.

The Chinese immigrants were usually limited to the craft or occupation which brought them to the country, but among the descendants of this race there was a broader choice of occupation.

39

CHINESE, DUTCH, AND ENGLISH IN THE EARLIER DAYS

THE principle here adopted is the same as that followed for the other countries of Southeast Asia, namely, that interest in the Chinese is reserved for them from the time when they formed more or less settled communities in the region, and little account is taken of trading voyages or the visits of isolated travellers.

Generally speaking, the Chinese came later to the seas of the Archipelago than the Arabs, Hindus, and Persians; they did not venture on visits abroad until after they had received regular visits from foreign traders, and they did not settle abroad in large numbers until after the establishment of European power had created stable conditions. Nor is this general proposition discounted by such facts as the finding in 1345 or 1356 by Ibn Batuta, the Arabian traveller, of Chinese junks at Calicut in one of which he embarked for Sumatra. As far back as the ninth century Chinese traders are known to have visited Java, and Chinese contact with Borneo is believed to have anticipated the founding of the Malay kingdom. However, Pigafetta (who had been with Magellan) does not mention their being in the port of Brunei, or 'Borneo Proper,' when he visited it in 1521, though (as Crawfurd suggests)[1] this may be accounted for by the time of year—the month of July—which would be after the sailing of the junks on their return voyage with the southwest monsoon. He mentions, however, the silks and porcelains of China which he saw in Borneo and he notes the adoption by the natives of the weights and money of China, facts sufficient to prove the existence of a trade which was afterwards known to have yearly employed four or five junks of large burden. Another curious fact attests the existence of the trade and proves it to have been of some antiquity. That is the finding among the aboriginal inhabitants of Borneo of Chinese vases 'of an ancient pattern which cannot now be imitated'. These vases were preserved by the Dyaks as sacred heirlooms.[2]

[1] John Crawfurd, *A Descriptive Dictionary of the Indian Islands and Adjacent Territories* (London, 1856), p. 62.
[2] The present writer has examined a number of these vases or jars preserved in the Sarawak museum at Kuching. Those he saw were of provincial design and coarse workmanship.

Horace St John[3] states that when the Dutch first landed in Java they found a scattered population of Chinese working in every province of the island; Amry Vandenbosch remarks that the Chinese were in Indonesia before the Dutch and have always outnumbered them;[4] and Cator says, 'Although the Chinese had had contact with the Indonesian islands for centuries and had formed a number of permanent settlements, they did not here as elsewhere, take up their abode in any large numbers until after the Dutch began to establish themselves'.[5]

Before the arrival of the Dutch in Java there is practically no material for an account of the Chinese settlements: their denizens were anonymous, their years unmarked except by the alternation of the monsoons, and their record to us is little but an inventory of merchandise such as Linschoten and his contemporaries retail.[6] But with the coming of the Dutch fleet to the Archipelago in 1596 and the establishment of their power in Java in the second decade of the seventeenth century begins an association that has continued for well over 300 years, and of the contacts and conflicts of these two very diverse peoples is born a fascinating history from which all sorts of political and economic lessons can be drawn.

The English writer, however, who takes it upon himself to retell the story, seeing as he must through the glass of his own reading and experience, is under obligation to examine his authorities with care. Many of the standard works in English date from the period when there was strong Anglo-Dutch rivalry, and often enmity, and the histories of Raffles, J. H. Moor, and Horace St John (to mention but three), though valuable for reference, have often an anti-Dutch bias, apparent or concealed. Clive Day, an authority of half a century ago, remarks in the preface to his book on Indonesia,[7] 'When I was first drawn into a study of some of the features of Dutch policy in Java, I was surprised by the wide divergence between the descriptions of the policy current in English and the facts as they appear in the writings of Dutch historians and in the original documents'. This is a warning which should be borne in mind.

At this point an impressionistic history of the Dutch in Indonesia is

[3] The Indian Archipelago (London, 1853), ii. 1.
[4] The Dutch East Indies (Berkeley, 1941), p. 100.
[5] The Economic Position of the Chinese in the Netherlands Indies (Oxford, 1936) p. 193.
[6] Jan Huygen van Linschoten, Voyage to the East Indies. Eng. trans. 1598 (London, Hakluyt Soc., 1885), lxx, lxxi, 124: 'Those of China trafficke with these islands (Philippines and Indies) and bring thither all sortes of commodities out of their country, as al silkes, cottons, porselynes, powder for shot, sulphur, brimstone, iron, steele, quicke silver, and other metals, coper, meal nuttes, chestnuttes, bisquit, dates, al sorts of lynnen cloth, diskes, and such like, and of al curious things that may be found. . . .' To China they took in return pepper, tin, spices, &c.
[7] Clive Day, The Policy and Administration of the Dutch in Java (N.Y., 1904), preface.

called for as a back-drop. The following may serve.[8]

The Dutch first reached the Indies in 1596; the Dutch East India Company was founded in 1602, the first Governor-General was appointed in 1609, and the city of Batavia was founded in 1619. Operations were begun against the Dutch by the British in February 1810, but Java remained in Dutch hands until 1811, when the Netherlands were incorporated in the empire of Napoleon I.[9] The Dutch East Indies were consequently seized by the British but were restored by them to the Netherlands in 1816 after the final defeat of Napoleon. The rule of the Dutch in Java and the Moluccas was established at an early date, but it was not for a great many years that the whole of the Archipelago was placed under effective Dutch control. By the middle of the seventeenth century the Portuguese influence was at an end in Indonesia except in Timor. After the interval of British rule in 1811–16 when Java was administered by Sir Stamford Raffles, England retained some posts in Sumatra. By 1876 the greater part of Sumatra was under Dutch administration, though the Achinese in the north were conquered only after long wars which ended in 1904. The new Governor-General appointed in that year, van Heutsz, undertook military patrols of nearly all the islands, and when he resigned in 1909 conquest was complete and Dutch administration largely consolidated.

Long before Jacatra (Djakarta) was conquered by the Dutch under Jan Pieterson Coen in 1619 and Batavia founded, the Chinese were installed at Bantam and other places in Java. In the Moluccas Chinese, Arabs, and Bugis came to Dobo to buy tripang (bêche-de-mer), mother-of-pearl, turtles, birds of paradise, and edible birds' nests. In the beginning of the seventeenth century the Dutch made an attempt to take part in the pepper trade of Banjermasin which was mainly carried on by Chinese. Their ships met with a hostile reception; some of the Dutch traders were captured and members of their crews were killed.[10]

Spices, especially pepper, nutmegs, and cloves, were in great demand in Europe where, before the introduction of winter feeding-stuffs in the eighteenth century, cattle had to be killed off in the autumn and the meat was likely to become tainted before the following spring. There was a deadly rivalry between the Portuguese, the English, and the Dutch for the trade. The feeling among the English and the Dutch was that the Chinese were reaping greater profits from the trade than they were. Says John Jourdain in his Journal of 1617: 'Notwithstandinge soe much money as is brought to Bantam yearlie by us and the Dutch, which wee paye for pepper, there is a great scarcitie of money, by reason that the

---

[8] Derived from RIIA, *Netherlands Overseas Territories* (1941), p. 24.

[9] It may be noted that the East India Company of Great Britain had held posts on the west coast of Sumatra without a break since the late seventeenth century, and these were not ceded to the Dutch till 1824.

[10] E. S. de Klerck, *History of the Netherlands Indies* (Amsterdam, 1938), i. 112, 245.

Chinese junkes carrie itt yearlie to China'.[11]

During this period the Dutch often treated the Chinese as enemies and were not above carrying out piratical raids upon their shipping. There is news of such a raid in 1607 when the Dutch Admiral Matelief was reported to have seized a Chinese junk trading at Ternate with the Spanish, bartering linen and wearing apparel for cloves and *reals*. The admiral is said to have removed her cargo and to have given the junk to the people of Gilolo.[12] Another letter (this time from Captain Christopher Harris to the East India Company, dated on board the *Peppercorn*, 25 August 1617)[13] relates that the Dutch had again seized the junks of the Chinese 'for while they rode in the road they took their junks and sent their men ashore'. There was talk, too, of the English themselves engaging in this piracy, though the report that Sir Edward Michelborne had in 1606 taken a Chinese junk was not brought home to him.[14]

Most English and Dutch agree, it seems, in having a low opinion of Chinese honesty (though Captain So Bing Kong became a personal friend of J. P. Coen). Speaking of Andrea Dittis, the Captain of the Chinese in Firando (Japan), George Bell, the English East India Company's agent at Bantam, writing to Richard Cocks at Bantam on 9 June 1617 says,

his endeavours are had in suspicion and accounted as bent to none other than to deceive you, and it disagrees not with my opinion, for never yet, having dealt with many, could I find an honest and faithful Chinesa [*sic*]; and it is not to be marvelled at, their serving so faithless and fraudulent a master, father of deceit, cannot but have inspired his disciples with his rules of perdition.[15]

George Cockayne, another of the company's servants, speaks of 'Chinese and other rogues',[16] and in 1615 there is a reference in these same letters to the 'dishonest dealing of the China merchants of Bantam, who are indebted to the Worshipful Company to the quantity of 16,000 sacks of pepper'.[17] The 'Flemings' (Dutch), we are told, have had the same experience in dealing with the Chinese.

---

[11] Cited by Cator at p. 6 from *So Bing Kong*, by B. Hoetink. In a letter to the East India Company of 5 Oct. 1614 Jourdain says that there was a shortage of money among both the Dutch and English (*Letters Received by the East India Company from its Servants* (London, 1897–1902), ii. 315).

[12] Letter from Gabrial Towerson from Bantam to the English East India Company dated 16 Dec. 1607 (ibid. (1896), i. 6).   [13] Ibid. vi. 89.

[14] *The First Letter Book of the East India Company* (London, 1893), p. 135 n. Michelborne said he paid for all he took. 'Thereafter they fought a little with a Chinish [*sic*] ship, from which they took some silks, giving twice as much in exchange; but learning soon after from some Hollanders that the King of Java would assault the English merchants of Bantam because of the taking of the Chinish ship, whereby the King of Bantam had lost his custom, Sir Edward thought it would be very dangerous for the English merchants if he remained in those parts so determined to return home' (Purchas, ii. 347, cited by G. B. Harrison in *A Jacobean Journal 1603–1606* (London, 1941), p. 320).

[15] *Letters Received by the East India Company* . . . (1617), vi. 13.

[16] Ibid (1617), v. 168.   [17] Ibid. (1615), iii. 262.

But what is admitted elsewhere by these downright English merchants of the ruthless, pioneering days is evidence that the Chinese had at least some virtues. Richard Cocks (writing home to the company) gives his opinion that Captain Jourdain need not be afraid of the company's lending money to the Chinese, and he mentions that when the Chinese themselves lend money they do so at 20 per cent per annum, whereas no Japanese would lend at less than 33 per cent, and would demand double the security into the bargain![18] On another occasion we find the company's servants doing their best to persuade the Chinese to accept their goods on credit to be paid for in pepper 'at the vintage'.

The English realized that whatever their shortcomings the Chinese were great merchants and that they bought very much more of their merchandise than the Japanese did. Therefore it was obviously good policy to treat them well. Thus Richard Cocks, writing to Captain Jourdain at Bantam, on 25 February 1615, repeating the letter to the agents at Patani and in Siam (Ayuthia), gives instructions that the Chinese 'may be kindly used, and not beaten and misused as heretofore'.[19]

The Dutch treatment of the Chinese, according to their rivals, the English company, was not good. They robbed their junks, seized their crews, and at Patani their ill-usage of the race had driven all the junks away to Singora.[20] The Malays also treated the Chinese in a violent manner, which, combined with a storm, kept their junks from reaching Musulpatam for a whole year.[21] Altogether the large profits gained by the Chinese merchant venturers were well earned, for in addition to the ill-usage they often received from the Europeans, especially the Portuguese and the Dutch, they were in danger of being captured and made into slaves.[22] But they were not deterred from their trade: in July 1615 George Cockayne reports the arrival of a Chinese junk at Macassar ('it being the first that ever came to this place') with a great cargo of raw silk, woven silks, porcelain, and all other Chinese commodities, and for sale at cheaper prices than at Bantam.[23]

When the Dutch came to Bantam they found the Chinese quarter surrounded by a strong palisade and a moat, containing the finest, *and the most insanitary*, houses in the town, and the only stone building. Most of the inhabitants of the quarter were traders, but in the suburbs there were also cultivators of pepper and rice. There were Chinese likewise at Djakarta where they imported rice and made arrack. In Nieuhoff's work[24] there is a pictorial map of the seventeenth century showing the Chinese

[18] Ibid. (1617), v. 14.   [19] Ibid. iv. 52.
[20] Ibid. v. 168.   [21] Ibid. iv. 28.
[22] John Browne writing to John Jourdain on 19 August 1616 mentions the arrival of a Borneo junk in Patani roads with 140 men on board her, 'whereof most being slaves taken at sea, both Chaynnemen [sic] and Javaes: amongst whom, as they say, were two Chaynemen [sic] were employed by the English in Bantam'.   [23] Ibid. iii. 136.
[24] Johan Nieuhoff, *The Embassy of the Netherlands East India Company to the Great Tartar Cham* (1655–67).

quarter outside the main palisade of the town at the western corner by the water's edge. In the same volume there is an engraving of three Chinese of a superior class. Many of them owned slaves.[25]

Bantam is described in a contemporary English account quoted by Purchas (and he incidentally provides an early estimate of the Chinese and Javanese character):

... This town of Bantam is about three English miles in length and is very populous. The houses of the Javans are altogether built of great canes, but at one end of the town is the China town, for the most part built of brick, every house square and flat overhead. ... The Javans are exceeding proud but extremely poor, for not one in a hundred will work, for that the Chineses being frugal, suck away all their wealth from them. ... They are a dull, blockish people, whereby all strangers overreach them, and especially the Chinese, who are a very crafty people in trading, using all sorts of cozening and deceit.[26]

That the Chinese quarter of Bantam was insanitary need not be doubted when we remember the general condition of such enclaves for the next three centuries, but in any case we have explicit contemporary evidence on the subject for Nicholas Downton, at sea homeward bound, on 20 June 1613 records:

... three days after I passed the Straits half my people were disabled for labour, some with flux, some with fever, and many with sore legs, for I hold that he that escapes without disease from that stinking stew of the Chinesa's part of Bantam must be of a strong constitution of body, or else of a temperate and well governed life.[27]

The belief was common that the old natives of Java were sprung from the Chinese who had escaped to the Indies in the path of the Mongol conquest of the thirteenth century, and we also find this contemporary belief regarding the natives of Macassar.[28]

A striking account of Bantam is given by Sir Thomas Herbert[29] whose travels to the Indies began in 1621. Herbert says:

The town [Bantam] of its own growth affords little save rice, pepper, and cotton-wool; albeit pepper for the greatest part brought thither by the infinitely industrious Chyneses, who each January come to anchor in multitudes at this port, and unload their junks or praws from Jamby in Sumatra, Borneo, Malacca, and other places, making Bantam their magazine; out of which, for *rials*, or by exchange for other commodities, they supply the English, Dutch, and other nations.

The Chyneses are no quarellers, albeit voluptuous, venereous, costly in their sports, great gamesters, and in trading too subtle for young merchants, oftimes so

[25] K. Verboeket, 'Geschiedenis van de Chineezen in Nederland Indië, . . .' *Koloniale Studiën*, nos. 5 & 6 (1936).

[26] Purchas, ii, 496–502 (cited by Harrison, *Jacobean Journal*, p. 302).

[27] *Letters received by the East India Company* . . . (1613), i. 260.

[28] Nieuhoff, *Embassy to the Great Tartar Cham* (quoted by Verboeket, p. 9).

[29] The text here is taken from Crawfurd, *History of the Indian Archipelago* (Edinburgh, 1820), i. 136 (from *An Itinerie of Some Years Travaile through divers parts of Asia and Africke, with the description of the Orientall Indies etc.* (1634)).

wedded to dicing, that, after they have lost their whole estate and wife and children are staked; yet in littel time, Jew-like, by gleaning here and there, are able to redeem their loss; if not at the day, they are sold in the market for most advantage.

Internal evidence suggests that Herbert is prone to exaggerate for effect (e.g. the staking of wife and children), but another passage in his *Travels* regarding the Siamese and their alleged homosexual habits gives the impression that at times he can be a gaudy if entertaining liar. None the less there is enough of truth in his description of the Bantam Chinese to give it verisimilitude.

During the siege of Jacatra (Djakarta) in 1619 Chinese were employed, using the Chinese language as a medium, to act as intermediaries in arranging the capitulation to the Dutch by the Pangeran or native ruler, as nobody in the fort knew how to read or write the Javanese language.[30] Very soon after the foundation of Batavia the Chinese established themselves outside the walls, and in spite of wild beasts and molestation applied themselves to agriculture, planting rice and sugar-cane and making market-gardens.[31] The citizens of Batavia who were not in the service of the company and who were known as *vrijburghers*[32] were unable to compete with the Chinese. From the beginning the Governor-General, Coen, declared that there was no people he desired to have more than the Chinese and that there could not be too many of them in Batavia. Following the practice of the Portuguese in other parts of the Indies, and indeed that of all the great marts of the East where each people had its own ruler, a native Captain was appointed for the Chinese of the new city.[33] There were no more than 350 of them at the time.

Governor-General Coen set out in a letter to the company what he considered to be the wise policy for the settlement. The Company, he said, should limit its trade to that of 'a mighty wholesale dealer'; the burghers should be active as middlemen, whereas retail trade should be

[30] Verboeket, *Koloniale Studiën* (1936), p. 9, quoting L. H. W. van Sandick, *Chineezen buiten China* (The Hague, 1909), p. 165.

[31] De Klerck, *Neth. Indies*, pp. 260, 268.

[32] Europeans who were *compagnies-dienaren* were not *vrijburghers*.

[33] Simsuan and Lak Moei are mentioned as early *towkays*, or leaders, in Bantam, and So Beng Kong (known to the Dutch as Bencon) was the first Kapitan China in Batavia (Verboeket *Koloniale Studiën* (1936), p. 11). So Beng Kong was unanimously selected by the Chinese community as their Captain. Shortly afterwards he was given a seat on the magistrate's bench and in the closing years of his life was elected one of the official executors. He had the monopolies of gambling and coining, and he was the overseer of the weigh-house so that all Chinese goods passed through his hands. He was in addition a merchant, ship-owner, and public contractor. He was also an intermediary with Bantam. He retired in 1636 to Formosa (*not* China for obvious reasons), but returned in 1639 to Batavia. He died in 1644. His successor was a Muslim Chinese named Lam Luk Ko (d. 1645). A Lieutenant China was first created in 1678 and a second Lieutenant in 1685; also Ensigns and Sergeants in 1678 (but these lasted only a short time) (C. R. Boxer, 'Notes on the Chinese Abroad in the late Ming and Early Manchu Periods, compiled from contemporary European Sources, 1500–1750', *T'ien Hsia Monthly* (1937), pp. 447–68). There is a photograph of Bencon's grave at Batavia in *Netherlands Indies*, iii (1930), pp. 283–91, and in the same issue another of seventeenth-century Chinese houses in the same town.

left to the Chinese ('retailers who in this connexion, and even as merchants, far exceed ours in ability').[34] As far as the Chinese were concerned, the scheme succeeded to an extent that called forth laments from some of Coen's successors.[35]

The Dutch East India Company under Coen's prompting proposed to secure to itself the monopoly in buying and trading in native products (pepper, tin, spices) and it was vindictively indignant when the Chinese attempted to compete with it in these preserves. At the same time the intention was to give the Chinese as much encouragement as possible without allowing any interference with the company's monopoly. In particular, the Chinese were to be encouraged to maintain shipping between Java and China. To protect the company's monopoly, as early as 1620 an ad valorem duty was levied on all imports and exports, but a good deal of latitude was allowed to Chinese trading to Batavia with their junks, and the duties in their case were not strictly levied. In 1643 a regulation was made freeing them of 'all vexations' on payment of an overall sum of 550 *reals* a junk.[36]

Before the Dutch came, the demand for sugar had been greater than the supply, and the Dutch had set themselves to encourage cultivation in their own territories, especially by Chinese immigrants. It was the latter who had introduced the real cane-sugar industry to Java, although the natives had prepared sugar in a somewhat primitive way. Shortly after the foundation of Batavia, sugar-mills had been established there under Chinese who knew their business. They pressed the cane between mill-stones turned by oxen or by water-power.[37] In 1637 the excise duty was remitted and it was decided to make advances to sugar manufacturers. The result was that the output which previously had been only 196 piculs rose by 1653 to 12,000 sold by the Chinese Captain, Jancon, to the company. As usual, the company lowered prices when supplies increased, but it would not fix the quantity it would pay for, although growers had to supply the company with all they grew. But the company's control over sugar was not so great as its control over coffee, which in this century was grown only by the natives, since there was a large local demand for the former, and, moreover, it was required in the manufacture of arrack which was an important article of commerce in the interior. As Furnivall remarks: 'Thus the Chinese cultivators were in a

[34] H. T. Colenbrander, *Koloniale Geschiedenis* (The Hague, 1871), ii. 181 (quoted by Cator at p. 7) and *Jan Pietersz Coen* (The Hague, 1919), ii. 181.

[35] C. Robequain, *Le Monde malais* (Paris, 1946), p. 91, gives 1632 as the date at which the company began officially to encourage the Chinese. 'Does this [asks Dr Vlekke] refer to the slight improvement in the status of the Chinese in judicial affairs (viz. their testimony admitted in the courts in certain cases)? Governor-General J. P. Coen always showed his respect for the Chinese by accepting invitations to dinner from the Chinese Captain So Bencon and the Company's officials "encouraged" the Chinese long before 1632.'

[36] Cator, *Economic Position of Chinese*, p. 9.

[37] Compare the method of sugar refining followed by the Chinese in Province Wellesley in the nineteenth century (Purcell, *The Chinese in Malaya*, p. 47 n).

stronger position than the natives who grew coffee and, being Chinese, had a keener economic sense and greater powers of resistance.'[38]

Gradually the number of sugar refineries in the vicinity of Batavia increased, so that in 1710 there were 130. Then followed a slump caused by exhaustion of the soil, scarcity of labour, the pillaging raids of the Bantamese, and finally, by the events following on the revolt of the Chinese in 1740. In Daendels' time only thirty mills remained. All sugar had to be delivered to the company.

Tea came originally not from China direct but from Japan. As demand for it increased the Dutch East India Company tried to obtain it from China, but on the whole it was found more convenient to buy it from the Chinese junks which came to Batavia. The usual price paid was $60 a picul, but when in 1717 an attempt was made to reduce the price to $40 a picul, the Chinese junks stayed away, much to the chagrin of the company's directors of Amsterdam, who never forgot this unfortunate attempt to 'buy cheap'. Later a factory was established at Canton. There was no question of a monopoly, for other European nations also had factories at Canton through which tea was procured.[39]

Though Coen had wished to make Batavia as soon as possible the 'largest commercial town of the entire Indies', particularly by encouraging the settlement of Chinese engaged in commerce, industry, and agriculture, the intention did not make much headway in the early years of the Dutch regime.[40] This was mainly due to the continued war with native States. In spite of the steady arrival of Chinese immigrants (2,000 in 1629 and Valentijn records another 2,000 newcomers in 1706), the Chinese population of Batavia which in 1619 had amounted to 400 had increased to 2,000 in 1629, but did not reach 10,000 until after 1725. In 1706 the number of immigrants per junk was limited to 100.

Coen used both fair means and foul to achieve his end of peopling his newly created metropolis with Chinese, for on the one hand he held out inducements to those in the neighbouring Bantam to remove themselves to Batavia (as did Francis Light later to the Chinese of Malacca to remove themselves to the neighbouring settlement of Penang), whilst on the other, he carried out a series of piratical raids on the coasts of Fukien and Kwangtung in an endeavour to seize large numbers of able-bodied Chinese for transportation to Batavia, Amboyna, and Banda.[41]

Meanwhile, Valentijn records under the year 1625 the arrival of the

[38] J. S. Furnivall, *Netherlands India; a Study in Plural Economy* (N.Y., 1944), p. 41.
[39] W. H. van Helsdingen and others, ed., *Mission Interrupted* (Amsterdam, 1945), p. 35.
[40] Cator, *Economic Position of Chinese*, p. 11. Compare the situation in Malacca under the Dutch where the population was 852 in 1678, did not rise to 2,161 until 1750, and had dropped to 1,390 by 1760 (Purcell, *Chinese in Malaya*, pp. 30, 36).
[41] Boxer, *T'ien Hsia Monthly* (1937), pp. 447–68. Compare the kidnapping tactics of Chinese slave dealers in Sumatra in the 1840s as described by G. F. Davidson in his *Trade and Travel in the Far East* (London, 1846), p. 87. According to Davidson the traffic was with Dutch connivance, but confirmatory evidence is lacking.

first Chinese in Amboyna.[42] They were charged a head-tax of eleven rix-dollars a year. In 1631 the Captain of the Chinese, Herman, so named after a previous Dutch Governor, who was a Christian, was murdered by a Chinese whom he had refused to help in a just cause, and was succeeded by another Christian Chinese who took the name of Artus Gysels after the then Dutch Governor. Valentijn mentions the Chinese in Ternate in 1665.[43]

Seventeenth-Century Impressions of the Chinese in Indonesia

From the beginning the company's policy (like that of the British in Malaya) was to interfere with the life of the Chinese only in matters in which it had a direct material interest, and beyond that to leave them to their own devices and the management of their own affairs. The intermediaries between the Dutch and the Chinese were headmen of the latter community (appointed by the Dutch) whose title was later 'Captain or Chief of the Chinese'.

The community was to adhere to its own usages and customs under which heading were generally included religious observances. But in 1651 (ordinances of 7 March and 28 November) the intolerant Governor-General Reyniersz issued an order that natives and Chinese were not to be allowed to follow their religion even outside the town limits, which so far had been allowed on sufferance, though, needless to say, he had little success in enforcing the order.[44]

But it should not be inferred that this was typical of Dutch policy. During the whole of the seventeenth and eighteen centuries *all* non-protestant religions (Mohammedanism, the Jewish religion, and also Roman Catholicism) were forbidden *on paper* (by ordinances) both in Holland and in the Indies, but *in practice* they were all tolerated. When a short-sighted man like Reyniersz tried at a particular moment to put these ordinances into practice, he succeeded only for a very short time or not at all. The last attempt in Batavia of the Calvinist clergy to enforce the paper prohibition against 'false and fallacious religions' was made under Governor-General Camphuijs (1684–91), but they received a rebuke from the Governor-General who answered that they, the *kerkeraad*, should redouble their efforts to get the heathens and Mohammedans baptized and thereby render any measures by Government of the sort asked for unnecessary.[45]

The surgeon-traveller Wouter (Gautier) Schouten (1638–1704) (to be distinguished from Joost (Justus) Schouten who was a company's official in Siam and Malaya) takes note of the 'idolatrous Chinese merchants',

---

[42] François Valentijn, *Oud en Nieuw Oost-Indien; Ambonsche Zaken* (Dordrecht, 1726), i. 55.   [43] Ibid. p. 140.   [44] De Klerck, *Neth. Indies*, i. 255.
[45] F. de Haan, *Priangan* (Batavia, 1910), i. 431 ff.

natives of Bantam, who had been permitted to reside in Batavia.[46] On 23 January 1659 they celebrated their New Year with many superstitions, monkey-tricks (*singeries* in the French translation), and idolatries.

Among other things [he says] this degenerate race, degenerated from the Chinese who are their ancestors, held great festival. They erected scaffolds and theatres like those of our own countries, and gave representations of their most famous heroes with gestures most appropriate to their humour, which went on all night for nights on end. They also had buffoons disguised, as at Mardi Gras at home, as wild animals and fabulous beasts, with much beating of drums. Those who were more religious lit candles while others celebrated the New Year by gambling.

The worst disgrace that could happen to any Chinese, remarks Schouten, was, when he had lost everything else, to lose the hair of his head, which was very long. When at length it was cut off their whole countenance was changed and they were covered with infamy to such a point the other Chinese refused to speak to them or even to help them in their direst need, so that at last in an attempt to recover some money they even came to staking their own persons and freedom, and when they lost they became slaves. The Regency at Batavia had not failed to make the most rigorous regulations to stop this abuse.

Schouten has a good deal to say about the nature and customs of these strange beings whom he compares, on account of their acquisitiveness, to the Jews (a comparison frequently to be made during the centuries to come—even in a series of newspaper articles written by King Vajiravudh (Rama VI) of Siam, see p. 120). He repeats that not all of them were born in China. They married natives and have transmitted to their posterity the greater part of their manners, customs, and religious culture. With a penetrating and subtle spirit and full of the wiles of commerce they were able to deceive the Christians. They were good seamen, loved aromatics, spices, and flowers—above all flowers with a powerful scent. They had (as he has already made clear) an extreme passion for gambling, and for women, of whom they had a considerable number. What was deplorable about them was the cursed cult of theirs which had rendered devotion to the Devil.

Chinese children (continues our informant) ran about naked until seven or eight years of age, then they put a piece of cloth round their middles. When they suffered some injury or from some defect they were rubbed from head to foot with Borreborri, which was a kind of Indonesian saffron which they mixed with coconut oil, sandal wood, and other things. When they became older they received a very good education. They learnt to read, to do arithmetic, and to keep books of account, using all their written characters for this purpose. They learnt trades

---

[46] *Voyage de Gautier Schouten aux Indes Orientales. Commencé l'an 1658 et fini l'an 1665* (Rouen, 1725), i. 35 (trs. of *Aanermerklijcke Voyagie, Gedaan door Wouter Schouten naar Oost-Indiën* (1676)).

and they became expert in making things. The girls were taught to sew, to embroider, and to knit, to ply the distaff, and even to engage in trade, 'as are girls of our country'.

There follows a description of the Chinese dress. Although the Ming dynasty had fallen in China, the Ming costume was still *de rigueur* in the Nanyang—especially the way of doing the hair before the pigtail had been adopted. To help us visualize the detail and the effect there is extant an engraving (previously mentioned) in Nieuhoff's book which shows three Chinese of the headman class at Batavia. The Chinese of Batavia, says Schouten, and those of the greater part of the other places in the Indies, dress in shirts of white or blue cotton with wide and hanging sleeves which they call *Cabaïes*, and they put them on over naked shoulders, but they pass them over their drawers or pants. Some wear them long and reaching down to their feet: others wear them shorter. Their footwear consists of sandals which have no leather band passing over the foot; they have only a piece of wood in the form of a button or of a peg which passes between the big toe and the others.

The hair (says Schouten) is plaited and fixed behind the head like that of our women. They pull out their beards, leaving only a few hairs on the lower lip. Some of the more important persons among them wear a woven cap or a silk *ress* on the head. This cap covers the head from the forehead to the back and keeps the hair, which appears sideways, in position. It is their hair which is their principal ornament: its tresses are rubbed with coconut oil, or some other oil, to make it more lustrous and smooth. They also wear on their heads a needle of gold or silver, ivory, brass, &c. 'In fine, those who have never seen Chinese before do not fail at first to take them for women, and it has often happened that lascivious sailors have seized them in error.'

The women, on the other hand, do not plait their hair: they do it up at the back of the neck with a button or with a cord. Some of them have red gorgets of cotton cloth, or of very light-coloured cambric, which hang down and half cover their naked bosoms. Others have their bodies naked from the middle upwards, except for the piece of cloth or taffeta which they twist round their waists. This they wear higher than the other women of the Indies, and sometimes the swathes pass over the ends of the breasts. The lower part of this sort of dress reaches to the feet.

Most of the Chinese are white enough: their wives, however, are browner, and some are quite black. The greater number of the women are from the Island of Bali, where the Chinese men go to buy them as slaves, and afterwards often make them their wives.

The Chinese houses at Batavia are substantial but not very clean, for the simple reason that the women are not clean in their habits, however rich they may be.

Wouter Schouten then proceeds to describe the domestic arrangements and eating habits of the Chinese, and notes the fact that rice is eaten at the end of the meal.

The dress of the Chinese as described here did not, except for the manner of doing the hair, alter substantially for centuries. During the third quarter of the seventeenth century the pigtail was adopted, and it had a political significance. We read in the instructions of Governor Bort of Malacca to his sea-captains of the Koxinga Chinese who wore their hair in the old Ming fashion, and of the Chinese who had yielded themselves to Manchu rule and who had their hair shaved or cut short to the crown of the head leaving a long plait or unplaited tress.[47]

In Tavernier's *Voyages*[48] is an amusing account of the way in which the Batavia Chinese of this period got even with the Dutch soldiers who helped themselves to refreshment intended for the ghosts of the Chinese departed. After a Chinese funeral the kindred and friends of the deceased gathered round the coffin.

. . . Besides that they put money in a little Box, and bury it by the deceas'd; and leave good store of victuals upon the Grave, out of an opinion that they rise and eat. Which the souldiers of Batavia observing, us'd to fill their Bellies at these Graves every time they walk'd their rounds. But when the Chinese perceiv'd it, they poysoned the victuals to spoil the Dutchmen's feasting. . . .

The townsmen took the soldiers' part in the ensuing unpleasantness and accused the Chinese of poisoning several of the Dutch, but the Chinese pleaded that if the soldiers surfeited themselves with what was left for the dead to eat, "Twas none of their fault; for that they did not leave their victuals for the souldiers; and besides that, among all the multitudes which they had buried, they had never had the least complaint before of any one that ever came at any harm by eating their food . . .' The matter was hushed up and the pilfering stopped.

In the year 1685 Father Guy Tachard (*c.* 1650–1712) of the Jesuits came to Batavia on his way to Siam, where he was to take part in the embassy sent by Louis XIV to the Siamese court.[49] The number of Chinese in the city and environs he puts at from 4,000 to 5,000, of which the greater part, he says, had retired to Batavia in order to avoid submitting themselves to the Tartars when the latter made themselves masters of China. Of this community he remarks:

---

[47] *JRASMB*, v, pt. 1 (1927), pp. 187–8. See also Purcell, *Chinese in Malaya*, p. 32. Stavorinus, 'Account of Java and Batavia', in *Pinkerton's Voyages*, ii. 179, describes the Chinese men's dress about 1790: 'They shave their heads all round, leaving a bunch of hair in the middle of the crown, which is twisted with a ribbon, and hangs down the back. Their dress consists of a long robe of nankeen, or thin silk, with wide sleeves, and under it they wear drawers of the same which cover their legs.'

[48] *The Six Voyages of Jean Baptista Tavernier, a nobleman of France now living, through Turky into Persia and the East Indies, finished in the year 1670* (London, 1678), iii. 173.

[49] *Voyage de Siam des pères jésuites, envoyés par le roy, aux Indes et à la Chine* (Amsterdam, 1687).

Since the Chinese are industrious and clever, they are of the greatest value at Batavia and without their help it would be difficult to live at all comfortably. They cultivate the land; there are scarcely any artisans excepting Chinese; in a word they are nearly everything. There are many rich men among them and we were informed that one of them who died a short time ago left a million in silver money.

Hearing from a Catholic soldier that the Chinese had their temple and their cemetery at about half a league from Batavia, Father Tachard and his companions requested him to take them to witness something of their ceremonies. They came first of all to a burial-ground in an ornamental wood not far from the little fort of Jacatra which was used for the burial of Chinese 'of low birth', but later they were taken to a second cemetery where the bonzes interred the 'people of quality' of the nation. They saw several small and grotesque idols hanging from the branches composing the roof of the rustic lodge to which the priests invited them. Here, it was said, the priests prepared the feasts for the dead. Most of the tombs were small mausoleums, very pretty and well kept. The graves were very much alike, except that some had dragons and others lions, and with steps that varied in number and in height in proportion to the magnificence of the tombs. The party, hearing the sound of kettledrums and hand-bells, repaired to the temple, where the Chinese and their priests were assembled to make a sacrifice.

Since the Chinese appeared astonished to see Father Tachard and his friends, the Jesuits explained that they were priests of the God of heaven and that they were going to China to preach the one and true religion, and in reply the Chinese bonzes said that they knew that in their country there were many Fathers who were very clever savants and who were held in great esteem by the Emperor and the great men of the empire. Father Tachard would have waited to the end, but hearing that the service, which was intended to drive the devil away from the body of a sick person, would last until evening, he stayed nearly an hour and then he and his companions withdrew 'with a feeling of much compassion for the blindness of this people, and a great desire to work for the conversion of their compatriots'.

About three years after Father Tachard's visit to Batavia we can take another peep at the Chinese as they were in these parts through the eyes of the celebrated William Dampier,[50] the ex-buccaneer and discoverer. It was at Achin (Atjeh) that he saw them, and though this part of Sumatra was not to come under the effective control of the Dutch for many years, it is nevertheless within the region we now call Indonesia, and the Chinese at Achin were the kith and kin of the Chinese of Batavia.

But of all the merchants that trade to that city [says Dampier] the Chinese are the most remarkable. There are some of them live here all the year long, but others

---

[50] William Dampier, *Voyages and Discoveries* (London, 1931), p. 195 (quoted by Crawfurd in his *History*, ii, 136–7, from the original edition).

only make annual voyages hither from China. The latter come hither sometimes in June, about ten or twelve sail, and bring abundance of rice and several other commodities. They take up houses all by one another, at the end of the town by the sea: and that end of the city is called the Chinese Camp . . . they brought with them several mechanics, viz. carpenters, joiners, painters, &c. These set themselves immediately to work, making of chests, drawers, cabinets, and all sorts of Chinese toys; which are no sooner finished at their working houses, but they are presently set up in shop, and at the door for sale. So for two months or ten weeks this place is like a fair. . . . As their goods sell off they contract themselves to less compass . . . if not at work they had as lieve be without victuals as without gaming. If before their goods are all sold, they can light on chapmen to buy their ships, they will gladly sell them also, or at least some of them, if any merchant will buy, for a Chinese is for selling everything. [Having sold their ships] they return as passengers with their neighbours. . . . They commonly go away about the end of September.

Dampier also tells us of the Chinese trick of making Europeans drunk while they keep sober themselves (no doubt with mercantile motives).

We see, then, that in spite of the Dutch policy of encouraging their immigration, and of the fact that wherever the company set up military establishments the Chinese followed close behind and set up trading posts, the Chinese community in Java at the end of the seventeenth century was still small.

40

BEFORE AND AFTER THE TROUBLES OF 1740

THE sentiment of the Dutch from early days was always hovering between two opposite opinions as to the advantages or disadvantages of the presence of the Chinese who followed the Dutch settlements wherever they were established. On the one hand, they were useful as intermediaries in the sale of the company's own imported goods; on the other hand, they were deeply involved in smuggling the native products over which the company claimed a monopoly. Moreover, they had imported with them a criminal element that was always a menace to law and order.[1] It was nearly two centuries before Schlegel's revelations of the nature and activities of the Heaven and Earth Society, but it is possible that the secret societies were responsible for some of the earlier outbreaks of disorder. The Dutch also realized in time that their policy of utilizing the Chinese as middlemen meant that the latter were by their

[1] Cator, *Economic Position of Chinese*, pp. 11 ff. The Dutch, however, made full use of the Chinese. Beeckman (see p. 419) in June 1714 at Arabaya in Madura saw two Chinese who called themselves *Shabanders*, 'which signifies Governors of a port, who were serviceable in keeping the natives in subjection, and managing the whole trade of the place'.

money-lending and their manipulation of mortgages and land leases extending their control over the native villages, with a consequent dislocation of the native economy.

Dr Cator says that during the two centuries of the company's existence the Chinese enjoyed many advantages from the latter's 'well-nigh permanent friendliness'. Certainly the tragedy of 1740 was an interruption of the ordinary relations between the two. Before that, on the whole, they prospered, some making great fortunes in sugar, and preserving the even tenor of their ways. Though not more than 100 were allowed in each ship coming to Java their numbers by 1733 had risen to 80,000 in the Batavia district alone. This sudden rise was due to the great increase in clandestine immigration which the Dutch failed to check.[2]

But the friendliness of the company's policy was one thing and the relation between Dutch officials on the spot and the Chinese was another. The Dutch police for their part oppressed the Chinese through extortion, and there was a general feeling that the rise of the community in wealth and importance, as well as to the turbulence of its hooligans, was a threat to Dutch rule. In 1740 the Dutch decided to send as slaves to Ceylon any Chinese who could not prove that they were making an honest livelihood. This action brought to a head the rising discontent among the Chinese and resulted in rebellion, followed by a massacre. 'The Chinese bandits from the outer districts', says Dr Cator, 'raised the standard of revolt and began to attack the forts around Batavia, while many Chinese from the town now also joined the armed groups wandering about in the vicinity.'[3]

The Government seems to have lost its head, and, being unable to bring the situation under control, initiated a promiscuous slaughter in which thousands of Chinese were killed.

A tragedy of this scale has naturally been the subject of conflicting accounts and varying judgments, in which national prejudices have at times played a great part. Horace St John, a British writer of the mid-nineteenth century, for example, censures the Dutch administration and its treatment of the Chinese in these words.[4]

The Dutch discouraged the Chinese in every possible way. They imposed crippling taxes on them and their trade, inflicted arbitrary punishment upon them, executing them in hundreds, and subjected their residence in Batavia to a series of harsh rules. To settle there the Chinese were supposed to have written permission from the Resident, and to pay a fee of ten shillings. They were forbidden to ride out beyond the jurisdiction of the city under a penalty, unless given express permission to do so by the Dutch commissary appointed to supervise the interests of the

---

[2] De Klerck, *Neth. Indies*, i. 362. According to Horace St John (*Indian Archipelago*, ii. 1, 2), the expulsion of the Chinese in the Philippines at the beginning of the eighteenth century had driven crowds of them to Java.

[3] Cator, *Economic Position of Chinese*, p. 18.

[4] St John, *Indian Archipelago*, ii. 1 ff.

natives. All who, when called upon, could not explain the origin of their subsistence, were arrested and sent to China. Bare suspicion was sufficient grounds for imprisoning a Chinese.[5]

The modern Dutch historian, E. S. de Klerck, states, on the other hand, that up to about 1727 the Chinese had always enjoyed much 'leniency' at the hands of the company.[6] They were appreciated as quiet and industrious inhabitants and were therefore favoured to some extent above the natives. The latter were protected by the Government, and so, incidentally, were the Chinese, so that little by little they spread over all the north coast of Java, and from Japara to Sidayu there was scarcely a factory that was not managed by Chinese. Eventually the Government took measures to restrict the number of immigrants, stipulating that each ship coming from China to Java should bring in no more than 100 men at a time. However, this regulation was often evaded or was not enforced, and the result was that there was great and growing unemployment among the Chinese. The Government became concerned and stiffened its policy towards this immigrant race. Chinese were forbidden to go wandering in search of work, the keeping by them of *waroengs* (i.e. little shops) in the interior was no longer allowed (though it was still possible by bribing the company's officials), and many were deported to Banda, Ceylon, or the Cape of Good Hope. 'For the flattering treatment of former days [says de Klerck] cruel persecution was substituted, and it therefore hardly could cause surprise that the Chinese rebelled'.[7]

In July 1740 van Imhoff, the leader of the political faction opposed to Governor-General Valckenier, proposed in the Council that all Chinese suspected of plotting against the Government should be arrested. This proposal caused much difference of opinion and led only to a resolution which was not carried out. In November of that year a revolt of the Chinese started. A rumour had been circulated that a number of Chinese who were sentenced to banishment had instead been flung overboard from the vessels transporting them. The rumour was without foundation, but many Chinese who believed it left Batavia for fear of meeting a similar fate. They joined the groups of their unemployed countrymen roaming the countryside and with them formed gangs, which used the sugar plantations as rallying-places. Fearing a general Chinese attack, the Governor-General recommended in Council that the town of Batavia be cleared of Chinese. This decision was finally taken, and the attempt to

---

[5] Before this period the conditions to which the Chinese were subjected seem to have been less rigorous, though de Klerck (*Neth. Indies*, i. 416) mentions that in 1717 the Governor-General compelled the Chinese tea traders to reduce their prices by one-third and Beeckman in 1714 says, 'A certain annual toll is imposed on the Chinese here [in Batavia] for the liberty of wearing their hair, which brings in no small income to the Government' ('A Voyage to and from the Island of Borneo, 1718', in *Pinkerton's Voyages*, xiv. 105).

[6] De Klerck, *Neth. Indies*, i. 363.

[7] Ibid. p. 364.

carry it out led to the 'deplorable and horrible massacre' which is known in Dutch colonial history as the 'Batavian Fury'.

Ni Hoe-kong, the Captain China, attempted to escape disguised as a woman, but was captured, tortured, and banished to Amboyna. The Captaincy lapsed, but was revived in 1743.[8]

De Klerck (p. 364) says that over 10,000 Chinese were killed by the enraged mob. But Cator states[9] that after the excitement 3,431 Chinese still remained, including 1,442 merchants, 935 cultivators and gardeners, 728 workers in sugar and timber, and 326 craftsmen. So the massacre did not amount to a complete extermination of the race in those parts.

Without going more deeply into the rights and wrongs of the matter, or the degree of provocation given by the Chinese, we may with safety accept the judgment of the Dutch historian Temminck.[10] He sums up:

> The impartial historian must agree, with M. van Hoevell,[11] that this catastrophe must be imputed only to the ineptitude, to the negligence and the arbitrariness of the Governors-General who were invested with power from 1725 to 1740, and without whose administration the elements of this revolt would never have been formed. . . .

But Temminck adds, 'the Chinese were nevertheless the aggressors . . . and if they had succeeded in their design all the Europeans would have been massacred'. Of this there can be no doubt either. The crime lay in the wanton slaughter after all effective resistance had ceased.[12]

The above was written before the author had had access to J. Th. Vermeulen's elaborate and authoritative work on the troubles of 1740,[13] but although this study brightly illuminates the background and provides detailed information not available to the earlier authorities, the above facts remain substantially correct. Dr Vermeulen confirms the judgment of Temminck and says that for the massacre of innocent Chinese in Batavia the blame must certainly be laid at the door of the weak Dutch Government. This, divided into two parties, was headed by an irresolute and tactless person, who in the crisis was unable to take command of the situation and who deliberately neglected to resist an outburst of unrighteous fury on the part of the Dutch and others in Batavia.[14]

Their first rage having subsided, the Dutch began to think of their trade and of what the Emperor of China would say when he heard of the

---

[8] Boxer, *T'ien Hsia Monthly* (1939), p. 465, quoted from B. Hoetink, 'Ni Hoe Kong Kapitan der Chineezen te Batavia in 1740', *Taal, land en volkenkund v. Nederl. Oost Indië*, lxxiv. 74, 447–518.   [9] Cator, *Economic Position of Chinese*, p. 18.

[10] *Coup d'œil général sur les possessions néerlandaises dans l'Inde archipélagique* (Leyden, 1847), i. 4.   [11] Quoting *Batavia in 1740* (Batavia, 1840).

[12] J. Chailley-Bert, not remarkable for his sympathy for Oriental peoples, and a strong critic of the Chinese, refers, however, to the '*cruauté inutile*' of the Dutch authorities (*Java et ses habitants* (Paris, 1901), p. 127).

[13] J. T. Vermeulen, *De Chineezen te Batavia en de Troebelen van 1740* (Leyden, n.d.).

[14] Ibid. p. 106.

affair. Valckenier, behaving as the Spaniards had done in like instance after their massacre of the Chinese at Manila in 1603,[15] dispatched warships to meet the trading fleets expected from China, and sent a letter to the Emperor couched in humble and submissive terms. But when the Emperor showed but little interest in the matter, Valckenier changed his tone and began to bluster. He accused Imhoff of opposing his will and had him arrested and sent to Holland. The story raised a storm in Europe. Valckenier followed Imhoff at a short interval but was arrested at the Cape, and, investigation into his conduct being protracted for several years, he died a prisoner.

Meanwhile the Chinese troubles continued in Java. Survivors from Batavia retreated into the east of Java. Here they opened negotiations with the Susuhunan (Susu) of Mataram, who longed to break the Dutch yoke. Some Chinese became Mohammedans to secure the goodwill of the Javanese. The insurrection continued until 1742, but in the end it was crushed by the Dutch.

After the rebellion (if it can fairly be so called) had been suppressed and things had settled down again the Chinese resumed their function as middlemen and extended their operations. Their numbers were soon made up further by clandestine immigration. The sugar industry, however, had been practically ruined in the troubles.

One of the principal causes of the Chinese penetration of Java was the farming-out by the Dutch to the Chinese of the right to levy taxes. This had been done even under the native rulers before the Dutch arrived, and the first Captain China, Bencon, was a large holder of these monopolies.[16] The principal method, however, by which the Chinese increased their hold over the people and the land was to obtain the lease of large territories (entire villages or even districts) from the native rulers. The native princes and chiefs, on behalf of the entire population of the leased districts, contracted to deliver stated quantities of produce, to provide labour (regulated by statute) as agreed, and to pay land rent to the lessee, either in money or in kind. The lessee usually maintained control as a kind of feudal lord. This system was responsible to a great extent for the disrepute in which the Chinese were held by the natives. By 1768 discontent had grown so strong that the people begged the Government of Batavia to depose the Sultans and to establish direct Dutch rule over the whole territory. They believed that this would protect them from the extortion of the Chinese. However, their request was refused.[17]

During the second half of the eighteenth century the Chinese gained in strength. They had in fact become necessary to both Dutch and natives

[15] See p. 514.
[16] See p. 395 n. Also Cator, *Economic Position of Chinese*, p. 18 and *passim*.
[17] B. H. M. Vlekke, *Nusantara: a History of the East Indian Archipelago* (Cambridge, Mass., 1943), p. 206.

as middlemen, and it was no longer possible, even if it had been desir-able, to root them out.[18] Towards the end of the century the company took to farming out to them large areas, and in 1796 out of 8,536 villages (*negorijen*) belonging to the company, 1,134 were leased out to Chinese.[19] This example was followed by the regents. On the Chinese estates near Batavia the people were better treated than elsewhere, but in the villages leased to them for only a short period the people were most miserable; for the Chinese were not landowners, but overlords: it was not the *land* that was leased or mortgaged to them but the *jurisdiction*, and the land went with the people and not, as in Europe, the people with the land; so (in Furnivall's analysis) they were able to exercise quasi-sovereign powers and the people were wholly at their mercy. Moreover, when the regent leased land to the Chinese, *his tribute to the company had to be made good from the remaining villages*, and the company was liable to suffer loss. This may explain why the company was so sensitive to the sufferings of the natives on these Chinese farms, and why in official reports the Chinese are consistently referred to with disfavour. One of such reports calls them 'a pest to the country' (a phrase borrowed by Raffles in the extract given below).[20]

Stamford Raffles, who was Lieutenant-Governor of Java during the British occupation of that country (1811–16), has recorded his im-pressions of the Sino-native and Sino-Dutch relations as he saw them in his time when the system had reached full development.[21]

The Chinese, in all ages equally supple, venal, and crafty, failed not to recom-ment themselves to the equally crafty, venal, and speculating Hollanders. They have, almost from the first, been the agents of the Dutch, and in the island of Java in particular, they have almost acquired the entire monopoly of revenue farms and government contracts. At present many of the most respectable Dutch families are intimately connected with the Chinese in their contracts and speculation, and it is only very lately that Marshal Daendels sold the whole province of Pasuki [Besoeki] to the Capitan China, or head Chinaman of Surabaya. It is even rumoured that this is not the only instance in which the Marshal has assigned whole provinces over to the unfeeling oppression of the Chinese, for the purpose of raising temporary resources in money. The Chinese have, in Java, been generally left to their own laws, and the regulation of their own chiefs: and being merely temporary residents in the country, they devote themselves entirely to the accumulation of wealth, without being very scrupulous concerning the means. When therefore, they acquire grants of land they always contrive to reduce the peasants speedily to the condition of slaves.

. . . A late report from the Counsellors of Batavia on this subject, accordingly states that 'although the Chinese, as being the most diligent and industrious settlers, should be very useful, they are, on the contrary, a very dangerous people,

18 Furnivall, *Neth. India*, p. 47.
19 Bergsma, ii. 297, quoted by Furnivall at p. 46.
20 Van Hogendorp, *Schets of Proeve*, ii. 152, cited by Furnivall at p. 46.
21 *Memoir of the Life and Public Services of Sir Thomas Stamford Raffles*, by Sophia (Hull) Lady Raffles. Letter to Lord Minto dated from Malacca, 10 June 1811 (London, 1830), p. 72.

and are to be remarked as a pest to the country; and there appears to be no radical cure for this evil but their extermination from the interior, a measure which cannot now be effected.'

This opinion of Raffles, it should be noticed, dates from *before* his experience as Lieutenant-Governor of Java, and is therefore obtained second-hand, though he had had an opportunity of observing the Chinese in Penang, and to a less extent in Malacca, but under entirely different conditions and where the abuses referred to regarding land tenure did not exist. In the same letter he adds, 'The Chinese must, at all events, be admitted to be industrious: but the Arabs are mere drones, useless and idle consumers of the produce of the ground'.[22]

When he undertook the administration of Java, Raffles resumed a number of tracts that his predecessor had leased to Chinese. But Daendels himself, to do him justice, had early set his face against the alienation of villages to Chinese, and during his first year he redeemed 56 which had been mortgaged for a sum averaging only 13 rix dollars. But he was the victim of circumstances. He was compelled against his principles to sell land to Chinese because Javanese produce could not find a market abroad as all ships, other than American, had been driven off the seas by the British.[23]

But the Dutch generally, in their projects for reform from late in the eighteenth century onwards, had the Chinese in mind as the chief fomenters of abuses. Measures were introduced forbidding the alienation of villages, and it afterwards remained a fixed rule of Dutch policy that land should not be alienated to non-Indonesians, including the Dutch themselves. This rule, Furnivall points out, gave protection to the natives, but it emphasized the plural aspect of society. This cut both ways. The Chinese were, on the one hand, prevented from obtaining a monopoly of the land and dispossessing the Javanese: on the other hand, any progress towards the assimilation of the Chinese into the Javanese community and making it a single homogeneous society was arrested.[24]

In addition to land, the company farmed out to the Chinese tolls and

[22] D. van Hogendorp's other strictures on the Chinese include: 'The lessees, like bloodsuckers, took as much as they could get' (*Berigt van den tegenwoordigen toestand der Bataafsche besittingen in Oost-Indiën*, 2nd ed. (Delft, 1800), cited by Cator, *Economic Position of Chinese*, p. 21). 'The Chinese have been made the owners of Java', *Coup d'œil sur l'île de Java et les autres possessions néerlandaises*, 2nd ed. (Brussels, 1830).

[23] 'The Chinese were forbidden (by Daendels) to lease any *dessas* (villages) even to reside in the interior; and what was probably not less necessary, the sultans were also forbidden to let out *dessas* to Chinamen' (M. L. van Deventer, *Daendels–Raffles, Governors of Java*, trans. from *Indische Gids* by George G. Batten (London, 1894), p. 26). Daendels, however, initiated a project in 1810 for the encouragement of Chinese colonization in the Preanger Regencies in order to obtainmore regularity in the supply of coffee, but it was a failure (Cator, *Economic Position of Chinese*, p. 21). See also *Staat der Nederlandsche Oost-Indische besittingen, ouder het bestuur van den gouverneur-generaal Herman Daendels . . . in de jaren 1801–11* (The Hague, 1814). Daendels, like Raffles, appreciated the essential part played by the Chinese in the economy of the Indies.   [24] *Neth. India*, p. 47.

C.S.E.A.—O 2

taxes, including the customs duty. By Raffles's time their control of these farms had been reduced, though, as he remarks, 'in the native provinces they are still farmers of the revenue, having formerly been so throughout the island'.

After the Treaty of London had restored Java to the Dutch (he was actually relieved of his post some months before the handing-over) Raffles set himself to compose a *History of Java*, in which he set down his considered opinions of Dutch policy.

In all their eastern settlements the favourite policy of the Dutch seems to be to depress the native inhabitants and give encouragement to the Chinese, who, generally speaking, are only itinerants and not children of the soil and they follow the almost universal practice of remitting the fruits of their industry instead of spending them where they are acquired. The Chinese, in all ages, equally subtle, venal, and crafty, failed not, at a very early period . . . [and here Raffles repeats the passage he had included in his letter of June 1811 to Lord Minto, before cited].

Raffles's recipe for checking the Chinese was 'by bringing forward the native population of Malaya and Javanese and encouraging them in useful and industrious habits'.[25]

At the beginning of the nineteenth century the Chinese had an almost uncontrolled command of the Javanese market for foreign commodities. Almost all the inland commerce was in their hands, for, possessing considerable capital and frequently speculating on a large scale, they bought up the principal articles of export from the native growers, conveyed them to the maritime capitals, and in return supplied the interior with salt and the principal articles imported from foreign countries.[26]

In the earlier days the Javanese merchants held their own with the Chinese, as some enterprising merchants still do in Minangkabau.[27] Fortune had favoured the Chinese rise to prosperity as well as their industry and acumen. Jacatra (Djakarta) was of very small importance as a trading centre before the Dutch came, and they were quick to see the advantages of using the Chinese as their agents. For one thing, the Chinese already had trade relations with the rice-producing East Java and they could obtain rice where the Dutch could not. When the Dutch suppressed the trade of the native merchants of East Java the Chinese were at hand to take their place.

The Chinese [says Furnivall] were mostly immigrants, naturally men of enterprise and character, with a long tradition of commercial affairs and craftsmanship, and it was not strange that they got the better of a mass of an oppressed peasantry in every economic transaction in which the two parties engaged. From the beginning they were playing against the natives with loaded dice.[28]

The Dutch East India Company had been long in decay, and owing partly to its policy of monopoly, partly to its parsimony in dealing with

[25] *Memoir*, by Lady Raffles, p. 72.
[26] Cator, *Economic Position of Chinese*, pp. 8, 9.
[27] Furnivall, *Neth. India*, p. 47.   [28] Ibid. pp. 47–8.

its servants, which encouraged corruption, and partly to other causes, it had been declared bankrupt in 1798 and its assets had been taken over by the newly created Batavian Republic from 1 January 1800. Some reforms had been initiated by the Dutch when the British occupation of Java put the policy of the country once again into the melting-pot. After its restoration to the Dutch in 1816, domestic policy had to be reconsidered all over again, and this resulted in far-reaching developments in which the Chinese community were naturally involved. But before dealing with these developments it will be profitable to turn back for a few decades to see how the Chinese community was progressing, considered rather as a social organism than an intermediary or entrepreneur.

41

CHINESE SOCIETY IN THE LATER DAYS OF THE DUTCH EAST INDIA COMPANY

WE are dealing, it is well to remember, almost entirely with the Hokkiens in the first two centuries of the Dutch connexion with the Indies. An impetus was given to emigration from the province from which the Hokkiens came in the second half of the seventeenth century when the Manchu conquest of China was completed and the civil war bore particularly hard upon it. In the second half of the nineteenth century the impetus was to come from the T'aip'ing rebellion and the resulting disorder, but this time other provinces besides Fukien suffered the depredations of the warring sides. The early Hokkien stock from the region of Amoy was very hardy and active, and their descendants still form the aristocracy among the Chinese in the Southern Ocean.

Crawfurd (whose experience dates from the early years of the nineteenth century) states that the Chinese who came to Java, &c, were from Canton and Fukien province, and adds: 'Those from the latter have a much better character than those from the former. They are rarely from the lower orders of society, and they are less gross and abject in their manners.'[1]

The Chinese have, as a whole [according to Duyvendak[2]] never been a seafaring people with the love of enterprise and adventure which has characterized some of the Western nations and which has made them conquerors in so many parts of the world. The spirit of adventure was really not at all in keeping with the Chinese

---

[1] *History*, i. 137.
[2] J. J. L. Duyvendak, 'Chinese in the Dutch East Indies', *Chinese Soc. & Pol. Science R.*, xi (1927), pp. 1–13.

attitude to life. The ideal life was rather the one of filial piety and it was difficult to reconcile personal love of adventure with the fulfilment of duty towards one's parents.[3]

Although in disregarding the Confucian precept the sea-going Hokkiens showed themselves unfilial, they were nevertheless more imbued with the culture of China than the immigrants of other provinces of a later period. They came, generally speaking, from a better class of society. They knew something about, and therefore valued, the ancient civilization of their homeland, and, once in the Indies, they learned the value of the Indonesian civilization as well. In preserving the cultural treasures of Java many Chinese, descendants of seventeenth- and eighteenth century immigrants, had a part. The immigrants of the late nineteenth century and early twentieth century came mostly from Kwangtung and belonged to quite another class of people.[4] This judgment is borne out by other recent testimony.[5] The author of an article on Java pays tribute to the taste and culture of the settled Hokkien families of the country in these words:

As many of the Chinese came from China centuries ago and have not ceased to hold intercourse with their native country, the houses of the wealthier men among them are often rich in ancient specimens of Chinese art. The special exhibition organized by Henri Borel and other enthusiasts showed how much of value in this matter might be brought together in spite of the reluctance of the owners to commit the sacrilege of exposing to public gaze the images of their ancestral gods and heroes. Borel has given exquisite examples of images of Kwan-yin, of Buddha, of the ghoulish god of literature, of Lie-Tai-Peh (the Chinese poet who has gone to live in the planet Venus) &c in illustration of his papers in *L'Art flamand et hollandais* (1900), a translation of his monograph published in Batavia.

This aspect of the Overseas Chinese in Indonesia is in rather sharp contrast with the indifference of some of the other communities in Southeast Asia to the refinements of their traditional civilization. In Malaya, for instance, there are very few houses where objects of vertu, images, hangings, &c, are to be found in any number, except in Malacca which also is an ancient Hokkien settlement.

We have already had a glimpse through the eyes of Wouter Schouten at the education that was carried on among the seventeenth-century Chinese of Batavia. It was, it seems, mostly of a domestic nature and not carried on in formal schools. Indeed, it was not until 1900 that the first school was established on modern lines by the Tiong Hoa Hwe Koan in Batavia and it was the first in the whole of the Indies. However, educa-

---

[3] Duyvendak mentions a recorded saying of Confucius that a son should not travel while his parents are alive, that he should not climb to high and dangerous places, and that he should be careful not to incur any harm or so much as scratch his skin. For if he were to die or sustain an injury it would cause grief to his parents and prevent him from caring for them in their old age.   [4] Vlekke, *Nusantara*, p. 330.
[5] *Encyclopaedia Britannica*, 13th ed. (1926), xv. 294.

tion was given for centuries before that, mostly through home instruction. De Haan says,[6] 'The Chinese have always had schools, to the annoyance of the Council of Church Elders (*Kerkeraad*) because it meant that the Chinese boys received instruction in them at home'. A separate school building for Chinese and other non-Christian children was added to the Chinese Hospital in 1729 by the Government when the hospital was rebuilt—a remarkable proof (says de Haan) of the progress in the spirit of tolerance among the Dutch. The school, of which the Chinese Captains and other officers bore the cost of upkeep, was on the side of the hospital opposite the Company's school for the poor.

In 1753 the Dutch authorities decided to place some Dutch boys in this Chinese school in order that they might learn the Chinese language, which it appears the authorities regarded as an easy task.

Later in the century the school, which from thirty to forty pupils had formerly attended at one time, ceased to function owing to mismanagement, and in 1787 the Chinese Lieutenants wanted to open a new school at Klenting.[7]

Confucianism, Buddhism, and Taoism remained the religion or social code of the majority of the Chinese immigrants, but a number of them became Mohammedans. There is a mosque in Batavia which was built by the Mohammedan Chinese in 1786. Near this mosque is the grave of the wife of its Chinese architect: it is ornamented with Chinese designs and inscribed with Chinese characters which would be regarded as sacrilege by an orthodox Muslim. The number of Mohammedans was small, but at Macassar it became considerably larger than anywhere else in the Indies and this town later became the seat of a Chinese Muslim Party, the Partij Tionhoa Islam Indonesia.[8]

Since the immigrant males married native wives they generated a mixed race 'inferior in energy and spirit to the original settler, but speaking the language, wearing the garb, professing the religion, and affecting the manners of the parent country'. 'The Chinese settlers', continues Crawfurd[9] (adding yet one more European judgment of the Chinese to the scores that sprinkle the pages of Southeast Asian history), 'may be described at once as enterprising, keen, laborious, luxurious, sensual, debauched, and pusillanimous'.

(The statement that the descendants of the Chinese settlers spoke the

---

[6] F. de Haan, *Oud Batavia*, 2nd ed. (Bardung, 1935), p. 392 (cited by Nio Joe Lan in 'De eigen onderwijsvoorziening der Chineezen', *Koloniale Studiën*, no. 1 (Feb. 1939), p. 67).

[7] *Oud Batavia*, p. 392, cited ibid. nos. 5 & 6 (1936), p. 68.

[8] Kwee Kek Beng, 'Het cultureele leven der Chineezen in Nederlandsch-Indiën', citing de Haan, *Oud Batavia*, i. 396 and ii. n. 16. Dampier (*Voyages and Discoveries*, p. 96) tells of 'a Chinese Renegado (Renegade) who was Captain of the China Camp (at Acheen) who got himself so entangled with the law that he would have been ruined had he not disentangled himself by turning Mohammedan, whereupon he was carried in great state through the city of Acheen on an elephant, with one crying before him that he had turned Believer.

[9] *History*, i. 135.

language of their forebears requires modification, for many lost their ancestral language altogether. They became, indeed, like the Babas of Malacca, speaking Malay which was often a Malay of their own.[10] This fact resulted in the coming into being of Malay-speaking theatrical companies which gave Chinese plays in Chinese costume with Chinese music and according to Chinese stage technique—but the actors and actresses spoke Malay instead of Chinese!)

Opinions of the Europeans held by the Chinese are, on the other hand, very few and far between—not, we may be sure, because the latter refrained from forming opinions, but because they rarely recorded them. One important exception is the book by Ong Tae-hae in Chinese published in the 56th year of Ch'ien Lung (1791) and referring to the author's experiences some years before in Java.[11] He lived ten years in the Indies, first at Batavia, then at Semarang, after that at Pekalongan, and then returned to Batavia. Medhurst says:

> The author appears to have been a man of education and observation, equal to the generality of his own countrymen. His distorted views and occasional mistakes are to be ascribed to his early habits and partial information: considering the circumstances under which he wrote, however, his remarks display not a little good sense and good feeling.

He was a Hokkien by birth. His book has three prefaces by Chinese scholars other than his own, and is accompanied by a map of the Nanyang which has to be seen to be believed. A European child of six would have made a far better attempt at cartography.

Ong Tae-hae gives a long and factual account of the Indies and the Dutch and their administration, and his statements appear to be substantially accurate. The territory of Batavia, he tells us, originally belonged to the Javanese, but the Dutch, having by stratagem and artifice got possession of the revenues, proceeded to give orders and enact laws, until, squatting down all along the sea coast, they have exacted duties, issued passports, guarded ingress and egress, put down robberies, and brought the natives under their entire control. The Hollanders have long noses and red hair. The Chinese rich merchants and great traders amass inexhaustible wealth, whereupon they give bribes to the Hollanders and are elevated to the ranks of great Captain, Lieutenant, Commissioners of Insolvent and Intestate Estates, or *Boedelmeester*, Secretary, Choo-kat-tat, and suchlike appelations, but all of them take the title of Captain (or Ca-pit-tan). When the Chinese quarrel or fight they represent their cause to the Captain, before whom they make a low bow without kneeling, and refer to themselves as 'juniors'. The rights and wrongs, with the crooked and straight of the

---

[10] Purcell, *Chinese in Malaya*, p. 293.
[11] Ong Tae-hae, *The Chinaman Abroad: an Account of the Malayan Archipelago*, trs. by W. H. Medhurst (Shanghai, 1844).

matter are all immediately settled either by imprisonment or flogging without giving the matter a second thought. With respect to flagrant breaches of the law and grave crimes, however, together with marriages and deaths, reference must invariably be made to the Hollanders. Those Chinese who journey by water or by land must all be provided with passports to prevent them going or coming in an improper way. From this may be inferred how strict the Hollanders are in the execution of the laws, and how minute in the levying of duties.

The Chinese is perplexed, however, by the Dutch method of investigating crimes of violence and by their criminal procedure. For example, in China when a dead body upon which violence has been committed is found, the nearest inhabitants are apprehended and are required to deliver up the culprit. (This was strictly in accordance with the Chinese theory of corporate responsibility.) Ong Tae-hae laments that this is not also the practice in Java. The Dutch instead lay great stress on evidence, requiring the witnesses to submit to examination and to take an oath by cutting off a cock's head (in the Chinese manner) before they will give judgment in any matter. But when a man meets with a violent death, his body is either thrown out into the streets or suffered to float down the streams, and nobody dares to come forward as a witness. Alas! Alas! exclaims our author, that human life should be treated so lightly!

The Dutch are very much like the man who stopped his ears up when he was stealing a bell.[12] Regarding them by the rules of reason, they possess scarcely one of the cardinal virtues[13]—husbands and wives separate, with permission to marry again, and before a man has been dead a month his widow is allowed to go and live with another man. Thus they have no rectitude. They make no distinction between superior and inferior, and men and women are mingled together. Thus they are without propriety. They are extravagant and self-indulgent in the extreme, and thus they bring themselves to the grave without leaving any inheritance to tranquillize and aid their posterity. They have no wisdom, but of the single quality of sincerity, however, they possess a little.

Every seven days, says Ong Tae-hae, there is a day of ceremony, or a sabbath, when from nine to eleven in the morning they go to their place of worship and mumble charms, the congregation hanging down their heads and weeping as if there were something very affecting about it all.

[12] Insinuating that they try to hide their vices from themselves and imagine that they are equally concealed from others. They have a story in China that while a man was stealing a bell he stopped up his own ears to prevent himself from hearing the noise and imagined that others would be deaf to the sound (Medhurst's note).

[13] The Chinese cardinal virtues are benevolence (or humanity), *Jen*; the duty of man towards his neighbours, *I*; politeness, *Li*; sagacity, *Chih*; and sincerity, *Hsin* (see Purcell, *Problems of Chinese Education* (London, 1936), p. 37).

But after half an hour's jabber they are allowed to disperse, and away they go to their garden-houses and spend the remainder of the day in amusement without attending to any business. They you may see the dust of their carriages and the pacing of their horses all along the road, presenting a very lively scene.

The book further tells us that in their habits the Europeans aim at being polite and affect an elegant air. They seem delighted at meeting their friends and are lavish in their compliments to one another. If a man should become poor and call upon them for help they will not turn him away; whether he be of the same clan or only distantly connected they will not look upon him slightingly.

In stating this, Ong Tae-hae is admitting that the Dutch possess one further virtue in adding to a tincture of sincerity and that is *I*, or the duty of a man towards his neighbours. But the Chinese interpretation of the virtue is somewhat different and does not involve responsibility to anyone outside his own clan.[14]

This small book of only eighty pages in the English translation is taking up a good deal of our space, but this is justified by the fact that it is undoubtedly genuine (as is proved by internal evidence), that it belongs to the period contemplated by our sub-title, and that it represents a unique attempt of a Chinese to regard foreigners objectively and not to apply to them the cast-iron judgments of a 'three-legs essay'. And in addition to revealing a great deal of the frame of mind of an immigrant Chinese, it gives valuable information about their affairs.

When any Chinese is appointed a Captain by the Dutch, a dispatch asking for permission to do so (says Ong Tae-hae) is sent to Holland. Having received notification of his appointment, the new Captain selects a lucky period and assembles his relatives and friends, the guests of the family, and visitors from the villages, amounting to a score or so of persons. Then on the appointed day the Hollander appears bringing with him the order for the appointment. An elaborate ceremony ensues, there is an interchange of compliments, 'and this', says our author, 'is the way the Dutch get our people into their net'.

We are further told that the power of the Captains in Batavia was divided and that the profits of the appointment were uncertain; whereas in Samarang the Captain's authority was fixed and his profits were more regular. The boiling of sea water to make salt and the cultivation of the fields to produce revenue were both perquisites of the Captain, and he was thus enabled to amass a great deal of wealth.

The habit of the Chinese of the Nanyang was to prefer for sons-in-law those who were born in China, and not to regard those born in the

---

[14] It must be borne in mind that all this criticism was uttered at a time when the Chinese code had fallen into a state of great ritualism and ossification.

country with great esteem. In the case of a China-born bridegroom a pair of wax candles would suffice as a marriage portion 'which was most delightfully cheap'.

The visitor from Fukien includes a striking picture of the luxurious lives of the richer Chinese in these parts. They lived in fine houses with gardens planted with splendid shade-trees, they were waited on by scores of female slaves, and the food they ate was of the finest quality. In Pekalongan the Chinatown faced the hills and bordered the sea. It consisted of a row of houses—perhaps fifty or sixty of them, with high stories, joined to one another. Towards the west was the Captain's residence, to the right of which was a garden of perhaps an acre in extent beautifully shaded with trees. In the garden was a pavilion called the 'pavilion of floating clouds' in which the Captain relaxed. (Ong Tae-hae describes how he himself was entertained to dinner by the Captain.)

The book includes several short biographies of eminent Chinese sojourners in the Nanyang, starting off with the famous Ong Sam-po.[15] One of the celebrities was the wife (presumably a Javanese) of a Chinese. The Chinese returned to China, and his wife, hearing of his death, braved the seas to come to China in order to look after his impoverished relatives. Another was Tan P'ak-kung, first cousin of Yang, Captain China of Samarang. When Yang died he was succeeded by one Kh'eng. The author describes a visit to Kh'eng by a native chief, the Temenggong, who came in a great procession accompanied by several hundred horsemen. The Chinese Captain sat exalted and apart and received the Javanese chief with only a slight inclination of the head. That he should have attained such a lofty position in a far land, says Ong Tae-hae, 'shows what our Flowery Chinese are capable of'.

We see, then, these two races, the Dutch and the Chinese, of widely separated homelands combining together to administer and exploit a great territory but with no great degree of sympathy with, or understanding of, one another. Their common interests were exclusively material. There was indeed a mutual respect based on an appreciation of the other's administrative or commercial qualities as the case might be, but nothing more. Dutch opinions of the moral nature of the Chinese were almost invariably unflattering: we have seen from Ong Tae-hae above that the Chinese, for their part, were not willing to concede much in the way of virtue to the 'red-haired'[16] conquerors.

As an example of the extent to which prejudice and ignorance could reach, we could not improve on the libels of the Dutch Admiral

---

[15] R. J. Wilkinson says that Chêng Ho's name is often wrongly given by the Chinese of the Straits as Ong Sam-po, the Ong really being the clan name of his second-in-command (see 'The Malacca Sultanate', *JRASSB*, xiii, pt. 2 (1935), p. 25).

[16] To the Chinese the Dutch were always the 'red-haired race'.

Stavorinus (even though some of them are of the kind that Gibbon usually relegates to Greek footnotes).[17]

Stavorinus is by no means, however, a stupid or an unobservant man, and to him we owe fresh sidelights on the social life of the Chinese in the later eighteenth century. He tells us, for instance, that the few Chinese who in the 1790s lived within the city of Batavia had very wretched houses. Most of them dwelt in the southern or western suburbs which were together called the Chinese Campong. Before the revolt of 1740 they had the best quarters in the city allotted to them, to the west of the great river, but when, in that commotion, all the houses were burnt to the ground, the whole quarter was made into a *pasar*, or market. The Chinese were taxed, he says, at the monthly rate of half a ducatoon (one ducatoon equals 36 stivers or 6 shillings sterling). Women and children and those who had no trade were exempted from the tax which brought in a total revenue of 40,000 rix dollars a year. A flag was hoisted at the door of the Chinese Captain in the 1st or 2nd of every month and the Chinese who were liable to the tax had to come and pay it. Most of the sugar-mills, he records, were run by Chinese.

It is when he comes to the Chinese in commerce, their religious observances, and their alleged immoralities that Admiral Stavorinus reveals his prejudice and his credulity. In business, he says, they are 'like the Jews in Europe'. He describes the images (or *Joostyes*) in every house, painted on Chinese paper and hung up in a niche, in front of which one or more lamps were kept always burning, and the incense made into thin tapers. Their idol is depicted as an old man with a square cap upon his head and with a female, designed for his wife, next to him. He also notes the practice of throwing lots with sticks in the temples. He says 'It is worthy of observation, that whilst the practice of the most abominable idolatry is allowed, the Roman Catholic Religion is obstinately prohibited'. (From which the presumption is that Stavorinus is a Catholic.) He ends up with the passage to which reference has already been made: 'The Chinese are of a very lustful temper. They are accused of the most detestable violation of the laws of nature and it is even said that they keep swine in their houses, for purposes the most shameful and repugnant.'

There is nothing to encourage the belief that either Europeans or Chinese in the Indies took any real trouble to understand one another. This is true of the Straits Settlements in the first century of their existence as it is of the Dutch East Indies. The Chinese were regarded as materially useful and left to their own devices as much as possible. It was not until 1877 in the case of the former and 1900 in the case of the latter

---

[17] Account of Java and Batavia from the voyages of Stavorinus in *Pinkerton's Voyages*, xi. 159 ff. Johan Splinter Stavorinus (1739–88) was writing of the period 1768–71 (see *Biografisch Woordenboek* (Leyden, 1912), vol. ii).

that there came into being a department of experts whose business it was to acquaint themselves as closely as possible with the Chinese outlook, and to advise as to the best methods of dealing with that important community.

42

THE CHINESE IN THE OUTER ISLANDS[1]

DISREGARDING earlier contacts and several smaller and often intermittent settlements,[2] the serious Chinese penetration of west Borneo began in 1760 (or in 1770 according to Veth[3]). About this time the Chinese gold-miners employed by the Sultan of Sambas rebelled against him and took over the management and the working of the gold mines for themselves. It is said that the extortionate and tyrannous behaviour of the Sultans of Sambas precipitated this revolution.[4] After this the Chinese miners took little further notice of the Sultans but the tribute agreed upon was still paid more or less regularly. Nor did their action deter the rulers from ceding tracts of territory to them. But when disputes arose between the Chinese and the Dyak population the rulers declined to intervene. There were many conflicts with a great deal of bloodshed.

The Chinese in Borneo did not confine their activities to mining. To begin with they came at long intervals and in small numbers. They carried out their usual systematic procedure, clearing large tracts of land, cultivating pepper, and laying out vegetable gardens. From clearings near the mouths of rivers they wandered into the interior and began felling the timber trees and floating them down stream to primitive docks they had erected. They built large and solid junks from this timber which they steered for China loaded with their merchandise. When they had disposed of the merchandise for considerable sums they sold their junks, secured inferior craft for their return journey, and then started the

---

[1] For the sake of convenience the various Chinese settlements in Southeast Asia are here dealt with according to the political divisions of the territories. The Chinese in Sarawak, Brunei, Labuan, and British North Borneo are therefore discussed separately since they come within the British area, but the account should be read in conjunction with the present one of the Chinese in Dutch Borneo since the history of the two communities is connected though the former, generally speaking, belong to a later period.

[2] Daniel Beeckman, who visited Borneo in 1714, says: 'The Chinese who live among them [the Borneans] are the only persons that have ships tolerably well furnished: they set them off with coarse chintz, calicoes, bastees, tea, drugs, china-ware, and many things—the current money is dollars, half, and quarter dollars: leaden cash as small change, in strings' ('A Voyage to and from the Island of Borneo' (1718), in *Pinkerton's Voyages*, xi. 125).

[3] Prof. P. J. Veth, *Borneo's Western-Afdeeling, 1854-6* (Zaltbommel, 1854-6).

[4] Cator, *Economic Position of Chinese*, pp. 139 ff.

process all over again.[5] A Mr Jesse who visited Borneo about 1774–5 reported to the (English) East India Company that he had himself seen a junk of 580 tons laid down in a Chinese building-shed at Brunei at the beginning of March that was launched at the end of May. He mentions that the Chinese artificers built her and completed her at an outlay of $4,250 or, to use his own words, 'about 30 shillings a ton, an example of cheap shipbuilding without a parallel in any other country'.[6]

Thomas Forrest (whose work is quoted in the first footnote below) gives a vivid impression of the animated commerce of Borneo town (Brunei, or Borneo proper) in the year 1776. He tells that the town stood about three or four miles up the river Patatan, consisting of about a hundred houses on the water-front. Above the town were many pepper gardens belonging to the Chinese in a delightful country-side. Regarding Borneo's market, 'Imagine', says Forrest, 'a fleet of London wherries, loaded with fish, fowls, grain, &c, floating up with the tide from London Bridge towards Westminster: then down again, with many buyers floating up and down with them; this will give some idea of the Borneo market'. Great quantities of blackwood for furniture were bought at about $2 a picul and sold for $5 or $6. Also rattans, dammer (*damar*), cloves, swallo (bêche-de-mer), tortoiseshell, edible birds' nests, &c. The best camphor sold for $10–$12 a Chinese catty. Seven junks were in port when Forrest arrived.

Forrest has a note, too, on Chinese pepper-growing which it would be interesting for the agriculturist to compare with other notes of Chinese pepper-growing at various times and places:[7]

They do not let the vine, which bears the pepper, twist round a chinkapin tree, as is the custom in Sumatra; but drive a pole, or rather short stout post, into the ground, so that the vine is not robbed of its nourishment. The Chinese keep the ground very clean between the rows of vines; and I have seen them pull off the vine leaves; saying they did it that the pepper corn might have more sun. I have counted 70, sometimes 75, corns of pepper on one stalk—more than Sumatra.[8]

Our English traveller tells us that the Chinese here in Borneo were very active and industrious. They brought with them all sorts of Chinese manufactures and kept shop on board their junks as well as on shore. But the Borneans did their best to prevent them dealing with the Muruts,

---

[5] 'At Borneo town the Chinese sometimes build junks which they load with the rough produce of the Island of Borneo, and sent thence to China. I have seen a dock close to the town in which a Chinese junk of 500 tons has been lately built, worth 2,500 taels, and 8,000 in China. Could these junks come readily at our (British) woolens, they would distribute immense quantities through the northern parts of China' (Thomas Forrest, *A Voyage to New Guinea and the Moluccas etc. performed in the Tartar Galley belonging to the Honourable East India Company, during the years 1774, 1775, and 1776* (London, 1780), p. 382. Though the title reads thus, it appears that it was a galley named the 'Tartar' (10 tons burden!) and not a 'Tartar Galley' which Forrest navigated.

[6] 'The Chinese in Borneo' (anon.), *China (Quarterly) R.*, vii (July 1878–June 1879), p. 4.

[7] See Purcell, *Chinese in Malaya*, p. 45, re Penang; p. 180 above, re Indochina.

[8] Forrest, *Voyage to New Guinea*, p. 382.

wishing to reserve the trade to themselves. The Muruts did not plant pepper: this was the monopoly of the Chinese and all their produce went to China.

As for the Chinese junks, it gave a European pleasure to see the regularity and cleanliness on board them. The fact that they did not use tar contributed not a little to the latter condition. They had instead an art of putting a mixture of lime and oil into the seams of their decks which hardened them and kept them tight. This was much cleaner than pitch, but if the deck 'worked' at sea, Forrest apprehended that the caulking would break open and the junk prove leaky. The tanks for water were sweet and clean: the cooking galleys remarkably neat; the crew all ate off china. In harbour everyone was employed without noise on his own business.[9]

But the Europeans were well aware of the existence of this trade and had for centuries regarded it with jealousy. The Portuguese first, and after them the Dutch, made treaties with the Malay princes which allowed them to undersell the junk masters. And, says Hunt, 'these powers went further; by setting at ports in Borneo their *guardas de costas*, they compelled the traders of Borneo to send their produce calculated for the China market to Malacca or Batavia, which at length completely cut up the direct trade with China by means of the Chinese junks'.[10]

The Kongsis

De Groot and Schlegel date the Chinese arrival in Borneo from the arrival of a Chinese junk during the reign of Sultan Omar Alamudin (*c.* 1772). 'The Chinese deputation, pale and exhausted by the misery suffered during the long and difficult crossing of the sea, directed its steps humbly towards the Sultan's palace and threw themselves on his magnanimity, praying for the grant of a small portion of his territory where they might settle.'[11] Their prayer was answered and they were assigned the district of Larah. For long they were regular in the payment of their taxes, industrious, and peaceable. They intermarried largely with the Dyaks. But the tyranny and the inexhaustible thirst for riches of the Sultan brought about a change in their attitude. As their numbers increased the Chinese formed themselves into so-called *kongsis*, and thus, gradually feeling their power, they backed out of their obligations.

Schlegel traces their origin to rural and village associations of China which make the base of the political constitution of China. Absolutely

---

[9] Compare, however, the experiences of Dr Ruschenberger in Siam, *c.* 1833, when he found the Chinese junks kept in a filthy condition (see p. 98).

[10] 'The Chinese in Borneo', *China R.*, vii (July 1878–June 1879), p. 5.

[11] J. J. M. de Groot, *Het Kongsiwezen van Borneo: eene Verhandeling over den Grondslag en den Aard der Chineesche Politieke Vereeningingen in de Kolonien mit eene Chineesche Geschiedenis van de Kongsi Lanfong* (The Hague, 1885). Reviewed in Prof. G. Schlegel, 'L'Organisation des Kongsis à Borneo', *R. Coloniale Internationale* (Amsterdam, 1885), i. 448–65. See also Raymond Kennedy, *The Ageless Indies* (N.Y., 1942), p. 48.

republican in government, they made a real counter-poise to the auto-cracy of the sovereign.[12] The *kongsis* formed, as it were, petty republican communities, which, though occasionally in strained relations with one another, had one thing in common which was that they cared little for the authority of the native princes or, later, when it was established, that of the Dutch Government.

The founder of the original *kongsi*, Lanfong, whose name was Lo Fong-phak, went to Borneo in 1772 with 100 members of his family. (The Lanfong, like the T'ien Ti *kongsi*, was exclusively agricultural and had nothing to do with mining.)

At the time of the arrival of the Chinese, native affairs seem to have been in a very fluid state, but soon afterwards the first Sultan Abdul Rahman succeeded in attracting round him several groups of Chinese, Bugis, and Malay settlers, and built a town. Soon after, in 1786 (says Hunt),[13] the Dutch appeared with two brigs and fifty troops to establish their factory.

The early Chinese establishments in Borneo were all on the fringe: there was no settlement of the huge interior. In the map accompanying Raffles's *History of Java* (1817) Borneo is described as a 'blank'.

About 1812 the principal gold-mines were at Sambas and thirty-odd of them were worked by the Chinese. There were about 300 coolies on each mine. The pay of each coolie was on an average $4 a month. The mines were rented from the Raja at the rate of 50 bunkals of gold per mine per annum, besides a capitation tax of $3 per head for each Chinese. There were 30,000 Chinese in the Sambas district: in addition about 12,000 Malays and Dyaks.[14] At Salako, up a river 15 miles south of the Sambas river, and lying nearly 40 miles up it, was a settlement where 20,000 Chinese were engaged in mining. At Montrado there were (says Hunt) about 50,000 Malays, Dyaks, and Chinese. At Mandor, where many Chinese were settled, their numbers were annually increasing. There were Chinese in the Songo district and also in Matan. The mine at Tampasuk was a very valuable one. The Chinese settlement, 'Campo China', at Pontianak contained 2,000 souls. The town of Borneo proper (Brunei), 'situated 15 miles up one of the finest rivers in the world', had a population of 15,000 including Chinese, Malays, Muruts, &c.

Hunt's comment on the situation in Borneo is:

Living as the Chinese do, under the rapacity of despotic and ferocious free-booters, who are actuated by no principle of honour, justice, or good faith, it is

---

[12] Schlegel, p. 456; Cator, *Economic Position of Chinese*, pp. 148 ff.
[13] J. Hunt, *Sketch of Borneo or Pulo Kalamantan*. Communicated in 1812 to the Hon. Thomas Stamford Raffles Esq., Lt.-Governor of Java. Printed as Appendix IV to *The Expedition to Borneo of H.M.S. Dido for the suppression of piracy*, by Capt. Hon. Henry Keppel, R.N. (N.Y., 1846). Hunt's sketch supplies most information about this period, but Crawfurd questions its reliability.   [14] Hunt, p. 390.

their interest to conceal the riches they amass, not only to preserve themselves from the clutches of these tyrants, but as the most compact substance to transport to their native shores.

The effect of the Dutch policy in diverting all trade via Batavia was that the transport of *gruff* (coarse) goods—rattans, sago, cassia, pepper, ebony, wax, &c—was too expensive. But the loss of direct intercourse with China had even more fatal effects:

. . . it prevented the arrival of large bodies of annual immigrants arriving from China and keeping up the prosperity of the country by commerce, handicrafts, and tillage. The old Chinese settlers by degrees deserted these shores, and to fill up the chasms in their revenues . . . the Rajahs have been tempted to turn their views to predatory habits, and have permitted their lands to run to jungle, by dragging wretched labourers from agricultural to maritime and piratical enterprises.[15]

After the conclusion of the Napoleonic Wars had restored to them their Indonesian dominions, the Dutch were resolved to establish direct control over Borneo. They were attracted in particular by the Chinese mines, and were assisted in their designs by the appeal of the Sultan Abu-Bakar-Tajudin to them in 1818 for assistance against the *kongsis*.[16] The Dutch obtained authority from the Sultan of Sambas to purchase mines, and sent several expeditions to Borneo beginning in the year 1816. But the invasion of the Chinese sphere was at first defeated by such weapons as poisoned water. Though between two enemies, the natives and the Dutch, the Chinese held out for years. In 1826 intervention was interrupted for a long period by the Great Java War. Finally, Chinese obstinacy was defeated by Dutch phlegm. The year 1854 saw the 'complete extinction' of the *kongsis*. However, the Captain Liou A Sin of the Lanfong *kongsi*, was granted independence until his death by the Dutch in return for services rendered, but when he died in 1884 and the Dutch Government took possession of his territory there was a serious revolt.

There are extant at least two contemporary accounts of the *kongsis* during the height of their power, one Dutch and one English. Temminck tells us that the *kongsis* were democratic communities formed with the object of exploiting for their profit the gold and diamond mines. They were divided into public associations of which three accounted for the greatest number of members and these three *kongsis* occupied the leading position and exercised control over the smaller ones distributed through the interior. All Chinese belonging to the *kongsis* shared in the gains and the losses of the mining enterprises. The Lanfong *kongsi* in the Sambas Residency had an armed force of 6,000 fighting men: the Taykong and the Lara Sin-ta-kiou *kongsis* in the Sambas Residency had 10,000 and 5,000 fighting men respectively.[17]

[15] Hunt, p. 385.
[16] Schlegel, *R. Col. Int.* (1885), i. 450.　　　[17] *Coup d'œil général*, ii. 399.

In February 1834, a report having been brought to Singapore that the people of a Chinese colony on the west coast of Borneo were anxious to establish a permanent commercial intercourse with the British Settlement, some merchants of Singapore dispatched Mr G. W. Earl in the schooner *Stamford* to that part with a cargo of opium, tea, and other commodities to exchange for the product of the gold-mines of Borneo.[18] He found the Chinese colony between two small Dutch settlements on the banks of the principal rivers, one at Pontianak and one at Sambas. Sinkawan, the chief seaport of the Chinese, was not down in the charts. It was defended by a barricade of stakes. He saw the Chinese boiling sea water to make salt. He was given an audience by the *kongsi*, and found the court-house filled with half-naked Chinese 'each of which considered himself authorized to join in the discussion which ensued, and endeavoured to make himself heard above his neighbour'. The noise at last became perfectly deafening and Earl was glad to escape under the plea of wishing to inspect the town. The Chinese were vexed and some bad feeling ensued. The town he found to consist of a single street of low wooden houses, the front rooms of each being shops for the sale of grain, meat, groceries, &c, or rooms appropriated to opium-smoking. The court-house, which was detached from the town, contained a large room for the transaction of public business, and several apartments which were occupied by the *kongsi* and their families. It was surrounded by a low turf wall with a gate opposite to the town near which several long *jingals*, or swivel guns, carrying balls of about one pound weight, were placed muzzle up, leaning against the wall. Many of the women were Chinese, though the majority were Dyaks.[19]

The *kongsi* at Sinkawan hesitated to open the port for trade for fear of a breach with the Dutch and wished Earl to wait until they could communicate with the Chinese Governor who dwelt at Montradok, the capital, about thirty-five miles in the interior. Earl, however, decided to make arrangements with the Dutch at Sambas and thereupon proceeded to that place. The Dutch representative, Mr Rumswinkle, informed him that he must make use of Sambas which had lately been a free port to vessels of all flags.

Before the arrival of the Dutch, says Earl, Sambas was a nest of pirates. In 1812 it was destroyed by the British, but in 1823 the Dutch again settled in Pontianak. They purchased the monopoly of the diamond mining from the Sultan for $50,000 and dispatched troops to take possession of the Chinese mines. The Chinese poisoned the wells and harassed the invaders by cutting off their supplies, and finally forced

---

[18] G. W. Earl, *The Eastern Seas, or Voyages and Discoveries in the Indian Archipelago in 1832–33* (London, 1837), p. 28.
[19] The Dyak women were shapely: the Chinese women were all 'large-footed' (i.e. their feet were not bound) (ibid. pp. 272, 292).

them to evacuate the territory. But the Dutch still held the trump card, and this was the control of the sea. It was clear the Chinese would eventually have to come to terms. The Dutch derived their revenues from salt, opium, customs duties, and a capitation tax on all Chinese who arrived in or left the country. Before the Dutch took possession of the west coast in 1823, 3,000 Chinese used to arrive annually, but immigration had now almost entirely ceased.

Earl estimates the total number of Chinese in west Borneo to have been 150,000—about 90,000 in the Chinese districts and the remainder in districts under the control of the Dutch. The Malays he puts at 50,000, the Bugis at 10,000, the Arabs at 400, the Javanese and Amboynese at 150, the Dutch at 80, and the Dyaks in the neighbourhood of 250,000. The Chinese were 'chiefly of the tribe which forms the lowest class at Canton, being, I believe, of Tartar origin' (namely, Hakkas [Khehs]).

The belated Dutch victory was an empty one. For years they had had control of the main ports such as Pontianak and had refused to trade with the Chinese except through these ports. The Chinese, though virtually shut off in the interior, had refused to yield to coercion and had learnt to exist without commerce. Immigration from China practically dried up.

Nor did the extinction of the *kongsis* bring about a cure of the political and economic ills of Borneo. De Groot and Schlegel (and they make a powerful combination) are agreed as to the nature of the trouble. This is how Schlegel expresses it:

De Groot says: after the end of the wars against the *kongsis* they [Sambas, &c] were reduced to poor agricultural districts, mines nearly abandoned. We entirely share his opinion that the abolition of the *kongsis* and the diminution of the Chinese population resulting from this abolition, have dealt to the development of Borneo a blow from which perhaps she will never recover.[20]

De Groot asks why the Government leave the Javanese their communal institutions and take away those of the Chinese. Why, he repeats, this sinophobia, this fear of a population which has never given any reason for fear to the Netherlands Government?

The fact was that without their *kongsi* organization the Chinese became much as a nest of white ants becomes when its central ganglion, or brain, the 'queen', is removed. (Or with such a useful community as the Chinese it would perhaps be more fitting to resort to the bees for an analogy!) But the Chinese, as ever, had strong powers of recuperation.

At this point it will be convenient to leave Borneo for a time while we resume the story of the Chinese in other parts of Indonesia.

Sumatra and the Rhio (Riouw) Archipelago

Chinese immigration to Sumatra is comparatively recent. Trading contacts were, of course, of ancient date, and the account of the annual

[20] De Groot, *Het Kongsiwezen van Borneo*, p. 163; Schlegel, *R. Col. Int.* (1885), i. 458.

visits to Achin (Acheh) by Dampier in 1689 has already been given. Captain Forrest, who visited Achin in 1762, 1775, and 1784, found no Chinese there, though he adds 'Chinese were there in Commodore Beaulieu's time'.[21] There was also a very early settlement of Chinese at Palembang.[22] Marsden, too, speaks of the Chinese at Bencoolen in his *History of Sumatra*. He mentions in particular Kee Soon, 'one of the most able cultivators among the people who worked the ground with indefatigable pains and dunged high', and who nearly had his heart broken by struggling against nature, the soil being so ungrateful, and he would have become bankrupt had it not been for the help of the (English) East India Company.[23]

It is said that the Dutch East India Company bought tin from the Sultan of Palembang as early as 1710, and the directors of the company signed a contract with this Malay potentate in 1722. By doing so the Dutch obtained a trade monopoly.[24]

The native rulers of Palembang soon discovered that the skill of the Chinese miners was superior to the primitive methods of their own subjects. They therefore sent their recruiting agents to the southern provinces of China to enlist workers for their mines at Bangka. In 1812 the Sultan of Palembang ceded his mineral rights in Bangka and Billiton to the King of England. From this time onwards a representative, first of the British and then of the Dutch, resided in Bangka and contracted with the Chinese miners. When the Dutch took over from the British in 1816 the mines became the property of the Netherlands Indies Government.[25]

The Chinese miners continued with their own primitive methods until after the middle of the century, after which Western experts began to modernize the mining operations. In Billiton the native population managed very cleverly for a long time to conceal the richest mining deposits, but these were eventually worked by the Billiton Maatschappij and after 1923 by the Netherlands Indies Government.[26]

In extension of this account by Mr Braake, we may quote from Dr Cator who says that when a representative of the Netherlands Indies Government in 1825 restarted mining the tin deposits in Billiton, there

---

[21] *Voyage to Mergui Archipelago*, p. 59.

[22] On 21 May 1687 Dampier's vessel overtook at Pulo Condore a great junk from Palembang, laden with pepper. It was full of little rooms or partitions 'like our well-boats' (Dampier's 'Account of the Philippines', in *Pinkerton's Voyages*, xi. 2). Beeckman (ibid. p. 147) in 1714 found at Palembang 'some Mohammedans and a few Chinese'.

[23] William Marsden, *The History of Sumatra, containing an Account of the Government, Laws, Customs, and Manners of the Native Inhabitants, &c.* (London, 1784). James Lancaster visited Achin in June 1602, but did not find any Chinese there. He mentions Gujarats, Bangalis, Malabaris, Peguans, and Patani Malays (see Hakluyt Soc., ser. 2, lxxxv (1940), p. 90).

[24] Alex. L. ter Braake, *Mining in the Netherlands East Indies* (N.Y., 1944), Bull. 4, p. 36.

[25] 'The Dutch employ Chinese miners to whom they pay 6 dollars for every pecul (picul) of tin delivered on the coast in a pure state, which they sell in Java for 16 dollars a pecul' (Davidson, *Trade and Travel*, p. 87).   [26] Ter Braake, p. 36.

was no other mining enterprise in the whole island. Nor were any mining operations going on in 1851 when extensive surveys were made. It may be assumed, therefore, that before 1851 there had been no real exploitation of these fields, though the existence of deposits was widely known. To begin with, free Chinese coolies were employed, but owing to the rivalry of the Bangka mines it was decided in 1853 to solve the problem by sending recruiting agents to China: in consequence, 253 men were brought from Hong Kong and Whampoa.[27]

Bangka's history is somewhat similar to that of Billiton. The Chinese settlements in Sumatra were relatively inconsiderable until the third or fourth decade of the nineteenth century. Collet says that the epoch of the foundation of Singapore fixes the period of this new immigration, but it was not until the development of the tobacco cultivation at Deli, Langkat, and Serdang (1864–70) that there was an inflow sufficiently considerable, taking the good years with the bad, to compensate for the losses due to death and, above all, to repatriation.[28]

The above are the main facts concerning the Chinese in this area during the period under review: the rest are miscellanea explaining or high-lighting them. Temminck tells us that by order of the Sultans the Chinese in the town of Palembang were not allowed to live on land; they were compelled to live on the river in boats and on rafts.[29] We learn from Davidson of the disgraceful traffic carried on in the 1830s and 1840s by Chinese between Padang and Nias. They visited the island of Nias and purchased hundreds of its inhabitants for whom they found markets all along the coast. Those brought to Padang were not, indeed, sold as slaves, but they were registered in the Resident's office and held as 'bond-debtors' for terms ranging from 7 to 15 or even 20 years. During this period of servitude they were treated as slaves but were free at its expiration. They also had the option of buying their liberty in the meantime if they could raise the money.[30]

But as an offset to this example of callous Chinese rapacity (remembering, however, that slavery still existed in other parts of the globe, including America, and was not abolished in the Dutch East Indies until 1860) Earl in 1834 (or early 1835) gives us a picture of Ban Ok, the Captain China of Rhio, 'whose hospitality and benevolence were exercised indiscriminately to all who approached him, without distinction of country or colour'.[31]

Chinese labour in Sumatra in the second half of the nineteenth century is referred to in the following chapter.

[27] Cator, *Economic Position of Chinese*, pp. 184 ff.
[28] J. A. Collet, *Terres et peuples de Sumatra* (Amsterdam, 1925), p. 193.
[29] *Coup d'œil général*, ii. 46.   [30] *Trade and Travel*, p. 87.
[31] Ban Ok, a plump, good-humoured looking man, advanced towards Earl and his companions, and, 'after giving each a hearty shake of the hand, called for chairs and bottles of Hodgson's pale ale' (Earl, *Eastern Seas*, p. 140).

As regards the Chinese in Eastern Indonesia, as long as the Dutch monopoly of the spice trade was maintained (until 1854) the Chinese were not wanted in that area. After that time there was no inducement for the Chinese to go there for the Moluccas were now poor. There were no plantations; therefore coolies were not needed. The same was true of the Celebes and the Lesser Sunda Islands from Bali to Timor. There was some trading with the natives of the smaller islands and of the New Guinea coast, but this was not considerable, for the whole area remained infested with pirates until the last quarter of the century.[32]

43

NINETEENTH-CENTURY DUTCH ECONOMY AND THE CHINESE

AFTER the resumption of Dutch rule in 1816 many changes were made and strong pressure was put on the natives to produce for export. During the brief English occupation of 1811–16 Raffles sought to introduce the system of peasant proprietorship prevailing in British India, using the village headman as his agent.[1] In doing so he was following a policy already advocated by Dirk van Hogendorp, the protagonist of a colonial administration on liberal lines. The machinery at the disposal of Raffles was insufficient, and the peasants he established fell in many cases into the hands of Chinese money-lenders. The system, with many other of Raffles's reforms, did not long survive the British administration, but the tradition of a liberal policy on the lines of van Hogendorp's proposals and the Raffles experiments survived and bore fruit in the last decades of the century.[2]

The famous 'culture system' was formally inaugurated in 1830 by Governor-General van den Bosch. Under this scheme native cultivators were exempted from the ground-tax, but they were compelled to devote one-fifth of their land to crops indicated by the administration, and to hand over the yield in lieu of taxes. Under van den Bosch himself the scheme seems to have worked fairly well, but, involving as it did a com-

---

[32] It has been suggested with some show of reason that the Chinese need a developing community as an economic environment and that a decaying area does not attract them.

[1] In this section RIIA, *Neth. Overseas Territories* is followed.

[2] On this passage Dr Vlekke comments: 'The problem of peasant proprietorship retained the attention of the Dutch administration. The number of proprietors grew gradually. I do not think that Raffles "established" any. He indicated a line of policy (which was easier to indicate than to carry out) and, as always, tried to suggest that his ideas had been realised. Therefore there was no relapse after his departure. Most of Raffles' reforms were retained after 1816. Even under the Culture System they were not abolished.'

bination of the *métayer* and the forced labour system, it was liable to great abuses, which increased until the home Government took action in 1854, when the whole colonial system was overhauled. The Regulations for the Government of Netherlands India promulgated in that year mitigated the despotic character of the administration and paved the way for the progressive reduction of servitude of all kinds, including the culture system. Extensive agrarian reforms were delayed until 1870. By that time the compulsory cultivation of pepper, cochineal, and indigo for the Government had already ceased, and from 1878 onwards the sugar plantations, at that time cultivated by forced labour, by the reforms of de Waal, the then Minister of the Colonies, were restricted and compulsory cultivation ceased altogether in 1890.[3]

The de Waal agrarian reforms prepared the way for the steady development of native agriculture which went on until the Japanese invasion in the next century. Not only was the peasant protected against economically stronger groups by the prohibition of the expropriation of his land, but also assistance was provided for the sale of the product. Native ownership of land was in many cases hereditary and individual, but part of the land was the common property of the village.

Simultaneously a sound foundation was laid for estate agriculture which did not encroach on native-tilled land but was mainly established on hitherto unused Crown lands, obtained on long lease from the Government. The estates, however, could in the case of some export crops, notably sugar and tobacco, rent native land, and later on the greater part of these two crops was grown on rented land. Government policy was in the direction of preventing the rise of non-native agrarian groups and the prevention of the formation of a rural native landless proletariat.[4] Exceptions to this occurred in special areas, particularly in west Bangka where large Chinese holdings came into being.

In 1848 the *Grondwet*, or fundamental law of the Netherlands, recognized, for the first time, the responsibility of the Dutch nation for its colonial dependencies. The *Grondwet* involved certain important changes which were embodied in an Act passed in 1854 and commonly known as the Regulations for the Government of Netherlands India. They reformed the judicature, introduced elementary education for the natives, and abolished slavery in Java as from January 1860.

The remainder of the nineteenth century from the beginning of the disappearance of the 'culture system' is known as the 'Liberal period', and is characterized by the development of private Western enterprise, mainly Dutch. The Chinese in this period made even greater progress

---

[3] 'A delusive appearance of prosperity under the "culture system" was given by the immense increase in exports, and the great profits made by European and Chinese manufacturers, contractors, and officials. . . . The native population increased by some 50 per cent. (1870–1900) but decreased in average wealth' (Sir Alan Pim, *Colonial Agricultural Production* (London, 1946), p. 21).   [4] RIIA, *Neth. Overseas Territories*, p. 47.

than the Europeans, though they did not increase so rapidly in numbers.[5]
There were already nearly 150,000 of them in Java and Madura alone by
the middle of the century, and by 1900 there were 277,000 in Java and
Madura and some 250,000 in the Outer Provinces.

Reference has already been made to Raffles's reforms: they demand
further mention at this point since they have an important bearing on the
economic position of the Chinese in the succeeding decades. The plan of
requiring, not a fixed amount, but a proportion of the average crop,
while it seemed to promise the Government the maximum that it could
fairly demand, led to difficulties and frauds.[6] When Raffles wrote his
minute of 1814 in which he had adopted the system of individual settlement as the normal, he had had actual experience of this form of settlement only in its application in districts formerly subject to Chinese
farmers. It was said that the new system, when introduced into a district
in Pekalongan formerly under Chinese, gave a net revenue nearly four-
fold that formerly received, which was collected with perfect ease. On
the other hand de Salis, in his report on Pekalongan and Kedoe, 1816,
said that one district that was formerly leased to Chinese and was now
under individual settlement, was always in arrears.[7] Raffles also proclaimed the abolition of internal duties and ordered that the market tolls
should be administered directly by the Government instead of being
farmed out to Chinese, but his regulations had little practical effect.
Even in his own time, it is said, new toll gates were established where
none had existed before, and the existing revenue-farmers persisted in
their abuses.[8] After the restoration of the Indies to Holland in 1816 the
predominant position of the Chinese in the economy of the islands was
maintained for many years, for, although imports of most kinds were no
longer in the hands of the Government, the sale of salt and opium and
buying up of sugar, tobacco, coffee, indigo, &c, at first remained almost
exclusively in its hands, but the Chinese were often used as intermediaries. Moreover, the system of farming out taxation (poll-taxes,
slaughter-house taxes, bazaar taxes, opium monopoly, &c) continued
until after the middle of the nineteenth century, so that the Chinese, as
farmers, retained their influence.[9]

The Chinese were the obvious contractors, for, as van den Bosch
remarked, the Dutch themselves 'could not be beaten out of their home
(in Holland) with sticks. "Gentle pressure" had to be exerted to induce
even the Chinese in some cases to accept the onus of being middlemen,
and in the 1830s a leading Chinese was warned that he could not expect

---

[5] Furnivall, *Neth. India*, p. 213.
[6] Furnivall points out that Raffles required the payment of taxes in money with the result
that 'cultivators unused to handle money but faced with a demand for the payment of revenue
in money, mortgaged their crops, their cattle and their land, so that more land passed to the
Chinese than under the former practice'.   [7] Day, *Policy and Administration*, p. 183.
[8] Ibid. p. 201.   [9] Cator, *Economic Position of Chinese*, p. 97.

to succeed his father as the Chinese Captain unless he accepted a contract. After vainly offering $5,000 for a substitute he had to comply, and within a few years he was the wealthiest man in Java.'[10]

The position had been consolidated by the middle of the century and, as Mr Jan O. M. Broek says, 'generally speaking, the natives form the agrarian base, the Chinese and Arabs the commercial middle class, and the Westerners the small but ruling apex of the socio-economic pyramid'.[11] Standing between Europeans and natives, and necessary to both classes, the Chinese were able to levy toll on both. So much of the newly created wealth as went to the Javanese passed immediately to the Chinese as holders of all the opium shops, pawnshops, and gambling houses. Furnivall points out that while in 1900 the natives were buying much less cloth per head than in 1880, the revenue from opium had risen from fl. 10·5 million in 1867 to fl. 1,817 million in 1897 and, during the same period the pawnshop revenue rose from fl. 365 thousand to fl. 1·23 million, the gaming revenue from fl. 365 thousand to fl. 844 thousand, and the excise revenue (also largely collected through the Chinese) from fl. 112 thousand to fl. 7·37 million.[12] At the same time the Chinese profited on a similar scale from the growth of trade, both wholesale and retail. All that the natives sold to Europeans they sold through Chinese, and all that the natives bought from Europeans they bought through Chinese. Chinese, too, were at hand to supply the demand for clerks, accountants, salesmen, or artisans and at rates which commerce and industry could pay. This race took part in the organization of native production so much so that an inquiry into the *batik* (cloth) industry in 1892 revealed that the replacement of native cloth by imported cloth, which the *batik* workers bought through Chinese, had resulted in the transfer of the whole industry to the Chinese, 'with native workmen in a position not unlike slavery'.[13]

With their undoubted energy and acumen it may be wondered why it was that the Chinese did not threaten to oust the Europeans from their supremacy as capitalists. They did indeed compete with the latter in production, many of the large estates (*particuliere landerijen*) having passed before 1900 into their hands and they were conspicuous in the timber business.[14] But the bulk of the larger undertakings continued to be European. There seems, indeed, to be a limit to the ability of the Chinese to organize on the big scale, a limit arising perhaps from the family system and making them less capable of running large joint-stock enterprises with the anonymous character of their shareholders. They seem to lack, says Clive Day, the breadth and boldness of conception

---

[10] Furnivall, *Neth. India*, p. 107.
[11] Jan O. M. Broek, *The Economic Development of the Netherlands Indies* (N.Y., 1942), p. 5.
[12] Ibid. p. 213.　　　　　[13] Furnivall, *Neth. India*, p. 213.
[14] In Sumatra the timber *Panglongs* in the forests were a Chinese monopoly and their trade was with Singapore.

that would enable them to enter upon large enterprises as rivals of the Europeans, but between the Dutch and the natives they have an assured position. Even in retail trade they did not everywhere have things their own way, and in the Outer Provinces the Chinese played a minor role. Here the native retained the initiative and reaped the profit, whereas in Java he was all too often simply a cog in the complicated machinery of Western trade.[15]

No two authors (in Clive Day's opinion) can agree in describing the moral characteristics of the Chinese, and certainly there is a great deal of contradiction in the accounts that have been preserved for us. Schlegel said that the Chinese were easy to govern; Temminck tells us that in west Borneo 'the Chinese miners formed the most boorish, the most turbulent, and the least tractable part of the population'.[16] He admitted, however, that they were regular enough in their family morals and in their marriages with women of the country, and their establishments were always tranquil and well regulated. But, like the Jews, they were always greedy of gain. G. W. Earl, writing in the 1830s, is critical of their function and their value to the community as a whole:

By some persons [he says] the Chinese are supposed to confer great benefit on Java, but on closer examination it will be found that their settlement on the island has been productive of very injurious effects. That they have enriched themselves and contributed to the aggrandisement of the Europeans cannot be doubted, but the interests of the natives have suffered proportionately . . . the accumulation of wealth forms their sole object, and being more energetic, and also more crafty than the Javanese, they have also managed in their commercial transactions to trammel the latter with debts from which they can rarely afterwards extricate themselves. . . .

Earl (and he seems a reliable witness in spite of the comparative shortness of his stay in the Indies) tells us that the Chinese adopted an artful and ungenerous system in their dealings with the native cultivators. They prevailed upon the cultivators to take goods in advance to be paid for by the produce of the ensuing harvest at a stipulated price, always much below its real value.[17] The following year the price of goods supplied by the Chinese would be augmented and that to be paid for the produce reduced, and the cultivator was nearly certain ever afterwards to be in debt and a slave to his creditor. The minor Government imports were farmed exclusively by the Chinese, and since these included all the smaller articles consumed by the natives the impositions pressed hardly upon those who were least able to support them. A hawker of sweet-meats or of fruit could not follow his calling without a daily *chop* or licence which had to be purchased from the farmer, and numbers of

15 Broek, *Economic Development*, p. 35.   16 *Policy and Administration*, p. 301.
17 Dr Vlekke notes, 'Was not the advance sale of the harvest customary in Indonesia—and probably in other parts of the world? It certainly existed in the Spice Islands before the arrival of the Europeans.'

Chinese were always prowling about ready to pounce and carry off to prison any unfortunate beings who tried to avoid the imposition. It was not surprising, said Earl, that the natives detested the Chinese, for they saw in them the active agents of a system of oppression by which they were frequently reduced to beggary.[18]

Immigrant Chinese arriving in Indonesia usually brought nothing but a bundle of clothes, a mat, and a pillow. When they made money, as so many did, they were careful not to flaunt the fact in the faces of those from whom they made it. 'The main streets', says Earl of Javanese towns, 'were appropriated by the Chinese merchants, who, however, make not outward display, since, from the mean appearance of their shops, a stranger could never for a moment suppose that the occupants were rolling in riches.'[19]

No one, however, speaks with greater asperity of the Chinese and their role than the ardent French colonialist and defender of European pretensions, J. Chailley-Bert, writing of the situation as it was at the end of the nineteenth century. 'Who other than the Chinese', he asks, 'would mix with the natives, speak their language, take part in their life, capture their confidence, condescend to the most disgusting details, harshly exact their due and sometimes more than their due, and take advantage of the least infraction of the letter of a contract to impose harsher conditions?' (He cites as an example the case of the farming out to the Chinese of cattle slaughtering, by which three florins went to the farmer for every animal slaughtered.) The Chinese admitted no moral obligation whatsoever, and there was everywhere evidence of their 'harshness, their immorality, and their work of demoralisation'.[20]

Yet the privileged position that they held in the economy of the Indies did not entail any great improvement in their civil liberties. They were still confined to certain towns and to certain areas of these towns; they could not land without a permit, and they could not travel in the interior without a pass.[21] The restrictions on immigration, however, were slackly enforced. But in one respect their position improved, for in 1855 they were brought under the European Civil Code in most of their commercial transactions, and this gave them a higher social standing than the natives. But nevertheless they continued in all other ways to be a race apart from both natives and Europeans.

Chinese Labour in Sumatra

New currents of Chinese immigration were flowing into the Indies before the end of the century and from different tribes of Chinese. This

[18] *Eastern Seas*, pp. 30, 31.
[19] Ibid. p. 28. But as against this we have the evidence of Raffles, and Ong Tae-hae and others, of the ostentation shown by the Chinese of Indonesia in their luxurious houses and fine equipages.   [20] *Java*, p. 113.
[21] Temminck, *Coup d'œil général*, p. 301; Furnivall, *Neth. India*, p. 213.

was notably the case in Sumatra's East Coast. In 1870 there were only about 150 Javanese in the East Coast region of Sumatra, the majority of the 4,000 labourers being Chinese.[22] From 1864 onwards thousands of Chinese coolies were recruited for the tobacco plantations. After the question of the protection of labour had attracted attention, recruiting was done either through the (British) Protector of Chinese, Singapore, or through the official bureau in Swatow.[23] Later on this Chinese labour on rubber and tobacco plantations was largely replaced by Javanese labour.[24]

Between 1888 and 1931 some 305,000 Chinese landed at Belawan. The great majority came from Swatow or Hong Kong where the Association of Deli Planters (D.P.V.) had recruiting offices. Between 1864 and 1888 the labourers were obtained through coolie-brokers in Singapore. From 1890 to 1914 German shipping companies transported Chinese labourers backwards and forwards between Belawan and south China, but from 1914 to 1931 ships of the K.P.M. brought the labourers to Sumatra.

For some sixty years the tobacco planters of Sumatra relied on Chinese labourers, but in the 1920s the number of Chinese declined while that of Javanese increased. The recruiting and importation of labourers from China stopped on 31 December 1931 on account of the high immigration fee, which was raised to 150 guilders when the penal sanctions against labourers were dropped.

Number of 'Field' Labourers employed by Sumatra Tobacco Estates[25]

1930: 21,000 Chinese 'field' labourers; 5,000 Javanese
1931: 19,000   „   „   „   6,000   „
1939: 8,000   „   „   „   10,000   „

---

[22] A. D. A. de Kat Angelino, *Colonial Policy* (The Hague, 1931), p. 504.

[23] Pickering, the Singapore Protector of Chinese, made himself unpopular with the Deli (Sumatra) Planters' Committee over charges he made against them of repudiating contracts made by their agents in the Colony, and he spoke of the substitution of inferior men for those brought to engage at the Protectorate. This charge was denied in a pamphlet, *The Deli Chinese Question* (1882).

[24] Measures for the control and protection of Chinese contract labour in Sumatra are contained in *Eerste Verslag van den Dienst der Arbeidinspectie in Nederlands-Indië* (Batavia, 1913) and *Derde Verslag van den Dienst der Arbeidinspectie en Koliewerving in Nederlands-Indië* (Weltevreden, Filial, 1914).

[25] See Karl Pelzer, *Arbeiterwanderungen in Südostasien* (Hamburg, 1935), pp. 90–96, from which these details are taken.

44

THE EVOLUTION OF THE CIVIL STATUS
OF THE CHINESE

THROUGH the Chinese headmen the company transmitted its orders to the Chinese notables for execution, and these officials for their part kept the Government informed as to what was going on in their communities. They served as petitioners, confidants, and representatives of their group, while at the same time they filled a semi-official position. It was the policy of *laissez-faire* so long as peace and order prevailed, but it was also one of indifference, and with the evolution of ideas as to governmental responsibility was regarded as being one of neglect.[1]

Up to 1824 in Java the civil affairs of the Chinese were dealt with by the European courts of justice (*Raden van Justitie*); their criminal affairs by the *Landraden* (courts of justice for the natives) in the inner territories (*binnenlanden*), and in the districts of Batavia, Samarang, and Surabaya by the Raden van Justitie. The private law applied was in the case of the Raden van Justitie the European law (with a few exceptions as to Chinese law of inheritance), and in the case of the Landraden customary (i.e. Indonesian, Chinese, or Arab) law. But the Chinese did not bring their marriage and divorce disputes before the courts.

By a 'publication' of 1824 (that is to say by an Order of the Governor-General van der Capellen in Council published in the *Staatsblad*, or Government Gazette) it was ordered that the Chinese all over Java in their civil and criminal affairs should be judged by the native courts. Those who complained of this were not the Chinese but the Dutch merchants who were of the opinion that their disputes with the Chinese were better dealt with by the Raden van Justitie than by the Landraden.

The East Indian Government Act[2] of 1848, whereby foreign Orientals were placed on the same footing as natives, did not alter the position of the Chinese in Indonesia, which position was confirmed by the Koninklijk Besluit Bepalingen van Wetgeving (Royal Decree on the Principles of the Law). In the same decree permission was given to individual non-Europeans to submit themselves to European law for some definite transaction (e.g. for a contract of sale or hire, &c) and this was extended

[1] Vandenbosch, *Dutch East Indies*, pp. 356 ff., and compare the situation in Malaya in Purcell, *Chinese in Malaya*, pp. 142 ff. and chap. 29 of the present work.
[2] This apparently is a translation of 'Indisch Reglement' of 1848 ('The Indisch Reglement is a Code of Police and Criminal Procedure for natives', Furnivall, *Neth. India*, p. 214).

later—in 1917—to allow a person to submit himself to the whole of European civil law.

By an ordinance of the Governor-General of 1855, made at the request of the Dutch merchants of Batavia, the Dutch law of property, contract, commerce, torts, and of testamentary succession, as laid down in the Netherlands Indies Civil Code, was declared applicable to foreign Orientals, which meant that when questions in these fields of law arose they had to be judged in the European Courts. Whereas most of the legal disputes which were brought before the courts were matters of contract, torts, or property, it may be said that from 1855 onwards the ordinary jurisdiction in Chinese civil matters was by the Raad van Justitie.

The Chinese never complained of this ordinance of 1855 which in the long run proved to be a great benefit to them, although it was intended by its originators to benefit the Batavian merchant.

The great grievance of the Chinese was that in *criminal* matters they had to be judged by the Landraad and not by the Raad van Justitie. After 1918 the criminal law for Europeans, Chinese, and natives was substantially the same though, as we shall see, the law of procedure differed.

Simultaneously with the growth of the belief in the minds of the Dutch Government that they should take a closer interest in Chinese affairs, the Chinese themselves were becoming conscious of their own nationality. Hitherto those who went abroad and deserted the graves of their ancestors were looked upon as unfilial rascals, but towards the end of the century there was a complete reversal of the official attitude. In 1894, in China, the ban on emigration (so long a dead letter) was officially removed, and this was followed up by a series of acts designed to bind the Chinese more closely to their mother country. The Chinese in the Indies became increasingly resentful of the fact that they were classed with 'other foreign Orientals' and were tried in the same courts, and that to them was applied the same law of procedure, whilst Europeans and others assimilated to them were tried by the European courts with much greater procedural protection. That by being so classified they retained the application of Chinese custom, appeared to them as of less and less consequence as time went on. The recognition in 1899 of the Japanese as Europeans in their legal relations, while the Chinese in most of their activities were left under the native courts, the Chinese received as a slight upon themselves.

The special object of Chinese dislike was the *politie rol*, a court having jurisdiction over minor offences and conducting preliminary examinations.[3] Here an officer of the local civil service often sat as a judge.[4]

---

[3] Vandenbosch, *Dutch East Indies*, 410.
[4] This was true also of Malaya until the 1930s when a newly created Colonial legal service began to take over the magistracies. This was, however, because of the development of

According to Fromberg it was a court

deeply penetrating into the life of the people, in which the administrative power in the person of the chief of police, without obligation to hear witnesses, and, if he hears them, without obligation to place them under oath, sentences in accordance with his finding of the facts, with an immediate execution of sentence, which originally was not suspended even when an appeal was made for pardon.

Often (said Fromberg) acts were punished that were punishable under no existing law, and cases were brought before the *politie rol* which no one dare bring before the *landraad*.[5]

The *landraad*, the intermediate court for natives and foreign Asiatics, was also the object of criticism both from Orientals and Europeans, because it was composed of a legally qualified chairman, usually a European, two native active or pensioned officials, a native officer of justice, a Chinese adviser, and a clerk. 'The non-jurist character of the layman and the recruitment of his service from the official class subjected the court to much the same criticism as was brought against the *politie rol*.'[6]

Another grievance of the Chinese was that, like the natives, they were often subjected to a long confinement before trial, and in house-search and criminal pleading the Europeans had far greater protection against arbitrary action.

Chinese agitation, assisted by the unification policy of van Deventer and other Dutch Liberals, led in 1914 to the abolition of the *politie rol* and in 1917 to a measure which permitted individual non-Europeans to submit themselves to European law, thus participating in its benefits.

Commenting on this, de Kat Angelino in his monumental work says:

The abolition of the police roll [*politie rol*] in Java was also caused to no small extent by a desire to end some disagreeable dualism in matters of justice and to purify it from the appearance of putting Indonesian and other groups as Asiatic populations behind Europeans. In the Residency Court there was a procedure which gave better guarantees than under the police roll. The more fully conscious Chinese group has especially, since about 1905, protested continually against this system. The reform of 1914 was, therefore, important in principle for more than one reason.[7]

Subsequent legislation from 1917 to 1925 had the effect of removing the Chinese completely from the civil jurisdiction of the *landraad*, but by

---

government on the lines of specialization—not through the influence of the principle of the 'separation of powers'.

[5] J. H. Fromberg, *Verspreide Geschriften verzameld door Chung Hua Hui* (Leyden, 1926). This collection of the writings of the champion of the Chinese with a *prae-avis* written on his death-bed fills over 800 pages.

[6] Vandenbosch, *Dutch East Indies*, p. 356.

[7] De Kat Angelino, *Colonial Policy*, ii. 154.

the time of the Japanese invasion their demand to be placed on the same legal footing as Europeans in criminal procedure as well had not been granted.[8]

In 1928 a new regulation passed by the *Volksraad* abolished the jurisdiction of the Chinese headmen.[9]

The legal position of the Chinese in Indonesia is thus summarized by Professor R. D. Kollewijn:[10]

... The Civil Code for Europeans was declared applicable to the Chinese in 1855 in Java (and later in the Residencies of the Outer Islands) as far as the law of contracts, torts and property and of testamentary succession were concerned, and it may be said that this has never given any great difficulty either in or out of the Courts. However, in 1919 for Java and certain of the Residencies in the Outer Islands, and in 1924–25 for the whole of the Netherlands Indies, the European family law (with the exception only of the Chinese law of adoption) and the law in intestate succession were also declared applicable to the Chinese who were Netherlands subjects (i.e. Chinese born in the Netherlands Indies of domiciled parents) and we cannot be easy in our minds about the social effect of these legal measures. It is already certain, for instance, that in one of the important centres of Chinese population in the Netherlands Indies, West Borneo, this statute law has not been able to drive out the law of custom, while there is also justified doubt about the following of the provisions of the European family and inheritance laws in other places.

With respect to the foreign Chinese (*foreign* according to the definition of the nationality law in the Netherlands Indies) the Netherlands Indian judges, according to Netherlands Indian private law, in questions of status and competency, dowry and property law must apply their national laws. Since these Chinese almost without exception come from Chinese provinces where the new Chinese Civil Code is being effectively applied *by the judges*, this implies therefore the modern codified Chinese law.

The comment of another jurist of note is that the European Dutch law was applied to the Chinese by the Dutch in the fixed belief that it was in their best interests, as, for example, when they were brought under the European commercial law in 1855.

Where the European law was inadequate to secure justice, the legislature included a special provision for the Chinese (e.g. *Adoptie*).[11]

It has been suggested that the adoption of the European law was not consistently beneficial. For instance (according to one writer in *Mission Interrupted*) the application to the Chinese of the Dutch Commercial

---

[8] The explanation given to the present writer when he visited The Hague in September 1946 was that the creation of the additional courts necessary to deal with the Chinese on an equality with Europeans was still at the moment a practical impossibility.

[9] De Kat Angelino, ii. 154.

[10] R. D. Kollewijn (Professor of International Law, Batavia, later at Leyden), *A Suggestion for the Undertaking of Research Work in the Field of Private Law by the Institute of Pacific Relations (in Particular the Application of Western Private Law to Chinese*, mimeo. [c. 1938].

[11] M. H. van der Valk, 'De Rechtspositie der Chineezen in Nederlandsch-Indië', *Koloniale Studiën*, nos. 5 & 6 (1936), p. 30.

Code had, by the end of the nineteenth century, 'severely shaken the old Chinese business morals'.[12] Professor Kollewijn considers, however, that there is no reason for believing that this was so. Again it is said that although the company, and after it the Netherlands Government, wished to leave the Chinese in undisturbed enjoyment of their own institutions and customs, they had sometimes erred through inadvertence in their interpretation of Chinese law. In support of this contention it is stated that under the company there had already been an effort to codify the Indonesian and Chinese law of inheritance; nevertheless it had been held that Chinese husbands and wives were not married 'in community of goods' so that the Chinese law of inheritance had been ignored, for according to the old Chinese patriarchal law, far from having no property, the wife herself was the husband's property. If this is stated (says Professor Kollewijn), it must also be added that this ordinance supposed that *all* the property was owned by the husband and that if the wife contended that she was the owner of any particular piece of property she had to prove her claim by way of a deed drawn up by a notary. So that in practice the ordinance conformed very well with the Chinese customary law. (The divergences of the new law of 1917–25 from the old law were much greater, but so also were those between the new Civil Code in China and the old law.) Nor is it correct to say that as a result of the interference with the old Chinese customary law a 'so-called Indo-Chinese customary law developed which varied from place to place, or rather was interpreted differently by different courts according to the lights of the various "experts" consulted'.[13] There were some differences in the opinions of the courts, and even the highest Court of Justice (*het Hooggerechtshof*) did not always adhere to its own precedents, but these differences must not be overestimated.

Emancipation of the Chinese from Restriction of Movement

In 1900 the Chinese could in principle live only where there were Chinese quarters (or *ghettoes* as they have been termed). For every trip he wished to make into the interior a Chinese merchant had to obtain a pass. The system was relaxed in 1904 by the grant of passes valid for a year instead of for a single journey, and in 1910 the right was conceded of free passage along the main highways without a permit, and Chinese notables were exempted from the obligation to obtain a pass. Thus for the first time since their arrival in Indonesia some hundreds of years before (and it must be remembered that restrictions were even more severe under native rule) the otherwise privileged Chinese were allowed to move about at will like free men.

[12] Helsdingen, *Mission Interrupted*, p. 63.
[13] De Kat Angelino, *Colonial Policy*, i, 162.

National Status and the Growth of National Feeling

It is often said that the Chinese became national minded only after the impact of Western nationalism upon their country. Before then they had merely a sense of family, clan, district, or province. It is indeed true that strong localism prevented them for long from thinking or acting as a nation, and that the natives of one province were quite willing to assist a foreign enemy operating in another province;[14] but at the same time they were conscious at all periods in their history that they were the Black-haired Race of the Middle Flowery Kingdom and that all others were 'Outside Barbarians'. It was probably due more to a sense of race consciousness than to rising nationalism that the Chinese regarded it as a slight upon themselves that they still had the status of foreign Orientals. At the same time it is unlikely that the feeling would have had any great strength or direction had it not been for the ferment already in process in their ancestral country and for the impetus given to it by Mr Fromberg. Hitherto they had asked for nothing except the opportunity to improve their own economic position, and had accepted their unequal legal position with equanimity or with resignation.

When with the help of guns and rifles China was opened up to Western trade, the Chinese could not help but remark the importance the Europeans attached to the protection of their own nationals. How very different from their own traditional indifference to the Chinese beyond the seas! And these barbarians had shown themselves superior at least in material strength. There must be some virtue and use in exiled nationals. Her statesmen, too, were able now to see that a great source of strength resided in the Western colonies whose obvious counterpart for China was the Chinese Overseas. But before this great arsenal in the battle with the West could be mobilized it was necessary to defeat the die-hard conservatives on the home front. In 1894 the prohibition of emigration was removed, and those who had gone overseas during the centuries were pardoned. In 1898, when the young Emperor tried to engineer a *coup d'état* to oust the entrenched forces of reaction and to modernize the educational system, he was defeated by the Empress Dowager and interned on an island in the Imperial Palace. Nevertheless, the reform movement gathered strength and when in 1905 the old examination system was finally abolished the way towards educational reform and the modernizing of China was open; but it was not until after the Revolution of 1911 that the new movement gained momentum.

China's new-found interest in her overseas children manifested itself in many ways—some of which were to be obnoxious to the Dutch

[14] Classic examples of this are the coolies recruited by the British in Canton to help them in their advance against Peking in the Second China War (1857–60), and the welcome given to Lord Elgin during the same war by the Chinese notables of Singapore (see Purcell, *Chinese in Malaya*, p. 85).

Government. As early as 1887 the Chinese Government had sent a committee to the Indies to study the commercial relations of China with that country. Permission to send the committee was obtained through diplomatic channels by way of The Hague, and the Netherlands Indies Government received the members as visitors from a friendly State. Then in 1891 the Peking Government requested permission to collect funds among the Chinese in the Indies for flood relief in China. Again in 1906 a Chinese official made a protracted visit to Java for the purpose of bringing about greater uniformity among Chinese commercial societies.[15] In 1907 the Assistant Secretary of the Department of Agriculture, Yang Shih-tshi,[16] visited the Indies to study commercial problems, and as a result of his visit many addresses and petitions were sent to Peking for the Chinese in Indonesia. These were some of the earlier Chinese missions with an allegedly commercial purpose, but already there had been Chinese emissaries with an avowed interest in education, a subject that was to be the source of much controversy and feeling between the two Governments, an important matter which is dealt with in a separate chapter.

As the Chinese Revolution grew nearer, the increasing sense of unity and nationalism among the Chinese began to bring matters to a head. In 1908 Wang Kang-ky, secretary to the Chinese legation at The Hague, travelled in the Indies for several months. At Surabaya he held a semi-official census and recommended that Chinese residents in the Netherlands Indies should choose between Chinese and Dutch nationality. In 1909 two Chinese cruisers appeared in the harbour at Batavia carrying Wa Ta-cheng, Secretary of the Department of Education, who spent some time in Java for the alleged purpose of studying commercial conditions. In 1910 Chao Ts'ung-fan, Adviser to the Department of Agriculture, Industry, and Trade, came for the same purpose.[17]

Against a background of growing nationalism and increasing diplomatic activity the question of national status assumed a new importance. The Dutch law on the subject was not at all clear, and in view of the controversies which were developing with several States it was necessary that it should be clarified.

The East Indian Government Act of 1854 referred to all persons living in the Indies as 'inhabitants', but as a qualification for Government service it demanded Dutch citizenship, and referred to the laws of the Kingdom of the Netherlands for the definition of such citizenship. Of these laws there were two, one of which regulated public law citizenship and the second, civil law citizenship. Under the first citizenship

[15] Vandenbosch, *Dutch East Indies*, p. 359.
[16] This is the name as given by Vandenbosch, but *Tshi* is not an accepted rendering of any sound in the English romanizations (Wade, &c). This is perhaps the Dutch rendering?
[17] Vanderbosch, p. 360.

C.S.E.A.—P 2

were included all persons born in the Netherlands and their descendants. The latter could not lose their citizenship by residence in Dutch territory outside Holland. Thus the descendants of Dutch citizens born in the Indies remained Dutch citizens. Under the civil law, citizenship included all persons born in the kingdom and the colonies of persons domiciled there. *Natives and Chinese born of parents there were specifically included.* Natives and Chinese could therefore sue in the courts of Holland as Dutch citizens, a right they did not enjoy in European courts in the Indies. A law of 1892 put an end to this duality of citizenship, but did nothing to clarify the status of natives and of the children of foreign Asiatics domiciled in the East Indies. Article 12 of the Act even designated them as foreigners, and at best they were regarded only as inhabitants of or residents in Dutch territory, and this had the effect of making their status abroad uncertain. It affected, for example, those Chinese from the Indies living in Siam who wished to claim Dutch citizenship in order to avoid the special tax system applying to the Chinese.[18]

Whatever were the grounds for claiming a Chinese as a Dutch citizen, they were bound to conflict with the Chinese law of nationality (until 1909 unwritten) which was based on the *jus sanguinis* and claimed all persons of Chinese descent through the male line as Chinese. This fact delayed a consular convention between the two countries and it was not signed until 8 May 1910.[19] Although the Chinese strenuously objected to the Dutch nationality law they had to accept it as the price of the right to consular jurisdiction in the East Indies. By a subsequent exchange of notes it was agreed that the East Indian legislation would be conclusive in determining Dutch or Chinese nationality.

But it was not to be assumed from this agreement that the Chinese Government, especially after the Revolution on the eve of which the consular convention had been signed, had abandoned its claim to the moral support, if not the technical allegiance, of all of Chinese race in Southeast Asia.

To continue this technical but essential description in Vandenbosch's words:

The law of 1910 dropped the classification of Dutch citizens and foreigners, and substituted for it that of citizens and subjects. The law adopted the *jus soli* and declared all children born of parents vested [domiciled] in the Dutch East Indies were Dutch subjects even if not Dutch citizens. The status of Dutch citizens would be lost through nationalization in a foreign State, marriage with a foreign man, government or military service under a foreign State without the consent of the

---

[18] See pp. 138-9.
[19] The first permanent Chinese legation was appointed to London in 1877. The minister was accredited to London and Paris. A Chinese legation was opened at Washington in 1878, in Tokyo the same year, in 1879 at St Petersburg. Consuls were appointed in various ports abroad in the next decade or so (see Dr Tung Ling, *An Historical Study of the Establishment of Chinese Diplomatic Organs* (Leyden, 1946)).

Governor-General, and by sojourn in a foreign State without registration with a Dutch consular official within three months of arrival, and, in the case of continuing sojourn, failure to register within the first three months of each calendar year.[20]

Fromberg criticized the law on two grounds—first, that it sought to put under Dutch jurisdiction as many as possible of the inhabitants of the country, and secondly, it allowed the status of subjects to lapse as quickly as possible when outside Dutch territory. The law (says Vandenbosch) does indeed have the aspect of forced naturalization and must frequently create a dual nationality, for no provision is made for repudiation on attainment of majority. The requirement of repeated registration was very unfair to the natives abroad, especially when they were employed at some distance from a consulate, and, as might be expected, many failed to register. The defect was remedied in 1929 when the law was revised to exclude the indigenous peoples of the East Indies from this provision.[21]

To the Chinese of the Indies this law was a great disappointment, for it conferred no rights, benefited them but little, and yet removed them from the protection of the Chinese consuls.

45

DUTCH-CHINESE RELATIONS, 1900–42

In the preceding chapter the questions of status under the law and the nationality of the Chinese of Indonesia have been discussed: in this chapter it is intended to cover a wider field, bringing in Dutch-Chinese and Indonesian-Chinese social and economic relations, though legal questions of a similar or related character will again arise.

In the nineteenth century Raffles, van der Capellen, and van den Bosch had all tried to attack the position of the Chinese, but these had always responded by finding new means of livelihood and growing richer and more powerful. We have seen, too, that during the Liberal period it was the Chinese who made the greatest material advance proportionately with the new-found freedom of enterprise. When in 1900, however, there was a decline in profits, the jealousy of the Europeans was directed to the Chinese who were enabled to trade successfully by reason of their lower standard of living, which meant a lower wages bill. Their strong economic position in the Indies (much stronger than in

---

[20] *Dutch East Indies*, p. 363.

[21] 'Chinese and Indians in Malaya who are Dutch subjects but have not reported to the Netherlands Consul-General since the liberation must do so before 30 April, otherwise they will cease to be Dutch subjects' (*Straits Times*, 2 Feb. 1948).

1850) was held to be due to their exploitation of the improvidence and vices of the natives.

Indeed, with both Europeans and natives the Chinese of this period had an unsavoury reputation. They were accused of exploiting the natives and of dishonesty in trade with the Europeans. They were also known to be prominent in the bribing of officials with handsome gifts at New Year and on other festivals. But it should have been clear that, whatever their guilt in these several respects, it was not the Chinese who invented the system, nor had they a monopoly of the abuses. Theirs was the unenviable position of middlemen, exposed to the animosity of two opposed forces, the natives and the Europeans, though useful as a buffer between them. In any case, high officials of the period gave support to the theory of the detrimental role of the Chinese in Indonesian society, and many regarded them as the 'main cause of the diminishing welfare of the Javanese'.

The Indies were now on the eve of the inauguration of the 'ethical policy', when, as a result of what is sometimes called a 'change of heart', the Dutch suddenly became acutely aware of their responsibilities towards the native peoples of their empire.[1] Since the Chinese were thought to be inimical to the welfare of the natives, many officials interpreted their duty of protecting the natives as necessarily meaning baiting the Chinese. The Dutch Colonial Minister, Fock (who, incidentally, made a fortune as an advocate of the Chinese in Batavia), shared the common view as to the baneful nature of the Chinese, and in his Report on measures for the relief of the Indies placed in the foreground the pressing need for stricter control over Chinese problems. 'It is unnecessary', he said, 'to argue that they exercise a pernicious influence in the interior.'[2]

The year of the Boxer rebellion was a significant one for the Chinese of the Indies since it was marked by several governmental acts of great importance to them. In that year the farming of opium was abolished and a Government monopoly to restrict the use of opium substituted; the decision was made to extend the Government monopoly of pawning throughout Indonesia; and in the same year the Government began its system of agricultural credit banks with the object of furnishing cheaper credit to the farmers and rescuing them from the clutches of the

[1] The 'ethical policy' is usually dated from 1901. In a speech from the throne that year by Queen Wilhelmina occurred the following significant passage: 'As a Christian Power the Netherlands is obligated in the East Indian archipelago to regulate better the legal position of native Christians, to lend support on a firm basis to Christian missions, and to imbue the whole conduct of Government with the consciousness that the Netherlands had a moral duty to fulfil with respect to the people and these regions. In connection with this the diminished welfare of the population of Java merits special attention. I desire to institute an investigation into this.'

[2] D. Fock, *Beschouwingen . . . van den economischen toestand der inlandsche bevolking van Java en Madoera* (1904), cited by Furnivall, *Neth. India*, p. 240.

usurers.[3] These measures were all detrimental to the interests of the Chinese, for in one case they took away a business that had been theirs for centuries, and in the other they created competitors to them backed by all the capital and resources of the Government.

From this year, too, dates the establishment of the Bureau for Chinese Affairs to meet the need keenly felt by the Netherlands Indies Government for expert advice. The personnel of the Bureau underwent a long period of preparation in Holland, China, and the Indies and had a thorough acquaintance with the Chinese languages and customs. The Bureau, which kept in close touch with movements in China and among the Chinese community in the Indies, furnished information and advice to all branches of the Government, prepared a bi-monthly report on the Chinese and the Chinese-Malay press in the Indies, and gave special attention to Chinese schools. 'Appointed originally as a watch-dog against Chinese aggression', says Furnivall, 'the Adviser on Chinese affairs has come to function rather as a Protector of Chinese.'[4] To assist in these matters the Governor-General had also the advice of an expert in international law.

Fock's proposals for dealing with the Chinese problem proved impracticable, but in any case the Indies Government was becoming increasingly aware of the rapid changes taking place in the international situation, and towards the Chinese it adopted a policy of conciliation by which most of their civil disabilities were removed. In 1911 it made an important concession to Chinese sentiment by recognizing Chinese consuls; in a succession of orders between 1914 and 1916 it allowed them a greater freedom of residence and movement; in 1919 it abolished all restrictions on their place of residence within Java, and in 1926 it extended the order to the Outer Provinces. Thus, since 1900, the whole policy of segregation had been abandoned. In legal status, too, as we have seen in the preceding chapter, the Chinese advanced more and more towards complete equality with the Europeans. But Chinese nationalism was now getting into its stride and creating a state of mind which allowed of no compromise with its slogan of 'Once a Chinese always a Chinese'. Dutch policy had conserved a plural society: an external force claimed one of the members of the society as an extension of itself, however mingled in blood it might be.

The Volksraad

In 1911 the foundation of the Chinese Republic aroused intense enthusiasm among the Chinese of Indonesia, not only among the large

[3] De Wolff van Westerrode was the pioneer both in the initiation of the 'paddy banks' and of Government pawnshops. In the Government pawnshops the people could raise money on more advantageous terms than when they resorted to Chinese pawnshops, there was a fairer valuation, the rates of interest were lower, the clients were assured of the protection of their interests, and better care was taken of pledges (Furnivall, p. 359).

[4] This statement is, however, strongly contested by some Indonesian Chinese to whom I have spoken (V. P.).

number of recent immigrants, but also among Indonesian Chinese, who, thanks in part to Dutch separatist policy, were more Chinese than Indonesian. Regarding the introduction of the symbols of a foreign country as a threatened invasion of their sovereignty, the Dutch discouraged the display of the new Republican flag (the 'five-barred' flag) which the Chinese were everywhere flaunting, and this led to boycotts and riots which had to be suppressed by force. Yet, in spite of these demonstrations, the Indonesian Government pursued a policy of courting the goodwill of the local Chinese.

It is indicative of the real situation that the Sarekat Islam (Javanese Muslim Society) was founded, before 1914, mainly as a defence against the economic encroachment of the Chinese. At the same time the nascent native movement had been stimulated by the example of the Chinese. The Javanese saw that Chinese agitation had been followed by concessions, and they also saw themselves being pushed farther and farther into the background as the Chinese grew stronger. And in its current form of an active protest against the exploitation of the natives by the Chinese, the new movement gained much sympathy from the Europeans. However, as events developed, it was the Europeans and the Chinese who were to be drawn into an unrecognized, but none the less real, alliance against the developing pretensions of native nationalism.

From at least the beginning of the century the Dutch had had in mind the gradual introduction of some measures of self-government in their huge Indonesian territories. It was not an easy matter with such a diversity of administrative units. There were in the period immediately preceding the Japanese invasion eight main units in Netherlands India— three Provinces and five Governments. Of these, three Provinces and two Governments were in Java and Madura. Finally, there were important Native States, covering large areas, within the Province or the Government, which had a certain autonomy of their own. The three Governments outside Java and Madura—Sumatra, Borneo, and the Great East—were constituted only in 1938. These large units were divided into Residencies, each under a Dutch Resident, and in Java these again were divided into Regencies, varying much in size and importance, each under the charge of a Native Regent. Usually the office of Regent descended from father to son. The governmental system was one in which the administration was nominally in the hands of the native hereditary Regents, assisted by a Dutch Resident and his assistant. Under the rule of the company the main function of the Resident was to ensure the collection of the produce. In more recent times he was 'charged with securing the welfare of the inhabitants and in exercising "gentle pressure" to secure efficiency in administration'.[5] The Regent had under him a native civil service. The Resident's supervisory influence

5 RIIA, *Neth. Overseas Territories*, p. 26.

was great, though the development of the specialist technical departments such as agriculture, public health, labour, &c, had meant a lessening in his responsibilities.

The ultimate unit in Javanese life was the *dessa* or village community in which local affairs were conducted under a council of leaders and a village chief; but here again there had been increasing interference with the *dessa* due to the growth of centralized technical administration.

In Java a beginning was made towards responsible government in 1903 with the creation of local municipalities, and this system was afterwards extended. The pre-war policy of the Dutch was to provide the provinces of Java and important group communities in the Outer Islands, such as Minangkabau in Sumatra, the Bandjar in Borneo, and others, with Municipal and Regency Councils, mainly elected by a limited franchise, but with some nominated members. The powers and functions of Councils were being steadily increased.

The government of Netherlands India was in the hands of the Governor-General assisted by the Council of the Netherlands Indies (*Raad van Indië*). In 1914 it had four members, of whom three were Dutch and one was Javanese. Finally, as a measure towards eventual self-government, a parliament, the Volksraad, came into being in 1918. It was an advisory body, but on certain subjects, including the key question of finance, the Governor-General had to act in agreement with it. It had power to amend Government Bills and to initiate legislation.

Representation in the municipal and legislative bodies was on a communal basis. Of the 61 members of the Volksraad no fewer than 3 and no more than 5 might be Chinese, and they held about the same number of seats proportionately in the provincial, regency, and municipal councils. Since the other seats were about equally divided between Europeans and natives, the Chinese should have held the balance of power in all these bodies, but most of the Chinese were Dutch-nominated. For a few years after 1918, when the Volksraad was established, there was a group of Chinese who opposed the acceptance of Dutch citizenship in any form and who opposed accepting representation in the Volksraad. Though many of these were Indonesian-Chinese of the third and fourth generations, they talked of being in the Indies only temporarily. This group of irreconcilables wished to be Chinese subjects and to enjoy a kind of extraterritoriality. Affecting to regard the Dutch as a passing phenomenon, some of them affiliated themselves with the more extreme movement of the Indonesian nationalists; others held aloof and interested themselves only in the politics of China. A large number, however, demonstrated a willingness to co-operate with the Government. For the most part the Chinese and native movements followed along different though parallel lines. 'Only in 1925 did the Chinese and native

movements intersect, when, for a short time, Chinese and Javanese Communists were associated, but the association broke down owing to the
difference in their aims.'[6] The association whilst it lasted led to a series
of strikes. In the 1930s new parties were formed, and those parties which
were based on the association of all races for the common welfare collapsed. Political parties were organized more and more on racial and
religious lines.[7]

The question of military service should here be mentioned. Even
those Chinese who wanted complete assimilation to the Dutch wanted
it without the concomitant obligation of military service. Most of the
Chinese who had accepted voluntary assimilation did not answer the
call-up, but the Indies Government never pressed the matter. It felt, no
doubt, that, as the Chinese outnumbered the Europeans by four to one,
it would be dangerous to take into the army such an uncertain quantity.
Greater certainty and reliability would be required in the event of a
crisis.

In 1940 there was still a very strong Chinese nationalist sentiment,
although among the Indonesian-Chinese[8] there was a tendency to align
themselves on the side of the Indonesian nationalists. Many Chinese,
however, were unable to make up their minds whether their interests lay
on the side of the Dutch or of the natives. Those whose resentment of the
Dutch led them to sympathize with the Indonesians reflected at the same
time that as a race they were not liked by the Indonesians, partly for
economic reasons and partly because of the 'superiority complex' common among the young Chinese nationalists, and felt that their interests
therefore might not receive as favourable consideration under a native-
controlled Government as they did under the Dutch. As regards allegiance to the Netherlands a few Indonesian-Chinese could be found who
were *plus royalistes que le roi*. Moreover, these Indonesian-Chinese were
more and more being orientated towards Dutch culture. Large numbers
received their higher education in the Netherlands. While in Holland they
were ardent Chinese nationalists, but on their return to the Indies
they increasingly attached themselves to the Europeans, both because
they now felt more at home with them, and also for the protection of
their interests against the natives and the Indonesian nationalists.[9] Very
few had a speaking or reading knowledge of Chinese.

These considerations pave the way towards a discussion of the key
question of education, but before proceeding to this it would be well if
we could find a Chinese spokesman to express the Chinese frame of
mind in this period. This fortunately can be done in the person of Mr

[6] Furnivall, *Neth. India*, pp. 241, 242.
[7] Vandenbosch, *Dutch East Indies*, p. 366 and *passim*.
[8] I have avoided the commonly used term 'Indo-Chinese' because of its suggestion of
natives of Indochina.   [9] Vandenbosch, *Dutch East Indies*, p. 366 ff.

Oey Kang-liu, though it must be borne in mind that his feeling is probably stronger and his expression more articulate than was the case with most of his fellows in Indonesia.[10]

As a community [says Mr Oey] the Chinese pay most of the taxes without any representation in the Government Councils. There is on every side discrimination against the Chinese. Every Chinese on arrival in the Indies has to pay fl. 150: if he fails to produce the sum he is promptly arrested and deported. Everyone in the Netherlands Indies pays an income-tax of 8 per cent. On paper the Chinese are treated on an equal basis, but in practice there is a big difference from theory— namely he is required to pay 15 per cent extra. For example, a Government officer comes to a Chinese merchant to ascertain his annual income. He is told that it is $5,000. On principle the revenue officer refuses to accept the statement of a Chinese, and proceeds to settle the question in quite a simple manner: he arbitrarily fixes the amount of taxable income by doubling or trebling the amount stated, and his decision is final, for there does not appear to be any way of appealing against this haphazard, even when not unjust, decision. But Chinese merchants who understand the psychology of these officers and their little weaknesses will tell you that more often than not a little 'greasing of the palm' will reduce the amount of income to the figure originally proposed by the payer. But here comes the rub. The following year the same officer will as a matter of routine raise the amount of the income of the harassed merchant who must again repeat the process of 'palm-greasing'. And so the farce goes on from year to year.[11]

Another grievance is that for the privilege of trading in the Indies the Dutch charge a business licence fee which is determined by the officials in such a manner that the Chinese pay more for their licence fees than the Dutch engaged in similar business. Even a firm registered as a Dutch company and managed by a foreigner has to pay twice the amount charged for an ordinary business licence if the principal shareholders happen to be Chinese.

The Chinese [Mr Oey concludes] are in fact treated as a subject race. The Dutch, in fact, regard all Chinese in the Colony on the same footing as the Javanese, a fact that is clearly indicated in the policy of discrimination against the Chinese and also in subjecting them to the jurisdiction of the courts specially reserved for the Javanese.[12]

As a footnote to a chapter on Dutch-Chinese relationships it would be fitting to give an extract from the opinions of another Chinese, this time an Indonesian-Chinese educated in Holland and resident there during

[10] Oey Kang-liu, 'The Chinese in the Dutch East Indies', *China Weekly R.* (7 Jan. 1933).
[11] Dr Vlekke comments: 'The assertions of Mr Oey Kang-liu ought to be checked. I cannot do this but I am sure that the tax settlements he complains about were not so arbitrary as he contends. It all sounds (except for the charge of bribery) curiously similar to the complaints I have heard many times of small business men in Holland a few decades ago when strict book-keeping was not so regularly attended to, who would maintain to their last breath that they really did not earn a worthwhile profit. Once a proper account was made it usually proved that they had enjoyed a considerable income and were most indignant at being taxed on the full amount.' Chinese human nature is, in fact, not very different from other kinds of human nature.
[12] An eloquent summary of Chinese disabilities in Java is given by Dr Liem Twan Djie, *De Distribueerende Tusschenhandel der Chineezen op Java* (The Hague, 1947), p. 40.

the German occupation of 1940–4, possessed of an affection for the Dutch and for Dutch civilization, yet at the same time fully conscious that he is a Chinese. This is Mr Tjan Tjoe-som, the president of the Chung Hwa Hui, addressing the Association in Leyden in April 1946.[13]

The Chinese, says Mr Tjan, had from the beginning of their settlement in the Indies been middlemen. As such they had in the course of time developed qualities of peacefulness, 'a kind of consummation of their inborn instincts', which had gradually made them the perfect type of quiet citizen. In Indonesia the middle-class man, who was *par excellence* the Chinese, enjoyed appreciation for his industry, frugality, and reliability: on the other hand he had been reproached for lacking interest in the country in which he lived, and at the same time, for having an undue interest in the country he had come from. The reproach, however, that the Chinese were indifferent to the fate of their foreign home must be seen and judged against the background of the social and political conditions under which they lived. It was common knowledge that the Chinese, having the status of, and being treated as, 'foreign Orientals', did feel themselves to be foreigners, and did feel that their interests were not sufficiently taken to heart and that their rightful wishes were not regarded. The opinion that as middle-class men the Chinese would acquiesce in any condition provided that it still left them room to earn money gave a highly distorted picture of their character. It is improbable that any human being could be found willing to suffer any sort of humiliating discrimination with gladness if only his mercenary activities were allowed, and with the Chinese it was certainly not the case. Mr Tjan continues:

As the sons of the culture the age of which is unparalleled by any extant one, of a country the past of which contains long and numerous periods of glory and beauty, of wisdom and richness, and the future of which holds the most immense possibilities, the Chinese may be excused for a pride that does not rest on hollow imagination alone. In their heart of hearts any act of injustice, wrong or inhumanity is resented as an injury to the Heaven-ordained norms of right, justice, and humanity. From across the oceans, China's age-long traditions of morality and ethics still had their hold on its wandering sons. . . .

There would have been no Chinese movement in Java if the Chinese had been content with the opportunity granted them to earn their bread, and in many cases to earn their bread handsomely. It was the failing on the part of the authorities to recognize that the Chinese is not the *homo economicus* all over, which gave rise to much misapprehension, much bitterness, and much resentment. The Chinese came to the conclusion, from their view naturally, from the others' view incomprehensibly, that the Government did not practise the *wang tao*, the kingly way, but the *pa tao*, the way of the oppressors. That they did not in this case feel inclined to abolish their attitude of being foreigners is a thing probably to be deplored but is not altogether unintelligible.

---

[13] *Chung Hwa Hui Nederland*, Brochure no. 2, Lustrum Speech, 15 Apr. 1946, 'Luctor et Embargo', Leyden.

We shall not venture any judgment until we have considered the experiences of the Chinese of Indonesia in the field of education and have ascertained as nearly as possible their economic position at the time of the outbreak of the war with Japan in 1942, both of which are essential factors to a proper understanding of our subject.

46

EDUCATION AND THE CHINESE IN INDONESIA

In this chapter we shall be dealing with three main streams of education —the Western, the Chinese traditional, and the Chinese post-revolutionary. In Indonesia the first two streams flowed side by side for nearly 300 years, albeit in tiny volume: the second stream, already freshened somewhat by the advance waters of the third stream, overflowed in some quantity in the first years of the present century to fertilize the mind of the Indonesian Chinese. The third of the waterways was a branch of the original river, but changed from it in character, and so reinforced by the freshets of the West that its advent was like the Yellow river once more changing its course.

For many centuries the Chinese traditional system of education had been in a state of stagnation. The written language, which had diverged so long from the spoken word that the two were entirely distinct, had become the preserve of scholars who had turned it into a means more of obfuscation than of information. At the same time an examination system had grown up by which the bookworms with prodigious memories and a morbid reverence for authority were selected to administer the vast Flowery Kingdom. Under the impact of the West, Japan had modernized itself whereas China resisted modernization with all its stored-up resources of inertia. Reluctantly, however, it consented to adopt Western sources of strength if this could be done without disturbing its own inviolable values. Thus there was a school for teaching telegraphy long before there was any modern school system. But, warned by the threat of China's dissolution if it did not adapt itself to a changing world, the reformers were active before the end of the century, and educational reform marched hand in hand with the Revolution. But in spite of great changes in the curriculum the old written language, *Wenli*, remained an unwieldy obstruction to progress till in 1917 Dr Hu Shih made a startling proposal. He suggested that *Wenli* should be dropped as the medium of primary and secondary instruction, and reserved for advanced study, and that the written form of the mandarin vernacular should be used in its place. This written vernacular, or *pai hua*, had been used for centuries as a vehicle for romances, was distended and verbose as compared with *Wenli* and had none of its refinements, but was nevertheless easily understandable and far easier to learn. Hu Shih won his way, and in 1920 mandarin, now known in its modified form as *Kuo Yü*, or the National Language, became the official medium of instruction in all Chinese schools.[1]

Everywhere they went the Chinese carried with them their reverence for learning. The pioneers were many of them illiterate, but of the Hokkien merchant class who predominated in the sixteenth and seventeenth centuries it is likely that a high proportion had received some schooling. We have glimpses of the high standard of practical instruction in their more prosperous centres from the pen of Wouter Schouten,[2] and there was in addition to home instruction at least one school in eighteenth-century Batavia with thirty to forty pupils. But all they learnt in such schools was the use of the abacus, to get by rote the Four Books —the Analects, the Doctrine of the Mean, the Great Learning, and Mencius—and to write a conventional letter. The curriculum in a Batavia Chinese household or school was probably not a whit different in the time of the first Captain Bencon in 1620 from what it was in 1890. Even of this kind of schooling it is certain that not more than a very small proportion reaped the benefits—even less so in the Outer Islands than in Java. Nor did they receive instruction in any medium other than Chinese.

Only after the restoration of Netherlands rule in 1816 was education given any consideration. In 1818 it was decreed that Indonesians should be permitted to attend Dutch schools. This regulation, however, was applied in such a manner that only a few natives could take advantage of it because of the very rigid entrance requirements of family background, environment, and tuition. The most difficult requirement was that the applicant must understand sufficient Dutch to be able to follow the instruction intelligently.[3]

The Regulations for the Government of the Netherlands Indies of 1854 laid down that the Governor-General should encourage the establishment of schools for the native population. The primary purpose in establishing these schools, however, was to train native officials. The schools when established were divided into native schools of the second class for the children of officials of low rank and for the middle class generally, and native schools of the first class for children of officials of high rank and of well-to-do persons. This system continued until towards the end of the century when, under the influence of the 'ethical'

---

[1] See the present writer's *Problems of Chinese Education, passim. Wenli* is a foreign-invented term formed from *Wen* = literature and *li* = principles.   [2] See pp. 399–400.

[3] R. L. Djajadiningrat, Director of Education and Public Worship in the Netherlands Indies, *From Illiteracy to University; Educational Development in the Netherlands Indies* (N.Y., 1942), p. 10 and *passim*.

movement in Holland, a policy was laid down for nation-wide education not merely in the interests of the Government.

Nothing, however, had been done for the education of Chinese children, for the above-mentioned article in the Regulations of 1854 was interpreted not to apply to children of peoples assimilated to natives. No subsidies were given to Chinese schools, and Chinese children were permitted to enter the lower native schools only if there was room for them and if they knew sufficient Dutch to follow the instruction, and upon payment of higher school fees.[4] Education in these schools led normally to employment in the Government service, but from even the lowest ranks of this the Chinese were excluded.

About 1900, under the stimulus of the reawakening spirit of China, and stirred to greater self-preservation by the Government measures regarding opium farms and the credit system, the Chinese of Indonesia began to assert themselves to improve their position. Education and the press were the chief means employed. School societies were organized and schools opened. With the knowledge, and even with the support and encouragement, of the Chinese Government, Chinese teachers were sent to Indonesia where Tiong Hwa Hwee Koan schools (schools established by Chinese Associations and by the trading society *Siang Hwee*) were organized with a strong Chinese nationalistic character. Preference was expressed for Dutch as the language medium, but since school societies could not afford the high-salaried Dutch teachers, English was chosen, for the reason that English-speaking Chinese instructors could be cheaply obtained from Singapore, and, in addition, English had the advantage of being the commercial language of the East. The Chinese press in the Indies meanwhile strengthened the unity and the national consciousness of the community and pressed the Chinese grievances with the Indies Government. 'The Chinese in the Indies', so wrote the press, 'are step-children neglected by the Indies Government, but are once again recognized by their own father, China, who after being asleep all these years, is now reawakened.'[5]

Contemporaneously, several elementary and secondary schools were established in China supported by Government and private funds to which the Chinese colonists were invited to send their children.

So far, though, the stream was but a trickle. But the Dutch Government, realizing that if it did not take things into its own hands the Chinese almost certainly would, began to make education easier for the Chinese to procure. Chinese were admitted to native schools on the same basis as natives, and the erection of Government schools for Chinese, the so-called Dutch-Chinese schools, was begun in 1908, and in 1909 private Chinese schools were granted Government subsidies.

[4] Vandenbosch, *Dutch East Indies*, p. 358.
[5] Ibid. p. 359.

The curriculum of the Dutch-Chinese schools was the same as that of the European elementary schools, with Dutch as the language medium, but they were intended exclusively for children of Chinese origin. In special cases children of other groups of the population might be admitted, but only with the permission of the Director of Education. However, applications for entry by non-Chinese were rarely made.

In order to meet the demand for a knowledge of English in business, courses in English were included in the curriculum of these schools when so desired by the parents.

As these schools were conducted exclusively for Chinese children, it was not demanded of the pupils that they should have some knowledge of the Dutch language before entry. The only prerequisite was some degree of social standing. Nevertheless, since the courses were given in Dutch, a knowledge of the Dutch language was necessary in order to follow the instruction. Therefore a preparatory Dutch class was included. It was calculated that as the number of Dutch-speaking families increased among the Chinese population, the preparatory classes would gradually disappear, as the children would learn Dutch at home.

It was soon evident that these schools had the support of the Chinese community and every year more schools were established. The greatest difficulty was to obtain sufficient teachers, and normal schools were opened to train them. Students of both sexes were admitted to these, and to begin with the number of students applying for enrolment was satisfactory, but then it fell off because the product of the Dutch-Chinese schools were finding it more profitable to enter business. The situation could not be met by increasing the salaries of the teachers because, in the first place, Indonesian teachers trained in equivalent normal schools would demand comparable salaries, thus making the Dutch-Chinese schools too expensive to support, and secondly, because it was impossible to compete with business as an employer, especially in times of prosperity. This placed the authorities in a dilemma. Many Chinese urged that the Dutch-Chinese schools be transformed into national schools open to every Chinese child. This demand could not be granted since the number of teachers necessary was not available. Besides, the environment, development, and culture of different parts of the Chinese community varied greatly. If children of all these different groups were admitted to the same school the student body would be too heterogeneous to maintain education at the desired level. So argued the Dutch education authorities. For this reason Malay-Chinese schools were organized along the same lines as the six grades of the Indonesian schools, with Dutch as a subject. General business courses were included in the curriculum.

The establishment of the Dutch-Chinese schools was in the nature of preferential treatment for the Chinese, and the Indonesians were not slow to recognize it. Their schools had nothing like the same facilities for obtaining a Western education.

The elementary education in the Dutch-Chinese schools connected up with secondary, higher, and vocational training. The graduates of the Malay-Chinese school could, it appears, obtain admission to the secondary system through the continuation schools (for learning the Dutch language), and the connecting schools.[6]

One effect of this great and novel expansion of opportunities for a Dutch education was naturally that, as has been mentioned,[7] a much larger proportion of Chinese received higher education in Holland, with the result, very often, that they conceived a warm regard for Dutch thought and European culture generally, but did not necessarily feel more reconciled to the status of the Chinese in Indonesia. A similar fact was noticeable among Indian students who attended the universities of Great Britain. Furnivall remarks that some graduates of the Chinese schools (presumably the Dutch-Chinese schools?) contributed learned articles to European periodicals, and some wrote treatises in Dutch that would stand comparison with the works of their European fellow subjects —for example the standard treatise on the land revenue system was by a Chinese. Many Chinese were trained as doctors in Dutch centres.[8]

What has been gleaned from publications such as Mr Djajadiningrat's *From Illiteracy to University* is illuminating enough, but we should be going far wrong if we assumed that it accounted for the whole of the education of the Chinese in Indonesia. According to Dr R. van Diffelin,[9] of 200,000 Chinese children between the ages of six and fourteen, in the year 1936, about 98,000 received education of some sort. Of these some 45,000 were educated in schools conducted by the Tjong Hwa Hak Tong (Overseas Chinese Association); 23,000 in public and subsidized Dutch-Chinese schools; 13,000 in native primary schools and Malay-Chinese schools; 2,500 in the European schools (six grades); and 13,500 in the 'special' Dutch-Chinese and other 'wildcat'[10] schools under private

[6] Dr Vlekke comments: 'The Dutch-Chinese schools never reached a large section of the Chinese population. The efforts to spread a knowledge of Dutch among Chinese or Indonesians were only half-hearted and often opposed by lower officials on the spot. In 1930 there were only 8,772 Chinese in the Indies who could write Dutch (*Visman Report*, i. 66). Only a very few Malay-Chinese schools were ever in operation. Part of the complicated East Indian school system existed only on paper, that is to say of several 'school-types' there existed so few establishments as to make the whole type of no importance. Moreover the statistics are incomplete as schools not coming under Government supervision (e.g. all Mohammedan schools!) were not included in the survey. In 1930, 71·1 per cent of the Chinese in Indonesia were illiterate.' [7] See p. 529; also Furnivall, *Neth. India*, pp. 418, 419.

[8] The Yang Seng Hospital in Batavia was the only hospital outside China founded, financed, and administered by Chinese (though there were a number of Chinese hospital foundations (e.g. the Tan Tock Seng Hospital, Singapore)).

[9] Dr R. van Diffelin, 'Het Onderwijs voor Chineezen', *Koloniale Studiën*, nos. 5 & 6 (1936), p. 42, quoting Loe Ping Kian, article reproduced from *Sin Po* (25 Apr.–13 June 1936).

[10] In the Straits Settlements and F.M.S. alone there were 91,534 pupils in Chinese schools in 1938 (Purcell, *Chinese in Malaya*, App. VI).

management. That is to say, that about 50 per cent of Chinese youth received education.[11] He further mentions that according to income-tax figures 32,000 Chinese have an income of at least $50 a month—that is to say, the minimum subsistence limit which entitles them to have their children admitted to the Dutch-Chinese schools.

No information appears to be publicly available regarding the schools conducted by the Tjong Hwa Hak Tong, but from experience elsewhere in Southeast Asia it is safe to say that, subject to Dutch official inspection and control, the curriculum had a purely Chinese nationalist character. That is to say, that through the medium of *Kuo Yü*, from textbooks produced by the Commercial Press or the Chung Hua Press in Shanghai, the doctrines of Sun Yat-sen (that China is the only country where 'race' and 'nation' are the same, that 'we are the wronged races', 'to save China we must certainly promote Nationalism', &c, &c) were being inculcated day after day, either in so many words or indirectly, and that, whatever the results for the 52,000, the 45,000 were irretrievably lost to Indonesia and the Dutch as citizens or subjects. And that is in addition to anything the Communists may have been teaching during the same period and of which so little is known.

It is not difficult to see that the Chinese in Indonesia were split by reason of their varying educational background. Divided first of all into *Peranakans* and *Sinkhehs*, according to whether they were born in Indonesia or in China, they were further divided into Dutch-, Malay-, or Chinese-educated. There do not appear to be any statistics as to how *Peranakans* and *Sinkhehs* were distributed among these school groups, but while it is safe to assume that children of the former attended the Dutch and Malay schools rather than the Chinese ones, and that the China-born showed a preference for the Chinese type of education, it is probable that, as in Malaya, the Chinese schools had captured many of the children of the *Peranakans*. The reasons for this were partly that the Chinese schools provided nearly half the primary education available to the Chinese of Indonesia,[12] partly the appeal of Chinese nationalism, and partly that the European type of education had produced a surplus of clerks, &c, and the Dutch-Chinese schools did not offer the same economic advantages as before.

[11] But compare this statement of van Diffelin with that of Vlekke, p. 455 n.

[12] The statement in *Island India Goes to School*, by Edwin R. Embree and others (Chicago, 1934), p. 53, in the section on Dutch-Chinese schools, that 'there are also a few schools, outside the Government system, organized and supported by the Chinese themselves with their language as the medium of instruction', does not at all agree with Dr R. van Diffelin's figure of 45,000 Chinese pupils in a total of 98,000 attending such schools. But then in Mr Djaja-diningrat's book (which can be taken as official, as he was Director of Education) I can trace no mention at all of these Chinese schools. Such are the pitfalls that beset the path of the investigator. The *Statistical Pocket Book of Indonesia, 1941*, gives (table 32, p. 22) the total number of 'Other Asiatic' pupils in all schools in Indonesia as 43,817 for 1933–4 and 49,695 for 1939–40, and thus appears to ignore altogether the pupils in Chinese schools in which Chinese was the medium of instruction.

Christianity made surprisingly little advance in the Netherlands Indies. *The Netherlands Indies*, by John Rauws and others,[13] gives a total of only 5,841 Chinese Christians for the whole of the islands.

47

PRE-WAR ECONOMIC POSITION OF THE CHINESE

RAFFLES writing in 1817 estimated the wealth of the Chinese at ten times that of all the Europeans put together.[1] This, however, must have been very much in the nature of a guess. But the modern investigator is only comparatively in a stronger position than Raffles was, for the extent of the wealth of the Chinese cannot even now be ascertained very closely. Mr Callis estimated the total entrepreneur investments in Indonesia in 1937 at 1,411 million United States dollars (at 40 cents to the guilder), of which the Dutch held 1,040 million, the British 200 million, and the Americans 95 million. He goes on to say:

It should be expressly said that available information in the case of the Netherlands Indies is such that island-Chinese investments cannot be separated from Dutch holdings. But on the basis of what is known of the Chinese population in the islands, their general economic position, their holdings in neighbouring countries in Southeast Asia, and their family remittances from the archipelago to China, the guess can be made that Chinese business capital is worth about 150 million United States dollars at the present time.[2]

In conjunction with this overall figure of investment we may consider the following table of national income according to race for the year 1936:[3]

	Number assessed	Total income in millions of guilders
Europeans	65,000	266
Indonesians	27,000	50
Chinese	37,000	82
Other Foreign Asiatics	3,000	9

When the sugar industry was dominating the economic life of Java until the world depression of 1929, when the market almost disappeared, the annual income of the island amounted to about 2,500 million

[13] (N.Y., 1935), p. 162 and App. X.
[1] Cited by Furnivall, *Neth. India*, p. 47.
[2] H. G. Callis, *Foreign Capital in Southeast Asia* (N.Y., 1942, mimeo.). Above 900 guilders per annum is, generally speaking, non-agricultural income.
[3] Helsdingen, *Mission Interrupted*, p. 246.

guilders. About 450 million guilders of this left the country in the shape
of profits and interest and to pay for capital goods, 300 million going to
Europeans and 250 million to Chinese.[4] The collapse of the sugar
industry greatly altered the picture.

But though the Chinese are consistently charged with a lust for gold,
auri sacra fames (on the assumption, perhaps, that this is a vice from
which other races are exempt), and although many of their number
certainly have a talent for acquiring it, it is nevertheless not proven that
the gold is equally distributed. Many poor Chinese in Indonesia believe
that it is not. Here is what the Federation of Chinese Associations in
Batavia has to say about it:

> Chinese living in Indonesia are generally considered as a wealthy group. This is
> a myth which is easily refuted by tax statistics. A few hundred families have indeed
> succeeded in amassing wealth, among whom may be counted a few millionaires; on
> the other hand there exist hundreds of thousands whose income is barely sufficient
> to make ends meet. Further, the number of Chinese working class and paupers is
> increasing daily.[5]

The Chinese were to be found in every economic stratum of Indonesian society, as large capitalists, bankers, and agricultural conces-
sionnaires as well as the humblest labourers, but their function in the
economic life was *par excellence* that of middlemen. Of the total Chinese
population of 1·233 million, 470,000 were in 1930 engaged in a trade
or profession: roughly 145,000 in raw material production, 94,000 in
industry, 185,000 in trade and commerce, 3,000 in Government service
(note the small figure), and 43,000 in other occupations. The Chinese in
Java were most numerous in trade; those of the Outer Islands as mining
or plantation coolies. Apart from their peculiarly Chinese function of
middlemen, the manufacture of rattan and other furniture, carpentry,
and, with the Arabs, the extension of small loans, usually at an usurious
rate, were some of the occupations which were almost exclusively theirs.
In the Outer Islands they were to be found in large numbers as contract
labourers in the mines of Bangka and Billiton and the European plantations of the northeast coast of Sumatra, and in northwest Borneo as
independent farmers. It was here centuries ago that numbers of Chinese
came in search of gold, and when gold-mining became unprofitable they
settled down to agriculture, which, after all, was the traditional occupation of the Chinese in their homeland.

(It is unfortunate that the figures available are so out of date, for the
picture was considerably changed by the trade depression of 1929–32
and again by the Japanese invasion of 1942–5. A similar great change

[4] Vandenbosch, *Dutch East Indies*, p. 28.
[5] *Memorandum outlining acts of violence &c*, compiled by Chung Hua Tsung Hui (Federation of Chinese Associations) (Batavia, 1947), p. 2. Only 32,000 Chinese had an income of
50 guilders a month or over. Official income-tax figures are given on p. 567.

had taken place between 1900 and 1930, a change to which reference is made below.)

With the great development of European trade and banking in the decades preceding 1930 the Chinese had found employment in European firms and as assistants in European shops, and later had become more prominent in professional work as teachers, dentists, and doctors, and in the technical grades of the mining industry. More than most Oriental races, the Chinese had taken kindly to learning modern technical methods, though not then on a large scale. In journalism they had gained a large share, and this included a share in the control of the native press.

Timber has been exported from Java for centuries, the trade having been mainly in Chinese hands. In 1938 the total value of timber and timber wood products exported amounted to over four million guilders.

Modification in the function of the Chinese in Indonesia 1900–30

In 1900 the bulk of the Chinese wealth came from opium shops, pawn-shops, and usury. The Government measures abolishing the opium shops and establishing State pawnshops and facilities for credit had a revolutionary effect on the Chinese economy. The Chinese had obviously to look for new outlets for their capital and energy. These they found in a number of less dubious activities with a resulting change in their position within the Indonesian community. This process is characterized by Furnivall as 'From Parasitism to Construction'.[6]

Having a monopoly of opium, the Chinese vendors were in a position to push the sale of this harmful drug—an opportunity of which they took full advantage. As pawnbrokers they fixed their terms for loans 'with reference to the need of the borrower rather than to the value of the pledge he offered'. The pawnshops were often illicit opium dens. In other forms of money-lending their operation was equally 'unconscion-able':[7] they aimed to get the native officials in their power and used this power to oppress cultivators. Even when ostensibly engaged in commerce, they were equally engaged in money-lending, and they had such a stranglehold on the *batik* industry in particular that the native crafts-man was little better than their bond-slave. Regulations made by the Government to protect the native from these forms of extortion and oppression were rendered largely inoperative by the combination of the Chinese among themselves through their secret trade organizations to defeat their ends. It was for this reason that the Government abolished the monopolies and developed State money-lending.

The first form of popular credit was the Government pawnshop

[6] See Furnivall, *Neth. India*, pp. 412 ff.

[7] 'unconscionable' is placed in inverted commas to indicate that the writer does not neces-sarily endorse the judgment it contains—he merely quotes it from contemporary foreign usage. A spirited defence of the Chinese trade-lender is in Sim Ki Ay, *De Chineesche Neder-zetting in Nederlandsch-Indië*, extra number of *Chung Hwa Hui Tsa Chih* (n.d.).

service, which in the more advanced areas maintained some 500 shops having a legal monopoly of the right to lend sums up to 100 guilders against the security of movable goods. This was found to be a useful institution for a population who traditionally kept much of their wealth in the form of jewellery, gold coins, ornaments, &c.[8] The rate of interest was high, and the proceeds of the service formed a considerable item in the Government revenue.

The second measure was the establishment of rural credit banks which were divided into *dessa lumbungs*, or village granaries, lending paddy to be repaid in rice at harvest time, and into *dessa* banks making small money advances, usually repayable in ten weekly instalments. Efforts were made to incorporate the co-operative principle into these institutions, but, up to the time of the Japanese invasion, with no great success.

The third medium of credit, for the lending of larger sums, was originally organized in the form of Divisional and Regency credit institutions, mainly in Java, under the direction of Dutch and native Government officials, but these were merged in 1934 into the *Algemeene Volkscredietbank*, and after that they acted only as branch offices. The average loan was stated to be 53 guilders in Java and 134 guilders in the Outer Islands.

A certain amount of rural credit was also provided by co-operative societies.[9]

To what extent all these efforts delivered the native out of the hands of the Chinese and other money-lenders is not certain. Speaking of the *Volkscredietbank* in 1938 Dr Th. Fruin said: 'Such large-scale efforts to relieve debt are by no means without attendant difficulties. What the results thereof will be—particularly the lasting results—time alone can show.[10]

Outside opium and pawnbroking, Chinese investment had hitherto been mainly in sugar and timber and then only on a moderate scale. The first outlet they sought for their idle capital was in land speculation, in the purchase of large private estates (*particuliere landerijen*). These estates had for the most part been granted by Raffles in the first place, and more and more of them passed during the nineteenth century to Chinese. When in 1900 their channels for investment were more circumscribed than before, they sought to increase their holdings. The Fock report of 1904 suggested the repurchase of the estates as one means of enhancing native welfare and diminishing Chinese influence. There were, however, difficulties in the way, and it was not until 1910 that the Dutch parliament sanctioned the purchase of one estate, and the following year pro-

---

[8] Phoa Liong Gie, 'De Economische Positie der Chineezen in Nederlandsch-Indië', *Koloniale Studiën*, nos. 3 & 6 (1936), p. 97 and *passim*.
[9] Details of credit facilities derived from RIIA, *Neth. Overseas Territories*, pp. 35, 36.
[10] Cited ibid. p. 36.

vision was made for the resumption of others at an estimated cost of fl. 400 million of the whole area under this form of tenure. By 1930 648,000 hectares had been resumed at a cost of fl. 81·3 million, leaving 503,000 hectares still in private ownership.[11]

Land speculation, therefore, offered a rapidly diminishing outlet for Chinese capital, but up to 1915 it was still possible to describe the Chinese as investing mainly in sugar, timber, and land speculation. It was only after the First World War that they began to build up a strong banking connexion and to lead the way in the development of local industry. Thus by force of events have they been redirected from often parasitical activities towards constructive ones.

Before about 1870 the Chinese were almost the only holders of private capital (as distinct from Government undertakings) in the Indies, but after that date they were displaced from their position by the entry of European capital and the establishment of large agricultural and industrial enterprises. For 1921 an estimate shows that of a total invest-ment of fl. 3,200 million (fl. 1,820 million invested in large-scale planta-tions and fl. 1,380 million in wholesale trade, industry, transport, and banking), the Dutch holding was fl. 2,350 million (73·4 per cent), the Chinese fl. 340 million (10·6 per cent), and the British fl. 300 million (9·4 per cent).[12] Part of the capital belonged to Chinese living in Singa-pore and Hong Kong.

One of the items of the wholesale trade in which the Chinese pre-dominated was rice, imported from Siam and Indochina, in which countries the Chinese had a practical monopoly of both the wholesale and intermediate trade. Of sugar they bought in 1924 4 million piculs as compared with 8·6 million piculs bought by Japanese and 5·5 million piculs bought by Europeans. After the failure of sugar in the crisis of 1930 the whole picture changed. Other products in which the Chinese traded were cassava, pepper, groundnuts, kapok, &c, and, in the Outer Provinces particularly, rubber and copra.

Dependent mainly upon the internal trade and consequently affected by even the slightest fluctuation in the purchasing power of the native population, the Chinese of Java suffered a severe setback during the trade depression that set in after 1929. In every branch of Chinese activity—sugar factories, wholesale, intermediate, and retail trade, credit business, the *batik* industry, &c—the full weight of the depression made itself felt. Moreover the resumption by the natives of old-time methods of production and distribution (barter) in consequence of the crisis also had a bad effect on the Chinese trading interests.[13]

---

[11] Furnivall, *Neth. India*, p. 314.
[12] Cited from E. Helfferich, 'Vreemde Kapitaalsbelegging', in *Economisch Statistische Berichten* (1924), p. 859, by Cator, *Economic Position of Chinese*, p. 64.
[13] Ibid. pp. 121 ff.

But in spite of their increasing competition with Europeans, accentuated during the years of recovery, the Chinese really did not constitute
the political danger that was often made out. For the most part they
were content to acquiesce in the powers of government being held by
others so long as they had an opportunity to make money. In the words
of the metaphor that has become a cliché, they did not mind who held
the cow so long as they milked it. And the milking, after all, was not
organized as it might be by a great American dairy corporation with
mechanical milkers and a chain-belt collection. For the most part the
Chinese in Indonesia were in charge only of second-rate businesses. A
few families had large interests, but the old Chinese family morality was
still strong, and this made the successful operation of a limited liability
company difficult. They had not the organizing power of the Europeans,
who, moreover, were far better equipped in commercial, scientific, and
industrial technique. The Europeans were able to build up firms which
grew stronger with the passing years, whereas a Chinese business usually
collapsed when its founder died.[14] The result of this limitation was that
they did not make the headway that might have been expected in the
accelerating tempo of local economic life, a fact which was lamented by
the Chinese press of the Indies. Also it meant that in the realms of big
business they were losing ground to a new competitor—the Japanese.

A generation ago practically the only Japanese in Indonesia were
a few photographers, barbers, and prostitutes; and in the preceding
centuries, when the Chinese were circulating and settling in the Nanyang
in their thousands and tens of thousands, only an occasional Japanese
navigator drifted into these tropical waters. Then when the Meiji Revolution had restored the Emperor to his power and Japan began to gaze
outwards with the hard eyes of an imperial ambition, her emissaries
came south to see what outposts could be seized by peaceful means. But
they came not, like the Chinese, in random multitudes, but in groups of
expert trade executives directed from home. Very soon they gained a
position analogous to that of the Europeans, but differing from it in the
fact that while the latter used the Chinese middleman as their natural
complement, the Japanese dealt with the native consumer and producer
direct. But before the outbreak of the war in the East this process had
not gone very far comparatively speaking, and the small number of
Japanese immigrants—farmers, fishermen, and shopkeepers—had to
meet competition, especially from the Chinese, who were much their
superiors as retailers and middlemen.

The 'Manchurian Incident' took place in 1931, and the fourteen years
of struggle between China and Japan had begun; but in spite of attempts
on the part of patriots to organize a boycott of the aggressors, the time

[14] The story of 'three generations, clogs to clogs', is very common indeed among the
Chinese of Southeast Asia.

for such to be effective was not yet. To the Chinese traders in the Indies business was business: politics were outside their sphere. Thus when about 1931 the Dutch introduced quotas to stem the spate of Japanese textiles which was threatening to swamp the market and to drive the European mills out of business, the Dutch merchants found that the Chinese merchants were still importing Japanese cottons, and they themselves had to import Japanese cottons or nothing.

Chinese Labour and Immigration

The demand for labour in the Outer Islands was met for a long time by indentured labour, i.e. by the engagement of coolies, mainly from Java and China, under contracts enforceable by penal sanctions: that is to say, labourers were liable to arrest and punishment if they broke their contract ar left their work. This system of contract and recruitment gave rise to severe criticism not only in the world at large, but in Holland olso. Some free labour ordinances date from 1911. The tobacco planters gave up the penal sanction in 1931 on account of the new American Tariff Act which prevented the importation of agricultural commodities grown by indentured labour which could be produced in the United States. This excluded tobacco produced by indentured labour in Sumatra but not rubber or other tropical commodities that could not be grown in the United States. (Tobacco growers in Massachusetts, Connecticut, and the South were responsible for this provision, but they failed to gain their objective since the Sumatra planters gave up the penal sanction clause in labour contracts. Even as late as 1941 there were coolies still under penal sanction on non-tobacco estates.)

On the east coast of Sumatra the recruitment of Chinese coolies for estates was considerable from 1888 onwards, but it ceased entirely in 1934. In east Sumatra the Labour Inspectorate was created in 1904 to prevent abuses on the estates, and much legislation for the protection of labour was enacted in the ten years preceding the war in Asia. Penal sanctions were abolished completely in 1941 before the Japanese invasion of the Indies began.

The regulations divided the coolies into several classes—*Singkhehs* (*Sinkhehs*), or newcomers, who were put on contract for three crop-years, never longer than three calendar years; *Laukhehs*, or old hands who had at least one contract behind them, were given special terms; *Kongsikangs*, or labourers on daily pay, and *Noempangs*, or piece-work labourers who signed contracts for periods not greater than six months, after which they were free to go to other plantations.[15]

One of the activities supervised by the new Labour Inspectorate was the *Panglongs*. These were concerns for the exploitation of timber run by

[15] *Verslag van den Dienst der Arbeidsinspectie en Koeliewerving*, East Coast of Sumatra (Batavia, 1913 & 1914).

Chinese along the east coast of Sumatra and in the Rhio Residency
—including beam-cutting mills, saw-mills, firewood mills, and charcoal-
burning plants. In spite of enactments passed since 1882, Government
interference with these undertakings was almost non-existent. They
were often in uninhabited regions and extremely difficult of access.[16]
Very bad conditions were said to prevail in the Panglongs of Bengkalis
in the 1920s.[17] About 3,000 men were employed in this type of work.

In the table below is set out the labour position in the Outer Islands
at the end of 1938.

Number of Coolies employed in the Outer Islands on
31 December 1938[18]

	Chinese	Javanese		Total*
		Men	Women	
SUMATRA				
Contract labour	7,752	7,733	3,219	18,704
Free coolies	17,400	177,857	96,826	299,753
BORNEO				
Contract labour	..	58	..	58
Free coolies	915	7,638	1,248	13,924
Total				
Contract labour	7,752	7,791	3,219	18,762
Free coolies	18,315	185,495	98,074	313,677

* Including other nationalities than Chinese and Javanese.

The influx of Chinese into Indonesia, which at one time, when China
was very unsettled by civil war, had threatened to become a real invasion
that it would be impossible to absorb, was checked by two forces.[19] The
excessive flow of labour into the Outer Islands was reduced by diminution of the demand, and the invasion of shopkeepers and other middlemen generally was checked by the imposition of a head-tax which was
payable by every Chinese entering the Indies. From 1924 to 1931 the tax
was between 50 and 100 florins, and after 1931 it was 150 florins a head.

In Bangka and Billiton where the tin-mining had for so long been
done by manual labour, employing respectively 40,000 and 20,000
Chinese coolies, the mining administration mechanized the industry by
the introduction of dredges. Consequently, a few thousand labourers
were now all that was required.[20] In Deli on the east coast of Sumatra

[16] Cator, *Economic Position of Chinese*, pp. 217 ff.
[17] De Kat Angelino, *Colonial Policy*, i. 583.
[18] *Neth. Overseas Territories*, p. 39.
[19] Ordinances of 1 Oct. 1911 and 20 June 1915, although they did not specify any nationality,
were intended in effect to protect Chinese coolies and encourage their immigration. I.L.O.,
Legislative Aspects of Asiatic Migration (July 1927), p. 19.
[20] An American expert who read this, questions its accuracy.

the decrease in the number of labourers employed by the tobacco plantations was due to a decline in markets which necessitated a reduction in
production. Other plantations, such as rubber, oil-palm, tea, and sisal,
used Javanese labourers even before the tobacco plantations began
to employ Javanese in place of Chinese. In the oil industry Chinese
labourers and artisans continued to be used in large numbers, but
other undertakings became more and more mechanized. In the Outer
Islands the large number of contract coolies was becoming a thing of
the past.

That the large immigration of Chinese in the years following the First
World War was regarded with apprehension by the Indonesians is shown
by a resolution, introduced by an Indonesian member in the Volksraad
in 1932, to raise the immigration fee to 250 florins. In countering the
proposal the leading Chinese member pointed out that the export of
Java sugar might suffer through a retaliatory boycott on the part of
China. Upon the urgent request of the majority of the members the proposed resolution was withdrawn, and a resolution requesting the Government to undertake a general study of the whole problem of immigration
was passed in its stead.[21]

The flow of *new* immigration into Indonesia from 1932 to 1938 (i.e.
excepting residents returning to Indonesia who are not included) may
be gauged from the following figures (to the nearest thousand).

	1932	1933	1934	1935	1936	1937	1938
Chinese	12,000	9,000	12,000	15,000	19,000	31,000	20,000[22]

Of the 1938 figures, 3,000 were males below 12 years of age and 8,000
over 12; and 2,000 females under 12 and 6,000 over 12.

From 1920 to 1930 the immigration of Chinese into Indonesia had
been at the rate of over 40,000 a year. In 1921 it was about 43,000, and
in 1928 about 41,000. The average from 1900 to 1930 was rather over
28,000.[23]

Chinese Politics in Indonesia before the Japanese Invasion

There were three happenings which had strong repercussions among
the Chinese of Indonesia. The first was the Revolution of 1911, the
second was the rise of the KMT and the purging of its left-wing elements
in 1927, and the third was trouble between China and Japan which began
anew in 1931.

As we have seen, the Chinese and Javanese Communists came together for a time in an uneasy alliance in 1925. After the purge in
1927 there was a permanent split between Chinese Communists and

[21] Vandenbosch, *Dutch East Indies*, p. 368.
[22] Including those whose sex was not specified.
[23] Cator, *Economic Position of Chinese*, p. 38.

C.S.E.A.— Q

Nationalists. At this period the Chinese were coming to the Indies at the rate of about 50,000 a year, and the strongly nationalistic quality of the immigrants who were from the provinces round Canton gave some anxiety to the Government of the Netherlands Indies. The KMT exercised great influence through its well-disciplined branches, such as the *Shü Pō Shé* (Cantonese rendering) or reading clubs, the Ten Men League, the Boycott Pickets, and the Iron and Blood Brigades. Fortunately for the Indies Government, the Chinese mentality was little inclined to translate abstractions into deeds, but, nevertheless, overt acts were not lacking.[24] During the time that Sun Yat-sen was in intermittent control of Canton and under the influence of Borodin, there were disturbances in the Indies which reflected the attitude of the militant Kwangtung Nationalists. Feeling against Japan had been bitter amongst the Chinese since the Twenty-One Demands which were made when the European Allies were fully occupied in fighting the Germans in Europe, and the Sino-Japanese conflict of 1931–2 arising from the Manchurian Incident caused a new wave of anti-Japanese feeling to run through the Chinese community. A boycott was instituted and in some places was enforced by terrorist tactics, but on the whole it was singularly ineffective at this time because the Chinese merchants and shopkeepers found it very profitable to deal in Japanese textiles, and their zeal for business confounded both their own patriots and the Europeans who desired the exclusion of Japanese goods for rather different reasons from those of the Chinese patriots. The Government warned several Chinese newspapers against articles inciting to violence and took precautions against outbreaks against the Japanese. Luckily the number of Japanese in the Indies was small, so that the opportunity for demonstrations was limited.

The Imperial Government of China had awakened, towards the end of its existence, to the advantages of cultivating China's settlements overseas, and the Nationalist Government intensified these efforts to obtain sympathy, support, and, not least, money from China's exiled children. It sent numerous missions to the Nanyang with variously described objectives but with one unvarying motive. In the 1930s it was demanding a new consular treaty with the Netherlands which should ensure the assimilation of Chinese to Europeans in the Indies. A point of friction between the Governments was the registration of overseas Chinese. Every new consul arriving in the Indies received instructions from his Government to register all Chinese in the Indies—*Peranakans* as well as *Sinkhehs*, the residents of three hundred years as well as the China-born. The Government of the Netherlands Indies sent circulars to the residents prohibiting the practice, and repeatedly informed the consuls that this was not permissible under the consular treaty. Such

[24] Vandenbosch, *Dutch East Indies*, p. 366.

abolition of the pass system, the recognition of the Dutch-Chinese schools, and the improvement in their legal status have given the Chinese new opportunities. These they have turned to good account. The Chinese have always been wealthy in comparison with the natives, and even in comparison with most Europeans. But a new feature of the present century was the use to which they put their riches. Now they were intimately associated with capitalist production, and this had brought them into close alliance with the European community. The new combination of Chinese and European interests, together with the improvements in the schools and the changes in the legal status of the Chinese, had given the Chinese community an increase in power greater than in proportion to its growth in numbers. And the Chinese community was now more Chinese, just as the European community was more European. National aspirations and the improvement in means of communication had strengthened the Chinese and their home country. The Chinese of 1900, if he received any kind of education, had usually been to a Dutch or native school: now he had been to a Chinese school under Chinese masters with a strong tradition of Chinese culture, and read periodicals which kept him in touch with his fellows in Singapore and China.[2]

The diversion of the Chinese to banking and to the development of local industry in late years had, however, meant that their economic life was no longer parasitic but constructive. Nevertheless, continues Mr Furnivall, they still formed a sectional, isolated community competing on rigidly economic lines with the European and native sections. Despite their diversity of race and occupation, taken altogether, they formed one section of a plural community with interests common to some extent among themselves and in many ways opposed to the interests of other sections. It is true that as middlemen they served both the Europeans and the natives, but they also competed with them, and on advantageous terms.[3] In some cases they were strong enough to tax European firms for the benefit of Chinese schools.[4] They could handle goods which allow too small a margin of profit for Europeans, and could undertake more risky ventures (because the penalties of bankruptcy are lighter for the Chinese than the European), thus sharpening the edge of economic corruption and tending to lower the standard of commercial morality; again, it was the Chinese who broke the European ring against Japanese exports. Natives could not

[2] This, I feel, is too sweeping considering that only half the Chinese children attending school received an education through the medium of the Chinese language. It would have been truer of Malaya.

[3] The Europeans reproached the Chinese for ruining their market by offering articles similar to theirs at a much lower price (which they were enabled to do by a far less expensive way of living) (G. Angoulvant, 'Les Indes Néerlandaises, leur rôle dans l'économie internationale', Le Monde Nouveau (Paris, 1926), i. 192).

[4] i.e. by putting a 'cess' on some commodity they control, e.g. rice. This was true of Malaya also.

find employment in a Chinese shop or other business,[5] and the attempts of natives to develop industrial activities were strangled by Chinese competition; it was the natives who first started kapok factories, but within a few years they were ousted by the Chinese; again, when the natives built up a new industry in the manufacture of native cigarettes, there was a long struggle before they could secure their ground against Chinese rivals who imitated their methods. In the economic sphere the Chinese were encroaching on the European world and they were building up an even more formidable barrier against native aspirations. Yet the cultural contact between the Chinese and the Europeans was no closer than before and nationalist sentiment is widening the gap, while the conflict of economic interest placed an increasing strain on the plural society to which they belonged.

Finally Mr Furnivall quotes Dr Boeke[6] on the subject of the Western and the Westernized element of the economy of the Netherlands Indies:

There is a materialism, rationalism, individualism and a concentration of economic ends far more complete and absolute than in homogeneous Western lands; a total absorption in the Exchange and Market; a capitalistic structure with the business concern as a subject, far more typical of capitalism than one can imagine in the so-called 'capitalistic' countries which have grown up slowly out of the past and are still bound to it by a hundred roots.

The above analysis seems on the face of things to be a fair one, except that the writer would quarrel with the word 'parasitic' as describing the activities of the Chinese in Indonesia prior to 1900. They were merely acting as revenue agents of the Dutch Government. The function, then, of the Chinese in Indonesia was mainly the creation of Dutch policy. This fact will be of the first importance when we come to consider the developments during the Japanese occupation and after the war when the Indonesian Republic came into being.

[5] 'It is only very recently that non-Indonesian enterprise, including Chinese capital, has accepted Indonesians into higher administrative posts' (*Recent Developments in the Netherlands East Indies*, speech delivered 16 Sept. 1942 by Dr Charles O. van de Plas, formerly Governor of East Java, Netherlands, and N.I. Council, I.P.R.). But still on a very small scale, I fear (V. P.).

[6] 'Dualische Samenleving', in *De Economist* (1935), p. 773, quoted by Furnivall, *Neth. Indies*, at p. 452.

49

AFTERMATH OF THE SECOND WORLD WAR

UP to 1949 there seemed remarkably little material available to write the history of the Chinese in Indonesia during the Japanese invasion and during the occupation. As regards the occupation, when Indonesia was cut off from the observation of the world, the Europeans, who are usually much more interested to record what they see than are the Oriental races, were isolated in concentration camps. No doubt a fairly connected story could be constructed from the narratives of individual Chinese and Indonesians, but the state of the country in 1949 did not facilitate efforts in this direction. The people were too engrossed in their attempts to repair war damage and to reconstruct their economy to dwell on the years of the occupation. The following main facts, however, emerge.[1]

All the efforts of the Japanese up till August 1943 were aimed at the organization of the indigenous population of Indonesia in aid of their own war effort. The non-indigenous Orientals, first and foremost the Chinese, were left unregimented. As the Chinese in the Netherlands Indies depended on the fully developed Western capitalism in the islands, it can be readily seen that this section of Indonesian society, which was predominantly middle-class, was heavily hit when the Japanese occupation of the Indies was completed. Resentment of the Japanese which had been acute for many years was not reduced on this account.

The Japanese established an office for Chinese affairs called the Kakkio Han (in Chinese Hua Ch'iao Pan) in Batavia. This was directed by a single Japanese, one Toyoshima: the remainder of the staff were Chinese. In Batavia and every other Chinese settlement there was a Hua Ch'iao Tsung Hui, a Chinese association, which was responsible to the local Japanese commander and which through its headquarters in Batavia was a channel for the communication of orders by the Kakkio Han. The Japanese used this organization to convey their new regulations which included (1) the reintroduction of the internal passport system which had been abolished by the Dutch, (2) the payment of a registration fee of $100 for Chinese males and $80 for Chinese females, (3) the establishment of the Chinese guards (police) for protection of their community

---

[1] Based on the unpublished doctoral dissertation, *Political Development in the Netherlands East-Indies during and immediately after the Japanese Occupation*, by Dr Janus Poppe (Georgetown Univ., Washington, D.C.), p. 95.

against possible violence on the part of the Indonesians, and (4) collection of money from the Chinese for war purposes.

Before the occupation there were practically no Chinese who supported the Nanking puppet Government of Wang Ching-wei: most Chinese support was for the KMT and its leader Chiang Kai-shek whose regime was recognized by the Netherlands Government. The Japanese had interned a large number of prominent Chinese, both *Peranakans* and *Sinkhehs*, under the impression that the backbone of resistance would thus be broken. This assumption proved to be mistaken; dissatisfaction among the Chinese residents became so great that another attitude had to be adopted. After observing the signs of a resistance movement, the Japanese in August 1943 induced a few pro-Nanking Chinese to form an organization with the intention of bringing all Chinese activities under its surveillance. Its directors were without exception appointed by the Japanese authorities. A similar course was adopted with the Eurasian community in the following month. These measures at least may have had the effect of preventing the resistance movement coming to a head and resulting in an uprising.

Allied intelligence concerning Indonesia during the occupation was more meagre than in the case of any other area in Southeast Asia. No Office of Strategic Services (OSS) or Allied intelligence teams were operating in the larger islands. After the surrender, Dutch internees and prisoners-of-war were either too biased or too out of touch to offer a fair index of the real state of affairs; unbiased Indonesians were as difficult to find, and the Chinese and Eurasian minorities were too afraid of either the returning Dutch or of the Indonesians to speak freely.[2]

There is, however, a document extant which, when due allowance is made for the circumstances under which it was written, affords some evidence of the experiences of the Chinese during the occupation.[3] This document (to which further reference is made later in this chapter) states that when the Japanese landed in Java Chinese residents were the main victims of robbery by the natives. In the majority of cases the trouble started with the robbing of one or two houses by a few bandits. When no police appeared and no resistance was encountered, the whole of the inhabitants of the town or village, who in the past had never committed robbery or any other criminal act, participated in the looting. Moreover, now that civilized controls were removed, a number of excesses occurred and there was murder and rape.

During the Japanese occupation Chinese-Indonesian relations were adversely affected by the memory of the looting in the early stages, by

[2] Charles Wolf, Jr., *The Indonesian Story* (N.Y., 1948), p. 10.
[3] Chung Hua Tsung Hui, *Memo. outlining acts of violence.* More than one person who read this section in manuscript (including Dr Tsoa Sik-ien), described the Chung Hua Tsung Hui as 'pro-Dutch', and an American authority remarked that it was 'an extremely non-objective and partisan source'.

the economic offensive undertaken by the Indonesians, with Japanese support, to supplant the Chinese, by political differences due to the fact that the Chinese were pro-Ally while the Indonesians were 'completely pro-Japanese', and by the haughty attitude of certain Indonesian officials who gained favour with the invaders.[4] When the Japanese capitulated and the Indonesian Republic was proclaimed, the Indonesians suddenly assumed a conciliatory attitude towards the Chinese. In the *bersiap* (preparatory) period following the proclamation of independence, when Dutch nationals were being hunted down and killed, a Chinese flag, displayed in front of a house or worn on the chest, proved a sufficient protection in even the most isolated spots.

After the Japanese surrender, the British Commander-in-Chief, who was sent by the Supreme Allied Commander to disarm the Japanese in Java, did not side with either the Dutch or the Indonesians, but confined his occupation to a few enclaves—Batavia, Bandung, Samarang, Surabaya—and from there tried to contact the rest of Java which was in the hands of the Republicans. The situation was similar in Sumatra where only Medan, Palembang, and Padang were occupied by the British, the remaining territory being left under Republican authority.[5]

The Chinese in Southeast Asia generally had anticipated that the liberation of these countries would be carried out by Chinese troops. It was widely rumoured that Chiang Kai-shek had made a radio speech in which he had promised to give armed support to those countries which had not yet won their independence. The fact that it was British and Indian troops who entered Indonesia was a disappointment to many Chinese nationalists, and the Mohammedan troops were later accused by the Dutch of siding with their fellow Muslims against the re-established Dutch regime.

The Indonesian attitude towards the Chinese began again to undergo a change. The 'neutrality' adopted by the Chinese did not satisfy the Indonesians who wanted the Chinese to carry out an economic boycott of the Dutch. When the Chinese began supplying goods to the Dutch, and some others received monetary and other aid from the Dutch Government and began working in Dutch offices, the community as a whole began to be regarded as definitely siding with the Dutch.[6] Resentment at this supposed partiality soon produced a number of 'incidents'.

At first a few Chinese were kidnapped or their dwellings were looted. The Chinese flag no longer afforded protection but instead incited animosity, and was often torn to shreds. Then the members of Chinese families who had thus been victimized 'took an understandable, but regrettable, course: they enlisted in the Dutch forces in order to wreak

---

[4] Ibid. p. 3.
[5] Neth. Information Bureau, N.Y., *The Political Events in the Republic of Indonesia* (1947), p. 8.   [6] *Memo. outlining acts of violence &c.*

C.S.E.A.—Q 2

vengeance'.[7] Thus Chinese-Indonesian relations became exacerbated. Yet Indonesians who were alienated from the Republican cause through ill-treatment on suspicion of helping the Dutch, and who had in some cases also joined the Dutch forces, were many times greater in number than the Chinese who enlisted under the Dutch flag. There was ill feeling, too, over the Chinese use of the new currency issued by the Dutch in March 1946—but then, as the Chung Hua Tsung Hui *Memorandum* points out, Indonesians living in Allied-occupied territory also used it.

During the hostilities that were destined to continue intermittently for some years to come, the Chinese were in a particularly unfortunate position. Suspected by the Indonesians of pro-Dutch sympathies and by the Dutch of pro-Indonesian inclinations, they received harsh treatment on both sides, especially from irresponsible Indonesian groups. The Indonesians seem to have overlooked the fact (says the *Memorandum*) that as business men it was impossible for Chinese living in Allied territory to boycott the Dutch, as this would have amounted to economic suicide. In the same manner, Chinese living in the Republic have closely co-operated in economic matters with the Republic, for they had no other course to follow if they were to maintain their position.

To prevent unpleasant repercussions for the Chinese living in the islands, China sought a middle-of-the-road position which would antagonize neither the Dutch nor the Republic.[8]

In December 1945 a punitive expedition against the village of Bekasi was undertaken by the British in consequence of atrocities committed against R.A.F. personnel and Indian troops. The greatest sufferers by the expedition were the Chinese. Some of their houses were inadvertently burnt with the rest of the village, and when the Indonesians returned, the Chinese were subjected to intimidation and violence.[9] But the first really serious incident occurred in June 1946 in a Chinese settlement west of the Tangerang River.[10] The *New York Times* of 6 June reported that 600 Chinese, suspected by the Indonesians of co-operation with the Dutch, had been slain and their villages set on fire. The massacre did not end until 8 June. On 10 June the Chinese Foreign Office was reported as having protested to both the Dutch and the Indonesian Republic.[11]

The Chung Hua Tsung Hui *Memorandum* says that according to the minutes of a meeting held in Tangerang on 28 May, prepared by Junadi, executive member of the Indonesia Republic Cabinet, the People's Band had conceived a plan of carrying out a holy war (*Perang Sabil*) in disregard of the instructions given by the T.R.I. (Republican Army) Com-

[7] *Memo. outlining acts of violence, &c.*, pp. 3 and 4.   [8] Wolf, *Indonesian Story*, pp. 160, 161.
[9] David Wehl, *The Birth of Indonesia* (London, 1948), p. 80.
[10] About 20 miles from Batavia.
[11] *New York Times* (6 June), p. 8, col. 5; (8 June), p. 9, col. 1; (10 June), p. 14, col. 6. Refugees reported more slain (17 June), p. 9, col. 5.

mander to establish a no-man's-land, in line with the agreement reached
with the Dutch.

As might be expected in the emotional stress, the Chinese accounts are
elaborated with details of horrible atrocities, including the burning alive
of women and children. The mere fact of the massacre, however, is
terrible enough.

In short [says the *Memorandum*] the suburbs of Tangerang have been turned into
a hell for the Chinese who for many years had lived so amicably with the Indonesians
and adjusted themselves to their environment so well that foreigners could hardly
distinguish them from real Indonesians. As the Chinese of this area have practically
become assimilated, it is incredible that they were so treated.

According to the report received by the Jang Send (Red Cross) in
Batavia, 653 Chinese were murdered in Tangerang and neighbourhood,
including 136 females and 36 children. There were approximately
25,000 refugees in Batavia from the area. 1,268 Chinese dwellings were
burned down, and 236 otherwise destroyed.

A further massacre was reported on 18 September at Bagan Si Api
Api when 200 Chinese are said to have been killed,[12] 20 more were
killed at Bangko, 34 at Telok Pulau, and 75 at Jembra. Another outbreak
at Palembang in Sumatra in January 1947 resulted in the death of
another 250.

Meanwhile, in November 1946, the Linggajati Agreement, which was
to have settled the differences between the Netherlands and the Republic,
was negotiated and was signed by both parties on 25 March 1947. This
agreement never became effective, and each side accused the other of
violating its terms. Finally, 'in order to put an end to the intolerable
chaos and to create conditions for the building of a State that would
bring renewed hope and fulfilment to the Indonesian people', the Dutch
from the night of 20–21 July 1947 until 4 August undertook military
action.[13]

Long before this 'police action' was started it was common knowledge
that the Republic would adopt a scorched-earth policy to hamper the
Dutch operations. Knowing that the Chinese community would be endangered if fighting occurred, the Chinese consul-general had, as early
as December 1946, endeavoured to establish safety zones where the
Chinese could gather in times of danger. The Republic wanted to know
what guarantee could be given that these zones would not be used to the
disadvantage of the Indonesians, and when the reply was given that such
guarantee would only be given if the Chinese were armed adequately to
uphold the neutrality of the zones, the Republic objected to such a course.
Another proposal to establish safety zones to be guarded by a mixed

[12] *Memo.*, p. 6.
[13] Neth. Inf. Bureau, *Political Events*, p. 30.

force of Indonesian-Chinese-Dutch police was disapproved by both the Dutch and the Indonesians.[14]

When the situation deteriorated and the outlook became critical, the Chinese consul-general, Mr Chiang Chia-tung, issued instructions to Chinese residing in Republican territory that they should decline to be evacuated outside the city limits, and when they were in immediate danger they should gather together in the buildings of schools or associations hoisting both the Chinese and the Red Cross flags.

According to the Chung Hua Tsung Hui *Memorandum*, between 21 July and 21 August 1947, 293 Chinese were killed and over 6,000 were missing. Reports received up to mid-September showed that 912 houses and factories had been burned. As a rule, prior to the arrival of the Dutch troops, Chinese living in Republican territory were unharmed, although they were exposed from time to time to arrest on spy charges. In the face of the Dutch advance, looting and arson were carried out by the Indonesian troops. In the process of effecting the scorched-earth policy industrial plants, official and private offices, and big buildings in general were the 'preferred objectives'. Most privately-owned big buildings belonged to Chinese. In addition to the destruction carried out under orders from the Indonesian High Command by special squads, native freebooters joined in the burning and looting. The *Memorandum* recites in considerable detail the separate acts of murder, rape, kidnapping, and destruction of property, usually with the names of the victims.[15]

On 25 July a memorandum expressing the Chinese Government's regret at the outbreak of hostilities in Indonesia and its grave concern as to the welfare and safety of the Chinese nationals in the Dutch East Indies was handed to the chargé d'affaires of the Netherlands embassy by the Chinese Ministry of Foreign Affairs. In this memorandum the Chinese Government asked what effective measures had been taken to safeguard Chinese lives and property.[16] On 31 July Dr George Yeh,

[14] *The Voice of China* (Chinese (official) news service, short-wave radio) (Nanking, 6 Feb. 1947) reported that the Netherlands authorities had agreed in principle to establish zones for the Chinese in Indonesia and to give emergency relief to Chinese who suffered losses in the armed conflict between the Netherlands and Indonesian troops from 1 to 5 Jan. in Palembang.

[15] Mr E. N. van Kleffens on 26 Aug. 1947 in addressing the Security Council of the U.N. said: 'Ten days ago, intelligence reached our lines in northern Sumatra that Republican elements had herded together in a cemetery near a place called Pankalan Brandan approximately four thousand Chinese, without food, without water, without shelter of any kind, who were thus exposed to certain death' (Neth. Inf. Bureau, N.Y., *The Other Side of the Medal* (1947)).

Most of the information relied upon above, it must be emphasized, is from Dutch or pro-Dutch sources. As against this, Dr Tjoa Sik-ien, a Chinese of standing from Java who supports the Indonesian point of view, expressed to the author his disagreement with the Chung Hua Tsung Hui *Memorandum* and stated that in his view it distorted or misinterpreted the facts. The Indonesians harboured no ill will against the Chinese. In normal times the latter lived peacefully in the Republican area without molestation. It was only during military operations that they suffered. The Dutch had magnified the differences between Indonesians and Chinese for their own purposes. He did not think that the Dutch affection for the Chinese was sincere.   [16] *Voice of China* (25 July 1947).

Vice-Minister of Foreign Affairs, made a statement in which he said that the Chinese Government viewed with grave concern the repeated acts of arson and violence inflicted on innocent Chinese nationals by the Indonesian army which constituted a serious offence against international law and humanity. It might be recalled, he continued, that, during the hostilities that took place prior to the conclusion of the Linggajati Agreement, the Chinese communities in the Netherlands East Indies had already sustained irreparable losses in lives and property. This had occurred in spite of the fact that throughout the period of fighting the Chinese communities, in accordance with instructions from the Chinese Government, had observed strict neutrality, and that the Chinese population there had been intimately associated with the development and prosperity of those islands for over three hundred years.[17]

The Indonesian Republic, of course, took a different view of the Chinese question from that of the Dutch. The Chinese, for their part, living as they did partly in Dutch and partly in Republican territory, tended naturally to adapt themselves to the situation as far as was expedient and to be conciliatory towards those exercising authority. *Indonesian Information* of 25 October 1947[18] stated the Republican position in the matter:

> Chinese nationals are the largest minority in the Indonesian Republic. Out of a population of about seventy millions, Chinese make up approximately one and a half millions. Naturally, therefore, they have to a certain extent shared in the general misery of the country, and in spite of all the efforts of the Republican Government, have suffered a certain amount of privation as a result of the two years' blockade. However, official Chinese sources have recognized the fact that the Republic is doing all in its power to help the Chinese communities.

The same publication at different times gave examples of the good feeling existing between the Chinese and the Republic, e.g. the Chinese deputy consul-general had stated at Kediri in East Java that the living conditions of the Chinese nationals in Republican territory were quite satisfactory 'except when Dutch provocations succeeded in provoking strife'; on the occasion of the Chinese National Day (10 October) Chinese planes had been given permission to fly over Republican territory to drop leaflets and pamphlets bearing goodwill messages to the Chinese inhabitants of the country; the Chinese inhabitants of Muntilar, near Jogjakarta, had contributed 18,000 rupees (Republican currency) for the defence of the Indonesian Republic, &c.

During a press interview in Singapore on 28 October 1947 Haj Agoes Salim, Foreign Minister of the Republic, explained the position of the Chinese in the existing situation in Indonesia.

[17] Ibid. (31 July 1947).
[18] i/4, published by the representative in Britain of the Government of the Republic of Indonesia.

To all appearances [said Haji Salim] it seems that it is the Chinese who are suffering most from the scorched-earth policy which is being forced on the Republic by the Dutch military action. However, if we know our Indonesia, we realize that in places such as Malang and Sourabaya, for instance, it is the Chinese who own most of the property, and so, when there is an assessment of damage in these places obviously the Chinese seem to be the ones most affected. We tend to forget, as we contemplate the figures of damage done to Chinese properties, that the few Indonesian properties have suffered just as much, and the Indonesian owners feel the oss just as keenly as the Chinese owners.[19]

Chinese property, the Foreign Minister insisted, was not singled out for any special attention, and so long as the conditions of war demanded the application of the scorched-earth policy, economic scruples must be sacrificed to military advantage. The only way to end the damage to Chinese property was to end the war.

This, of course, was cold comfort to the Chinese to whom the continuance of the civil war meant only loss of life and property.

In West Borneo there had been no conflict between the interests of the Chinese inhabitants and those of the other groups of the population for several years—not even in the agrarian sphere which was in many respects common ground. Nor was there any outbreak during the time of the serious incidents elsewhere in Indonesia.[20]

After the 'police action' was completed and the troubles of the Chinese community had died down, both the Chinese and the Indonesian Government made practical demonstrations of their sympathy with the victims. The Executive Yuan appropriated one million florins for the relief of the sufferers,[21] and the Republican Government five million rupees for the same purpose.[22] Republican leaders such as Sjahrir and Sjarifouddin made broadcast speeches regretting the massacre of the Chinese and expressing sympathy for the sufferers from the scorched-earth policy. Though the Republic of Indonesia Information Service made no attempt to hide the extent of the Chinese casualties (it quoted the Chinese consul-general, Chiang Chia-tung, as stating in Singapore that 1,000 Chinese had been killed and 100,000 rendered homeless since the Dutch opened hostilities in Indonesia),[23] it stressed that the incidents had occurred only in the areas of military operations. Sumatra and other islands were quiet and the Chinese consul-general had visited Jombang in East Java and had stated that he was now satisfied with the living conditions of the Chinese in all the Republican areas.[24] The Republicans made much of the fact that the Chinese within the Republican area had demonstrated their sympathy with the Republic and their General

[19] *Indonesian Information*, i/12 (12 Nov. 1947).
[20] *Economic R. of Indonesia* (Batavia, Oct. 1947), p. 171.
[21] *Thien Sung Yit Po* (Batavia, 12 Aug. 1947).
[22] *Sin Po* (Batavia, 15 Aug. 1947).
[23] Indonesian News Service (N.Y., 25 Sept. 1947).   [24] Ibid. (3 Oct. 1947).

Association had even made a collection of comforts for dispatch to the Republican troops at the front.[25]

Controversy now turned on the subject of the establishment of *Pao An Tui*, or Chinese protection corps. These bands of armed Chinese were intended to protect the Chinese community during times of trouble. The Dutch sanctioned their formation. Some Chinese newspapers actually recommended that China should send troops for the protection of the Chinese in Indonesia, but would the Dutch (one paper asked rather naïvely) permit them to land?[26] The supporters of the KMT were in favour of the *Pao An Tui*, but the leftist papers were not. The Jogjakarta authorities compared them with the military forces maintained by the Western powers in the old treaty ports in China, and characterized them as an attempt to create a Chinese extraterritoriality in Indonesia. In this attitude they received leftist support, and Mr Gromyko attacked the *Pao An Tui* in the Security Council. The controversy was taken up in the Convention of Chinese Associations held in August.

The *Sin Po* of 6 September quoted two views on the situation—one that the scorched-earth policy of the Indonesian troops had been carried out with the intention of destroying the economic foundations of the Overseas Chinese, and the other that the Dutch wished the two peoples, the Chinese and the Indonesians, to hate one another.

The misfortunes of the Chinese during the Dutch-Indonesian hostilities were not sufficient to create a solid pro-Dutch anti-Indonesian attitude on the part of the community, though it is likely that a majority favoured the Dutch. Nevertheless, there were then and still in 1949 several Chinese holding important positions in the Republican Government itself, such as Mr Tan Ling Djie, the secretary of the Socialist Party, and a leading Komitie Nasional figure, and Mr Ong Eng Djie, former Vice-Minister of Finance and director of the Republic's Banking and Trading Corporation.[27] The *Sin Po*, in an editorial of 13 September, reported that among the international volunteers who had come to Sumatra to fight for the Republic of Indonesia there were some Overseas Chinese. 'This action is not welcome to us', commented the newspaper. 'When the Indonesian rioters choose to murder the Overseas Chinese and burn their property what will the volunteers do then? Will they look on or take part in the atrocities?'

Many Indonesian Chinese, too, felt that their community was isolated from other Chinese communities in the Nanyang. Although there had been all these murders of Chinese in the Indies, there had not been a single voice of sympathy from the Chinese newspapers in Malaya.[28]

When the Security Council's cease-fire instructions had failed to end

[25] Ibid. (5 Oct. 1947).   [26] *Seng Hwo Pao* (8 Aug. 1947).
[27] Wolf, *Indonesian Story*, p. 161.
[28] Editorial in *Thien Sung Yit Po* (Batavia, 25 Aug. 1947).

hostilities in Indonesia the Council on 25 August appointed a Committee of Good Offices to do its best to mediate between the parties. The committee and its staff arrived in Batavia on 27 October. They chose as a neutral meeting ground U.S.S. *Renville*, a navy transport, which sailed into Batavia bay on 8 December. The truce was accepted by both parties on 17 January with acceptance of six additional principles two days later.[29]

1949–63[30]

The vicissitudes suffered by the Overseas Chinese in this period, consequent on the new pattern of forces operating in the region, were more painful in Indonesia than in any other country in Southeast Asia. Having been sandwiched between the Dutch and the Indonesian revolutionaries and having suffered accordingly, after independence they were the victims not only of nationalist aspirations towards equality (or 'levelling down') but were also persecuted as 'capitalists', and as such were denied the effective protection of Communist China.

As a result of the Round Table conference held at The Hague from 23 August to 2 November 1949, complete and unconditional sovereignty was transferred to the Republic of the United States of Indonesia. From this transfer, Netherlands New Guinea ('West Irian' to the Indonesians) was excluded, its status being left for determination through subsequent negotiations between the Netherlands and Indonesia. (In 1962 the Dutch agreed to transfer it to the control of the United Nations, who would eventually transfer it to Indonesian sovereignty.) In 1954 the proposed Union between the Netherlands and Indonesia was dissolved by mutual consent.

In 1950 the federal system which had come into being during the struggle between the Indonesian nationalists and the Dutch in 1946–8 was abolished and a unitary State was re-established.

The Chinese community had come in for much unpopularity with the Indonesians during the war for independence, being accused by the latter of collaboration with the Dutch and being subject to retaliation and even to massacre in consequence, and now that full independence was an accomplished feat their future status was a matter of considerable anxiety to them.

The question of citizenship came to the fore once again between 1946 and 1949 when the Dutch established a chain of States in East and West

---

[29] *United Nations Bulletin*, iv/5 (Mar. 1948), p. 163.

[30] Since the first edition of this work was published, the results of detailed research on the status of the Chinese in Indonesia have become available. See, in particular, G. McT. Kahin, *The Political Position of the Chinese in Indonesia* (Stanford, 1946); G. W. Skinner, ed., *Local, Ethnic, and National Loyalties in Village Indonesia; a Symposium* (N.Y., 1959); D. E. Willmott, *The National Status of the Chinese in Indonesia, 1900–58*, rev. ed. (N.Y., 1961), and *The Chinese of Semarang* (N.Y., 1960); and L. E. Williams, *Overseas Chinese Nationalism: the Genesis of the Pan Chinese Movement in Indonesia, 1900–16* (Glencoe, Ill., 1960).

Java, Madura, and the 'Outer Islands' (as they had been called before the war). The system of government was parliamentary and elective, but the Dutch retained control of policy. These States were joined together into a Federation. Chinese were appointed as members of the governing bodies of the States and Federation and many entered the civil service during this period.

Early in 1948 the constitutional committee of the Federal Consultative Assembly agreed that all persons of foreign descent who were born in Indonesia and had resided there for more than two years should be regarded as Indonesian citizens, but since the proposal did not allow *Peranakans* to opt for Chinese citizenship, there was a good deal of opposition to it within the Chinese community and a final decision was consequently deferred. But as Indonesia progressed towards complete independence these discussions became a dead letter.

Anticipating that a Government to embrace the whole of Indonesia under purely Indonesian control would soon be formed, the Chinese decided at this juncture to form a new political association for their protection. This was brought into being as the 'Persatuan Tionghoa', or Chinese Union, in May 1948. Its main purposes were to promote the interests of Indonesia and to co-operate with other nations, to protect the interests of the Overseas Chinese without sacrificing those of the masses, and to strive for the principles of democracy. Although the Chinese Union was composed mostly of *Peranakans* it aimed to include the *Totoks* (*Sinkhehs*) as well, and in a bid to secure their support it passed a resolution to the effect that those Chinese who did not wish to accept Indonesian nationality should be free to select one of their own choice. The Union further recommended that China and Indonesia should sign a treaty as soon as possible whereby their respective nationals residing in the other's country should be given the same treatment as nationals of the 'most-favoured nation'. The Persatuan Tionghua, however, proposed that in general the Chinese should accept Indonesian citizenship and the responsibilities attached to it, but insisted that the Chinese minority should retain their own culture and be allowed to maintain their own schools.

With the ratification of the Round Table Agreement by the legislature of the former Republic of Indonesia and the several Federal legislatures, a new citizenship law was automatically adopted. Under its provisions, Chinese *Peranakans* from all over Indonesia were given two years (until 27 December 1951) in which they might, if they so wished, reject Indonesian citizenship and become nationals of China—in effect the same system as had applied to Chinese living in the Republican territory between 1946 and 1948, so that the Chinese were faced with the necessity of making a choice between the two citizenships all over again.[31]

[31] Willmott, *National Status*, is followed in this section.

The citizenship provisions of the Round Table Agreement, however, were only on general principles, and when the new unitary constitution was promulgated in August 1950, it laid down that matters of citizenship and naturalization were to be regulated by law. In the meantime Indonesian citizenship would be determined by the provisions of the Round Table Agreement and anyone whose nationality was not defined by this agreement but who had acquired citizenship under a previous law of the Republic would remain an Indonesian citizen.

Pending the enactment of the new citizenship law there was a good deal of confusion regarding the legal position of the Chinese. In some parts of Java, for example, the local authorities were of the opinion that a *Peranakan* was not to be considered a citizen unless he could produce a certificate of citizenship, and in the Bandung area Chinese born in Indonesia of parents who had never obtained certificates of permanent residence during the Dutch period were officially (but mistakenly) considered as Chinese citizens, together with their parents. But the drafting of a citizenship bill was clearly going to involve some bitter controversy.

While the Government was still striving to standardize the policies of the central and local Government departments regarding nationality, it was simultaneously attempting to find a solution to the dual nationality question with the People's China. Indonesia made the first *démarche*, proposing to the People's Government that they should negotiate a treaty regarding nationality, delaying the finalizing of its own citizenship bill until it had been able to come to terms with China. But although the People's Government accepted the proposal early in 1954 it was in no hurry to proceed with the matter, its Foreign Ministry being preoccupied with the Geneva conference. In the meantime Mr Chou En-lai, the Chinese Prime Minister, while on a visit to India, was reputed to have told Mr Nehru that China was ready to give up its claim to the citizenship of Overseas Chinese possessing dual nationality, and when he visited Burma the Prime Minister also raised the question of the dual nationality of Chinese in that country.

The draft constitution of the People's Republic of China was adopted in September 1954, and Article 23 provided that the National People's Congress should include deputies elected by 'Chinese residents abroad'. Then on 23 September Chou En-lai in his report to the First National People's Congress made the following statement:

For our part, we are willing to urge Overseas Chinese to respect the laws of the governments and the social customs of the countries in which they live. It is worth pointing out that the question of the nationality of Overseas Chinese is one which the reactionary governments of China in the past never tried to solve. This placed Overseas Chinese in a difficult situation and often led to discord between China and the countries concerned. To improve this situation, we are prepared to settle this question, and are ready to settle it first with the Southeast Asian countries which have established diplomatic relations with us.[32]

This declaration prompted what no doubt was a competing bid from Chiang Kai-shek in Formosa. On 25 October Chiang expressed his hope for the loyal support of the Overseas Chinese in regaining mainland China, and the next day the KMT ambassador to Canada, Liu Chieh, stated at a United Nations committee that according to the present Chinese (Nationalist) law, Overseas Chinese were not considered Chinese nationals if they obtained the citizenship of another country.[33]

A start to put the principles of the People's Government into operation was made with Indonesia. Negotiations began at Peking in November 1954 and were concluded in December. Then in March 1955 they were continued in Jakarta. The Indonesian delegation was headed by Mr Woijopronoto, head of the Asian and Pacific Affairs Section of the Indonesian Foreign Ministry, and the Chinese delegation by the Chinese ambassador to Indonesia. Finally, a treaty was signed at Bandung between Mr Sunario, the Indonesian Foreign Minister, and Mr Chou En-lai on 22 April 1955, in the middle of the Asian-African Conference. The treaty was to come into force after ratification by the two countries—but this did not take place for another five years (for reasons that will in a moment be explained).[34]

The purpose of the treaty was to eliminate dual citizenship and to prevent its occurrence in the future. Most of its provisions applied to persons who were at the same time citizens of Indonesia and of the People's Republic of China. This included all persons of Chinese descent who had acquired Indonesian nationality under the Act of 1946 and the Round Table Agreement. It did not include those who were born in China and were never naturalized as Dutch subjects or those who rejected Indonesian citizenship during the periods of option of 1946–8 and 1949–51. These latter, being Chinese citizens only, were given no further choice in the matter.

Under Section II, all persons who had come of age (i.e. attained 18 years) when the treaty came into effect, must choose their nationality within two years. Under Section V, persons who failed to choose within two years—would, if their fathers were of Chinese origin, be deemed to have chosen Chinese nationality (and *mutatis mutandis* for Indonesians). If such persons had no legal relationship with their fathers or if their fathers' nationality was not ascertainable, provided their mothers

---

[32] *People's China*, 16 Oct. 1954, p. 24 (cited by Willmott, *National Status*).

[33] Which is quite opposed to the writer's experience as a Protector of Chinese in Malaya before the war. Several Chinese who were British subjects through birth in the Straits Settlements tried to renounce their Chinese citizenship through the official channels in China but none succeeded.

[34] See V. Purcell, 'The Dual Nationality of the Chinese in Southeast Asia', *India Quarterly*, xi/4 (Oct.–Dec. 1955), for the full text of the treaty.

were of Chinese origin they should be considered as having chosen Chinese nationality (and *mutatis mutandis* for Indonesians).

In the future, all children born in Indonesia of alien Chinese parents would acquire Chinese citizenship, while those born in China of Indonesian parents would be Indonesian.

One of the final provisions of the treaty was of the highest importance politically and represented a complete break with pre-war KMT policy, namely that

(XI) With a view to improving the conditions under which citizens of one country reside in the other, the high contracting parties agree to encourage their own citizens residing in the other country to respect the laws and social customs of the country in which they reside and not to take part in the political activities of that country. Each high contracting party affirms its willingness to protect according to its laws the proper rights and interests of the citizens of the other party residing in its territories.

When the conclusion of the treaty was announced it was hailed by nearly all parties in Indonesia as a great success. The PNI (Nationalist Party) issued a statement declaring their full support, as did also the Communist Party (PKI). Nevertheless, the treaty also met with a great deal of opposition when its text was released. Even some Government supporters criticized various aspects of it, and the opposition parties were outspoken in their condemnation. Masjumi said that the treaty was contrary to the provisional constitution, the Political Manifesto of 1945, the Citizenship Act of 1946, and the Round Table Agreement of 1949; that it would sacrifice to China many Chinese whom the Indonesian Government had hitherto considered as friends, and that the registration of over a million Chinese would involve tremendous difficulties. The Indonesian Socialist Party had similar objections to the treaty, and the Catholic Party (Partai Katolik) and the Protestant Party (Parkindo) were also against it on a number of special grounds of their own.

So much for Indonesian reaction. But what of the reception of the treaty by the local Chinese? Articulate *Peranakans* had almost unanimously opposed the draft citizenship bill which had been made public a few months earlier, but they were not so sure about the treaty. For one thing, the two-generation *jus soli* provision which they had objected to in the draft bill was absent from the treaty, and for another it did promise a final resolution of the thorny problem of dual nationality which no unilateral legislation could do. The anti-Communist *Kuangpo*, a Semarang newspaper, opposed the treaty, and the two most important *Perankan* newspapers in Jakarta took opposite sides. While differing on the merits of the treaty itself, *Peranakans* were unanimous in their fear that the signing of the treaty might raise uncertainties about their rights as citizens, at least until the end of the two-year option period. They were unanimous, therefore, in their desire for the Government to issue a directive guaranteeing their full rights as citizens in spite of the uncertainties of the treaty.

Both the Chinese and the Indonesian Governments wanted to have the goodwill of the Chinese, and as a means of overcoming difficulties there was an interchange of notes in 1955 between them resulting in a supplement to the treaty which was to be ratified and to come into effect with the treaty itself. This supplement was intended to remove ambiguities, including those regarding the status of Indonesian citizens of Chinese descent before the option period and after the twenty-year term of the treaty. For China's part, the Dual Citizenship Treaty was ratified by the Standing Committee of the National People's Congress on 30 December 1957, but it was not until two years later that the exchange of ratifications finally took place. This was due to a disagreement in Indonesia as to the 'option' provisions of the treaty. The debate in the legislature on 21 and 25 November 1957 revolved round certain points— the status of the pro-Kuomintang Chinese whom the Government was treating as 'stateless', the issue raised by a Masjumi member that 'recognition of Chinese as Indonesian citizens would endanger the Indonesian nation', and the demand that the debate on the treaty be postponed until after parliament had passed a bill on citizenship and naturalization. There was also the question whether voters should be exempted from having to exercise options. Finally, after five years of debate, deadlock, and unsuccessful compromise, the supporters of the active option system at last overcame the dogged opposition of the Chinese community and a major, if not a predominant, section of parliament.

Meanwhile the 1958 Citizenship Act had been passed.[35] The Act opens by affirming that all persons are Indonesian citizens who have become such under laws, agreements, or regulations promulgated since Indonesia's independence on 15 August 1945. Section 4 contains a two-generation *jus soli* provision whereby an alien born and residing in Indonesia whose father was also born and resides there can apply for Indonesian citizenship,

if, upon the acquirement of the Republic of Indonesia citizenship, he has no other citizenship, or if he submits a statement which under the legal provisions operative in his country of origin divests him of any other citizenship he may possess under the legal provisions operative in his country of origin, or under the provisions of an agreement in settlement of dual citizenship entered into between the Republic of Indonesia and the country concerned.

Since, however, there was no way whereby a person of Chinese descent could divest himself of his Chinese citizenship under Chinese law, except during the option period provided for in the Dual Citizenship Treaty, none of the Indonesian Chinese would be able to take advantage of this

[35] The text is given as App. V of Willmott, *National Status*.

provision of the 1958 Act. The 1958 Act makes it virtually impossible for dual citizenship to arise in the future. Apart from minor exceptions, the Act follows the principle of *jus sanguinis*. In fine, it can be said that the Act confirmed the citizenship status which the Chinese had acquired through the 1946 Act and the Round Table Agreement, but made it impossible for Chinese aliens or their descendants to become Indonesian citizens after the option period provided for in the Dual Citizenship Treaty with China.

Neither the 1958 Citizenship Act nor the Dual Citizenship Treaty did anything to clarify or settle the status of pro-KMT Chinese aliens. By the Government agencies they were considered to be 'Stateless', which they naturally preferred to being considered citizens of the People's Republic of China—which was the only alternative in a country which did not recognize the Government of Chiang Kai-shek. Pro-KMT Chinese who were born in Indonesia did not reject Indonesian citizenship during the 1949–51 option period because they feared that to do so might put them under the jurisdiction of Communist Chinese consuls. No opportunity was given them under the Dual Citizenship Treaty to reject Indonesian citizenship in favour of Nationalist Chinese citizenship.

The prolonged discussions, divergence of views, and resort to compromises must not be allowed to obscure the fact that the Treaty of Dual Citizenship was an achievement of great historical importance. For the first time, China had relinquished her traditional claim that all persons of Chinese descent remain Chinese citizens even when they acquire another citizenship—the principle of 'once a Chinese: always a Chinese' which had aroused such fears of Chinese expansionism during the KMT period and had caused such resentment in Southeast Asia. If other countries sought and obtained similar treaties (as Chou En-lai had practically invited them to do), an outstanding source of friction between China and the Southeast Asian countries would have been removed.

The question of dual citizenship, however, was not the only problem to be solved in harmonizing Sino-Indonesian relations and the relations between Indonesia and its ethnic Chinese minority.

The first question that arose was how many Indonesian Chinese remained Chinese and how many became Indonesians by operation of law. The answer is very hard to arrive at. To begin with, it is not known how many Chinese gave up their Indonesian citizenship in the option periods 1946–8 and 1949–51. Unofficial reports gave a wide range of estimates. Mr Willmott (who has carefully investigated the subject) estimates the following local percentages of Indonesian-born Chinese who repudiated their Indonesian citizenship—Djakarta 25 per cent; Jogjakarta 25 per cent; Surakarta 20 per cent; and Semarang 10 per cent.[36] He further calculates that from 40 to 45 per cent of the Chinese living in

<hr />

[36] *National Status*, p. 69.

Indonesia in 1955 were considered Chinese subjects. He adds: 'Whether the new round of options called for in the Dual Citizenship Treaty will substantially change this picture is a matter for speculation. But it appears that, under any circumstances except mass deportation, there will soon be one million alien Chinese in Indonesia.'[36]

Before 1954, under the Republic, the alien Chinese were subjected to very little supervision or control, but as the internal situation deteriorated official and public suspicion and distrust of the Chinese deepened. Pro-Peking Chinese were distrusted by Government officials and army officers who disliked their Communist ideas and loyalties, while pro-KMT Chinese were accused of activities detrimental to the State. Added to this were reports in the press that the Sumatra rebels were obtaining aid both from Taiwan and from the Chinese in Singapore. The consequence was a spate of control measures directed against the Chinese.

These alien-control measures covered immigration, the press, the foreign schools, the imposition of the 1957 Aliens Tax, and restrictions on the economic activities of alien Chinese. New immigration laws passed in 1950 had virtually prohibited further Chinese immigration (though clandestine immigration continued on a limited scale). In 1952 a special department of the Ministry of Education was established to supervise foreign schools, most of which were Chinese. In April 1958 a military decree banned all Chinese-language newspapers and magazines on the ground that the military authorities responsible for national security had not adequate personnel to supervise such publications, though in May selected Chinese-language papers were allowed publication under close military supervision. The consequence of the foreign schools regulation was that Chinese schools were reduced from over a thousand to a few hundred confined to a handful of towns. In 1957 an Aliens Tax of 1,500 rupiahs was imposed. The restrictions on the economic activities of the Chinese were complicated and extensive.

Summarily stated, those restrictions were as follows. Remittances by Indonesian Chinese to their families in China were stopped. The reason for this was the difficult economic position of Indonesia in post-war years and the shortage of foreign exchange, and, moreover, the Government took the view that profits made by foreign business men in Indonesia should be spent or invested in Indonesia and not sent abroad. The Minister of Economic Affairs, Iskaq, then announced that concerns owned by aliens would receive only 15 per cent of the available foreign exchange, and that only by turning over 50 per cent of their capital to native Indonesian business partners could foreign Chinese firms avoid this limitation. Again, foreign Chinese were excluded from certain activities to be reserved for Government development. To begin with no serious steps were taken to oust the foreign Chinese from fields in

[36] Ibid.

which they were entrenched, but later these too were invaded. For example, in 1954 and 1955 licences for the importation of textiles were granted only to firms that were preponderantly Indonesian-controlled, and foreigners were forbidden even to hold shares in rice-mills. These were only a few of a continuous series of measures directed against the alien Chinese, with the result that there was a considerable slump in their business activities, though to a certain extent they were able to find a way round the restrictions by bribing officials or operating behind Indonesian 'licensees'. In January 1958 a law concerning the employment of foreign personnel was promulgated, the result of which was greatly to discourage the employment of foreigners, and the law might at any time be used to eliminate foreign workers from any type of employment.

Indonesian citizens of Chinese descent were also subjected to considerable restrictions on their activities, with the intention of eliminating their association with Chinese rather than Indonesian culture and of reducing the economic importance of the Chinese community as a whole. In the early 1950s more than half of the Chinese *Peranakans* attended Chinese-language schools, another large fraction went to Catholic or Protestant schools, and only a minority attended the Government schools. In an effort to temper and modify the drive against Chinese as a medium or subject of study, BAPERKI (Badan Permusjawaratan Indonesia), the chief *Peranakan* association, declared against all schools conducted exclusively for specific groups, including both foreign Chinese schools and the Government's experimental schools for Chinese, proposing to establish schools of their own with a 'national' curriculum. But the Ministry of Education was intent on decisive action and so thorough-going were its measures that by the end of 1957 virtually all the children of Chinese race but Indonesian nationality were in schools in which the national curriculum was taught through the medium of the Indonesian language.

In the economic sphere, the Government claimed to be non-discriminatory in its treatment of Indonesian citizens whatever their racial origin, but the measures taken by them had brought the Chinese in general to disbelieve this claim. Preference was given always to 'indigenous' Indonesians.

By one measure, a Dutch law of 1875 prohibiting the alienation of land to persons of foreign descent had been perpetuated by the Indonesian Government so that with few exceptions Indonesian citizens of Chinese descent could not buy farm land. It was not that the majority of the Chinese *wished* to buy farm land (and many admitted that without this law a highly undesirable problem of landlordism might arise) but they argued that if the Government really were non-discriminatory it would protect the farmer from losing his land to native Indonesian landowners as well as Chinese.

More important than this, however, was the proposal of the Ministry of Economic Affairs that Chinese entrepreneurs, *of whatever citizenship*, should find Indonesian business partners and make them co-directors and joint-owners of their firms. The statutes of such firms should lay down that at least 50 per cent of the shares should be owned by native Indonesians. Since most native Indonesian partners would not have enough capital to pay for their shares at the outset, they should be allotted their full 50 per cent on the undertaking to pay for them gradually out of their share of the profits. Furthermore, the *Peranakans* should arrange for the employment of native Indonesian personnel in their firms and undertake their technical training. The scheme was to be 'voluntary' —but the Minister of Economic Affairs had considerable powers to enforce it by the allotment of foreign credits.

Indonesian pressure on the several groups of Chinese was exerted in different ways. The KMT Chinese, for example, were associated with the rebellions against the Government in 1959 and suffered accordingly. In March 1959 an influential Indonesian M.P. urged that all KMT Chinese be deported and asked the Government to seek Red Cross or U.N. assistance in effecting this. 'As long as KMT Chinese remain in Indonesia [he said] they will continue to disturb security as they have done during the rebellion.'

The year 1959 saw a stepping up of measures directed against the Chinese. In mid-year it was forecast by the Indonesian Chamber of Commerce that 25,000 traders, mostly Chinese, would be affected in 1960 by an Indonesian trade ban on aliens conducting businesses in small towns and villages. It was estimated at the time that there were 75,410 alien businesses in Indonesia—45,740 in Java and 29,670 in the other islands. One-third of these were in the villages; the remaining two-thirds in the main cities would not be affected by the ban. The method of closing down Chinese businesses would be the refusal to renew licences; 300,000–400,000 Chinese were in consequence expected to be displaced and deprived of the means to earn a livelihood. In October the Chinese trek from the villages to the towns had begun.

What was Peking's reaction to these drastic measures against aliens of Chinese race and maybe also of Chinese nationality? On 17 November 1959 it was reported that the Indonesian Foreign Minister, Subandrio, had had a ninety-minute talk with the Chinese ambassador, Huang Chen, in which the Foreign Minister had said that the Chinese merchants were 'not only capitalistic but monopolistic', but added that Indonesia would absorb the alien Chinese with pleasure if only they would adjust themselves to a socialist Indonesia.[37] It was clear, then, that the People's Government were being appealed to to regard the issue as a politico-economic and not a racial one. Nevertheless, Sino-Indonesian friendship was at stake.

[37] *New York Times*, 22 Nov. 1959.

Following the line that Sino-Indonesian disaccord was fomented by 'imperialist' propaganda, the *Hsinhua* News Agency (25 November) urged that the question of Chinese nationals be solved between China and Indonesia in accordance with Bandung principles and through friendly consultation. The banning of the operation of alien small and retail trade in the areas outside the Indonesian capitals was calculated to injure good relations between the two countries, and from the angle of humanitarianism or friendship or international law the Chinese People's Republic had the right to ask for protection of the proper rights of its nationals resident in Indonesia.

On 26 December 1959 the Chinese Foreign Minister, Marshal Chen Yi, in a letter to the Indonesian Foreign Minister, said:

> The overwhelming majority of the Overseas Chinese in Indonesia are working people. For generations they have lived amicably with the Indonesian people and have played their part in the economic development and the cause of national independence of Indonesia. They are fundamentally different from the Colonialists backed up by gunboats and harbouring the aim of oppressing and plundering another country. It is true that a very small number among the Overseas Chinese do not behave well. But it would be unfair, merely on account of this, to describe the entire Overseas Chinese community as a monopoly group which hinders Indonesia's economic development and to make them the main target of discrimination and attack.[38]

The letter went on to say that to adjust the economic position of the Overseas Chinese to the development of Indonesia's national economy was a complicated question. It had been mutually agreed that the economic resources of Chinese nationals in Indonesia would still play a useful role in the economic development of Indonesia, and that the Indonesian Government should take suitable steps to turn Chinese capital step by step from trade to industry. Unfortunately the regulation on the prohibition of small or retail trade by aliens in rural areas had (the letter said) been utilized to make a concentrated attack on Overseas Chinese, and even to force their evacuation on a large scale, so that tens of thousands of Overseas Chinese had lost their homes and property.

The People's Government, however, did not demand that the laws should be rescinded (that would have been anti-Marxist) but asked for compensation for those Chinese who were rendered destitute and undertook to repatriate them to China. Yet in this unpromising situation the People's Government were successful at least in damping down the fires of dissension and in coming to an understanding with Indonesia on some important international questions. Marshal Chen Yi paid a visit to Indonesia from 28 March to 2 April 1961. 'Identical views' were officially reached and a treaty of friendship and a cultural co-operation agreement between the two countries were signed.

[38] Press Release, Chinese Chargé d'Affaires, London.

During 1960 the Chinese *Hsinhua* News Agency reported the repatriation of batches of displaced Chinese from Indonesia to China. For example, on 5 March representatives of a number of Indonesian people's organizations were said to have called on the displaced Overseas Chinese of West Java who had assembled in Djakarta to wait for ships to return to China. These organizations included the Indonesia-China Friendship Association, the Indonesian Women's Movement, and the Committee of Indonesian Mothers against Atomic and Hydrogen Bombs. These representatives told the displaced Overseas Chinese that the Indonesian and Chinese peoples were friends for ever and presented the Chinese with coffee, tea, medicines, and soap. The displaced Chinese (some of whom were of families who had lived in Indonesia for generations) were said to have been greatly moved by the concern for them shown by their Indonesian friends.

Simultaneously there was news of the reception of batches of displaced Chinese on their arrival in China—e.g. (4 March 1960) that more than 300 Chinese who had 'returned' to Fukien Province in the previous two months had been suitably settled for work or study and those who were in difficulty because their belongings had been confiscated in Indonesia before they left had been fitted out by the State authorities. Two Chinese displaced women (the new report said) 'expressed great joy' when they began working in the farm's sewing group. They remarked, 'We women are now really emancipated. There are community dining rooms and kindergartens and there is work for all of us.'

The numbers of repatriated displaced Chinese mentioned in these reports are only two or three hundred in each batch, so if the total number displaced by the new laws is 300,000–400,000 it is certain that the majority still remained in Indonesia at the end of 1962, and that the problem of disposing of the excess Chinese nationals in Indonesia was still a long way from solution. The notable feature of the Chinese attitude was that the claims to protection on racial or national grounds of the alien Chinese in Indonesia were ignored in the negotiations with the Indonesian Government on the ground of their 'bourgeois' function in Indonesian society, but their claims to be absorbed into Chinese society as members of 'the Chinese People' were recognized.

PART VIII

THE CHINESE IN THE PHILIPPINES

50

DEMOGRAPHY

The Philippines Economic Handbook, 1960 states that 'among the aliens are some 130,000 Chinese'. The figure most often cited for Chinese nationals registered with the Immigration Bureau under the Alien Registration Act is 140,000.

Birth in the Philippines did not confer automatic Philippine citizenship on those of Chinese race. By Article IV, section 1 of the Philippines constitution (1935), the following were citizens of the Philippines.

1. Those who were citizens at the time of the adoption of the Constitution.
2. Those born in the Philippine Islands of foreign parents, who, before the adoption of the Constitution had been elected to public office in the Philippine Islands.
3. Those whose fathers are citizens of the Philippine Islands.
4. Those whose mothers are citizens of the Philippine Islands and, on reaching the age of maturity, elect for Philippine citizenship.
5. Those who are naturalized according to the law.

The Retail Nationalization Act, however, did not apply to American citizens.

The figures commonly given for the number of Chinese in the Philippines varied greatly and were usually high (sometimes through uncertainty as to the facts, but often through political motivation)—e.g. '500,000 Chinese residents' (*Weekly Graphic*, Manila, 12 Dec. 1962; '920,000' (*Free Press*, Manila, 3 Nov. 1962). It happened, however, that the results of the 1960 Census were coming to hand at the time that this chapter was being revised and they for the first time provide us with some definite information.

The Census was being published in separate volumes for each province (56 in all) and some 47 of those were available at the time this was written. A table giving an abstract of the results so far as they affected the Chinese is given below (p. 495). It will be seen from this table that a much larger number of persons claimed to owe allegiance to China than claimed Chinese as their 'mother tongue'. In Manila, for example, 69,337 persons claimed to be Chinese nationals, but only 61,599 had Chinese as their 'mother tongue'. In a number of the provinces the discrepancy was much greater—e.g. in Zamboanga del Norte 1,036 'Chinese' as compared with only '430' who spoke Chinese in their childhood.

The advance provincial totals issued by the Bureau of Census and Statistics, Manila, became available at the moment that this was written. One of the break-downs of population was by 'citizenship' and 'mother-tongue'. As to citizenship, the explanation of the Census stated, 'A person's citizenship depends on the country to which he owes allegiance. The enumerator was instructed to accept the statement of a person on his citizenship, unless he had reason to doubt the veracity of the answer, in which case the respondent was required to produce his citizenship papers.' 'Mother tongue' was defined as 'the language or dialect spoken in the person's home in his childhood'.

The table below gives an abstract of the results from the Provincial Reports available at the time of writing.

Total population	27,087,685
Total Chinese citizens	181,626
(male	103,569
female	78,057)

The figures given above are for the present day: those that now follow relate to the early Spanish periods onwards and are intended to give historical perspective.

In 1590 there were 3,000–4,000 Chinese in the Chinese quarter of Manila, not counting the 2,000 visitors during the trading season, with a total of 6,000–7,000 for the islands and by 1602 the number had increased to 30,000; the revolt and massacre of 1603 reduced the number to very few, and it did not revive to 8,000 until 1609; just before the second revolt and massacre of 1639 the total had increased again to 20,000–30,000 but the community was once more reduced to an extremely small figure when blood had ceased to flow. In 1662 there was once more a settlement of 15,000 in the Chinese quarter of Manila, the Parián, and although the ultimatum delivered to the Spaniards by the Chinese pirate, Koxinga, resulted in a drive against the Chinese, a large-scale massacre was averted, and some thousands were left in the Parián when the trouble had died down. In 1740, 20,000 were reported in Manila. A royal order for the expulsion of all Chinese was received in 1741 and again in 1747, but the orders were suspended in both cases.

Philippines: Census of 1960

(Abstracted from reports by province in arbitrary order as they became available)

	Chinese Citizenship				Chinese Mother Tongue			
	Total population all races	Male	Female	Chinese (Both sexes)	Male	Female	Both sexes	Per cent of total population
Quezon	653,426	2,569	2,077	4,646	1,834	1,065	2,899	0·4
Zamboanga del Norte	47,596	557	479	1,036	290	140	430	0·2
Masbate	335,971	472	404	876	212	70	282	0·1
Cebu	1,332,847	5,290	4,125	9,415	3,960	2,855	6,815	0·5
Oriental Mindoro	228,998	692	548	1,240	420	189	609	0·3
Sorsogon	347,771	846	712	1,558	515	299	814	0·2
Palawan	162,669	318	262	580	159	78	237	0·1
Mindoro Occidental	84,316	86	36	122	59	6	65	0·1
Surigao	67,718	940	904	1,844	431	265	696	0·2
Iloilo	966,266	1,918	1,418	3,336	1,275	757	2,032	0·2
Davao	158,316	3,586	2,630	6,216	2,280	1,329	3,609	0·4
Sulu	326,898	730	587	1,317	657	442	1,099	0·3
Manila	1,138,611	40,450	28,887	69,337	37,728	23,871	61,599	5·4
La Union	293,330	409	298	707	244	133	377	0·1
Batangas	681,414	577	367	944	406	174	580	0·1
Bulacan	555,819	477	261	738	314	84	398	0·1
Camarines Norte	188,091	680	522	1,202	467	245	712	0·4
Bataan	145,323	44	12	56	24	1	25	—
Aklan	226,232	158	107	265	122	56	178	0·1
Antique	238,405	127	101	228	60	33	93	—
Abra	115,193	4	49	53	46	20	66	—
Ilocos Sur	338,058	450	355	805	—	—	—	—
Rizal	1,456,362	11,683	9,217	20,900	8,468	4,815	13,283	·09
Bukidnon	194,368	165	91	256	96	28	124	0·1
Agusan	271,010	568	350	918	370	164	534	0·2
Ilocos Norte	287,333	407	287	694	262	147	409	0·1
Mountain Province	435,839	1,145	925	2,070	601	280	881	0·2
Nueva Vizcaya	25,569	250	157	407	160	91	251	0·2
Isabela	442,062	1,421	1,079	1,500	568	291	859	0·2
Nueva Ecija	608,362	793	682	1,475	423	195	618	0·1
Tarlac	74,294	1,090	741	1,831	712	303	1,015	0·2
Romblon	131,658	165	162	327	53	30	83	0·1
Zambales	213,442	772	647	1,419	361	173	534	0·3
Negros Oriental	104,643	887	729	1,616	454	229	683	0·1
Negros Occidental	1,332,323	2,552	2,223	4,775	1,237	670	1,907	0·1
Marinduque	114,586	334	276	610	187	112	299	0·3
Agusan	271,010	568	350	918	370	164	534	0·2
Camarines Sur	819,565	1,623	1,262	1,885	881	458	1,339	0·2
Albay	514,980	1,216	863	2,079	720	397	1,117	0·2
Catanduanes	156,329	223	164	387	109	38	147	0·1
Capiz	315,079	203	130	333	98	52	150	—
Batanes	10,309	..	..	..	..	..	..	..
Cavite	378,138	393	211	604	239	81	320	—
Cagayan	445,289	836	621	1,457	615	366	981	0·2
Bohol	592,194	436	426	862	150	85	235	—
Misamis Occidental	248,371	612	505	1,117	439	386	825	0·3
Misamis Oriental	388,615	1,416	1,244	2,660	850	553	1,403	0·4

— = Nil or negligible.   .. = No return.

When in 1755 the order was renewed attempts were made to put it into effect, and after the British had occupied Manila many of the Chinese remaining in Luzon were massacred in 1763 for having sided with the enemy. In 1778 the expulsion order of 1769 was revoked and in 1804 it was decreed that only Chinese who were agriculturists or artisans should remain. Massacres, albeit on a much smaller scale than the wholesale killings of 1603 and 1639, continued as late as 1819 and 1820, and by 1828 Spanish policy had reduced the number of Chinese in the Philippines to 5,708, exclusive of mestizos, of whom 5,279 were in Tondo. By 1850, however, they had surpassed their former numbers, and there were said to be over 50,000 in the whole of the Philippines, including nearly 30,000 in the capital. The next great increase was between 1876 and 1886 when the figures rose from about 31,000 to 94,000.

It is at this point, however, that controversy intervenes. The Spanish census of 1886, as we see from the table on p. 503, showed 93,567 Chinese in the Philippines. Reyes Lala, *The Philippine Islands* (N.Y., 1899), pp. 104–6, says that there were at that time about 100,000 Chinese in the Philippines of whom 40,000 were in Manila. As against this, *The Census of the Philippines, 1903* (Washington, 1905) states as follows (pp. 38–39):

Carlos Palanca, a Christian Chinaman, the most prominent Chinese merchant in the islands, and for forty-three years a resident, stated that he had twice been appointed Chinese captain, or headman of the Chinese, and prior to American occupation was acting Chinese consul; and that he had 40,000 Chinese under him, which included all in the Philippines, of whom 23,000 were in Manila at that time, June, 1899. As every Chinaman who arrived in or left the Islands was registered by the Chinese captain, these figures were probably correct.

Only four years after this the Americans conducted the Census of 1903 which gave the number of Chinese in the Philippines as 41,035, and the Census Report remarked (p. 38), 'it is probable that the margin of error in the number of civilized Filipinos, Chinese, and other foreigners does not exceed a fraction of one per cent'.

When the United States army took over control of the islands, the exclusion laws applying to Chinese in the United States were almost immediately extended to the Philippines and were continued after the end of the military period when the civil government took over in 1902. The effect of these laws was to prohibit Chinese immigration except for such groups as merchants and students, who were allowed temporary stay; but Chinese residents could bring in their families, and 'family' was liberally interpreted. Thus, when in 1940 a new immigration law was passed limiting to 500 a year the number of aliens of any one nationality to be admitted, the new law was regarded as much more restrictive than the old.[1]

[1] The exclusion laws were repealed in the United States in 1943 (see K. S. Latourette, *The Chinese; Their History and Culture* (N.Y., 1946), p. 508).

The Census of 1903, the first under the American regime, gave the number of Chinese in the Philippines as 41,035; that of 1918 placed their total at 43,802. If these censuses were anything like correct, then the estimate of 100,000 at the end of the Spanish period must have been very much out. It is scarcely conceivable that the Chinese population dropped by nearly 60 per cent in the space of five years. The Census of 1939 put the Chinese at 117,487 and, for reasons already given, it can be accepted as being not very far short of the truth. At the end of 1947 an official estimate of the Bureau of Immigration put the number at 100,971, a reduction of nearly 17,000 since before the Pacific War.[2]

In 1939 the Chinese consulate-general in the Philippines carried out a general registration of all Chinese resident in the islands. The registration fees were to have been used in the construction of a new consulate and therefore the registration was considered to have been more or less complete. The total Chinese counted are said to have been about 130,000, including 50,000 in Manila.[3]

Miss Catherine Porter says that at least a million Filipinos have Chinese ancestors.[4]

There has at all times been a large amount of illicit immigration into the Philippines, some of it via Borneo, and some via the northern tip of Luzon, as well as by other routes. After the Japanese surrender, UNRRA assembled and examined Chinese displaced by the war from Southeast Asian countries, and of these 7,600 were certified by them and by CNRRA as bona-fide pre-war residents of the Philippines. However, it was contrary to the policy of the Philippines Government (which was completely independent from 4 July 1946) to allow the mass entry of displaced Chinese who had, therefore, to take their turn on the small annual quota of 500. A good many of these persons have made their way back to the Philippines by devious and illicit means, and there is reason to suspect that Chinese Communists in considerable numbers were smuggled into the islands between 1946 and 1949 to soften up the political ground as a prelude, if possible, to revolution.

In addition to the illegal entry, there is a considerable amount of passing to and fro via the recognized ports. The abstract in the table on p. 498 gives a good idea of the outward flow of migration in the years 1930–46.

Data were presented in the 1939 Census Report for the brown, yellow, and white peoples. Separate data were also given for American negroes,

[2] Mr Paul McNutt, former United States ambassador to the Philippines, said that in August 1947 there were 200,000 Chinese in the Philippines, but he gave no evidence in support of his estimate (*North China Daily News* (14 Aug. 1947)). It is possible that the Spanish and the Americans adopted different definitions of 'Chinese'.
[3] This information I received from Mr Chu-pei Chen who tells me that he himself checked the figures at the consulate in 1939 (V. P.).
[4] *Crisis in the Philippines* (N.Y., 1942), p. 97.

C.S.E.A.—R

negritos (aborigines), and mixed (mestizos). The Census enumerators were instructed to classify as mixed or mestizos only persons whose fathers and mothers belonged to different races. The Chinese of mestizo parents were to be reported not as mestizos but according to their predominant race.[5]

The Philippines: Aliens coming from Foreign Countries by Nationality, 1930–46[6]

	Total	Immigrant	Non-immigrant	Total	Immigrant	Non-immigrant
	1930			*1931*		
Total	26,622	12,323	14,299	20,348	7,036	13,312
Chinese	20,878	8,143	12,735	16,878	5,525	11,353
	1932			*1933*		
Total	21,389	7,427	13,962	20,293	7,155	13,138
Chinese	18,271	6,079	12,192	16,727	5,641	11,086
	1934			*1935*		
Total	19,596	7,381	12,215	19,727	6,046	13,681
Chinese	15,458	5,533	9,925	15,017	4,127	10,890
	1936			*1937*		
Total	25,649	8,445	17,204	30,036	10,620	19,416
Chinese	18,717	5,485	13,232	20,242	5,170	15,072
	1938			*1939*		
Total	22,998	9,551	13,447	13,002	2,670	10,332
Chinese	16,316	6,064	10,252	7,830	750	7,080
	1940			*1941 (1 Jan. to 30 June)*		
Total	13,124	2,169	10,955	7,848	634	7,214
Chinese	9,138	1,382	7,756	5,669	422	5,247
	1945			*1946*		
Total	3	2	1	400	8	392
Chinese	2	2	..	216	4	212

For centuries the Chinese intermarried freely with the native community (following the general practice in the early days in Siam, Indonesia, and Indochina) and produced large groups of citizens of Filipino-Chinese blood which have been absorbed into the general population of the country. The number of Filipinos with a notable mixture of Chinese blood amounted in 1949 to at least three-quarters of a million.[7]

---

[5] J. R. Hayden, *The Philippines; a Study in National Development* (N.Y., 1942), p. 695. Through the centuries many Chinese mestizos have Hispanicized their names, e.g. Limjap, Cojuangco, and Golayco. The names of the President of the Chinese Chamber of Commerce in 1948 was Alfonzo Z. Sycip. The great patriot and martyr, José Rizal, was of Chinese mestizo origin.

[6] Abstracted from *Yearbook of Philippine Statistics, 1946* (Manila, 1946), p. 231.

[7] The distribution of Chinese in the Philippines in 1918, 1933, and 1939 is set out in the table on pp. 504–5 below.

The residents of the islands were in the 1939 Census Report classified according to the country of which they were citizens. That is to say that, since the Philippines did not claim a Chinese as a citizen, there were none of the complications of dual nationality such as we encounter in Siam and Indochina, for the description deriving from the *jus sanguinis* is ethnic as opposed to national. But it must be added that Philippine law recognizes the husband or wife of a Filipino as a Philippine citizen except when the spouse's native State has a law to the contrary. A Chinese remains a Chinese even after marriage until the Ministry of the Interior approves his or her application to renounce citizenship. (Such approval, if it has ever been given at all, must be very rare.)

In 1939 over 39 per cent of the total Chinese population in the Philippines was resident in Manila, and 45·4 per cent in Manila and the surrounding area. The only other communities over 3,000 strong were in Cebu, Davao, Iloilo, Leyte, Quezon (Tayabas), Rizal, and Zamboanga; in twenty of the other provinces the figure was from 1,000 to 2,000, but smaller communities were dotted all over the islands, and only one of the fifty-two provinces, Batanes, is shown to be without Chinese in the censuses and estimates from 1918 to 1947.

In 1939 citizens of China constituted the largest group of non-Philippine citizens, and they accounted for 70·9 per cent of all foreigners in the Philippines. A large proportion of the group being males, most reported as married were married to Filipinos.[8]

The Chinese in the Philippines were about 75 per cent Hokkiens (Fukienese) and about 25 per cent Cantonese. The former predominated in all lines of business except grocery stores, hotels, and restaurants, in which undertakings the Cantonese were in the forefront.

In the Philippines the proportion of Chinese females to males was about the same as in the other countries of Southeast Asia. In Siam in 1939 it was roughly 1 : 3, and in Malaya about the same; in Indonesia in 1930 it was 1 : 1·6 and in the Philippines it was only one female to every 3·3 males. The table on p. 500 sets out the position.

Though the sexes of the Chinese were unbalanced, the ratio had greatly improved in the preceding two decades. In 1918 it had been about 1 : 13; in 1933, 1 : 5, and in 1939, 1 : 4. But while this could be described as a definite 'improvement' in the sex ratio in the case of, say, Malaya, where there was practically no intermarriage between the races, and the preponderance of males had produced unstable social conditions, the increase of Chinese females was a very doubtful improvement in the

[8] Mr Chu-pei Chen remarks: 'Actually most Chinese in the Islands, though reported single, are married and have a family in China. With them early marriage is a common practice. In pre-war days, many Chinese bachelors in the islands went back to China to be married and then returned to the Philippines bringing their wives. It was generally believed that this practice was due to the fear of their parents, or close relatives, that if they married Filipino women their ties with the family would be loosened.'

case of Siam, Indonesia, and the Philippines, where there had been considerable intermarriage for centuries and assimilation was now being diminished by the importation of Chinese brides, and by the rise of nationalism which tended to discourage marriage with other races. This, as we now know, is very much a repetition of the story for the remainder of Southeast Asia.

Citizens of China classified by age-groups and sex for the Philippines, 1939

Age-group	Both sexes		Males		Females	
	No.	Per cent.	No.	Per cent.	No.	Per cent.
Total	117,487	100·0	90,007	100·0	27,480	100·0
Under 5 years	11,224	9·6	5,872	6·5	5,352	19·5
5–9 ,,	10,083	8·6	5,756	6·4	4,327	15·7
10–14 ,,	9,360	8·0	6,050	6·8	3,310	12·0
15–19 ,,	12,495	10·6	10,001	11·1	2,494	9·1
20–24 ,,	13,774	11·7	11,516	12·8	2,258	8·2
25–34 ,,	31,022	26·4	26,009	28·9	5,013	18·2
35–44 ,,	19,205	16·3	16,463	18·3	2,742	10·0
45–54 ,,	5,004	4·1	3,826	4·3	1,178	4·3
55–64 ,,	3,588	3·1	2,957	3·2	631	2·3
64 plus ,,	1,708	1·5	1,536	1·7	172	0·6
Age unknown	24	..	21	..	3	..

Chinese in the Philippines. Their Numbers and Circumstances at Different Periods[9]

(B & R = Blair & Robertson, *The Philippine Islands*)

Year		Authority
1570	'In the town lived 40 married Chinese and 20 Japanese', (i.e. in the native town of Manila).	Anonymous contemporary account, B. & R. iii. 101.
c. 1572	'In Luzon the Chinese, all of them, number about 150.'	B. & R. iii. 167.
1588	'Over thirty vessels have come here from that land China, bringing so many people that together with those living here, there are over 10,000 Sangleys now in this city.'	Letter from Manila Audiencia to Philip II, 25 June, 1588, B & R. vi. 316.
1589	'About 4,000 men of that land [China] are here as a general rule, including merchants and workmen.'	Santiago de Vera to Philip II, 13 July 1589, B & R. vii. 89.
1590	'The Sangleys who live in this Parián number ordinarily between 3 and 4,000 not counting the 2,000 and more who come and go in ships. These, together with those residing in Tondo, and the fishermen and	Bishop Salazar to Philip II, 24 June 1590, B & R. vii. 230.

[9] Compiled by the present writer.

Year		Authority
	gardeners who live in this neighbourhood, number, according to the Dominican fathers who have them in their charge, from 6 to 7,000 souls.'	
1591	'The Chinese quarter of Parián contained some two hundred shops and a population of about 2,000.'	Report of the Encomiendas in the islands in 1591, B & R. viii. 97–8.
1597	'. . . the large number of Sangleys here (somewhat over 10,000)' (i.e. in Luzon).	Letter from Francisco Tello to Philip II, B & R. x. 259.
1599	(re the Parián) 'Its growth has increased to such an extent that more than three hundred houses of wood and cane have been built and, in them are more than 3,000 Sangleys.'	id., B & R. x. 42.
1600	'more than 15,000 Chinese live outside its [Manila's] walls.'	Oliver van Noordt (information obtained from a Chinese pilot) 24 October 1600, B & R. xv. 305.
1603	'There are always 8 to 10,000 of them.'	Benavides to Philip II, B & R. xii. 108.
	'The Chinese were more than 16,000; and these, added to those in the fleet, when it came from China, amounted to 20,000.'	Two letters from ecclesiastics, 15 December 1603, B & R. xii. 253.
	'Although it was agreed that there should not be more than four thousand Sangleys, yet there were found in the rising more than 18,000.'	Don Pedro de Acuña, 23 December 1603, B & R. xii. 168.
	Deaths in the insurrection '22–24,000' according to anonymous contemporary Spanish account. (Acuña, attempting to explain away the massacre in a letter to the Viceroy of Fukien, says the number killed was less than half the 30,000 alleged. B & R. xiv. 45.) Argensola, *Conquista de las Malucas* (B & R. xvi. 295) says 'more than 23,000 Chinese died and only five hundred are left for the galleys'.	B & R. xxix. 249.
1602 and 1622	Laws of these years limit the number of Chinese in the Philippines to 6,000 and that of Japanese to 3,000.	
1605	1,500 'infidel Chinese' allowed to remain for rebuilding the burnt part of Manila. 'This number not to be exceeded.'	The licentiate Manuel de Madrid y Luna, 5 July 1605, B & R. xiv.
1606	'Not over 6,000 Chinese in the Parián.'	Ramón Jordana y Morera, *La Inmigración China in Filipinas*, 1888.
1609	'in the Alcayceria "more than four hundred shops and generally 8,000 men who trade therein".'	Argensola's *Conquistas*, published 1609, B & R. xvi. 296.
1621	'there are now more Chinese in the	Serrano to Philip,

Year		Authority
	country than there were sixteen and a half years ago, when they revolted.'	30 July 1621, B & R. xx. 96–7.
1627	'Fire caught at one o'clock at night on March 13, in the Parián or Alcayceria of the Chinese, where more than 12,000 Chinese live.'	Relation of 1628–9 (unsigned), B & R. xxii. 211.
1634	'. . . between one of the churches (which is called Minondo [Binondo]) and the church of the Parián is generally a settlement of 20,000 or more Sangleys during the year.'	Salamanca to Philip IV, 10 August 1634, B & R. xxiv. 328.
1635	'in one village alone, which they call Parián, an arquebus-shot from the said city, more than 20,000 Chinese Indians called Sangleys have all come out from Great China and Japan.'	Juan Grau y Monfalcón to the King, 1635, B & R. xxv. 49.
1637	'so many Chinese are now in Manila that there are two villages: one that of Vinondoc [i.e. Binondo], which is near the city, and composed of married Christians, and the other the Parián in which live those who bring merchandise.'	id., memorial of 1637, B & R. xxvii. 114.
1638	'4–5,000 Chinese now paying the general licence fee of nine pesos less one real now living in the islands.'	Corcuera to Philip IV, 10 June 1638, B & R. xxvi. 140.
	In Parian 'usually 10,000 Chinese and at times as many as 20,000'.	Aduarte's *Historia*, B & R. xxxii. 76.
	25,000 to 30,000 (see under 1644).	Fiscal Don Sebastián Cavallero.
1639	Second great Chinese insurrection. 'Those who make the most careful estimate of the deaths of both sides state that the number of Spaniards who died in the war were about 40 or 45, and of Indians 300 . . . on the side of the enemy, they make the deaths approximately 22,000 to 24,000—including those who died in the provinces.'	Anon. Nov. 1639, B & R. xxix. 249.
1644	The privilege of remaining on the islands 'brings his Majesty according to the number of the Sangleys now, 120,000 pesos annually; in the years 1638 and 1639, when there were 25 or 30,000 Sangleys . . . these licences amounted to 230,000 pesos'.	Fiscal's Report on Sangley licences, 1644, B & R. xxxv. 190.
c. 1649–61	'Usually 15,000 Chinese live there in the Parián.'	Bartolomé de Letona, *Description of the Philippine Islands*, La Puebla, Mexico, 1662, B & R. xxxvi. 200.
c. 1678–90	'the number of Sangleys is less than ever . . . for it is supposed that their numbers do not reach the 6,000 which the royal decrees allow.'	*The Augustinians in the Philippines, 1670–1694* (Manila, 1718), B & R. xlii. 252.
1662	Koxinga's ultimatum. Third insurrection, large-scale massacre averted by Governor; 2,000 Chinese pursued and killed in six months by Spanish and Tagálogs.	

Year		Authority	Total population
1686	Insurrection. Wealthy Chinese remain loyal.		
1693	3,000 in Parián; formerly 4,000.[10]	Giovanni Gemelli-Careri.	
1740	'in the city of Manila it is said that there are at least 20,000 Chinese who constantly reside there.'	Anson's *Voyages* (Walter).	1,000,000 (1735) (Fray Juan de San Antonio est.)
1745	'Insurrection' falsely reported.		
1747	Royal order for expulsion of Chinese received, but suspended.		
1755	Order for expulsion reissued (515 Chinese Christians plus 1,000 who 'pretended to be studying the Chinese doctrine' exempted).		1,350,000 (Arguelles, est.)
1762–4	British occupy Manila.		
1763	Massacre of Chinese for supporting the British.		
1766	Chinese survivors rounded up for expulsion.		
1769	Many Chinese expelled under order of this year.		
1785 (25 Feb.)	New order for expulsion of the Chinese.		
1785 (1 April)	Order approving Chinese colonization in certain islands.		
1790 (14 May)	Capitation tax of six pesos ordered for Chinese.		
1788	Order of 1769 revoked.		
1804	Order that only Chinese who are agriculturists or artisans may remain in the Philippines.		
1807	4,700 Chinese on the registers, but with those 'wandering about' the total was estimated at 7,000.	Thomas de Comyn (1820).	1,741,000 (Census 1805) 2,593,000 (Acafo 1818, est.)
1828	5,708 Chinese in the Philippines: 5,279 in Tondo, the rest in Cavite and other parts of Luzon.	Manuel Buzeta, cited by 1903 Census Report, 135.	
1842	10,000 Chinese in the Philippines and 240,000 Mestizos de Sangley.	Sinibaldo de Mas, *Informe sobre el Estado de las Islas Filipinas en 1842*, p. 138.	3,815,878 (Census 1850) 4,500,000 (est. 1860)
1876	30,797 Chinese in the Philippines.	Ramón Jordana y Morera.	4,712,000 (Census 1870)
1886	93,567 Chinese in the Philippines.	Census.	5,985,000 (Census 1886)
1899	40,000 Chinese in the Philippines; 23,000 in Manila. Census Report 1903, p. 39, says 'these figures were probably correct', but Reyes Lala, *The Philippine Islands* (New York, 1899) pp. 104–6, says 40,000 in Manila and 100,000 in the Philippines.	Carlos Palanca (Chinese captain) cited in 1903 Census Report (pub. 1905) i. 38–9.	
1903	41,035 Chinese in the Philippines.	Census.	6,988,000 (Census)

[10] Very likely an underestimate, but is included as by a contemporary observer. But see p. 523 n. 15 regarding Gemelli-Careri's credibility.

Year		Authority	Total population
1918	43,802 (40,704 males: 3,098 females).	Census.	10,314,000 (Census)
1933	71,638 (59,054 males; 12,584 females)	Bureau of Health.	
1939	117,487 (90,007 males; 27,480 females).	Census.	16,000,000 (Census)
1947	100,971.	Immigration Bureau.	19,511,000

Total population is given in round figures.

Chinese in the Philippines. Distribution 1918, 1933, and 1939; and estimated total for 1947

Provinces	1918		1933		1939
	Males	Females	Males	Females	Both Sexes
Abra	18	1	29	3	66
Agusan	59	5	154	25	351
Albay	1,153	82	1,063	210	1,895
Antique	124	2	291	146	215
Bataan	21	..	30	3	55
Batanes	..	..	..	..	..
Batangas	318	15	420	64	741
Bohol	255	29	360	109	840
Bukidnon	5	..	34	2	106
Bulacan	207	13	329	64	464
Cagayan	692	53	1,082	441	1,404
Camarines Norte	1,037	38	301	109	1,220
Camarines Sur			990	207	2,087
Capiz	284	41	408	100	715
Cataduanes	227	4	210	28	..
Cavite	456	17	509	36	1,204
Cebu	1,509	153	2,215	482	6,117
City of Baguio	*	*	343	101	*
Cotabato	146	5	567	75	1,591
Culion I. Colony	†	†	36	2	†
Davao	743	19	1,706	213	3,595
Ilocos Norte	105	4	284	31	424
Ilocos Sur	245	6	472	66	717
Iloilo	1,560	133	3,578	321	3,511
Isabela	472	29	635	72	1,778
La Union	160	18	297	84	458
Laguna	946	21	1,171	269	1,939
Lanao	117	27	169	51	567
Leyte	2,147	99	1,986	571	3,076
MANILA, City of	16,136	1,624	23,357	5,502	46,233
Marinduque	189	20	263	114	557
Masbate	184	19	299	68	731
Mindoro	108	1	248	49	513
Misamis Occ.	621	71	483	74	1,049
Misamis Ortl.			686	142	1,512
Carried forward	30,244	2,549	45,005	9,834	85,731

* Included in the Mountain Province.   † Included in Palawan.

Provinces	1918		1933		1939
	Males	*Females*	*Males*	*Females*	*Both sexes*
Brought forward	30,244	2,549	45,005	9,834	85,731
Mountain Province	180	10	54	14	1,212
Negros Occ.	824	34	1,481	129	2,679
Negros Ortl.	385	7	637	127	1,125
Nueva Ecija	442	34	761	134	1,361
Nueva Vizcaya	10	..	69	14	273
Palawan	128	1	142	36	368
Pampanga	473	28	588	70	1,301
Pangasinan	643	50	823	180	1,800
Quezon (Tayabas)	1,208	66	2,117	627	4,069
Rizal	623	22	1,529	226	5,431
Romblon	113	6	158	48	214
Samar	1,451	57	1,052	135	1,956
Sorsogon	892	26	854	178	1,451
Sulu	687	67	666	391	1,294
Surigao	395	17	522	108	1,115
Tarlac	326	34	677	112	1,359
Zambales	395	30	143	74	581
Zamboanga	1,280	60	1,776	147	4,167
Total	40,699	3,098	59,054	12,584	90,007 males 27,480 females
	43,797		71,638		117,487

1947 Total Chinese in the Philippines 100,971.

1918, 1939 figures from Census of these years.

1933 figures from an unpublished report of the Philippines Bureau of Health, based on house-to-house investigations reported upon by district health officers in the provinces, and the chief of police, Manila.

1947 total from an official estimate of the Philippines Bureau of Information.

51

THE CHINESE UNDER THE SPANISH REGIME, 1570–1603

CHINESE intercourse with the Philippines goes back at least 700 years.[1] The *Ming Shih* (chap. 323, p. 11a) relates that in 1405 the Emperor Yung Lo sent to Luzon a high officer who was to govern the country. Berthold Laufer remarks,

[1] Hayden. *Philippines*, p. 692.

C.S.E.A.—R 2

How long Yung Lo's delegate remained in the island and what character his jurisdiction was are not narrated, but it is not at all incredible that the ambitious Yung Lo exercised a kind of supremacy, or at least claimed a prerogative of protection, over the Philippine Islands; for since its establishment the rule of the Ming dynasty had been characterized by a tendency towards expansion, from a desire to extend its fame over land and sea to the furthest extremities of the world.[2]

Laufer also says that there can be no doubt that there was a colony of Chinese on Luzon before the arrival of the Spaniards, as is clearly stated in the *Ming Shih* (chap. 323, p. 11b)[3] and indeed (see chronological scheme, p. 500) a small colony of forty Chinese is noted in Manila by a Spanish eye-witness of 1570. However, the nature and extent of Chinese pre-Spanish connexion with the Philippines are a matter of dispute among the experts, and it is convenient for us to start our narrative with the arrival of the Spaniards.[4] Our sources are to be almost exclusively European, mainly Spanish, from the establishment of Manila in 1571, for, in the words of Professor C. R. Boxer:

Confucian scholars would have scorned to chronicle the adventures of stray coolies or fisher-folk amongst the hairy barbarians of the West so we cannot expect to find anything of importance in the Chinese annals. It is to European sources that we must turn exclusively for information about the doings of the Celestial waifs and strays in the Outer World during the late Ming and early Manchu periods.[5]

Which is no doubt an exaggeration (as we see from the writings of Laufer, Duyvendak, and others), but it correctly reflects the indifference

---

[2] 'The Relations of the Chinese to the Philippines', *Smithsonian Miscellaneous Collections* (Washington, 13 Sept. 1907), B & R, l. 257.   [3] Ibid. p. 258.

[4] The following extracts from the booklet by H. Otley Beyer, *Early History of Philippine Relations with Foreign Countries, especially China* (Manila, 1948), will be of interest to the student of this question, for Mr Beyer has been able to rely, *inter alia*, on archaeological work done in the Philippines in the twenty years preceding 1948.

'It is improbable that many Chinese ships were engaged in this trade during the early period (at least before the late 11–12th century part of it), and it is unlikely that there were any Chinese resident in the islands at that time . . .' (p. 4). [re 12th–14th centuries] 'Chinese merchant colonies began to establish themselves in a few places where a fairly strong or well-organized native government gave prospect of protection' (p. 5). 'With the death of Cheng Ho, however, and the passing of the Yung Lo regime, this Chinese attempt at dominion overseas also passed away . . .' (p. 6). [re A.D. 1430–50] 'As Mohammedan influence spread eastward through the southern Philippines, and northward from Borneo into Luzon, the Siam and Indo-China trade was at first cut off, while the Chinese merchant vessels were forced to seek new trading routes leading around the eastern side of Luzon, and into the eastern Visayan Islands etc., where Islamic beliefs had not yet penetrated' . . . (p. 7). 'While the Chinese settlers intermarried freely in the country, built good houses, and taught their families better ways of living, they were not otherwise interested in converting or spreading new ideas among the native folk. Their influence was chiefly economic, and aside from the brief period of Yung Lo's empire, they made no attempt to meddle or interfere with native political institutions, social customs, or beliefs . . .' (p. 8).

[5] C. R. Boxer, 'Notes on Chinese Abroad in the late Ming and Early Manchu Periods', *T'ien Hsia Monthly* (1939), p. 447–8.

of the Chinese mandarinate to the unfilial and (to them) impersonal emigrants.

Miguel Lopez de Legaspi landed at Cebu on 27 April 1565 and established the city of Manila in June 1571. The first conflict between the Spanish and the Chinese was at Mindoro in May 1570. The Chinese junks came out side by side with their foresails up, beating on drums, playing on fifes, firing rockets and culverins, and making a great warlike display. But they were defeated in the affray and about twenty of the Chinese were killed.[6] In November 1574 the Chinese outlaw, Lim Ah Hong, usually known as Limahon,[7] in command of sixty-two war junks, captured a Chinese merchant vessel off the coast of Luzon. From the crew he gained information about the wealth of Manila and its military weakness due to the temporary absence of the Spanish forces on a distant expedition. The Chinese landed at Parañaque, eight miles south of Manila, surprised and killed the Spanish captain Goiti, and were prevented from taking Manila only by the arrival of the Captain Juan de Salcedo who relieved the Spanish garrison besieged in the citadel. Limahon established himself in a fortified camp in the delta of the Agno river in the province of Pangasinan but he was driven out by Salcedo. Through mismanagement, the Spanish failed to follow up their success and the Chinese eventually departed from Luzon.[8]

The following year (1575) two ships arrived from the Viceroy of Fukien with an envoy named Omocon. The mission was received by the Spanish Governor, Labezares, who considered it his principal task to entertain peaceful and amicable relations with an empire whose very pirates were able to rock the Spanish power in Asia. Laufer says that the commander (Omocon), charmed with the chivalrous character and generosity of the Spaniards, offered to take Spanish envoys over to China in his ship. The embassy sent in consequence of this invitation consisted of two military officers and two Augustinian friars, Martín de Rada and Jerónimo Marín. They were, however, unsuccessful in their mission although they humiliated themselves so far as to perform the kowtow before the Viceroy, and they returned to Manila in October 1575 accompanied by the Chinese envoy, Omocon, and three Chinese captains who had come to take Limahon back to China in chains. These officers brought rich presents for Labezares, but as he had now been succeeded as Governor by Francisco de Sande the Chinese refused, without due authority from their Viceroy in China, to hand their gifts

---

[6] E. H. Blair and J. A. Robertson, *The Philippine Islands, 1493–1898* (Cleveland, 1903–9), iii. 75.

[7] His name was (in the mandarin dialect) Lin Tao-K'ien or Linfung; Lim Ah Hong was the form of the latter in the Amoy dialect (Laufer, *Smithsonian Misc. Coll.* (1907), B & R, l. 259).

[8] W. C. Forbes, *The Philippine Islands* (Cambridge, Mass., 1945), p. 24. Francisco de Sande himself, in his Relation of 7 June 1576 (Blair & Robertson, iv. 38 ff.) gives an account of the Limahon affair from which the last statement above is extracted.

over to de Sande. Offended at this, he from that day showed such an antipathy towards everything Chinese that he endangered the interests of the Spanish crown by his narrow-minded policy.[9]

Labezares said that the Chinese were 'mean, impudent, importunate, and deceitful'. Omocon wanted de Sande to write to China saying that Limahon was dead, but the Governor replied that the Castilians did not know how to lie, and that he could not discuss such trivial matters.[10]

The Chinese were known to the Spanish at a very early period as Sangleys, which (according to Laufer) is from the Amoy word *Sengli*, meaning 'trade'.[11] They had been carrying on trading voyages with the Philippines for many years before the Spanish occupation, but the number of these greatly increased as a result of the arrival of the Spaniards. Bishop Salazar, writing to Philip II of Spain in 1590, stated that the Parián, or Chinese quarter, contained a population of between 3,000 and 4,000 in the ordinary way, not counting the 2,000 and more who came and went in the annual shipping season. The total in city and suburbs was from 6,000 to 7,000 souls.[12]

The Chinese were the principal artisans and labourers and built many of the old churches, convents, and forts which were still standing up to the closing phases of the Second World War, while Chinese carpenters, tailors, cobblers, and craftsmen were mainly responsible for supplying the daily household wants of the Spanish community. It is probable, too, that a Chinese was the first printer in the Philippines.[13]

[9] Ibid. p. 260–1, apparently following Gaspar de San Augustan, *Conquistas de las Islas Filipinas* (Madrid, 1698) via F. Blumentritt, *Die Chinesen auf den Philippinen* (Leitmeritz, 1879).   [10] Blair & Robertson, iv. 49.

[11] But the author has seen a fine Spanish manuscript volume of 1590, the property of Prof. C. R. Boxer, in which, obviously by a Chinese hand, there is a coloured picture of Chinese with the title 'Sangleys' and in Chinese 常來., which means 'frequently coming' (see C. R. Boxer, 'A Late Sixteenth Century Manila MS.', *JRAS*, pts. 1 & 2, 1950). This alternative explanation, however, though based on this undoubtedly contemporary evidence, does not appear a reasonable one to the author, while the one given in the text above is certainly so.

[12] Blair & Robertson, vii. 32. But from the chronology on p. 500 it will be seen that writing in 1588 the Manila Audiencia had estimated the total Chinese, during the trading season, at over 10,000. The Chinese were transferred to the Parián by Diego de Ronquillo, Governor *ad interim* 1583–4.

[13] Boxer, *T'ien Hsia Monthly* (1939), pp. 458–9, says: 'Books printed included works in Spanish, Chinese, and local dialects such as Tagal.' See also *Doctrina Christiana, the first book printed in the Philippines*, Manila, 1593, with an introd. by E. Wolf (Washington, 1947).

Salazar (letter of 24 June 1590, Blair & Robertson, vii. 226) says: 'What has pleased us all has been the arrival of a bookbinder from Mexico. He brought books with him, set up a bindery, and hired a Sangley who offered his services to him. The Sangley secretly, and without his master noticing it, watched the latter bind the books, and lo, in less than [blank space in original] he left the house, saying that he wished to serve him no longer, and set up a similar shop. I assure Your Majesty that he had become so excellent a workman that his master has been forced to give up the business, because the Sangley has drawn all the trade. His work is so good that there is no need of the Spanish tradesman. At the time of writing, I have in my hand a Latin version of Nabarro, bound by him, and it could not be better bound, even in Seville.'

Bishop Salzar's *Relación*, or Report to his royal master, of the year 1583, illustrates the narrow policy of the civil authorities in a striking manner, as may be seen from the following extract:[14]

Commerce with the Sangleys has always been considered of the first importance, on account not only of its value in supplying provisions to this town and for maintaining its foreign connexions, but also because of the expectations for the future to which it gives rise, namely, that through it we may even obtain a foothold in that great realm [China] which is the end desired by us beyond all other things. This commerce has, however, failed so dismally that we fear that next year the Sangleys may not return, or if they do, it will not be in such great numbers as heretofore, or that even if they do come they will not want to sell their merchandise at the same prices as before because of the ill-treatment they have suffered here—and because of the disorder there has been.

During the last two years they have become more and more irritated, the reason being that whereas they had paid nothing in taxes before, an anchorage tax was afterwards imposed on them. This tax was imposed more as a recognition of their presence than with any hope of gain. Last year and this they were required to pay three per cent, from which demand has proceeded many of their grievances. The long and the short of it was that they were ordered to repair to a palisaded house which was turned into a tax-collecting office. They went there very much against their will, and were made by the shops to pay higher prices than they would have had to have done outside. A warder was placed over them with power of punishment, and in this place, according to what they say, they suffered many wrongs, and were much molested; indeed, for very little cause they were put in the stocks and fined, and they were fined furthermore for going out to buy provisions by night, or for not keeping their quarters and equipment clean. Under the pretext of exacting dues for Your Majesty, they were forbidden to sell anything without first registering it, and since the best of what they had was taken away from them when they went to register it, and they were compensated for this at prices fixed by the inspector or his registrar, they hid some pieces of silk in order to sell them at a better price or to persons to whom they had been promised. As a result they were heavily penalised as if they had been under this obligation for many years instead of being only the first or second time they had heard of it.

The bishop goes on to refer to a case when Don Antonio Yofre, the Treasurer, ordered a Chinese who had hidden certain pieces of silk to be arrested and then sentenced him to a hundred lashes and a fine of 75 tostons. The brother of the Chinese had gone to the bishop, and upon the latter's plea the lashes had been remitted, but the Chinese had had to pay the fine before he could leave the prison. 'So many suffer from personal wrongs', says the bishop, 'that I am sorry for them.' Other impositions suffered by the Chinese included the forcible confiscation of their merchandise by officers who kept it for themselves; other Chinese were given in exchange for their goods official *vales*, or promissory notes, which were later dishonoured. The result of all this was that although

[14] Based on a trans. of *Relación de las cosas de Las Filipinas hecha por Fr Domingo de Salazar, Primer obispo de dichas islas, publicada ahora por primera vez* (Madrid, 1847), by H. D. Purcell, compared with that in Blair & Robertson, v. 236 ff.

twenty Chinese junks had arrived that year, a larger number than had
been seen in Manila for some time, China goods were available only at
excessive prices. A piece of stain which used to cost 10 to 12 tostons had
fetched up to 40 or 45, and even at that price had not been easy to come
by, even for the church, which was in dire need, for it had not been
possible to get enough silk to make ornamental hangings. And it was the
same with all the other things that used to come from China and were
sold freely in the streets.

The evil (said Bishop Salazar) did not stop here, for the Chinese
traders were compelled to perform sentry duty, just as the soldiers did,
and in order not to leave their goods to be stolen they paid a soldier
1 toston (the equivalent of 4 reals) for his services as sentry. The latest
imposition, which was really the last straw, occurred when a galley was
being sent to Japan and the Spaniards seized twenty or thirty of the
Chinese who had come to Manila that year and put them forcibly to the
oars. Many went to the bishop to complain, saying that they had come
to Manila in order to earn something wherewith to feed their children,
and, since they were not allowed to do so, could they please go back to
their own country. 'But this talk', says the bishop, 'profited neither myself nor them, for though they went back to China they soon returned.'
With all this the prosperous settlement of Chinese which used to be on
the other side of the river had practically ceased to exist.

As Jan Pietersen Coen, the founder of Batavia, did half a century
later, the Spaniards impressed Chinese into their service just as it suited
their convenience. The Governor, Santiago de Vera, in a letter to Philip
II, dated 26 June 1588,[15] reporting that he had had a galley built, stated
that he had tried to keep up its crew by hiring men, but the natives were
such a despicable lot of people that they were of little use for the purpose, nor had they sufficient strength for rowing. On hearing the report
of an arquebus they threw themselves on the ground, and did not even
rise at the sting of the lash! De Vera then selected 300 Chinese, who
were stronger, and who, if allowed liberty to quit this work at their
pleasure, would nevertheless bind themselves to work in the galleys.
'But', he adds, 'though earnest endeavours have been made to teach
them, they row very badly and have as little energy as have the natives
of these Islands.' (A case, it seems, of sixteenth-century Chinese
ca'canny.)

De Vera's enlistment of Chinese was, according to him, not forcible,
but his successor, Gómez Pérez Dasmariñas, a year or two later, having
a large army ready for the conquest of the Moluccas but not enough
rowers for his galleys, seized by force any Chinese he could lay hands on
in the Parián, and had them chained to the oars of the galleys.[16] Later on,

[15] Blair & Robertson, vii. 52.
[16] Antonio de Morga, *The Philippine Islands* (London, Hakluyt Soc., 1868), p. 35.

however, these Chinese working under the lash rose to a man, and the Governor and his companions were all killed.[17]

The Chinese, resorting to Manila in such numbers and expanding their trade among the natives of the Philippines, soon aroused the anxiety of the Spanish authorities. Governor Dasmariñas (who later came to so sad an end), writing to King Philip in June 1592, said: 'With Your Majesty's permission, I must state that I regret the trade of the Chinese, for it seems to me injurious. It might be forbidden them on the ground of the great sums of money taken from the islands to foreign countries.[18]

Most of the trade was in cotton stuffs, the raw cotton being taken from the Philippines to China and brought back woven. The Governor had already confirmed an ordinance issued by the city of Manila forbidding the 'Indians' (Filipinos) to wear Chinese stuffs.[19] In justification it was pointed out that when the Spanish discovered the islands the natives wore no other garments than those made there, planting cotton for their own use, and continued to do so for many years. But they now used Chinese stuffs and silks. Formerly, where the Chinese carried away in payment for their clothing 30,000 pesos annually, they now took annually 200,000 pesos. 'This money leaves the realm of His Majesty, and is carried to a foreign country, in violation of the royal edicts.' This could all be prevented if the natives were forbidden to clothe themselves in these Chinese textiles. Native stuffs, it was argued, were in any case better woven and more economical than the Chinese. Moreover, if the natives were to apply themselves to other things, instead of producing raw cotton for the Chinese, there would be something for the Spanish to export. This was the purport of the evidence of Filipino witnesses examined in relation to the new ordinance.

The difficulty (said Dasmariñas) in dealing with the problem of the Chinese trade was the interference and obstruction of the bishop and the clergy.[20] No sooner was it decreed that the 'Indians', in order that they might cultivate and weave their own cotton, since it was so abundant in the country, should not wear Chinese silks and other stuffs, than the bishop declared that 'nothing could be worse'. No sooner was the excise, or the 'merchant's peso', or the 2 per cent duty imposed, than the bishop would declare the order to be against the Papal bull *De Cena Domini* ('Of the Lord's Supper'). It was a hard life for a Governor in a State where the clerical arm was so powerful.

When Bishop Salazar arrived in Manila he found that in Tondo, then

---

[17] The *Ming Shih* (History of the Ming Dynasty) under the 8th month of the 21st year of the period Wan-li (1593) records that a Chinese, P'an Ho-wu, stabbed the Philippines Governor, Dasmariñas (Laufer, pp. 261, 262).

[18] Blair & Robertson, viii. 269.   [19] Ibid. p. 78.

[20] Dasmariñas says, of the Bishop, 'I have never seen a man more peculiar or inconsiderate and obstinate in his opinions, who even does not hesitate to oppose the right of patronage, the jurisdiction, and the exchequer of Your Majesty' (Blair & Robertson, viii. 276).

a village across the river from the Spanish town of Manila, many Chinese were living, some of whom were Christian but most infidels. In Manila itself there were some shops kept by the Chinese, but these people had no special quarter assigned to them and were scattered among the Spaniards until Don Gonçalo Ronquillo allotted them a place to live in, built under the guns of the fort. It contained four 'great quarters' to be used as a silk market (the Alcaycería,) and it was called the Parián.[21] All Chinese, except such as were married to Filipino women, were required to live and conduct their business there. Here many shops were opened, commerce increased, and more Chinese came to the city. 'Anxious for the conversion of the people', says the bishop, 'I soon cast my eyes upon them, and took precautions to see that they were well treated.'[22]

The early writers are fond of repeating that from China came not only finished silks and costly wares which in part were destined for the trade to New Spain and Europe, but also cattle, horses and mares, foodstuffs, metals, fruits, and even ink and paper. 'And what is more', says Chirino, 'from China come all who supply every sort of service, all dextrous, prompt, and cheap.' The Chinese were everything from physicians to bakers and porters; they were the tailors and shoemakers, the metal workers, the silversmiths and sculptors, the locksmiths, the painters, the masons, and the weavers, and they performed 'every kind of service in the commonwealth'. They made chairs, bridles, and stirrups of so good a quality and so cheaply that some merchants wished to load a cargo of these articles for Mexico.[23] They baked bread at low cost, and also sold fowls, eggs, and fish, and wood split for fuel.

The story as it unfolds in the Philippines is one that will be repeated in essence throughout Southeast Asia: that is to say, of an initial welcome to the Chinese, on the part of the metropolitan Power because of their undeniable qualities of energy and skill, followed by fear and suspicion; the two attitudes afterwards alternating or being adopted simultaneously. Bishop Salazar, as we have seen, favoured the Chinese, and, before him, Salcedo, on his first punitive expedition to Mindoro, when he found a Chinese junk which had gone ashore on the west coast, was careful to rescue the voyagers and return them to their own land with a friendly message inviting trade relations. Governor Labezares invited Chinese friendship and intercourse, but the hostility of de Sande, his successor, was engendered against them for reasons above related.

In 1597 we find the Governor, Francisco Tello, writing to the King:

When I came to the government I found the Sangleys had been given a free hand and jurisdiction on the administration of the *cabildo* [municipal council]. Considering the troubles that might result and the large numbers of Sangleys here (some-

---

[21] Alcaycería (silk market) was often used by metonymy for the whole of the Parián.
[22] Blair & Robertson, vii. 220.
[23] Bishop Salazar letter of 24 June 1590 (ibid. vii. 212–38).

what over 10,000) I took away and withdrew their power in the administration, leaving, however, a governor among them as was formerly the custom. I have expelled from the country a large number of Sangleys who were here, and I shall soon order others to go, leaving only 3–4,000 men who are necessary for the service of the country.[24]

In May 1603, not long after one of the numerous great fires in the Parián, three Chinese mandarins arrived at Manila. (Usually thirty ships or more came during the season, but this year there were only fourteen.) The mandarins sent a letter to the Governor stating that a Chinese named Tio Heng had told their Emperor that in the port of Cavite there was a hill of gold which had no owner, and the Emperor had sent them to ascertain the truth. They landed on 23 May, wearing all their badges and other signs of office as they were accustomed to do in China, and were attended by alguacils, executioners, and other officers with wands and cords, and when they landed they received much reverence from the Chinese population. They also had a box in which they carried their seals and patents of their appointments.[25] The three mandarins behaved exactly as if they were on Chinese territory and administered a flogging to any one of their race they considered deserving of it. However, the Governor was angry with Jerónimo Salazar y Salcedo, the Fiscal, for petitioning the Audiencia to stop the mandarins flogging Chinese.

This absurd mission inflamed the already active suspicions of the Spaniards, who expected that the arrival of the mandarins foreshadowed a Chinese attempt to oust them from the Philippines, while the Chinese in their turn felt that the Spaniards were on the point of attacking them.[26] On the eve of St Francis's Day, at about 11 p.m., the Chinese of the Parián revolted. Banners were raised and war gongs were beaten. The rebels chose for a leader a Christian Chinese named Juan Untae, or Juan Bautista de Vera. That night the pueblos of Quiapo and Tondo were burned and many Spaniards were murdered. Chinese gathered on the other side of the river to the number of 10,000 to 12,000. They burned several houses and the orchard of a citizen, Estevan de Marquiña, killing him and his wife and four children, and several servants. Two Spaniards, Luís Pérez Dasmariñas and Tomás Bravo, who had gone across the river to quell the revolt, and about one hundred other Spaniards were slain. Drawing lots to ascertain whether their attack would succeed, the Chinese insurgents decided to advance against the city. But their assault was thrown back (the priests said it was owing to the apparition of St

[24] In the same letter (29 Apr. 1597) the Governor mentions that about two months before the Parián had been burned with a large amount of property in it. Fires were frequent in the Parián during the Spanish period (B & R, x. 42).
[25] Blair & Robertson, xii. 83.
[26] See C. B. Elliott, *The Philippines to the End of the Military Regime* (Indianapolis, 1917), p. 170.

Francis on the walls), they were dislodged from their earthworks, and a general slaughter ensued. About 23,000 Chinese are said to have been killed.[27]

Immediately their blood lust had subsided, the Spanish dispatched letters to the Chinese Emperor explaining away the massacre, stating that the Chinese revolted without provocation. These letters were apparently sent through the Portuguese at Macao, but it seems that they were not delivered. Later the Emperor demanded redress, but he did not seem to attach too much importance to the loss of a few thousand disloyal exiles. By February 1605 we find that the Spaniards had recovered their self-confidence (if they had ever lost it), for a formal complaint was made against the Chinese by Archbishop Benavides, supported by the depositions of several witnesses. The Parián, it appears, had now been rebuilt, and was again peopled by 'infidel Sangleys'. The Chinese (said the complaint) were idolatrous and exceedingly licentious and vicious, and in both these respects were demoralizing the natives and drawing them away from the Catholic faith. The Chinese, moreover, were inclined to avenge themselves on the Spaniards for the slaughter of 1603, and this was a constant source of danger. The Archbishop recommended that they be driven out of the city except that they be allowed a space where they could live during the months while the ships for the Mexican trade were being unloaded and reloaded, but that they should not be allowed to hold intercourse with the natives. The Japanese (the complaint adds), who lived not far away from the Chinese, were equally vicious and dangerous.[28]

Backing up the extreme view of the flagitious nature of the Chinese and their deleterious influence, a contemporary Spanish writer says that the Sangleys are the people who, 'the less they are admitted, the better will it be for us in every respect'.[29]

Archbishop Benavides, however, later relented, and in June 1605 appealed to the Audiencia to accede to the demands of the Chinese Emperor (which apparently had now been made) by making restoration to Chinese merchants of their property which, left in Manila at the time of the insurrection, had been sold to the Spanish, and by sending back

[27] See chronology, p. 501. The authorities for the rebellion are notably Antonio de Morga's *Sucesos* (Blair & Robertson, xv. 273) and Argensola's *Conquistas* (ibid. p. 295). See also *Relación verdadera del levantamiento de los Sangleyes en las Filipinas, y el milagroso castigo de su rebelión,* &c, by a soldier who found himself in these islands at the time, retold by Miguel Rodríguez Maldonado (Seville, 1606).

[28] Blair & Robertson, xiii. 271. Colonel Fernandez de los Rios, who in 1603 was in China as the ambassador of the Governor of the Philippines, wrote the following to Manila, '. . . it seems that every Sangley is a fiend in human form, for there is no fraud or evil deed to which he will not stoop. This is brought out in my daily experience' (Ramón Jordana y Morera, *Inmigración China en Filipinas* (Madrid, 1888), p. 26). De Morga, on the other hand, is sensible of the value of the Chinese and says that 'after the end of the war the need of the city began, because of not having Chinese who worked at the trades, they had no food, no shoes to wear, not even at excessive prices'.

[29] *Sucesos de las Islas Filipinas* (Mexico, 1609). Trans. in Blair & Robertson, xvi. 173.

to their own country those Chinese survivors of the rebellion who had been sentenced to the galleys. At the same time a letter sent to Acuña in March 1605 'by a Chinese official' was now answered by the Governor in a letter in which he blamed the Portuguese for not having delivered the letter containing excuses after the insurrection and massacre. The Governor renewed the excuses, emphasized the kindness of the Spanish Government to the Chinese, and asserted that they revolted without provocation.[30]

After the massacre of 1603 the Spaniards felt the loss of the Chinese, not only because they relied on them for all trades and services, but also because the Filipinos (as de Morga lamented) were unable to replace them even in agriculture, and had forgotten much of their husbandry, the rearing of fowls, flocks, and cotton, and the weaving of clothes, which they used to do in the time of their paganism.[31]

Soon the Chinese in the Parián were nearly as numerous as before.

A word or two may be said here regarding the Chinese in the Philippines and the Christian religion.

To the Spanish, as to the Portuguese, the conversion of the heathen in their eastern possessions was second not even to their hope of worldly gain. Thus (as Bishop Salazar states in his letter to Philip II, quoted above) the Philippines were important, not only for the opportunity that their possession afforded for saving the souls of the natives, but also as a stepping-stone to the 'great kingdom' of China.

In 1588 the Governor, Santiago de Vera, complained that the friars had neglected his commands to learn the Chinese language and to instruct the Chinese who lived in these islands in Christianity. The Dominicans alone had entered this field and had achieved great results; there was already among the Chinese 'a village of Christians', and many more would be converted (said de Vera) if it were not for the bishop's order that the long hair of the converts should be cut off.[32] Only a few years after the foundation of Manila the Augustinians had made a bold attempt to gain entry into China to preach the gospel. They had, indeed, as proof of their zeal, offered to become slaves to the Chinese merchants visiting Manila in return for being given a chance of entry into China. Not one of their attempts, however, being successful, they prayed God to reveal to them a better way of achieving their purpose.[33]

---

[30] Blair & Robertson, xiv. 45.
[31] Laufer, p. 278.   [32] Blair & Robertson, vii. 304, 308.
[33] *Histoire du Grand Royaume de la Chine situé aux Indes Orientales*, trans. from the Spanish of Juan Gonzales de Mendoza of the Order of St Augustine (Paris, 1600), p. 111. (Reference is to the voyage of Jerónimo Marín and Martín de Rada, 1575.)

52

THE CHINESE UNDER THE SPANISH REGIME, 1605–1700

THE Chinese trading with, or emigrating to, the Philippines caused anxiety not only to the Spanish but also to the authorities at home. The *Tung Hsi Yang K'ao*, published in 1618, states:

> Our people at home were anxious lest the emigrating class might be too numerous there, and after their return home breed rebellion. It was ordered that each junk should carry only 200 men, and that the number of junks sailing should not exceed a fixed number. Returning home and sailing out again, the number of men increased to 400, the number of ships remaining the same. When our people put out to sea many gave a false name, and figured only as a number. While their investigation was going on they suddenly escaped in the midst of it and went back to that country.[1]

These measures, like many others, proved ineffective as regards the Philippines, as did similar measures to restrain Chinese from resorting to the other countries of Southeast Asia.

In the Philippines the Chinese were subjected to many restrictions. They were, for example, not allowed to travel in the islands, nor to go two leagues from the city without a written licence, nor could they remain overnight in the city after the gates were closed, on penalty of their lives. They had their own alcalde, judge, tribunal, and gaol. Infidel Chinese were separated from the converts as much as possible. On the north side of the river Dominican friars who had learned the Chinese language had erected a mission and a hospital. There was a separate Barrio (district) for the baptized Chinese and their families to the number of about five hundred.[2]

At different times laws for the regulation of the Chinese were enacted or decreed, and the following is a summary of the more important of them in chronological order:[3]

Law III
(Philip II, Madrid, 11 June 1594)

Since the bishops do not permit Chinese who have been converted in the Philippine Islands to our Holy Catholic faith to return to their own country, so that intercourse with and living among the gentiles [infidels] may not cause them to

---

[1] *Tung Hsi Yang K'ao*, 'Investigations regarding the Eastern and Western Oceans' (1618), cited by Laufer, p. 279.

[2] D. P. Barrows, *History of the Philippines*, rev. ed. (Yonkers-on-Hudson, 1924), p. 158.

[3] Based on Blair & Robertson, xxii. 151 ff. and a trans. by H. D. Purcell from *Biblioteca de legislación ultramarina en forma de diccionario alfabético* (Madrid, 1844), v. 398–401.

suffer the danger of apostasy, and recognizing that these same Christian Chinese have no means of livelihood other than their dealings in the local market, buying provisions in order to supply the community, and that the Governor does not allow them to leave Manila without a pass, which is a great stumbling-block to the conversion of others; we now order that the said permits shall be issued to them free of charge, and moreover that the Governor should show great consideration and care in preventing inconvenience or obstruction to them in their free passage through the Islands.

Law IX
(Philip II, Madrid, 1594)

Whereas Sangleys who come to trade in the Islands are subject to having their goods valued and a wholesale price fixed for them by officers deputed for the purpose (which is called *pancada*) and these goods are then left with them under guarantee that they will not dispose of them without the Governor's order, no price being attached to the goods that are classified as 'various' (except in the case of some of the more important and costly kinds); we order that those Chinese who return to these Islands shall be subject to all the laws and regulations that may be in force with respect to these and other matters, but that the *pancada* shall be applied to them only in the gentlest fashion so that they may have no grievance and no reason for ceasing to come here to trade.

Law X
(1596)

That no wrong or injury be done to any Sangley in the Philippines, and that they be well treated in every way, especially by Spaniards and officials.

Law XIII
(1598)

That the Governor and Captain-General shall not allow any inhabitant of Manila to have Sangleys in their houses, that he should forbid them to sleep inside the city, and that the judge of foreigners should severely punish all who disobey this law.

Law VI
(1603 and 1614)

That the alcaldes-mayor of Manila shall try the suits and causes of the Sangleys jointly with the Governor.

Law VI
(1614)

Insomuch as the alcaldes-mayor of Manila have claimed the right to try suits and causes of the Chinese who live in the Parián, jointly with the Governor, we consider it fitting to order the ruling of ley XXIV, título iii, libro v, which concedes the first instance exclusively to the governor of the Parián with appeal to the Audiencia. Now it is our will, and we order the President, Governor, and Captain-General, and the Audiencia, not to allow any ordinary judge or one who has received a commission, to try civil or criminal suits or causes of the Sangleys in the first instance, even if they be auditors of that Audiencia, who shall be performing the duties of criminal alcaldes; neither shall they try cases regarding the locations or inspections of shops or their trade (for it pertains exclusively to the governor of the Parián to try such), except it be a case so extraordinary, necessary, and requisite that it becomes advisable to limit this rule.

Law XI
(1619)

That the practice of forcing the Chinese to give so many fowls a year to the judges and members of the Audiencia at a price lower than the market price be discontinued.

Law IV
(1620)

That no personal services be demanded of the Sangleys.

Law VIII
(1620)

That Chinese converted to Christianity who are married to Filipino women be given grants of certain uncultivated lands in the suburbs.

Law I
(1606 and 1622)

That the number of Chinese in the whole of the Philippines be limited to 6,000, and that of the Japanese to 3,000.

Law II
(1625)

That licences issued by the Government of the Philippines to Chinese shall be issued under the authority of the royal officials, that the money obtained therefrom shall be paid into the royal treasury, and a separate account of the payments shall be kept.

Law VII
(1627)

That Sangleys converted to the Catholic faith shall not be liable for the payment of tribute for the first ten years after their conversion, and that after that time they shall be required to pay at the same rate as natives.

Law XII
(1627)

The Sangley Chinese of the Philippines have a treasure-box with three keys in which each Sangley deposits 12 reals a year in order to create a fund from which dues to the royal service shall be paid. The King commands that any balance there may be at the end of the year shall not be withdrawn but carried forward to the credit of the Sangley for the following year.

By this last decree of 10 September 1627 the King ordered that a Protector of the Chinese be appointed who should not be the Royal Fiscal.

The royal decrees and the report to the King by which the decrees were inspired were vigorous or tolerant according to whether the policy of the mailed fist or the velvet glove was in the ascendant. A further decree of 1627 (19 November) referred to the oppression that the Chinese in the Parián suffered by the compulsory cutting off of their hair when they became Christians and by the levying on them of an extortionate tax, and ordered that 'both these vexations be abolished'. The Governor Tavora advised that the Chinese should be tried and punished by the methods in vogue in their own country, and that they should not be allowed to appeal to the Audiencia. This was followed by a decree of the following year (1628) ordering the Governor of the Philippines to protect the Chinese from extortion and forced contributions, and directing that permission be granted them to travel in the islands. At the same time the King referred back for the Governor's consideration a demand made by the Manila Spaniards that all Chinese except the married Christians should be strictly confined within the Parián. In 1629 the King ordered the Governor to ascertain whether the Chinese needed a protector, and, if so, to send him a list of persons from whom an official might be chosen by the Council of the Indies.[4]

The Chinese paid annually at that time 64 reals in silver to the King for the privilege of living in the islands, plus 5 reals as the ordinary tribute, plus 12 reals for the King's Treasury, 'spent in assessments for affairs of my service'.[4]

In 1639 occurred the second Chinese revolt. It lasted nearly four months and caused a great loss of property to the Spaniards and of lives among the insurgents. Most of the Chinese population of Luzon were exterminated, thanks to their lack of firearms and to the 'special protection of Our Lord over the army'. Twenty-two to twenty-four thousand Chinese were killed as against 45 Spaniards and 300 Filipinos. The Chinese were armed with spears or with bamboos hardened by fire, and on these were fastened the knives with which they were wont to harvest the rice. After the suppression of the rebellion the *Te Deum* was sung in the churches of Manila; there was a great pageant of victory headed by the Governor Don Sebastián Hurtado de Corcuera, with drums, trumpets, and halberdiers of the guard, and with a standard bearing an image of the blessed Christ from Antipolo mounted on a staff. There had been a sickening record of slaughter, caused by a blind panic, fear of the house servants and other Chinese of Manila, and there were also several thousands of Chinese killed in Cavite.[5]

After another period of depopulation the Parián again miraculously renewed itself as from a Fortunatus's purse of Chinese. In 1644, less than five years after the second rebellion, we find the Royal Fiscal reporting on

[4] Blair & Robertson, xxiii. 287. The King, we observe, already in 1627 had given orders for the appointment of such an official. A colonial administrator is bound to remark on the wide range of matters that had to be referred back to the King of Spain for decision, which, especially considering the very long time required for an answer to a dispatch or a memorial, must have been a great handicap to the Philippines administration.

[5] See Blair & Robertson, xxxv, Preface, 17, 208.

the licences granted to the Chinese allowing them to reside in Manila. The amounts payable for the licences had apparently been increased by the Governor, Corcuera, as a punishment for the rising of 1639. The increase, the Fiscal reported, was not justified. He said that the new taxes had damaged the entire colony, since they had prevented the Chinese from leaving the Parián to cultivate the rice fields and to engage in similar productive occupations. In support of his charge he cited the great increases in price of both commodities and labour due to the new tax on the Chinese.[6]

Corcuera again came in for censure from His Majesty's Fiscal in the Royal Audiencia of Manila, Don Sebastián Cavallero, when he recommended that the issue of licences called 'fortification licences' (an increase of 11 reals to be added to general licences) be suspended as the Governor had no authority to impose the increase.[7]

Mistrust in the Spanish mind continued regarding the irrepressible Sangleys who insisted, in spite of everything, on filtering into the pool of the Parián as it was periodically drained. There were insurrections among the Filipinos, too, and the Chinese were blamed for supporting them. 'It cannot be denied', says the historian of the Discalced Augustinian Fathers, 'that the nation fomented and maintained with aid and cunning the rebellions of the Indians which we have just related.'[8] One had occurred in Pampanga and the other in Pangasinan. When the alcalde-mayor, Don Francisco, was killed in Pangasinan, there were found among the rebels some Sangleys who contrived that under cover of the small boats they might capture the large vessel in which the alcalde-mayor was defending his life very gallantly, and on the arrival of the Spanish fleet to explore the beach at Lingayen there were many armed men consisting of Sangleys and Indians.[9] The complicity of the Chinese was further proved by many bodies of Sangleys which were found in the field whenever there was an engagement with the rebels, for on occasions (says Fray Pedro) they served the Indians as auxiliaries.[10]

China itself by this time had been for many years in a state of great and increasing disorder, the empire having passed into the throes which portended the end of the Ming dynasty and the Manchu conquest. Piracy and buccaneering expeditions, by which thousands in the maritime provinces flourished exceedingly, gave the Spanish colonists an idea that the Chinese were dangerous fellows to be watched and repressed wherever they settled. Added to this fear on the part of the Europeans was the jealousy of the native Tagals who found themselves ousted from

[6] See Blair & Robertson, xxxv, Preface.   [7] Ibid. xxxv. 185.
[8] Fray Pedro de San Francisco, *General History of the Discalced Augustinian Fathers* (refers to 1661–90) (Saragossa, 1756), Blair & Robertson, xli. 85.
[9] Father Santa Cruz, *The Dominican History of the Philippines*, Blair & Robertson, xli. 85.
[10] This refers to the rebellions of 1661–2.

every lucrative pursuit the moment they were subjected to competition by the Chinese.[11]

We are now past the middle of the century and the next notable event, the ultimatum of Koxinga to the Spanish, is imminent. It would be well if we paused here for a moment to take one of our periodic glimpses at the Chinese in the Parián of Manila, since from such successive glimpses we can convince ourselves how little the tragic upheavals we have described affected the ordinary life of the capital, or that of the Chinese community within it. Here is what the Franciscan, Bartolomé de Letona, saw about the year 1661.[12]

On the Eastern side of the city, but outside of it and in front of its walls, at the distance of a musket-shot, is a silk market which they call Parián. Usually 15,000 Chinese live there; they are Sangleys, natives of China, and all are merchants and artisans. They possess, allotted among themselves by streets and squares, shops containing all kinds of merchandise and all the trades that are necessary in a community. The place is very orderly and well arranged, and a great convenience to the citizens. It is an indication of their [the Towkays'?] greatness that although they are so few, they have so many workmen and servants assigned to their service. The Sangleys live in wooden houses; they have a governor of their own nation, and a Spanish alcalde-mayor and other officers of justice, with a notary, and also a gaol. They have a parish church where the sacraments, the divine word, and the burial rites are administered to the 4,000 Christians among the Sangleys; the rest of them are heathen.

Koxinga (his real name was Cheng Cheng-kung, 1624–62), the famous corsair and supporter of the Ming dynasty, now in process of being driven out of China by the victorious Manchus, had expelled the Dutch from Formosa. In 1662 he sent a letter to the Spanish Governor of the Philippines, de Lara, in which he accused the Spanish of oppressing the Chinese, and demanded that they should submit to his rule immediately or be wiped out. The demand, as was to be expected, was rejected by the Spaniards, and the Chinese in Manila, fearing evil to themselves, and hearing of their intended expulsion from the islands, began to flee from the Parián and other neighbouring settlements in a blind endeavour to save their lives. The Jesuit missionaries at Santa Cruz hastened to the Government to secure pardon for the Chinese, and other priests seconded their efforts. Meanwhile, the other Sangleys in the Parián were so terrified that many were drowned in trying to swim across the river, others committed suicide, and most of those who remained fled to the hills. The Spanish in Manila, in fear of attack from the Chinese, were ready to slay them all, and a repetition of the horrors of the Chinese insurrections of 1603 and 1639 was averted only by the

[11] F. W. Williams, 'The Chinese Immigration in Further Asia', *American Historical R.*, v/3 (April 1900), p. 503.
[12] Description bound in with author's *Perfecta religiosa* (Mexico, 1662), Blair & Robertson, xxxvi. 189.

good sense of the Governor, Manrique de Lara, who, with mingled firmness and humanity, calmed the fears of the Chinese and the anger of the Spaniards. Granting protection to all who returned to Manila by a certain day, he ordered a specified number to remain there for the aid and service of the Spanish residents, and obliged the rest to return to China. Fugitives who did not take advantage of the amnesty and return to Manila were hunted down and slain by Spanish troops aided by the natives. The Chinese leaders of the Sangleys in their flight were captured and executed in public. Forced labour was being used in the feverish fortification of Manila and Cavite when news was received of the death of Koxinga.[13]

After the seventeenth century the Philippines were declining in prosperity and the Chinese preferred the Dutch colonies for the investment of their capital and for trade and residence. Nevertheless, they remained numerous in the Philippines, especially in Manila, where they continued to monopolize the trade and commerce of the place. This was quite contrary to the original intention of the Spaniards, who had allowed them to enter the islands only to cultivate the soil or to work in the handicrafts.[14]

Most of this history is derived from Spanish documents and very little from Chinese, so the *tu quoque* which is such a healthy corrective to the opinions of one race as expressed by another is altogether absent. Nevertheless, the Spanish themselves in their voluminous documents and histories provide some of the qualifications to their own charges. An excellent illustration of this is to be obtained from the exhaustive and meticulous index to the fifty-five volumes of Blair and Robertson's monumental collection of books and documents on the Philippines, where Spanish opinions of the Chinese are classified and references given to the pages of the text. The 'mental (negative)' qualities (as the index puts it) take up about double the space of the 'mental (positive)' qualities. Here are some of the former:

barbarous, mean, impudent, importunate, deceitful, unwarlike, cowardly, avaricious and greedy, addicted to sodomy and secret sins, tyrannical, ignorant, superstitious, vicious, intemperate, lustful and sensuous, polygamous, disloyal and faithless, evil-minded and wicked, mercenary, covetous, timorous, suspicious, cautious, cunning, unchaste, treacherous, shameless, vile, addicted to gambling, addicted to bribery, unscrupulous, rascally, cruel (in tortures, penalties, etc.), conscienceless, nomadic, fond of litigation, commit perjury, have tendency to revolt, inconstant, proud, talkative, extortionate, not spiritually-minded, inclined to sorcery. . . .

With this must be contrasted the 'mental (positive)' qualities of which the following is the complete list:

[13] Academia Real de la Historia, Madrid; Blair & Robertson, xxxvi.
[14] Ibid. li. 228.

civilized, humble, polite, ingenious, intelligent, imitative, careful of women, industrious, valiant and spirited, shrewd (generally in trade), generous, able and discreet, kind, honourable, tractable and docile, simple and unsophisticated, clever, possess good memories, not hostile to foreigners, grateful, religious, respect old age, legally minded, sensible and prudent, energetic, enterprising, fond of learning, cultured, respectful, sober, patient, peaceable.

It will be seen that the two lists are to a large extent contradictory and cancel one another out. Some epithets are favourable or derogatory descriptions of the same thing, e.g. fond of litigation, legally minded. In any case they convey the opinions of the Spanish regarding the Chinese over a period of 335 years, and are a warning to those who tend towards downright judgments of races other than their own.

As the seventeenth century draws to a close we will round off our impressions of it by a final glimpse at the Chinese in the Parián—this time more in paraphrase than in quotation. Our authority is a wealthy Neapolitan dilettante, who made a voyage round the world in 1693–9 (his figures of the numbers of the Chinese in the Parián are, however, not to be trusted).[15]

... within a musket-shot of the gate of Parián is the habitation of Chinese merchants called Sangley, who in several streets have rich shops of silk, purcellane and other commodities. Here are found all the arts and trades, so that all the citizens are worth runs through their hands, through the fault of the Spanish and Indians who apply themselves to nothing. There are about 3,000 in this suburb, and in many more about the Islands; which is permitted them, if not as Christians, at least in the hopes that they may become such, though many are converted for fear of being banished. There were formerly 4,000, but abundance of them were put to death in tumults they raised at several times, and particularly that on St Francis' Eve in 1603, and they were afterwards prohibited staying in the Islands by his catholic Majesty. The order is very little observed, for there always remain behind hid many of those who come every year in forty to fifty *Chiampans*, loaded with commodities; the profit being very great at Manila, which they could not find in China, by reason of the small prices the manufactures bear. The merchants or Sangleys of Parián are governed by an *alcalde*, to whom they allow a good salary, as they do to the solicitor their protector, to his steward, and other officers. Besides all the duties and taxes to the King, they pay His Majesty 100,000 pieces of eight a year for the privilege of playing at *metua*.... The Spanish keep these Chinese very much under, not suffering them to be in Christian houses at night, not obliging them to be without their houses or shops, to break them of the abominable vice that nation is inclined to.[16]

[15] Giovanni Gemelli-Careri, 'A Voyage Round the World', in *Churchill's Voyages* (1744). See also C. R. Boxer, *T'ien Hsia Monthly* (1939), p. 405. Gemelli-Careri was a credulous person. He believed the estimates of the Jesuit missionaries in China which placed the population of Nanking at 32 million, and in the Philippines he saw leaves 'which when they come to a certain pitch of ripeness, become living creatures with wings, feet, and tail' (see M. Macmillan, *The Globe Trotter in India two hundred years ago* (London, 1895)).

[16] Boxer, p. 459. The ascription of unnatural vice to Orientals by Europeans is very common, e.g. Sir Thomas Herbert so accused the Siamese and Admiral Stavorinus the Chinese in Java.

We see, then, the Chinese in Manila submitting to conditions of life which would have been intolerable even to a people used to a capricious despotism in their own country had it not been that the rewards were very high. The question of national or personal dignity did not, however, come into the reckoning. The Chinese, like all other Orientals, understood and accepted the rule of power, and had as yet but faint glimmerings of the idea of the rule of law. It was still a far cry to the Three Principles of Nationalism, Democracy, and People's Livelihood.

53

THE CHINESE UNDER THE SPANISH REGIME, 1700–1898

THE question as to whether the Chinese were a blessing or a menace to the Philippines had agitated the Spaniards throughout the seventeenth century and the consensus of opinion was that they were the latter. What the critics of the Chinese particularly disliked was the silk trade. As far back as 1628 it had been argued that it was pernicious to allow the importation of the silk of China, both to the Indies and to Mexico, for although not more than 250,000 pesos 'of Tipuzque' were allowed to be taken from Mexico to the Philipinnes annually, an incalculable sum in pieces of eight was exported in addition. The Chinese would accept no other currency, nor would they exchange their silk for other merchandise. Consequently, they managed to carry away annually the greater part of the eight-real pieces that were coined in New Spain in exchange for 'grass, which is the substance of that coarse and hard silk which is so plentiful among the Chinese. . . . Thus they weaken our strength and increase their own; and consequently, they can make war on us whenever they wish, without any cost to them as far as we are concerned.'[1]

The controversy continued into the eighteenth century. The people of Seville urged severe restrictions on the Manila–Acapulco trade on the ground that the wealth of Mexico was being drained off by the Chinese. In consequence of this agitation the King, in 1718, decreed that the trade in Chinese silk goods be thenceforth prohibited. But the following year the Viceroy of Mexico, de Valero, remonstrated against the prohibition

[1] Juan Velasquez Madr^co, *Economic Reasons for Suppressing the Silk Trade of China in Spain and its Colonies* (1628) (Blair & Robertson, xxii. 279). The reference (say Blair & Robertson) is probably to a plant called 'China grass' (*Boehmeria nivea*), a shrub indigenous to India. China grass, *Chu ma* (ramie), is considered a textile substance of the first rank. (Swatow-grass cloth is a famous product of China, outwearing linen by years. V. P.)

on behalf not only of the Filipinos but also of his own subjects, most of whom were too poor to purchase Spanish piece-goods from which to manufacture the clothes they wore, and who therefore depended on Chinese materials. Memorials ensued from Manila and Cadiz respectively, each endeavouring to justify its own side in the controversy. At one stage Cadiz offered Manila the spice trade of Mexico as the equivalent of the latter's traffic in Chinese textiles. A decree of 27 October 1720 addressed to the Marquis de Valero, Viceroy of Mexico, laid down that two ships only should go annually from the Philippine Islands to Nueva España (Mexico), each of 500 tone-ladas. The value of the lading which the said ships were to carry to the port of Acapulco might be up to the amount of 300,000 pesos which must come invested strictly and solely in the following kinds of merchandise: gold, cinnamon, elephants, wax, porcelain, cloves, pepper, cambayas and linens woven with colours (*lienzos pintados*), chitas, chintzes, gauzes, lampotes, Hilicos blankets, silk floss and raw spun silk, cordage, and like commodities. These ships were prohibited from carrying silken fabrics. Manila protested against the injury done to the islands by this decree, and eventually on 8 April 1734 a decree was promulgated increasing the amount of trade permitted to Manila to 500,000 pesos of investment and 1 million of return.

In the long run Manila interests had triumphed over those of Cadiz and Seville.[2]

Spain was involved with England in the 'War of Jenkins' Ear' (1739–1742), and again in the Seven Years War (1756–63). In the former the celebrated Admiral Lord Anson appeared in these waters on his circumnavigation of the globe and captured the Mexico–Manila treasure ship. His chaplain, Richard Walter, who was to become the historian of the voyage, has left on record his information regarding Manila, which can be regarded as substantially accurate:

The trade carried on from this place to China and different parts of India is principally for such commodities as are intended to supply the kingdoms of Mexico and Peru. These are spices, all sorts of Chinese silks and manufactures, particularly silk stockings, of which I have heard that no less than fifty thousand pairs were the usual number shipped in each cargoe; vast quantities of Indian stuffs, such as calicoe and chints, which are much worn in America, together with other minuter articles, as goldsmith's work &c, which is principally wrought in the city of Manila itself by the Chinese, for it is said that at least 20,000 Chinese constantly reside there, either

---

[2] Blair & Robertson, xliv. 227 ff., 266, 286; xlv. 57–8. The arguments recorded in Blair & Robertson to the effect that the China trade ruined the Philippines are almost equalled in number by others to the effect that the trade benefited the islands. Meanwhile in 1709 many Chinese had been banished from Manila on the charge of carrying off the public wealth, and prosecutions of this kind led to their settling in smaller places on Luzon during the eighteenth century. In 1747 a royal order was received for the final expulsion of the Chinese but the execution was suspended.

as servants, manufacturers, or bakers. All these different commodities are collected at Manila, there to be transported to the port of Acapulco in the kingdom of Mexico.[3]

Walter remarks that Chinese silks coming directly to Acapulco could be sold there considerably cheaper than any European commodities of equal goodness, and, he adds, 'the cotton from the Coromandel coast makes the European linens useless'.

Governor Don Gasper de la Torre, whose governorship generally was an unfortunate one, became affected with melancholy and chronic dysentery (perhaps the order should be reversed) which were aggravated by the news that the village of Balayan had revolted, and finally a supposed revolt of the Sangleys caused him to depart this life. There was a rumour that the Chinese were about to enter the city of Manila and, despite his illness, he prepared to go out to meet the insurgents. The rumour turned out to be a fabrication put abroad to vex him, but the Governor became so feverish from the shock that he died a few days afterwards on 21 September 1745.[4]

When a new Archbishop of Manila, Don Fray de la Santísima Trinidad (Pedro Martínez de Arizala), arrived in the Philippines on 27 August 1747 he brought with him a decree by which His Majesty the King committed the Government to the expulsion of the Chinese from the islands. The expulsion already ordered had not yet been effected on account of the personal interests of the Governors, but Pedro de Arizala thought it well not to make the decree known until a better opportunity offered because he found that Señor Arrechedera, the Commissary of Inquisition, who had been acting Governor *ad interim*, was himself greatly devoted to the Chinese.[5]

Then once more, on 30 June 1755, Governor Arandía, in obedience to instructions received from the King, ordered that all Chinese should be expelled from the Philippines, excepting 515 Christian Chinese, and a thousand more 'who pretended to be studying the Christian doctrine'.[6] The Christian Chinese could remain so long as they confined themselves to agriculture—actually most of them engaged in trade notwithstanding. After Arandía's death in 1759 Chinese immigration and residence were again allowed.

A few years after this new order for expulsion, when Spain was involved in war in Europe, the English captured Manila in 1762 and held it until 1764. At the time of the capture the Chinese who still remained in the Philippines took sides with the English, whereupon Simón de Anda, the Lieutenant-Governor, ordered that all Chinese in the

[3] R. A. Walter, *A Voyage Round the World in the Years 1740–44 by Lord Anson*, 3rd ed. (London, 1930), p. 220.   [4] Blair & Robertson, xlviii. 142–3.
[5] Ibid. p. 146. 'Events in the Philippines 1739–62, compiled from Martínez de Zúñiga, Concepción, and Montero y Vidal.'   [6] *Census of the Philippines, 1903*, i. 319.

islands should be hanged. This order was to some extent carried into effect by the Spaniards in 1763.[7]

In that same year 6,000 Chinese are said to have been massacred by the Spaniards in Pangasinan alone for siding with the Filipinos in a conspiracy to oust the Spanish regime.[8]

In 1766 the survivors were rounded up and in 1769 the order of expulsion was put into effect.[9] Yet soon after Le Gentil is saying: 'I do not know any Spaniards who did not sincerely regret the departure of the Chinese, and who did not frankly admit that the Philippines would suffer for it, because the Indians were not capable of replacing the Chinese.' (This an echo of de Morga's lament after the insurrection of 1603.) In 1778 the order for expulsion was revoked, but only Chinese workmen were encouraged to immigrate.

A decree of 17 April 1766 ordered that all Catholic Sangleys who had committed excesses during the time when the British had occupied Manila should be expelled from the Philippines, only true Christians being allowed to remain. The latter were not to be allowed to carry weapons of any sort and were to be employed only in agriculture and the trades. They were not allowed to leave their respective villages without permission of the police, governor, or alcalde-mayor, under penalty of perpetual exile from His Majesty's dominions.[10]

The order of expulsion of the Chinese was revoked in 1788.[11]

Most of the interest in the Chinese during the Spanish period centres on the residents of Manila, but their compatriots were also present in considerable numbers in other parts of the Philippines.[12]

In 1775 (says Captain Forrest) many Chinese resided in the town of Selangan, near the mouth of the Mindanao or Cotabato river; many also resided on the tongue of land between the Matampay and the main stream. They were mostly carpenters, arrack distillers, and millers. They ground the husk off the rough rice (paddy) between two stones much more expeditiously than the Maguindanao (Mindanao) people were able to do in a wooden mortar. In that part of the town of Coto Intang which borders on the Melampy lived a few Chinese, but there were many

[7] Laufer, p. 273.
[8] See Li Mei-ping, 'A Historical Survey of the Development of Sino-Philippine Relations', *New Age in Asia*, i 7-8 (Dec. 1947), pp. 16-22 (in Chinese). (This journal is considered authoritative in this field of study.)
[9] 'By a Royal Warrant of 17 April 1766, all the Sangleys in the Islands, including Christians, were to be expelled. For, during the occupation of the town by the English they committed infidelity, apostasy, and other ugly abominable excesses. Only the true Christians were to remain' (Jordana y Morera, *Inmigración*, p. 16).
[10] Blair & Robertson, l. 253.   [11] Ibid. p. 65.
[12] Joaquín Martínez de Zúñiga, in his *Historia* (Sampaloc, 1803), p. 19, says that in some districts Indians (Filipinos) are found who are whiter than others '... doubtless descendants of some Chinese or Japanese who were shipwrecked on these coasts, the Ygorrotes (Igorotes) in particular. Their eyes, similar to those of the Chinese, prove that they were mingled with the companions of Limahon who fled to the mountains when Juan de Salcedo had besieged him in Pangasinan' (Blair & Robertson, xliii. 113).

Mindanao mechanics, vessel builders, and merchants. The Chinese in
Mindanao were not allowed to settle higher up the river than Boyan, the
Mindanoese being jealous of their superior abilities in trade.[13]

Captain Forrest explains that the coarse Chinese cloth ('kangans')
used in the Pulangi delta generally came via Sulu to Cotabato, for the
Spanish had long hindered Chinese junks bound from Amoy to Mindanao
from passing Zamboanga. This was the cause of there being so little
trade at Mindanao, no vessels sailing from India thither, and the little
trade that there was being confined to a few 'country' Chinese, called
'Orang Sangley', and a few natives of Sulu who came here to buy rice
and paddy, bringing with them Chinese articles, for the rice crop at
Sulu could never be depended upon. (Rice was the usual currency in the
market at Mindanao, and it used to be reckoned that a prow, a house, &c,
was 'worth so many slaves'. But Chinese cash was also used at Mindanao,
though Forrest found it scarce.) Many Chinese articles, especially
'kangans',[14] beads, gongs, Chinese basins with red edges, deep brass
plates—five in a set, deep saucers—three and four inches in diameter,
brass wire, and iron were carried from Sulu to Mindanao.

The Sulus told Forrest (and their claim has been repeated often since)
that their island was formerly part of the ancient Borneo empire founded
by Chinese, many of whom were settled among them, who had taught
the Sulus the art of grafting and improving their fruits, but the fruits of
Mindanao, on the contrary, had remained of indifferent quality.[15] The
industrious Chinese used teak leaves and leaves of a fruit called *madang*
to line the baskets of cane and bamboo in which they packed the 'swallo'
(bêche-de-mer) which they exported in great quantities from Sulu. 'The
Chinese must gain handsomely from their trade thither', Forrest remarks, 'else they would not put up with the rough usage they sometimes
received from the sturdy barons, the Datoos' (i.e. *Datoks*).[16]

*List of articles that generally compose the cargo of a Chinese junk,
of which two come annually from Amoy to Sulu (January 1776)*

	Cost in China in dollars	Sell for (sic) in Sulu
2,000 galangs (salvers of brass) seven to a picul .	40	70
100 piculs iron, in small pieces, like Bengal iron .	4	8
Sugar candy, a quantity, per picul . . .	7	10
50 raw silk, ditto	400	600
3,000 pieces black kowsongs, a kind of nankeen, per piece	0¾	1

[13] T. Forrest, *A Voyage to New Guinea and the Moluccas Performed on the Tartar Galley
belonging to the Honourable the East India Company, during the Years 1774 and 1776* (London,
1780), pp. 179 ff.   [14] One kangan was equal to 160–180 cash.
[15] *Voyage to New Guinea*, p. 323.
[16] The student of Eastern economic history may find interest in the above (ibid. p. 325).

5,000 pieces of kampow, white strong linen . .	0¾	1
500 Kangans, 25 in a bundle, called gadangs per gadang	7	10
200 quallis, an iron pan, 3 foot diameter each .	1	2
500 nests of quallis, 3 in a nest . .	1	2
One million pieces of chinaware, consisting of small 'terrenes' and basins in nests, big and small, plates and basins with red edges for Mindanao, &c, &c, per hundred	1	2
200 pieces of flowered silks, per piece . .	6	10

The merchandise taken from Sulu was in the shape of the following articles:

	Cost at Sulu	Sell for in China
Black swallo per picul	15	30
White swallo „ „	10	20
Wax	15	25
Teepye, or pearl oyster shells	1½	5
Birds' nests per catty	6	9
Tortoiseshell, price uncertain	..	..

Also agar-agar, carooang oil, clove bark, black wood rotans, sago, various barks for dyeing, cassia, pepper, native camphire (camphor), sandalwood, curious shells for grottos, pearls, etc., and spices.

There was a law both at Mindanao and at Sulu, that no Chinese could be made a slave, but at either place for a sum advanced by a *Dato* (chief) to a Chinese (and such advances were often forced on them) they were obliged to pay every twelve months a high rate of interest, perhaps 25 or 30 per cent, the lender often refusing to receive back the principal at the end of the year, unless indeed the Chinese made it appear that he was going to return to his own country, in which case repayment was never refused.[17] 'The industrious Chinese [says Forrest] seems to be excluded from the benefit of law.'[18]

Another of our peeps at the Parián of Manila is afforded by de Guignes, Resident of France in China in the last quarter of the eighteenth century. The year of this visit was 1797. There were then, he says, about 3,000 Sangleys there. A very strict watch was kept over them, and an alcalde and a number of Spanish officers had the superintendence of police and exacted from the Chinese, it was reported, considerable sums of money, chiefly at Chinese New Year, the licence for playing *metora* (or *metua?* = fan-tan?) alone being purchased by them at the rate of $10,000 a year. San Sebastián likewise, says de Guignes, had some good houses. In this suburb there was a large causeway, raised by the Government as a promenade for the inhabitants, whither Spanish ladies, in

[17] Ibid. p. 327. He accuses the Chinese *per contra* of defrauding pearl fishers.
[18] Ibid. p. 277 n.

particular, resorted in their carriages. The Chinese were said to have defrayed the expenses of making this causeway or wall with money extorted for exemption from certain disabilities imposed upon them by the Spaniards; the wall was a pleasant one, shaded by a number of areca trees, and commanded a fine prospect over the country.

'The Chinese who inhabited Manila [our French informant continues] profess Christianity, but this is only for form's sake, for when they leave Manila they throw their images and chaplets into the sea and cease to be Christians as soon as they lose sight of Mirabel Point.'[19]

Spanish policy in the early nineteenth century was to confine the Chinese as far as possible to agricultural pursuits. In 1804 it was ordered that only Chinese in the provinces who were agriculturists or artisans should be allowed to remain in the islands.[20] Later on, in 1828, various royal decrees were obtained for the promotion of agriculture, manufactures, and other industries, and for obliging the Chinese to be grouped under headmen (as were the Filipinos) whose function was to collect the taxes. (This 'headman' system was, however, not acceptable to the Chinese, as will shortly be seen.) As regards clothes, the Filipinos could manufacture cotton goods themselves, providing they knew how to dye them properly and had the machinery necessary for manufacturing cotton thread, and Chinese imports could then be dispensed with.

Meanwhile, the influence of the Chinese immigrant had already been felt in Filipino cultivation, for their plough was of Chinese origin, having one handle, no coulter or mould-board—the upper part of the share, which was flat, being turned to one side to perform this function.[21]

The Chinese in the second decade of the nineteenth century paid a poll-tax of 6 dollars (48 reals) each; the mestizos paid 3 dollars (12 reals). The tax was generally farmed out. In 1817 the Chinese paid $30,000 in a total revenue of $1,449,760 of which $639,000 came from poll-taxes, and $811,000 came from rentals (monopolies, opium farms, &c).[22]

By this time the Philippines were in none too happy a state. Robbery and piracy were rampant in the neighbourhood of Manila; justice was neglected or corrupted. The Church insisted on so many holidays that the farmers neglected their fields. 'Until very recently [says the Englishman—a naval officer—cited above, writing of the period 1819–22] these rich islands have been a constant burden to the crown of Spain, money having been annually sent from Mexico to supply their expenses.' As in the case of the Moors in Spain, blame was laid mainly at the door of the Chinese for drawing off the wealth of the country. How much they had in reality 'drawn off' is, however, uncertain. De Comyn estimates that

---

[19] M. de Guignes, *Voyages à Pékin, Manille (&c.), faits dans l'intervalle des années 1784 et 1801* (Paris, 1806), iii. 401.   [20] *Census of the Philippines, 1903*, i. 320.
[21] *Remarks on the Philippine Islands by an Englishman* (Calcutta, 1828) (Blair & Robertson, li. 128).   [22] Ibid. pp. 120, 121.

between 1565 and 1820 Spanish America exported to Manila 400 million silver dollars. 'The Sangley mestizos [de Comyn goes on] have amassed immense sums in specie; but it would be impossible to point out the amount, distribution, or the secret places in which they are hoarded.'[23] The Chinese merchants were, moreover, accused of fraudulent practices.

At the beginning of the nineteenth century the Chinese in the Philippines paid each a capitation tax of 6 pesos a year.[24] In addition each had to pay to the public treasury a surtax to cover the expenses of maintaining the hospital, the church, the police, and other administrative expenses connected with the Parián.

A new agitation against the Chinese got under way in 1828. There were (says Crawfurd) only 5,708 Chinese in the whole of the Philippines, of whom 5,279 were in Tondo. By a new decree of 6 April the Chinese merchants, shopkeepers, and artisans were divided into three classes— (1) merchants of the first class who paid an annual tax of 120 pesos; (2) merchants, &c, who paid 48 pesos annually; (3) smaller merchants, &c, who paid 24 pesos annually. A fourth class, paying 12 pesos annually, was introduced in 1830. When the taxation was applied it was found that there were only 7 Chinese merchants of the first class, while 166 belonged to the second class, 830 to the third class, and 4,509 to the fourth class. On account of age, 191 were exempted from taxation altogether. The Chinese were to be gathered into villages, as were the 'Indians' (Filipinos). Their 'heads of barangay' were to collect the tribute due from them.

These taxes, it appears, were payable in addition to the capitation tax of 6 pesos.[25]

According to Crawfurd, when these new rates were approved the Chinese refused to accept them or to be concentrated in villages. Eight hundred returned to China; 1,083 fled to the mountains, where they were hospitably received by the native population; 453, not having the means of defraying the cost of their passages back to China, were seized and condemned to penal labour as defaulters. 'The effect of this action', says Crawfurd, 'is observable a decade or so later when the Chinese enrolled did not exceed 6,000, while their capitation taxes amounted to over $100,000 per annum, and those of the native inhabitants, exceeding 3,000,000, did not equal eight times that amount.'[26] The intendant, in

[23] Tomás de Comyn, *Estado de las islas Filipinas* (Madrid, 1820) trans. from the Spanish by William Walton (London, 1821), p. 76. Charles Robequain, *Le Monde malais* (Paris, 1946), p. 97, says: 'De Comyn estime que, de 1571 à 1821, l'Amérique Espagnole a exporté à Manille 400 million de dollars d'argent, *dont la moitié peut-être est passé en Chine*.' Which does not appear to represent de Comyn correctly. M. Robequain seems to have copied Laufer's version of de Comyn (Laufer, p. 277) which is from the *Chinese Repository*, viii. 173.
[24] The royal decree ordering this was dated 14 May 1790 (Blair & Robertson, l. 65), 'Events of 1764–1800' compiled from Montero y Vidal, *Historia de Filipinas* (1887). But *The Census of the Philippines, 1903* says (p. 359) that the tax, which had hitherto been 8 pesos, was reduced to 6 pesos in 1799.   [25] I am not certain about this (V. P.).
[26] Crawfurd, *Descriptive Dictionary of the Indian Archipelago* (1856), p. 97. Commenting on this, Mr Ifor B. Powell (to whom I am indebted for a most careful scrutiny of this Part and

view of the difficulty of collecting the taxes, explained to the government
the expediency of modifying the enactment and this was done in 1834.[27]

Chinese engaged in agriculture were taxed on a different scale. In 1834
Chinese were allowed to engage in any occupation under permit. In 1849
the regulations were elaborated and amended by Governor Corcuera.
Transient Chinese could now remain only three months: residents could
stay as long as they liked.

Already in 1843 a Spanish official of standing had recommended that,
since capitalists and workers were needed in the Philippine Islands, there
must be governmental and administrative reforms in order to attract
them, and that the heavy tribute exacted from the Chinese must be
reduced to not more than 12 reals per annum for those engaging in
agriculture. Europeans, Chinese, and mestizos should be encouraged to
go and live in the islands in greater numbers.[28] In 1850 Chinese agriculturists were granted the same privileges as Filipinos of the same class
and paid only a tax of 12 reals a year.[29] After 1852 every Chinese, except
tillers of the soil, paid a head-tax of $6, and, in addition, an industrial
tax of $100, $60, $30, or $12.[30]

After 1852 Chinese mestizos paid a poll-tax of $3 a year. The Filipino
woman married to a mestizo of this class paid the same tax as he did
during marriage, but if she became a widow she paid only at the same
rate as a Filipino widow. But mestizos who cultivated the soil with their
own hands paid only the same amount as the natives. (The mestizos
formed their own 'Barangays' where 25 or 30 of them lived together.)

It was recommended in some quarters that dowries or marriage
bonuses be paid by the Government at the following rates—to a Chinese
mestiza marrying a Filipino, a sum of 100 pesos; to a Filipino woman
marrying a Chinese mestizo, 100 pesos; to a Chinese mestizo marrying a
Spaniard, 1,000 pesos; to a Spaniard marrying a Chinese mestiza, 2,000
pesos; to a Spanish woman marrying a Filipino chief, 3,000 to 4,000
pesos. This was regarded by reformers as an impulse towards the
amalgamation of the races! But it does not seem that these recommendations were adopted.

The Spanish Government maintained almost to the end the theory (it
was hardly more than an empty theory) that Chinese immigration to the
Philippines was being regulated to constitute a stimulus to agriculture.[31]

To prevent illegal entrance via the Sulu Archipelago and Borneo, and

for the correction of a number of mistakes, both my own and those of my authorities)
remarks: 'Buzeta says regarding the 800 odd that they were 'prepared' to go to China, and
another Spanish writer says that they 'opted' to go. But did they ever go ' Though I have
consulted Sinibaldo de Mas (from whom Crawfurd draws much of his information) I have
not yet found the answer.   [27] See Blair & Robertson, li. 53–54 and p. 53 n.

[28] *Communication from the Intendant of the Army and the Treasury* (*Intendente de Ejercito y
Hacienda*) *of the Philippine Islands, Don Juan Manuel de la Matta* (Blair & Robertson, liii. 91).

[29] Blair & Robertson, lii. 53.   [30] Ibid. lii. 58.

[31] J. A. Leroy, 'The Philippines 1860–1896' (ibid. lii. 144).

to remove the lucrative Moro trade from the hands of the Chinese who fairly monopolized it even in the first half of the twentieth century, a decree of the Governor-General of January 1886 forbade the Chinese to live permanently in the provinces, and absolutely prohibited them from engaging in trade with the Moros; a further decree of July 1886 forbade all Chinese to live in Mindanao.[32]

Notwithstanding the liberal counsels of officials and publicists, the opposition to the Chinese continued to be strong. In 1859, when Señor Norzagaray gave up his command in the Philippines, he wrote an extensive paper on the Chinese question in which he argued that it would be better for Spain to be impoverished by taking energetic measures against the Chinese than that the Philippines should be ruined by foreign absorption.[33] In 1866 a new campaign for Chinese exclusion was started by Spanish merchants and business men, together with a programme for fostering immigration of Spaniards into the Philippines, especially into Mindanao and Palawan. The campaign continued with varying intensity, but with no practical effect so far as reducing the numbers of the Chinese went, right to the end of the Spanish period. It was backed by strongly-worded articles in the local press, and in the controversy that ensued the sole champion of the Chinese was the newspaper *El Commercio*, while against them were *El Boletín de Avisos*, *El Diario de Manila*, and *La Oceania Española*. A writer of the 1880s says[34] that the extraordinary increase in Chinese immigration into the Philippines during the previous few years had with great force attracted the attention of people of thoughtful habit and patriotic sentiment who saw in this a grave peril to Spanish interests in the region. He quoted a pamphlet of two years previous to this,[35] to the effect that after deduction of the mortality applicable to each case the Chinese population of the archipelago had grown during the period 31 December 1876 to 23 May 1886 from 30,797 to 93,567, this being a multiplication by three in one decade. Another Spanish writer says of the Chinese:

The Chinese, whose peculiar racial characteristics allow them to resist successfully climatic rigours without number, are notwithstanding a terrible threat to peninsular immigration.... They multiply at a startling rate and not content, as they were once, with the trade in certain specified articles, they now want to embrace the whole scope of the traffic. If this goes on it will not be surprising if they also want to handle the plough and the hoe, monopolizing agriculture to the detriment of the natives who get their living in this way.[36]

[32] *Census of the Philippines, 1903*, p. 491.
[33] *Report of the Philippine Commission to the President* (1899–1900), i. 151.
[34] Ramon y Morera, *Inmigración*, p. 10.
[35] Series of articles in *La Oceania Españ, published in pamphlet form as *Los Chinos en Filipinas* (Manila, 1886).
[36] Eduardo Casal y Ocha, *Questiones filipinas: estudio político-social* (Madrid, 1888), p. 24. I think that 'peninsular immigration' must refer to the Iberian Peninsula. Or am I wrong? (V. P.).

At the present moment (the writer continues) the Chinese considered his position insecure and he was not therefore an element to inspire fear, but later on, if his immigration were guaranteed, he would become almost the only immigrant, especially as he was willing to work at a wage so low that no European could compete with him.

Such remained the suspicion and fear of the Chinese among the Spanish up to the day when Commodore Dewey destroyed the Spanish fleet in Manila Bay in 1898 and the regime which had lasted for well over 300 years was about to come to an end. There were at that time estimated to be 40,000 Chinese in the Philippines, though one Spanish writer at least places it at 100,000. For reasons stated in Chapter 50, the writer is inclined to accept the former figure as being nearer the truth.

Cultural prejudice preceded 1850, but nation-wide economic competition between Chinese and Filipinos, marking the birth of Filipino nationalism that was to be directed eventually against the Chinese, and the beginnings of formal political relations between the Philippine Chinese and China, are all phenomena of the late nineteenth century.[37]

54

THE CHINESE UNDER THE AMERICAN REGIME, 1898–1946

WAR was declared upon Spain by the United States on 25 April 1898. On 1 May Commodore Dewey steamed into Manila Bay; by noon he had put the weak Spanish squadron out of action, and by August hostilities were over. At the peace conference a few months later Spain ceded the Philippines to the United States, and $20 million were paid by the United States to Spain for public works built in the islands during the three centuries of her occupation. Until 1902 the Philippines remained under a Military Government and by that year most of the Filipinos who had declared their own republic had yielded to American arms, but the Moros continued under military government until 1913. In 1934 the islands became a Commonwealth, and, after the Japanese occupation of them from 1942 to 1945, the Philippines were declared absolutely independent, as the Republic of the Philippines, on 4 July 1946.

As is always the case in Southeast Asia, the Chinese in 1898–9 suffered from native animosity while disorder continued. The Tagálog leaders Braganza, Vicente Ursua, and others ordered the killing of all

[37] Edgar Wickberg, 'Early Chinese Economic Influence in the Philippines', *Pacific Affairs*, xxv/3 (Fall 1962).

Spanish and Chinese at Minalabag, Pasacao, Libmanan, and Calabanga.[1]

To the Americans who took over the reins of government in 1898 the Spanish laws in force for the control of the Chinese seemed inadequate, for they were thinking in terms of Pacific Coast sentiment, and within a month after the occupation of Manila the laws relating to the admission of the Chinese into the United States were by an order of the Military Government under Brigadier-General Otis made applicable to the Philippines.[2] In 1902 Congress extended the Chinese exclusion laws to the island territory under jurisdiction of Congress, and directed the Philippines Commission to make necessary regulations under the law effective.[3] These laws amounted to the exclusion of the Chinese from the Philippines.[4]

Before the American occupation the records of arrivals and departures of Chinese showed an increase in the number of residents of 36,250 in the years 1889–93. In the first five years of the United States occupation, 1899–1903, the excess of arrivals over departures was 8,624. The Census of 1903 (published in 1905) gave the total number of Chinese as 41,035 (though private estimates put it at over 100,000 in 1898 and at a similar figure in 1903). Between the Spanish and the American figures there is an obvious discrepancy.

Under Spanish rule, as we have seen, an effort had been made to admit Chinese only for unskilled labour, the lower kinds of service, and agriculture. Immigrants were forbidden to engage in any trade. Chinese brought in for tobacco-growing were not taxed. But the fact was that the Chinese did not like agriculture (though so many of the immigrants had been peasants at home) for the simple reason that it did not pay as well as trade.

Opinion was divided as to the wisdom of the exclusionist policy, though anti-Chinese feeling was far more vocal and influential than advocacy for the encouragement of the race. Señor Gabriel Garcia Ageo, in his memorandum to the Schurmann Commission of 1899,[5] said that he believed that the leniency of the Spanish Government towards the Chinese in the past had been to the detriment of both the Spanish and the Filipinos.[6] He suggested that heavy duties be imposed on Chinese

---

[1] D. C. Worcester, *The Philippines Past and Present* (N.Y., 1930), p. 181.

[2] Elliott, *Philippines*, pp. 438, 439.

[3] Ibid. Wu Ting-fang immediately protested against this action on behalf of the Chinese Government. For the pros and cons of the Chinese immigration question as argued in 1899 see *Report of the Philippine Commission to the President* (Schurmann Commission), (1899–1900) i. pt. 10, pp. 150 ff.

[4] The laws were based on the limited treaties of 1880 and 1894 between the United States and China, both of which modified the general treaty of 1868. The 1868 treaty was for the reciprocal immigration of Chinese and Americans into America and China respectively. But the agitation of the 1870s led to a limited suspension of the treaty of 1880.

[5] Report of Schurmann Commission, ii. 432.

[6] The Spanish policy towards the Chinese may have been weak and vacillating, but it can scarcely be said to have been lenient. V. P.

goods, and that the Chinese should be prohibited from engaging in agriculture. The Philippine Commission of 1900–3 thought it would be unwise to admit Chinese skilled labourers to the islands in unlimited numbers. It admitted, however, that there was not sufficient skilled labour among the Filipinos to meet the construction immediately necessary for the development of the islands. The introduction of a limited number of Chinese for a period of five years, during which a Filipino apprentice should be employed for every Chinese admitted, would secure a sufficient number of skilled labourers among the Filipinos at the end of that period.[7] When the United States Senate was debating the future of the Philippines the question came up again for discussion. The following extract from the record will give an idea of how these arguments tended, and will throw some light on the economics of the Philippines.[8]

> *Senator Rawlins.* If the Chinese are admitted that will be a phase of the question.
> *Governor Taft.* The commission has expressed the opinion as to what ought to be done in the matter of the admission of the Chinese. It is a very definite political question in the Islands, not due to competition in labor, but to competition in trade.
> *Senator Hale.* Do you think it a possibility or probability that in expending this large amount of money on public works you will be driven to the necessity of bringing in the Chinese?
> *Governor Taft.* That is what the contractors say.
> *Senator Hale.* You think it may come to that?
> *Governor Taft.* I hope not. Some of the quartermasters of the army think it is possible by care to secure labor and teach it constancy. But if you will talk with the business man in Manila, who is usually not very friendly towards the Filipino, he scouts the idea; and I think possibly you have already had a petition from the American Chamber of Commerce of Manila to allow the entrance of Chinese, because the labor of the Filipinos is so unsatisfactory. . . .
> *Governor Taft.* The Chinaman comes into this country and labors, say, at 12 silver dollars a month. Out of that, the local saying is, he saves $16 or $18. At any rate, he is not there for more than three to four months before he has capital to set up a store, and when he sets up a store the Filipino who has a store next to him is driven out of business.
> *Senator Carmack.* Is it not true that one of the greatest obstacles to the pacification of these Islands has been and is, the fear of bringing Chinese labor to the country, and the fear of sudden and excessive exploitation, and the belief that the United States want the Islands purely for the purpose of such exploitation?
> *Governor Taft.* Certainly there has been, if one can judge by the proclamation of the insurgents and by the statements of the insurgent leaders, a very considerable attempt to make the public believe that it is the purpose of the Americans. Now, with respect to the effect of Chinese importation, possibly that goes with it.

Pressed by Senator Carmack as to whether it would be necessary to throw open the doors to Chinese immigration in order to secure a supply

----

[7] U.S., Bureau of Insular Affairs, War Dept., *Reports of the Philippine Commission, the Civil Governor, and the Heads of the Executive Departments of the Civil Government of the Philippine Islands (1900–1903)* (1904), p. 291.

[8] U.S., *Hearings before the Committee on the Philippines of the United States Senate in Relation to the Affairs of the Philippines* (1902), pp. 96 ff.

of efficient and helpful labour for the development of the country, Governor Taft replied that he was 'profoundly hopeful' that this might not be the case. In certain parts of the archipelago, he said, the admission of Chinese labour without permission to trade, keeping the immigrant a labourer and requiring those who brought him in to take him out again, would doubtless aid the development of islands like Mindanao where the population was sparse, but in Luzon, Panay, and Negros, the thickly populated islands, he was hopeful that they could gradually give the people a motive for labour and that, so encouraged, the labour might become more efficient than it was. Asked whether all Filipinos were opposed to Chinese immigration, Governor Taft replied that generally they were, but that the Tabacalera, the largest company in the Philippines and controlled by Spaniards, had been pressing the Government to allow them to bring in Chinese *skilled* labour for the construction of warehouses and other buildings on the tobacco installation.

'The burning question of the hour', Dr Doherty proclaimed in his pamphlet printed by order of the United States Senate, 'is this: shall Chinese labour be brought into the Islands or not? The Manila papers which are printed in English howl for it, and the foreign commercial interests of Manila and Iloilo beg for it, but the civil government is averse to it, and the Filipino people are opposed to it, and look on in dumb despair as they see the net slowly drawn around them.' It was, thought the Doctor, a wrong to the Filipino people, and they should make the question their Thermopylae.[9]

In public life the importation of Chinese labour had few advocates, but some individuals outside the Philippines urged that favourable consideration be given to the idea. Thus at the very beginning of the American regime an article was written 'in the sincere hope that the preceding lines may help in influencing legislation to encourage Chinese immigration', and quoted Sir John Bowring as saying, 'There is no colonizer who, under intelligent control, may be more useful than the Chinese.' His advocacy, however, was for the importation of Chinese *agriculturists* (though they had hitherto shown little inclination towards this type of employment) and he pointed out that the Philippines had a very similar temperature to that of the fields they generally immigrated from round Amoy, Swatow, &c. 'The Archipelago', he declared, 'would soon turn from an uncultivated field to an El Dorado.'[10]

Another British writer quoted Jenks's report of 1902 to the Secretary of War in favour of the admission of Chinese labour on the ground that the measure would result, with here and there an individual exception,

[9] U.S., 50th Congress, 2nd session, *Conditions in the Philippines*, by D. M. Doherty, Senate Document no. 170 (27 Feb. 1904).
[10] Juan Mencarini, 'The Philippine Chinese Labour Question', *JRAS*, China Branch, xxxiii (1899–1900), p. 157.

not at all to the disadvantage of the Filipino, but indeed to his benefit
through the improved conditions in the islands which would furnish
him not only with a better market for his produce but also a better
opportunity of engaging in the kind of work for which he was best
suited and which most closely accorded with his tastes.[11]

These arguments are here set out at length because they give the pros
and cons of the whole Chinese question in Southeast Asia, and they are
not likely for long to get out of date. But the anti-Chinese labour
advocates won the day in the Philippines, and the exclusion laws remained. In 1909 Mr Russell M'Culloch Story sums up the situation by
saying that to admit the Chinese at this stage 'would be to invite a disturbing social, political, and economic factor into the life of the Islands'.
The existing number of Chinese, however (he continued), was not a
menace to the peace and industry of the archipelago and would soon be
absorbed into the population of the islands. The danger lay in the coolie
class, who in their struggle to advance themselves would hinder the
upward course of the Filipino.[12] (Mr Story, like most others, did not
foresee the rise of Chinese nationalism!)

We have no means of knowing how far the Spanish censuses or the
American Census of 1903 were out in their enumerations, but, assuming
the latter to have been nearly correct, the number of Chinese in the
Philippines tripled between 1903 and 1909. This is certainly a striking
commentary on the effectiveness of the 'exclusion' laws, for the second
figure cannot have been mainly due to natural increase. There can be
little doubt that the unquestioned multiplication of the race has been due
to illicit entry. One common route was by way of the Borneo coast;[13]
another, more direct, via the northern tip of Luzon.

The history of Chinese admixture with the native community follows
much the same general pattern as for other parts of Southeast Asia. For
centuries the Chinese intermarried freely with women of the country and
produced mestizos of Chinese-Filipino blood whose descendants were
absorbed into the general population of the country. The number of
Filipinos with a noticeable admixture of Chinese blood probably
amounted in the 1940s to more than three-quarters of a million. These
Chinese mestizos formed 'one of the most capable, prosperous and
powerful elements of the Filipino people'.[14] Yet, as we have remarked in
the case of Siam, a high proportion of Chinese blood in an individual is
no guarantee of his sympathy with the Chinese community, and, as
Filipino nationalism developed, the leaders who declaimed against the

[11] A. Ireland, *The Eastern Tropics* (N.Y., 1905), p. 232.
[12] R. M. Story, 'Problem of the Chinese in the Philippines', *American Soc. & Pol. Science
R.*, iii/1 (Feb. 1909), p. 30.
[13] The Moros of Zamboanga are said before the war to have charged 150 pesos, or $75, for
each Chinese they took in their *vintas* (F. Horn, *Orphans of the Pacific* (N.Y., 1941), p. 147).
[14] Hayden, *Philippines*, p. 695.

Chinese most violently had almost invariably Chinese blood in their veins.[15]

It is probable that the Chinese benefited from the change-over from Spanish to American control more than any other element of the population of the Philippines. The exclusion laws may have prevented the mass immigration of the race, but it managed, nevertheless, to multiply its numbers by about three. In the time of the Spanish control the legal disabilities imposed on the Chinese were arbitrary and unpredictable; under the Americans these disabilities were removed, and the reform of the administration meant that the Chinese were not subjected to exactions, except in some localities where they still had to pay a certain amount of tribute to minor political authorities.[16]

In 1904 a Chinese Commercial Council was established, which later developed into the Chinese General Chamber of Commerce.[17] This was to become the centre of Chinese business and social organization. Members were divided into two types—the score of rice merchants, grocers, second-hand dealers, &c, into which the Chinese Manila business community is divided, and Chinese business firms and individuals. The activities of this powerful organization were divided again into two categories, business and civic. On the business side the chamber collected and disseminated information about trade conditions, investigated and guaranteed the credentials of Chinese business men, arranged for the display of China products, conducted research into the problems and methods of business, and in any crisis or critical period provided a forum for discussion and machinery for action. On its civic side the chamber organized the collection of funds for charitable purposes, with an emphasis, no doubt, on causes favouring the Chinese, and after the outbreak of war with Japan relief for 'China distress' was the major object of the collections. But at the same time it raised funds on a considerable scale for Philippine undertakings such as the Red Cross, hospitals, &c. For the Chinese community itself the chamber maintained a school system,[18] a social club, a modern hospital, and a cemetery.

With the Chinese consul-general and the Philippine branch of the KMT the Chinese General Chamber of Commerce formed a trinity of organs for voicing views upon questions affecting the Chinese community to the Chinese Government as well as to the Philippine authorities and the public.

[15] 'There may well be over 1 million Chinese mestizos, including the very politician who wants to legislate the Chinese out of business' (Horn, p. 143).

[16] Hayden, *Philippines*, pp. 695 ff.

[17] Ibid. (Hayden is relied on in this chapter except where indicated.)

[18] Many Chinese children in the Philippines suffered under the double system whereby they learnt history, geography, arithmetic, &c, through the medium of Chinese in the morning, and the same, or similar, subjects through the medium of English in the afternoon. The strain was great and the minds of the children were confused and dulled in the process.

It is estimated that, before the systematic invasion of this field by the Japanese after 1932, the Chinese in the Philippines conducted between 70 and 80 per cent of the retail trade and a large percentage of the internal commerce of the islands. Approximately the same proportion of the commercial credit facilities was likewise in their hands. Regarding the situation immediately preceding the Pacific War, Mr Helmut G. Callis provides information which may be summarized as follows:

> Chinese predominate in the retail trade with U.S. $25 million investment; they own 75 per cent of the 2,500 rice-mills which are scattered throughout the islands. They control ten per cent of the capital invested in the lumber industry. Their influence in banking is not negligible. The total resources of the China Banking Corporation in Manila was $27 million in 1937, representing mainly capital of Chinese residents. About fifty new Chinese companies came into existence in 1937-9, with a capital of 1·5 million pesos—surpassed only by new registrations of American and Philippine companies. A great sum of money is said to have been invested by the Chinese in immovable property during this period, probably representing investments of Chinese profits which were not sent to China because of the war. Though statistical data are not available, it has been estimated that the total Chinese investments in the Philippines reach U.S. $100 million, which would give them the second place among nations doing business in the islands, Americans holding first place.[19]

The Chinese commercial and credit system covered virtually every business, and reached from Manila to the remotest corners of the archipelago. The trade organizations (which were members of the Chinese General Chamber of Commerce) were the old Chinese guilds adapted to Philippine laws and conditions. As has happened in other Southeast Asian countries, the control of these guilds over wages and conditions of labour has been replaced by State legislation, and trade secrets have also largely disappeared, but the associations have a wide scope for their activities in enforcing agreements regarding competition, credit, and wages, and for the promotion and protection of the interests of their members.[20]

Chinese wholesale business, with its salesmen and buyers covering every corner of the Philippines, supplied the Chinese provincial merchants and the smallest Chinese retailer. Behind the business houses, which were conducted either by an individual or by a family, were two Chinese banks, one of them, opened in 1939, being a branch of the Bank of Communications owned by the Chinese National Govern-

---

[19] H. G. Callis, *Foreign Capital in Southeast Asia* (N.Y., 1942, mimeo.), p. 21. Mr Callis estimates the total foreign investments in the Philippines, other than Chinese, at about U.S. $315 million (p. 21). In 1932 the Bureau of Insular Affairs estimated Chinese investments in the Philippines at 162,932,000 pesos, exclusive of real estate. This figure, says Hayden, was probably a great deal too low. At about the same time the Chinese consul-general put the figure at 201 million pesos (U.S. $100,500,000). A good deal of Chinese money was lost in the stock exchange collapse of 1937, most of it invested in worthless mines (Horn, *Orphans of Pacific*, p. 210).   [20] Hayden, *Philippines*, p. 698.

ment. There were also two other Manila banks in which a large amount of Chinese capital had been invested. In normal times there were approximately 15,000 Chinese mercantile and industrial firms in the Philippines, though in the years preceding the war with Japan, Japanese and Government-subsidized Filipino competition had reduced the number of Chinese firms. As in Siam and Indochina the Chinese largely financed the growing of rice, and to a great extent controlled its milling and distribution. This was a hold that the Philippines Government was trying to break. Chinese, too, practically controlled the retail trade in lumber and cut 40 per cent of the timber put on the market annually.[21]

As the undeveloped country in the Philippines was opened up the Chinese were in the van of those seeking for new commercial opportunities. In Cotabato, at the mouth of the Rio Grande de Cotabato, which drains an enormous territory in fast-developing Mindanao, most of the firms were Chinese. Chinese had traded throughout the Sulu Archipelago centuries before the Filipinos voluntarily entered that area. 'From these and other centres [says Hayden] Chinese traders penetrate to the uppermost reaches of jungle rivers, travel the remotest forest trails, and reach the most isolated coastal villages. Carrying in cotton and assorted trade goods, they bring out copra, hemp, gutta percha, and other native products.' They did not take up land partly because public land was not alienated to foreigners and partly because Chinese agricultural immigration was now forbidden.[22]

[21] Hayden, p. 699. But the actual share of the Chinese in the trade is not known.

	Imports from Philippines		Exports from China to Philippines		Total trade	
	Haikwan taels	Index no.	Haikwan taels	Index no.	Haikwan taels	Index no.
1868	280,700	100·0	163,197	100·0	443,897	100·0
1878	112,842	40·2	242,499	148·6	355,341	80·1
1888	68,402	24·4	314,249	192·6	382,651	86·4
1897	75,887	27·0	132,095	80·9	207,982	46·9
1898	14,133	5·0	85,718	52·5	99,851	22·5
1908	1,806,726	643·6	175,078	107·3	1,981,804	446·5
1918	3,193,324	1,137·7	2,153,227	1,319·4	5,346,751	1,204·3
1928	5,775,932	2,057·7	5,848,357	3,583·6	11,624,289	2,618·7
1933	2,730,000* (*U.S. $4,254,000)	972·6	3,497,000* (*$5,449,000)	2,141·6	6,228,000* (*$9,903,000)	1,403·0

From Ho Ping-yin, *The Foreign Trade of China* (Shanghai, 1935), p. 569.

[22] Hayden, *Philippines*, pp. 699, 700 says: 'Only very courageous men would live the lives of many of these Chinese traders. In 1931, the author travelled by river boat, horseback, and on foot across Mindanao from Cotabato to Davao over a route now traversed by a modern road. Through the centre of the Island the trail, which in places had to be hacked open by Bolos, wound through virgin forests inhabited by primitive peoples. Philippine officials insisted upon providing a constabulary escort for the expedition. In the heart of this wild

The Americans continued the land policy of the Spanish, so that in
1940 the Filipino still owned 90 per cent of the land of the islands. At
the same time it was observed that the Chinese were increasingly
anxious to obtain possession of soil which had yet to be tilled. As evidence of this an article in the *China Economic Journal* of January 1941
called attention to the opportunities that would be offered to Chinese
investors and settlers by an independent Philippines, and also to the ease
and cheapness with which Chinese born in the islands could obtain land
there even now. In Mindanao the Director of the Bureau of Non-
Christian tribes warned that the Chinese were already adopting a device
which the Japanese had successfully used in Havao, namely, marrying
pagan or Moro women and acquiring public land in the names of their
wives.[23]

Accentuation of the Chinese Question

It was not to be expected that the substitution of the go-ahead,
democratic control of the Americans for the languid, semi-feudal, and
semi-clerical regime of the Spanish would dispose of age-old problems in
a night. Indeed, when the United States had terminated its rule of forty-
eight years at least two notable problems of the Philippines, the agrarian
question and that of the Chinese, were still far from solution.

Outbreaks against the Chinese occurred under the American Government, but there was, of course, nothing to compare with the holocausts
of 1603 and 1639. The ruling power took no part in instigating or carrying out attacks on the Chinese, but, on the contrary, was stern in their
repression. Minor outbreaks of this sort were a feature of Philippine life,
but the most serious disorder between 1898 and 1950 occurred in 1924.
It is said to have originated in a rumour, entirely without foundation, to
the effect that a number of Filipino students had been killed by Chinese
in Canton or Hong Kong, and the feeling excited in the Philippines
brought forth one more story, that a Filipino baby had been killed by
local Chinese and parts of its body used as charms or medicine—a
counterpart, in reverse, of the Tientsin rumours of 1870, when similar
allegations were made by Chinese against Europeans. The first riot was
at Cabanatuan in Luzon, where the Chinese control of the business and
agriculture of a great rice region had made the area ripe for demonstrations of resentment. Further outbreaks took place in Manila and in other
Chinese centres, and the Philippine constabulary had to be used to

country was found a small *tienda*—just a counter, a dozen shelves and a place to sleep. The
proprietor, a Chinese, was absent, but we met him on the trail, returning from Davao with
two Manobo *cargadores* who carried on their backs his slender stock-in-trade. Few Americans,
Japanese, or Filipinos would have been willing to face the isolation and danger to which he
was cheerfully returning. This pioneer merchant was typical of the enterprise and determination which have brought such a large proportion of the trade of the frontier areas of the Far
East into their hands.'   [23] Ibid. p. 703.

restore order. Another attack upon the Chinese of more than average seriousness took place at San Pablo in February 1931.

But quite apart from their immediate causes or excuses these disturbances were indicative of the widespread feeling of hostility towards the Chinese, based on the conviction that they were an alien people endangering the livelihood of the Filipinos by their competition and against whom an occasional display of spleen was both legitimate and a temperamental necessity. The ordinary people required the moral support of indignation derived from a fable or alleged sharp practice before they would attack the Chinese, but Filipinos of the better-educated classes constantly thought of the Chinese as a sort of nagging pain in the Philippine economy. Many officials considered that redress through exactions from the Chinese shopkeepers and merchants in the shape of special licence fees by municipal councils or by demanding 'open-date credit' from them was not at all unreasonable, and when the Chinese acquiesced in the exactions as the price of their being left alone they were publicly accused of corrupting Filipino officialdom!

Much more serious than the sporadic outbursts of popular feeling were the Book-keeping Act of 1921 and other legislation directed specifically against the Chinese business community. The Book-keeping Act required that every merchant in the Philippines should keep accounts of his business in English, Spanish, or a local dialect.[24] The aim of this legislation was officially declared to be to put an end to the defrauding of the public treasury of millions of pesos annually by the 15,000 small Chinese shopkeepers, which had been made possible because of the inability of Filipino officials to check their books. The Chinese, quite naturally, were immediately 'up in arms'. The effect of the legislation, they declared, would be to compel every little Chinese barrio to employ a Filipino clerk and to reveal to their competitors all their trade secrets. Its motive, they said, was to feather the nest of certain politicians by forcing the Chinese to bribe them to prevent the law being carried into effect. The last allegation, ironically enough, was responsible for dissuading Filipino politicians who regarded the law as unjust from voting for its repeal since, if they did so, their opponents would say that they had been bribed by the Chinese!

The Chinese business community of the Philippines, regarding the Book-keeping Law as the test case *par excellence* of their right to carry on trade under conditions of justice, marshalled their forces to fight the matter and to their aid rallied their compatriots in China, the United States, Canada, the Netherlands, and in the business centres of Southeast Asia. European counsel were employed to state the case against the Act with all their resources of legal argument. At the request of Governor-General Leonard Wood, the Philippine legislature postponed the

[24] Hayden, *Philippines*, pp. 705 ff.

execution of the statute, but refused to modify it in any substantial degree. Failing to secure the repeal of the law, or its annulment by Congress, the Chinese took the case to the Supreme Court of the United States, which declared the Act unconstitutional.

In their official memorandum for the information of the Supreme Court, the Philippine Chinese declared that the matter was vastly more than local, more than a domestic regulation. It had, they said, an international character of profound importance. If the law were allowed to go into effect (the memorandum continued) it was not unreasonable to suppose that retaliation would result. China might pass a law requiring American merchants to keep their books of account in Chinese, which would be an end of American business in China.[25]

The Philippine legislature was, however, not prepared to accept the Supreme Court's decision as a final defeat. In 1926 it enacted a new Book-keeping Law, drafted so as to meet constitutional requirements; but Chinese opposition again made it inadvisable to enforce it, nor did amendments passed in 1934 make the measure workable. In 1935 the Philippines became a Commonwealth, and the following year the Government, resuming the battle, introduced a new amendment to the law which permitted commercial books to be kept in a language other than a native language or English or Spanish, but required that all entries therein should be translated into one or other of the three recognized languages, and certified under oath by the book-keeper or manager of the company concerned. Again, the Chinese through their Chamber of Commerce intervened to delay the bringing into force of the law, with the result that President Quezon prevailed upon the legislature to grant a year before it should become effective.

Legislative acts to keep the Chinese under control were one set of weapons against the Chinese; the Government-stimulated or subsidized organizations to compete with them were another set, and, on the face of it, much more promising of results. For years previously, privately sponsored organizations had sought to stimulate Filipino production for Filipino consumption. The Ang Bagong Katipunan in 1930-1 and later the National Economic Protective Association conducted campaigns to this end. Early in 1940 the National Trading Corporation was established and provided with capital from Government funds. This activity was an extension of the provisions of the constitution of the Commonwealth of the Philippines (art. xii, sect. 1) which limited the exploitation

[25] 'What (asks Hayden) would the suggested retaliation have been if the outraged Chinese had been dealing with an independent Philippine Republic instead of the United States of America ' (Chinese accounts, I can state from experience when I was official assignee and liquidator of companies, Penang (1926-9), kept by shopkeepers and small traders are not complicated. There are a day-book and a ledger and (usually but not invariably) a stock-book. The Chinese are very jealous of their trade secrets, and in Malaya were opposed to registration of partnerships. V. P.)

of the islands to citizens of the Philippines or to corporations of which at least 60 per cent of the capital was owned by such citizens, and (art. xiii) which made similar provision with regard to public utilities.[26] The object of the National Trading Corporation was, as its president declared, to 'break the stranglehold of foreign retailers' upon the Philippine trade.

Action closely parallel to that taken in Siam in 1947 was taken in the Philippines in 1941 when the Manila Municipal Board passed an ordinance prohibiting all persons from engaging in any form of business in the public markets except citizens of the Philippines or the United States, three years' grace being granted to alien holders of market stalls. Chinese were the holders of practically all these stalls, and the ordinance was therefore immediately followed by a protest from the Chinese consul-general to the United States high commissioner, declaring that the ordinance violated treaties between China and the United States and would throw thousands of Chinese out of work. Although supported by a suggestion from the high commissioner that apart from its legality the ordinance 'might have an unfavourable effect in the field of international relations', the protest was disregarded and the law remained.

It must not be concluded, however, that the attitude of the Commonwealth was altogether uncompromising. So far as establishing the Filipino trade went, it was resolute in its principles, but it strove to avoid provocation of the Chinese. President Quezon explained in a speech that 'foreigners, aside from their rights recognized in international law and our own laws . . . have the further right to be treated with equity and justice, because they have helped in the development of our country when our own people were not engaging in business enterprises'.[27] What, however, the Filipino business men had the right to expect from their Government, and what it was creating for them (President Quezon went on) was banking institutions, facilities for trade and communication, and new opportunities to engage in trade and industry. But the Filipino must stand on his own merits. He must make his way through earnest, intelligent, and determined effort; he must be prepared to meet fair competition. At the same time the Government could not adopt a policy that in any way might be interpreted as antagonistic to foreigners.[28]

In his annual message to the National Assembly in 1941 President

---

[26] Hayden, *Philippines*, pp. 838, 840, app. ii.

[27] Address at the inauguration of the Philippine Chamber of Commerce (29 July 1938) (ibid. pp. 708 and 945 n. 20).

[28] In 1933, when Tomas Confesor, Director of the Bureau of Commerce, had stated that if Filipinos were to supplant the Chinese by 'legitimate' (i.e. non-political) means they would have to develop the economic efficiency of the Chinese and perform for the community the services now performed by the Chinese, he had brought upon his head a storm of Filipino indignation (see ibid. p. 700).

Quezon found himself able to state that Filipino participation in the retail trade of the country had increased from between 15 and 20 per cent at the time of the inauguration of the Commonwealth to approximately 37 per cent in 1939. Filipinos, he declared, now outnumbered the merchants of all other nationalities in the retail trade and controlled a greater number of retail stores.[29]

As has been remarked, and should be repeated, the Filipino politician who finds himself impelled to declare that 'something must be done about the Chinese' is very likely to proclaim by his eyes and by the bone structure of his face that one or more of his ancestors was Chinese. The same anomaly is found in Siam. But what may be an historical or philosophical irony may also be a practical irrelevance, since racial antecedents are of small importance beside national sentiment and political expediency. Pressed as to his case against the Chinese, the Filipino politician would say that the Chinese were too numerous, that they had more than half of the retail business in their hands, that they charged too high prices, cheated in weights and measures, and made high profits. Should it be objected that if this were so all the Filipino had to do was to open up a *tienda* on his own and put the Chinese out of business in the village, the politician would probably shift his ground. He would now say that the Chinese standard of living is deplorably low; the owner of a Chinese *tienda* is willing to live in a small corner of his store, he eats almost nothing and works day and night; so does his family and his assistant as well if he has one. The Chinese in Manila, he says, persistently disregard the eight-hour law. In fine, the charge now is that the Chinese runs his business with too little, not with too great, overhead expenses and profits. If this is true, then the Chinese give excellent service to the community as distributors. The Filipino can buy cheaply because the Chinese live so meagrely.[30]

This argument is followed up by an appeal to the fear in the listener of the Chinese power. If they used their control of the retail trade as a weapon they could paralyse the economy of the country in a single night. (This does not seem actually to have happened in the Philippines, but it did happen in Bangkok in 1910.)

Then there is the charge of usury. The Chinese who keeps the local *tienda* lends money to the Filipino at extortionate rates of interest. The result is that the Filipino is everlastingly in debt to the Chinese. That the Filipino is always in debt to the Chinese is undoubtedly true, but the evidence is all to the effect that the Filipino *cacique* is even more oppressive and usurious.

---

[29] On the other hand, the provincial commercial supervisor of Pangasinan, a rich province of central Luzon, reported that in December 1938, only 2 per cent of the retail trade and of the wholesale dealing in the staple crops was in the hands of Filipinos (ibid. p. 711).

[30] The above is summarized from Horn, *Orphans of Pacific*, pp. 142–3.

Finally the politician's charge is that the Chinese own the country's rice-mills. It is probable that before the Pacific War 75 per cent of the Philippine rice-mills were owned by Chinese. The *tao* (peasant) sells rice to the mill which often acts also as a banker and money-lender. Frequently the Chinese mill is the only buyer of rice in a given locality and the price given is what the mill will pay.[31] The cure for this, in any case, would not be Filipino-owned rice-mills but something in the nature of marketing co-operative organizations set up with Government aid and encouragement.[32]

In this vexed question of the Chinese domination of the rice trade, there is some expert evidence forthcoming which tends to refute the assertion that the excessive profits of the middleman explain the low returns to the grower and the high cost of rice to the consumer. In a study of the marketing of rice in Nueva Ecija conducted by the college of agriculture at Los Baños not long before the war with Japan it was found that comparing prices paid to farmers by Cabanatuan mills with the wholesale price of rice in Manila the difference, on margin, was relatively small. In terms of the wholesale price of rice in Manila, the farmer in Nueva Ecija received on the average 87 per cent, while the Chinese rice merchant received a margin of 13 per cent. Of this margin 4 per cent represented milling costs, and 3·9 per cent railway freight, 2·1 per cent marketing costs, and 3 per cent profit to the miller or wholesaler.[33] The same authority continues:

The results of the survey show that the Chinese merchants are performing essential marketing services at a fairly low cost. It is therefore evident that for the Filipinos to displace the Chinese in the rice trade they must be able to render marketing services at margins equal to, or still lower than, those now received by them. For co-operative marketing by farmers to be successful the same condition obtains.

The Chinese engaged in the business even before the Spanish regime in the Philippines. They have the experience and trade ties with other Chinese in neighbouring countries. It seems that the Filipino is not by nature so good a business man as the Chinese, though Government officials, from President Quezon down, have been optimistic regarding the ability of the Filipino to learn the rice business within ten years from *c.* 1941 after which complete nationalization was foreseen.[34]

Considering how popular fury had so often been worked up against the Chinese retailer 'drawing off the riches' of the country and squeezing out the native Filipino by his relentless competition, it is curious to note

---

[31] The same complaint would apply to tobacco areas where the Tabacalera is the sole buyer.
[32] Horn, *Orphans of Pacific*, p. 145.
[33] H. H. Miller, *Principles of Economics Applied to the Philippines* (Boston, 1932), pp. 198–9, cited in California, Food Research Inst., *The Rice Economy of Monsoon Asia* (1941), p. 182.
[34] In 1936 the National Rice Corporation (NARIC) was created.

how unimpressive the ordinary Chinese *tienda* is. This is also true of the country shops and booths of the Chinese in other parts of Southeast Asia. The average Chinese shop in the Philippines is a miserable little *nipa* shack[35] with small stocks of food and cheap household articles. (There is an aroma, too, about it of shrimp paste, kerosene oil, and dried fish.) The Chinese shopkeeper does not look at all prosperous and he cares less for his clothes and his cleanliness than does the average Filipino. Yet it is certain that he is not as poor as he looks, and it is probable that a large percentage of the villagers owe him money.

The balance-sheet of the value or detriment of the Chinese to the Philippine Islands, so far as we can ascertain it, consists of debit or credit items presented by detractors or apologists. Each item calls for careful scrutiny in the light of the facts and the motive of the person stating it, and at the end the reader should be able to decide whether the balance should be written in black ink or red.

The Chinese memorandum to Congress on the occasion of the appeal against the Book-keeping Act does not neglect the appeals of rhetoric, of which the basis was derived from the Chinese themselves and which was given by expert American advocates the form and finish that would appeal to American elder statesmen. Here is an example:

> The Chinese merchants are not newcomers. They are as much a part of the Philippine Islands as the hills and valleys and streams of that beautiful archipelago. No one knows when they came, as they came at a time when the memory of man runneth not to the contrary. . . . When the Spaniards came to the Islands first, in 1520, they found Chinese merchants doing all the commercial business of the Islands. It is hardly possible to call them foreigners—they are a part and parcel of Philippine life. They have never failed to answer any call for public service. They constitute the commercial class of the Islands just as the Filipinos are the official and the farming class. The existence of one is just as essential as that of the other for a proper functioning of the life of the Philippine Islands. Each has his task to perform. The officials govern; the farmers produce; but it is the merchants who pay the bills, because the greater part of the taxes for the maintenance of the Government comes from them. . . . The Chinese merchant is more than a merchant; he carries on the commercial end of the Philippine industrial life. These merchants, thus scattered throughout the provinces, loan money to the Filipinos to aid them in growing and marketing their crops. The Chinese merchant buys their crops. He exports them and brings to them in return the commodities they need. Chinese merchants constitute the very essence of the commercial life of the Islands. No complaints are heard of their dealings. They are universally recognized as fair, honest, and square. Their reputation is higher than the reputation of any similar body of merchants to be found elsewhere in the world. . . .

The memorandum pointed out that the Chinese merchant is not peculiar to the Philippines. He is to be found throughout Oceania, in the Nether-

---

[35] So Florence Horn observes, but a critic, commenting on this, remarks, 'This is going much too far!'

lands Indies, in Malaya, in French Indochina, and in other quarters of the globe. In no other instance than this 'had sovereignty presumed to enact such an unconscionable and unendurable law'.[36]

So much for the very understandable Chinese point of view. Sympathy, however, must not altogether be denied to the Filipino statesmen in their avowed political goal of the creation of a representative democracy. 'The domination of the business of the country [says Dr Hayden] by a powerful and unassimilable foreign element in the population does not make this admittedly difficult task any easier.' This outstanding authority on the politics of the Philippines before the Second World War continues in these words:[37]

What would be the effect upon American local, state and national government, were three-quarters of the 'business men', including the bankers and the 'produce merchants' engaged in the distribution of the basic foodstuffs of virtually every city, county, town, and village in the land, aliens who had no votes, no interest in government save to protect themselves from it or to use it, and no devotion to the political institutions of the nation? What would American politics be were 75 per cent of all taxes on business to be paid by this same group of aliens who possessed no legitimate control over government agencies for levying and collection of taxes and the regulation of business? Few, indeed, would say that the prospects of good government or democratic government would be bright under such conditions. Yet in the Philippines, which until three decades ago, was an autocratically governed Spanish colony, precisely such conditions exist.

In the Philippines the Chinese were, and are, the easiest political target. The Americans and the Spaniards had a far larger share of the profits from the islands, but concerning them the Filipino politicians were generally silent; it was the Chinese who were the scapegoats for oratory and the objects for discrimination. In November 1939 Manuel Quezon devoted an entire speech to threats against the Chinese and to promises to set up the Filipinos in business. At just about the same time Quezon was offering haven to 10,000 Jewish exiles from Europe! They were to be settled in an agricultural colony in Mindanao. The Chinese wondered at this generous hospitality. They knew, no doubt, that, like themselves, the Jews ended up in trade no matter how they started life in any country.[38]

Finally, the Chinese (as elsewhere) were accused of drawing off capital from the country. After the outbreak of war between China and Japan

[36] Hayden, *Philippines*, pp. 709–10.   [37] Ibid. p. 711–12.
[38] See Horn, *Orphans of Pacific*, p. 146. This was speedily exemplified. The following is an extract from the *North China Daily News* of 29 Jan. 1947: Jews who came to the Philippines before the war as refugees from Nazi rule were recently found to have violated the conditions upon which they were admitted. A Department of Justice official said that these Jews were admitted into the country by the late Commonwealth President Manuel L. Quezon on condition that they settle only in sparsely populated areas and engage in agricultural pursuits. Contrary to this condition, the official said, most of them settled in Manila and other commercial centres and are at present engaged in business other than agriculture.

they contributed to Chiang Kai-shek's war chest as well as to the support of their families at home. It was estimated that sums exceeding U.S. $6 million had gone out of the Philippines to China between 1937 and 1941. One close observer of Philippine affairs remarks that these remittances appear to have been the only real drain which the Chinese have made on the economy of the Philippines and a control of them not only would prevent the Chinese sending wealth from the country 'out of proportion to the economic benefits which their presence brings', but also would provide a simple, indirect, and (at least on the surface) non-discriminatory means of controlling immigration. The difficulty would be to make the estimation required by the phrase italicized.

On 2 May 1940 the Philippine National Assembly passed an Act providing that not more than 500 'quota immigrants of any one nationality' might be admitted into the islands in any one calendar year. This law established a national 'non-discriminatory' immigration policy designed to protect the Philippines from mass immigration. The Filipino action was taken in face of 'grave warnings' from the Government of Japan issued directly to the Commonwealth (and, it was reported, repeated to Washington) and a milder protest from the Chinese consul-general in Manila. President Roosevelt, ignoring Japanese objections, granted approval to the law.[39]

The Philippines are nearer to the China ports than other Southeast Asian countries. In the old days migration between the Philippines and China was not so frequent as it has since become. Many of the richer Chinese used to maintain one household in Canton or Amoy and another in Manila or Cebu, but in the immediate pre-war years this was ceasing to be the case, and China was becoming the sole family centre with increased ties with the ancestral country, and more and more Chinese merchants retired to China. It was estimated, too, that before the Japanese war more than two hundred children of Chinese business men were sent annually to the mainland for education. Chinese nationalism was thus increasingly claiming the Philippine Chinese as its own, though the majority of them were still born of Filipino mothers and most of their descendants continued to be absorbed eventually into the Filipino people.[40]

No view of the Chinese which tries to take in both sides of the medal will find favour either with the Chinese or their critics. The former regard themselves as persecuted or unreasonably differentiated against, and will

[39] Hayden, *Philippines*, p. 691.
[40] Ibid. pp. 697, 712. Claude A. Buss in his article on the Philippines in L. A. Mills and associates, *The New World of Southeast Asia* (Minneapolis, 1949), p. 21, says: 'For some unaccountable reason, the children of mixed marriages between Spanish and Filipinos (like Quezon) or between Chinese and Filipinos (like Sergio Osmena) have come to be regarded as distinct social assets, while children of mixed marriages between Americans and Filipinos or illegitimate children of the liberation are often faced with unpleasant social barriers ,

accept no other solution than that they should be subjected to no restrictions or regulations of any sort which do not equally apply to Filipinos. The Filipinos, for their part, have no difficulty in finding a moral as well as a legal justification for their legislative or administrative actions. These rigid partisan attitudes (as is always the case in politics) cut across the human instinct for compromise. In the villages, the peasant who regards the Chinese traders as his oppressors and the authors of his misfortunes is yet, consciously or subconsciously, aware that they provide a distribution service which he himself could not reproduce either in this generation or the next, and, while he resents the Chinese proprietor of the *tienda*, he would think himself very lucky to obtain him as the husband for his prettiest daughter, for with him as *pariente* the whole family would never be in want. He knows him to be frugal and economical where he himself is shiftless. In the words of Hayden (p. 712), 'A permanent settlement of the issues involved can be reached only by applying the principle of equity, as well as of law; by exercise of patience and caution; and by a mutual recognition of conflicting points of view'. Unfortunately such a solution is likely to be found only when a completely impartial authority is holding the scales of justice. But even when under the Commonwealth the Americans still had a large measure of final control, they were able only to soften the impact of the Filipino offensive; after July 1946, when the complete independence of the Philippines was promised, the tribunal of power was likely to be influenced by political considerations, and the Chinese were likely to be in a worse plight. Politicians are never their own masters, at liberty to obey the dictates of their own consciences or to adopt the abstract standards of justice and humanity; to remain in power they must play up to the prejudices of their electorates. As it turned out the Chinese received little benefit from the advance of Philippine democracy.

55

BEFORE AND AFTER INDEPENDENCE

THE Pacific War created an entirely new pattern in Southeast Asian politics—so much so that the observer who was fairly closely in touch with the situation in 1940 would, if he did not return to Southeast Asia until 1948 and had not kept himself up to date with a close study of

---

[1] Mr Chu-pei Chen informs the writer that while the majority of the Chinese living in the islands are adherents of the Roman Catholic faith, ancestor-worship is also carried on in the average Chinese family. On All Souls' Day Chinese Christians, Catholic or Protestant, join their relatives in ancestor-worship at the Chinese cemetery, and are distinguished from the non-Christian Chinese only by not burning incense and not kneeling before the tomb or shrine.

reports, find himself almost unable to recognize what he saw. The basic elements, perhaps, had not changed, but some of them had developed so disproportionately, and the arrangement was so different, that the change amounted in effect to one of kind.

In the Philippines the situation of the Chinese may conveniently be described under three heads, (a) political, (b) economic, and (c) the immigration and repatriation questions.

Before the war the activity of the Chinese Communists in the islands was slight. The Chinese 'left-wingers' had their centre in Manila known as the Tion Hwa Tian (China Hall) located in Alvarado Street. It was believed that their membership did not exceed 1,000. They denied that they were Communists. Their mouthpiece was the *Kim Kuo Press* (bi-monthly) with a minute circulation. During the first year of the Japanese occupation the Chinese Communists began to get to work and created anti-Japanese organizations without at first revealing their political affiliations. They had at least one underground newspaper, and organized students and young shop assistants, especially the latter who were disgruntled because the shops in which they worked were closed. Later on they filtered into the neighbouring provinces and started a military training base. Classes on guerrilla warfare were held. A considerable group of officers who later organized the Hwa Chi combat units and joined the Hukbalahaps and the United States armed forces during the liberation were products of these military training classes. During the occupation a Communist guerrilla unit travelled Luzon playing hide-and-seek with the Japanese.[2]

Meanwhile the KMT also organized three guerrilla units, namely the Philippine Chinese Volunteer Corps under the command of Sy Yat-sien, the head of the KMT, the COHEM (*Hsüeh Kan Tuan*) headed by Li Hai-jo, and the Philippines Chinese Youth Corps under Lin Cho-mei. Li and Lin had been sent to the Philippines to organize the San Min Chu I Youth Corps shortly before the war. However, these three KMT units did not co-operate very well and were not engaged in active combat. They were mostly occupied in underground anti-Japanese propaganda activities. Only after the liberation were some of Sy Yat-sien's and Li Hai-jo's men incorporated into the U.S. armed forces in mopping up Japanese remnants near Baguio and other regions.

During the battle for Manila in the last phase of the war both the Communist and KMT guerrillas aided the Americans, acting as guides and providing guards for bridges against Japanese dynamiters. The two units each set up a headquarters, but that of the Communists had much the more militant appearance. Both units obtained recognition from the

---

[2] The commanders of the left-wing guerrilla forces were Uy Kiat, Chua Kien-hua, Tan Chon-sien, chief of staff, and Ong Seh-hsiün, commander of the Hwa Chi 48th Unit, later incorporated into the Hukbalahaps.

United States army by sending new forces to the front, but both soon incurred the displeasure of the high command by engaging in rival political action within the local community.

With the Japanese removed from the scene, the Communists came into the open, taking over the campus of the Philippine Chinese high school as headquarters of the League of the Philippine Anti-Japanese and Puppets, and they placed all Communist-affiliated organizations under their control. This was now the centre of left-wing activity in Manila. At the same time a 'people's court' was set up to try persons accused of collaboration. The first persons summoned before it were Yu Khethai, pre-war supreme leader of the Chinese community and president of the Resist-the-Enemy Association, and Justo Cabo Chan, the last puppet president of the Chinese Association, who had survived the assassination drive of the Communist guerrillas. Yu, however, did not answer the summons, and Chan, being under the custody of the Americans, could not come.

In the post-war Chinese community of the Philippines, the most vexed issue was that of wartime 'collaboration' with the Japanese. It was precisely similar to the situation in other Chinese communities in the Nanyang, notably Malaya. In the long period of three years under the Japanese many prominent, law-abiding Chinese had been forced to join the puppet Chinese Association. It is true that most of them were inactive and reluctant to participate in any activity under the association, such as Yu Khe-thai, the Sycip brothers, and others; but in the eyes of the left-wingers they were all collaborators and should be punished accordingly. Between the *Great China Daily News*, the post-war KMT paper, and the *Chinese Guide*, the Communist official organ, a desperate press war now ensued. The Communist organ also attacked Roxas and a number of other Filipino officials.

Meanwhile the Communists were intent on taking the law into their own hands. In the early days of the liberation a ring known as the Hing Han Chu Chien Tuan, whose aim was the liquidation of Chinese collaborators, swung into action. It was believed that Tan Tien-hon, secretary of the Chinese Association, Go Co-lai, first president of the association, and Ty Han-kee, Go's successor, were victims of this ring. The leader was an unidentified bloodthirsty Communist military leader who was known as the 'Flying Tiger'. Other victims of the ring were Chan Chin, a student consul of the Chinese consulate in Manila, who was believed to have been a collaborator in the Japanese 'buy-and-sell' scheme, and Uy Ken-sien, connected with Nishimura's Kempeitai (military police), who were assassinated immediately after the liberation.

During the occupation the Chinese Communists had established contacts with the Filipino Communists. After the liberation, the Hwa Chi 48th Combat Unit, commanded by Captain Ong Seh-hsiün (who was believed to have been connected with the 8th Route Army in China, and who was a very able man) was incorporated into the Hukbalahaps, the Filipino agrarian insurgents who were now in a state of open rebellion against the Government.[3] In Batangas, in Luzon province, the constabulary seized a number of Chinese Communists in one raid. It is believed that they had 'cells' in other parts of Luzon, especially in the northern tip, which is the landing point of junks smuggling Chinese immigrants into the islands as well as into other islands of Southeast Asia.

Young men and girls were organized and indoctrinated through a 'research society', a 'debating society', a 'library society', and other branches. These novices were required to live in the premises of the organization so as to be completely under its influence and without any outside contamination.

Besides these activities, the Chinese Communists were suspected of assassination and terrorism. A clerk of the Chinese consulate, who worked for the Japanese during the occupation and was one of the only two survivors of the Japanese massacre of the Chinese consular staff, was shot within two weeks of the liberation—by Communist agents, it was alleged. The same body assassinated two wealthy Chinese who had served as chairmen of the Chinese Association during the occupation.[4]

These internal dissensions in the Chinese community continued with increasing bitterness. When the Philippines became an independent republic there would be a reorientation of policy, and, though the Philippines would remain within the American diplomatic and economic orbit, it was likely that the Government would be more vigorous than before in dealing with disturbances among the Chinese in the Philippines. In September of that year, sixty-one Chinese were detained some hours for questioning, and raids were conducted on the *Chinese Guide* and the *Chinese Commercial Bulletin* (newspapers that termed themselves independent), the Chinese Labour Federation office, a Chinese Y.M.C.A. school, the Hung Kwong Institute, and the Chinese Union high school. This action the police called 'crime investigation'.[5]

These raids threw the Chinese community into an 'apprehensive

---

[3] 'Philippine economy is rooted in the feudal economy of sixteenth-century Spain, which the conquistadores implanted on Philippine soil. The half-century of American occupation brought about a substantial advancement in education, public health, self-government, and an increasing national income, but it did not create a middle class of any size, and the bulk of the newly created income went to the Government, the landlords, and the urban areas. In spite of large schemes for nationalizing land, little was done in effect to ameliorate conditions among the feudal peasantry or to replace the backward agricultural economy.' So says Hernando J. Abaya, *Betrayal in the Philippines* (N.Y., 1946), pp. 206 ff. During the Japanese occupation there came into being the Hukbalahaps or militant peasant army of the resistance movement. The name is from the Tagalog *Hukbo Ng Bayan Laban Sa Hapon*, or People's Anti-Japanese Army.

[4] The report of Mr Arthur M. Goul, United Press correspondent in the Philippines, published in the *North China Daily News* of 7 Apr. 1948, has been closely followed in the above account.   [5] *New York Times* (6 Sept. 1946).

furore', since they were the climax of a long period of acute political tension among the Chinese of the Philippines which reflected divisions in the Chinese homeland. It seemed that each of the two, or several, factions had been 'informing' the police against the other or others. Certain Chinese generals living in the Philippines were declared by ultra-conservative Chinese groups to be subversive, and these groups requested Zulueta, the Secretary of the Interior, to deport them. Other elements in the Chinese community decried such a move. Right-wingers also charged the Chinese left-wingers with aiding the Hukbalahaps, but at that time no responsible authority in the Philippine Government could confirm the charge. On 7 September it was reported that indiscriminate raids by the military police on the Chinese were halted by President Roxas because of the possibility that they might be misinterpreted by the Chinese or by their sympathizers abroad. A Government spokesman explained that the raids resulted from complaints that some individuals frequenting the offices of Chinese newspapers were connected with lawless elements, and with a kidnapping ring which had been preying on prominent members of the Chinese community.

Although for the first two years, or thereabouts, after the liberation no positive evidence came to light of any association between the Chinese Communists and the agrarian revolt, it was clear that the Communists in general intended as a policy to support and make use of every dissident movement in countries which were not under a Communist Government. But until such evidence was forthcoming, the foreign observer of liberal mind was inclined to regard the charge as part of an attempt in Southeast Asia to identify all nationalist or liberation movements of whatever sort with Communism. In the Philippines it was well known that the agrarian unrest was to some extent the natural and justifiable result of the grievances arising from an obsolete system of land tenure inherited from the Spanish regime, and one which the Americans had not succeeded in replacing. But in the latter months of 1947 reports that the Chinese Communists were in league with the Hukbalahaps were not easily dismissed.

Early in September Major Napoleon Valeriano, commander of the military police commandos widely known as the 'skull unit', and acting military commander of Pampanga, declared that he had positive proof of the existence of an all-Chinese Hukbalahap squadron acting in and around Manila.[6] It was believed that most of the arms possessed by the Communists and the rebels were obtained from the Japanese, though some were served out by the U.S. forces.

[6] *Manila Bull.* (2 Sept. 1947).
The present writer passed through Hukbalahap country in November 1947 when attending the United Nations Conference at Baguio. The Government provided a heavy military escort, for ambushes were fairly frequent.

The taking of justice into their own hands by the Communists and their 'people's court' after the liberation had, as in Malaya, prejudiced the action that the properly constituted authorities were in the meantime undertaking or contemplating. In Communist eyes any person who accepted employment or public appointment under the Japanese was a 'collaborator'. The effect of this attitude was that almost every Chinese who had been at all prominent or had held any property before the war was put in this class, for the simple reason that only those who had no stake in the country and had no family to protect or support could take to the hills and join the guerrillas. The Communists were ready besides with accusations and 'evidence' against anyone they happened to dislike, and of their charges authorities were naturally suspicious. The net result was that many who had been guilty of collaboration escaped punishment. But action against suspected collaborators did continue in a desultory way, and in November 1947 fifty Chinese-born persons, naturalized Filipinos, were 'screened' to decide whether or not they should be prosecuted for treason during the Japanese occupation. In the following January the screening by the Philippine constabulary was extended so as to cover, it seemed, the whole of the Chinese population; but how far this action had anything to do with suspected collaboration with the Japanese, and how far it was a round-up of Communists and others is a matter of opinion. In the meantime, in November, a clash between Chinese Communists and KMT supporters was expected at any moment.[7]

About this time Alfonso Z. Sycip, president of the Chinese Chamber of Commerce, was ordered to conduct a census of Chinese residents, and to submit a report. Five Chinese, black-listed by the provincial (? Pampanga) command, were already under investigation. Faction fights among the Chinese Nationalists, who had indiscriminately accused their opponents of being Communists, had stirred the constabulary to action. There were, however, enough genuine Communists in Manila and elsewhere to keep the police busy. In March 1948 Senator Salipada Pendatun, speaking in the Philippines Senate, and quoting a secret report of Government intelligence agents, asserted that there were now 10,000 Chinese Communists in Manila and the provinces. He accused them of the murder of 200 Chinese since the liberation. He mentioned incidentally that 45 Russians were registered with the Bureau of Immigration, and that 150 other Russians were classified as 'Stateless'. He claimed that the purely Russian group was under the control of 'an invisible hand' in Manila, and he asserted that during the meeting of the U.N. Economic Commission for Asia and the Far East, held at Baguio in November and December, the Russian Communists in Manila had made contact with the Russian delegates to the conference.[8]

[7] *North China Daily News* (2 Nov. 1947).   [8] Ibid. (18 Mar. 1948).

It seemed inevitable, with the transition from underground to open action by the Communists in Malaya, Burma, and in Indonesia in the middle months of 1948 that, if these operations were successful, or even if they were not, the Philippines would not in the long run be omitted from the campaign.

This Communist activity belongs to what might be called the horizontal splitting-up of society according to affiliations of its layers with either the bourgeoisie or the proletariat, as distinguished from the vertical splitting which arose from differences of race, tribe, and clan. The Philippines authorities were conscious of this grid interaction, and, while they could depend on some support from the Chinese trading class in their offensive against the Communist elements, they were hostile to the KMT which was still angling for power. Thus it was that when the old question of holding elections among the Chinese residing in the Philippines in connexion with the elections in China, which had been a source of friction for years between the Governments of Southeast Asia and the National Government of China, came again to the fore, the Philippines Government was prepared to take a strong line. In October 1947 Quirino, the Secretary for Foreign Affairs, advised a Chinese delegation that the Philippine Government would not allow local Chinese to hold elections.[9] The Chinese minister to the Philippines, Mr Chen Chih-ping, advised the Nanking Government to this effect, and on 22 October Dr George Yeh, Vice-Minister for Foreign Affairs, told a press conference at Nanking that new regulations covering the participation of Overseas Chinese in the coming national elections would shortly be published, as a result of protests from the Philippines, Siam, the United States, and other countries. It had been represented in the diplomatic exchanges (Dr Yeh said) that China's attempt to hold its elections on foreign soil constituted an infringement of the sovereignty of these countries. China, he said, had a particular problem because of the overwhelming number of Chinese nationals who would be represented in the National Government. The question of dual nationality had already been raised, and no Chinese would be allowed to vote unless he had already been registered at the Chinese consulate and had formally renounced his citizenship of the country he was living in.

Simultaneously 'a well-informed Foreign Office source' confirmed that a notification had been sent to the local Chinese legation to the effect that the holding of an election by Chinese nationals in the Philippines would be regarded as an infringement of the sovereignty of the Philippine Republic. However, the same spokesman said, the Philippine Foreign Office would have no objection if local Chinese nationals were to conduct their elections in the same manner as the United States armed forces in the Philippines cast their votes at the Presidential elections. The

[9] *Manila Bull.* (23 Oct. 1947).

course that would be acceptable to the Philippine Foreign Office would be for the Chinese Government to send their nationals the ballots and forms to be filled in, and that these should be sent back to China for counting. The Philippine Government, it was understood, would not countenance the local holding of election meetings, rallies, and campaigns by Chinese nationals for their forthcoming national elections.[10]

It is doubtful, however, whether Filipino public opinion took these political questions half as seriously as it did the economic pressure of the Chinese. It was always possible to arouse the intensest resentment by any mention of the latter subject. As early as October 1945 a trade nationalization bill aimed at the Chinese was stopped only by the presidential veto. The Press Secretary, Mauro Mendez, explained that President Osmena had favoured the measure, but had been forced to reject it because he 'couldn't afford to antagonize the Chinese Government so long as that Government remains friendly to the United States, which controls our foreign policies'.[11]

Though Brigadier-General Manuel Roxas, when candidate for the Presidency of the Philippine Republic, disavowed any anti-Chinese animus in his statement to the representative newspapers, one of his own organs, the *Daily Star*, was an outspoken baiter of the Chinese, indicating the likelihood of this sentiment becoming a campaign issue.[12] One newspaper correspondent stated at this time that 'a miasma of Axis ideology still hovers over ground ostensibly liberated nearly a year ago' and was responsible for a rising tide of animosity against resident Chinese and other national minorities, and suggested that the traditional Filipino aptitude for study had not been dormant during the three years of Axis indoctrination.[13] Scarcely a day passed in Manila without some expression of resentment against alien participation in the social and economic affairs of the nation. Though the Chinese were the primary target, the aim was spreading in the use of such expressions as 'foreigners' and 'aliens'. The next most openly attacked group after the Chinese were the Jewish refugees.[14]

In March 1947 a proposed Sino-Philippines treaty of amity was halted on the verge of signature. The question of sovereign rights came into the dispute, but the rights of Chinese nationals to engage in trade within the Philippines was the real sticking-point between the two countries. Vice-President Quirino had sought to eliminate a reference to this type of trade, reserving it for inclusion in a separate treaty of commerce, but in

[10] *Manila Bull.* (23 Oct. 1947).   [11] *Christian Science Monitor* (12 Jan. 1946).
[12] Assemblyman Sato, whose grandfather was pure Chinese, started an anti-Chinese league. During the post-war Presidential elections he was a strong supporter of Manuel Roxas. When the latter became President he entered the National Assembly and introduced several anti-Chinese Bills including one to reduce the immigration quota for Chinese from 500 to 50. His league supported by Filipino lawyers, had a membership of over 1,000.
[13] *Christian Science Monitor* (12 Jan. 1946).   [14] Cf. p. 121.

reply to this, the Chinese Minister, Mr Chen Chih-ping, said that the right of Chinese to engage in trade in the Philippines could not be classified as international commerce, and properly belonged to a treaty of friendship rather than a commercial pact.

The treaty was finally agreed upon and signed on 18 April 1947. It did not meet the Chinese demands for the raising of the immigration quota nor for protection against discrimination, but provided in rather vague terms for peace and friendship, exchange of diplomatic and consular personnel, and for the right of the nationals of either party to travel and reside in the territory of the other, but only in conformity with the existing laws. The treaty was ratified by the Executive Yuan in China, but only with difficulty by the Philippines legislature. A proposed treaty of commerce and navigation was postponed.

In spite of all the agitation and the measures taken against them, the Chinese continued to retain their hold on the trade of the islands. The figures for trade in the Philippines for 1947, showing a percentage of trade done by traders of different nationalities, indicate the share of the Chinese in the total commerce.[15]

	Imports	*Exports*	*All trade*
Americans	28·00	42·97	33·59
Chinese	39·14	24·08	33·51
Filipinos	23·48	21·38	22·70
Others	9·38	11·57	10·20

Tied up with the resentment of Chinese possession of the lion's share of the Philippines internal trade was the long-standing charge that the Chinese corrupted Filipino officials. This charge was frequently renewed, and in March 1947 the executive secretary of the Chinese Chamber of Commerce gave an interview in reply to it. It took two, he said, to accomplish bribery. If the Filipino was susceptible to Chinese bribes it was hardly the responsibility of the Chinese. He quoted the New Testament in pointing his argument—'As Peter said, with the exception of Jesus Christ all men are sinners'.[16]

The highest feeling ensued from the action of Manila municipal authorities in ejecting Chinese from the stalls in the Manila markets. The ban was to become effective on Monday, 12 January 1948. The Chinese Market Vendors' Association, on hearing of the proposed move, had immediately petitioned the Supreme Court for a writ of prohibition against the city treasurer. A move to evade the measure by the construction of private markets was frustrated by the refusal of the mayor, Manuel de la Fuente, to approve applications for permits to establish

[15] *Manila Post* (11 Mar. 1947).
[16] 'A.S.B.O.', 'The Philippine Islands', *The World Today* (Nov. 1948).

such businesses. While the application of the Republican Act No. 37 (giving the Government power to take action against the stallholders) was suspended during the hearing of the petition by the Supreme Court, the Chinese minister complained that the city of Manila had put its own ordinance into effect. The Chinese stallholders in Manila were compelled to leave their places of business. Even if the Supreme Court should decide in their favour, said the minister, the damage done to them would hardly be reparable. His own solution was, that Chinese who were already holding stalls (some had been doing so for twenty years) should be allowed to continue to do so, but that no new applications should be entertained.[17]

While the Manila city authorities were resolutely persevering in their measures against the Chinese stallholders, an obstacle to the complete fulfilment of their programme was the lack of Filipino applicants qualified to take over the stalls. Contrary to general opinion, the running of small retail businesses of this sort was an expert job. The city treasurer, Mr Sarmiento, said that the (City?) Department of Finance had ordered 1,400 stalls to be vacated, but only 1,000 would be available for raffling to Filipino applicants by 12 January, the date set.[18]

The third burning Chinese question was that of immigration. The Chinese population of the Philippines had dropped from 117,000 in 1939 to 101,000 in 1947; 7,600 Chinese certified by UNRRA and by CNRRA to be bona-fide pre-war residents of the Philippines were at China ports waiting for permission to return to the Philippines. The President of the Philippines now refused to accept the repatriation of these Chinese as a group because of the 'acute housing, food, and unemployment problems confronting the country'. Permission for re-entry would be considered on the merits of each individual case by the Philippine consul at Amoy, where the majority of displaced Chinese were assembled.[19] Chinese who were refused reconsideration of their cases by the consul could return to the Philippines only as a part of the 500 annual quota. In April the Immigration Commissary, Mr Engracio Fabre, had reported to the President that it would not be advisable to allow these 7,600 Chinese to 'acquire *en masse* residence in the Philippines . . . considering the present housing and food problems, the high cost of living, and the number of unemployed'. The return of the Chinese, he said, would mean competition in the Philippines, especially among the labouring classes who were now struggling for a livelihood.[20]

This attitude was based on economic grounds (reinforced, no doubt, by political considerations) but the Government of the Philippines supported it by the legal argument that since the Chinese, driven out of the country by the enemy, had failed to return to Manila within the time

[17] *Manila Bull.* (7 Feb. 1948).   [18] Ibid. (8 Jan. 1948).
[19] *Voice of China* (23 May 1947).   [20] *North China Daily News* (20 Apr. 1947).

prescribed by law, they had automatically forfeited their right to come back.[21] Nor could the Chinese who were born in the Philippines rely on the *jus soli*, for the Supreme Court decision of 17 September held that this did not apply to the Philippines.

In spite of the *non possumus* attitude of the Philippine Government it was fairly certain that the Chinese community in the Philippines was recouping itself for its losses in numbers by illicit immigration. The official reports gave the number of them now (1947) in the islands as 101,000, but Mr Paul McNutt, former United States ambassador to the Philippines (as we have seen, p. 497 n.) said that their number was 200,000, adding 'thousands have entered during the Japanese occupation'. This estimate, however, was probably in excess of the facts, and Mr McNutt was not giving his opinion as a diplomat but as a private person, he having resumed, or being on the point of resuming, his legal practice in the United States. Nevertheless, it would not have taken very long, if the existing rate of illegal entry were sustained, for the numbers of the Chinese to come up to this figure. The Communists were undoubtedly playing a big part in the smuggling of their supporters into the islands.[22] A grave view was taken by the Philippine authorities of the increase in smuggling, and in April 1947 President Roxas had told a special Cabinet meeting at Baguio that the Philippines must be firm in their attitude towards illegal entry of foreigners.[23]

1949–63

Roxas died in 1948 and was succeeded by Vice-President Quirino. He headed the so-called 'Liberal Administration' which (says Georges Fischer) 'was characterized by corruption, falsified elections, and economic and financial difficulties'.[24] Meanwhile, much of Manila and other towns was still in wartime ruins, few of the demolished bridges had been replaced, the agrarian problem remained untouched, and the Huk insurrection was daily gaining in force. To distract attention from the abuses of the Government and rural distress, great publicity was given to the repressive legislation repeatedly passed against the small Chinese minority. With their large share in the retail trade, money-lending, and so on, they were alleged to be draining off the wealth of the country and depriving thousands of Filipinos of the chance of earning a living in business.

[21] Ibid. (3 May 1947).
[22] Five Chinese were arrested for subversive activities in connexion with the smuggling into the country of 67 Chinese at Sanchez Mira, Cagayan, in August (*Manila Bull.*, 9 Sept. 1947). Another batch of 68 deportees arrested earlier were to be deported to Amoy, and the Immigration Bureau was asking the Chinese authorities to shoulder the expenses of their deportation (*North China Daily News*, 4 to 10 Apr. 1947). These are but two examples among many.   [23] *North China Daily News* (4 Apr. 1947).
[24] *The Political Evolution of the Philippines* (1956).

C.S.E.A. — T

It was, of course, the American people who were footing the bill, and by 1950 their pressure on their Government persuaded it to send the Bell Mission to the Philippines to investigate. The Mission's report[25] was a terrible indictment of the Liberal régime—it found that incompetence in the administration, both central and local, was general, and that corruption was universal. Yet in order to secure any improvement in economic and social conditions further subsidies were demanded from America. The Bell Mission recommended these—but only on condition that the Philippines, now in its fifth year of independence, adopted some drastic financial, social, and economic reforms and submitted to a degree of supervision of its finances. To wield the new broom, a new man was wanted, and this was found in the person of the new President, Magsaysay, elected in 1953.

Magsaysay was free from the taint of collaboration with the Japanese, and had worked in the Resistance with the Americans. He was a man of action and believed in direct contact with the people. In due course he produced a programme of radical reform—but his plans were defeated by landlord interests in Congress which succeeded in emasculating them.

On 17 March 1957 Magsaysay was killed in an air accident, and was succeeded by Carlos P. García. García was a retiring personality who represented the 'old guard' in politics, and as such was unlikely to do anything to displease the ruling élite. Since 1907, this élite had remained continuously in power. They were *caciques* (chiefs), very often of mixed Spanish-Filipino blood, who as landlords enjoyed virtually feudal authority. They had originated as a class in the Spanish period, their power had been confirmed by representative institutions on the American model, and their economic interests had been consolidated by the part they played in the production of raw materials for the American market. In addition to this, they benefited politically from the fact that for many years suffrage was confined to those who could read and write, so that only about half the adult population voted in 1957.

In December 1961 Diosdado Macapagal (Liberal), who had been elected Vice-President in 1957, was elected President in a contest with the former President, Carlos García. But his election did not appear to promise any radical change in the general situation. The Philippines remained an integral part of the United States Pacific strategic system, and were held firmly inside it by the dependency of the Philippine economy on the United States. The Filipinos nevertheless considered themselves as Southeast Asians (they claimed to be a 'Malay' people) and, while the Spanish and American régimes had in many respects isolated them from the rest of the region, the frequent visits of Philippine missions to Southeast Asian countries (especially Thailand and Malaya)

[25] U.S. Economic Survey Mission to the Philippines, *Report to the President of the United States* (1950).

and the various agreements for cultural and economic co-operation with them were evidence of a nostalgia for pre-European associations.

It is against this background that we must view the fortunes of the small Chinese minority. Philippine nationalism continued to press upon them with undiminished vigour. In particular, the existence of some 168 Chinese schools with some 50,000 pupils was regarded as an indigestible element in Filipino society. Some Filipino congressmen wanted them closed on the ground that they retarded the assimilation of the Overseas Chinese. The Chairman of the House Committee on Good Government declared that Chinese schools 'violate Philippine sovereignty much more than United States bases'. Nevertheless, the move to close Chinese schools lacked solid support among Filipinos generally. The Secretary for Education, José Romoro, maintained that Chinese schools should not be closed simply because they were Chinese—any law nationalizing or closing them must apply also to schools run by Americans, Spaniards, and other foreigners.[26]

According to the Philippines Census of 1948,[27] there were 135,494 commercial establishments in the islands, employing 456,495 persons. Their total assets were calculated at P 1,210,209,981 and their gross receipts at P 3,149,080,997. The assets were distributed as follows:

Nationality	Assets in 1,000 pesos	Percentage of total
Filipino	558,546	46·2
Chinese	282,049	23·3
American	156,450	12·9
Spanish	43,040	3·6
Norwegian	8,173	0·7
Hindu & Pakistani	6,996	0·6
Swiss	5,625	0·5
British	4,660	0·4
French	1,595	0·1
Swedish	1,565	0·1
Italian	1,028	0·1
Others	138,777	11·0

The same Census classified 128,984 retail establishments by nationality of their owners as follows: 113,866, or 88 per cent, Filipino-owned; 12,274, or 10 per cent, foreign-owned; 2,844 corporations, partnerships, and associations, or 20 per cent. Of the foreign-owned, Chinese controlled 12,007; Americans 88; British 14; Hindus and Pakistanis 42;

[26] *Japan Times*, 13 Jan. 1961 (report from Ernesto Mendoza, Reuter's correspondent in Manila).   [27] See *Philippine Economic Handbook, 1960*.

Spanish 8; others 35. The gross sales were as follows:

	Gross sales (1,000 P.)	Percentage of total
Filipinos	467,364	43·2
Chinese	*294,894*	*27·2*
American	4,544	0·4
Hindu-Pakistani	922	0·1
British, Spanish, &c.	4,327	0·4
Corporations	310,251	28·7
Total	1,082,302	100·00

Although the Chinese holding in retail trade was very large in proportion to their small numbers, it did not approach being a monopoly. Nevertheless in the long-standing clamour of Filipino merchants for protection against the competition of alien retailers, the Government finally enacted Republic Act No. 1180 (1954), commonly called the 'Retail Nationalization Act', the objective of which was the eventual elimination of aliens from the retail trade of the country. The Act, however, permitted the alien to continue his retail business 'until his death or voluntary retirement from the said business', in the case of individuals, and for a period of ten years from the date of approval of the Act or until the expiration of the term of association or the corporate existence of the corporation, whichever came first, in the case of juridical persons.

By the end of the 1950s the Chinese had practically been legislated out of the retail trade. In 1958 87 per cent of the retail stores were owned by Filipinos, with 61 per cent of the total capital, while the Chinese owned only 13 per cent with 37 per cent of the capital.

Altogether the Chinese minority in the Philippines were in a very difficult and unenviable position in the 1950s and 1960s. Many Chinese traders who were not protected under the Retail Nationalization Act managed for some years to carry on business behind a Filipino figurehead who held the trading license (in the same way that their fellows had got round Indonesian and Thai restrictive laws), but the law was being tightened against them and they found it increasingly difficult to circumvent it. The Chinese of the Philippines suffered also from other disabilities—(like the Indonesian Chinese) they could not remit money to dependants in China and it was impossible to obtain a visa for Hong Kong unless they could obtain a previous guarantee of employment there. They could only, therefore, with extreme difficulty, escape from the pressures exercised upon them in the Philippines by emigrating.

CONCLUSION

ANY 'conclusion' regarding the Chinese in Southeast Asia can in the nature of things be only an interim one, and must be shaped to take account of the conceptions concerning them current at the time of writing. Thus the Conclusion to the first edition of this work was concerned to appraise the position of the Overseas Chinese community at a time when China itself, having for many years been in the throes of civil war was at last unified again under an apparently stable regime. The attempt must now be repeated after more than a decade of the People's China.

In the Western world, and to a more limited extent inside Southeast Asia itself, the current concept of China is of a giant that within the foreseeable future will be compelled by the pressures of its rapidly growing population to overflow its frontiers. The 'Yellow Peril' is, of course, no recent scare, but it has assumed a new significance as a feature of the Cold War between the two rival world blocs. In the maintenance of present Western policy it is politically desirable that the other nations of Asia shall be constantly reminded of the danger in which they stand from an imminent Chinese expansion. And to the extent that the reality of this threat is accepted, the attitude of the indigenous peoples of Southeast Asia towards the Chinese minorities in their midst largely depends. Economic rivalry and social friction further influence this attitude. An assumed fact lies at the root of this policy.

In late 1963 the evidence for active 'expansionism' on the part of the People's China was confined to the frontier fighting with India and to alleged political machinations on the part of the Chinese Communists in Southeast Asia, especially in Thailand and Singapore. There was also said to be a certain amount of illicit immigration of Chinese into Burma, though so far on a comparatively small scale. The case for a new 'Yellow Peril', therefore, would have to depend upon evidence of China's *intentions* to expand—deliberately or through political necessity.

The arguments for the political necessity for Chinese expansion are based on population trends and on the alleged inability of the Communist system to produce enough food to feed the rapidly increasing population of the country.

A full examination of this evidence would entail investigations beyond the scope of this study, but the ostensible situation late in 1963 can be briefly stated.

In spite of the great increases in agricultural production up to 1950, the Chinese Government had itself showed its awareness of the population problem. Towards the end of 1956 a birth-control campaign was officially launched by the Chinese Minister of Health, but by the end of the year the campaign had stopped. The reason seems to be that the Chinese Communists had now embarked on the 'Great Leap Forward' and the shortage of manpower which this effort was producing was not consistent with a birth-control campaign. The latter must wait its turn. As it happened, the 'Great Leap Forward' was followed by three years of bad harvests and natural calamities and the Communists were forced to switch their emphasis in planning from heavy industry to agriculture which was now given first priority. In the meantime the Communists claimed that they had been able by use of their powerful methods of mass suggestion to reduce the annual rate of population increase to 10 million, which was a number China could provide for by increased production and by the development of the underpopulated two-thirds of the country (e.g. by migration into Sinkiang). But whether this optimism was justified or not would be demonstrated within the next two or three decades.

An imminent overflowing of population, however, might be expected to produce immediate portents. Where were these to be found? Not, as we have seen, in any actual emigration in significant numbers. If anywhere, we must look for them in political activity among the Overseas Chinese inspired from Communist China. Only by political preparation could these communities be turned into a 'spearhead' or 'fifth column' for Chinese expansion.

In nearly all of the Southeast Asian countries the Chinese were in a minority—in most cases a very small minority (e.g. Burma, Indonesia, the Philippines). Only in the Federation of Malaya and Thailand did their numbers bear an important relationship to total population, and in one small State only were they in a majority. A physical 'take-over', therefore, without armed assistance from the People's China, was out of the question everywhere except in Singapore.

The preponderance of Chinese over other races in Singapore (about 80 per cent) gave emphasis to the importance of the 'Greater Malaysia' movement of the early 1960s. In the addenda to the histories of the Chinese in the Federation, Singapore, and the Borneo territories we have already seen how the fear that the Communists might gain control of Singapore and, through the Chinese community, extend this control to the Federation, had predisposed both the Alliance Party in the Federation to the 'Greater Malaysia' proposals. By agreement between the British Government and the Federation of Malaya, Singapore, Sarawak, and North Borneo, the Federation of Malaysia came into being in September 1963.

The birth of Malaysia was attended by strong opposition to the Federation on the part of Indonesia, and (in a lesser degree) of the Philippines, the latter putting forward a historical claim to North

Borneo. A rising had taken place in Brunei in December 1962, with Indonesian support, and Brunei for the time being decided to remain outside Malaysia. But in spite of meetings between the representatives of Malaya, Indonesia, and the Philippines at Manila, where agreement seemed to have been reached, President Sukarno greeted the establishment of Malaysia with hostility. It was, he declared, the product of neo-colonialism inspired by Britain. The Cobbold Commission had reported earlier in the year that a majority of the inhabitants of Sarawak and North Borneo were in favour of the Federation, but to satisfy President Sukarno's demands, the coming into being of Malaysia was delayed in order to permit a United Nations Commission to investigate the wishes of the people. The latter confirmed the Cobbold findings, and Malaysia was created on 15 September 1963. Indonesia then declared a policy of 'confrontation' to Malaysia, and followed it up by a trade boycott against the new Federation and by taking over British firms in Indonesia.

The attitude of Indonesia towards Malaysia accentuated the problems of the Overseas Chinese. As early as July 1945, President Sukarno had made it clear at the meetings of the Japanese-sponsored Committee for the Preparation of Indonesia's Independence that he dreamed of a 'Pan-Indonesia' that would include Malaya, New Guinea, and the Philippines. His hope now seemed to be that by increasing economic pressure against Malaysia, which would mainly hit the Chinese of Singapore, he might create pro-Communist disaffection among the Chinese and thereby increase a fear of the Chinese on the part of the Malays and induce them to throw in their lot with Indonesia. The immediate effect of the policy, however, was to consolidate Malaysian resistance to Indonesia, and to convince the several communities of the necessity of a united front.

The effectiveness of any 'fifth-column' plan would depend also on the solidarity of the Overseas Chinese with the People's China. As we have seen, the regaining by China of its position as a 'Great Power' through the instrumentality of the Chinese Communist Party had given the People's Government great prestige in the eyes of the Overseas Chinese. But this did not mean that a majority of them had been converted to Communism. A large number of the Overseas Chinese merchants, retailers, &c might by now be indifferent towards the Chiang Kai-shek regime in Taiwan, but they were still functioning as capitalists within a capitalist framework and their interests were tied up with the economy of the country in which they lived. It was therefore consonant with their continued prosperity that in politics they should maintain a strict neutrality, and this they tended to do. And while a great deal of the power in Overseas Chinese affairs had passed to the labour-unions, the old *towkays* were by no means impotent in their 'reformed' guise.

Taking all the above points into consideration, there seemed little reason in 1963 to anticipate that the position of the Chinese in Southeast

Asia would be greatly changed within the next decade or so. China was unlikely (short of global war) to embark on any expansionist adventure, utilizing the Overseas Chinese as a 'fifth-column'. The immigration of Chinese into Southeast Asia (so great in 'colonial' times) had virtually stopped since the end of the Second World War, and there was no reason to suppose that their overall rate of natural increase was any greater than that of the indigenous peoples. The latter numbered some 220 million to the 12 million or so Overseas Chinese in Southeast Asia and, although divided into a number of separate countries, each of those countries was intensely nationalistic and any attempt at Chinese expansion would be met with resolute opposition.

What then of the prospects of assimilation of the Overseas Chinese?

The obstacles to intermarriage remained much the same that they were a decade before. In the Muslim countries there was still the absolute barrier of religion; in the Buddhist countries assimilation proceeded slowly but surely as before. As regards cultural assimilation, the lack of a common education continued to be the greatest obstacle. A large proportion of the Overseas Chinese were still intent on educating their children in the Chinese language and the reservation of 'Education' as a subject of State government in the State of Singapore within the Federation of Malaysia was one indication of this. As against this, the PAP Government had accepted Malay as the official language of Singapore and has also accepted a Malay Head of State (Yang di-Pertuan Negara). The Prime Minister (Mr Lee Kuan-yew) in particular evinced an awareness of the necessity for the Malayan Chinese to identify themselves with the Malays, Indians, &c. as 'Malayans'. But apart from the continued use of English in administration and of Malay as a *lingua franca* in the ordinary daily contacts, the intercultural influences between the communities remained weak. Perhaps the principal seat of cultural interplay was the amusement parks where a Malay *bangsawan* (burlesque), a Cantonese opera, or an Indian play might attract more than a sprinkling of the other races to vary their cultural intake. Such processes of cultural interaction were always slow in any case throughout history.

The main obstacle to the finding of a *modus vivendi* between the Overseas Chinese and the other races was the continuance of the Cold War. If the artificial alignment of humanity consequent upon this could be removed, it was likely that the presence of Overseas Chinese in Southeast Asia would become increasingly less a 'problem'. But it could not be denied that the conflict between China and India over their common frontier had reawakened fears of an intention on the part of China to overflow its frontiers into the Southeast Asian countries.

THE SOUTHERN DIALECTS OF CHINESE

BY R. A. D. FORREST, M.A.

(Lecturer in Tibeto-Burman languages in the University of London)

WHAT are commonly known as the dialects of Chinese are confined practically to the coastal provinces of Kwangtung, Fukien, Chêkiang, and Kiangsu; but there are not inconsiderable extensions into the adjoining areas of Kwangsi, Kiangsi, and Anhwei. Within the Northern Chinese ('Mandarin') area there are indeed districts in which important differences from the standard speech still exist, but these districts are largely under the influence of the speech of the capital of the later dynasties, Peiping, from which the southern coastal regions have been protected by their distance and by natural obstacles. The same forces have had the effect that within this relatively small part of China the differences from dialect to dialect are in many cases as great as those which divide the dialects as a whole from the standard language; and not less than those which separate distinct national languages in other parts of the world.

It is in fact the case that, apart from the phonetic archaisms by which these dialects are placed closer to Ancient Chinese (the standard dialect of the capital, then at Sian in Shensi, as interpreted by Bernhard Karlgren in 1915), they have little in common which they do not also share with the northern forms of Chinese. The outline of the history of the main groups which follows will make this plain, as well as the causes by which it has been brought about. The archaisms consist in the retention of the old final consonants -*k*, -*t*, and -*p* (throughout a major part of this area); of a fuller form of certain initial combinations in a number of words; of the distinction between final -*n* and -*m*; and of a more complete tonal system. All these features existed in the Ancient Chinese of the sixth century, but have been universally lost in the great Northern Chinese region.

If we exclude from this survey the Wu dialects (spoken in the ancient kingdom of Wu, around the mouth of the Yangtze), the speakers of which do not contribute largely to the numbers of Chinese emigrants, the remaining forms of speech in this area may be divided into three main groups of dialects: Cantonese, Hakka, and the Fukien dialects.

I. Cantonese, itself with several well-marked sub-dialects, chief among which is the Se-Yap group of the western delta of the Canton River, is commercially the most important of the southern forms of Chinese. It is spoken by the majority of the population of Kwangtung, at least as a second language, though its actual area of usage is not very great; the numerousness of its speakers is due to its being the speech of the great commercial centres of Hong Kong, Canton, Fatshan, Macau, Wuchow (in Kwangsi), as well as a number of smaller towns; and its speakers have tended to form colonies in the areas of other dialects in the trading ports all over the south, as in Kweilin, Fuchow, and Chiungchow. It is probably the oldest-established form of Chinese in the southern provinces, and has developed independently of the Northern language at least since the tenth century of our era, and in all probability since much earlier. Cantonese has kept the full range of eight tones of Ancient Chinese, and has even added a ninth by subdivision of one of the others, whereas the tendency in the north has been consistently towards their reduction. With a much fuller consonantal system than the Northern dialects, it has had less need to resort to compound words to distinguish homophones, and so expresses meanings with greater economy of syllables. Its divergence from Northern Chinese is mainly due to its preservation of an older phase of the language, its independent innovations being few and chiefly in the matter of tones and vocalism. In vocabulary—differences in vocabulary between Chinese dialects affect mainly the pronouns and particles—it has more affinity with the forms of Northern Chinese in use along the lower Yangtze than with other southern dialects, except Hakka.

II. The Hakkas, speakers of the second most widespread dialect of Kwangtung, entered the province from the northeast about the thirteenth century, leaving on their way a number of now-isolated colonies in Kiangsi and northern Fukien. There is no clear boundary between Cantonese and Hakka, as the two peoples tend to occupy separate villages in the same areas; in urban districts Hakka is losing ground to Cantonese, bilinguals being mostly Hakkas. They occupy a broad belt of country beginning a short distance north of Canton city and running east and west, and many have penetrated into Hainan, adding to the linguistic complexity of that island. Hakka, like Cantonese, differs from standard Chinese particularly in being more archaic, but its archaism is less pronounced, and it distinguishes itself by peculiar tonal developments resulting in a much greater proportion of aspirated consonants than in other dialects, and moreover prefers aspirates to fricative consonants; a number of Hakka words, for example, begin with *kh* (i.e. aspirated *k*) where Cantonese has *h* or *f*. It keeps the final stop consonants, but tends to substitute final *t* for *k* in certain cases. The tonal system is very vigorous, overshadowing even syllable stress.

III. Sharply defined against the two great dialects of Kwangtung are those which, however they differ between themselves, have in common an origin in a very old stratum of Chinese spoken, probably since the Han dynasty, in Fukien province. This older stratum is marked by great aversion to fricatives, and so retains the initial *p*- in a large class of words in which all other dialects show a development to *f*-. It is less conservative of final consonants than are the dialects dealt with above, and tends to show a nasalized vowel in place of the final nasal consonants. The local patois of the northern half of Fukien have gone much further in reduction of final consonants than have the remainder of this group. Common to the whole group is also a peculiar vocabulary; in place of the words for 'son', 'die', 'love', 'house', and many other basic ideas, where the remaining dialects have words which, however different their phonetic evolution, are derived from the same ancient Chinese forms, Fukien dialects have a series of words peculiar to themselves.

The Fukien group is conveniently divided into four sub-groups:

1. The most distinctive in many ways are those spoken in the southern parts of the province and, as a result of modern emigration, on the island of Taiwan, as well as in the immediately adjacent parts of Kwangtung. The chief varieties recognized are those of Amoy, Swatow, and Chaochow. The most remarkable feature of this group is a double pronunciation of its vocabulary. An illustration is the case of the English words 'cattle' and 'chattel' on the one hand, 'capital' on the other; these are in origin the same word, but the last may be regarded as a learned pronunciation of the two former (specialized, of course, in meaning). The duplication in the southern Fukien dialects is of this kind, but it extends to the full range of the large Chinese vocabulary to the degree that the words are used in the colloquial language at all. What are called the literary forms are the only forms used in reading, but in the

course of time considerable numbers of literary forms have, in certain phrases, spread into the colloquial language, generally with slightly different meanings from those of their popular counterparts. The origin of this wholesale duplication is itself interesting. During the T'ang dynasty (A.D. 618–906) a new standard dialect was introduced into China, having its roots in an area in the province of Shansi, where certain of its peculiarities still survive in the local speech. On the downfall of that dynasty, north China reverted to the old tradition, and it is on this that modern Northern Chinese is based. But it appears that in a resinicization of Fukien towards the end of T'ang its court dialect was imposed as a literary language on the population of the province; and there its peculiar features, chief of which is the substitution of initial g-, d-, b- (in some dialects k-, t-, p-) for earlier ng-, n-, m-, still make the literary pronunciation, and in some few cases (as in the word be for 'horse', where every other dialect has something like ma) have penetrated into everyday speech.

2. The northern dialects of the province agree in their loss of final consonants, and in little else except their derivation from the early pre-T'ang stratum of Chinese. Excluding Fuchowese, to be separately treated, the chief among them are those of Kienyang and Kienning.

3. The Hainanese dialect was obviously carried to Hainan by immigrants from the south of Fukien, as its basis is the old dialect of that province; but in its new home it has evolved peculiarities of its own which place it apart from the rest of the group. Whereas other Fukien dialects avoid fricative sounds, Hainanese develops an f- sound from aspirated p-; but its strangest characteristic is the radical transformation of initial dentals. Here all initial sibilants have become t-, while a new s-sound has evolved from the aspirated affricate, ts- or tsh- (i.e. English ch-). On the other hand, the initial aspirated t- is represented by h-. These changes, which give a very peculiar aspect to the language, are curiously reminiscent of similar changes in the Se-Yap subdialect of Cantonese on the mainland opposite.

4. The dialect of Fuchow city, said not to be understood farther than some forty miles from Fuchow itself, is isolated among the dialects of the province. Here again a foreign dialect has been superimposed on the original Fukien stratum, but in this case it is the standard Northern Chinese, in a rather antique form, and not the T'ang standard speech with its d- for n-, &c. This Northern Chinese dialect has been accommodated to the phonetic habits of the northern half of Fukien, with the result that final consonants are seriously reduced, all distinction between the final nasals on the one hand, between final stops on the other, being lost.

The complicated linguistic pattern of Fukien province, itself due to the difficulty of communications in a country so cut up by natural accidents, probably accounts for the fact that the modern standard Chinese, the 'National Language' (kuo yü), has made more progress there than in Kwangtung, where the commercial value of Cantonese as a lingua franca has so far protected it from displacement.

RECENT ARCHAEOLOGICAL RESEARCH

BY ALASTAIR LAMB

THE Chinese contact with Southeast Asia can be traced back to before the opening of the Christian era; but, with the exception of parts of Vietnam, the Chinese did not begin to settle in significant numbers in Southeast Asian regions until many

centuries later. Recently the references in Chinese literature to early Chinese relations with Southeast Asian states have been re-examined and the pioneer researches
of scholars like Pelliot have been extended and modified. In this context should be
mentioned Wang Gungwu, 'The Nan-hai Trade', *Journal of the Malayan Branch of
the Royal Asiatic Society*, 1958, Paul Wheatley's *The Golden Khersonese*, and O. W.
Wolters' *Early Indonesian Commerce and the Origin of Srivijaya* (University of
London Ph.D. thesis, 1962). These works all make it abundantly clear that, except
in those districts actually adjacent to Chinese territory, the Chinese initially came
to Southeast Asia as merchants rather than as settlers. It is now certain that many
of the diplomatic exchanges between Southeast Asian states and China which are
described in the Chinese texts were in fact little more than trading ventures.

Early (pre-Ming) Chinese trade with Southeast Asia can now be seen to fall into
two categories. On the one hand the Chinese exchanged their manufactures, their
ceramics and textiles, for local Southeast Asian products, tin, spices, jungle resins,
and the like. On the other hand the Chinese found that some Southeast Asian
regions, by virtue of their geographical position astride the sea routes between the
Middle East and the Far East, became the sites of entrepôts of political and economic
importance where Chinese merchants could meet merchants from the west. Chinese
relations with states like Srivijaya were certainly a product of Chinese interest in
this entrepôt trade. Both categories of Chinese commercial contact with Southeast
Asia, the local trade and the entrepôt trade, are capable of being investigated by
archaeological methods. One of the major Chinese exports at all periods since at
least the end of the Han dynasty has been ceramics, and this is a category of artifact
which is most durable. Hardly a region of Southeast Asia exists where Chinese
ceramics of Sung and later date cannot be found; T'ang and earlier wares, however,
are not so common, and their distribution clearly related to the patterns of early
Chinese maritime commerce. In the entrepôt sites Chinese ceramics are sometimes
found in association with glassware and manufactured objects from India and the
Middle East. Here again the plotting of the distribution of categories of finds may
throw much light on patterns of trade.

To date the potentialities of this kind of archaeological research have not been
exploited to a significant degree. Investigations, however, of sites yielding pre-Ming
Chinese wares have been carried out in Indonesia, Cambodia, Vietnam, Sarawak,
Thailand, the Philippines, and Malaya under more or less scientific control in the
years since the end of the Second World War. (Some of the problems and possibilities of this kind of research are discussed in A. Lamb, 'Miscellaneous Papers on
Early Hindu and Buddhist Settlement in Northern Malaya and Southern Thailand',
Federation Museums Journal 1961.) No general synthesis is as yet available, but the
following conclusions would seem to have emerged:

1. By Sung times Chinese ceramics were being exported in large quantities to the
remote corners of Southeast Asia; and even aboriginal tribes in the mountain jungles
of New Guinea had learned to cherish vessels of Chinese porcelain which they used
for ritual purposes.

2. This Chinese export trade stimulated rulers in what is now Vietnam and
Thailand to attempt to compete by developing local ceramic industries. By the Yüan
period wares from kilns in Annam were being widely exported, and at some point
in the fourteenth century kilns in central Thailand, perhaps based on the experience
of a few Chinese potters specially imported, began to produce on a large scale.

3. From T'ang times onwards Chinese merchants were meeting merchants from
the Middle East at entrepôts in the general region of the Malacca Straits. In sites
here, like Takuapa on the Isthmus of Kra and Pengkalan Bujang in Kedah in Malaya,

archaeology has revealed Persian and other Middle Eastern ceramics and glass in association with Chinese wares. The Middle Eastern wares are virtually unknown in Southeast Asia to the east of the Malacca Straits, thus suggesting that here was a boundary to the Chinese monopoly of the local trade.

It should be possible on the basis of archaeological evidence to work out a detailed picture of the extent and nature of Chinese commercial penetration into Southeast Asia from the T'ang period onwards; but a great deal of research and of publication is still required.

SELECT BIBLIOGRAPHY

I. WORKS IN EUROPEAN LANGUAGES

1. SOUTHEAST ASIA: GENERAL

Abramowitz, Z. The economics of Asian minorities. *Far Eastern Economic R.*, xxiv 22 (1958).

Alers, Henri J. *Dilemma in Zuid-Oost-Azië; een anthropo-geografische interpretatie van de Chinese penetratie in Zuid-Oost Azië.* Leyden, 1955.

Boxer, C. R. Notes on the Chinese abroad in the late Ming and early Manchu periods; compiled from contemporary European sources, 1500–1750. *T'ien Hsia Monthly*, ix (Aug.–Dec. 1939).

Bush, J. D. The overseas Chinese as an economic factor. *China R.* (Sept. 1922).

Butwell, Richard. *Southeast Asia today and tomorrow: a political analysis.* N.Y., 1961.

Callis, Helmut G. *Foreign capital in Southeast Asia.* N.Y., 1942.

Campbell, P. C. Chinese coolie emigration. London Univ., M.Sc. (Econ.) thesis, 1932, unpubl.

Carnell, F. G. Southeast Asia and the modern world. *India Q.*, xiii (Apr.–June 1957).

Chen Su-ching. *China and Southeastern Asia.* Chungking, 1945.

Cheng, T. C. The education of overseas Chinese. London Univ. thesis 1949, unpubl.

Ch'iao-wu pao. Answers to questions concerning education and employment of returning overseas Chinese students. U.S. Consulate, Hong Kong, *Extracts from Chinese Mainland Magazines*, Aug. 1959.

Cornell University Library. *Southeast Asia accessions list*, compiled by Giok Po Oey. Vol. v: 1962–3. Ithaca, N.Y., Dept of Asian Studies, Southeast Asia Program.

Du Bois, Cora. *Social forces in Southeast Asia.* Rev. ed. Cambridge, Mass., 1959.

Durdin, Peggy. Reappraisal of the overseas Chinese. *N.Y. Times Magazine*, 15 May 1955.

Duyvendak, J. J. L. *Ma Huan re-examined.* Amsterdam, 1933.

—— The true dates of the Chinese maritime expeditions of the early fifteenth century. *T'oung Pao* (Leyden), xxiv (1939).

Economic problems of the Overseas Chinese. *Bank of China Monthly Economic R.* (Jan.–Feb. 1960).

Edinger, George Adolphus. *The twain shall meet.* N.Y., 1960.

Elegant, Robert S. *The dragon's seed; Peking and the overseas Chinese.* N.Y., 1959.

Emerson, Rupert. The Chinese in Malaysia. *Pacific Affairs* (Sept. 1934).

—— *Representative Government in Southeast Asia*, with supplementary chapters by Willard H. Elsbree and Virginia Thompson. Harvard, 1955.

Fa Hsien Fo Kuo Chi, trans. by Abel Rémusat as *Relations des royaumes boudiques* (Paris, 1836); by Samuel Beal as *An account of Buddhist countries* (Oxford, 1869); by L. Legge (1886); by H. A. Giles (Cambridge, 1923).

Fang Fang. How the returning emigrants and emigrant families are exerting all their efforts and forging ahead together with all the Chinese people. *Tsiao-pao*, iii (1958).

—— Second Plenary Session of the Overseas Chinese Affairs Communities. U.S.

Consulate, Hong Kong, *Extracts from Mainland Magazines*, clxxvi (13 July 1959) (from *Ch'iao-wu pao*).

FitzGerald, C. P. Overseas Chinese in South East Asia. *Australian J. of Politics and History*, viii/1 (May 1962).

France, Direction de la Documentation. L'Émigration chinoise dans le sud-est asiatique: son importance politique et économique. *Notes et études documentaires*, nos. 2035–6 (21 & 23 June 1955).

Frankel, J. The governments of South East Asia and the Chinese. London Univ., Ph.D. thesis, 1950, unpubl.

Freedman, Maurice. Colonial law and Chinese society. *J. Rl. Anthrop. Inst.*, lxxx (1950). (Publ. 1952.)

——Chinese communities in Southeast Asia. *Pacific Affairs*, xxxi/3 (Sept. 1958).

—— The family in China, past and present. *Pacific Affairs*, xxxiv/4 (1961–2).

—— *Lineage organization in Southeastern Asia*. London School of Economics, 1958. (Monographs on Social Anthrop., 18.)

—— The handling of money: a note on the background to the economic sophistication of the overseas Chinese. *Man*, lix (1959).

—— Religion and society in south-eastern China. *Man*, lvii (Apr. 1957).

—— and Willmott, William E. Recent research on race relations: South-East Asia, with special reference to the Chinese. *International Social Science J.*, ii (1961).

Fried, Morton H. *Colloquium on overseas Chinese*. N.Y., 1958.

Gardner, C. T. Amoy emigration to the Straits. *China R.* (Hong Kong) (1896).

Gosling, L. A. P. Migration and assimilation of rural Chinese in Trengganu. *Festschrift for Sir Richard Winstedt* (in preparation).

Gottwaldt, H. *Die überseeische Auswanderung der Chinesen und ihre Einwirkung auf die gelbe und weisse Rassen*. Bremen, 1903.

Gull, E. M. The Chinese in South-East Asia. *Asiatic R.*, xiv (1948).

Gützlaff, Karl. *Journal of three voyages along the coast of China in 1831, 1832 and 1833, with notices of Siam, &c*. London, 1840.

Hall, D. G. E. *A History of South-East Asia*. N.Y., 1955.

Han Suiyin. The two Chinas and the overseas Chinese. *Eastern World*, ix. (Mar. 1955).

Hanrahan, Gene Z. Recent Chinese communist publications on Indochina and Malaya. *Pacific Affairs*, xxvii (Dec. 1954).

Heinisch, Heinz H. *Südostasien; Menschen, Wirtschaft und Kultur der Staaten und Einzelräume*. Berlin, 1954.

Helbig, Karl. Das chinesische Element in Südostasien. *Erde; Zeitschrift der Gesellschaft für Erdkunde zu Berlin*, ii (1950).

Hinton, Harold C. The overseas Chinese and Peking. *Far Eastern Economic R.*, xix (Oct. 1955).

Hirth, F. and Rockhill, W. W., trans. *Chau* (or Chao) *Ju-Kua, his work on the Chinese and Arab trade in the twelfth and thirteenth centuries*. St Petersburg, 1911.

Ho Hsiang-ning. Rising patriotism of overseas Chinese. U.S. Consulate, Hong Kong, *Current Background* (15 July 1957).

Hudson, G. F. Chinese in South-East Asia. *Eastern World* (Oct. 1947).

Inst. of Pacific Relations. *Government and nationalism in South-East Asia*; pt 1 by R. Emerson; pt 2 by L. A. Mills; pt 3 by Virginia Thompson. N.Y., 1942.

Kahin, G. McT. *The Asian-African Conference, Bandung, Indonesia, April 1955*. Ithaca, N.Y., 1955.

Kong Yu-leong. Asian overseas Chinese thinking. *China Critic* (Shanghai), xii/3 (16 Jan. 1936).

Lee, Rose Hum. The Chinese abroad. *Phylon*, xvii (3rd quarter, 1956).

Leifer, Walter. *China schaut südwärts*. Würzburg, 1961.

Lu Yu-sun. *Programs of communist China for overseas Chinese*. Hong Kong, 1956.

Lyman, Stanford. Overseas Chinese in America and Indonesia. *Pacific Affairs*, xxxiv/4 (1961–2).

MacNair, H. F. *The Chinese abroad*. Shanghai, 1924.

McVey, Ruth T. *The Calcutta Conference and the Southeast Asia uprisings*. Ithaca, N.Y., 1958.

Majonica, Ernst. Eine asiatische Grossmacht; die Überseechinesen. *Das Parlament*, ix/4 (1959).

Malory, Walter H. Chinese minorities in Southeast Asia. *Foreign Affairs*, xxxiv (Jan. 1956).

Mende, Tibor. *South-East Asia between two worlds*. London, 1955.

Miles, G. T. The Chinese in South East Asia and the East Indies. London Univ., M.A. thesis, 1932, unpubl.

Mitchison, Lois. *The overseas Chinese*. London, 1961.

Ong Tae-hae. *The Chinaman abroad: an account of the Malayan Archipelago*, trans. by W. H. Medhurst. Shanghai, 1849.

Overseas Chinese students in Free China. Taipei, 1956.

Pauker, Guy J. *The Bandung Conference*, Cambridge, Mass., 1955.

Pickering, W. A. Chinese secret societies. *JRASSB*, i & iii (1878–9).

Purcell, Victor. Co-existence: the two great cultures that live side by side but do not clash. *Asia Magazine* (Hong Kong) (Oct. 1962).

—— *The Colonial period in Southeast Asia*. N.Y., 1953.

—— The Dual nationality of the Chinese in Southeast Asia. *India Q.*, xi (Oct.–Dec. 1955).

Pye, Lucian W. *Some observations on the political behaviour of overseas Chinese*. Mass. Inst. of Technology, Center for International Studies, 1954.

Revised statute for investment within China by overseas Chinese. *Bank of China Economic R.* (Mar.–Apr. 1960).

Roll, C. Peking und die Auslandchinesen. *Aussenpolitik*, x (1959).

Simoniya, N. A. *Overseas Chinese in Southeast Asia: a Russian study*, trans. by U.S. Joint Publications Research Service. Ithaca, N.Y., 1961. (Cornell Univ., Southeast Asia Program.)

Skinner, G. William. *Report on the Chinese in Southeast Asia, Dec. 1950*. Ithaca, N.Y., Feb. 1951. (Cornell Univ., Southeast Asia Program.)

—— Overseas Chinese in Southeast Asia. *American Academy of Political and Social Sciences Annals*. (Jan. 1959).

Solich, Eduard J. Die Chinesen in Südostasien. *Zeitschrift für Geopolitik*, xxvi (1955).

—— *Die Überseechinesischen in Südostasien*. Frankfurt-am-Main, 1960.

Ta Chen. Chinese Migrations with Special Reference to Labour Conditions. U.S. Bureau of Labour Statistics *Bulletin* (Washington), no. 340 (July 1923).

—— *Emigrant communities in South China*. N.Y., 1940.

Tan Kah-kee. Closing address before conference on overseas Chinese affairs. U.S. Consulate, Hong Kong, *Current Background* (25 June 1956).

—— Opening Address at the Returned Overseas Chinese Federation Session. *Peking R.*, ii (22 Dec. 1959).

Tay Ehr Soon. The Chinese in South-East Asia. *Race* (Nov. 1962).

Teng Chih-hsiung. Überseechinesen. *Zeitschrift für Geopolitik* (Mar. 1954).

Toledo, R. Chinese in America and Southeast Asia. *Far Eastern Economic R.*, xxi/6 (1956).

Tregonning, K. F. Kublai Khan and South-east Asia. *History Today* (7 Mar. 1957).

Tsai Chutang. Chinese nationality law. *American J. of International Law*, lv (1910).

Uchida, Naosaku. Economic activities of the Chinese in Southeast Asia. *Asian Affairs* (1 Mar. 1956). Same title in *Far Eastern Economic R.* (8 Nov. 1956).

—— Problems of overseas Chinese in Southeast Asia. Paper read at Symposium on Economic and Social Problems of the Far East, Golden Jubilee Congress, Hong Kong Univ., 1961.

—— Overseas Chinese problems in Southeast Asian nations. *Asian Affairs* (Oct. 1960).

—— *The overseas Chinese; a bibliographical essay with supplementary bibliography by Eugene Wu and Hsüeh Chün-tu.* Stanford Univ., 1959. (Hoover Inst. Bibliog. ser. vii.)

Van der Kroef, Justus M. China in Southeast Asia. *Current History* (Dec. 1957).

Vandenbosch, A. The Chinese in Southeast Asia. *J. of Politics*, ix (Feb. 1947).

—— Chinese thrust in Southeast Asia. *Current History* (Dec. 1939).

Wang Gungwu. Adaptability: can the Nanyang Chinese remould their lives in Southeast Asia? *Asia Magazine* (Hong Kong) (7 Oct. 1962).

—— The Nanhai trade. *JRASMB*, xxxi/2 (1958).

—— *A short history of the Nanyang Chinese.* Singapore, 1959.

Wapler, René J. L'Émigration chinoise dans l'Asie du sud-est. *R. de défense nationale*, n.s. xix (Oct. 1954).

Wee, A. Chinese-Malay relationships: the conflict of social values in a plural society. In *Symposium on Economic and Social Problems of the Far East.* Hong Kong, 1962.

Weightman, George H. Comparisons of the American-Chinese with other overseas Chinese communities. *Philippines Sociological R.*, iii (July 1955).

Wiens, Harold J. *China's march towards the tropics; a discussion of the Southward penetration of Chinese culture, peoples and political control in relation to the non-Han peoples in South China and in the perspective of historical and cultural geography.* Hamden, Con., 1954.

Williams, Frederick W. Chinese immigration in further Asia. *American Historical R.*, v/3 (Apr. 1900).

Williams, Lea E. The Chinese in Indonesia and Singapore under Raffles. *Far Eastern Economic R.*, xxxiii (July 1957).

Wong Po-shan. The recent changes in the economic situation of overseas Chinese in Southeast Asia, Code no. 4.3.1. *Symposium on Economic and Social Problems of the Far East, Golden Jubilee.* Hong Kong Univ. 1961.

Yuyitung, Rizal C. K. Citizenship, nationalization and the overseas Chinese community. *Chinese Weekly* (Manila) (26 Feb. 1961).

Zvieli, Elizer. The Chinese in South-East Asia. *Hamizrah hedadash* (The New East), vii/1 (1956). (In Hebrew with Eng. summary.)

2. BURMA

Brant, Charles S. Kuomintang Aggression against Burma. *Guardian*, ii (Feb. 1955).

Chao Feng. Once more I hear the heart-warming word 'paukphaw'. *Chinese Literature*, xii (1960).

Clubb, Oliver E. *The effect of Chinese Nationalist military activities in Burma on Burmese foreign policy.* Santa Monica, Calif., 1959 (Rand Corporation paper P-1595.)

Coryton, J. Trade routes between British Burma and western China. *JRGS*, 1875.

Gordon, Robert. *Trade routes from Bhamo to Yunnan through the Chinese Shan States*. Calcutta, 1869.

Huber, Édouard. Une Ambassade des Chinois en Birmanie en 1406. *BEFEO*, iv/142 (1904).

Imbault-Huart, C. Histoire de la conquête de la Birmanie par les Chinois. *J. asiatique*, vi/12 (Feb.–Mar. 1878).

Leach, Edmund. The frontiers of 'Burma'. *Comparative Studies in Society and History*, iii/1 (Oct. 1960).

Lin Win. Chinese in Burma. *Guardian*, ii (Nov. 1954).

Luce, G. H. Chinese invasions of Burma in the eighteenth century. *JBRS*, xv/2 (1925).

Verma, S. L. *The Law relating to foreigners and citizenship in Burma . . .*, with a foreword by U San Maung. Mandalay, 1960.

Whittam, Daphne E. The Sino-Burmese boundary treaty. *Pacific Affairs*, xxxv/2 (Summer 1961).

Wilbur, C. Martin. Southeast Asia between India and China; Burma's peaceful co-existence policy. *J. of International Affairs*, x/1 (1956).

Yin T'ang-chang. The 'Kha-khu' area; a geographical study of the undemarcated borderland between China, Burma, and India. *Tsing Hua J.*, n.s. i (June 1956).

3. SIAM (THAILAND)

Coughlin, R. J. The status of the Chinese minority in Thailand. *Pacific Affairs*, xxv (Dec. 1952).

—— Double identity; the Chinese in modern Thailand. Hong Kong, 1960.

—— The Chinese in Bangkok: a commercial-orientated minority. *American Sociological R.*, xx (1955).

—— The pattern of the Chinese in Thailand. *J. of South Seas Soc.* viii (June 1952).

Freyn, Hubert. The Chinese in Thailand. *Far Eastern Economic R.*, xxx (29 Dec. 1960).

Garivaite, Savite. La Condition des Chinois en Thailande. Paris, Doctorate thesis, 2 Mar. 1959, unpubl.

Giles, F. H. Absorption of the Chinese by the Siamese. *J. of Siam Soc.*, xx/3 (1927).

Landon, K. P. *The Chinese in Thailand*. London, 1941.

—— The Problem of the Chinese in Thailand. *Pacific Affairs*, xii/2 (1940).

Li, M. H. Overseas Chinese Economy in Thailand. *Far Eastern Economic R.* xxiii/21 (1957).

Lin Yu. Twin loyalties in Siam. *Pacific Affairs*, ix/2 (1936).

Rebrikova, Nina Vasil'evna. *Ocherki noveishei istorii Tailanda, 1918–59*. Moscow, 1960.

Skinner, G. W. *Chinese society in Thailand; an analytical history*. Ithaca, N.Y., 1957.

—— Chinese assimilation and Thai politics. *JAS* (16 Feb. 1957).

—— *A study of Chinese community leadership in Bangkok, together with an historical survey of Chinese society in Thailand*. Michigan, Ann Arbor Univ. Microfilms, 1954. 2 pts.

Tsan, Y. H. Chinese in Siam. *China Press Weekly* (Shanghai) (Sept. 1935).

4. VIETNAM (NORTH AND SOUTH), CAMBODIA, AND LAOS

Chieu-nguyen-Huy. Le Statut des Chinois en Indo-Chine. Paris Univ., law thesis, 1939, unpubl.

Deschamps, René. La Main-d'œuvre en Indo-Chine et l'immigration étrangère. Poitiers Univ., Faculté de Droit, 1908, unpubl.

Dubreuil, R. *De la condition des Chinois et leur rôle économique en Indo-Chine*. Bar-sur-Seine, 1910.

Fall, Barnard B. The international relations of Laos. *Pacific Affairs*, xxx (Mar. 1957).

FitzSimmons, Thomas, ed. *Cambodia; its peoples, its society, its culture*. New Haven, Conn., 1957.

Gaspardone, Émile. Bonzes des Ming réfugiés en Annam. *Sinologia* (Basle), ii/1 (1949).

Halpern, Joel Martin. *The role of the Chinese in Lao society*. Los Angeles, Univ. of Calif., 1961.

Janse, Olov R. T. *Archaeological research in Indo-China*. Cambridge, Mass., Harvard U.P., 1947. 2 vols.

Klopotov, K. K. *Ocherki narodnogo khoziaistva Demokraticheskoi Respubliki V'etnam*. Moscow, 1956.

Lancaster, D. *The Emancipation of French Indo-China*. London, 1961.

Le Bar, Frank M., and Suddard, Adrienne, eds. *Laos, its people, society, and culture*. New Haven, Conn., 1955, 1960.

Nguyen-the-Phuong. Le Poisson dans l'alimentation du Vietnamien. *Soc. des Études Indochinoises, Bull.*, xxxv (1960).

Mazaev, Al'bert G. *Agrarnaia reforma v Demokraticheskoi Respubliki V'etnam*. Moscow, 1959.

Phan-van-Thinh. Les Chinois au Vietnam. Paris Univ., Doctoral thesis, Faculté de Droit, 1954, unpubl.

Schneyder, P. L'Immigration chinoise en Indochine. *Encyclopédie mensuelle d'outre-mer* (1956).

United Nations, Economic Survey Mission to the Republic of Vietnam. *Towards the economic development of the Republic of Vietnam report*. N.Y., 1959.

United States, Joint Publications Research Office. *Indochina: the ethnic minorities of North Vietnam*. Washington, 1958.

Vietnam, Republic of. Some aspects of the legal situation of the Chinese in Viet-Nam. *Vietnam I* (1956), 5–22 (in French); 110–26 (in English).

Way Tsung-to. Overseas Chinese in Vietnam. *Far Eastern Economic R.*, i (1958).

5. Malaya and Singapore

Awbery, S. S., and Dalley, S. W. *Labour and trade union organization in the Federation of Malaya and Singapore*. Kuala Lumpur, 1948.

Barnett, A. Doak. *Notes on three growing forces among Singapore Chinese: political parties, students, and workers*. American Universities Field Staff, ADB-9-35 (1955).

Biographies of prominent Chinese in Singapore, ed. Victor Sim. Singapore, 1950.

Blythe, W. L. Chinese societies in Malaya. *Corona* (July 1949).

—— Historical sketch of Chinese labour in Malaya. *JRASMB*, xxi (1947).

—— The interplay of Chinese secret and political societies in Malaya. *Eastern World* (Mar. & Apr. 1950).

Brimmell, J. H. *A Short history of the Malayan Communist Party*. Singapore, 1956.

Butwell, Richard. A Chinese university for Malaya. *Pacific Affairs*, xxvi (Dec. 1953).

Chapman, F. Spencer. The Chinese in Malaya. *Geographical Mag.*, xxiii (Jan. 1951).

—— *The Jungle is neutral*. London, 1949.

Ch'en, Joseph Tao. *Postwar problems of the Chinese in Malaya*. Berkeley, Calif., 1958.

Chen, L. M. The Chinese in British Malaya. *China Quarterly R.*, iii (1938).

Ch'en, Su-ching. The Chinese in Malaya. *Pacific Affairs* (Sept. 1948).

Chiang Liu. Glimpses of Chinese in Sitiawan. *J. of South Seas Soc.* (June 1952).

Chin Kee Onn. *Malaya upside down*. Singapore, 1946.

—— *Silent army (Marai-ee)*. Singapore & London, 1952.

Chinese Students at Singapore. *Far Eastern Economic R.*, xxi (Oct. 1956).

Chong Seck-chim. The Development of the Kuala Lumpur district. *Malayan J. of Tropical Geog.*, iii (1954).

Chou Kai-ren. The Post-war trend of capital formation in Malaya against the background of Southeast Asia. London Univ., Ph.D. thesis, 1955.

Comber, Leon. *Chinese ancestor worship in Malaya*. Singapore, 1954.

—— *Chinese magic and superstitions in Malaya*. Rev. ed. Singapore, 1955.

—— *Chinese secret societies in Malaya; a survey of the Triad Society from 1800 to 1900*. Locust Valley, N.Y., 1959.

—— *Chinese temples in Singapore*. Singapore, 1958.

Coope, A. E. The Kangchu system in Johore. *JRASMB*, xiv/3 (Dec. 1956).

Cowgill, J. V. Chinese place names in Johore. *JRASMB*, ii/3 (1924).

Ee, J. Chinese migration to Malaya. *J. of Southeast Asian History*, ii/1 (Mar. 1961).

—— Chinese migration to Singapore, 1896–1941. *J. of Southeast Asian History*, ii (1961).

Elliott, J. A. *Chinese spirit-medium cults in Singapore*. London School of Economics, 1955. (Social Anthrop. new series.)

Fang Siew. Malayan Chinese literature: its development and periodization. *J. of South Seas Soc.*, xvi (1960).

Fenn, William P., and Wu Teh-yao. *Report on Chinese Education [in the Federation of Malaya]*. Kuala Lumpur, 1951.

Firth, Raymond. *Report on social science research in Malaya*. Singapore, 1948.

Fistié, Pierre. *Singapour et la Malaisie*. Paris, 1960.

Freedman, Maurice. *Chinese family and marriage in Singapore*. London, 1957.

—— 'Nan Yang': Chinese Southeast Asia. *Asian Horizon*, i/3 (1948).

—— The Sociology of race relations with special reference to British Malaya. London Univ., Ph.D. thesis, 1948, unpubl.

—— The growth of a plural society in Singapore. *Pacific Affairs*, xxxiii (June 1960).

—— Overseas Chinese associations: a comment. *Comparative Studies in Society and History* (The Hague), iii (1961).

—— Immigrants and associations; Chinese in 19th-century Singapore. *Comparative Studies in Society and History*, iii (Oct. 1960).

—— and Topley, Marjorie. Religion and social realignment among the Chinese in Singapore. *JAS.* xxi/1 (Nov. 1961).

Gamba, Charles. Labour and labour parties in Malaya. *Pacific Affairs*, xxxi/2 (June 1958).

—— *The Origins of trade unionism in Malaya*. Singapore, 1962.

Goodrich, B. W. F. Secret societies. *Malaya* (Mar. 1959).

Jackson, R. N. *Immigrant labour and the development of Malaya, 1786–1920*. Kuala Lumpur, 1961.

Kaye, Barrington. *Upper Nankin Street, Singapore; a sociological study of Chinese households living in a densely populated area*. Singapore, 1960.

Lee Ah-chai. Policies and politics in Chinese schools in the Straits Settlements, 1788–1941. Malaya Univ., M.A. thesis, 1957, unpubl.

Lee Kuan-yew (Prime Minister of Singapore). *The battle for merger*. Singapore, 1962.

Lee Yong-hock. A history of the Straits Chinese British Association. Malay Univ. B.A. (Hons.) thesis, 1959, unpubl.

Li Dun-jen, ed. *British Malaya: an economic analysis.* N.Y., 1955.

Malayan Chinese Association. *Memorandum on Chinese education in the Federation of Malaya.* Kuala Lumpur, 1954. (Chinese & Eng.)

Middlebrook, S. M. Pulai: an early Chinese settlement in Kelantan. *JRASMB*, xi/2 (1933).

—— Yap Ah Loy, 1837–85, with an introd. and three final chapters by J. M. Gullock. *JRASMB*, xxiv/2 (July 1951).

Mills, J. V. Malaya in the Wu-pei Chih charts. *JRASMB*, xv/3 (1937).

Newbold, T. J. The Chinese secret Triad Society of the Tien-ti-huih. *JRAS*, iv (1841).

Newell, William H. Family quarrels in a north Malayan Teochiu Chinese vegetable-growing community. *American Anthropologist*, lix (1957).

—— *Treacherous river; a study of rural Chinese in north Malaya.* Kuala Lumpur, 1962.

Ng Siew Yoong. The Chinese Protectorate in Singapore, 1877–1900. *J. of Southeast Asian History*, ii/1 (Mar. 1961).

Png Poh Seng. The Kuomintang in Malaya. *J. of Southeast Asian History*, ii/1 (Mar. 1961).

Purcell, Victor. *The Chinese in modern Malaya.* 2nd ed. Singapore, 1960.

—— Fédération de Malaisie et Singapour; fin d'une insurrection. *Civilisations*, ix (1959).

—— *The Chinese in Malaya.* London, 1948.

—— The Crisis in Malayan education. *Pacific Affairs*, xxvi (Mar. 1953).

—— The Position of the Chinese community in Malaya. *JRCAS* (Jan. 1953).

Robinson, K. Recent developments in Chinese education in Singapore. *Oversea Education*, xxix (1957).

Siah, U Chin. The Chinese in Singapore. *J. of Indian Archipelago and East Asia*, ii (1848).

Soh Eng Lim. Tan Cheng-lock: his leadership of the Malayan Chinese. *J. of Southeast Asian History*, i (1960).

Song Ong Siang. *One hundred years of history of Chinese in Singapore.* London, 1923.

Tan Cheng-lock. Federation problems of Malaya. *Eastern World* (Oct. 1947).

—— *Malayan Problems.* Singapore, 1947.

—— *Malayan problems from a Chinese point of view.* Singapore, 1947.

Tan Seng-huat (Mrs). The early Chinese newspapers of Singapore, 1881–1912. Singapore Univ., M.A. thesis, 1962, unpubl.

Tan, T. H. The Chinese in Malaya. *Eastern World*, vii (Nov. 1953).

Thio, Eunice. The Singapore Chinese Protectorate: events and conditions leading to its establishment, 1823–77. *J. of South Seas Soc.*, xvi (1960).

Topley, Marjorie. Chinese women's vegetarian houses in Singapore. *JRASMB*, xxvii (1954).

—— Ghost marriages among the Singapore Chinese: a further note. *Man*, lvi (1956).

—— Immigrant Chinese female servants and their hostels in Singapore. *Man*. lix (1959).

—— The emergence and social function of Chinese religious associations in Singapore. *Comparative Studies in Society and History* (The Hague), iii (1961).

Tregonning, K. G. P. The Chinese and the plural society in Malaya. *Symposium on Economic and Social Problems of the Far East, Golden Jubilee*, Hong Kong Univ., 1961.

Tregonning, K. G. P. Malaya, 1959. *Australian Q.*, xxxii (June 1960).
—— The Chinese and the plural society in Malaya. In E. Szczepanik, *Symposium on Economic and Social Problems of the Far East*. Hong Kong, 1962.
—— Penang and the China trade. *Malaya in History*, v (1959).
Valentijn, François. Account of Malacca in 1726, trans. by Muller. *JRASSB*, xiii (1884) & xxi (1890).
Vaughan, J. D. *Manners and customs of the Chinese of the Straits Settlements*. Singapore, 1879.
Ward, J. S. M., and Stirling, W. G. *The Hung Society*. London, 1925. 2 vols.
Westerhaut, J. B. Notes on the Chinese of Penang. *J. of Indian Archipelago*, viii (1854).
Wheatley, P. Tun-sun. *JRAS* (1956), pp. 17–30.
—— Ancient books containing references to Malaya. *Malayan Library Group Newsletter*, 1/2 (Oct. 1955).
—— *The Golden Khersonese*. Kuala Lumpur, 1961.
Wynne, W. L. *Triad and Tabut*. Singapore, 1941.

6. SARAWAK, NORTH BORNEO (SABAH), AND BRUNEI

Baring-Gould, S., and Bampfylde, C. A. *A History of Sarawak under its two white Rajahs, 1839–1908*. London, 1909.
Chinese in Borneo. *China Quarterly R.*, vii (1878–9).
Dickson, M. G. *Sarawak and its people*. Rev. ed. Kuching, 1956.
Fortier, David H. The Chinese in British North Borneo: ecological factors in cultural change. *N.Y. Academy of Sciences Transactions*, ser. ii/19 (Apr. 1957).
Harrisson, Tom. The Chinese in Borneo, 1942–6. *International Affairs*, xxvi/3 (1950).
—— *The Peoples of Sarawak*. Kuching, 1959.
Hwang, James P. The Chinese in Sarawak. *China Critic* (Shanghai), xxix/6 (1940).
Irwin, Graham. *Nineteenth-century Borneo; a study in diplomatic rivalry*. The Hague, 1955.
Li Dun-jen. *British Borneo; an economic analysis*. N.Y., 1955.
Liu Chiang. Chinese pioneers, A.D. 1900: the new Foochow settlement of Sarawak. *Sarawak Museum J.*, vi (1956).
T'ien Ju-k'ang. *The Chinese of Sarawak; a study of social structure*. London School of Economics, 1955. (Monographs on Social Anthrop.)
—— with Barbara E. Ward. *The Early history of the Chinese in Sarawak*, being App. I to 2nd impression of above, 1956.
—— A Hakka kongsi in Borneo. *J. of Oriental Studies* (Hong Kong), i/2 (1954).
Tregonning, K. G. *Under Chartered Company rule: North Borneo, 1881–1946*. Singapore, 1958.
Ward, Barbara E. A Hakka kongsi in Borneo. *J. of Oriental Studies*, i (July 1954).

7. INDONESIA

Bastin, Joh. The Chinese estates in East Java during the British administration. *Indonesië*, vii (July 1954).
Bertling, C. T. De Chineezen op de oostkust van Borneo. *Koloniale Studiën*, i (1925).
Boeke, J. H. Dualistische samenleving. *De Economist* (1935).
—— *Economics and economic policy of dual societies, as exemplified by Indonesia*. Haarlem, 1953.

Bool, H. J. *De Chineesche inmigratie naar Deli*. Utrecht, 1904.

Broek, Jan O. M. *The Economic development of the Netherlands Indies*. N.Y., 1942.

Bruin, A. G. de. *De Chineezen ter oostkust van Sumatra*. Leyden, 1918. (East Coast of Sumatra Inst., i.)

Cator, W. J. The economic position of the Chinese in the Netherlands Indies. Oxford, 1936.

Chailly-Bert, J. *Java et ses habitants*. Paris, 1901.

Diffelin, R. van. Het onderwijs voor Chineezen. *Koloniale Studiën*, xx (1936).

Djie Ting Liat. *De economische positie der Chineezen op Java*. Semarang, 1933.

Donnithorne, Audrey G. The Chinese in Indonesia. *Eastern World*, vii (Apr. 1953).

Duyvendak, J. J. L. Chinese in the Dutch East Indies. *Chinese Social and Pol. Science R.*, xi (1927).

Freedman, Maurice. Overseas Chinese in America and Indonesia. *Pacific Affairs*, xxiv/4 (Winter 1961–2).

Fromberg, J. H. *Verspreide geschriften verzameld door Chung Hua Hui*. Leyden, 1926.

Groeneveldt, W. P. *Historical notes on Indonesia and Malaya, compiled from Chinese sources*. Jakarta, 1960.

—— Notes on the Malay Archipelago and Malacca. *Verhandelingen van het Bataviaasch Genootschap van Kunsten en Wetenschappen*, xxxix (1880). (Reprinted for *JRASSB*, London, 1888.)

Groot, J. J. M. de. *De Lijkbezorging der Emoy-Chineezen*. The Hague, 1853.

—— *Het kongsiwezen van Borneo*. The Hague, 1885.

—— *Les Fêtes annuellement célébrées à Émoui* (Amoy). Paris, 1896.

Hoetink, B. Ni Hoe Kong, Kapitan der Chineezen te Batavia in 1740. *Bijdrage tot de Taal-, Land- en Volkenkunde v. Ned. Oost-Indië*, lxxiv.

—— So Bing Kong. *Bijdrage tot de Taal-, Land- en Volkenkunde v. Ned. Oost-Indië*, lxxiii (1917).

Humbaraci, Arslan. Anti-Chinese feelings in Indonesia. *Far Eastern Economic R.*, xxvii (10 Sept. 1959).

Indonesia. Government issues text of Indonesia's reply to China on repatriation of overseas Chinese. *Djakarta Dispatches* (1 Apr. 1960).

Kahin, George McT. The Political position of the Chinese in Indonesia. Stanford Univ., M.A. thesis, 1946, unpubl.

Kat Angelino, A. D. A. de. *Colonial policy*, tr. by G. J. Renier. The Hague, 1931. 2 vols.

Kielstra, E. B. Bijdragen tot het geschiedenis van Borneo's westafdeeling. *Indische Gids*, xi/1.

Kwee Kek Beng. Het cultuureele leven der Chineezen in Nederlandsch-Indie. *Koloniale Studiën*, v/6 (1936).

Lasker, B. The role of the Chinese in the Netherlands Indies. *Far Eastern Q.*, v/2 (1946).

Lee Thung-liang. The Unreality of Chinese nationalism in Indonesia; an apologia and a reorientation. *Indonesia R.*, ii (Jan.–Mar. 1954).

Liem Twan Djie. *De Distribueerende tusschenhandel der Chineezen op Java*. The Hague, 1947.

MacDougall, Colina. The Chinese in Indonesia. *Far Eastern Economic R.*, xxii/8 (1961).

Nio Joe Lan. De eigen onderwijsvoorziening der Chinezen. *Koloniale Studiën*, xxiii (Feb.–Mar. 1939).

Oey Kang-liu. The Chinese in the Dutch East Indies. *China Weekly R.* (7 Jan. 1933).

Pernitzch, M. G. *Die Chinesen in Nederlandsch-Indiën*. Berlin, 1934.

Phoa Liong Gie. De economische positie der Chinezen in Nederlandsch-Indië. *Koloniale Studiën*, xx (1936).

Roll, C. Die antichinesische Kampagne in Indonesien. *Aussenpolitik* (May 1960).

Schlegel, G. L'Organisation des kongsis à Borneo. *R. Coloniale Internationale* (Amsterdam), 1 (1885).

—— *Thian Ti Hwui or Heaven-Earth-League*. Batavia, 1866.

Skinner, G. W., ed. *Local, ethnic and national loyalties in village Indonesia; a symposium*. New Haven, Conn., 1959.

—— Change and persistence in Chinese culture overseas: a comparison of Thailand and Java. *J. of South Seas Soc.*, xvi (1960).

Somers, Mary F. The Influence of Indonesian nationalism on the Indonesian Chinese. Thesis in preparation, 1963.

Tan Giok-lan. *The Chinese community in a Sundanese town; a study in social and cultural accommodation*. Ithaca, N.Y., 1961.

Tjan Tjoe Som. De culturele positie der Chinezen in Nederlandsch-Indonesië. *Indonesië* (July 1947).

Valk, M. H. van der. De Rechtspositie der Chinezen in Nederlandsch-Indië. *Koloniale Studiën*, v/6 (1936).

Van der Kroef, J. M. Minority problems in Indonesia. *Far Eastern Survey*, xxiv/9 & 11 (1955).

Veer, W. de. *Chineezen onder Hollandsche vlag*. Amsterdam, 1908.

Verboeket, K. Geschiedenis van der Chineezen in Nederlandsch-Indië. *Koloniale Studiën*, v/6 (1936).

Vermeulen, J. T. De Chineezen de Batavia en de troebelen van 1740. Leyden Univ., Doctor of Letters thesis, 1938.

Veth, P. J. *Borneo's wester-afdeeling*. Zaltbommel, 1854–6.

Vishal Singh. The Problem of Chinese traders in Indonesia. *International Studies*, i (1960).

Vleming, J. L. *Het chineesche zakenleven in Nederlandsch-Indië*. Batavia, 1926.

Williams, L. E. *Overseas Chinese nationalism: the genesis of the pan-Chinese movement in Indonesia, 1900–16*. Glencoe, Ill, 1960.

Willmott, Donald Earl. *The Chinese of Semarang: a changing minority community in Indonesia*. Ithaca, N.Y., 1960. Rev. ed. 1961.

—— *Sociocultural change among the Chinese of Semarang, Indonesia*. Michigan, Ann Arbor Univ. Microfilms, 1959.

——*The National status of the Chinese in Indonesia, 1900–58*. 2nd ed. Ithaca, N.Y., 1961.

8. The Philippines

Ageo, G. G. Memorandum on the Chinese in the Philippines. In *Report of the Philippines Commission*. Washington, 1900.

Alip, Eufronio Melo. *Ten Centuries of Philippine-Chinese relations; historical, political, social, economic*. Manila, 1959.

Appleton, Sheldon. Communism and the Chinese in the Philippines. *Pacific Affairs*, xxxii (1959).

—— Overseas Chinese and economic nationalism in the Philippines. *J. of Asian Studies*, xix/2 (Feb. 1960).

Barrows, David P. *History of the Philippines*. Yonkers-on-the-Hudson, 1924.

Beyer, H. Otley. *Early history of Philippine relationships to foreign countries, especially China*. Manila, 1948.

—— The Philippines before Magellan. *Asia,* xxi (1921).

Blair, Emma H. and Robertson, J. A. *The Philippine islands, 1493–1898.* Cleveland, Ohio, 1903–9. 55 vols.

Ch'en, Paul Ching-szu. The contribution of the Chinese nationals to the Philippine economy. *J. of East Asiatic Studies* (July–Oct. 1954).

Los Chinos en Filipinas. Reprinted from *La Oceania Española,* 1886.

Constructive channelling of tensions in the Philippines. World Brotherhood, Philippine Chapter, Report no. 4, Inst. of Economic Studies, Araneta Univ. Manila, Aug. 1961.

Fischer, Georges. *The Political evolution of the Philippines.* 1956.

Fonacier, Tomás S. The Chinese exclusion policy in the Philippines. *Philippine Social Services & Humanities R.,* xiv (Mar. 1949).

—— The Relations between China and the Philippines. Stanford Univ., microfilm of typescript, 1958.

Forbes, W. Cameron. *The Philippine islands.* Harvard, 1945.

Horsley, Margaret Wynant. *Sangley; the formation of anti-Chinese feeling in the Philippines: a cultural study of stereotypes of prejudice.* Michigan, Ann Arbor Univ. Microfilms, 1950.

Isidro, Antonio. Chinese education in the Philippines. *Far Eastern Economic R.,* xxi (18 Oct. 1956).

Jensen, K. K. M. *The Chinese in the Philippines during the American regime.* Michigan, Ann Arbor Univ. Microfilms, 1956. (Abstracted in *Dissertation Abstracts,* xvi/11 (1956), 2143.)

Jordana y Morera, Ramón. *La inmigración china en Filipinas.* Madrid, 1888.

Liao, S. C. *Investment, employment in Chinese enterprises and the economic development of the Philippines.* Manila, Univ. of the East, Chinese Students Ass., 1959.

Manuel, E. Arsenio. *Chinese elements in the Tagálog language.* Manila, 1948.

Marcos, M. P. Foreign investments in the Philippines and the problem of alien minorities. *Far Eastern Economic R.,* xx/8 (1956).

Ravenholt, Albert. Chinese in the Philippines; an alien business and middle class. *Asian R.,* xii (1955).

Reyes, Teofilo D., jr. The social and economic adjustments of the Chinese minority in the Philippines. *Commerce,* lii (Sept. 1955).

Story, Russell M'Culloch. Problem of the Chinese in the Philippines. *American Social & Pol. Science R.,* iii/1 (1909).

Tan-Gatue, Belen. The social background of thirty Chinese-Filipino marriages. *Philippine Sociolog. R.,* iii (July 1955).

Weightman, G. H. Community organization of Chinese living in Manila. *Philippine Soc. Sciences & Humanities R.,* xix (Mar. 1954).

—— *The Philippine Chinese: a cultural history of a marginal trading community.* Michigan, Ann Arbor Univ. Microfilms, 1960.

—— A Preliminary ecological description of the Chinese community in Manila. *Philippine Sociolog. R.,* iii (Nov. 1955).

Wickberg, Edgar. Early Chinese economic influence in the Philippines, 1850–98. *Pacific Affairs,* xxxv/3 (Fall 1962).

Wu Ching-hung. A Study of references to the Philippines in Chinese sources from earliest times to the Ming dynasty. *Philippine Social Sciences & Humanities R.,* xxiv/1 & 2 (1959).

Zaide, G. F. The Economic development of the Philippines and the contribution of foreigners. *Far Eastern Economic R.,* xviii/1 & 2 (1955).

II. WORKS IN CHINESE AND JAPANESE
Compiled by Hugh D. R. Baker under the author's direction

1. BIBLIOGRAPHIES

Note: The bibliographies listed here are referred to subsequently
by the initials given after them in brackets

Ch'üan-kuo hsin-shu-mu. Peking, Wen-hua pu, 1957—(monthly). (Copy in British Museum.) (*HSM*).

Ch'üan-kuo tsung shu-mu. Peking, Wen-hua pu, 1949–54 cumulatively and thence annually. (Copy in British Museum.)

Chung-kuo shih-hsüeh lun-wen so-yin. Peking, K'e-hsüeh ch'u-pan-she, 1957. 2 vols. (*CKS*).

Fairbank, John K., and Kwang-ching Liu. *Bibliography of modern China.* Harvard, 1950. (F & L).

Feuerwerker, A., and Cheng, S. *Chinese communist studies in modern Chinese history.* Harvard, East Asian Research Center, 1959. (F & C).

Giok Po Oey. *Survey of Chinese language materials on Southeast Asia in the Hoover Institute and Library.* Ithaca, N.J., Cornell Univ., 1953. (*HL*).

Hua-ch'iao wen-t'i tzŭ-liao mu-lu so-yin, Ch'iao-cheng ts'ung-shu, Nos 4 & 7, Chung-kuo Ch'iao-cheng hsüeh-hui. Taipei, Hai-wai ch'u-pan-she, 1956 & 1957. (*HCW*).

Irikura, James K. *Southeast Asia: selected annotated bibliography of Japanese publications.* New Haven, Yale Univ. in association with Human Relations Area Files, 1956. (SEA Studies.) (*SEA*).

Kokuritsu Kokkai Toshokan, Ippan Kōsabu. *Tōnan Ajia kankei shiryō sōgō mokuroku.* Zōho kaitei-ban, 1958. (*TNA*).

Kyōto Teikoku Daigaku, Keizai Gakubu Kenkyūshitsu. *Nampō shiryō bunken mokuroku.* Kyoto, [1942?].
  Bibliography of Southeast Asia citing Japanese and Chinese publications.

Nihon Takushoku Kyōkai. *Nampō bunken mokuroku,* 1943. (*NBM*).
—— *Zōho Nampō bunken mokuroku.* Osaka, Daidō Shoin, 1944.
  Revised bibliography of Southeast Asia.

Uchida Naosaku. *The overseas Chinese.* Colorado, Calif., Stanford Univ., 1959. (Hoover Inst. Bibliographical ser. vii.) (*TOC*).
  A bibliographical essay with supplementary bibliography by Eugene Wu and Hsüeh Chün-tu. (See p. 578.)

Wu, Eugene. *Leaders of twentieth-century China.* Stanford Univ., 1956. (*C20*).

2. SOUTHEAST ASIA: GENERAL

Asaka Sueki. *Nampō kōekiron.* Tokyo, Chigura Shobō, 1943. (*SEA*).
  Position of Chinese in the industry of Southeast Asia is discussed in the first section.
—— *Nanyō keizai kenkyū.* Rev. ed. Tokyo, Chigura Shobō, 1941. (*SEA*).
  Discussion of the Chinese in regard to each of the countries of Southeast Asia excluding Burma.

Bukkyō Kenkyūkai. *Nampōken no shūkyō.* Tokyo, Daitō Shuppansha, 1942. (*SEA*).
  Includes discussion of Chinese and religion in Southeast Asia.

Chang Cheng-fan. *Chin liu-shih nien lai Nanang hua ch'iao chiao* (History of overseas Chinese education in the Nanyang in the last sixty years). Taipei, Chinese Cultural Service, 1956. (*HL*).

Chang Chün-mai. *Wo tui-yü hai-wai ch'iao-pao chih i-chien.* Shanghai, 1926.(*TOC*).
A short account of attitudes in China to the Overseas Chinese.

Chang Feng-ch'i. *Yün-nan wai-chiao wen-t'i.* Commercial Press, [1936]. (*HL*).
A very good study of Chinese interests in Indochina and Burma.

Chang Hsiang-shih. *Hua-ch'iao chung-hsin-chih Nan-yang.* Hai-K'ou, Hainan, Hai-nan Shu-chü, 1927. (*HL*).
The economic conditions and activities of the Chinese in the Indochina peninsula and Malay archipelago.

Chang Hsü-kuang. *Chung-hua min-tsu fa-chau shih-kang.* Kweilin, 1943. (*TOC*).
A history of the expansion of the Chinese race.

Chang Li-ch'ien. *Chung-nan pan-tao.* Chungking, Commercial Press, 1943. (*HL*).
Geography of Indochina, Burma, Siam.

—— *Tung-Hsi-Yang K'ao-chung chih chen-lu.* Hsin-chia-p'o Nan-yang shu-chü, 1947. (Nan-yang yen-chiu ts'ung-shu ser.) (*HL*).
A study of the historical geography of Southeast Asia.

Chang Wei-hua. *Ming-tai hai-wai mao-i chien lun.* Shanghai, Shang-hai jen-min ch'u-pan-she, 1956. (F & C).
China's trade with Southeast Asia in the Ming dynasty.

Chang Yin-tung, tr. *Nan-yang Hua-ch'iao yü ching-chi chih hsien-shih.* Shanghai, 1946. (*TOC*).
The economics of the Chinese in Southeast Asia.

Chang Yung-fu. *Hua-ch'iao yü ch'uang-li Min-kuo.* Shanghai, Chung-hua shu-chü, 1933. (*HL*).
Sun Yat-sen's revolutionary movement in Southeast Asia.

Chao Ju-K'ua. *Chu fan chih chiao chu.* Peking, Chung Hua Shu-kuan, 1956.
A gazetteer of foreign countries, 960–1278.

Ch'en Ch'in-hsien, ed. *Nan-yang hua-ch'iao sheng-huo shou-ts'e.* Singapore, 1939. (*TOC*).
A handbook on the life of Southeast Asian Chinese.

Ch'en Chung-hsing. *Chung-kuo-jen tao tung-nan-ya.* Tzu-yu ch'u-pan-she, 1957[?]. (*HCW*).
The Chinese in Southeast Asia.

Ch'en Hsiu-ching. *Nan-yang yü Chung-kuo,* Ch'ing-hua yin-shu-kuan. (Copy in Shih-ta t'u-shu-kuan). (*HCW*).
The relations between China and Southeast Asia.

Ch'en Kung-lu. *Chung-kuo chin-tai-shih.* Shanghai, Commercial Press, 1935, 1948. 2 vols. (*HL*).
An extensive survey of modern Chinese history including information on Burma and Annam in ch. 7.

Ch'en Li-t'e. *Chung-kuo hai-wai i-min shih.* Shanghai, Ku Shu-sen, printed by Chung-hua shu-chü, 1945. Li-shih ts'ung-shu ser. (*HL*).
The spread and history of Chinese colonies abroad from the T'ang dynasty onwards and their political significance.

Ch'en Lun-chiung. *Hai Kuo Wen Chien Lu.* [Author's preface 1730, rev. by Ma Chün-liang and Lin Ping-lu 1793.] 2 *chüan,* 2 *ts'e.* (*HL*).
Geographical description and maps of Southeast Asia.

Ch'en Pi-sheng. *Tien-pien san-i.* Commercial Press, 1941 [app. dated 1939]. (Yü-Kung ser., ed. by Wang Yün-Wu.) (*HL*).
> A collection of essays by the author on the land, peoples, government of Yunnan, Burma, and Indochina.

Ch'en Shou-p'eng. *Nan-yang yü Tung-nan-yang ch'ün tao chih-lüeh.* Shanghai, Cheng-chung shu-chü, 1946. (*HL*).
> Geographical and historical data on Southeast Asia and the Pacific.

Ch'en Sung-kuang. *Hsiang-kang ching-chi chin-jung yü Hua-ch'iao.* Hong Kong, 1957. (*TOC*).
> Hong Kong's economy and finance and their relation to the Overseas Chinese.

Ch'en Ta. *Nan-yang Hua-ch'iao yü Min Yüeh she-hui,* ed. by Wang Yün-wu. Commercial Press, 1938, 1939 (*HL*).
> A sociological analysis of the influences of the Overseas Chinese on the mode of living in Fukien and Kwantung provinces.

—— *Lang chi shih nien.* Chungking, Shanghai, Commercial Press, 1946. (*HL*).
> Reminiscences of 1934–45. Southeast Asia, chs. 2–4.

Chen Tung. *Chung-kung tsen-yang tui-tai Hua-ch'iao.* Kowloon, 1953. (*TOC*).
> The attitude of the Chinese Communist Party towards the Overseas Chinese.

Cheng Yen-fen. *Ch'iao-pao ti tung-hsiang yü lu-hsiang.* Taipei, 1952. (*TOC*).
> The future of the Overseas Chinese.

—— *Ko-ming ling-hsiu tui hai-wai kung-ts'o ti chih-shih* (Revolutionary leaders and their activities overseas). Taipei, Hai-wai ch'u-pan-she, 1956.

Chiang Ch'en-hua. *Jih-pen tsai T'ai-p'ing-yang shang-chih ching-chi-chan.* Nanking, Cheng-chung shu-chü, 1934. (*HL*).
> Japan's position in the Pacific and Southeast Asia.

Ch'iao-pao chiao-yü. Hsing-cheng-yüan hsin-wen-chü yin-hang, 1947. (*HL*).
> Report on education among Overseas Chinese.

Ch'iao-wu pao-she, comp. *Ch'iao-wu cheng-ts'e wen-chi.* Peking, 1957. (*TOC*).
> Essays on policy towards Overseas Chinese.

Ch'iao-wu wei-yüan hui. *Hua-ch'iao hui-kuo tou-tzu yao lan.* Taipei, Committee on Overseas Chinese Affairs, 1957. (*HL*).
> Survey of investments by Overseas Chinese repatriates.

Ch'iao-wu wei-yüan-hui ti-san ch'u. *Hua-ch'iao yü k'uang-chan tung-nan-ya mao-i wen-t'i.* Taipei, 1957. (*TOC*).
> The Overseas Chinese and problems of trade expansion in Southeast Asia.

Ch'iu Han-p'ing *and* Chuang Tsu-t'ung. *Hua-ch'iao wen-t'i.* Commercial Press, [preface dated 1936]. (Hsien-tai wen-t'i ts'ung-shu ser.) (*HL*).
> Problems of the Overseas Chinese in all parts of the world, including discriminatory regulations and the judicial position in each country.

Chou Ch'i-kang. *Hai-wai wen-t'i yen-lun hsüan-chi.* Hai-wai yüeh-k'an, 1935. (Hai-wai ts'ung-shu ser., No. 3.) (*HL*).
> Essays on the Overseas Chinese in relation to the Chinese government.

Chu Ch'i. *Nan-yang chih kuo-ch'ü yü chiang-lai.* Peking, Pei-ta she-hui k'o-hsüeh chi-k'an, June 1930. (*CKS*).
> Chinese settlements in Southeast Asia and their future.

Chu Chieh-ch'in. *Ya-chou ke-kuo shih.* Canton, Kuang-tung jen-min ch'u-pan-she, 1958. (*HSM*).
> A history of the countries of Asia.

Chu Hua-yü. *Hua-ch'iao she-hui sheng-huo yü chiao-yü*. Canton, 1937. (*TOC*).
Education in Overseas Chinese societies.

Chu K'o-ching. *Jou-yuan hsin-shu*. [Preface dated 1884.] 4 *Chüan*, 4 *ts'e* in 1 *t'ao*. (*HL*).
A collection of passages from the classics made up by Liu Yün-chi pertaining to foreign peoples. Only one essay on Southeast Asia.

Chung-hang yüeh-k'an (Bank of China Monthly). Shanghai, Bank of China, Research Dept., July 1930–.
Deals *inter alia* with Overseas Chinese remittances.

Chung-hua min-kuo hsien-hsing fa-kuei ta-ch'üan. Shanghai, Commercial Press, 1934.
A comprehensive compendium of the laws and regulations of the Republic of China. Under Executive Yuan, sub-category 2 is on foreign relations and Overseas Chinese affairs.

Chung-kuo chih-kung tang. *Chung-kuo chih-kung tang tang-chang*. Hong Kong [?], 1947. (*TOC*).
The regulations of the Chih-kung Tong, a political party with some activities in Southeast Asia.

Chung-kuo ching-chi nien-chien (Chinese economic yearbook). Shanghai, Min. of Industries, 1934. 3 vols.
Chapters on economic conditions of Overseas Chinese.

Chung-wai yüeh-chang tsuan-hsin. Shanghai, Shih-chung shu-chü, 1904. 10 *chüan*, 10 *ts'o*. (*HL*).
A collection of Chinese and foreign treaties, 2 regarding Thailand, 1 regarding Malaya, and 2 on the Haiphong–Yunnanfu railway.

Dai Tōa tōkei sōsho. Tokyo, Kokusai Nihon Kyōkai, 1942. (*SEA*).
Vol. x deals with the Chinese.

Feng Ch'eng-chün. *Chung-kuo Nan-yang chiao-t'ung shih-hsü*. Shanghai, Commercial Press, 1937. (Chung-kuo wen-hua-chih ts'ung-shu ser.) (*CKS*).
A history of China's intercourse with Southeast Asia.

—— *Chung-kuo Nan-yang chih chiao-t'ung*. Shanghai, Tung-fang tsa-chih, Apr. 1937. (*CKS*).
China and Southeast Asia.

—— ed. *Hai Lu chu*. Changsha, Commercial Press, 1938. (*HL*).
An annotation of Yang Ping-nan's *Hai Lu*. Attempts to identify names and romanize them.

Feng Li-san. *Hsin-wen chiang-hua*. Singapore, 1951.
Talks on journalism.

Feng Tzu-yu. *Hua-ch'iao ko-ming k'ai-kuo shih* (The Overseas Chinese, the revolution, and creation of the Republic: a history). Chungking, Commercial Press, 1946. (*HL*).

—— *Chung-hua min-kuo k'ai-kuo ch'ien ko* (History of the revolution before the founding of the Republic). Taipei, 1954. (*HL*).

—— *Ko-min-i-shih* (Reminiscences of the revolution). Taipei, 1956. 2 vols. (*HL*).

Fu-chien ch'iao-hsiang pao-she, ed. *Ch'iao-wu cheng-ts'e wen-ta*. Foochow, 1957. (*TOC*).
Mainland China's policy on the Overseas Chinese discussed by the Fukien Overseas Chinese Association.

Fukuda Shōzō. *Kakyō keizairon*. Tokyo, Ganshōdō, 1940. (*NBM*).
A fairly comprehensive study of the economy of the Overseas Chinese in Southeast Asia.

Gaimushō Ajiakyoku Daisanka. *Tai, Biruma, Indoneshia ni okeru kakyō no genjō.* Tokyo, Gaimushō Ajia kyoku Daisanka, 1952. (*TNA*).
The Chinese in Southeast Asia and their present position.

Gaimushō Oakyoku Daisanka. *Nanyō to Kakyō.* 1940. (*NBM*).
Foreign office report on Southeast Asian Chinese.

Gotō Asatarō. *Nanyō no Kakyō.* Tokyo, Takayama Shoin, 1942. (*SEA*).
Survey of the Chinese in Southeast Asia.

Habu Misao. *Nampō no minzoku.* Tokyo, Kōfūkan, 1944. (*SEA*).
The peoples of Southeast Asia.

Haga Takeshi. *Tōa kyōeiken to Nanyō Kakyō.* Tokyo, Tōkō Shoin, 1941. (*SEA*).
Survey of Chinese in Southeast Asia.

Hai-wai ch'u-pan-she. *Chin-jih ch'iao-ch'ing.* i–iv. Taipei, 1954–7. (*TOC*).
The Overseas Chinese at the present day.

—— *Chung-kung tsen-yang chieh-to Hua-ch'iao.* Taipei, 1955. (*TOC*).
'How the Chinese Communists rob the Overseas Chinese', by Nationalist writers.

—— *Hua-ch'iao ching-chi tao-lun.* Taipei, 1956. (*TOC*).
A guide to the economic position of the Overseas Chinese.

—— *Kung-fei ching-chi yin-mou yü Hua-ch'iao.* Taipei, 1957. (*TOC*).
Secret economic plans of the Chinese Communists with regard to the Overseas Chinese, according to Nationalist writers.

—— *Ti fang hsiao chih.* Taipei, 1958–.
Local gazetteers, compiled by the Committee of Foreign Library Resources. Includes Saigon, Cholon, Nanyang, Malacca, Hanoi, Haiphong, Manila, Kuala Lumpur, Djakarta, Rangoon.

Hai-wai wen k'u pien-chi wei-yüan-hui Taipei. *Hua ch'iao hsing-shih hsien-lieh chuan* (Biographies of eminent clan ancestors among the Chinese). Taipei, Hai-wai wen Ku, 1961–. (*HL*).

Higashi Hikarubuzo. *Nanyō to kakyō.* Takayama shoin, 1941. (*NBM*).
The Chinese in Southeast Asia.

Higashionna Hiroatsu. *Tai, Biruma, Indo.* Tokyo, Dai Nihon Yūbenkai, 1941. (*SEA*).
Primarily a travel book, the second section deals in part with the Chinese in Southeast Asia.

Higuchi Hiromu. *Nampō ni okeru shihon kankei.* Tokyo, Mītō Shooku, 1942. (*SEA*).
Details of Chinese business firms in Southeast Asia.

Hirano Yoshitarō *and* Kiyono Kenji. *Taiheiyō no minzoku seijigaku.* Tokyo, Nihon Hyōronsha, 1942. (*SEA*).
Ch. 4 deals with Overseas Chinese.

Ho Chao-fa. *Ya-chou ke-kuo hsien-tai-shih chiang-i.* Peking, Kao-teng chiao-yü ch'u-pan-she, 1958. (*HSM*).
History of the countries of Asia; vol. ii, 1945–55.

Ho Han-wen. *Hua-ch'iao kai-k'uang.* Shanghai, Shen-chou kuo-kuang-she, 1931. (*HL*).
Discussion of problems of the Overseas Chinese all over the world and the attitude of the Chinese government towards them.

Ho I-wu, ed. *Hua-ch'iao ching-chi ts'ung-shu*. Taipei, Ch'iao-wu wei-hui ti-san-ch'u, Hai-wai ch'u-pan-she, 1956–. 17 vols proposed. (*TOC*).

> Relevant to Southeast Asia are 7 vols. *See under*: Indo-China: Chang Wen-ho; Burma: Hsü Yen-shao; Philippines: Huang Ming-te; British Borneo: Sung Che-mei; Indonesia: Tai Hung-ch'i; Malay & Singapore: T'ang Shih-ch'ing; Thailand: Tseng Chien-ping.

Ho Ping-hsien. *Chung-kuo-ti kuo-chi mao-i*. Shanghai, Commercial Press, 1937. (*HL*).

> A comprehensive work on Chinese international trade, 188 pp. devoted to Southeast Asia.

Horiuchi Kazuo. *Nanyō kiryo*. Yokkaichi, 1933. (*SEA*).

> First section contains references to the Chinese in Southeast Asia.

Hsiang Ch'eng. *Chung-kung ch'iao-wu yin-mou-ti hsin tung-hsiang*. Taipei, 1958. (*TOC*).

> A Nationalist writer discusses 'the new direction of Communist China's secret plans regarding the Overseas Chinese'.

Hsieh Mou-hung. Ch'ao-hsien chan-cheng ch'ien-hou-ti tui ch'uan ya-chou-ti ch'in lüeh. Peking/Shanghai, Shih-chieh chih-shih-she, 1950. (*HL*).

> A Communist warning against the threat of American imperialism in Asia.

Hsieh Tso-min. *K'ang-chan yü Hua-ch'iao*. Chungking, 1939. (*TOC*).

> The Overseas Chinese and the war of resistance to Japan.

Hsü Chi-yü. Ying huan chih lüeh. [Preface 1848.] (*HL*).

> A famous work on the geography of the world. Southeast Asia is discussed in *chüan* 1 & 2, 10 *chüan*, 6 *ts'e*, in 1 *t'ao*.

Hsü Mou-yung. *Ya-chou-ti min-tsu chieh-fang yün-tung*. Hankow, Chung-nan jen-min ch'u-pan-she, 1951. (*HL*).

> Communist book on revolutionary movements in Far East and Southeast Asia.

Hsüeh Tien-tseng. *Pao-hu ch'iao-min lun*. Shanghai, 1937. (*TOC*).

> Protection of the Chinese Overseas discussed.

Hu Han-min, ed. *Tsung Li Ch'uan Chi* (complete works of Sun Yat-Sen). Shanghai, 1930. 4 vols.

Hua-ch'iao chih pien-tsuan wei-yüan-hui, ed. *Hua-ch'iao chih-tsung-chih*. Taipei, 1956. (*TOC*).

> General Gazetteer of the Overseas Chinese with much information on their economic position.

Hua-ch'iao ching-chi ts'an-k'ao tzu-liao. Ed. & publ. by Ch'iao-wu wei-yüan-hui ti-san-ch'u. Taipei, 1956–8. 7 vols. (*TOC*).

> A monthly publication of the Overseas Chinese Affairs Commission in Formosa, giving up-to-date economic data on the Overseas Chinese.

Hua-ch'iao ts'an-cheng-ch'üan ch'üan-an, compiled by Liu Shih-mu. Shanghai, Shang-hai Hua-ch'iao lien-ho-hui, 1913. (*HL*).

> The right of participation by the Overseas Chinese in the Chinese government.

Hua-ch'iao wen-chiao hui-i, Taipei, 1955. *Wen chiao hui i, yeh wu pao kao, wen chiao pao kao*. Taipei, 1955.

> Conference on Chinese Education, reports.

Huai Shu. *Chung-kuo ching-chi nei-mu*. Hong Kong, Hsin-min-chu ch'u-pan-she, 1948. (*HL*).

> Deals with Chinese economy but some information *re* Nanyang Tobacco Co. and Ch'en Chia-keng (Tan Kah-kee).

Huang-ch'ao fan-shu yü-ti ts'ung-shu. Shanghai, Wen-jui-lou, 1903. 48 *ts'e*, 6 *t'ao.* (*HL*).
A compilation of works on countries surrounding China.

Huang Ching-ch'u. *Nan-yang Hua-ch'iao.* Shanghai, 1930. (*TOC*).
A short description of the Overseas Chinese in Southeast Asia.

—— *Hua-ch'iao ming-jen ku-shih lu.* Shanghai, Commercial Press, 1940. (*C20*).
Collection of biographical sketches of Chinese in Malaya and Indonesia.

Huang Ching-wan. *Nan-yang pi-li Hua-ch'iao ko-ming shih-chi.* Shanghai, Wen-hua mei-shu t'u-shu kung-ssu, 1933. (*HL*).
Sun Yat-sen's revolutionary activities among the Chinese in Southeast Asia.

—— *Hua-ch'iao tui tsu-kuo ti kung-hsien.* Shanghai, 1940. (*TOC*).
Remittances from the Overseas Chinese to China.

Huang Fu-luan. *Hua-ch'iao yü Chung-kuo ko-ming.* Hong Kong, 1954. (*TOC*).
Connexions of the Overseas Chinese with the Revolution in China.

Huang T'ien-chüeh. *Hua ch'iao ching chi wen t'i* (The economic problem of the Overseas Chinese). Taipei, 1962. (*HL*).

Huang Tse-ts'an. *Hua-ch'iao hsien-shih.* Shanghai, 1934. (*TOC*).
The contemporary position of the Overseas Chinese.

Ide Kiwata. *Genka no Kakyō gaikan.* Tokyo, 1940. *See under* Tōyō Kyōkai, Chōsabu. (*SEA*)

—— *Kakyō.* Tokyo, Rokkō Shōkai, 1942. (*SEA*).
The Overseas Chinese with discussion of Chinese in Southeast Asia in particular.

—— *Nampō kaihatsushi.* Tokyo, Mikuni Seinen Kyōiku Kyōkai, 1942. (*SEA*).
History of development of Southeast Asia.

—— *Nampō Kakyōron.* Tokyo, Chuō Kōronsha, 1943. (*SEA*).
Outline of the Chinese in Southeast Asia.

Ide Teiichirō. *Ran-In, Ei-In, Futsu-In.* Tokyo, Sanseidō, 1942. (*SEA*).
Remarks on resident Chinese in Indonesia and Indochina.

Iizuka Shigeru. *Nanyō yūshi.* Tokyo, Manrikaku, 1929. (*SEA*).
Covers Southeast Asia in general.

Ishida Mikinosuke. *Nankai ni kansuru Shina shiryō.* Tokyo, Seikatsusha, 1945. (*SEA*).
Chinese historical materials on the South Seas.

Ito Ken. *Nanyō no minzoku to bunka.* Tokyo, Daitō Shuppansha, 1941. (*SEA*).
Peoples and cultures of Southeast Asia.

Kaneda Chikaju. *Nanyō oyobi Indo keizai kenkyū.* Tokyo, Kōbunsha, 1942. (*SEA*).
Second section contains discussion of Chinese society in Southeast Asia from an economic standpoint.

Kao Shih-heng. *Nan-yang-lun.* Shanghai, Nan-yang ching-chi yen-chiu-so, 1948. (*HL*).
A detailed account of the countries of Southeast Asia devoted to many topics but with accent on economics.

Kimata Seigo. *Nanyō Kakyō no atarashii jōsei.* Kaizōsha, 1942. (*NBM*).
The position of the Chinese in Southeast Asia.

Kobayashi Shinsaku. *Shina minzoku no kaigai hatten, Kakyō no kenkyū.* Tokyo, 1932. (*TOC*).
Research on the Overseas Chinese and the expansion of the Chinese abroad.

Kōbunkan, Shuppambu. *Nanyō sōran*. Singapore, 1920. (*SEA*).

Section 2 contains references to the Chinese in Southeast Asia.

Kokubō Kyōkai. *Nanyō kensetsu kōza*. Tokyo, Shōzambō, 1943. (*SEA*).

Lectures on Southeast Asia.

Kokumin seifu jitsugyō bu. *Kakyō keizai*. 1935. (*NBM*).

The economics of the Overseas Chinese.

Ku Chi-chung. *Pa-shih-wu-nien-chih Chung-Ying*. Shanghai, Hsin-min yin-shu-kuan, 1935. (*HL*).

History of 85 years of Sino-British relations, from Opium War. One chapter relates to the loss of Burma to the British; another deals with an incident in Singapore in 1927 when Chinese commemorating the death of Sun Yat-sen are said to have been fired on.

Kuan Shih-k'ai. *Hai-wai hua-ch'iao chih kuo-ch'ü yü chiang-lai*. Shanghai, Hsin Chung-hua tsa-chih, Oct. 1934. (*CKS*).

The future of the Overseas Chinese.

Kung Hsüeh-sui. *Chung-kuo min-tsu hai-wai fa-chan chuang-k'uang*. Shanghai, 1929. (*TOC*).

The expansion of the Chinese overseas.

Kuno Hōryū. *Nampō minzoku to shūkyō bunka*. Tokyo, Dai Ichi Shuppan Kyōkai, 1943. (*SEA*).

Second section includes chapter on religion of Chinese in Southeast Asia.

Nanyō to Kakyō, kaitei. Rev. ed. Tokyo, Sanseidō, 1943. (*SEA*).

Pt 2 considers Chinese in Southeast Asia under topical headings.

Kuo-jen tui-yü Jih-chün chan-ling hsin-tao hou-chih kan-hsiang chi hsi-wang. Shanghai, Chung-hua min-tsu fan ying mei hsieh-hui, 1942. (*HL*).

Pro Wang Ching-wei and Japanese Co-prosperity Sphere.

Kuwabara, Jitsuzo. *Chung-kuo A-la-po hai-shang chiao-t'ung shih*. Shanghai, Commercial Press, 1930, 1934. (*HL*).

A translation of an important study which appeared in a series of articles in the *Shigaku Zasshi* (Tokyo, Imperial Univ.). Sino-Arabic relations.

Kyōchōkai. *Nampō kyōeiken no rōdō mondai*. Tokyo, 1942. (*SEA*).

Discussion of the problem of Chinese labour immigrants in Southeast Asia.

Li Chang-chuan. *Nan-yang hua-ch'iao shih*. Chi-nan ta-hsüeh [copy with Hai-wai t'ung-hsün she]. (*HCW*).

A history of the Chinese in Southeast Asia.

Li Ch'ang-fu. *Chung-kuo chih-min nan-yang hsiao-shih*. Shanghai, Tung-fang tsa-chih, Mar. 1926. (*CKS*).

A short history of Chinese settlements in Southeast Asia.

—— *Hua-ch'iao*. Shanghai, Chung-hua shu-chü, 1927, 1929. (*HL*).

A study of the Overseas Chinese with a bibliography. Ch. 3 deals with the Chinese in Southeast Asia.

—— *Nan-yang hua-ch'iao i-chih-shih niao-k'an*. Nanking, Hsin Ya-hsi-ya yüeh-k'an, Jan. 1931. (*CKS*).

Short history of Chinese settlements in Southeast Asia.

—— *Nan-yang Hua-ch'iao-shih*. Commercial Press [author's preface dated 1933]. (Shih-ti hsiao-ts'ung-shu ser.) (*HL*).

History of the Chinese in Southeast Asia. Detailed histories of each of the Chinese communities with a long bibliography.

C.S.E.A.——U

Li P'u-sheng. *Hua-ch'iao fa-chan chien-shih* (A brief history of the Overseas Chinese). 1942. (*HL*).

—— *Ch'iao-pao ying ju-ho fan-kung*. Taipei, 1952. (*TOC*).
On the necessity of opposition to Communism by the Overseas Chinese.

Liang Shao-wen. *Nan-yang lü-hsing man-chi*. Shanghai, Commercial Press, 1924–5. (*HL*).
Account of author's travels in Malaysia and Indonesia.

Liang Tzu-heng. *Ch'iao-cheng kai-lun*. Taipei, 1956. (*TOC*).
An outline of Overseas Chinese government.

—— *Hua-ch'iao she-hui yen-chiu*. Hong Kong, 1958. (*TOC*).
Researches into Overseas Chinese society.

Lin Po-ai *and others*. *Nan-yang ming-jen chi-chuan*. Penang, 1922. (*C20*).
Collection of biographies of Chinese in Malaya and Indonesia.

Liu Cheng-ming. *Nan-yang Hua-ch'iao wen-t'i*. Chungking, 1944. (*TOC*).
Problems of the Chinese in Southeast Asia with discussion of the Coolie Trade.

Liu Chi-hsüan *and* Shu Shih-cheng. *Chung-hua min-tsu t'o-chih Nan-yang shih*. Nanking, 1935. (*TOC*).
A history of Chinese colonization in Southeast Asia.

Liu Shih-mu *and* Hsü Chih-kuei. *Hua-ch'iao kai-kuan*. Shanghai, Chung-hua shu-chü, 1935. (*HL*).
Detailed analysis of the Chinese abroad and their circumstances, with a bibliography appended.

Liu Tso-jen. *Nan-yang hsien-shih*. Canton [?], Chung-kuo wen-hua fu-wu-she, 1947. (*HL*).
Collection of reprints of articles by the author, financial, economic, etc. *re* Southeast Asia.

Liu Yen. *Chung-kuo chin-shih wai-chiao shih*. Shanghai, Hua-ch'ang yin-shua-chü, 1914. (*HL*).
Chs 6 & 7 deal with the loss of Chinese authority over Annam and Burma.

Mantetsu Chōsaka. *Nanyō ni okeru Shinajin*. 1926. (*NBM*).
The Chinese in Southeast Asia.

Mantetsu Tōa Keizai Chōsa Kyoku. *Kakyō*. 1927. (*NBM*).
The Overseas Chinese.

—— *Nanyō kakyō sōsho dai 1–6 kan*. 1940. (*NBM*).
A series on the economic position of the Southeast Asian Chinese.

Matsubara Tsutomu. *Namban Tsūkōshi*. Tokyo, Dai Nihon Shuppan Kabushiki Kaisha, 1942. (*SEA*).
A historical study of China's relations with Southeast Asia. Bibliography of Chinese sources appended.

Min-kuo chiu-nien-fen wai-chiao nien-chien, ed. by T'ung Chi-k'o of the Wai-chiao-pu. Peking, 1921. (F & L).
Second part contains references to foreign recruitment of Chinese labour.

Minami Manshū Tetsudō Kabushiki Kaisha, Shomubu, Chōsaka. *Nanyō ni okeru shinajin*. Dairen, 1926. (*SEA*).
A pamphlet on the Chinese in Southeast Asia based on field investigation.

Minami Manshū Tetsudō Kabushiki Kaisha, Tōa Keizai Chōsakyoku. *Nanyō Kakyō sōsho*. Tokyo, 1939–41. 6 vols. (*SEA*).
The Chinese in Southeast Asia: (i) in Thailand; (ii) in French Indochina; (iii) in the Philippines; (iv) in the Dutch East Indies; (v) in Malaya and Burma; (vi) in Southeast Asia as a whole.

Miyoshi Shunkichirō. *Nanyō kakyō ni tsuite.* Toā kenkyūsha, 1941. (*NBM*).
On the Chinese in Southeast Asia.

Naikaku, Kikakuin. *Kakyō no kenkyū.* Tokyo, 1939. (*SEA*).
Research on Overseas Chinese particularly in Indochina, Thailand, Malaya, Indonesia, and Philippines.

Nakai Kitarō. *Nanyōdan.* Tokyo, Tōgyō Kenkyūkai, 1914. (*SEA*).
Notes and comments on Southeast Asia with references to the Chinese.

Nakajima Kanji. *Nampō kyōeiken no bukkyō jijō.* Tokyo, Kōshisha Shobō, 1942. (*SEA*).
Discusses religion of Chinese in Southeast Asia.

Nampō Keizai Kondankai. *Nampō kensetsu no kihon mondai.* Tokyo, Naigai Shobō, 1942. (*SEA*).
One section on economic position of Chinese in Southeast Asia.

Nampō keizai shigen sōran. Tokyo, 1942–4. 12 vols. (*SEA*).
Survey of the economic resources of the South Seas. Vol. v contains material on the history, society, and economic position of the Chinese in Thailand. Chinese also discussed in vol. vi, Malaya; vol. vii, Burma; vol. ix, Philippines; vol. x, Indonesia; vol. xi, Borneo.

Nampō Kenkyūkai. *Nampō gaikan, shigen.* Tokyo, Shinkeizaisha, 1942. (*SEA*).
Discussion of Japan's policy towards the Chinese in Southeast Asia.

Nampō Nenkan Kankōkai. *Nampō nenkan.* Tokyo, Tōhōsha, 1943. (*SEA*).
Sect. 1, pt 8, devoted to Chinese in Southeast Asia.

Nampōken Kenkyūkai. *Nampō shinkensetsu kōza.* Tokyo, Ōsakayagō Shoten, 1943. (*SEA*).
Contains lecture on Japan's policy towards the Chinese in Southeast Asia.

Nan-ch'iao jih-pao, ed. *Hsin Chung-kuo yü nan-ch'iao.* Singapore, 1950. (*TOC*).
New China and the Southeast Asian Chinese.

Nan-yang Chung-hua hui-yeh tsung-hui nien k'an ti-erh chi (Nanyang Chinese Exchange & Remittance Association 1948 Annual). Singapore, 1948. (*HL*).
Articles on remittances to China by Overseas Chinese.

Nan-yang Hua-ch'iao, compiled by Wang Yün-wu and Li Sheng-wu. Shanghai, Commercial Press, 1933. (*HL*).
Collection of essays on the Chinese in Southeast Asia by different authors.

Nan-yang mao-i chih-nan. Shanghai, Tsu-hsiu ch'ou-k'an-she, 1940. (*HL*).
A handbook on Southeast Asian trade.

Nan-yang nien-chien. Singapore, Nan-yang pao-she, 1951. (*HL*).
Year-book of the Nanyang.

Nanyō Kakyō to kinyū kikan. 1917. (*SEA*).
The Chinese in Southeast Asia and their banking agencies.

Nanyō kyōkai. *Dai Nanyō ken.* Tokyo, Chū ō Kōronsha, 1941. (*SEA*).
Study of Southeast Asia including Overseas Chinese.

—— *Saikin no Nanyō jijō.* Tokyo, 1941. (*SEA*).
One paper on Chinese in Southeast Asia.

—— *Nanyō annai.* Tokyo, 1942. (*SEA*).
Section on Overseas Chinese in Southeast Asia.

—— *Nanyō no Kakyō.* 2nd ed. Tokyo, Meguro Shoten. 1942. (*SEA*).
First section is a general study of Chinese in Southeast Asia; second section consists of translations of works by these Chinese themselves.

Narita Setsuo. *Kakyōshi, zōho.* Tokyo, Keisetsu Shoin, 1942. (*SEA*).

Second section deals with relations of Chinese overseas with China and with the Overseas Chinese in Southeast Asia.

Negishi Tadashi. *Kakyō zakki.* 2nd ed. Tokyo, Osaka, Asahi Shimbunsha, 1942. (*SEA*).

The Overseas Chinese and their economic position in Southeast Asia.

Nihon Bōeki Shinkō Kabushiki Kaisha, Kikakubu. *Bōeki taisaku shiryō.* Tokyo, 1942–. 7 vols. (*SEA*).

Vol. i deals with the Philippines; vol. ii with Malaya; vol. iv with Thailand. Discussion of economic position of Chinese in each of the above.

Nihon Nampō Kyōkai. *Shigen kaihatsu to sono keiei, Nampō jijō.* Tokyo, Kyōiku Kenkyūkai, 1942. (*SEA*).

One lecture on Chinese in Southeast Asia.

Nihon Takushoku Kyōkai. *Takushoku sōsho.* Tokyo, 1941. (*SEA*).

Vols. i & iii contain discussion of the Chinese in Indochina and the Philippines.

Nomura Teikichi. *Nampō kyōeiken wo kataru.* Tokyo, Tsuru Shobō, 1942. (*SEA*).

Third chapter on Chinese in Southeast Asia.

Ogata Tadashi. *Nampōken no keizaiteki kachi.* 2nd ed. Taihoku, Nanyō Kyōkai, 1941. (SEA).

The economic value of Southeast Asia with discussion of the economic power of the Chinese.

Ōgata Tarō. *Nanyō Kakyō to keizai.* Tokyo, Seiki Shobō, 1942. (*SEA*).

The Chinese and the economy of Southeast Asia.

Oka Kanhei *and* Yamazaki Seizaburo. *Gendai kakyō mondai.* Seikatsusha, 1940. (*NBM*).

Problems of the Chinese in Southeast Asia.

Ōno Kyōhei *and* Satō Shirō. *Nankaku.* Tokyo, Maruzen Kabushiki Kaisha, 1915. (*SEA*).

Economic aspects of Southeast Asia with some references to the Chinese.

Ono Takashi. *Tōnan Ajia shisatsu hōkoku.* Tokyo, Tsūshin Chōsakai, 1940. (*SEA*).

Field report on Southeast Asia with discussion of the Chinese problem, especially the Hakkas.

Ōsaka Shiyakusho, Sangyōbu, Bōekika. *Nampō jijō.* Osaka, 1942. (*SEA*).

Vol. i contains a lecture on the Chinese problem in Southeast Asia.

Pa-jen. *Yüan-tung min-tsu ko-ming wen-t'i, She-hui k'o-hsüeh hsiao-ts'ung-shu,* i/6. Hong Kong, Nan-hai ch'u-pan-she, 1948. (*HL*).

(Pa-jen is the pseudonym of Wang Jen-shu.) Survey of revolutionary movements in the Far East, particularly in Southeast Asia.

P'an Kung-chao. *Tung-nan-ya ko-kuo nei-mu.* Shanghai, Shi-chieh chih-shih-she, 1948, 1949. (*HL*).

Economic, social, and political problems in India and Southeast Asia. Communist slant.

Sakamoto Tokumatsu. *Nampō bunkaron.* Tokyo, Ōsakayagō Shoten, 1942. (*SEA*).

The sociology of Chinese in Southeast Asia.

Sanseidō. *Nampō bunka kōza minzoku oyobi minzoku undō hen.* Tokyo, 1944. (*SEA*).

Supplementary section describes character, distribution, and history of Chinese in Southeast Asia.

Shibata Kenichi. *Nampō hatten no chishiki.* Tokyo, Seinen Shobō, 1942. (*SEA*).

Second section contains discussion of Chinese in Southeast Asia.

Shih-chieh nien-chien (World yearbook). Shanghai, Ta-t'ung, 1931. 3 vols. (R 9316/4162.)

Vol. iii refers to Chinese abroad.

Shirasaka Yoshinao. *Nanyō seiji chiri shikō.* Tokyo, Tanaka Seikōdō, 1943. (*SEA*).

Geopolitics of Southeast Asia with one chapter devoted to the Chinese.

Shu Shih-cheng. *Chung-Fa wai-chiao-shih.* Shanghai, Commercial Press, 1928. (*HL*).

History of Sino-French relations.

Ssu-fa hsing-cheng pu. *Tiao ch'a chu kung fei hsien chieh tuan ti ch'iao wu kung tso* (The present state of Communist activities in Overseas Chinese affairs). Taipei, 1960.

Su Hsi-wen. *Chiang tsung-t'ung yü Hua-ch'iao.* Hong Kong, 1958. (*TOC*).

Chiang Kai-shek and his dealings with the Overseas Chinese.

Suyama Takashi. *Kakyō shakai.* Tokyo, 1955. (*TOC*).

An account of Overseas Chinese society.

Taiheiyō Kyōkai. *Taiheiyōken, minzoku to bunka.* Tokyo, Kawade Shobō, 1944. (*SEA*).

The peoples and cultures of the Pacific. Sects. 1, 2, & 3 deal with Southeast Asia and the Chinese.

Taiwan Ginkō, Chōsaka. *Nanyō ni okeru Kakyō.* Taihoku, 1914. (*SEA*).

The Chinese in Southeast Asia and their economic position.

Taiwan Sōtokufu, Gaijibu. *Nampō Kakyō yūryokusha meibo.* Taihoku, Nampō Shiryōkan, 1942. (*SEA*).

Directory of prominent Chinese in Southeast Asia.

—— *Nampō Kakyō dantai chōsa.* Taihoku, 1943. (*SEA*).

Chinese societies in Southeast Asia.

Taiwan Takushoku Kabushiki Kaisha, Chōsaka. *Nanyō Kakyō to sono taisaku.* Taihoku, 1942. (*SEA*).

Southeast Asian governments' policies relative to Overseas Chinese.

Takeda Kōji. *Nampō no gunsei.* Tokyo, Senryudo, 1943. (*SEA*).

Military government in Southeast Asia with some general discussion of the Chinese population.

Takei Jūrō. *Waga Nanyō bōeki wo sogai suru Kakyō no shinsō.* Tokyo, Tōa Keizai Chōsakyoku, 1932. (*SEA*).

Strongly anti-Overseas Chinese account of trade in Southeast Asia.

—— *Nampō kensetsu to minzoku mondai.* Tokyo, Kokusai Nihon Kyōkai, 1942. (*SEA*).

Contains discussion of Chinese in Southeast Asia and their culture.

—— *Nampō minzoku to seiji taisaku.* Tokyo, Tōkō Shoin, 1943. (*SEA*).

The impact of and exploitation by the Chinese in Southeast Asia is discussed.

Takumushō, Takumukyoku. *Nanyō saibai jigyō yōran.* Tokyo, 1935. (*SEA*).

Survey of agricultural industries in Southeast Asia, 1934, with discussion of Chinese residents.

Tamura, Jugen *and* Hamada, Tsuneichi. *Nan-yang Hua-ch'iao yü ching-chi-chih hsien-shih,* trans. by Chang Yin-t'ung in the Nan-yang ts'ung-shu ser. Chungking, Shanghai, Commercial Press, 1946 (*HL*).

The development and contemporary position of Chinese colonies in Southeast Asia.

Teng Tzu-sen (Tang Chisum). *Hua-Ying ho-pi shih-chieh pu-ming.* Singapore, P'u-i kung-ssu, 1922. (*HL*).
Place-names in Chinese and English with special attention to Southeast Asia.

Teo Eng-hock. *Nanyang yü ch'uang-tsao Minkuo* (Nanyang and the Creation of the Republic). Shanghai, 1933.

Ti-erh-tz'u shih-chieh ta-chan-hou chih-min-ti yü pan-chih-min-ti jen-min chieh-fang tou-cheng, trans. by Kuo Tr'ung-chou and Nan Chih-shan. [App. dated 1950.]
Collection of translations of reports submitted to the Economic Inst. of the Russian Academy of Sciences and the Pacific Inst. in June 1949.

T'ien Ju-k'ang. *17–19 shih-chi chung-yeh Chung-kuo fan-ch'uan tsai Tung-nan Ya-chou.* Shanghai, Shang-hai jen-min ch'u-pan-she, 1957. (F & C).
Chinese ships in Southeast Asia in 17–19 centuries.

Tōa Kenkyūjo. *Nanyō kakyō chōsa no kekka gaiyō.* Tokyo, 1941. (*SEA*).
History, economy, and anti-Japan movements of the Chinese in Southeast Asia.

Tōkyō Furitsu Shōkō Shōreikan, *Nampōken sōgō kōza.* Tokyo, Kenshinsha, 1943. (*SEA*).
Vol. ii contains a lecture on Overseas Chinese.

ōyō Kyōkai, Chōsabu. *Genka no Kakyō gaikan.* Tokyo, 1940. (*SEA*).
Outline of the situation of the Chinese in Southeast Asia at the time of writing (actual work of Ide Kiwata).

T'u K'ai-yü. *Hua-ch'iao.* Shanghai, Commercial Press, 1934. (*HL*).
First chapter deals with the Chinese in Southeast Asia.

Tung-fang pei-ya-p'o min-tsu chieh-fang wen-t'i, compiled by Chung-kuo Kuo-min-tang Che-chiang-sheng chih-hsing wei-yüan-hui. Che-chiang Hang-chou yin-shua-chü, 1930. (*HL*).
An extensive political treatise on the Asiatic countries under colonial rule; Communist slant.

Wai-chiao kung-pao. Peking, Wai-chiao-pu, 1921–8 (monthly). (F & L).
Diplomatic documents, some relating to Overseas Chinese.

Wai-kuo chuan, compiled by Yu T'ung (Ch'ing dynasty). 8 *chüan,* 4 *ts'e* in 4 *t'ao.* (*HL*).
Geography of many countries. Southeast Asia is discussed in first few *chüan.*

Wang Pi-ch'en. *Ko-kuo tai-yü Hua-ch'iao ho-li kai-yao.* Shanghai, Wang Yün-wu, 1933. (*HL*).
Restrictive measures against Chinese overseas.

Wang Ta-chu. *Lun Nan-yang hua-ch'iao chih fa-chan chi ch'i ch'ien-t'u.* Hua-ch'iao lun-wen chi ti-i-chi, 1955. (*HCW*).
Past development and future of the Chinese in Southeast Asia.

Wang Yün. *Mei-ti ch'in-lüeh-hsia-ti Tung-nan-ya.* Peking/Shanghai, Shih-chieh chih-shih-she, 1951. (Ta-chung shih-chieh ts'ung-shu ser.) (*HL*).
Anti-U.S.A. survey of Southeast Asia.

Watanabe Takeshi. *Nampō kyōeiken to Kakyō.* Tokyo, Shigensha, 1942. (*SEA*).
The Chinese in Southeast Asia and their economic position.

Wei Yüan. *Hai-kuo t'u-chih.* [Editor's preface 1842.] 100 *chüan,* 24 *ts'e* in 4 *t'ao.* (*HL*).
This famous work includes accounts of Indochina, Siam, Burma, Malaya, Indonesia, and the Philippines.

Wen-hui pao, ed. & pub. *I-ch'ien san-pai wan Hua-ch'iao ti kuang-jung.* Hong Kong, 1956. (*TOC*).

'13 million Overseas Chinese' and their relations with Mainland China.

Wu Chi-hsien. *Tung-nan-ya ching-chi kai-kuan.* Shanghai, Chung-hua shu-chü, 1951. (*HL*).

A Communist study of the economy of Southeast Asia and conditions under colonial rule.

Wu T'ieh-ch'eng. *Hsüan-wei Nan-yang pao-kao-shu.* (*HL*).

Report of the author's goodwill trip to Southeast Asia in 1940.

Ya-chou Ao-chou ko-kuo kung-yün chieh-shao, compiled by Chung-hua ch'üan-kuo tsung-kung-hui. Peking, 1949. (*HL*).

A Communist survey of labour movements in Asia and Australia, of which five chapters deal with Southeast Asia.

Ya-chou chih-min-ti jen-min-ti chieh-fang yün-tung, compiled by the Chung-nan jen-min ch'u-pan-she. Hankow, 1951. (*HL*).

A collection of newspaper articles discussing the revolutionary movements in Southeast Asia.

Yang Ping-nan. *Hai lu.* 2 *ts'e*, with 2 additional *ts'e* entitled 'Hai-tao i-chih Chai-lüeh', by Wang Ta-hai, and 'Hung-mao-fan Ying-Chi-li K'ao-lüeh', compiled by Wang Wen-t'ai. [Preface by Wang Liu, 1862.] (*HL*).

Description of travel, marvels, and curiosities in Southeast Asia, etc.

Yao Nan. *Chan-hou Nan-yang ching-chi wen-ti.* [Preface by H. H. Kung.] Chung-king, 1945; Shanghai, Commercial Press, 1946. (*HL*).

An economic study of post-war Southeast Asia.

—— *Chung-nan pan-tao hua-ch'iao-shih kang-yao.* Chungking, Shanghai, Chung-kuo nan-yang hsüeh-hui, 1945, 1946. (*HL*).

The Chinese in Indochina, Burma, and Siam.

Yao Nan *and* Hsiu Yü. *Ku-tai Nan-yang shih-ti ts'ung-k'ao.* Peking, Shang-wu yin-shu-kuan, 1958. (*HSM*).

Southeast Asia in historical times.

Yao ts'eng-yiu. *Kuang-tung-shang-ti hua-ch'iao hui-kuan.* Academa Sinica Inst. of Social Sciences, 1943. (Monograph ser, 18.) (*HL*).

A study of the system of remittances made by the overseas Cantonese to China (more information *re* remittances from America than from Southeast Asia).

Yen Ch'ing-p'ing. *Nan-yang ching-chi ti-li.* Chungking, Cheng-chung shu-chü, 1942, 1943. (*HL*).

Economic geography of Southeast Asia.

Yokohama Shōkin Ginkō, Chōsabu. *Nampō Kakyō shōrai no sangyō bunya to sono hatten no kanōsei.* Yokohama, 1944. (*SEA*).

The future industrial influence of the Chinese in Southeast Asia.

Yoneda Shizuo. *Taikoku oyobi Futsu-In no kaiun.* Tokyo, Kimura Shoten, 1944. (*SEA*).

The maritime trade of Thailand and French Indochina and the place of the Chinese residents.

3. BURMA

Biruma Kenkyūkai. *Dai Birumashi.* Tokyo, Sanseidō, 1944. 2 vols. (*SEA*).

Vol. ii includes discussion of the history and organizations of the Chinese in Burma.

Chang Cheng-fan. *Mien-tien te hsien-chuang yü hua-ch'iao.* Chung-yang wen-wu kung-ying-she, 1954. (*HCW*).
The Chinese in present-day Burma.

—— *Mien-tien hua-ch'iao shih-hua.* Taipei, 1955. (*TOC*).
A short history of the Chinese in Burma.

Chang Ch'eng-sun. Chung-Ying T'ien-nien chiang-chieh wen-t'i; Sino-Burmese frontier problem. *Yenching J. of Chinese Studies* (Peking), 1937. (Harvard Yenching Inst. ser. 15.) (*HL*).

Chao Sung-ch'iao. *Mien-tien ti-li.* Peking, K'e-hsüeh ch'u-pan-she, 1958. (*HSM*)·
The geography of Burma.

Chiang Yün-ch'ing. *Pao-wei hsien-shang-ti Mien-tien,* ed. by the Chün-shih wei-yüan-hui cheng-chih-pu ti-i-t'ing, 1942. (*HL*).
History of Sino-Burmese relations and geography of Burma for use of military forces.

Chou Kuang-cho. *Mien-tien nan-tuan mo-ting chieh ti'ao-ch'a pao-kao-shu.* Nanking, Han-wen cheng-kai yin-shu-chü [epilogue 1935]. (*HL*).
Report of the investigation of disputed frontier in Pan-hung area.

Chung-kuo hai-kuan yü Mien Tsang wen-t'i. Peking, K'o-hsüeh ch'u-pan-she, 1957. (Ti-kuo chu-i yü chung-kuo hai-kuan, vol. v.) (F & C).
The Imperial Maritime Customs and Burma.

Hsü Shih-yin. *Mien-tien Chung-kuo T'ung-meng-hui k'ai-kuo ko-ming-shih.* Ssu ming jih hsin shu-chü [preface dated 1931]. (*HL*).
The revolutionary movement among the Chinese in Burma, 1908–11.

Hsü Yen-shao. *Mien-tien Hua-ch'iao ching-chi.* Taipei, Hua-ch'iao ching-chi ts'ung-shu, ti-i chi, 1957. (*TOC*).
The economic position of the Chinese in Burma. [*See under* General: Ho I-wu.]

Hsüeh Fu-ch'eng. *Mien-tien hua-chieh t'u-shuo.* Wu-hsi, Ch'uan-ching-lou, 1902. 1 ts'e. (*HL*).
Collection of documents concerning border disputes with Britain.

I-p'ei. *Mien-tien.* Shanghai, Sheng-huo t'u-shu hsin-chih Shang-hai lien-ho fa-hsing-so, 1949. (*HL*).
A Communist account of Burma.

Liu Po-k'uei. *Chung-Mien chieh-wu wen-t'i.* Shanghai, Cheng-chung shu-chü, 1946. (*HL*).
Sino-Burmese border disputes.

Mien-tien Hua-ch'iao hsing-shang tsung-hui nien wu-chou-nien chi-nien t'e-k'an. Rangoon, 1936. (*HL*).
Commemorative publication of the Burma Chinese Trade Association; contains articles on Overseas Chinese trade with Burma.

Ogata Tadashi. *Biruma no genjō.* Taihoku, Nanyō Kyōkai, 1942. (*SEA*).
Includes discussion of Chinese in Burma.

Shu Shih-cheng. *Chung-Ying wai-chiao-shih.* Shanghai, Commercial Press, 1933. (Hsin-shih-tai shih-ti ts'ung-shu ser.) (*HL*).
Sino-British relations with discussion of Sino-Burmese border disputes.

Sun K'o-kang. *Mien-tien tang-k'ou-chih.* Shanghai, Shih-tai t'u-shu kung-ssu, 1946. (*HL*).
A Chinese war correspondent's story of the campaigns in the Burma theatre during World War II.

Taiwan Sōtokufu, Gaijibu. *Biruma jijo gaiyō*. Taihoku, 1943. (*SEA*).
Outline of Burma with references to the Chinese.

Tseng K'o-nien. *Chin-Hsin Mien-tien*. Rangoon, 1940. (*HL*).
Account of Burma.

Wang Po-leng. *Chung-Mien kuan-hsi-shih kang-yao*. Chang-chung shu-chü, 1944, 1947. (*HL*).
Historical relations between China and Burma based on Chinese material.

Watanabe Takeshi. *Gendai Biruma no keizai*. Tokyo, Shigensha, 1942. (*SEA*).
Economy of modern Burma with references to the Chinese.

Yoshida Minoru. *Indo-Biruma no kyōiku-shokumin seisaku*. Tokyo, Sankyō Shobō, 1942. (*SEA*).
Educational policies and the Chinese in Burma.

4. SIAM (THAILAND)

Akashi Jirō *and* Seki Yoshihiko. *Taikoku nōson keizairon*. Tokyo, Chūō Kōronsha, 1942. (*SEA*).
Thailand's agriculture and the Chinese.

Amada Rokurō. *Genchi ni miru Taikoku Kakyō*. Tokyo, Nanyō Kyōkai, 1939. (*SEA*).
Survey of the Chinese in Thailand.

Chiang Yün-ch'ing. *Chung-kuo chan-ch'ü-ti T'ai-kuo*. 1942. (*HL*).
Booklet issued as guide to Thailand for the use of Chinese military forces operating in the north of that country.

Chuang Hsin-tsai. *T'ai-kuo hua-ch'iao sheng-huo yü wen-hua*. Cheng-chung shu-chü, 1956. (*HCW*).
The Chinese in Thailand.

Hsin chung kung ssu, Tōkyō shisha. *Nanyō Kakyō no kenkyū*. Tokyo, 1937. (*SEA*).
General survey of Chinese in Southeast Asia with third section devoted to their conditions in Thailand.

Hua ch'iao chih pien-tsuan wei-yüan-hui, T'ai-pei. *Hua-ch'iao chih T'ai-kuo* (Overseas Chinese gazetteer: Thailand). Taipei, 1959.

Jiyū Bunka Jigyō Shuppansha. *Taikoku kakyō jimbutsushi*. Taikyō, Jiyū Bunka Jigyō Shuppansha, 1956. (*TNA*).

Kokusai Keizai Gakkai. *Tai, Futsu-In no kenkyū*. Tokyo, Tōkō Shoin, 1942. (*SEA*).
The Chinese in Thailand and their economic position.

Liang Wen-chung. *T'ai-kuo min-tsu yü hua-ch'iao*. Hua-ch'iao lun-wen chi ti-i-chi, Oct. 1954. (*HCW*).
The Overseas Chinese in Thailand.

Minami Manshū Tetsudō Kabushiki Kaisha, Tōa Keizai Chōsakyoku. *Shamu gaisei to sono kinjō*. Tokyo, 1937. (*SEA*).
Third section has some comments on the Chinese in Thailand.

Miyahara Takeo. *Yakushin Taikoku no zembō*. Tokyo, Aikoku Shimbunsha, 1941. (*SEA*).
Survey of Thailand with discussion of the Chinese residents.

—— *Aratanaru Tai*. Tokyo, Tosho Kenkyūsha, 1942. (*SEA*).
Discussion of the Chinese in Thailand.

C.S.E.A.—U 2

Narita Setsuo. *Taikoku Kakyō to kome*. Tokyo, Bunkyūdō, 1942. (*NBM*).
　　Chinese agriculture in Thailand.

Nihon bōeki shinkō kyōkai. *Taikoku no sangyō bōeki jijō*. Tokyo, 1942. (*SEA*).
　　Fourth chapter on the Chinese in Thailand.

T'ai-kuo hua-ch'iao kung-shang-yeh ch'üan-mao. Kung-shang chou-pao-she, 1951.
　　(In the *Ch'iao-wu wei-yüan-hui tzu-liao-shih*.) (*HCW*).
　　Chinese industry in Thailand.

Taiwan ginkō, Chōsaka. *Taikoku no kinyū narabi ni jūyō sangyō jijō*. [Taihoku?].
　　1941. (*SEA*).
　　The Chinese and the industry and finance of Thailand.

Taiwan takushoku kabushiki kaisha, Chōsaka, *Taikoku Kakyō*. Taihoku, 1939.
　　(*SEA*).
　　The Chinese in Thailand and the Thai government's oppression of them.

Tōa Keizai Kondankai. *Nampō no minzoku keizai*. Tokyo, Dai Tōasha, 1944. (*SEA*).
　　Second lecture discusses the Chinese in Thailand.

Tōa Kenkyūjo. *Taikoku nōmin to Kakyō*. Tokyo, 1941. (*NBM*).
　　The Chinese and their relations with the Thai peasantry.

Ts'ao Mien-chih. *Hsien-lo*. Hong Kong, Hsin-chung-kuo shu-chü, 1949 (Hsin-
　　chung-kuo pai-k'e hsiao-ts'ung-shu ser.) (*HL*).
　　An account of Thailand, the last four chapters dealing with the Chinese.

Tseng Chien-ping. *T'ai-kuo Hua-ch'iao ching-chi*. Taipei, Hua-ch'iao ching-chi
　　ts'ung-shu, ti-i chi, 1956. (*TOC*).
　　The economic position of the Chinese in Thailand. (*See under* General: Ho-I-wu.)

5. Vietnam (North and South), Cambodia, and Laos

An-nam ch'i-shou pen-mo, Chiao-pu, corrected and supplemented by Liu I-chang,
　　T'ao Feng-lou. Shanghai, photolithographed, 1937. 3 *ts'e*. (*HL*).
　　An account of Sino-Annamese relations from 1404–35, taken from the *Ming Shih-Lu*.

Andō Sei. *Mita mama no Minami Shina to Indoshina*. Taichū (Formosa), Taiwan
　　Shimbunsha, 1922. (*SEA*).
　　Discussion of Chinese residents in section on Indochina.

Chang Kuang-piao. *Ts'ung chih-min-ti tao tu-li-ti Yüeh-nan*. Peking, Shanghai, Shih-
　　chieh chih-shih-she, 1951. (Shih-chieh chih-shih ts'ung-shu ser. No. 65.) (*HL*).
　　Various aspects of the period following the declaration of independence in Vietnam.

Chang Wen-ho. *Yüeh-nan Kao-mien Liao-kuo Hua-ch'iao ching-chi*. Taipei, Hua-
　　ch'iao ching-chi ts'ung-shu, ti'i chi, 1956. (*TOC*).
　　The economic position of the Chinese in Vietnam, Cambodia, and Laos. (*See under*
　　General: Ho I-wu.)

Ch'en Hsiu-ho. *Yüeh-nan ku-shih chi ch'i min-tsu wen-hua-chih yen-chiu*. [Preface
　　Kunming, 1943.] (*HL*).
　　Ancient history of Annam, anthropology, situation before coming of French.

—— *Chung-yüeh liang-kuo jen-min te yu-hao kuan-hsi ho wen-hua chiao-liu*. Peking,
　　Chung-kuo nien-ch'ing ch'u-pan-she, 1957. (*HSM*).
　　Culture contact between China and Vietnam.

Ch'iao-wei-hui mi-shu-shih. *Yueh-nan hua-ch'iao kuo-chi wen-t'i tzu-liao*. Ch'iao-
　　wei-hui mi-shu-shih, 1956. (*HCW*).
　　Material on the nationality problem of the Chinese in Vietnam.

Chou Sheng-k'ao. *Yüeh-nan hua-ch'iao chiao-yu* (Overseas Chinese education in Vietnam). Taipei, Hua-Ch'iao, 1961 (*HL*).

Chu Hsieh. *Yueh-nan shou-hsiang jih-chi*. Shanghai, Commercial Press, 1946. (*HL*).
Account of the surrender of Japanese in N. Indochina to forces under General Lu Han.

Hemmi Shigeo. *Futsuryō Indoshina kenkyū*. Tokyo, Nihon Hyōronsha, 1942. (*SEA*).
First section contains discussion of Chinese in Indochina. Map of distribution appended.

Hsiao Yang. *Chieh-fang-chung-ti Yüeh-nan*. Shanghai, Ch'ün-lien ch'u-pan-she, 1951. (*HL*).
A Communist account of Vietnam and its recent history.

Hsin Tsu-k'ang. *Liao-kuo hua-ch'iao chiao-yu* (Overseas Chinese education in Laos). Taipei, Hai-wei, 1960.

Hsü Wei-nan. *Hu Chih-ming*. Shanghai, Commercial Press, 1950. (Ta-chung hsin-tu-wu ser.) (*HL*).
A short sketch of Ho Chi-minh's life.

Hua-ch'iao chih pien-tsuan wei yuan hui, Tai-pei. *Hua ch'iao chih-chien pu-chai* (Overseas Chinese gazetteer, Cambodia). Taipei, 1960. (*HL*).

Huang Tse-ts'ang. *Yüeh-nan*. Shanghai, Commercial Press, 1934. (*HL*).
Demography, history, economy, geography of Annam, with an account of the Chinese there.

Ide Asakame. *Futsu-In kenkyū*. Tokyo, Ōkoku Seinen Kyōiku Kyōkai, 1941. (*SEA*).
Contains discussion of Chinese in Indochina.

Juan Wen-kang. *Yüeh-nan tu-li yün-tung i-lan*. Shanghai, 'The Vietnam Residents' Association', 1946. (*HL*).
Eng. title: 'A Glance at the Annamite Independence Movement'. The book is in two parts, the Chinese text being fuller than the English. Topics dealt with are the geography of Vietnam and relations with China, economic, political, and cultural problems.

Kaneko Takanosuke. *Sosei Futsuryō Indoshina no zembō*. Tokyo, Aikoku Shimbunsha, 1941. (*SEA*).
History, distribution, economic and legal position of the Chinese in Indochina.

Kusaka Yorinao. *Hōjin wo matsu Futsu-In no hōko*. 2nd ed. Tokyo, Bummeisha, 1942. (SEA).
Discusses commercial position of the Chinese in Indochina.

Li Cheng-fu. *Chün-hsien shih-tai-chih An-nam* (Annam when it was a Chinese prefecture). Shanghai, Commercial Press, 1945.

Li Chuang. *Chien-pu-chai hua ch'iao chiao yü* (Overseas Chinese education in Cambodia). Taipei, Hai-wai, 1959.

Liang Chao-k'ang. *Yueh-nan ch'iao-ch'ing tzu-liao*. Ch'iao-wei-hui mi-shu-shih, 1956. (*HCW*).
The position of the Chinese in Vietnam.

Lü Ku. *Yüeh-nan jen-min fan-ti tou-cheng-shih*. Shanghai, Tung-fang shu-she, 1951. (Hsin-shih-tai ya-chou hsiao-ts'ung-shu ser. 2.) (*HL*).
A Communist treatment of the history of Vietnam and the people's struggles for independence.

Lü Shih-p'eng. *Yüeh-nan hua-ch'iao shih-hua*. Taipei, 1958. (*TOC*).
A short history of the Chinese in Indochina.

Mai Lang. *Chan-tou-chung-ti Hsin-Yüeh-nan*. Hong Kong, Hsin-Yüeh-nan ch'u-pan-she, 1948. (*HL*).
A collection of essays on Vietnam with an appendix which includes Ho-Chi-minh's address to the Overseas Chinese.

Mizutani Otokichi. *Futsu-In no seitai*. Tokyo, Okakura Shobō, 1942. (*SEA*).
First chapter: the Chinese in Indochina.

Mori Tokuhisa. *Futsu-In no nōgyō keizai*. Tokyo, Keizai Shimpōsha, 1943. (*SEA*).
The Chinese and the agricultural economy of Indochina.

Naikaku, Jōhōkyoku. *Tōa kyōeiken no ikkan to shite no Futsuryō Indoshina*. Tokyo, 1941. (*SEA*).
The strength of the Chinese in Indochina.

Nihon Bōeki Shinkō Kyōkai. *Futsuryō Indoshina to bōeki jijō*. Tokyo, 1941. (*SEA*).
Discussion of the position of the Chinese in Indochina in the first section.

Shu Shih-cheng. *Chung-Fa wai-chiao-shih*. Shanghai, Commercial Press, 1928. (Hsin-shih-tai shih-ti ts'ung-shu ser.) (*HL*).
Sino-French relations with discussion of Indochina.

Su Tzu. *Chin-jih Yüeh-nan*. Kowloon, Tzu-yu ch'u-pan-she, 1952. (*HL*).
Vietnam and the position of the Overseas Chinese.

Taiheiyō Kyōkai. *Futsuryō Indoshina, seiji-keizai*. Tokyo, Kawade Shobō, 1940. (*SEA*).
The economic and political position of the Chinese in Indochina.

Taiwan Takushoku Kabushiki Kaisha, Chōsaka. *Futsu-In no seikaku to kankyō*. Taihoku, 1941. (*SEA*).
The social, cultural, and economic position of the Chinese in Indochina.

Tazawa Takeo. *Futsu-In jijō*. Tokyo, Hata Shoten, 1940. (*SEA*).
Final chapter discusses the Chinese in Indochina.

Ti-i fang-mien chün ju-Yüeh shou-hsiang ching-kuo. (*HL*).
A document recording the surrender of the Japanese forces in Indochina to the Chinese army.

Yamakawa Toshikazu. *Futsu-In no jūmin to shūzoku*. Tokyo, Kaiseisha, 1942. (*SEA*).
The economic activity of the Chinese in Indochina.

Yao Nan. *Chung-nan pan-tao hua-ch'iao shih kang-yao*. Chungking, 1946. (*TOC*).
An outline history of the Chinese in Indochina.

Yüeh-nan hua-ch'iao kuo-chi wen-t'i yen-chiu, compiled and published by Hai-wai ch'u-pan-she, 1957. (*HCW*).
Problems of nationality of the Chinese in Vietnam.

Yüeh-nan wang-kuo-shih, told by Ch'ao Nan-tsu, ed. by Hsin-min ts'ung pao-she. Shanghai, Kuang-chih shu-chü, 1905. (*HL*).
Story of the loss of Indochina to France told by a refugee, in classical style.

Yüeh-nan wen-t'i, compiled and published by the Central News Agency, Nanking, 1940. (*HL*).
A collection of essays on Indochina dealing with its geography, history, the impact of the Japanese move on the Overseas Chinese amongst other matters.

6. MALAYA AND SINGAPORE

Chang Li-ch'ien. *Ma-lai-ya li-shih kai-yao*. Changsha, Commercial Press, 1939, 1940. (*HL*).
Summary of Malayan history.

—— *Ma-liu-chia shih*. Commercial Press, 1941. (Nanyang historical ser.) (*HL*).
A detailed illus. history of Malacca.

Ch'en Chia-keng. *Nan-ch'iao hui-i lu.* Singapore, Nan-yang, 1946. 2 vols. (*C20*).
Reminiscences of Ch'en Chia-keng (Tan Kah Kee).

Hai Shang-ou. *Ma-lai-ya jen-min k'ang-jih chün.* Singapore, 1945. (*TOC*).
Chinese Communist forces in Malaya in the fight against the Japanese.

Hsin-chia-p'o hua-ch'iao ming-jen chuan, ed. by Shen Wei-tse. Singapore, NanKok
Publication Co., 1950. (*HL*).
111 biographies of Chinese personalities in Singapore. English text also available but less
informative.

Hsin-chia-p'o Ku-ch'eng hui-kuan ch'i-shih-liu chou-nien chi-nien t'e-k'an. Singapore,
1949. (*HL*).
Commemorative publication of a four-clan burial association.

Hsü Su-wu. *Hsin-chia-p'o hua-ch'iao chiao-yü ch'üan-mao.* Singapore, Nan-yang
shu-chü, 1950. (*HL*).
Chinese education in Singapore.

Hsü Yü-chiao *and* Kao Meng-yün. *Nan-yang ssu chou fu hua-ch'iao shang-yeh chiao-
t'ung lu.* Ipoh, Kuang-ming yin-wu chü, 1928. (*C20*).
Biographies of Chinese in Malaya.

Hsün Lao. *Ma-lai-ya.* Shanghai, Sheng-huo, Tu-shu, Hsin-chih Shanghai lien-he
fa-hsing-so, 1949. (*HL*).
The geography, history, economics, anthropology, and politics of Malaya and Singapore.

Hu Wen-hu hsien-sheng liu-chih chin-wu shou-ch'en chuan-k'an, ed. & pub. by Star
News Amalgamated Ltd, Singapore, 1947. (*C20*).
A biography of Aw Boon Haw (the 'Tiger Balm King').

Huang Tso-ts'ang (Huang Che Tsang). *Ma-lai-ya.* Shanghai, Commercial Press,
1931. (*HL*).
Description of Malaya.

Li Chung-chiu. *Hsin-chia-p'o feng-t'u-chi.* Singapore, Nan-yang shu-chü, 1947.
(*HL*).
A description of Singapore in 1887 by the first Chinese Consul.

Li Jui-hua. *Ma-lai-ya hua-ch'iao.* Tzu-yu Chung-kuo ch'u-pan she, 1954. (*HCW*).
The Chinese in Malaya.

Liao Kang-lu. *Ma-lai-ya yü Chung-kuo li-tai kuan-hsi.* Tientsin, Kuo-wen chou-pao,
Apr. 1936. (*CKS*).
Historical connexions between Malaya and China.

Ma-kung tang-ch'ien min-chu kang-ling ch'ien-shih. Singapore, Ma-lai-ya ch'u-pan-
she, 1946. (*HL*).
A 30-p. document containing the directives of the Communist Party of Malaya drawn
up at the eighth plenum in 1946.

Ma-lai-a hua-ch'iao shih (trans. of Victor Purcell, *The Chinese in Malaya,* by Liu
Ch'ien-tu). Penang, Kuang Hua Jih Pao, 1951.

Nan-feng shang-yeh ch'u-pan-she. *Hsin-chia-p'o miao-yü kai-lan.* Singapore, 1951.
(*TOC*).
The temples of Singapore.

*Nan-yang Ying-shu Ma-liu-chia Ming-hsing chih-shan-she hsün-nan she-yüan ai-ssu-
lu.* Malacca, Ming-hsing chih-shan-she, 1949. (*HL*).
Commemoration of victims of Japanese cruelty in Malacca.

Ninomiya Mineo. *Marē Hantō jijō.* Tokyo, Naigai Shuppan Kyōkai, 1898. (*SEA*).
Discussion of the Chinese in Malaya, their culture and business activities.

P'an Hsing-nung. *Hsin-chia-p'o yu-lan chih-nan.* Singapore, Nan-tao ch'u-pan-she, 1946. (*HL*).
Travellers' guide to Singapore.

—— *Ma-lai-ya Ch'ao-ch'iao t'ung-chien.* Singapore, Nan-tao, 1950. (*C20*).
The Chinese in Malaya who originated in Ch'ao-chou.

Su Hsiao-hsien. *Chang-chou shih-shu lü Hsing t'ung-hsiang lu.* Singapore, Ch'iao-kuang, 1948. (*C20*).
The Chang-chou Chinese in Singapore.

Sung Yün-p'u. *Nan-yang Ying-shu hai-hsia chih-min ti chih-lüeh.* Peking, Nan-yang yün-hsing kung-ssu, 1930. (*HL*).
A study of the Straits Settlements.

Ta-chan yü Nan-ch'iao, Ma-lai-ya-chih-pu, compiled by Nan-yang Hua-ch'iao ch'ou-chen tsu-kuo nan-min tsung-hui, Singapore, 1947. [Preface by Tan Kah Kee.] (*HL*).
Activities and sufferings of Overseas Chinese in Malaya during war. Valuable material for history of Japanese occupation of Malaya.

Taiwan Sōtoku Kambō, Chōsaka. *Marē Hantō to Sumatora to no saibai kigyō hikaku.* Taihoku, 1929. (*SEA*).
Comparison of Malaya and Sumatra with references to the Chinese.

Taiwan Sōtoku Kambō, Gaijika. *Eiryō Marē to Kakyō.* Taihoku, [1935?]. (*SEA*).
British Malaya and the Overseas Chinese.

Tan Yeok-seong. *Nanyang Ti-i Pao-jen* (The first Newspapermen of the Nan-yang). Hong Kong, 1958.

T'ang Chih-yao. *Hua-ch'iao chih Hsin-chia-p'o.* Taipei, Hua-ch'iao wen-hua, 1960. (*HL*).
Overseas Chinese gazetteer, Singapore.

T'ang Shih-ch'ing. *Ma-lai-ya Hsin-chia-p'o hua-ch'iao ching-chi.* Taipei, Hua-ch'iao ching-chi ts'ung-shu, ti-i chi, 1956. (*TOC*).
The economic position of the Chinese in Malaya and Singapore. (*See under* General: Ho I-wu.)

T'ang Su-min. *Ma-lai-ya hua-ch'iao she-hui sheng-huo.* Hua-ch'iao wen-t'i lun-wen chi ti-erh chi, Oct. 1955. (*HCW*).
The Chinese population in Malaya.

—— *Ma-lai-ya yü Chung-kuo.* Taipei, 1956. (*TOC*).
Malaya and China (Formosa).

Tōa Kenkyūjo. *Marē no tsūka kinyū.* Tokyo, 1943. (*SEA*).
Money and banking in Malaya with discussion of Chinese banks.

Yao Nan *and* Chang Li-ch'ien. *Pin-lang-yü chih-lüeh.* Chungking, 1943, 1945; Shanghai, 1946. (*HL*).
Account of Penang.

Yao Tan. *Ma-lai-ya hua-ch'iao-shih kang-yao.* Nan-yang yen-chiu she, 1956[?]. (*HCW*).
An outline history of the Chinese in Malaya.

Yü Shou-hao. *Ma-lai-ya ku-chin t'an.* Singapore, 1953. (*TOC*).
Malaya past and present.

Yün Yü-min. *Hsin-chia-p'o Ch'iung-ch'iao kai-k'uang.* Hainan, Hai-nan shu-chü, 1931. (*HL*).
A study of the Chinese from Hainan in Singapore.

7. SARAWAK, NORTH BORNEO (SABAH), AND BRUNEI

Lo Hsiang-lin [1905–]. *Hsi P'o-lo chou Lo Fang-pai teng so chien kung ho kuo k'ao.* Hong Kong, 1961. (*HL*).

A historical survey of the Lanfang presidential system in western Borneo established by Lo Fang-pai and other Overseas Chinese.

Miho Gorō. *Hōjin shin hattenchi to shite no Hoku Boruneo.* Tokyo, Tōkyōdō, 1916. (*SEA*).

Discussion of the Chinese in North Borneo is included.

Sung Che-mei. *Pei-po-lo-chou Po-lo-nai Sha-lao-yüeh hua-ch'iao ching-chi.* Taipei, Hua ch'iao ching-chi ts'ung-shu, ti-i chi, 1957. (*TOC*).

The economic position of the Chinese in British Borneo. (*See under* General: Ho I-wu.)

——*Ying shu Po-lo-chou hua-ch'iao ch'iao-yü* (Overseas Chinese education in British Borneo). Taipei, Hai-wai, 1959. (*HL*).

8. INDONESIA

Aikoku Shimbunsha, Ran-in Jijō Kōshūkai. *Ranryō Indo sōsho.* Tokyo, 1940. 2 vols. (*SEA*).

Vol. ii considers the economic problem of the Chinese in Indonesia.

Chang Wen-ho. *Chih jih ti Yin-tu-ni-hsi-ya* (Present-day Indonesia). Hong Kong, Hsin-hsüeh shu-tien, 1958. (*HL*).

Ch'en En-ch'eng. *Fan-kung tou-shih Chang Hsün-i* (Chang Hsün-i, the anti-Communist warrior). Taipei, 1956. (*TOC*).

Ch'en I-ling. *Yin-ni hsien-chuang yü hua-ch'iao.* Taipei, Chung-yang wen-wu kung-ying-she, 1954. (*HCW*).

The Overseas Chinese in present-day Indonesia.

Ch'iu Shou-yü. *Tung-yin-tu yü hua-ch'iao ching-chi fa-chan-shih.* Cheng-chung shu-chü, 1947. (*HL*).

A study of the economic geography of Indonesia. Last chapter deals with the economic significance of the Chinese. Authoritative.

Chu Hsiu-hsia. *Yin-ni yü Chung-kuo.* Taipei, 1955. (*TOC*).

Indonesian relations with China.

Chung Lu-chai. *Chao yu san yüeh chi.* Hong Kong, Nan-hua ta-hsüeh, 1940. (*HL*).

Memoirs of a trip to Java in 1939.

Fujiyama Raita. *Nanyō sōdan.* Tokyo, Nihon Hyōronsha, 1927. (*SEA*).

Discussion on Southeast Asia includes Chinese in Indonesia.

Hua-ch'iao wen-t'i yen-chiu hui, ed. *Yin-tu-ni-hsi-ya Hua-ch'iao wen-t'i tzu-liao.* Peking, 1951. (*TOC*).

Problems of the Overseas Chinese in Indonesia.

Huang Su-feng. *K'o-hsüeh-ti Nan-yang.* Shanghai, Commercial Press, 1934. (*HL*).

Essay on science in the Nanyang islands; the first attempt at a scientific Chinese book on Indonesia.

Hsü Wei-han. *Tung-t'ang-chung-ti Ho-shu Tung-yin-tu.* Siam, Fen-tou ch'u-pan-she, 1940. (*HL*).

Account of Indonesia apropos of Japanese expansion to the south.

Ide Teiichirō. *Reimei no Nanyō.* Tokyo, Jumpū Shoin, 1929. (*SEA*).

Considers the Chinese in Java.

Kai-shan Ho-Yin hua-ch'iao tai-yü wen-t'i. Wai-chiao-pu Ou-chou-ssu yen-chiu-shih ts'ung-k'an, No. 3, 1943. (*HL*).

Classified report by Chinese Ministry of Foreign Affairs on treatment of Chinese in Indonesia.

Lai Chao-hua. *Yin-ni shou-ts'e.* Jakarta, 1954. (*TOC*).

An Indonesian handbook.

Masufuchi Sahei. *Nampō no hōko; Ran-In Sumatora.* Tokyo, Yoshida Shoten, 1941. (*SEA*).

Third section deals with Chinese in Sumatra.

Miyoshi Tomokazu. *Higashi Indo no dozoku.* Tokyo, Kanda, Nihon Kōronsha, 1943. (*SEA*).

Discussion of the livelihood of the Chinese in Indonesia.

Ogasawara Nagahiro. *Ran-In jijō.* 4th ed. Tokyo, Hata Shoten, 1941. (*SEA*).

Second chapter on economics and the Chinese in Indonesia.

Sambō Hombu. *Ran-In jijō.* Tokyo, 1941. (*SEA*).

Japanese General Staff survey of Indonesia with comments on the position of the Chinese.

Sano Minoru. *Nanyō shotō junkōki.* Tokyo, Nabeshima Yoshihiro, 1913. (*SEA*).

Discussion of the economic potential of the Chinese in Indonesia is included.

Tai Hung-ch'i. *Yin-ni Hua-ch'iaō ching-chi.* Taipei, Hua-ch'iao ching-chi ts'ung-shu, ti-i chi, 1956. (*TOC*).

The economic position of the Chinese in Indonesia. (*See under* General: Ho I-wu.)

Taiwan Ginkō, Batabiya Shisha. *Batabiya kakyō chōsa.* Batavia, 1939. (*SEA*).

The economic activities of the Chinese in Batavia.

Takei Jūrō. *Tōsa nijūsannen, fugen no Nanyō.* Tokyo, Hakubunkan, 1930. (*SEA*).

The economic sphere of the Chinese in Indonesia.

—— *Ranryō Indo wo kataru.* Tokyo, Heibonsha, 1935. (*SEA*).

Some discussion of the position of the Chinese in Indonesia.

T'ien-sheng jih-pao shih chou-nien chi-nien-ts'e. Batavia, Thien Sung Yit Po, 1932. (*HL*).

Anniversary volume of the *Thien Sung Yit Po* including articles on the Chinese in Indonesia.

Torigai Taichirō. *Oran no Nanyō shokuminshi.* Tokyo, Maruzensha, 1941. (*SEA*).

Discussion of Chinese disturbances in Indonesia.

Tzu-yu Yin-ni. Hong Kong, 1949. (Yin-ni hsiao-ts'ung-shu ser.) (*HL*).

A collection of eight Communist essays by various authors on the Indonesian struggle for independence.

Wang Jen-shu. *Yin-ni she-hui fa-chan kai-kuan.* Shanghai, Hong Kong, Singapore, 1948. (Hsin-shih-chi ts'ung-kan ser.)

The author afterwards became the first Chinese Communist ambassador to Indonesia. A Communist account of Indonesian nationalism.

—— *Lin-jen men* (Our Indonesian neighbours). Peking, 1950. (*TOC*).

Wu Fan. *P'u-shu Ti'wen hua-ch'iao chiao-yu* (Overseas Chinese education in Portuguese Timor). Taipei, Hai-wai, 1958. (*HL*).

Wu Shih-huang. *Yin-ni shih-hua.* Jakarta, World Publishing Co, 1951. Illus., maps. (*HL*).

History of Indonesia.

—— *Yin-tu-ni-hsi-ya shih* (trans. of an original Indonesian work by S. Pane, 1955). Peking, Shang-wu yin-shu-kuan, 1959. (*HSM*).

A history of Indonesia.

Yamada Fumio. *Higashi Indo keizairon.* Tokyo, Chigura Shobō, 1943. (*SEA*).
The Chinese and the economy of Indonesia.

Yokohama Shōkin Ginkō, Chōsaka. *Ranryō Higashi Indo.* Yokohama, 1919. (*SEA*).
The economic strength of the Chinese in Indonesia.

Yoshino Sakuzō. *Nanyō.* Tokyo, Minyūsha, 1915. (*SEA*).
Section on Indonesia includes discussion of the position of the Chinese.

9. The Philippines

Chao Hung-han. *Fei-lü-pin hua-ch'iao kai-k'uang.* Canton [preface 1928]. (*HL*).
Description of a trip to the Philippines to raise money for planes to fight Japan. The hostile attitude of the Filipinos towards the Overseas Chinese.

Ch'en Hsiao-yü, ed. *Fei-lü-pin yü hua-ch'iao shih-chi ta-kuan* (The Philippine Chinese Chronicle), v. ii. Manila, 1948. (*TOC*).

Ch'en Lieh-fu. *Fei-lü-pin hua ch'iao chiao yü* (Overseas Chinese education in the Philippines). Taipei, Hai-wai ch'u-pan-she, 1958.

Fei-lü-pin hua-ch'iao, Ch'iao-wei-hui yen-chiu pao-kao, MS. in *Ch'iao-wu wei yüan-hui tzu-liao-shih,* 1942. (*HCW*).
The Chinese in the Philippines.

Huang Hsiao-ts'ang. *Fei-lü-pin Min-li-la Chung-hua shang-hui san-shih chou-nien chi-nien k'an.* Manila, Chung-hua Shang-hui ch'u-pan pu, 1936. (*C20*).
First part gives biographies of Chinese in the Philippines.

Huang Ming-te. *Fei-lü-pin hua-ch'iao ching-chi.* Taipei, Hua-ch'iao ching-chi ts'ung-shu, ti-i chi, 1957. (*TOC*).
The economic position of the Chinese in the Philippines. (*See under* General: Ho I-wu).

Huang Yen-hsing. *Hirippin Kakyō* (The Chinese in the Philippines). Tokyo, Bunka Kenkyūsha, 1944. (*SEA*).

Kuei Hua-shan. *Fei-lü-pin yü-chung hui-i lu.* Shanghai, 1947. (*TOC*).
Reminiscences of prison in the Philippines.

Liang Shang-yüan. *Fei-lü-pin.* Hong Kong, Hsin-chung-kuo shu-tien, 1949. (*HL*).
General account of the Philippines.

Liu Chih-t'ien. *Hua-ch'iao yü Fei-lü-pin.* Fei-lü-pin kung-li-pao-she, 1955. (*HCW*).
The Chinese in the Philippines.

—— *Fei-lü-pin hua-ch'iao shih-hua.* Taipei, 1958. (*TOC*).
A short history of the Chinese in the Philippines.

Matsushita Masatoshi. *Firippin bunka.* Tokyo, Risōsha, 1941. (*SEA*).
Comments on the Chinese resident in the Philippines.

Minami Manshū Tetsudō Kabushiki Kaisha, Tōa Keizai Chōsakyoku. *Saikin no Hirippin.* Tokyo, 1936. (*SEA*).
Resident Chinese and China-Philippine trade discussed in Sect. 2.

—— *Waga nanshin seisaku wo meguru Hitō no seiji keizai dōkō.* Tokyo, 1941. (*SEA*).
Text discusses the political and economic activities of the Chinese in the Philippines.

Miyoshi Tomokazu. *Tōa kyōeiken to Hirippin.* Tokyo, Tōkō Shoin, 1941. (*SEA*).
The activities of the Chinese in the Philippines.

Nakahara Zentoku. *Firippin dokuritsu seishi.* Tokyo, Chūbunkan, 1944. (*SEA*).
The history of Philippine independence including a chapter on Chinese revolutionaries.

Nihon Bōeki Shinkō Kyōkai. *Hirippin no shigen to bōeki.* Tokyo, 1942. (*SEA*).
Second chapter discusses the Chinese and the economy of the Philippines.

Shih Liang. *Fei-lü-pin yen-chiu.* Shanghai, Cheng-chung shu-chü, 1947. (*HL*).
An account of the Philippines with some discussion on the Overseas Chinese.

Taiwan Sōtokufu, Taihoku Kōtō Shōgyō Gakkō. *Hirippin no tennen shigen narabi ni rōdō jijō to shōgyōkai genkyō ippan.* Taihoku, 1933. (*SEA*).
Third chapter deals with the Chinese and domestic trade.

Wang Shao-p'ing. *Fei-tao Ch'iung-yai yin-hsiang chi.* Hong Kong, Sheng-wu chi-lu, 1939. (HL).
Travel account of the Philippines and Hainan.

Watanabe Kaoru. *Nettai igaku to Firippin no zembō.* Tokyo, Takunansha, 1942. (*SEA*).
Survey of tropical medicine in the Philippines with discussion of policy towards Chinese.

—— and Matsuya Taichi. *Hirippin Kakyō shin yōroku.* Manila, Watanabe Kaoru, 1932. (*SEA*).
The commercial activities of the Chinese in the Philippines.

INDEX

Choisy, Abbé de, 89, 100.
Chola (Coromandel), 15.
Cholera, 95, 107, 111, 201.
Chooliahs, see Tamils.
Chou En-lai, xv, 77, 482 f.
Chou Ta-kwan, 14 f.
Christians, Chinese, 371 f., 450, 502, 516, 518, 521, 527, 551.
Christmas Island, 319.
Chu Fan Chi (Chao Ju-kua), 13 n.
Chulalongkorn, King, 116, 118.
Chung Hua Tsung Hui (Fed. of Chinese Assocs. in Indonesia), 458 n., 474-5.
Chung Hui Tang, 293.
Chung Hwa Hui (Neth.), 450.
Citizenship: Dutch policy on, 435-42; Siamese, 136; Malayan, 318-20.
Civil Code of Republic of China, 439.
Clan halls, 126 n.
Clark Kerr, Sir A., 301.
Clarke, Sir A., 265.
Clementi, Sir C., 300.
Clifford, Sir H., 257, 299-301.
CNRRA, 560.
Cobbold Commission, 381.
Cobbold, Lord, 354, 378, 567.
Cockayne, George, 392-3.
Cocks, Richard, 392-3.
Cocos-Keeling islands, 318.
Coen, J. P., 391 f., 395-6, 510.
College of Agriculture, Los Baños, 547.
Comintern, 301.
Commercial Council, Chinese (Philippines), 539.
Commercial Press, Shanghai, 280, 456.
Committee of Good Offices (UN), 480.
Commonwealth of the Philippines, 534, 544-5, 551.
Communist Liaison Committee (Malaya), 281 n., 340, 342.
Communist Party, Chinese (CCP), xiii, chs. 8, 18 f., 24, 31, 34 f., 37, 45, 49, 54 f., 158 f., and *passim.*
Communist Party (Malaya) (MCP): 301-3, chs. 31-35.
Communist Youth Corps (Malaya), 299.
Communist Youth Party, 299.
Communist Youth Section (Malaya), 302.
Compulsory Education Act (Siam), 151.
Comyn, Thomas de, 503, 530.
Concubinage, concubines, 31, 52, 202.
Confucius, Confucianism, 29 f., 141, 250, 412 f.
Congrégations, Chinese, in Indochina, 189, 213 n., 215.
Consuls, consulates, Chinese: in Indochina, 206, 213; in Indonesia, 445, 466, 475 ff.; in Malaya, 545; in Philippines, 539, 545, 550; in Siam, 113, 117 f., 148, 152-3; in Rangoon, 71, 73.
Consultative Committee (Malaya), 324-5, 327.
Convention, Anglo-Chinese, 64.

Convention of Chinese Assocs. (Indonesia), 479.
Coolie ships, 286-7.
Co-operative societies: in Indochina, 195, 198; in Indonesia, 459-60; in Malaya, 195, 198 f.; in Philippines, 547; in Siam, 133, 173.
'Co-Prosperity Sphere', 306 f.
Coromandel, 181, 237, 258.
Corvée, 72, 100, 117, 184.
Coughlin, R. J., 30 ff., 82.
Council of the Indies (Spanish), 519.
Council of the Netherlands Indies, 447.
Cowan, C. D., 265.
Cox, Capt. H., 52.
Crawfurd, John, 53 ff., 84, 94 f., 98 f., 365-6, 389, 411, 413.
Credit institutions (Indonesia), 459.
Crookshank, Mr, 369.
Crosby, Sir J., 115.
Crosthwaite, Sir C., 65 f.
Culture system, 428-9.

Daendels, Marshal H. W., 397, 408 f.
Daha (Kediri), 477.
'Dalforce', 303, 305 f.
Dalley, F. W., 337.
Dampier, William, 402-3, 426.
Damrong (Dhamrong) Nawasat, 154.
Damrong, Prince, 122, 142.
Danish officers, 108.
Daru, king of, 239.
Dasmariñas, see Pérez Dasmariñas.
Davis, J. L. H., 309-10.
Day, Clive, 390, 431.
De Haan, F., 413.
Del Tufo, M. V., 342.
Deli, 427, 464.
Democratic Party (Siam), 155.
Dennery, E., 192 ff.
Dent, Alfred, 364, 374.
Deventer, M. L. van, 409, 437.
Dewey, Commodore, 534.
Dhonburi, 91.
'Diem', see Ngo dinh Diem.
Diffelin, R. van, 455.
Discalced Augustinians, 520.
Discrimination against Chinese: in Indochina, 187 f., 204 f.; in Indonesia, 404, 409, 427, 433, 436, 439, 490-1; in Philippines, 509-10, 515-18, 523, 558 ff.; in Malaya, 291, 321-2; in Siam, 134 ff., 139-40, 143-147, 154-7.
Disraeli, Benjamin, 87.
Dittis, Andrea (Captain of Chinese), 392.
Djajadiningrat, R. L., 452 f., 455.
Djambi (Jambi), 388, 394.
Doherty, David M., 537.
Doll, W. A. M., 130, 135.
Dominicans, 501, 515-16.
'Double Seventh' (7.7.37), 293, 372.
Doudart de Lagrée, E. M. L., 86 n., 106, 186.

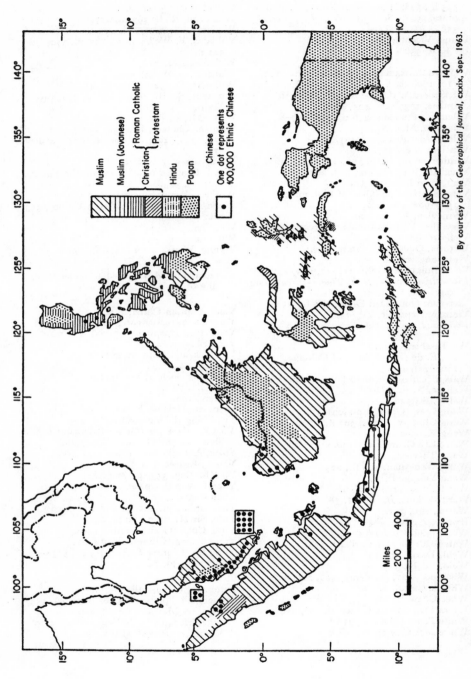

Muslim

Muslim (Javanese)

Christian { **Roman Catholic**
            Protestant

Hindu

Pagan

Chinese
One dot represents
100,000 Ethnic Chinese

Miles
0   200   400

By courtesy of the *Geographical Journal*, cxxix, Sept. 1963.

RELIGIONS PROFESSED BY MAJORITY OF INHABITANTS IN AREAS SHOWN

(based on map by Professor C. A. Fisher)